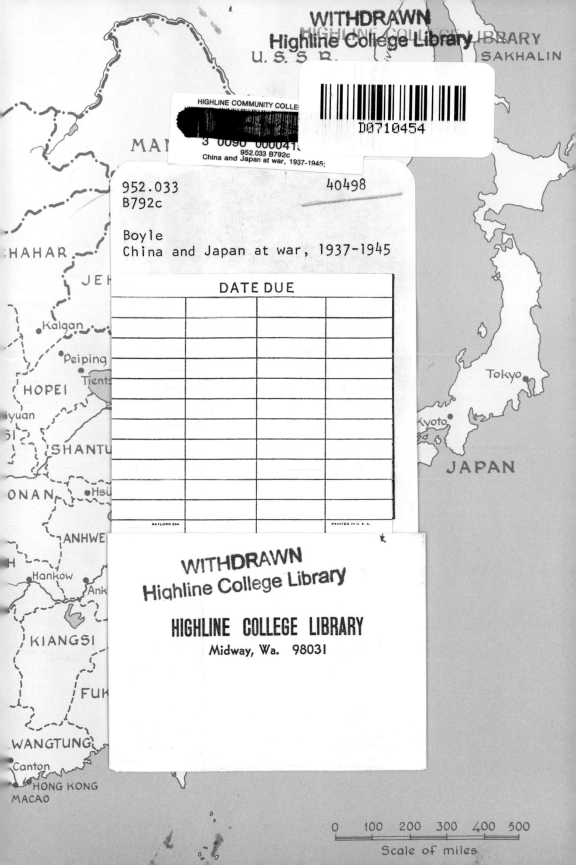

DATE DUE

GAYLORD 234   PRINTED IN U. S. A.

MANCHURIA

CHAHAR

JEHOL

Kalgan

Peiping

Tientsin

HOPEI

yuan

SHANTUNG

Hsu

ONAN

ANHWEI

Hankow   Ank

KIANGSI

FUKIEN

WANGTUNG

Canton

HONG KONG

MACAO

Tokyo

Kyoto

JAPAN

0   100   200   300   400   500

Scale of miles

China and Japan at War, 1937-1945

The Politics of Collaboration

China and Japan at War
1937-1945
The Politics of Collaboration

John Hunter Boyle

Stanford University Press, Stanford, California   1972

Sources of photos and illustrations:
1, 2, 6, 10, Mme. Tseng Chung-ming
3, 4, 12, 17, 19, 21, Misuzu Publishing Co., Tokyo, and Imai Takeo
5, Gombojab Hangin; 7, Ishii family; 8, Hara Publishing Co., Tokyo
9, 20, David D. Barrett Collection, Hoover Library
11, Nym Wales Collection, Hoover Library
13, 14, Ho Ping-hsien; 15, Kagesa family
16, Japanese Foreign Ministry Archives
18, Hoover Library.

Stanford University Press, Stanford, California
© 1972 by the Board of Trustees of the Leland Stanford Junior University
Printed in the United States of America
ISBN 0-8047-0800-2   LC 76-183886

FOR BARBARA

Preface

In 1971 a four-and-a-half-hour documentary movie, "Le Chagrin et la Pitié" (The Sorrow and the Pity) opened in Paris and began to shatter thirty years of wartime legends about the Resistance. The movie suggests that, far from being an exceptional phenomenon limited to a few craven Vichy officials and a handful of unpatriotic women who fraternized with the Wehrmacht, collaboration was a commonplace; and that if there had been a referendum in 1940, Pétain and a full armistice with the German invaders would have received a resounding mandate from the French people. "Le Chagrin et la Pitié" shows that, Gaullist myth-makers notwithstanding, France's Pétainist sympathies did not begin to change until Germany's fortunes of war were reversed at Stalingrad in the winter of 1942–43. "Only then," writes a *Le Monde* reviewer of the movie, "did the French begin to realize that collaboration was a sucker's game in which their German 'comrades' played not according to any rules but instead demanded, 'Hand over your watch—and I'll tell you what time it is.'"

The Chinese have not been so troubled with questions and doubts on this point. Certainly no Chinese equivalent of "Le Chagrin et la Pitié" has surfaced in either mainland China or Taiwan. Nor is any likely to. The whole matter has been submerged by the historic revolutionary upheaval that has preoccupied the Chinese people since the war years. And yet, occasionally, one hears that the memory of the once-crucial issue of collaboration and of China's Pétain, Wang Ching-wei, is still alive. Recollections of the dilemmas posed by the Japanese occupation of China are too vivid to disappear overnight. This point was driven home to me with particular force at a recent meeting of historians when a young Chinese prefaced his remarks on a paper about Wang Ching-wei by saying that to this day the mere mention of Wang was enough to divide his otherwise placid and harmonious family into two bitterly hostile factions and bring on weeks of stony silence between them.

It is the Japanese rather than the Chinese, at least at the level of scholarship, who have been exercised by the issue of wartime collaboration. The Japanese have been fumbling and groping for a century to determine whether they are a part of the West or a part of the East, or perhaps a bridge between the two. Many nations are concerned about their identity and self-image, but few are as compulsively introspective as Japan in this respect. As a consequence, in the past decade or so Japanese scholars and writers for the popular press have been evaluating and reevaluating the war with China, the Pacific War with the United States, and the once-shining vision of an East Asia Co-Prosperity Sphere.

But it is not the Chinese and Japanese alone who can profit from a re-reading of the history of their eight-year war. As we in America enter the eighth year of our own Asian war (the eighth, anyway, since the Gulf of Tonkin Incident), we too can surely usefully learn from the lessons of that earlier war and from the words of the Chinese military classic of the fourth century B.C., the *Sun-tzu*: "There never has been a protracted war from which a country has benefited." The *Sun-tzu*'s epigram may well be taken as the maxim that guided those who followed the road to collaboration in the Sino-Japanese War.

I am deeply grateful to the many men and women who have assisted me in the preparation of this book. To Kano Tsutomu, the editor of the *Japan Interpreter*, I owe a special vote of thanks. During the year 1969–70, when I served on the staff of that journal and did much of the research for this book, he took time from his crowded schedule to help me in more ways and on more occasions than I can enumerate here. Everyone writing a book on Japan should be so fortunate as to have a Kano-san as friend. I am also most thankful to Dr. Tsunoda Jun of the Diet Library for arranging interviews for me and for giving me the benefit of his surpassing knowledge of modern Japanese history.

Those who granted me interviews made an especially important contribution to this book, and I am happy to acknowledge their kindness here: Chang Chia-ao, Ch'en Chün-hui, Chin Hsiung-pai, Imai Takeo, Kao Tsung-wu, Li Sheng-wu, J. I. Lu, Matsukata Yoshisaburō, Matsumoto Shigeharu, Okada Yūji, Shimizu Tōzō (whose death in 1970 I am sorry to report), T'ao Hsi-sheng, Ushiba Tomohiko, and Yamazaki Jūzaburō. I am indebted to Ho Ping-hsien not only for granting me an interview, but also for taking the initiative in arranging my first meeting with many others on the above list, for providing me with photographs, for answering a flood of questions in correspondence, and for treating me and my family with great kindness during our stay in Hong

Kong. We shall not soon forget his hospitality. I am also grateful to Madame Tseng Chung-ming for granting an interview to my wife and for generously providing me with many of the photographs I have used. To all of these men and women, I want to say that I hope this book merits the trust they placed in me when they discussed what were, for some at least, exceedingly painful events to recall.

I wish also to thank the professors who read and commented on the thesis that led to this book: Thomas C. Smith, Lyman P. Van Slyke, and Claude A. Buss. To many good friends who have been generous with support and encouragement this acknowledgment is a long overdue and inadequate statement of appreciation; two of them—Ken Butler and John Barnett—must be singled out for a separate thank you. I am grateful to the staff members of the Lou Henry Hoover Library at Stanford for their assistance and cooperation, and to David Tseng and Allan Paul in particular for their special interest and help in acquainting me with the library's resources; to Baba Akira, Seiji Aizawa, Gombojab Hangin, and Henrietta Lo for a variety of favors; and to the Fulbright Commission for the financial assistance that permitted me to do research abroad.

To itemize all that I owe to my wife, Barbara Shipley Boyle, would burden the printer unduly. Still, I cannot conclude these acknowledgments without thanking her for her patience, understanding, and confidence. Had each been given in less than boundless measure, this book might not have been.

J.H.B.

Chico, California
March 1972

Contents

Eight pages of pictures follow page 162

China and Japan at War, 1937-1945

The Politics of Collaboration

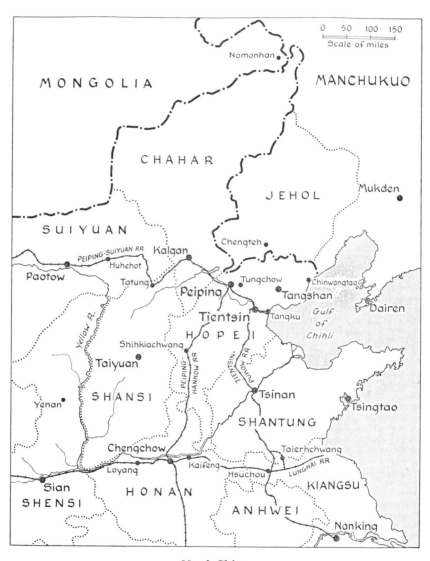

North China

CHAPTER ONE

Collaboration—Asian Style

NISHI YOSHIAKI, Tung Tao-ning, Kao Tsung-wu, Itō Yoshio, Matsu-moto Shigeharu, Inukai Ken, Horiba Kazuo, Ishiwara Kanji—Western students of Asian history would have to say that the one outstanding characteristic shared by these men is their obscurity. A standard textbook survey of modern East Asian history makes only a single passing reference to the last named.[1] And yet, Tsunoda Jun, the editor of the distinguished *Taiheiyō sensō e no michi* (The Road to the Pacific War) volumes, maintains that a knowledge of the activities and beliefs of this group is "indispensable" to an understanding of the Sino-Japanese War. "The aborted outcome of their efforts," Tsunoda writes, "is the key to an understanding of the war."[2] Speaking of the Japanese on the list, Tsunoda credits them with being the only men in Japan who developed any kind of a comprehensive and constructive plan for the adjustment of Sino-Japanese relations in the years after the Marco Polo Bridge Incident. He contrasts the relative clarity of their vision and above all their recognition of the danger and futility of a protracted war on the mainland with the official policies, which he describes with a list of uncomplimentary adjectives, including superficial, inconsistent, empty, and haphazard.

Of the group, Horiba and Ishiwara were military strategists whose calculations of an inevitable war with the Soviet Union led them to a single-minded preoccupation with efforts to modernize and rationalize the Japanese military establishment to prepare for that day. They were no less preoccupied with the necessity of avoiding conflict with China, and after the conflict erupted, of bringing it to a speedy conclusion with the minimum expenditure of Japanese military might, preferably via the conference table. Their views steadily lost ground, and by 1939 both had been relieved of their strategy-planning functions at the Center—Chūō—in Tokyo.*

---

* The Center is a vague term referring to a complex of several civilian and military officials in Tokyo. At different times it consisted of different officials, but in general

The remainder of the group was an assortment of subministerial-level bureaucrats, businessmen, and a newspaperman who constituted themselves as a "third force" of interested citizens attempting to bring about an end to the war. What began as the private peace efforts of this group ended with Wang Ching-wei's celebrated defection from Chungking in December 1939. And what began with Wang's defection from Chungking ended with the creation of a collaboration government under his leadership in Nanking fifteen months later. As the story of the creation of the Wang regime unfolds, it will be seen that there were close ties, both personal and ideological, between Ishiwara and Horiba on the one hand and the third force group on the other.

Ishiwara's belief was that Japan had every reason to foster—rather than resist—the growth of a strong, unified, and independent China. This view was as appealing to the third force group as it was disturbing to Ishiwara's Army colleagues. Had Ishiwara remained at the Center, his views might have been the determining factor in shaping the character of the Wang regime, in making it a viable independent government rather than a puppet government. But Ishiwara did not remain at the Center, and his ideas and those of the third force did not prevail. The denouement—"the aborted outcome of their efforts"—was in concrete terms the Wang Ching-wei regime and a host of other puppet regimes established by Japan on the China mainland from 1937 to 1940. This study, then, accepts Tsunoda's suggestion that an examination of the views and schemes of this group of men—in large measure a study of the politics of collaboration—is a useful way to illuminate that great historical watershed period in East Asian history, the Sino-Japanese War.

In the second chapter I take a look at the early career of Wang Ching-wei. Insofar as Wang is remembered at all by Chinese, whether of Communist or Nationalist persuasion, he is remembered by most as the arch-villain of modern Chinese history. At the outset, I ought to say that my purpose in writing this book is not to mobilize evidence in support of the majority contention that Wang was a traitor. Nor is it my purpose to side with those who find in him the qualities of unalloyed hero. Wang, along with most of those who joined him in collaborating with Japan, was as psychologically complex as the Nationalist and Communist leaders who did not collaborate. In short, Wang, like his critics, was motivated by mean and selfish considerations as well as by those that were

---

its members included the Premier, Foreign Minister, Finance Minister, Army and Navy Ministers, and Army and Navy Chiefs of Staff. Also included were certain second-level officials, such as Vice Chiefs of Staff and the Chief of the Military Affairs Bureau.

lofty and patriotic. In the second chapter we look at the pre-1937 years, when some of those varied motivations were generated, first, in the factional rivalries of the Kuomintang and, second, in the increasingly complex love-hate relationship that developed between China and Japan.

In chapters three and four, before moving on to a discussion of the various puppet regimes, I first attempt to put the whole discussion of puppet regimes in a broader perspective by analyzing the dispute that raged within Japanese military and government circles during the opening months of the war. This dispute concerned the means and terms by which Japan would terminate what was then known as the China Incident.* One of the key issues of that dispute was whether Japan should seek to solve the China Incident and determine the character of her future presence on the mainland by working out arrangements with the National Government or by relying on local regimes of her own creating.

The first option clearly implied an abandonment of some, if not all, of the special rights and powers Japan had laboriously acquired in China, especially in North China and the Inner Mongolian border provinces. For some, however, such self-denial had merit as a step in the direction of a realistic adjustment to the potential power of Chinese nationalism presaged by the events at Sian in December 1936. Moreover, it had appeal to the pure strategists who emphasized the perilous threat posed by the Soviet Union. In the event of a war with this adversary— which in their strategic estimate was not merely possible but inevitable —China would be indispensable as an ally or at least as a friendly neutral.

Nevertheless, the months between July 1937 and January 1938 saw a decisive erosion of the strength of those advocating this policy of accommodation. Whatever its merits, such a policy had to oppose a momentum that had gathered during the past two decades of empire-building in North China and Manchuria. Both promoting and capitalizing on disunity in China, Japan's militarists grew accustomed to success as they acquired for Japan the "paramountcy" in North Asia that her diplomats could never quite achieve. The war, then, offered to these militarists the ideal opportunity for establishing the puppet regimes that would divide China and ensure Japan's hegemony in the north of China. After months of contention in Tokyo the promoters of a divided China achieved a signal victory when Premier Konoe Fumimaro announced on January

---

* On September 2, 1937, the North China Incident (*HokuShi jihen*) became the China Incident (*Shina jihen*) by order of the Cabinet.

16, 1938, that Japan would cease all contact with the National Government. Instead, Konoe declared, Japan would look forward to the establishment and growth of a new Chinese regime with which she would adjust her relations.

The advocates of a divided China had not, in fact, awaited official sanction for their program but had begun creating local puppet regimes before the war was two months old. Not one but several regimes were created in Inner Mongolia, and these were grouped together in a loose federation in October 1937. In December a Provisional Government of the Republic of China was established by the North China Area Army in Peiping without perceptible concern on the part of the Japanese Government. Later, in March 1938, still another government, styled the Reformed Government of the Republic of China, with a base in Central China, was established by the Central China Expeditionary Army. Municipal administrations independent of any of these governments were also established in certain key centers.

Chapters five through seven describe the various puppet agencies, their origins, their special characteristics, their personnel, and their relationship to their sponsoring units within the Japanese Army. Careful study of these regimes from the standpoint of their Chinese participants would probably yield a wealth of information about the dynamics of political allegiance in China. My main reasons, however, for surveying these earlier and lesser puppet regimes are (1) to compare them with the ultimate product of Japanese puppet-making attempts, the Wang Ching-wei regime; (2) to examine the effect the prior existence of these regional regimes had on efforts to establish the Wang regime; and (3) to show how these governments realized the visions of the important segment of Japanese Army leadership that yearned for a divided, pliant China.

After an examination in chapter eight of the various options open to the Konoe government after the historic January 16, 1938, announcement, I turn to a discussion of the Wang Ching-wei regime in the remaining chapters. More than two years elapsed between the first known hints of an effort in that direction and the final establishment of Wang's Reorganized National Government on March 30, 1940. Without going into detail here on the events of those two years, I will simply state briefly the main theme of these final chapters: the significant shift in attitude on both sides regarding the purpose and character of the proposed new government. The Chinese side originally envisioned the Wang regime as a relatively independent government, operating in and gradually expanding from the unoccupied provinces in South China. However, as a result of misunderstandings, miscalculations, and a considerable amount of duplicity on the part of the Japanese, the Wang regime turned out to be something quite different. After nearly two years of negotiations between the Wang forces and the Japanese, the Wang government, situated in occupied China, signed a Basic Treaty that spelled out a decidedly inferior relationship with Japan.

The position of the Japanese side also underwent important changes during these two years. At no time during this period (and even after the establishment of the Wang Ching-wei regime) did Wang enjoy anything like the wholehearted support of the Japanese Government or even of the Japanese Army. There was, for example, constant pulling and hauling among a number of factions within the Army over the merits of collaborating with Wang as against various other policies. Some wished to maintain the existing ties with the regional puppet regimes or to establish new ones with warlords like Wu P'ei-fu. Others had grave doubts about the wisdom of dealing with Wang, feeling that any final solution of the "China problem" would have to be arranged with Chiang Kai-shek. Indeed, even among Wang's most ardent Japanese supporters there was no consistent or uniform view of the role he should play, whether he should be treated as an end in himself or only as a "bridge" to Chungking. The factors behind the uncertainties and changes in attitudes toward Wang will of course be treated at much greater length in the final chapters of this study.

Never far from sight in this book is the shadowed career of the man Wang Ching-wei. Though widely respected and situated at political stage center in much of the Republican era, Wang became more and more isolated from the sources of real power in the 1930's, and so was never in control of China's destiny. As we shall see, Wang's political adversary Chiang Kai-shek shared rather than opposed Wang's conciliatory approach to Japan in the late 1920's and early 1930's. The Sian Incident, however, forced Chiang into abandoning the appeasement policy, whereas Wang persisted in seeing merit in the regrettably necessary policy of conciliation. Wang, who lacked a military base of support in 1936 before Sian, now found himself increasingly estranged from political and popular backing, too, as the country became intoxicated with the spirit of resistance. Here then, for many, lies the answer to the paradox of the great patriot turned puppet. Wang, some hold, was "blinded by self-esteem and goaded by political frustration. . . . He brought his misfortunes to the Japanese. They, *faute de mieux*, accepted his aid."[3]

This argument—or accusation—begs a very basic question, which this book must attempt to answer. Put quite simply that question is: was Wang after all a puppet? Or, to reduce the question to even more

basic terms, how useful is the word puppet in describing collaborators—
a category that runs the spectrum from Vidkun Quisling, whose perfidy
was so universally recognized that his name, like Judas's, has stayed in
the language as a generic word for traitor, to Sukarno, who could freely
boast of his collaboration with the Japanese?

How useful is the term in the context of modern international relations, where cross-national purposes and interdependence are at the
core of every nation's policies and where only the fiction of international
law justifies the claim to complete independence? How useful is the term
in the context of Chinese history, a classic feature of which has been
the ability of the Chinese people to survive and even flourish under alien
rule? "It mattered little who the despot was," writes John K. Fairbank,
"as long as he fitted 'benevolently' into the system."[4] The history of no
other nation is as replete with the names of distinguished citizens
who found ways to live at peace with their conquerors. And why should
it be otherwise? Did not Chinese history offer a reassuring multitude of
examples demonstrating that the barbarian conquerors inevitably abandoned their alien ways, adopted the superior culture and life style of the
Chinese, and eventually lost their identity among the Chinese masses?

And finally, and most especially, how useful is the term puppet in the
context of an Asian setting in World War II, when collaboration with
Japan frequently meant—or was thought to mean—deliverance from
Western imperialist domination and from the specter of Bolshevization?
In such a context it would seem the stigma (or lack of it) that attached
to the collaborator had relatively little relationship to the degree to
which he was manipulatable. Rather, the stigma (or lack of it) was a
function of the way in which his collaboration was perceived in nationalistic terms. If cooperation with the "enemy" was compatible with—or
could be made to appear compatible with—nationalism, the "puppet"
suffered little discredit and, in some cases, was highly esteemed.

By way of introduction, some general remarks on "puppetry," with
particular reference to the phenomenon in recent Asian history, seem to
be in order.

The stigma attached to the Asian puppet was sometimes an ambiguous
one, as in the case of the Philippine *muñeco*. The ambiguity stemmed
in part from the ambivalence of Philippine feeling toward the Americans and the dubious value of exchanging American control (with its
promise of independence in 1946) for Japanese control (with its promise
of independence *within* the Greater East Asia Co-Prosperity Sphere).

Even more, the ambiguity derived from the performance of the muñeco: when Sergio Osmeña, whose responsibility it was to determine the fate of Philippine collaborators, landed with General MacArthur in Leyte he said that the measure of loyalty was not the mere act of serving the Japanese in an official capacity, but the motive in holding office and the conduct while in office.[5]

Manuel Roxas, for example, collaborated with Japan, but only on a selective basis: he was the director of the wartime rice procurement agency that supplied the Japanese Army, but he declined Japanese requests that he act as President; he was a member of the drafting committee of the constitution of the Republic sponsored by Japan in 1943, and his eminence lent prestige to that Republic, yet he also managed to strike from the preamble the reverent references to the Greater East Asia Co-Prosperity Sphere the Japanese had hoped for; and finally, when Japan demanded that the Filipinos declare war on the United States, Roxas convinced opponents they should "not make the mistake of defying Japan," but at the same time he helped see to it that Japan was denied her request for an army of Filipino youth.[6] When Roxas came face to face with MacArthur, who had vowed that he would "run to earth every disloyal Filipino," he received an "enthusiastic bear hug" from the General, with whose support he became the first President of the postwar republic in 1946.[7]

The ambiguity of the Filipinos' attitudes toward their muñeco is perhaps most dramatically illustrated in Jose P. Laurel, who served as President of the Japanese-sponsored "Republic." After the Japanese occupation ended, Laurel was indicted on more than a hundred counts of treason. Pardoned before his trial was called, he went on to become a Senator and was very nearly successful in the presidential contest in 1949. Today his portrait, inscribed simply "President Laurel," hangs with those of the other Presidents of the Philippines in the great hall of the Malacañan.[8]

In other Asian countries collaboration with the Japanese led to little or no stigma at all. In Indonesia, for example, the goals of the nationalists and the Japanese occupation authorities meshed well. The spectacle of Asians inflicting defeat on a European colonial power was psychologically satisfying. "We Indonesians learned in this way that [our] white masters and the white men in general were not by nature superior, and that Asians could easily remove them."[9] Indonesian nationalist leaders were permitted contact with the Indonesian masses on a scale that the Dutch had never countenanced; they were, for example, permitted to

tour the countryside and use the radio network. As Sukarno later recalled:

> When I requested permission "to write and travel in order to allevi-
> ate complexities in areas I cannot reach," he [General Imamura,
> the Commander-in-Chief of the army of occupation] placed news-
> papers and planes at my disposal. He allowed me mass rallies. Su-
> karno's face, not just his name, penetrated the archipelago. I have
> the Japanese to thank for that.[10]

The Japanese were of course bent on securing the nationalists' "help in
harnessing Indonesia more effectively to Japan's wartime economic requirements—in particular assistance in mobilizing forced labor and in
organizing peasant deliveries of rice."[11] Arriving with almost no military government personnel, the Japanese were obliged to turn to Indonesians to fill the formerly Dutch-staffed bureaucracy. As a result, as one
student of Indonesian history has written:

> It became apparent to many that the skills of the Dutch colonial
> official, who for so long they had been taught to regard as their
> superior, were well within the compass of their own abilities. This
> realization engendered a powerful self-confidence, which increased
> their belief in their ability to govern themselves.[12]

When toward the end of the war the Japanese were obliged to ask for
Indonesian help in the creation of a native auxiliary to fight off the
expected invasion of Allied forces, Sukarno and his colleagues were
happy to comply. Consequently, when the first Allied troops landed in
Java, ready to assist the Dutch in their return, they were amazed to find
the Indonesian Republic a going organization and the Indonesian Army
determined to resist Dutch recolonization. In the Indonesian context,
therefore, puppetry was a patriotic virtue of the highest order.

Similarly esteemed in spite of his collaboration was the Indian patriot
Subhas Chandra Bose, who formed the Indian National Army under the
aegis of the Japanese in 1943 with the intention of leading it into India
as part of a great Japanese offensive to drive the British out. His plans
were dashed by the defeats suffered by the Japanese in the Burma
theater, and he died in an airplane crash on Taiwan near the end of
the war, but he is still regarded as a national hero and is even thought
to be still alive by many of his countrymen; an Indian postage stamp
bearing his likeness and the Indian National Army's insignia was issued
in 1964. At the postwar treason trials of Indian collaborators both
Gandhi and Nehru testified that Bose had been a true patriot.[13]

In Burma, too, the ranks of the collaborationists include many an esteemed patriot, including Dr. Ba Maw, Aung San, and the military dictator, Ne Win, who came to power in 1962. Ba Maw, who headed a Japanese-sponsored regime in Burma from 1942 to 1945, writes with evident pride of his collaboration with the Japanese. He credits the Japanese officer who organized and led the Burma Independence Army with being the "most vivid and dynamic force" in rallying Burmese resistance to the British. Incredibly, he also gives credit to the same remarkable soldier for "stiffen[ing] the backs of the Burmese in dealing with the victory-flushed Japanese armies." Conceding that "Burmese notions of liberty and nationalism were altogether different from [Japanese notions]," and allowing that the Japanese often acted arrogantly and made harsh exactions on his countrymen, Ba Maw nevertheless upbraids his people for sometimes failing to appreciate what stakes they had in the war.[14] Obsessed with their own political aims, the Burmese "saw what the Japanese were taking from them to carry on the combat, but not what they were getting back from the Japanese in return."[15] He writes movingly of the debt he feels Burma—and all of independent Asia—owes to Japan. It is a debt that justifies and brings honor to Burmese collaborators:

> Nothing can ever obliterate the role Japan has played in bringing liberation to countless colonial peoples. The phenomenal Japanese victories in the Pacific and in Southeast Asia, which really marked the beginning of the end of all imperialism and colonialism; the national armies Japan helped to create during the war, which in their turn created a new spirit and will in a large part of Asia; the independent states she set up in several Southeast Asian countries as well as her recognition of the provisional government of Free India at a time when not a single other belligerent power permitted even the talk of independence within its own dominions ... these will outlive all the passing wartime strains and passions and betrayals in the final summing-up of history.[16]

To return to the historical setting of this study, wartime China, one had a wide range of choices when it came to applying the puppet epithet. The belief that Wang Ching-wei was the puppet of Japan was held by most Chinese and Westerners; but by the same token many Japanese, scholars as well as propagandists, believed with equal conviction that Chiang Kai-shek was the puppet of the Western imperialists. For them this was a notion grounded in Sun Yat-sen's theory of China as a "hypo-colony of Western imperialism," personified in the Western orientation of the Soongs and the Kungs, illustrated in trade and industrial statistics, graphically evident in the Westernized character of the coastline from the Shanghai Bund to the resorts at Peitaiho, and eventually "proved" by Lend-Lease and massive financial assistance; one did not need to be a Marxist to equate financial assistance with imperialist control and draw the logical conclusions about Chiang's beholden condition.

Even more widely believed, especially among Japanese military circles in the period after the Sian Incident, was the notion that Chiang Kaishek was a puppet of the Chinese Communists or the Soviet Union, or both; the distinction between the two was blurred, since for most, the Chinese Communists were merely puppets of the Russians. Here, two choices were available. One might argue that Chiang was basically a Bolshevik at heart, but this required magnifying the significance of his brief stay in the Soviet Union, wrenching ten-year-old statements from their context, and ignoring nearly everything he had uttered since the Shanghai terror of April 1927. More easily demonstrable was the view that Chiang, for reasons of expediency and survival, had accepted the aid of both the Soviet Union and the Chinese Communists. He had then allowed the management of the propaganda organs to slip into the hands of the Communists and thus lost the ability to control the direction of the war. The Communists, according to this view, were whipping the Chinese people into a furious state of anti-foreignism directed mainly at Japan, and encouraging the Nationalists into a futile resistance to the Japanese while they held their own forces in fresh reserve. Thus, it was all too clear to many Japanese leaders that Chiang was simply being used by the Communists, who would proceed with the "sovietization of China" as soon as the Nationalists and the Japanese forces had exhausted themselves.[17]

The foregoing should suggest caution in the use of the term puppet, especially in the Asian context. Still another reason arguing for wariness in this regard is that few of the "puppets" discussed in this book were in fact spiritless dummies, utterly responsive to the commands of their ventriloquists, utterly incapable of speaking with their own voices. By oversimplifying the complexities of human personality and political behavior, the image delivered by the word puppet is often misleading.

Japan's Manchurian puppet, the Emperor K'ang-te (Henry Pu-yi), is perhaps the only Japanese collaborator to whom that term can be applied without reservation. But the pathetic Pu-yi was a unique case by virtue of his background and personality. His palace-sheltered and eunuch-dominated upbringing, effete by even Chinese Monarchical standards, was an excellent training ground for the role of puppet; his autobiography[18] testifies to an enervating preoccupation with personal vanity, homosexuality, drug addiction, sadism, and an assortment of neurotic fears and compulsions, all of which combined to make the ideal configuration: a passive personality lacking the ambition, interest, and talent required for any positive self-assertion in government, and a vanity willing to exchange the substance of power for the emptiness of title and ceremony. Henry Pu-yi recalls that he "went wild with joy" when the Commander of the Kwantung Army informed him that the Japanese Government was about to recognize him as the Emperor of Manchukuo: "My first thought was that I would have to get a set of imperial dragon robes . . . , the robes I had been dreaming of for twenty-two years."[19]

None of the other "puppets" selected by the Japanese were as pliable as Henry Pu-yi. They were, first of all, men accustomed to power and authority and well-schooled in the techniques of acquiring them. Sometimes they bargained and gained concessions to their personal advantage or to the advantage of their cliques; sometimes they bargained with broader national interests in mind. More often, probably, they bargained with mixed motives, including all of these elements. Motivation is difficult to establish with precision; and, in any case, for the purposes of this discussion it is only important to establish that the Japanese were not always able to manipulate their collaborators freely.

Though the bargaining position of the collaborators was undoubtedly weak, theirs was far from a hopeless cause. An important factor on the Chinese side was the division of purpose and authority among the Japanese. In a situation that saw each of several regimes under a different Army headquarters jealously guarding its empire and prerogatives against encroachment by other headquarters and the Army's central authorities in Tokyo, the "puppets" found that the historic Chinese tactic of "playing one barbarian off against another" was feasible. An illustration of the bargaining leverage provided by this age-old ploy is afforded by the following American Embassy dispatch on the subject of Wang K'o-min, the head of the Provisional Government in North China, generally regarded as one of the most pliable of Japan's puppets. (In this case, the "barbarians" were Maj. Gen. Kita Seiichi and Lt. Gen. Terauchi Hisaichi of the North China Area Army and Gen. Doihara Kenji of the Army General Staff.)

> Although Kita and his (Wang's) other Japanese sponsors are reportedly tired of him because of his stubbornness, his elimination would mean a political defeat for them and victory for Doihara. As

an example of Japanese difficulties with him, . . . General Terauchi
and Kita have for some time been trying to persuade Wang to sign
a document "transferring" all North China railways to the Japanese Government for war expenditures. . . . This Wang has refused
to do and although he must conform to most of their general and
specific proposals . . . , he is known to quarrel with them constantly
over matters in which he sees some possibility of saving something
for the Chinese.[20]

In the long run, however, the device of pitting barbarians against each
other historically proved more ingenious than efficacious, and it would
be wrong to think that Chinese puppets were very successful in using
this tactic to manipulate their puppeteers. There was, nevertheless,
another advantage the Chinese possessed.

The Chinese were well aware that the Imperial Army was faced with
a dilemma as it attempted to convert its battlefield successes into total
victory. It could rely on its own personnel to pacify and administer the
areas under its control, but only by committing huge manpower resources to the task—and manpower was still sorely needed for the strictly
military aspects of the war. Moreover, notwithstanding the assertions
by prominent Japanese that the Army was being welcomed enthusiastically in China, the Imperial Army itself was realistic enough to appreciate that alien Japanese could not hope to administer China effectively. Still less could they hope to induce China to accept its place in
the "New Order in East Asia"—unless the inducement was channeled
through Chinese spokesmen and interpreters. Consequently, military
government was never seriously considered for China. From the very
beginning of the war the Imperial Army chose to rely heavily on Chinese
collaboration.

One of the purposes of this study is to analyze the negotiations and
agreements between the Chinese collaborators and the Japanese to see
to what purpose and how effectively each side pressed its advantages.
Was the Chinese advantage we have been discussing—the fact that Chinese partnership was needed—outweighed by the sheer military and financial superiority of the Imperial Army? To summarize our findings,
we might say, as Lyman Van Slyke has suggested, that there was a "threshold of effective collaboration."[21] To a certain degree, generally a very
limited one, Japan was willing to satisfy the requests of her collaborators.
Beyond that threshold, however, and in all matters the Army felt vital
to its own strategic requirements, collaboration ceased to be effective
or productive from the Chinese point of view.

A second major purpose of this study is to examine Japan's collaboration policies to determine what they reveal about wartime decision-making processes in Japan, about changing goals and purposes in the war with China, and about intra-Army and Army-civilian differences of opinion about that war. Above all, it is my hope that this effort will help to isolate what was constant and what was not in Japan's policies and attitudes on China, and to indicate what was feint and what was reality in the "New Order in East Asia."

CHAPTER TWO

Wang, Chiang, and the Threat of Japan

WHEN THE charismatic Sun Yat-sen died in March 1925, he left behind a magnificent legend—his own life—on which his followers might focus the patriotic attention of the nation in their efforts to build a new China. Since that time both Nationalist and Communist Chinese have found it useful to identify themselves with the memory of Sun, the former deifying him and the latter honoring him. No other figure in Chinese history is so esteemed by both camps as Sun, the Father of the Republic and, from 1949, a "Pioneer of the Revolution." The reason for this dual appeal is that Sun dreamed large, extravagant dreams for China without articulating programs for their realization that could lay him open to attack from either quarter. It is not easy to quarrel with Sun's vision of national unification, liberation from foreign control, social revolution, and economic modernization—goals on which he left behind a gospel composed of political tracts, manifestos, party programs, and, finally, a last testament so vague and ambiguous that Communists, Nationalists, and nearly everyone in between could interpret his views to their own satisfaction. Even in apparently concrete matters within his area of expertise, such as railway construction, Sun had a talent for creating monumentally impractical schemes, so impractical that even now, more than half a century later, China has not come close to putting them into effect.

Not the least important thing Sun failed to bequeath China was a successor. At his death, the Kuomintang's most urgent task was to wrest power from the dozens of warlords who still controlled a politically fragmented China. That goal seemed most remote. The Party represented the hopes of a loosely bound collection of disparate groups, running the spectrum from devout Bolsheviks to reformed warlords who sensed which way the historic tides were flowing. Injecting strength and cohesion and some clarity of means and ends into this group was a task calling for leadership at least as strong as Sun's. And yet Sun had lingered near death for weeks without revealing to his anxious followers his choice for a successor.

Of the several contenders for the position, two were in the forefront. Both Hu Han-min and Wang Ching-wei had been close personal friends of Sun—and of each other—for two decades. Both had helped Sun to weld the T'ung-meng Hui (United League) into an effective revolutionary movement capable of discrediting the Imperial claim to rule China and hastening the fall of the dynasty. Both had spent many years helping Sun to develop the T'ung-meng Hui's successor, the Kuomintang, into a vehicle for completing the work of the Revolution of 1911. But the claim of the senior contender, Hu Han-min, proved short-lived, for within six months of Sun's death Hu was indirectly implicated in a political assassination that damaged his reputation in the Kuomintang. He was forced to resign his Party posts and to accept a mission—in effect an enforced vacation—in the Soviet Union. With Hu abroad Wang slipped with comparative ease into positions that made him head of both the Party and the new Government proclaimed in July 1925. When the Second National Congress of the Kuomintang was convened in Canton on New Year's Day, 1926, Wang's commanding position was certified, and a substantial number of his followers were elected to important posts in the Party's controlling committees. As we shall see, Wang's effort to succeed to Sun's authority within the Kuomintang proved as short-lived as Hu's; but before discussing that turn of events, we should take a look at Wang's earlier career.[1]

Though Wang's ancestral home was in Chekiang province, he was born at Canton in 1883 and always considered himself Cantonese. The tenth and last child of a legal secretary to an official in the Imperial civil service, Wang was given the name Chao-ming. Despite his family's straitened circumstances throughout his youth, Wang acquired a conventional education in the Chinese classics, mostly at home. A father who acted as tutor and an uncle who opened the doors to his ample library were instrumental in providing the educational background that enabled the young Chao-ming to obtain the *hsiu-ts'ai* degree in 1902. Two years later he was able to take advantage of an energetic if woefully tardy educational reform measure instituted by the enfeebled Ch'ing dynasty, which had been persuaded that the old ways of China, including the Imperial institution, could be preserved if a generation of Chinese students could learn the secrets of Western strength. Still, for many Chinese students, among them young Wang, Japan offered a classroom almost as suitable and much closer to home than Europe and America. Arriving in Tokyo in 1904 on a government scholarship to study law and political theory, Wang was in the vanguard of a flood of students who went to Japan and eventually returned to become the leaders of modern China.

Wang learned Japanese and graduated from Hōsei University in 1906, but beyond those accomplishments he did not fulfill the expectations of his Imperial sponsors. Exposure to a rapidly modernizing country capable of overwhelming Russia in the war of 1904–5 helped to sharpen the contrast between the moribund homeland of the students and vital Japan. Anti-Manchu revolutionary activities began to flourish in the Chinese student communities in Tokyo and Yokohama, and Wang took a leading role in furthering these activities, joining the newly founded T'ung-meng Hui. At only twenty-two he became chairman of one of the three key councils of the organization. He lent his brilliant oratorical skills to the revolutionary cause; and he lent his already considerable polemic skills to a running literary debate with opponents of the Revolution, including that formidable defender of the Monarchy and of a gradualist approach to reform—Liang Ch'i-ch'ao. When the first issue of the revolutionary journal *Min-pao* (The People) appeared in 1905, it was Wang who contributed the first article, and it was he who "carried most of the journalistic burden in succeeding issues."[2]

Most students who analyze the speeches and literary output of Wang pay him high tribute for his expositional talent. Whether speaking or writing, he had throughout his life an outstanding talent for captivating audiences, large and small. Even his detractors customarily commenced their attacks on him by making concessions to his eloquence. "Persuasive," "brilliant," "polished," "dramatic"—these are the adjectives that are found repeatedly in the descriptions of Wang. So brilliant a polemicist was he that he was frequently deferred to by T'ung-meng Hui leaders many years his senior, a rare phenomenon in age-conscious China. Even Sun, seventeen years older than Wang, sometimes deferred to the youthful revolutionary. A Japanese journalist who knew Wang in his later years recalls his oratory: "He always spoke in a very, very low voice in small groups. He was very polite, would address you by your full name. But in a crowd of three thousand, he was just like a crazy lion! He was a great orator."[3]

These were precisely the assets needed by the revolutionists in Sun's circle. If the content of Wang's speeches and articles lacked the enduring theoretical integrity and depth of his opponent Liang, it is scarcely surprising. Wang had only a nodding acquaintance with Western political theory and, in any event, he gave only secondary importance to theorizing: he was an activist, not an ideologue.

In 1905, when Wang began to write for *Min-pao*, he followed Chinese tradition by adopting a new name, Ching-wei. (In Chinese mythology, the *ching-wei* is a bird that spends its life carrying bits of wood and rock to deposit in the sea. Wang's choice of this name is said to have indicated his determination to overthrow the Manchus; that is to say, he had no more concern about the impossibility of this task than the *ching-wei* has about the difficulty of filling in the sea.[4]) In the following year, 1906, the authorities at home took note of Wang's revolutionary activities by cutting off his stipend and placing a price on his head. During the next few years he accompanied Sun on trips throughout Southeast Asia, organizing chapters of the T'ung-meng Hui, lecturing, writing, and appealing for financial support from the generally wealthy Overseas Chinese communities, a preponderance of whose members were from Wang's and Sun's native province of Kwangtung. The Chinese Empire was clearly collapsing, and the question in those years was not if, but when and where. It was important to Sun and Wang—and presumably to many Overseas Chinese—that the revolutionary base be in their native province. The stereotype image of Cantonese Chinese as cliquish is justified by political as well as social behavior. Throughout his life Wang revealed a strong affinity to his native province, and many of his closest followers were Cantonese.

In spite of the energy and dedication of men like Sun and Wang, the T'ung-meng Hui suffered a series of setbacks. Poor planning, inexperience, a shortage of arms and ammunition, and bad luck dogged the movement and turned one invasion attempt after another into fiasco. Revolutionary stalwarts were arrested and executed, the morale of the organization degenerated, and factional contention began to grow; and suppression by the Japanese authorities further weakened the movement. In 1910 the fortunes of the T'ung-meng Hui were at their lowest ebb. It was at this juncture that Wang moved to restore hope and spirit to the revolutionary cause.

In the February 1, 1910, issue of the then clandestinely published *Min-pao*, Wang wrote an article reflecting the strain of anarchism that was prevalent among Japanese radicals at the time. In the article he advocated assassination as a means of sparking the overthrow of the Empire. Bent on putting into practice what he preached, Wang slipped into China incognito, bombs and the *Min-pao* sewed into his clothing, made his way to Peking, and drew up plans to assassinate Prince Ch'ün, regent for the four-year-old Emperor. Once again, however, bad luck foiled the revolutionaries' plans. Police sleuths discovered the bomb Wang had planted under a bridge over which the Prince's carriage was expected to pass, and within a few days Wang was apprehended, clapped in chains, and sentenced to death. Adversity was never more useful, as it turned out, for Wang was denied the martyrdom—torture followed by beheading—that he had every reason to expect for attempting to murder a royal relative; instead, the twenty-seven-year-old youth, unknown except to a hard-pressed handful of émigré anarchists and republicans, was suddenly catapulted to the status of an authentic national hero.

Wang's death sentence was commuted to life imprisonment for reasons that are still uncertain. The intended target's son, the Hsüan-t'ung Emperor, later wrote that Japanese intervention was instrumental in the regime's turnaround.[5] Another explanation, one that rings truer, has it that Manchu authorities, well aware of the weakness of the monarchy, considered it prudent to placate the revolutionaries. Still another explanation holds the Empress became enamored with the handsome youth and begged for clemency. Whether true or not this last explanation gained wide and durable credence: John Gunther cited it in *Inside Asia* twenty-nine years later.[6] It is undeniable that Wang's engaging personality was matched by an extraordinarily handsome face, as later photographs of him reveal. Few who have written of Wang from personal acquaintanceship fail to mention the strikingly delicate, smooth features of a man who still appeared boyish in his fifties. "When I met Wang Ching-wei, I gasped," wrote Gunther. "He is fifty-three; he looks twenty-eight, an extraordinarily handsome man.... He might almost be a schoolboy." To his detractors, like the tough Red Army general Chu Teh, he was as effeminate as a female impersonator in an old Peking opera.[7] To his admirers, however, and to those who knew him only in romantic legend, he was attractive enough to have beguiled the Manchu dowager.

Wang contributed to his own immortalizing process with poems and utterances about selfless sacrifice that could not fail to impress the Chinese, a people whose literature and theater are full of eye-moistening accounts of knights-errant ready to undertake impossible causes to rectify injustice with no thought of the personal consequences. Wang was one of two men arrested and sentenced to death for the attempted assassination. The other, Huang Fu-sheng was, like Wang, eventually freed from prison, and though he achieved a modest eminence in the Kuomintang in later years, his part in the act brought him nothing like the fame Wang earned—doubtless in good part because Huang's chief claim to fame was a simple knowledge of chemistry, which enabled him to construct a bomb. Wang's talents were more subtle and universal: the souls of his countrymen were stirred when they later read his soul-searching prison poetry and heard of his confession to his captors.* Pointing to

---

* The most famous of Wang's prison verses went as follows: "Among the crowds in Yen [Peking] I chant / Entering the prison with peace of mind / To die by the sword, what rapture / A fate truly worthy of this young head!"

articles he had written in *Min-pao*, Wang said: "These articles were written in ink; I wanted to translate them into blood."[8]

On October 10, 1911, a small uprising of soldier-rebels in Wuchang signaled the beginning of the end of Imperial China. Wang was released from prison the following month and immediately plunged into political activities. Indicative of the eminence of the twenty-eight-year-old Wang, he was soon engaged in a series of private discussions with the most powerful man in China, Yüan Shih-k'ai. Yüan's power rested in his control of China's only effective modern army, the Peiyang Army, for years the bulwark of the Empire's military strength. Yüan eventually made a superficial and transitory conversion from monarchism to republicanism, and when the Republic was inaugurated on January 1, 1912, he became the first Premier.

Wang declined that post and several others he was offered and, instead, withdrew from political activity, an action that further heightened his reputation.* There are few Confucian saints more honored than those idealists who eschew political office in order to preserve their own incorruptibility. Wang's motives, however, did not spring from Confucianism but from a commitment to the principles of the Chin-te Hui (Society to Advance Morality), which he helped found in 1912. An anarchist-inspired movement, the Chin-te Hui had no officers and encouraged its membership to accept no official governmental appointments. Beyond its anarchist roots, however, there was a profound reformist sense alive in the Chin-te Hui. There was an awareness, uncommon among Chinese revolutionaries of the day, that political revolution was meaningless without accompanying social reform. The corruption of the Manchu dynasty, the Society argued, did not stem so much from its political form as from the corruption of the whole of Chinese society. Members of the Chin-te Hui had to promise to avoid the three worst forms of corruption in the old China—prostitution, gambling, and the concubine system—in an effort to build a morality appropriate to the new China.[9]

One evidence of Wang's personal liberation from the ways of the old China was his marriage. Contrary to traditional Chinese practice he chose his own wife—Ch'en Pi-chün, the daughter of a prosperous merchant family from the Straits Settlement city of Penang. In 1908, when Wang and Sun were in Malaya, Ch'en Pi-chün, then still in her teens,

---

* Scalapino and Yu, p. 38, citing *Min-li pao*. According to James Shirley (p. 59), Wang's forbearance, with its Confucian "overtones of selflessness [and] disinterested refusal to be corrupted by office," earned him the sobriquet "The Saint" in a play about the Revolution of 1911.

became attracted to both the revolutionary and his cause, and without her father's permission decided to accompany Wang back to Japan. She was far from simply an admirer of the young revolutionary; she was an active accomplice as well. When Wang undertook his assassination mission to Peking in 1910, Ch'en Pi-chün accompanied and assisted him. From that time until her death in a Communist prison cell in 1959, she consistently and ardently defended every cause Wang Ching-wei espoused. She was by all accounts an extraordinarily assertive woman who did not shrink from political controversy and from taking unpopular stands. She pursued a public career of her own and by the 1930's was serving as a member of the Central Supervisory Committee of the Kuomintang. Wang relied on her for advice and counsel. As he later explained to a Japanese colleague: "She is my wife, but she is also my old revolutionary comrade, and for that reason I don't find it easy to make important decisions without considering her views."[10]

Following their marriage in 1912 Wang and his wife traveled to France, where they remained for the next five years, a period of chaos, treachery, and backsliding for the republican cause. While China moved into the turbulent era of the warlords, Wang enjoyed a period of comparative detachment from politics. A contemplative, poetic strain in his personality emerged in the leisurely interlude. Paradoxically, the organizer of a Chin-te Hui attuned to the reform needs of modern China, joined the Nan-she (Southern Society), a group of poets who sought literary inspiration in poetry of the T'ang period. Perhaps the paradox is more evident to Western than Chinese minds, for Mao Tse-tung, another revolutionist with more than a little competence as a poet, also draws on the styles of the classicists. The founder and leader of the Nan-she, Liu Ya-tzu, was a close personal friend of Mao.

Returning to China in 1917, Wang once again joined Sun and plunged into the task of strengthening the Kuomintang. Strengthening the Kuomintang proved to mean alliance with the fledgling Chinese Communist Party and reliance on aid from the only foreign power that demonstrated sympathy for Sun, the Soviet Union. The alliance of the Soviet Union, the Chinese Communists, and the Kuomintang was based less on shared goals and beliefs than on hatred of common foes, the Chinese warlords and Western imperialists. There was always an element of cynicism in the alliance, a suspicion that one of the parties was using another. Each of the parties was alert to the dangers to its own integrity and yet confident that it could avoid being victimized. Whatever the risks for the Kuomintang, its own weakness in 1923 necessitated the alliance. Russian rifles, a corps of Soviet advisers, the organizational and propaganda skills of Communists like Chou En-lai—these made the difference between the old and the new Kuomintang. The one was loosely united and directed, and lacked a power base of its own. The other—the Party that was beginning to take shape at the time of Sun's death—was moving toward discipline and power.

Inevitably, however, the united-front tactics of the 1920's deepened the tendency toward factionalism in the Kuomintang. Among its members, there were varying degrees of apprehension about the wisdom of cooperating with the new Communist allies. There were also varying views on the priorities of the revolution: whether to proceed with the task of reunifying the country or to embark on social reform programs. And if social reform, how much? And how much anti-imperialism? And directed at which nations? In addition to such ideological divisions, there was China's historic tendency toward factionalism based on regional or personal loyalties. Though the paramount position of the Wang Ching-wei faction was confirmed by the Second National Congress of the Kuomintang in January 1926, it was challenged by the rival faction of Chiang Kai-shek a short three months later.

There was no protracted struggle for power. In the space of a few hours on March 20, 1926, Wang's briefly held authority dissolved.[11] Until that day Wang had been the leader of both the Party and the Government and, as Chief of the Military Council, had represented civilian control over the military establishment. The events of the day, however, demonstrated that his lack of a real base of military power was decisive. The arbiter of the factional struggle within the Kuomintang proved to be the cadets of the military academy located on Whampoa Island, just outside of Canton. The Commander of the academy (and of the First Army) was Chiang Kai-shek. Before dawn on the morning of March 20, without consulting Wang Ching-wei, Chiang sent his detachments fanning out over Canton, to arrest the Communist commissars attached to various military units, confine Soviet advisers to their quarters, and disarm the Communist "strike committee" that had led an effective anti-foreign boycott in the city for the past nine months. Many of the details about Chiang's coup are still clouded in mystery. His enemies point to it as the first of a series of treacherous attacks on his revolutionary allies and the first of a series of sellouts to the imperialists. As one of them wrote of Chiang:

> He became what Karl Marx, referring to Louis Napoleon, once called "a man who did not decide at night and act during the day but decided during the day and acted at night." ... It was time, in

short, to cut the political wages of the Communists, to increase the political profits of the bourgeoisie, and to place at the latter's disposal the immense and still untapped capital reserves of the mass movement.[12]

Looking back on the event some thirty years later, Chiang defended the coup on the grounds that he "suspected at the time that the Communists were about to stage a revolt."[13] In other words, according to him the coup was a countercoup. The preponderance of scholarly research supports his suspicion that some kind of conspiracy was afoot and that his personal safety might well have been at stake. Chiang holds that the political situation in Canton at the time was incredibly complicated and has darkly hinted that the whole story of the Canton coup will not be known until after his death. Though he has never publicly blamed Wang for causing the incident, there is little doubt, both because of Wang's close ties with the Communists and because of the naked struggle for power between Wang and Chiang, that Wang was one of the intended targets and the chief victim of the coup. Chiang was quick to soothe the ruffled feelings of the Soviet advisers and the Chinese Communists, whose support was vital to the success of the Northern Expedition he was anxious to launch. But Wang, powerless and angered, resigned his official posts and soon went into Parisian exile for the second time in his career. For less than a year Wang had been in at least titular command of the Revolution. After March 20, 1926, the initiative in that Revolution began to slip into the hands of Chiang. It took him from 1926 to 1928 to complete the Northern Expedition and consolidate his control over Government, Party, and military forces. During the remainder of Wang's life, he often challenged but never seriously threatened the hegemony Chiang developed in those two years.

At the beginning of 1926 few could have guessed that Wang's position in the Revolution would be so swiftly jeopardized by Chiang, whose name had not yet earned a place in the *China Yearbook*. Like Wang, Chiang had gone to Japan and joined the T'ung-meng Hui in the last decade of Manchu rule. But while the expansive, brilliant Wang was giving program and passion to the revolutionary movement, Chiang was an obscure private second class studying in a Japanese military academy. The withdrawn, brittle officer candidate enjoyed little popularity among his fellow students. Much less did he enjoy the talents and personality to sway a revolutionary cause. Chiang was diligent or plodding, depending on how one chooses to characterize the man who endures the humiliating drudgery of barracks life in order to learn the latest that artillery science can offer and advance through the ranks. Wang was either inspirational or flamboyant, depending on how one chooses to assess the role he played in the Revolution of 1911. But the fact remains that while Wang was earning a reputation as hero and leader of the Revolution, Private Second Class Chiang was in Hokkaido "scrubbing down the horses" of the Thirteenth Field Regiment.[14]

In terms of closeness to the prestigious Sun Yat-sen, the difference between Wang and Chiang was also striking. By the time Sun died in 1925 Wang could claim two decades of association with the venerated Father of the Revolution. Despite Wang's years abroad and some clashes over policy with Sun, the names of the two were almost indissolubly linked in the minds of their countrymen. It was only natural that as Sun hovered between life and death in Peking, Wang should be at his bedside, and that when the time came for a political last testament to be composed, Wang should assume the task on behalf of the stricken leader. Thus, it was Wang who finally interpreted Sun for posterity and drafted the testament to which Sun assented with his last feeble signature.[15] For many, Wang's role in the deathbed drama of Sun was yet another compelling indication of Wang's worthiness to inherit the mantle of power.

And yet all of this counted for naught when balanced against the military power that persistence and maneuver had earned for Chiang. Unless one is prepared to bestow on Wang a Gandhian indifference to personal ambition and honor, it is impossible not to recognize that his enduring rancor at his eclipse in the decade after 1926 played an important role in his decision to collaborate with Japan in 1938. The task we face in later chapters is to examine the other reasons for that collaboration.

In late 1928, with the country nominally unified, the capital of China was established in Nanking. For the next decade, until Japan's full-scale attack on China in 1937, the task of reshaping Chinese society while warding off the threat from Communists within and imperial powers without was in the hands of the Nanking Government and the Kuomintang party dictatorship under Chiang Kai-shek. To delve very deeply into the history of that decade would exceed the scope of this study, but some observations are plainly in order.

The first is that Chiang's military power after 1928 was challenged from so many quarters that the Generalissimo—as the foreign press came to call him—could ill afford open hostility to all adversaries. Compromise and coalition were a hallmark of the Nanking decade. In addition, Chiang was fully aware of his deficiencies as a political leader. As one writer has commented, Chiang was "by nature introverted . . . not an accomplished orator or propagandist. He works best behind closed doors. He knows how to manipulate the politicians, but not how to move about in a crowd; how to coerce, but not how to convince, people."[16] Wang's strengths complemented the Generalissimo's weaknesses, as Hollington K. Tong, Chiang's official biographer, has pointed out: "Chiang had always been in need of a competent political colleague to keep him in touch with Party affairs and to expound the policy of the National Government to the Chinese public as well as to the outer world. Wang Ching-wei possessed this rare ability."[17]

As a result, Wang was sometimes in and sometimes out of the National Government during the Nanking decade. From 1928 to 1931, both from outside China in self-imposed exile and from inside the country, Wang strenuously opposed the growth of Chiang's power. In 1930, for example, he allied himself with Feng Yü-hsiang and Yen Hsi-shan, two northern warlords who were holding out against the Kuomintang's efforts to eradicate their private armies and gain control over their territorial bases. It was the kind of expedient alliance that Sun himself had more than once entered, but it proved futile. Nanking worked out its own warlord alliance with the Manchurian "Young Marshal," Chang Hsüeh-liang, and after some of the bloodiest fighting of the entire warlord era, the Wang-Feng-Yen coalition was defeated. Wang was expelled—"permanently"—from the Kuomintang and appeared to face a bleak future. The following year, however, brought new opportunity, this time in the south of China.

The 1931 challenge to Nanking was precipitated by the arrest of Sun's oldest and closest confidant and fellow Cantonese, Hu Han-min. Leading Kuomintang figures responded by calling for the impeachment of Chiang Kai-shek, resigning their posts in Nanking, and moving to Canton. Wang joined the dissidents, who possessed formidable muscle because of the participation of the powerful Cantonese warlord, Chang Fa-k'uei. Typical of the interminable shuffling and reshuffling of alliances in the period, Gen. Li Tsung-jen, who but two years earlier had been engaged in bitter warfare with Chang, joined the Canton rebels. Soon after, in May 1932, the new anti-Chiang allies called for the creation of a separatist National Government. Chiang Kai-shek, now surrounded by a scattering of enemies in North China and a solid coalition of enemies in the south, wisely chose to avoid the kind of showdown that had been militarily expedient a year earlier. Throughout the summer of 1931 an uneasy truce between the Canton separatists and Nanking prevailed. Wang, as usual, provided the phrasemaking flourishes that expressed the mood of many. "Unification through reconstruction" must replace the futile and destructive civil wars, he said. To that end, he announced his willingness to cooperate with Chiang.[18]

On September 18, 1931, the parties to the feud were given a compelling reason to hasten their reconciliation. On that day an explosion wrecked a section of track on the Japanese-owned South Manchurian Railway and, on the pretext that Chinese troops were trying to blow up the railway, Japanese soldiers began to fan out over all of the area known to the Chinese as the Three Eastern Provinces. The entire area was detached from China within a few months and in early 1932 was converted into the puppet state of Manchukuo. The Japanese action forced the feuding factions to set aside their differences in the interest of national security, and in January 1932 Wang assumed the office of President of the Executive Yüan.* The breach that had been widening between Chiang and Wang for nearly six years began to close.

For the next four years, until late 1935, the Generalissimo was preoccupied with a series of Extermination Campaigns to eradicate the pockets of Communist "bandits" that now loomed as a more immediate threat to national unity than the warlords. This left Wang free to play a major role in shaping the nonmilitary programs the Government initiated in those years. Throughout his career and especially in the watershed year of 1927 Wang was classified as a leftist, the leader of the Left Kuomintang. As slippery as such terms are, they were not without some substance. Wang, it is true, did not shrink from alliances with warlord generals—but then expediency had dictated that course of action to Comintern agents and Chiang Kai-shek alike. By and large Wang earned his Left Kuomintang reputation from his persistent reliance on aid from the Soviet Union. Eventually that earned him criticism as a "puppet" of Stalin. The fact is Wang was simply adhering to the Sunist proposition that reliance on one foreign power was a necessary evil to deliver China from the control of other foreign powers. When it became evident that Stalin intended to manipulate the Revolution for goals Wang could not abide, he swiftly severed ties with Moscow. The incident that precipitated the break was the famous disclosure of Stalin's telegram of June 1, 1927, by the Comintern representative M. N. Roy. Through Roy's indiscretion Wang learned of Stalin's orders for a pro-

---

* In law, the Executive Yüan was the highest executive organ in the National Government, but in terms of actual power it was overshadowed by various military agencies that ran parallel to the civil government. The highest military authority was the Military Affairs Commission, which was headed by Chiang Kai-shek from 1932 to 1946.

gram of land confiscation, the destruction of "unreliable generals," and the creation of an army of workers and peasants. Contrary to Roy's assumptions, Wang flatly refused to cooperate with Stalin's wishes and, instead, adopted a vigorously anti-Communist stance that endured to the end of his life.

It cannot be emphasized enough that, in trying to understand either Sun Yat-sen or his disciple Wang, one is in conceptually arid terrain where oases of consistency are seldom encountered. Theory changed from year to year and often seemed to have little relevance to practice. However, if class struggle and more specifically the use of peasant violence to dispossess rich landlords are regarded as the criteria for separating reform leftists from radical leftists, then Wang was clearly a reformer, not a radical. He and many of his chosen colleagues—as opposed to his allies of expediency—were by almost any definition of the day leftist. For example, Ch'en Kung-po, probably Wang's closest confidant and the chief theoretician of Wang's Reorganization Faction,* had helped found the Chinese Communist Party in 1921, and in 1925 had lent a militant hand to the boycotts and strikes that devastated British economic interests in the south of China for nearly a year. The members of the Reorganization Faction shared a genuine concern about the need for drastic social and economic change in China; but they were unwilling to unleash the peasantry to accomplish this aim—and, indeed, like all but a few in China, were unaware of the full extent of the furious energy that lay stored up in the peasantry.

When Wang returned to government office in 1932 many members of his Reorganization Faction were also allocated important posts. Ch'en Kung-po became Minister of Industry, and Ku Meng-yü, an economist and prominent figure in the May Fourth Movement, took command of the Railway Ministry and began the process of "reconstruction" Wang had called for. Thanks to Wang's reputation for incorruptibility, the scholarly background of many of the members of the Reorganization Faction, and a general feeling that the disastrous inertia of the past was at last passing from China, the Nanking Government began to enjoy an interlude of good press and relatively good relations with the Chinese intellectual community. Though Wang took an active role in the direction of domestic reconstruction projects, we must restrict our attention here to another area of his responsibility during the Nanking

* The Reorganization Faction (Kaitsu-p'ai) was an abbreviated version of the Association for the Reorganization of the Kuomintang (Kuomintang Kai-tsu T'ung-shih Hui).

decade, namely foreign relations, which for China in the early 1930's meant preeminently relations with Japan.

Sino-Japanese relations, tense and often on the edge of crisis in the 1920's, entered a fourteen-year era of almost unrelieved agony with the attack of Japan's Kwantung Army on Manchuria in September 1931. A wave of anti-Japanese resentment spread across China. Patriotic student organizations sprang up, intent on mobilizing the nation's resentment and intensifying it to the point where the Nanking Government would have to declare a policy of all-out resistance. Chinese merchants banded together to boycott the purchase, sale, and transportation of Japanese goods; those that failed to comply faced harassment by militant students. Chinese managers of Japanese firms resigned their positions. Thousands of Japanese businessmen, residents, and diplomats faced "No Japanese Allowed" signs and abusive treatment throughout China. The public clamor for resistance, however, did not slow down the headlong retreat of the armies of the Young Marshal, Chang Hsüeh-liang. By the end of the year the troops of the Kwantung Army had almost finished their fighting, and the political-minded colonels could turn their attention to the creation of a client state. The humiliating defeat of Chang's numerically superior forces delivered a stinging blow to Chinese pride, but the responsibility did not belong to the Young Marshal alone. The thirty-three-year-old Chang, a Peking socialite addicted to narcotics and to the company of glamorous ladies (including screen actress "Butterfly" Wu and Edda Ciano, the daughter of Benito Mussolini), pulled his forces south of the Great Wall on orders from Chiang Kai-shek. China would not fight, said Chiang, but would instead entrust its case to the League of Nations.

The Generalissimo explained, in one of the edifying lectures he regularly delivered on Monday mornings to the cadets of the Central Military Academy, that if his popularity were the only issue,

> it would be quite easy—I would only have to declare war against Japan. Then the whole nation would praise me and extol me to the skies. Then why do I not do so? Why, on the contrary, am I suspected of "nonresistance"? I do not fear death, but I cannot let the life of the country be lost, nor leave the nation at stake. I must think in terms of the future. I cannot sacrifice China for the sake of my personal reputation.[19]

The reason the "life of the country" was in danger of being lost, Chiang firmly believed, was communism. For Chiang the Communists were not merely political or military foes, but monsters who "took delight in killing by torture. . . . They made it a point to instigate conflicts among family members and among different families in the same village. They especially encouraged moral laxity among young people. In short, they declared war on Chinese family life and ethical concepts in general."[20] It was not that he was unmindful of the menace Japan represented, Chiang often repeated. "I give you my word that within three years we shall have beaten the Japanese to their knees. Believe me, go back to your schools and study hard," he instructed a delegation of angry students.[21] But it was useless to exhaust China's limited military resources in a struggle against Japan only to have the Communist forces take advantage of Nanking's diversion. For this reason, in Chiang's scale of priorities, internal pacification had to precede resistance to external aggression. Internal pacification, Chiang notes, was "proceeding satisfactorily" when Japan "came to the timely rescue" of the beleaguered Communists in September 1931.[22] As a result, some of Nanking's armies had to be diverted; but the main forces continued to be deployed in the Third Extermination Campaign against the pockets of Communist "bandits" in the mountains.

Anti-Japanese hostility reached a new peak of intensity on January 28, 1932, coincidentally the day on which Wang Ching-wei became President of the Executive Yüan. On that day tension over anti-Japanese boycotts in Shanghai erupted into open hostility when Japanese marines crossed into the suburb of Chapei and encountered resistance from the Nineteenth Route Army, which was quartered nearby. Shots were exchanged and, to the horror of the world, the Japanese responded by ordering an aerial bombardment to "punish" the Chinese forces. When the unchastised defenders refused to capitulate, Japanese warships were called into action, and additional troops were disembarked. Civilian refugee camps were attacked, atrocities were committed against Chinese, and foreigners were humiliated in what the world did not yet realize was a mere foreshadowing of events five years distant.

For thirty-four days the Nineteenth Route Army resisted the Japanese in fierce fighting that took place in crooked streets, in burned-out factories, and, finally, as the inevitable retreat occurred, in the suburbs. When it was over, the comic-opera image of the Chinese soldier had been put to rest. Overnight, the field commander of the Nineteenth Route Army, Gen. Ts'ai T'ing-k'ai, became a national, even an international hero, as world opinion lined up on the side of Chinese underdogs. Astonished Japanese commanders, who had estimated that one regiment would do the job, ended up throwing several divisions into the fracas. "The Nineteenth Route Army . . . redeemed China from shame, from dishonor," recalls authoress Han Suyin. "Even today, my throat gets stuck, my eyes prick up when the emotion of those days wells up from me."[23] Student groups rallied to the support of the Nineteenth, traveling from town to town in the neighborhood of Shanghai, "shouting slogans, distributing leaflets, haranguing streetcorner crowds, presenting plays, glorifying the heroic story of the Nineteenth, and rousing the people against Japan."[24] Volunteers, most of them students, joined the Nineteenth, and their spirited patriotism prompted one foreigner to observe: "Something new was born in the life of the nation when that army of ill-equipped fighters, with their cloth shoes and soft caps, stood against one of the best equipped armies in the world. . . . China can hold her head with pride among the nations that proudly point to their valiant sons who died bravely in the defense of their soil."[25]

The Nanking Government, however, was not in harmony with the pulse of the nation. While defense contributions poured into Nanking from individual Chinese and foreigners, the Government denied supplies and ammunition to the forces of General Ts'ai. His resistance was in violation of orders from Nanking, and when he was finally forced to withdraw beyond the line insisted on by a Japanese ultimatum, Nanking and Tokyo began to work out a settlement of the incident. The May 1932 "Peace Agreement" found Nanking assenting to the creation of a twenty-kilometer demilitarized zone around Shanghai in which Chinese troops would be prohibited. The Nanking Government was satisfied that, though the agreement was an affront to Chinese sovereignty, it would prevent Japan from launching any further attacks against the lower Yangtze area. More important, valuable time was won in the struggle against the Communists. As soon as accord with Japan had been reached, Chiang ordered a Fourth Extermination Campaign against the Reds.

The year 1933 brought new and more serious incursions by Japan. In January her troops captured the strategic Shanhaikwan corridor, the "Mountain and Sea Pass" between the easternmost end of the Great Wall and the Gulf of Chihli that gave access to the plains of North China. While troops of the so-called Tientsin garrison, stationed in North China since the Boxer Protocol to protect Japanese interests, maneuvered—both militarily and politically—in the North China provinces of Hopei and Chahar, the Kwantung Army commenced operations in Jehol province to the north of the Great Wall. The operations in Hopei and Chahar were complex, the beginning of a determined effort to create an autonomous North China. The operations in sparsely populated, mountainous Jehol were swiftly and successfully completed. The Chairman of the province, T'ang Yü-lin, "a warlord of the old type, fat with the profits of widespread opium cultivation in his province and patently not the stuff of which heroes are made," was instructed by Nanking to resist.[26] Neither troops nor planes were sent to assist him, however, and in ten days Japan conquered the entire province; the capital city of Chengteh fell to a force of 128 Japanese soldiers!

Once again came the call for resistance from outraged citizens. Soong Ch'ing-ling, widow of Sun Yat-sen, lashed out at the "opium general T'ang who opened the gate to let the Japanese troops enter China," but she reserved her sharpest attack for her brother-in-law, the Generalissimo: "Who is responsible for this traitorous activity? It is Chiang Kai-shek. Why? Chiang uses his power to fight the Chinese people, and appoints traitorous generals whom he refuses to dismiss. Also he is unwilling to arm the people, or to organize guerrillas to fight Japanese imperialism."[27]

Madame Sun accompanied her protests with appeals for an end to the Extermination Campaigns and incorporation of the Red guerrillas into a resistance effort. It was essentially a plea for national unity. Chiang himself constantly talked about the need for national unity. It was his dedication to the ideal of a harmonious social order, in fact, that inspired his inflexible determination to crush the Communists first as the most immediate threat to China's order. And so the full force of the modern military machine that Chiang was creating with the help of German advisers continued to be directed against the Communists. Given this weak response to Japanese incursions, it was only natural that Japan pressed for a settlement of the 1933 conflict on her own terms. The settlement came in May, when a "local" truce was signed at Tangku. The local character of the truce signified the weakness of the Nanking Government in the provinces in question and its desire to avoid the stigma of putting its own name to the humiliating agreement. Nanking exercised little more than titular control over the area in and around Peiping, which was still effectively under the rule of warlords. In May Chiang named his trusted friend and adviser Huang Fu Chairman of the Peiping Political Affairs Council, which had nominal jurisdiction over the provinces Japan sought to break away from the rest of China. It was Huang who signed the Tangku Truce, which in effect became the charter for the next four years of Japanese efforts to autonomize North China.

The most important provision of the truce provided for the creation of a demilitarized zone, thirty to forty miles wide, running from the

Great Wall south to the Peiping-Tientsin corridor. No Chinese troops were to be permitted in this zone. A Chinese police force was assigned the task of "maintaining peace," but secret clauses in the agreement specified that the police would have to be friendly to Japan. The truce further gave Japan control over the Shanhaikwan. It made no change in the status of the Boxer Protocol force—the Tientsin garrison—meaning that Japanese troops could remain in certain areas of a demilitarized zone forbidden to Chinese troops. The military leverage Japan gained in the truce afforded her increased political and economic leverage over local administrations and warlords in North China. As she moved to exploit that leverage to the fullest in the following years, Chinese criticism of the weakness of the Nanking Government grew apace.

That criticism was directed more and more at Wang Ching-wei. Wang was receiving medical treatment in France when the Jehol and North China crises erupted but returned in March 1933 and was soon appointed Foreign Minister, a post he held concurrently with the Presidency of the Executive Yüan for the next two-and-a-half years. There is little reason to doubt that Chiang and Wang were in complete accord about the necessity—the regrettable necessity—of Nanking's assent to the terms of the Tangku Truce. Wang's close friend Ch'en Kung-po, disturbed that Wang was receiving the lion's share of the criticism for defending the "weak" truce, suggested to Wang that he remind his critics of Chiang's approval of the arrangement. Wang refused, saying that as President of the Executive Yüan he had to accept full responsibility for the agreement. Wang's eulogy of Huang Fu, who died two years after signing the truce, contains a clear statement of the dilemma facing China in the early 1930's. He conceded that the truce had been certain to demoralize the people and generate "misunderstandings" between them and the government. But this danger had been carefully considered, and it had been decided that "empty words and false pride are useless." China was simply too weak militarily to defend the north against Japan, and if the north fell the "provinces south of the Yellow River would also be threatened." "Therefore," said Wang, "we decided to find a means of stopping the war temporarily." By signing the truce China could gain time,

> first, to unite the country politically and economically so as to form a united front against outside forces; second, to eliminate the Red bandits who have disturbed the safety of the interior and checked the armed forces from moving to the front . . .; and third, to strive diligently to reconstruct our material resources so as to strengthen and enlarge our capacity for a war of resistance.[28]

From his entrance into the Government at the time of the Shanghai Incident in 1932 on, the task of explaining and apologizing for the weak defense policy fell to the articulate and persuasive Wang. He quickly coined the slogan "resistance *and* negotiation" (*i-mien ti-k'ang i-mien chiao-she*) to summarize his position and to disarm critics who talked about the Government's policy of nonresistance. "Reconstruction *and* negotiation" was to join "unification through reconstruction" as enduring shibboleth in the Wang vocabulary. The slogan was not an empty cliché for Wang: in the battles for both Shanghai and Manchuria, he had advocated resistance and had taken the lead in cashiering generals (like the Young Marshal) who did not resist. But in both cases, when it became clear to him that resistance was futile—given the limited defense resources and the overriding priority set on the Extermination Campaigns—Wang turned to negotiations to salvage what he could of a desperate situation. Willingness to negotiate with the Japanese, he constantly explained to his countrymen, did not imply that China would someday acknowledge Japanese or Manchukuoan sovereignty in the Four Northeastern Provinces.* China would never recognize the fruits of Japanese aggression on Chinese territory, Wang promised. "China will never give up an inch of her land, and will never sign treaties derogatory to national honor, impairing national sovereignty, and violating territorial and administrative integrity, under whatever duress," he wrote in 1934. Nor, he said, did truce mean surrender. But it would give the nation time to achieve a united front (which then meant eradication rather than incorporation of the Communists). "The moment a united domestic front is achieved," Wang assured his readers, "China with her large population and extensive territory will be able to defend herself against Japan, however wealthy and militarily powerful the latter may be."[29]

In the meantime, however, China must ignore those who shouted about declaring war and "storming Tokyo." "Japan is a great naval Power. Do we possess enough naval strength to enable us to storm Tokyo?" Wang asked.

> At present our armaments compare to those of the Japanese like arrows to machine-guns, and if we should rashly declare war on Japan, we would experience a repetition of the disastrous Boxer Rebellion. . . . Japan can mobilize at short notice 2,500,000 troops

* Liaoning, Kirin, Heilungkiang, and Jehol, the provinces Japan invaded in 1931–33, which were incorporated into the puppet state of Manchukuo. The Chinese avoided the use of the name Manchukuo.

and reserves, and by the sea route she can transport her forces to China in two days, while it takes half a month for our troops to move from north to south because of lack of transportation and communication facilities.[30]

But despite China's critical predicament, there was no need for alarming talk about subjugation and defeat, Wang maintained. China was too big. The Japanese might be able to attack a few places, but they "will certainly be unable to extend their lines throughout the whole of our country. While our military forces may suffer temporary reverses, there is no awakened nation in the world which can be permanently subdued. So long as we persist in our preparations for self-defense, a time will inevitably come when the invaders will be exhausted, and the Powers will awaken to their obligations to the cause of Peace."[31]

In short, Wang pleaded for realism rather than wishful thinking, patience rather than rashness. Like Chiang, he appealed to history and mythology to buttress his arguments. Aesop's fable of the hare and the tortoise was frequently commended to audiences by the Generalissimo to convey his confidence that the Chinese tortoise would win the race with the Japanese hare. For his part, Wang liked to cite the precedent of the last years of the Ming dynasty, when the Ministers of State were prevented from shaping national policy in a responsible manner because of "popular clamor." "The result," Wang warned, "was the downfall of the Dynasty, and with the collapse of the Ming Empire died also all true patriots." As for the people who had clamored for war, they were forced to "accommodate themselves to the new regime." For Wang the lesson was clear. In measured antithetical phrases, he drove home the point that "high-sounding words are anathema. Pride kills victory; modesty averts defeat. We know full well that we cannot with advantage undertake offensive operations; but equally, we know that on the defensive we can resist with a fair measure of success."[32]

The time bought by the Tangku Truce began to produce results. Toward the end of 1934 Chiang's mounting pressure on the Communists forced them to abandon their Kiangsi base and commence the epic 6,000-mile Long March to safer territory around Yenan in the remote northwest of China. As Chiang concentrated on military affairs Wang became more and more preoccupied with the task of asserting and maintaining what control he could over the constantly deteriorating situation in North China. His opposite in much of the negotiations was Shigemitsu Mamoru, Minister to China and later Vice Minister of Foreign Affairs.

It was undoubtedly because of Shigemitsu's relatively conciliatory attitude toward China that Wang placed as much confidence as he did in the efficacy of diplomacy. The astute Shigemitsu would have diverted Chinese xenophobia from Japan to the Western imperial powers by assisting China to gain full, sovereign control over her maritime customs, her legal system, and her cities, including Shanghai, Tientsin, and other coastal areas where foreign concessions still existed. Though this almost certainly meant that Japan would have to abandon her own extraterritorial privileges in China and withdraw her forces from North China, Shigemitsu felt his country stood to gain much by such a policy of self-restraint. Instead of being a drain on Japanese resources, China, weak and in need of the kind of assistance a strong neighbor could offer, would inevitably become politically and economically dependent on Japan.

These incipient Pan-Asian notions constituted an appealing basis for possible Sino-Japanese understanding. The Shigemitsu policy was self-serving, to be sure, but what nation's diplomacy is not? And, of course, there were problems that were all but hopelessly irreconcilable. Manchukuo was perhaps the greatest of these; no important political or military figure in Japan, no matter how conciliatory to China, considered returning Manchukuo to Chinese sovereignty as an acceptable method of winning Chinese friendship. Still, from the Chinese point of view, a policy of Japanese self-denial in North China was a goal well worth the diplomatic effort. And as for Japanese assistance in bringing to an end the century of unequal treaty relationships with the Western powers—this was precisely the kind of interdependence Sun had in mind when he emphasized that, "without Japan, there would be no China; without China, there would be no Japan." Wang was fond of quoting that dictum to both Chinese and Japanese audiences to the end of his life.[33]

Shigemitsu's voice was not, however, the voice of the Imperial Army, which continued to think of China as an aggregation of warlord domains whose weakness and disunity invited exploitation. Few within the Japanese military hierarchy viewed the Kuomintang as the wave of the future, as a force capable of reversing the trend toward regional military separatism that had made China so vulnerable to pressure from Japan in recent years. The image of Chiang Kai-shek, then, was that of a mere warlord, stronger than most but, conveniently, weakest in the very part of China where Japan's greatest strategic interests were centered—North China. In 1931 the Japanese military moved into Manchuria in order to create a buffer against Soviet expansion; now, in 1934, the Imperial Army concluded that the buffer needed a buffer and, consequently, rejected the axioms of Shigemitsu. On December 7, 1934, in an important meeting of the Inner Cabinet,* the Army's opinion emerged triumphant, and it became the official position of Japan that the "principles of the National Government of China were fundamentally antagonistic to the China policies of Japan." Specifically with regard to North China, the Inner Cabinet decided that "Japan looked forward to a gradual reduction of the authority of the National Government in the political administration of North China."[34]

With the sanction of the highest decision-making body in the Imperial Government, the Army set about translating the decisions of December 7 into action. The on-the-scene work in North China was carried out by a trio of Army officers known for their skill at political intrigue. Using a variety of approaches, from cajolery to intimidation, they set the stage for the signing of agreements that obliterated not only the substance but also the symbols of National Government presence in much of North China. The highest ranking and best known was Maj. Gen. Doihara Kenji, who three years earlier had been responsible for resurrecting the pathetic Henry Pu-yi from obscurity and restoring him to a throne.

Doihara was building a reputation as the most political of Japan's political generals, and was developing an idée fixe on his own talents for manipulating tractable Chinese warlords. "As a person, he was a splendid gentleman," writes a Japanese contemporary. "But he never learned from the past and just went on repeating the same old anachronistic, corrupt operations."[35] Now, in 1935, Doihara's efforts were centered on the province of Chahar, which extended north and west from Peiping far into the Inner Mongolian steppes. The presence of Nationalist influence in Chahar could serve as an irritant to Japanese purposes in the nearby Peiping-Tientsin corridor; Nationalist troops could—and did—challenge the Japanese presence in newly acquired Jehol province, which shared a long common boundary with Chahar; and finally, Nationalist forces in Chahar were preventing the Kwantung Army from realizing still another of its imperialist ambitions, the creation of an autonomous federation of Inner Mongolian tribes in frontier provinces like Chahar and Suiyuan. In June 1935 Doihara signed an agreement with Gen. Ch'in Te-ch'un, a member of the Chahar provincial government who had been designated by the Generalissimo to nego-

---

* An arrangement used in the 1930's to bypass the more cumbersome meetings of the full Cabinet. Sometimes referred to as the Four Ministers' Conference (Shisō Kaigi), the four ministers being the Premier, the Foreign Minister, and the two service ministers. Occasionally the Four Ministers' Conference was expanded to a Five Ministers' Conference (Gosō Kaigi) through the addition of the Finance or Home Minister.

tiate with Doihara. Following the pattern of the Tangku Truce, the Ch'in-Doihara Agreement was a "local" agreement that allowed the Nanking Government to discount its importance while enjoying the temporary benefits that came from appeasement. It provided for the extension of the Tangku Truce line into Chahar province, thus resulting in the "demilitarization" of a broad stretch of the province. It also provided for the dismissal of officials offensive to Japan, restriction of Chinese immigration into the province, and dissolution of "anti-Japanese organs" (i.e., Kuomintang agencies of all kinds). In addition, Japan gained the right to send civil and military "advisers" to the provincial government; with their arrival in July, the plans for autonomizing Inner Mongolia began to move ahead.[36]

While General Ch'in was negotiating the Chahar settlement for Nanking, another emissary of the Generalissimo's was reconciling himself to the conclusion of an even more far-reaching agreement involving the metropolitan province of Hopei. This luckless envoy, doomed to become the target of student demonstrations and growing popular opposition to the Japanese schemes, was Ho Ying-ch'in, one of Chiang's most trusted military officers and from 1930 to 1944 the Minister of War. The secret agreement Ho signed with Lt. Gen. Umezu Yoshijirō, the Commander of the Tientsin garrison, provided for further withdrawals of Chinese troops from Hopei, the abolition of Kuomintang party organs, the dissolution of anti-Japanese secret societies in Hopei, and the prohibition of anti-Japanese activities throughout China.

As the terms of the secret Ho-Umezu Agreement became known to the public, the Nanking Government sought to ward off criticism by denying that any such understanding had been reached, but the evidence of its existence was too blatant to be concealed. As the Twenty-ninth Army withdrew south in accordance with the terms of the agreement, an atmosphere of despair and rage swept over North China. The loss of the Four Northeastern Provinces and the frontier province of Chahar had been humiliating, but it was a humiliation of an entirely different order than that involved in the new crisis. Fewer than two million people populated Chahar province, and a large percentage of them were not Han Chinese; about twenty-eight million lived in Hopei, for centuries the heartland of Chinese national life. Feeling themselves on the verge of being abandoned to an uncertain but undesired fate, the people of Hopei reacted with something approaching panic. Students of the great universities of Peiping, Tientsin, Yenching, and Tsinghua took to the streets, enraged (as an earlier generation had been in May of

1919) more with the venality and timidity of their own leaders than with the Japanese actions. Inevitably, their demonstrations prompted the Japanese to accuse the Chinese officials charged with carrying out the Ho-Umezu Agreement of acting in bad faith. Japanese demands of "prompt and vigorous action" to eliminate anti-Japanese activities caused Chinese soldiers and police to take even harsher measures against Chinese student demonstrators. As the spectacle of Chinese fighting Chinese and as reports of mass arrests, torture, and even murder of student demonstrators spread, the resentment of Government policy spread to the highest quarters of the Kuomintang itself. On August 7 the Central Political Council of the Central Executive Committee—the highest political organ in China—passed a resolution of no-confidence in the Foreign Minister, Wang Ching-wei. The following day Wang resigned.

The Generalissimo, however, was unwilling to accept the decision of the Party. He rushed back from his bandit-suppression activities, called a conference of important leaders in Lushan, and dispatched his close friend Chang Ch'ün to dissuade Wang from going through with his resignation. On August 22 Chiang assured the members of the Central Political Council that Wang had his "complete support" in the diplomatic line he was pursuing.[37] The next day the Council nullified its vote of no-confidence, and Wang withdrew his resignation. Satisfied that the appeasement policy would not be interrupted, Chiang returned to the front to complete the Fifth Extermination Campaign against a Communist force whose ranks had dwindled to a few thousand under the fire of Nationalist guns and the rigors of the Long March.

On November 1, 1935, the entire leadership of the Kuomintang assembled in Nanking for the convening of the Fifth National Congress. At 9:30 A.M., after the conclusion of the opening ceremonies, Wang and others were posing for photographers in front of Nanking's Ceremonial Hall. Suddenly, one of the photographers pulled a pistol out from behind his camera and fired three shots point-blank at Wang before being cut down by guards. The "photographer" turned out to be a newspaper reporter for the Ch'en Kuang News Agency who was enraged at the Wang appeasement policy. Because of the long-standing enmity between Chiang Kai-shek and Wang and because the Ch'en Kuang News Agency was said to be "connected" with the Generalissimo, Chiang was immediately suspected of being involved in the assassination attempt. Like so many other events related to the stormy Wang-Chiang rivalry, this one remains clouded. Wang himself never accused the Generalissimo of complicity, and given the convergence of views the two had recently achieved, it seems doubtful that Chiang had anything to do with the incident.*

Wang was critically injured in the attack. His wounds, complicated by old health problems, necessitated two surgical operations and a long period of recuperation. Even then he was not fully restored to health, for one of the bullets could not be removed and, as the unsuccessful surgeons predicted, later caused an infection and other complications that hastened his death in 1944.

Even more damaging to Wang's career than the assassin's bullets was the stigma he had unjustly earned as the architect of a policy of diplomatic appeasement. That the Kuomintang continued to support the diplomatic efforts Wang had begun is indicated by its election of Wang as Chairman of the Central Political Council shortly after the assassination attempt. And that Chiang continued to support that policy is indicated by his public statement of November 19, the tone of which was altogether forbearing and conciliatory toward Japan. The public reaction to the soft diplomatic policy, however, grew more and more hostile. In December 1935 the indignation of students in Peiping exploded in a series of demonstrations, organized and disciplined with unprecedented success, that asked the old question, "Why are we not fighting Japan?" The December demonstrations, it so happened, represented a turning point in the history of that question, for the demonstrations were staged with such dramatic force that it could no longer be ignored. Respected educators like Dean Hu Shih of Peiping University could no longer counsel his students to restrain themselves and "listen to the Government" without being booed off the platform.[38]

The Generalissimo was scarcely a man to be swayed by outbursts of public emotion—even if they were of patriotic inspiration. Even less was he moved by shouting student demonstrators who questioned his assertion that they could best serve China by trusting their leaders and returning to their studies. And still less was he inclined to look favorably on demands that threatened to breathe new life into his implacable foes, the Communists, whose extermination finally appeared to be nearing. Predictably, therefore, he pinned the label Communist on the December Ninth Movement (as the series of protests came to be called). As a result, the arrests of those who questioned Chiang's "internal pacification first" policy continued as before. But as the students gained their political voice and perfected their propaganda styles, the nation became

---

* Madame Wang, however, not only believed the Generalissimo was responsible for the assault on her husband but said so openly. Chin, *Wang cheng-ch'üan*, 2: 175.

acquainted (as it had not been until then) with the need for a "resistance first" policy. And as it did the name of Wang Ching-wei became more and more coupled with the invidious epithet *han-chien* (traitor). In December 1935 the Vice Minister of Foreign Affairs, T'ang Yu-jen, Wang's personal go-between in negotiations with the Japanese and long-time friend, was assassinated in Shanghai. In February 1936, when Wang set sail for a long period of recuperation in France, the prospect of returning to any kind of a political future must have seemed bleak indeed.

In the meantime Japanese ambitions for an autonomous North China congenial to Japan advanced another step. On November 24, 1935, in Tungchow, a city some twelve miles east of Peiping, once famous as the terminus of the Grand Canal, a declaration of independence, severing the northeastern third of the province of Hopei from the control of the Nanking Government, was issued. The new regime embraced twenty-two counties that had been demilitarized under the Tangku Truce and purged of Kuomintang influence under the Ho-Umezu Agreement. Within its boundaries were about five million people, the rich coal deposits at Kailan, and rail arteries leading from Manchukuo to the Peiping-Tientsin area. In proclaiming the new regime the founders announced their dissatisfaction with the Nanking Government's inability to rid China of communism. Thus, its name: East Hopei Autonomous Anti Communist Council. (The word Council was soon changed to Government.) For the next twenty-seven months, until the East Hopei regime was absorbed into a larger puppet regime, it represented the spearhead of the Imperial Army's drive to autonomize North China. When the Chairman of the Council, Yin Ju-keng, announced the establishment of the regime he made it clear that this was only the first step in the eventual amalgamation of China's five northern provinces into an autonomous government.* As with other such projects, the mainland commands of the Imperial Army had received vague, general sanction for their sponsorship of the autonomy movements. The Inner Cabinet decision of December 7, 1934, to weaken Kuomintang influence in North China had been reaffirmed just six weeks before the establishment of the East Hopei regime in terms broad enough to allow the Army's actions.

With the exception of a flag—the five-barred flag used in the early years of the Republican era—the East Hopei regime had few of the trappings of a government. Its headquarters was an ancient Confucian temple. Although no nation, including Japan, accorded it diplomatic

* The other provinces destined for inclusion were Shantung, Shansi, Chahar, and Suiyuan.

recognition, diplomatic affairs were placed under the control of Chairman Yin. Military affairs were likewise relegated to him. Military affairs meant the Pao-an Tui (Peace Preservation Corps), an overgrown militia recruited locally, trained by Japanese officers, and assigned to keep order. The Pao-an Tui had been serving Japanese interests throughout the Tangku Truce period. In the opening weeks of the new regime it was called on to prevent the contamination of East Hopei by the December Ninth Movement. The danger of relying on the loyalty of the Pao-an Tui became apparent in July 1937, when the Tungchow garrison rebelled and massacred about 250 Japanese and Korean residents of the city.

In addition to the obvious strategic importance of East Hopei, the area proved to be valuable as a means of putting economic pressure on the central government.[39] Smuggling operations on a vast scale had opened up in areas covered by the Tangku Truce, and now, under the benevolent eye of the East Hopei authorities, expanded enormously. Opium and other narcotics were transported into the area from Manchukuo and Chahar, where the cultivation of poppies was encouraged by Japanese authorities.[40] The trafficking was in the hands of Japanese and Korean *rōnin* (hoodlums), who became an offensive addition to the local scene after 1935.* Smuggling silver out of China through East Hopei reached such levels that it seriously undermined the efforts of the Nanking Government to stabilize its monetary system. In addition, in order to deny the Nanking Government the revenues it desperately needed and in order to bolster Japan's own sagging export market, Japanese authorities connived with the Tungchow authorities to look the other way as a veritable flood of goods funneled from Japan through East Hopei to markets in North China, untaxed and unregulated. When goods did pass through the customs barriers established by the East Hopei authorities, they were taxed at rates far below those charged by the China Maritime Customs.[41] Reliable statistics are difficult to obtain, but some indication of the scale of the smuggling can be seen in the strong protests delivered to Japan by countries whose loans and indemnities were secured by Chinese customs receipts.[42]

The East Hopei experiment earned Yin Ju-keng a reputation as the foremost *han-chien* in North China and vastly reduced Japan's chances

---

* Originally the word *rōnin* referred to a masterless samurai, that is, one who was cast adrift after the death of his lord. In modern times the term took on a sinister nuance when it began to be applied broadly to vagabond soldiers of fortune who engaged in smuggling, narcotics trafficking, and other illegal pursuits.

of convincing the Chinese of her sincerity in broaching a "Sino-Japanese partnership." The Japanese Ambassador in China, Ariyoshi Akira, was given the task of explaining Japanese intentions in North China to Chiang Kai-shek and his new Foreign Minister, Chang Ch'ün, a few days prior to the creation of the East Hopei regime. In answer to Ariyoshi's assertion that the autonomy movement was based on the "spontaneous will of the people" rather than Japanese insistence, Chang answered: "The plain fact is that if Japan would recall General Doihara . . . the autonomy movement would probably come to a sudden end."[43]

For the moment at least, the five-province autonomy scheme favored by Doihara and others in the mainland Army commands had to be set aside. East Hopei could be detached from China without provoking a major war, but the more grandiose plan of a Hua-pei Kuo (North China-land) was not yet feasible. A more modest plan, however, was being worked out by the mainland Army commands. It involved the creation of a Political Council in the provinces of Hopei and Chahar. Negotiations to that end went on throughout the turbulent months of November and December 1935 amidst a rising tide of demonstrations and assassinations of pro-Japanese officials and journalists. Chinese military power in the area was in the hands of Gen. Sung Che-yüan, who was subjected to pressure from the public on the one hand and from the Japanese Army on the other. After numerous visits from General Doihara, General Sung came to the conclusion that it would be easier to defy the students than the Imperial Army, and accordingly wired Nanking on November 30 that "the situation in North China is growing more and more tense, and it is now impossible to control it."[44] The import of the message was that Sung was about to bow to Japanese wishes and create a separatist government on the model of the East Hopei regime. Rather than allow Sung to create a completely independent North China, Nanking decided to dispatch its War Minister, Ho Ying-ch'in, to the area. After three-way negotiations involving Ho, Sung, and the Japanese, a compromise Hopei-Chahar Political Council was worked out. A tiny measure of Kuomintang dignity and presence in North China was to be preserved in exchange for Nanking's consent to virtual autonomy for the two provinces. Nominally, Nanking controlled the appointment of the Chairman and members of the Council, but in fact they had to meet the approval of the Japanese. As a result, the Council included several men who had been actively collaborating with the Japanese in administering the Tangku Truce territories. Some, in fact, had collaborated with the Japanese since the days of the infamous Nishihara loans.* In the Council there was a distinct atmosphere of the Anfu Clique, the notoriously pro-Japanese faction that flourished in North China in the heyday of the warlord era.

There were precedents for the Political Council device, most notably the Southwest Political Council that had been functioning for several years in Canton. Embracing the provinces of Kwangtung and Kwangsi, the Southwest Political Council was nominally an arm of the Nanking Government. Its armies were likewise nominally a part of the National Army, but in fact the authority of Nanking reached the southwestern provinces only to the extent that the self-appointed leaders of the Southwest Political Council tolerated it. In all except name it was a separatist regime. Both the Southwest and the Hopei-Chahar councils were thorns in the side of the Central Government, glaring evidence that the Communists were not the only obstacle to national unity. Both councils weakened the Nanking revenue base and undermined the Government's efforts at fiscal reform. The regime in the south could and did embarrass the Central Government by condemning its temporizing policies toward Japan; the regime in the north was a conspicuous manifestation of the results of those temporizing policies.

As the lines of political and military pressure bore in on Nanking in 1936 the irony of the "internal pacification first" policy became clearer and clearer: China could not be pacified until Japanese inroads into North China were blocked. Slowly, in 1936, China moved toward the united front policy and a reversal of the priorities that had allowed Japanese influence to spread unchecked into North China. Then, in December of that year, the dramatic Sian Incident settled the issue posed by Chiang Kai-shek's "unification before resistance" slogans.[45] Chiang, in Sian to unleash the Sixth Extermination Campaign against the Communists, was kidnaped by his own "bandit suppression" chief. For two weeks he was held captive. While the world awaited news of his fate, a remarkable spirit of national unity crystallized in China. There was a sudden awareness by leaders in Yenan, Sian, and Nanking that the murder of Chiang would plunge the nation into all-out civil war, and that only Japan would profit by the ensuing chaos. Even Moscow, alarmed by the recently concluded Rome-Berlin-Tokyo Anti-Comintern Pact, recognized the disastrous consequences of further division in China and

---

* Nishihara Kamezō was sent to Peking by Premier Terauchi in 1917 to negotiate a series of loans with the pro-Japanese government of Tuan Ch'i-jui. In return for loans totaling 145,000,000 yen—much of which was never accounted for by the recipients—Japan was given special concessions in North China.

helped to mediate the release of Chiang. On Christmas Eve, 1936, the Sian interlude ended when Chiang was freed. Though the Generalissimo had signed no papers to that effect, it is evident he gave tacit assent to his captors' demands for a cessation of the civil war against the Communists and the formation of a united front resistance effort against the Japanese.

On January 1, 1937, the American Ambassador in Tokyo, Joseph C. Grew, recorded in his diary that the new year had opened on "an ominous key."

> The Japanese nation seems to be somewhat thunderstruck by the sudden and unexpected determination of China to yield no more to Japanese pressure. The nation is, figuratively, scratching its head and wondering what it should do next. There has been some discussion in the newspapers of a reorientation of policy toward China, but there has been no indication of the direction which that reorientation will take. It is strange but true that Japan appears to have been the last to appreciate the changed conditions in China.[46]

CHAPTER THREE

General Ishiwara Versus the Expansionists

ONE OF THE more frustrating tasks the student of the Sino-Japanese War can undertake is to try to define who were the "expansionists" of that war and who the "anti-expansionists," or, in modern parlance, to separate the hawks from the doves. To assume that Army and Navy officers dominated the expansionist (*kakudai-ha*) camp and that civilian Cabinet members and bureaucrats were struggling to head off expansion does not do justice to the skills and influence of men like Hirota Kōki and Prince Konoe Fumimaro, who as Foreign Minister and Premier in a critical stage of the China Incident showed themselves to be on the side of the expansionists.

It is more useful to argue that the Army General Staff was anti-expansionist and the War Ministry expansionist. However, though such a construct holds true on many occasions, it too collapses, for there were too many exceptions and too many transfers from Ministry to Staff and vice versa. One Japanese specialist on the Sino-Japanese War holds that, if one insists on charting the factions, the following refinement is necessary: within the War Ministry, the Military Affairs Section (Gunmu-ka) was anti-expansionist and the Military Administration Section (Gunji-ka) expansionist; and in the Army General Staff, the anti-expansionists dominated the War Guidance Section (Sensō Shidō-ka), the expansionists the Operations Section (Sakusen-ka).[1] Even this scheme needs qualification as its author admits, but for the early years of the war it will serve as an approximate indicator.

The Chief of Staff at the time of the Marco Polo Bridge Incident and for nearly three years after was Gen. (Imperial Prince) Kan'in Kotohito, who was appointed at the time of the Manchurian Incident when conflicts within the Army were too bitter to allow the important post to go to a partisan general. Kan'in's royal ties placed him above feuds and debates and consigned him to a figurehead function. He presided over meetings, lending a dignified presence that helped to keep the sometimes stormy staff meetings within the bounds of military decorum. A much more important role was played by the Vice Chief of Staff, Gen. Tada Shun. Tada, however, was so preoccupied with resolving disputes and achieving a working consensus within his often divided staff, that his views do not always appear consistent. To see in sharper focus how the China Incident split the Army hierarchy into expansionist and anti-expansionist camps, it is best to examine the views and fate of the principal exponent of the anti-expansionist cause, Maj. Gen. Ishiwara Kanji, who at the outbreak of the war served as Chief of the First, or Operations, Division (Sakusen-bu) of the Army General Staff.

Thanks to brilliant achievements while at the Army War College—he was second in his class of 1918—and as a junior officer, Ishiwara was given a prestigious overseas study assignment in the mid-1920's. In Berlin he became a keen student of European military history; his notebooks and essays suggest that he was as familiar with names like Von Clausewitz and Scharnhorst as most Japanese officers were with Tōgō and Ōyama.[2] In 1928 Lt. Col. Ishiwara was assigned to the Kwantung Army, and in the next few years more than any other one man he helped give that Army its reputation as the spearhead of Japanese expansion onto the continent. Together with Col. Itagaki Seishirō, Ishiwara undertook the careful preparations necessary to effect a swift, successful extension of Japanese power throughout the vast area of Manchuria. They assessed the strength of Chinese forces, drew up operational plans to overwhelm those forces, and then set about convincing both their own commanders in the Kwantung Army and the military authorities in Tokyo of the wisdom of a Manchurian campaign. When the time for action came in September 1931, they were undaunted by the fact that their efforts at persuasion fell short of eliciting the unqualified endorsement of Tokyo military circles and ran completely counter to the aims of the Government. They viewed Manchuria as a fortress against China to the south and more important, the Soviet Union to the north.[3] In addition, they looked on it as a strategic supply base capable of supplementing Japan's inadequate mineral resources. Ishiwara and his colleagues in the Kwantung Army were not unaware of the circular reasoning in their Manchurian strategy: "feeding war by war" was the phrase they used to describe that strategy.[4]

In 1935 Ishiwara was called back to Tokyo and appointed to an important position on the General Staff, and in the following year he became Chief of its Operations Division. Thanks to his efforts, the Operations Division was charged with economic as well as military planning. For Ishiwara the two were intimately related. Ishiwara was not in the tradition of the typical Imperial Army officer, who emphasized the overriding importance of discipline, spiritual excellence, and Yamatoda-mashii (Japanese spirit), arguing that these assets could compensate for a lack of the modern paraphernalia of war. Unlike the majority of his colleagues, Ishiwara did not scorn the skills of the statistician and the economic planner. Quite the contrary, the central effort of his Division—and especially of its War Guidance Section—became the preparation of estimates of the Army's future needs and surveys of the strengths and weaknesses of the Japanese economy. From the painstaking studies of his staff, Ishiwara concluded that Japanese resources were woefully short of the levels necessary to underwrite a modern war. He further concluded that the Japanese economy could not be geared to meet the Army's immediate, predictable needs unless it was put on a total war footing. National economic priorities had to be completely reshaped in order to meet the demands of a modern, mechanized, and mobile Army operating far from the Japanese home islands. As a result of these conclusions, Ishiwara's staff drew up a comprehensive five-year plan for the years 1937–41, which provided for a vast expansion of the nation's industrial capacity. Airplanes, coal, steel, electrical power, rice—no deficiency was left unnoticed.[5]

Ishiwara was not merely a military strategist; he was also a historian and philosopher of war whose studies led him to postulate an apocalyptic world war (*sekai saishū sen*).[6] The views he formulated in the years just prior to the Manchurian Incident underwent many changes in the next two decades, but throughout there was the theme of a great ideological clash between two world blocs, the East and the West. At the root of the conflict was an enduring tension between the spiritual values of the East and the material values of the West rather than a simple competition for territories or markets. Once the epic war determined which civilization was superior, the peoples of the world would become united in eternal peace. In Ishiwara's first formulations of his theory in the late 1920's, his keen awareness of the importance of modern technology was evident. The war, he felt, would be brief because of the development of instruments of massive destruction; globe-girdling aircraft would also play a crucial role. As originally conceived, the final war would see the United States, which had emerged from World War I as the most powerful defender of the values of Western civilization, pitted against Japan, the champion of Eastern civilization. For Ishiwara Manchuria fit into the final war theory not only because the area itself was militarily useful, but also because expansion there was a first step in bringing unity to the people of East Asia. China was obviously incapable of unifying even herself, much less all the peoples of East Asia; Japan therefore had to take the lead in this process, so that the peoples of the East would be of one mind and heart in the epic struggles ahead.

In Ishiwara's view the Soviet Union was always a part of the West. At various times, however, it loomed larger or smaller as a potential adversary. By the mid-1930's, that is, around the time he joined the Army General Staff, Ishiwara had come to regard the Soviet Union as the most immediate threat to Japan. The more remote threat of the great final war became a secondary consideration in the face of the new challenge from Soviet communism in East Asia. For the time being, until the immediate danger from the Russians was eased, it would be necessary, Ishiwara held, to avoid tension with the United States and the European powers. The final war, in other words, was to be delayed as long as possible. The impending struggle with the Soviet Union was not something vaguely foreseen by Ishiwara. In 1936 his calculations placed the war with the Soviets as no more than five or six years in the future. It was the inevitability of this second Russo-Japanese war that loomed uppermost in the mind of General Ishiwara and his staff as they prepared their five-year plan, which would terminate on the eve of that war. Ishiwara was thoroughly convinced that Japanese military power was no match for the Soviet Far Eastern armies—a calculation that was borne out by test encounters in 1938 and 1939 at Changkufeng and Nomonhan, where Japanese forces were overwhelmed by superior Soviet equipment and logistical support.

Ishiwara's predictions of an inevitable Russo-Japanese war led him to completely revise his thinking about China. At about the time of the Manchurian Incident (1931), he believed that Japan had to consolidate an East Asia League (Tōa Renmei), a political and economic bloc encompassing Japan, China, and Manchukuo, by establishing control over China through force of arms. But by the eve of the Marco Polo Bridge Incident (1937), he had come to reject force as a means of knitting together the East Asia League and emphasized instead moral suasion and example as the means of obtaining Chinese participation in the bloc. His logic did not lead him to advocate relinquishment of Manchukuo, which had been won by force; rather, he proposed to make Japan-Manchukuo relations a model of harmony and mutual prosperity that would entice China into cooperation. This required that the Japanese Army relax its heavy-handed control of Manchukuo. At the same time, Japan must refrain from all military adventures in China proper—China to the south of the Great Wall.

For Ishiwara it was the sheerest folly for Japan to become stuck in the morass of a protracted war in China, a war that would leave her vulnerable to her real enemy, the Soviet Union. Japan dared not risk a war with the Soviet Union with a hostile China to her rear. Apart from that consideration, Ishiwara's revised views on China were shaped by a new, positive evaluation of the Kuomintang, along with a healthy respect for the force of Chinese nationalism, that was altogether uncommon among the officers of the Imperial Army. By the mid-1930's, in contrast to the prevailing view among the military, Ishiwara had come to feel that the Kuomintang was not simply another warlord faction but in fact the leader—or perhaps a follower—of an upsurge of nationalism, which Japan was resisting at its peril.

The Sian Incident and the subsequent formation of the united front in China impelled Ishiwara to push his views of China more vigorously. In January 1937, the month following the Incident, he and his staff prepared numerous memoranda emphasizing the need to abandon the past self-serving, "privilege-seeking" policies in North China and Inner Mongolia. For many within the Army the Sian Incident was an alarming sign that there was more involved than just the coalescing of the Nationalists and the Communists; a Sino-Soviet coalition aimed at Japan was also in the wind. Ishiwara, however, dismissed this analysis. "Although in its origins and development, the anti-Japan front has some relationship to a third Power [the Soviet Union], and especially to the Communist Party, it is really a variation of the Kuomintang. Essentially, it can be expected to change into a genuine campaign to construct a new China."[7] Whether the creation of a new China would be accompanied by a policy of hostility toward Japan or not—that, said Ishiwara, was a matter Japan alone would determine. The "determining factor," he concluded, was Japan's willingness (or refusal) to "discard her past policy of imperialist aggression and thereby display the sincerity of the true Japan." In another memorandum written at the same time Ishiwara urged "liquidation of the notion" that North China constituted some kind of a "special zone" distinct from the rest of China. Japan must cease her encouragement of independence for the five provinces of North China and must "make it clearly understood that the area presently being administered by the Hopei-Chahar regime is naturally a part of the territory of the Chinese Republic and must therefore be placed under the central government of China."[8]

Ishiwara's views contrasted with those of the expansionists, many of whom shared his belief in an impending war with the Soviet Union. From that premise, however, they came to a conclusion diametrically opposed to Ishiwara's, namely, that the menace of China should be militarily eliminated in order to free Japan's hands for the struggle with the Soviet Union. Where Ishiwara and the anti-expansionists saw the rising number of attacks on Japanese in China and the increasingly strident anti-Japanese atmosphere as evidence that a nationalism capable of creating a strong, united China was awakening, which Japan would do well to ally herself with, the expansionists saw the same attacks and the same wave of anti-Japanese feeling as evidence of Chinese "insincerity," proving only that Japan could never trust or work with the Kuomintang regime. The views of Lt. Gen. Tōjō Hideki well illustrate the response of the expansionists to the developments in China. On June 9, 1937, less than a month before the Marco Polo Bridge Incident, Tōjō, then Chief of Staff of the Kwantung Army, sent a top secret, urgent telegram to Tokyo in which he argued that Japan should not allow the Kuomintang regime to dissolve the political organs and special relationships Japan had established in North China in recent years. The Kuomintang regarded Japan with disdain, and any attempt by Japan to restore friendly relations with it would only enhance that disdain, said Tōjō. "From the point of view of military preparations against Russia," he concluded, "I am convinced that if [our] military power permits it, we should deliver a blow first of all upon the Nanking regime in order to remove this menace at our rear."[9]

The eruption of violence at the Marco Polo Bridge came as a shocking surprise to the anti-expansionists, whose representatives immediately commenced on-the-scene negotiations to settle the affair and prevent any spread of the fighting. Ishiwara was caught in a dilemma. As we have seen, he favored a complete mobilization of the nation to prepare for war against the Soviet Union; and the hostilities in North China seemed to offer precisely the kind of crisis needed to spur Japan onto a total war footing. Nevertheless, he opposed efforts to mobilize even a few Army divisions, recognizing that the expansionists on his own staff and in the War Ministry intended to use the newly mobilized troops to strike against China. On two occasions in the opening month of the war Ishiwara saw to it that mobilization orders were rescinded. As for the dispatch of troops to China proper, he was categorically opposed to such a move. "Not one soldier is going to be sent to China while I am alive," he is said to have told a conference at the Foreign Office one month before hostilities broke out.[10]

Ishiwara's resolution was not shared even by those in his own Division. The Chief of his Operations Section, Col. Mutō Akira, persistently challenged Ishiwara's efforts to prevent the mobilization and dispatch of troops to North China. In 1936 Mutō, then on the staff of the Kwantung Army, had taken a leading role in organizing the disastrous invasion of

Suiyuan province in defiance of Ishiwara's policy of befriending China.*
Ishiwara had responded by hurrying to Manchuria to persuade the
Kwantung Army to cease its attacks on Suiyuan and there had been confronted by an unyielding Mutō, who reminded him that, "We are simply
doing the same thing you yourself did in Manchuria at the time of the
Manchurian Incident."[11] Irony was thus added to Ishiwara's discomfiture
as he discovered that he was becoming the victim of the same type of
insubordination he himself had practiced in 1931. The loudest expansionist voices were heard in the China Section (Shina-ka) of the General Staff and the War Ministry's Military Administration Section,
under Col. Tanaka Shin'ichi. As Chinese resistance stiffened in the opening weeks of the war and as the conflict spread to Shanghai in August
1937, these voices drowned out the cautious advice of Ishiwara with talk
of a blitzkrieg campaign (or in Japanese terms, a *sokusen-sokketsu*, rapid
war, rapid settlement).

In the early days of the war, for example, the Chief of the China Section, Col. Nagatsu Sahijū, solemnly told Ishiwara that, "We need only
dispatch more troops and take Peiping, and the rest of the country will
be on its knees."[12] Two years after the Marco Polo Bridge Incident, in
a long interview with Prince Takeda Tsuneyoshi, Ishiwara set forth his
disagreements with the expansionists. "The Manchurian Incident had
given them an *idée fixe*, and they concluded that the war could be ended
in a hurry. I thought that this showed a shallow understanding of the
national character of the Chinese," he told Prince Takeda. Ishiwara declared he had become more than ever convinced "China would go all-out
for war" after he learned (via telephone wire-taps) that Minister of
Finance H. H. Kung was ordering an immense quantity of weapons from
abroad. Once hostilities began, it was inevitable that the war would be
protracted, Ishiwara told the Prince. The kind of "decisive showdown"
(*kessen*) the China Section had anticipated was "impossible." But the
members of the China Section had insisted that once Japan took North
China, China would be "economically bankrupt." "They even cited figures," Ishiwara continued. But they were always "basing their ideas on
the easy success we had in Manchuria."[13]

---

* In March 1936 Manchurian troops invaded Suiyuan, the domain of the warlord
Gen. Fu Tso-yi, and captured Pailingmiao. In November of that year, a more ambitious invasion of eastern Suiyuan was launched by the Pailingmiao-based troops,
now armed with Japanese weapons and supported by Japanese aircraft. General Fu's
neighboring warlord, Yen Hsi-shan, the Governor of Shansi province, threw his forces
into the fray, and the Japanese-inspired invasion attempt was repelled in December
1936. A good account of the invasion and its results can be found in Gillin, *Warlord*,
pp. 230–39.

As it became clearer in the summer and fall of 1937 that Ishiwara was correct, that there would be no easy, quick victory, the antagonism between him and his critics grew more and more pronounced. Unable to produce the victory they had confidently predicted and unable to concede that their calculations were in error, the expansionists called for campaign after campaign to bring the war to an end. Conversely, Ishiwara became more and more convinced that the resistance of the Chinese, far from being broken, was if anything becoming stronger, and cautioned his superiors that it was imperative to keep military operations and occupied areas to an absolute minimum.

Meanwhile, in China in the crucial month of July 1937 a series of conferences was under way at the summer capital in Kuling. Designed to cement the united front and provide training and indoctrination for several thousand selected Army personnel, the meetings were attended not only by Kuomintang figures, but by Communist leaders as well, among them Mao Tse-tung, Chou En-lai, and Chu Teh. On July 17 Chiang used this forum to make an unambiguous statement of China's determination to resist Japanese attempts to remove North China from Kuomintang control.[14] Chiang made it clear that China desired peace—but not peace at any cost. He declared that the Kuomintang Government wished to negotiate a settlement of the conflict, which was still confined to North China, but that the loss of even one more inch of Chinese territory was unacceptable to tolerate it would be an "unpardonable crime against our race." If Japan pushed China beyond the limits of her patience she would have no choice but "to throw the last ounce of her energy into a struggle for national survival regardless of the sacrifices." The address at Kuling was made public—it was a call to all of the people of China to unite and steel themselves for a long and difficult struggle to avoid "extinction." In both tone and content it was a dramatic departure from Chiang's previous speeches, which had emphasized the need for caution and conciliation.

In Tokyo the speech caused little reaction. "Hardly anyone paid attention to the grave significance of the speech," wrote diplomat Ishii Itarō. "It sounded like 'bluff.' "[15] Two days after the Kuling address Ishiwara was in the office of War Minister Sugiyama Gen pleading the case for caution. There was a great danger that the war was about to become a "general war," he said, and if it did Japan would become "bogged down in China exactly as Napoleon had in Spain."[16] To avoid that, Ishiwara advised that all Japanese troops in North China be pulled back into Manchukuo immediately. Further, he recommended that Konoe immediately fly to Nanking to undertake direct, personal talks with Chiang. There is little reason to believe that General Sugiyama, who was known by a number of nicknames, all of them indicating his dull wit,* had any appreciation of Ishiwara's well-chosen historical analogy. It is certain that he disapproved Ishiwara's plan for "settling basic problems" through direct negotiations with Chiang.[17] Those in the Army and the Government who favored a negotiated settlement of the China problem continued to think in terms of a local settlement that would exclude the Kuomintang from North China.

Ishiwara ignored the opposition that was building up to his policies and took his proposal to Premier Konoe. As the son of a well-known friend of China (Konoe Atsumaro) and as one relatively free of the contempt for the Kuomintang that was so common among Japanese political figures, Konoe was regarded by Ishiwara as the "one man" who could successfully negotiate with Chiang. In mid-July Ishiwara telephoned Konoe's Cabinet Secretary, Kazami Akira, and spelled out the details of his proposals. Before the day was out Konoe was convinced of the merits of the plan and, though ill, ordered an aircraft readied for the flight to Nanking. The plan, however, aroused a storm of protests from expansionists in the Army—and from civilian advisers like Saionji Kinkazu, who felt that Konoe could not depend on the Army accepting agreements worked out with Chiang. Saionji discounted Ishiwara's own influence in the Army. "For years," he told Konoe, "Generals Terauchi, Sugiyama, and Umezu have been trying to establish their 'line,' and Tōjō is their choice. To them Ishiwara is a 'nuisance.' He is treated by them as a stepchild. He is like a candle in the wind ready to be snuffed out at any moment."[18]

In the next few months Ishiwara's position was increasingly beleaguered. A friend of his, visiting the General Staff in September, was "shocked" to hear that "only Kawabe Torashirō [Chief of the War Guidance Section] and one or two subordinates agreed with Ishiwara's opinions. All the rest of the personnel were undermining [his] plans."[19] Colonel Mutō, head of the Operations Section, took a leading role in consolidating the opposition to Ishiwara and pressing for his transfer from the Center.[20] Gen. Homma Masaharu, of later "Bataan death march" fame, also generated much of the resistance in the General Staff to the moderate approach of Ishiwara. As Chief of the General Staff's Second, or Intelligence, Division (Jōhō-bu), Homma was responsible for assessing the fighting capability of the enemy. His staff contributed

---

* Two of them were *Guzu Gen* (Gen the dullard) and *Benjo no doa* (toilet door). The second suggests that Sugiyama lacked firm convictions and could be pushed from any (either) side. Kase, p. 11; NSGT, p. 48.

greatly to the inculcation in the military mind of the *Tai-Shi ichigeki ron*, the view that with "one [decisive] blow against the Chinese" their resistance would collapse.[21] This contemptuous estimate of Chinese strength and unbounded confidence in Japan's military might were best expressed when War Minister Sugiyama assured the Emperor that "the China Incident will all be over in a month."[22]

The strategic optimism that Ishiwara so deplored was also concentrated in the Kwantung Army, which set forth its "Essential Points for Managing the Situation" on August 14, 1937.[23] The Kwantung Army, no less than Ishiwara, was preoccupied with the menace of the Soviet Union, but took the view that Japan dared not face the Russians in combat as long as China remained at her back, unsubdued and hostile. The Kwantung generals emphasized the expansion of military operations, both in terms of "intensification of military force" and in terms of the geographical scope of the operations: "We must not only wipe out the Chinese Army and other [Chinese] military forces in North China, but also quickly occupy Shanghai . . . , secure a commanding position in Shantung, [and] prosecute an air war, and with these steps achieve our desired goals in a brief period of time and bring all resistance to a speedy conclusion." Diplomatic efforts to seek a solution were to be discarded "until the Nanking government ends its resistance and surrenders." Japan, the Kwantung Army felt, had to administer a "chastisement" (*yōchō*) to the enemy—a term and concept that appears repeatedly in the policy statements of the day.[24]

By the end of September 1937 Ishiwara's views were so out of step with the prevailing opinion in both the Center and the field armies that his enemies were able to secure his removal from the General Staff. On September 27 he was assigned to the Kwantung Army as Vice Chief of Staff (under General Tōjō). The transfer was tantamount to exile. Ishiwara's voice was henceforth muffled, heard by a group of comrades but largely ignored in the higher councils of the Army and the Government.

It is difficult to say at what juncture hopes for limiting the war on the mainland were dashed, at what stage Japan became committed to total war. James B. Crowley argues that such commitment came with the January 16, 1938, speech of Konoe, in which he announced the decision to cease dealing with the Kuomintang Government.[25] Chalmers Johnson postpones the "end of all attempts by the Japanese government to localize the China Incident" until the T'ungshan Operation (in effect, the Hsüchou campaign, April 1938).[26] Others would insist that there was still hope for limiting the war until the Hankow campaign in the summer and fall of 1938. Whichever view is correct, it is clear, at least in retrospect, that the absence of Ishiwara at the Center had a decisive effect on the policy pursued on each of these occasions.

On September 2, 1937, as we have seen, the Japanese Government took note of the expansion of the war by converting the name North China Incident to China Incident. Japan had sound reasons in international law for steering clear of an open declaration of war, but as an ex-Imperial Army general has written, there was actually little feeling among Army officers in the first few months that Japan was in fact involved in a war. Rather, most suffered from the "hallucination that just as always the China problem could be settled by the same old policy of intimidation."[27] Each new campaign brought fresh victories and drove the Chinese farther and farther from the great coastal cities, where the trade, industry, and financial wealth of Kuomintang China were concentrated. And yet the battlefield successes failed to bring about the expected and even predicted capitulation of the enemy. The Army drew lines and promised that it would not be necessary to go beyond them. According to Konoe's adviser Saionji, someone rushed into a meeting of the Premier's "kitchen cabinet" in the early weeks of the war with the "good news" that "the Army says it will not go beyond the Yungting River." Indeed, War Minister Sugiyama had to promise Emperor Hirohito that the river would not be crossed, writes Saionji, but the promise was broken, and the "Army tramped into North China."[28] Similar assurances were offered at the Yellow River, and when it too was crossed Sugiyama was said to have mumbled, "*Ten-chan* is going to be angry."*

By the end of November 1937 much of North China and the Inner Mongolian provinces was in Japanese hands, and the staffs of Gens. Terauchi Hisaichi and Ueda Kenkichi, the Commanders of the North China Area and Kwantung armies, were taking steps to create separatist puppet regimes for the areas under their jurisdiction. There had been little opposition to slow down the drives of the Imperial armies along the railroad lines deep into Chinese territory—little of the harassment from guerrilla troops that was to prove so costly to Japan in succeeding years. Shanghai too was in Japanese hands, though as in 1932 Chinese resistance had been stiff. All eyes were now turned toward Nanking, the Nationalist capital city. Vice Chief of Staff Tada Shun, who shared Ishiwara's concern about Japan being drawn little by little into a morass, ordered a halt to the Japanese advance on November 19. The field generals, however, pleaded that the capture of Nanking was abso-

---

* Saionji, p. 283. *Ten-chan* is a diminutive for the Emperor, which in this case would seem to suggest flippancy.

lutely necessary; and Col. Mutō Akira, now serving as Vice Chief of Staff of the Central China Area Army, voiced the opinion held by many that the fall of Nanking would mean the surrender of China.[29] In the end General Tada's objections were overridden, and the order went out to attack Nanking. As the Japanese troops closed in on the city in the early days of December they met surprisingly little resistance, and a wave of victory-by-the-end-of-the-year optimism gripped the Japanese Army and public alike. On December 13 Nanking fell, and the historic orgy of rape and looting began. When the news of the Imperial Army's most illustrious success reached Japan, the atmosphere was one of unrestrained joy. More than thirty years after the event, many Japanese still recall the lantern parades that took place all over the nation. In Tokyo thousands marched from the Marunouchi business district to the gates of the Imperial palace, where shouts of "Banzai" filled the air, and the reflections of hundreds of lanterns danced in the moat waters surrounding the palace.

But it was quickly evident that the fall of Nanking was not going to produce the predicted catastrophic effects on the morale and will to resist of the Chinese people. Again the expansionists and anti expansionists (now headed by General Tada) clashed over the wisdom of a further extension of the war front. This time their debate centered on the vital transportation center of Hsüchou. Once again the expansionists gained the upper hand: after the Japanese occupation of Hsüchou was successfully carried out in the spring of 1938, orders immediately went out to press on to Hankow in the west and Canton to the south.

Ishiwara railed against the folly of these campaigns. Back in Tokyo for a public address shortly after the fall of Hsüchou, he told his audience that the battle for Hankow about to be launched could not change anything. "Even if Hankow is captured, I regard it as highly unlikely that Chiang will fall. And even if Chiang falls, I hardly think that four hundred million Chinese are going to capitulate." He went on to tell his audience that the fault lay with the politicians, who had no knowledge of military strategy, no awareness of the strength of Chinese resistance, and no appreciation of Japan's unpreparedness to fight a full-scale war in China. Blaming the political leaders for expanding the war fronts in defiance of the Emperor's explicit commands, Ishiwara charged: "Politicians shouting 'Take Hankow!' and 'Take Canton!' are merely trying to cover up for their own incompetence. For politicians, [such invigorating war cries are] like an injection of morphine or an injection of camphor [given *in extremis*]. In the end, the people are riled up in this contrived fashion."[30]

The "riled up" Japanese people not unnaturally expected that the sacrifices the nation was making to prosecute the war would be re-warded, at least with victory but hopefully with compensation and in-demnification as well. Those who wished to "chastise" China encour-aged and magnified the public clamor for victory and compensation, and spoke darkly in the councils of government about the dangers of leaving the people discontented. As the public became convinced that Chiang was a mere local warlord, as their military and political leaders claimed, they inevitably came to expect a quick victory and harsh sur-render terms.

Such an atmosphere is easier to generate and exploit than it is to dis-pel. Once the official propaganda line caught on, it became increasingly difficult for Army and Government officials to promote a peace settle-ment on terms conciliatory enough to interest the Chinese. "No matter what sacrifices we have made (in the war), it will not do for us to make greed a part of our basic philosophy," Ishiwara warned. "It is base for us to argue that because we have lost a hundred thousand in the war we must grab some Chinese territory." The Allied Powers had inflicted a harsh treaty on Germany after World War I, Ishiwara said, but it hardly behooved Japan to behave in the same predatory fashion as the Euro-peans. Ishiwara's speeches are sprinkled with invidious comparisons be-tween the Western and Eastern nations. The nations of the West were powerful but lacked the spiritual resources of Japan. And yet Japan was ignoring her moral (*dōgiteki*) dictates, Ishiwara said, in seeking to pre-serve special privileges on Chinese soil and in failing to understand how the war was affecting the sense of dignity of the Chinese people.[31]

Ishiwara made more explicit what he saw as an immorality foreign to the Japanese tradition in a speech to the Concordia Society (Kyōwa-kai) in May 1938. He was concerned with the callously insensitive victory celebrations that Imperial Army units encouraged and sponsored in Manchuria and in Chinese areas under their control. "We Japanese are really something," he told his audience: "Manchuria is like an adopted child of Chinese and Japanese parents. Now the parents are fighting and the father says: 'We've taken Nanking and so it's time for festivities.' And so the sake is poured, the flags are unfurled, and we have lantern parades."[32] He was particularly distressed, Ishiwara went on, by the "mystified expressions" he saw on the faces of Chinese schoolchildren in Manchuria, who were mobilized to march in celebration of the exploits of the Imperial Army.

Still, Ishiwara claimed he had mixed feelings about the war. Though it saddened him, it also gave him "great pleasure" to realize that "our four hundred million Chinese brethren, since the Manchurian Incident and especially since this present incident, have come alive after being on the verge of death." China's people had opened their eyes, he said, "but now it is the Japanese who are dozing." With biting sarcasm, Ishiwara spoke of meeting an eminent Chinese intellectual and suggesting to him that Chiang Kai-shek award "China's highest medal" to a certain Japanese general who had played an important if unintentional role in awakening the Chinese to such vigor. "The Chinese gentleman agreed with me," Ishiwara added.[33] To understand how Ishiwara's caustic criticism of the war earned him a premature and involuntary retirement from the Army, one needs only to recall that remarks like these were made at a time when thousands of Japanese were dying in what had been officially proclaimed a holy war (*seisen*).

Over and over Ishiwara condemned Japan's leaders for being untrained to the tasks of piloting a modern nation through times of crisis. They merely responded to crises and lacked the kind of long-range vision necessary to avoid future ones. There were dangerous forces at loose within the Japanese military, and no men at the helm capable of controlling those forces, Ishiwara felt. "Everybody is going his own way and nobody is coordinating efforts." In other countries, however, "great leaders who combine political and military talent come along to direct their countries in critical times," wrote Ishiwara. For him Chiang Kai-shek was such a man, a figure who ranked with Napoleon and Ataturk. To compensate for Japan's inability to produce leaders of such a caliber, Ishiwara proposed that a greater effort be made to train the Emperor and members of the Imperial Family in military science and other matters, so that they could take a direct role in ruling the country.[34]

Ishiwara was also extremely critical of the training program for Japan's elite officers at the Army War College.* The War College taught tactics and taught it well, said Ishiwara. But officers emerged from their training "with no knowledge about fighting a long-range war." In the present war, for example, Japanese war capacity had to be balanced against the Chinese capacity for resistance; that alone was a complicated matter, he said, but in addition the strategist had to take into consideration the political and military power the Soviet Union, the United Kingdom, and the United States could exert on the Far East. The ability of Germany and Italy to counterbalance those forces also had to be con-

---

* The Army War College (Rikugun Daigakkō), sometimes translated as the Army General Staff College, provided advanced training for an elite segment of the officer corps. Most officers went no further than the Military Academy (Shikan Gakkō). The implications of this distinction are discussed by Crowley in "Japanese Army Factionalism."

sidered. "To synthesize all these elements and then decide on the basis
of that synthesis how much military power Japan can appropriate for
war in China—this kind of talent is necessary, and yet I don't believe
that there is anyone in the entire Army General Staff who can do it. All
they can do is handle local fighting."[35]

Ishiwara's criticisms are echoed in the recent comments of an officer
who studied in the Military Academy in the mid-1930's:

> The Chinese military academy at Whampoa—that had two sec-
> tions, a military section and a political one. But ours had only one,
> a military section. As a result we had no opportunity to study the
> important trends that were taking place in China in the 1930's. We
> now know that the currency reforms China undertook were a ter-
> ribly significant move in the direction of national unification, but at
> the time we didn't know a thing [*baka ni shite*] about currency re-
> forms. After the Sian Incident we had no notion of the significance
> of the united front to China. We went on thinking that China was
> a divided country and was going to stay divided, each region under
> its own leaders. If we had had any inkling of what was going on,
> we would have known that resisting Chiang was mad.[36]

Referring to the Italian campaign against the Ethiopians, Ishiwara
ridiculed those in Japan who looked forward to a quick military solution in China. "They are guilty of a grave error in likening four hundred
million Chinese to the savages of Ethiopia," he said. "There is no doubt
that as long as the Chinese have an inch of land—even on some remote
frontier—they are going to continue to resist us." Japan would need
"tens of divisions" and "tens of years" to subdue China.[37] And in the
meantime, as one of Ishiwara's disciples cautioned, "we will bring about
a fragmented China for many years [and impose] a tremendous drain
on the Empire's strength for a long time into the future."[38] Constantly
emphasized by Ishiwara and his followers was the theme that a divided
China was useful to Japan only if one assumed Japan wished to join
the imperialist nations in ravaging China. They maintained that if the
intent was to bring China into a viable East Asia League capable of
excluding the Western imperialists from the Orient, Chinese disunity
was plainly a liability rather than an asset. Most Japanese commentators
of the time agreed with Baron Ohkura Kimmochi in assessing Chiang
Kai-shek as an "ignominious outlaw" for "turning again toward the
Soviet Union" at Sian.[39] Ishiwara did not accept an interpretation of
the Sian Incident that focused on the Soviet Union, and he was far from
ready to accept the characterization of Chiang as an "outlaw."

In June 1938, as Japan prepared for a further escalation of the war by deciding to move against Hankow, Ishiwara summarized his feelings about the China Incident in four terse sentences:

1. China has a very strong and unified will to fight against Japan's use of armed forces.
2. Because of that it is unavoidable that we will fall into a protracted war unless we settle the situation now.
3. If we fail to devise an appropriate policy for resolving the conflict and instead continue to aimlessly pursue our own self-interests, we will forever hope in vain for peace in the Far East.
4. We must bear in mind that the Soviet Union is also our immediate enemy.[40]

Ishiwara had been troublesome at the Center, and he proved to be no less a thorn in the side of the Kwantung Army. He was soon removed from his staff position there, and in 1939 was given garrison duty in Kyoto. Two years later, on the eve of the Pacific War, he was reduced to the ranks of the inactive reserves. His charges of a misguided war policy and inept national leadership continued throughout the war and very nearly resulted in his imprisonment. As it was he spent the war under the surveillance of the military police (Kempeitai).

Ishiwara was an ardent believer in the Hokke (or Lotus) sect of Buddhism founded by Nichiren seven centuries earlier. Like Nichiren, whom he regarded as the greatest figure in Japanese history, Ishiwara was a man of great learning, a soldier of monumental self-discipline who lived life by strict rules and freely displayed his contempt for those who did not. "You admired him but you felt uncomfortable with him," was the way one contemporary put it.[41] Like the wrathful Nichiren, who stormed about Japan on the eve of the Mongol invasions warning the country of its national peril, Ishiwara belabored all who would listen with his latterday vision of national calamity. Neither man was known for his capacity for compromise or his agreeable disposition. Circumspection was not a part of their style. Neither feared clashing with authority but indeed seemed to find a certain strength in it. Both had a band of admirers who worshiped them for their integrity and insight, but both made far more enemies than friends. Their enemies looked on them as eccentric alarmists and despised them for their very un-Japanese individualism, for their disdain of consensus and the other instruments of graceful social behavior. Both of these Japanese Jeremiahs paid for their militant righteousness with banishment. For Nichiren it was a physical exile to the rugged island of Sado; for Ishiwara it was a professional exile to the ignominy of wartime retirement while yet in his fifties. Both eventually retired to a hermit's cabin in the rugged north of Japan to spend their last years in the company of their followers. Both died at the age of sixty-one. The dying Ishiwara was reportedly pleased at the coincidence. He was buried opposite his forerunner on a hill overlooking the Japan Sea.

This digression into the ideas and times of General Ishiwara is meant to show that there were Japanese—even at the highest levels of the General Staff—who regarded war with China as a monumental error, men who sought to prevent the war before it began and to find a peaceful solution for it after it started. In the following chapter we shall examine how Japan moved deeper into the morass of mainland warfare by creating puppet regimes in China and by deciding, on January 16, 1938, to cease all efforts at finding a solution to the war with the Kuomintang Government. In later chapters, however, we will come back to this lonely figure, for many of the Japanese who founded the Wang Ching-wei collaboration movement in the hope of breaking the impasse caused by the January 16 decision were strongly influenced by the ideas of Ishiwara.

CHAPTER FOUR

An Incident Becomes a War: Konoe's 'Aite ni sezu' Declaration

ON OCTOBER 1, 1937, Premier Konoe met with his Inner Cabinet, that is, his Foreign Minister and his two service ministers, to unveil a comprehensive China war policy. Such conferences frequently served as devices by which the Government committed itself to policies that had originated in the General Staff. The policy approved and presented to the Emperor on October 1 was no exception. The conclusions of the October 1 conference were contained in an "Outline of a Policy for the China Incident," which was the descendant of a document drawn up on August 8 by members of the War Guidance Section of General Ishiwara's staff.[1] That document called for a "moral settlement" to the war, which was then still confined to North China. In order to remove the major obstacles bedeviling Sino-Japanese relations over the past four years, it advocated the abolition of the East Hopei and Hopei-Chahar regimes, the abrogation of the Ho-Umezu and Ch'in-Doihara agreements, and the abandonment of the "special trade" relationships Japan had developed in East Hopei. The solution to the North China problem, it asserted, would be realized only when a "truly splendid area" was created in North China "under the sovereign control of the Nanking Government." A "truly splendid area" in North China was a cliché that had found its way into many official policy statements on China in recent years, but it was usually linked to statements calling for the exclusion of the National Government from North China. Now, in words that accurately reflected the aims of Ishiwara, the War Guidance Section put itself on record as favoring the presence of the Nanking Government in North China as the best way of "achieving concert and harmony between China, Japan, and Manchukuo."

During the remainder of August and throughout September, as the War Guidance Section's document shuttled from one staff and ministry officer to another for comments and necessary seals of approval, the hard-line advocates (kyōkō-ha) endeavored to write their own views into it.

The October 1 decision, however, showed that on the vital question of North China, the Government was determined to follow the recommendations of the August proposals—to abolish the agreements and regimes that were causing Sino-Japanese friction and allow the Kuomintang Government its rightful sovereignty over North China. The October 1 decision seemed to indicate that the counsel of Ishiwara and Foreign Office spokesman Ōta Ichirō had been accepted as national policy. During the period when the "Outline" of October 1 was being formulated, Ōta had warned that "Japan would regret for a thousand years" any attempts to establish regimes independent of Nanking and any support of reactionary "old-timers" like Wu P'ei-fu in their perennial effort to fracture Kuomintang power.[2]

Still, the views of the hard-liners were also represented in the document of October 1. In the section on "adjusting diplomatic relations" between Japan and China, the "Outline" spoke in fairly general terms about the need for China "to eliminate all obstacles that stand in the way of Sino-Japanese economic cooperation" and "cooperate with Japan to prevent communism." Though the "Outline" would probably have constituted a basis for fruitful diplomatic negotiations with China, it is clear from various "explanations" and "interpretations" of the document's language that the Inner Cabinet had veered sharply toward a set of hard-line terms, considerably dimming the prospects for successful negotiations in the months ahead. Taking note of the "expanded expectations of the people for fruits of victory," the official explanation of the "Outline" declared that the Japanese Government could no longer be content to negotiate on the basis of earlier and more generous terms of peace. Rather, Japan would have to consider demands for "material" compensation for the loss of life and the expenses she had incurred in the war. Specifically, the explanation called for indemnification for Japan's "direct losses." In addition, Japan demanded a host of special economic privileges in North China, including joint Sino-Japanese management of important railroads, shipping companies, and airlines and special rights to exploit underground mineral resources in North China. As one Japanese historian comments, it was scarcely accurate for Konoe later to attribute these demands for indemnities and special privileges to the "people's" expectations of compensation for wartime suffering.[3] That the Konoe Cabinet and the Army General Staff found the terms entirely congenial to their ambitions in North China can be seen in the enthusiastic way they set about organizing national policy companies (*kokusaku kaisha*) to exploit the economic potential of North China.

NATIONAL POLICY COMPANIES

The transfer of Ishiwara from the Center triggered a "sudden increase" in the General Staff's concern over the possibilities of economically exploiting China. Its "Tentative Plan for the Economic Development of North China," issued on October 16, 1937, laid the groundwork for later policies that would place all important industry, economic development, and exploitation of natural resources in occupied China under Japanese control.[4] In succeeding chapters we will discuss more fully the organization and operation of the national policy companies Japan established to that end. But first a brief word about the origins of Japanese wartime economic policy toward China.

In considering what the economic exploitation of North China involved, the General Staff concluded that a vast amount of private capital would be needed to finance the large-scale operations it envisioned. Consequently, it proposed the creation of a giant holding company to take charge of all major economic activities in North China. A model for such a company existed in the China Development Company (Kōchū Kaisha), which the South Manchurian Railway Company had created in 1935 to manage its affairs in North China. The General Staff proposed to separate the China Development Company from the South Manchurian Railway and transform it into a holding company, which would then funnel Japanese capital and managerial talent into North China.

On December 8, 1937, Ōtani Son'yū, a former Buddhist priest and chief abbot of the Nishi Honganji Temple in Kyoto who had taken a leave of absence from his priestly duties to become Konoe's Minister of Colonization, drew up a comprehensive plan that complemented the General Staff's "Tentative Plan."[5] It called for the establishment of a government in North China to operate with the aid of a Japanese "supreme guidance organ," for Japanese advisers to be sent to each of the several "autonomous" provinces in the proposed North China regime, and for the formation of giant national policy companies in both North and Central China to direct economic exploitation. Even South China, which was customarily ignored when economic development schemes were being devised, was included in Ōtani's vision: exploitation of the area was to be overseen by the Taiwan Colonization Company. In 1938 Ōtani was appointed president of the corporation he had proposed for North China.

The Army's "Tentative Plan" was approved at a Four Ministers' Conference on December 9. In the Ministers' words, it was "necessary to establish 'national policy organs' [*kokusaku kikan*] with the object of developing the economy in North China, the Shanghai area, and elsewhere so as to cope with a protracted war in China."[6] Specifically earmarked for exploitation were the transportation, communications, and metal-mining industries. A happy marriage was being arranged beween the ambitions of Japanese private capital for a role in the economic development of China and the strategic needs of the nation. The advocacy of such a program of economic privilege by the General Staff represented a decided shift in its policy; and by design or not, it also signified a further step toward the creation of puppet regimes, which alone could provide the kind of political and legal framework needed to make such a policy work. Given Japan's determination to make China's economy contribute to the prosecution of the war, the utterly subservient character of those regimes was a foregone conclusion. It was an irony that seems not to have disturbed the minds of the Ministers on December 9, this endorsement of economic privileges as necessary to the prosecution of a protracted war that was certain to be prolonged by those very privileges.

Eight days after the Ōtani plan was broached, the Government's Planning Board (Kikakuin) issued a definitive policy statement entitled "Policy for the Economic Exploitation of North China."[7] The recently created Planning Board, whose duty it was to advise the Premier on matters affecting mobilization of manpower and matériel, was simply "a detached organ of Army planners."[8] The Secretary of the Board, for example, was Lt. Col. Satō Kenryō, who was concurrently assigned to the Military Affairs Section of the War Ministry and was a "pioneer in advocating withdrawal of recognition from the Chiang regime."[9] The military control over the Planning Board and the extension of the Board's authority to North China affairs represented a serious erosion of the Foreign Ministry's influence in determining Japan's China policy. A reliable contemporary account states that the Foreign Ministry was disturbed by this turn of events, but "since it was all alone in its opposition and since the Army and Navy ministries were for it," it was "expected to come around."[10]

The Planning Board's policy provided for the establishment of a national policy company, later designated the North China Economic Development Company, whose task was to "exploit, manage, and regulate important industry [in North China] related to transportation (including harbors and highways), communications, mining, salt, and salt utilization." The control of this company was to extend not only to the industry Japan introduced but to existing enterprises as well. Any questions that might arise over the company's operations would be settled by negotiations with the Provisional Government of the Republic of China—established on December 14, 1937—or with local Peace Preservation Committees (Chian Iji Kai).

The North China Company was only one of many techniques designed to reduce the scale of Western economic penetration into North China, to create a yen bloc composed of Japan, Manchukuo, and North China, and to weaken the National Government. Another move that served all of these purposes was the disruption of the Maritime Customs Service, for long the mainstay of Nanking's international credit standing.[11] By 1937, though still under the direction of a British Inspector-General and staffed by an international force, the Maritime Customs had become well integrated into the overall financial structure of the National Government. China's staggering foreign debts were serviced from its receipts, and by the eve of the Marco Polo Bridge Incident efficient administration, together with expanding international trade, had given China an unprecedentedly good credit rating abroad. That credit was desperately needed, for China had to look abroad for much of her war matériel. The Japanese seizure of ports like Tientsin and Shanghai threatened the customs revenues and raised touchy international questions that put Western and Japanese diplomats at loggerheads.

In Tientsin, the Japanese pressed the local Customs Commissioner to deposit collections into a Japanese bank, retaining only a small portion to service some of the international debts and to meet expenses. He bowed to that pressure on October 22, 1937, and three days later a substantial portion of China's customs revenues began to flow directly into the Yokohama Specie Bank. Similar pressure was put on the Customs Administration in Shanghai, which under normal conditions collected half of all the Chinese customs revenues. This time, however, British diplomats demanded guarantees on debt servicing and other matters before consenting to Japanese wishes. In the end the complicated arrangements that were finally worked out in the spring of 1938 represented a compromise: Japan deferred to Great Britain by not seizing the administrative machinery outright, and in return was allowed to divert most of the customs revenues away from the Nanking Government. It was a lopsided compromise in which form was awarded to Britain and substance to Japan, but inevitably so, given the weak bargaining position of the British, who were unable to persuade the United States to join them in standing up to Japan.

Meanwhile in North China, to the surprise of few, one of the first acts of the new North China puppet regime was to appoint a Supervisor of Maritime Customs, who immediately revised downward the comparatively high tariff of 1934 in order to attract foreign shipping to the north. The beneficiary of the new rates was Japan, for among the selected commodities enjoying the lower rates were tea, silk, and paper products, exports for which the sorely depressed Japanese economy needed buyers. The loser was the Nanking Government, which lost not only the receipts collected in North China ports, but also the revenues from the trade diverted north by the new attractive rates. The United States and other nations filed stiff notes of protest with the Japanese over the illegal and discriminatory actions of the Peiping government, but Tokyo merely denied any responsibility for the actions of the North China regime.

Within two years of the Marco Polo Bridge Incident Japan had developed a powerful stranglehold over the economy of China—especially North China—through the national policy companies, tariff controls, and banking and currency schemes (which we will examine in the next chapter). When in 1939 the time arrived to negotiate an understanding with Japan's principal collaborator, Wang Ching-wei, there was no more thorny issue to resolve than the vested economic interests Japan had acquired in North China.

Still, though Japan was plainly staking out an economic future in China, she continued constantly probing diplomatic avenues to resolve the Incident. Neither China nor Japan was prompted to break diplomatic relations in 1937. In the early days of August, before the flames of the North China conflagration spread to the Shanghai area, Japanese Ambassador Kawagoe Shigeru held secret talks with the Asian Bureau Chief of the Chinese Foreign Office, Kao Tsung-wu, in an attempt to lay the basis for formal negotiations. Tokyo also instructed Funatsu Shinichirō, a man with both business and diplomatic experience in China and a personal friend of Kao's, to participate in the talks. The secret meetings got under way in Shanghai on August 9, with Kao warning the Japanese that the atmosphere in Nanking was extremely hostile to any form of conciliation with Japan. The "slightest weakness" was interpreted as treason, he told them.[12] Meanwhile, Saionji Kinkazu, who had been sent as a personal envoy from Konoe to sound out Chinese feelings, was hearing much the same from Chiang's brother-in-law T. V. Soong.* Said Soong:

* Saionji's fascinating account of his talks with Soong is contained in his "Kizoku no taijō," pp. 269–77. Saionji traveled to Shanghai to meet Soong under disguise. He was promptly arrested by Chinese military police, who accused him of being Japanese. He was released, however, after he explained, probably in the accents of Oxford where he was educated, that he was a California Chinese who spoke only English. He gained

Both the Chinese and the Japanese military have misunderstandings about themselves. The Japanese military still hold to their preconceived ideas about the Chinese Army. They think that if you hit us once we will surrender and do what you want. The Chinese Army has studied hard since the Manchurian Incident. It's been trained by the Germans, and we have spent much to modernize it. It knows that it is stronger, and it has the confidence that it won't be beaten this time. So, the Japanese Army underestimates the Chinese Army, and the Chinese Army overestimates itself. Here is where the great danger lies.[13]

Soong's concern about the difficulty of keeping the armed forces of both China and Japan from acting rashly out of an exaggerated notion of their own strength and the enemy's weaknesses was wholly justified, as events soon showed. In the second week of August a Japanese Navy Lieutenant, Ōyama Isao, was killed on the outskirts of Shanghai under circumstances that suggested he had in mind a one-man assault on the vital Hungjao Airport. For the most part the local Japanese military authorities responded with circumspection, offering apologies and canceling night patrols lest they inflame the tense situation.[14] Nevertheless, the premonitions of Soong proved correct when on August 14 Chinese planes struck at Japanese warships in the harbor at Shanghai. Both sides spoke of too long "enduring the unendurable" and the need for taking stronger measures against the other. The work of diplomacy became increasingly difficult once the war moved into a larger arena, and for the next two months diplomatic negotiations were stalemated.

In Japan the initial effort to break the diplomatic impasse came from the General Staff, on which the moderate Ishiwara still sat. On September 9, at the insistence of Ishiwara and Tada, War Minister Sugiyama went before the Emperor to assure him that the Army had no "territorial ambitions" in China, and that "somehow or other" it wished to use diplomatic channels to settle the war. In answer to the Emperor's query about the War Minister's ability to hold the lower ranking officers in line, Sugiyama said he would take that responsibility. At about the same time the General Staff decided to bypass the Ministry of Foreign Affairs and instructed the Japanese Military Attaché in Berlin, Gen. Ōshima Hiroshi, to sound out the Germans about acting as mediators. Germany, in fact, had two very good reasons for wanting peace

---

entrance to Soong's presence in his magnificent mansion, Saionji writes, only after he passed down a corridor "a couple of blocks long" and through a labyrinthine network of "ten or more doors, each secured by two pistol-bearing guards" (p. 273).

and stability in China: to safeguard the increased trade she was developing there and to divert Japan's animus toward the Soviet Union. Both China and Japan had cause to regard Germany as an honest broker, China as the recipient of German military aid and advice, Japan as a partner in the Anti-Comintern Pact. But the German Foreign Ministry made it clear to Japan that it had no intention of exerting pressure on China in any Sino-Japanese negotiations, and that for the moment at least Germany did not even wish to take an active hand in mediating the dispute. However, she would act as a "letter-carrier," if Japan so desired.

Japan agreed, and on November 3 Oscar Trautmann and Herbert von Dirksen, the German Ambassadors in Nanking and Tokyo, began their "letter-carrying" tasks. On that day Dirksen notified Berlin of a set of terms he had been given by Foreign Minister Hirota. Dirksen advised the German Foreign Office that he felt Hirota was sincere in wishing to make peace on the terms offered. He also felt Hirota was sincere in stating that if China refused to consider the terms, Japan would carry the war on until China was totally defeated and would then "exact far more difficult terms."[15] Berlin soon instructed Trautmann to convey to Chiang Kai-shek the terms, "which seem acceptable to us as the basis for the opening of negotiations." The terms the Ambassador passed on to the Generalissimo on November 5 were in conformity with the October 1 "Outline," minus of course the hard-line "interpretations" (such as the demand for indemnities). The newest Japanese proposals were as lacking in specific detail as the October 1 "Outline" had been: Inner Mongolia was to be autonomous, but the boundaries were not defined; North China was to be placed under the administration of the Central Government, but a demilitarized zone extending from the Manchurian border to a point south of the Peiping-Tientsin line was to be created; the Nationalist Government was to cease its anti-Japanese policies and commence a common struggle against communism, and so forth. The November 5 terms are often described as lenient because they neither mentioned indemnities and autonomous regimes in North China nor called for Chinese recognition of Manchukuo.[16]

From many different sources the Japanese Government had become fully aware that, whatever other points of difference might be negotiable, there was no possibility of inducing the Kuomintang Government to recognize Manchukuo. The best that could be hoped for was a kind of silent assent to its de facto existence. When Saionji had broached the issue of recognition to Soong, in the first month of the war, Soong had said that any such demand by the Japanese would "cause the fire to spread." If Japan was not interested in helping the Kuomintang regime save face, said Soong, the least it could do was "not to cause us to lose [it]." To Saionji's rejoinder that Japan might be willing simply to remain silent on the subject of Manchukuo, Soong replied that he would check with the Generalissimo. Two days later he reported back that Chiang had no objection to such a tacit, de facto recognition.[17]

When Trautmann handed the Japanese negotiating package to Chiang on November 5 the Generalissimo's response was swift and negative. He could not possibly accept the demands for several reasons, he told Trautmann. Any Chinese government that agreed to such demands would be "swept out by the tide of public opinion." Only if the Japanese were prepared to restore the *status quo ante* could he begin negotiations, he said. Furthermore, Chiang went on, for the time being it was necessary to ignore all Japanese proposals, because the Western powers were about to assemble in Brussels to consider what actions might be taken under the terms of the 1922 Nine Power Treaty. It behooved China to wait until it became clear whether they would vote to take some strong disciplinary action—such as economic sanctions—against the Japanese Empire.[18] The Powers met in the Belgian capital for three weeks beginning November 24. They "labored and brought forth a mouse," as one observer wrote.[19] The United States was isolationist, and Britain, France, and the Soviet Union preoccupied with the menace of Hitler; in short, none of China's sympathizers was willing to take the kind of action that might have inhibited Japan or made her soften her peace terms. As the American Ambassador in Tokyo, Joseph Grew, noted in his diary some days before the conference, it should never have been called in the first place, for it would only serve to demonstrate the "lack of unity and impotence of the Powers" and thus renew the confidence of the Japanese militarists.[20]

While Chinese hopes for meaningful international support were being dashed at Brussels, battlefield reports at home were adding to the general despair. On November 4, the day before Chiang rejected the proposals relayed by Trautmann, Lt. Gen. Yanagawa Heisuke's Tenth Army was ordered ashore at Hangchow Bay south of Shanghai. The landing was unopposed. Moving west and north units of the Tenth broke the defense of Shanghai and by the end of November had pushed to within sixty miles of Nanking. Germany continued to exert "friendly pressure" on China to respond to the Japanese overtures of November 5. In personal conversations with high Chinese officials, Trautmann conveyed his own conviction that "the time was ripe for settlement of the dispute." "During the Great War," Trautmann said pointedly, "Germany had various favorable opportunities to discuss peace, but was overconfident in her own strength, and thus refused to talk peace until she was forced to accept whatever terms were dictated to her at Versailles."[21]

As the battlefield situation grew more desperate, Chiang assembled his leading generals in the half-evacuated capital of Nanking on December 2 to discuss the Japanese peace proposals. Most of those attending the meeting heard for the first time the terms offered nearly a month before. Wang Ching-wei later released an account of the meeting in an attempt to justify his own peace efforts with the Japanese.[22] According to that account, after the Vice Minister of Foreign Affairs, Hsü Mo, briefed the assembled generals on the Trautmann mission and the November 5 terms, they asked him if there were any other terms the Japanese insisted on, such as limitations on Chinese armaments. Hsü replied that there was none. At that point the Generalissimo asked Gen. T'ang Sheng-chih, the Commander of the Nanking garrison who had vowed to achieve victory or die with the city, for his opinion; but General T'ang withheld his opinion for the moment. The Generalissimo next turned to Pai Ch'ung-hsi, one of the best Kuomintang generals and known for his vigorous resistance to Japan. His reply was, "If these and these alone are the terms, why should there be war?" Vice Minister Hsü once again assured the gathering that Trautmann had conveyed no other terms, and the Generalissimo continued to poll his generals. Gens. Hsü Yung-ch'ang and Ku Chu-t'ung found the Japanese terms acceptable as a basis for negotiations, and when General T'ang was asked again, he agreed with the others. Finally, the Generalissimo summarized the general sentiment, which held that the Japanese terms neither threatened the extinction of the nation nor denied authority to the Kuomintang in North China. German mediation should therefore not be refused, he concluded.

Accordingly, Chiang met with Trautmann late in the afternoon of December 2 and indicated his willingness to commence talks with Japan. Chiang's hope, nurtured by assurances from Trautmann, was that once China and Japan agreed to begin negotiations, Hitler would call on the belligerents to observe an armistice. A day later Ambassador Dirksen cabled the German Foreign Office from Tokyo to report that the Japanese Army General Staff was most concerned about the increase in war expenditures and the expanding war front, and anxious to conclude a peaceful settlement to the war.[23] His report was at least partially correct. Senior General Staff officers like Generals Tada and Kawabe felt that if negotiations were not commenced before the fall of Nanking the hand of the hard-line advocates would be greatly strengthened. "The notion that Japan should deny recognition to the Chiang regime was rampant" in the days before the fall of Nanking, recalls one General Staff officer.[24] On December 1 General Kawabe issued a policy statement that reflected the concern of the anti-expansionists on the staff:

> A denial of the Chiang regime would put it in an extremely desperate situation in which it would acquire the strength of a cornered rat [*kyūso hangetsu no ikioi*] in its struggle against Japan. Thus, whether we destroy it or not, in the end we would have brought about a China fragmented for many years ..., one that would be a tremendous drain on the Empire's strength far into the future. Moreover, it would represent a temptation to Britain and the United States all over the Far East.[25]

On the same day, however, the Imperial General Headquarters set forth a "Draft Proposal for the Solution of the China Incident."* This policy statement clearly indicated the extent to which the hard-line faction had come to the fore. It revised—in the direction of greater severity—the terms Trautmann had carried to Chiang less than one month earlier. Now, in addition to the earlier demands, the Imperial General Headquarters wanted Chiang's "official recognition of Manchukuo," "cooperation in the establishment of a 'new Shanghai,'" and "compensation ... for damages arising out of the Incident suffered by Japanese residents."

Still harsher was a set of "guarantee clauses" inserted into Section Four of the "Draft Proposal" as insurance that China would sincerely carry out all her obligations under the peace treaty. Until Japan was satisfied on that score, China must agree to demilitarize all areas into which Japanese armies had advanced; but Japan would withdraw her own troops from those zones only when "local peace was restored." Moreover, "in important areas of North China and around Shanghai," China would have to agree to a more permanent arrangement, with the garrisoning of Japanese troops and "Japanese control of necessary communications." A second form of guarantee called for Chinese recognition of a number of special economic privileges in the five provinces of

---

* "Shina jihen kaihatsū shori hōshin-an." For the text, see *Gendai shi shiryō*, 9: 51–52. The Imperial General Headquarters (Daihon'ei), a supreme war council with Army and Navy divisions (Rikugun-bu and Kaigun-bu), was created on November 17, 1937. Though its announced purpose was to facilitate cooperation between the Army and Navy general staffs, its real purpose, according to Baron Harada, was to control the recalcitrant mainland commands, which in the flush of victory were bent on overthrowing the Nanking Government and setting up regimes on the Manchukuo pattern. Jones, p. 64.

North China. The document did not define these privileges except to indicate that they would be concerned with customs and duties, development of natural resources, and transportation and communications. Finally, China must give Japan control over the "agencies that were required" to exercise and administer these privileges.

Throughout November it was the Japanese who made the overtures and the Chinese who saw fit to drag their heels on the peace negotiations. Meanwhile, Japan's military position improved to the point where the Imperial General Headquarters and many Japanese Government officials thought better of the "generous" terms of early November. Consequently, when Chiang Kai-shek finally notified Trautmann on December 2 that he was prepared to negotiate on the basis of the November terms, the response received an icy reception in Tokyo. To the astonishment of Dirksen, who conveyed the news of Chiang's acceptance to the Foreign Office on December 7—as the battle for Nanking was under way—Minister Hirota indicated he doubted whether it was still possible for Japan to negotiate on the basis of terms drawn up more than a month earlier. The military situation had changed in the past month, said Hirota, and as a result "public opinion" would no longer countenance the earlier terms; moreover, the "field Army had become more exacting in its demands."[26] Hirota refused to hand a new set of Japanese terms to Dirksen; the newest, the December 1 terms of the Imperial General Headquarters, had not yet been approved by the Government. During the next two weeks a flurry of Cabinet, Inner Cabinet, and Liaison conferences were convened to formulate more exacting peace terms.* In the same period Nanking fell and the puppet Provisional Government of the Republic of China was created in Peiping.

An internal change of great importance also took place. Adm. (Ret.) Suetsugu Nobumasa, one of the most consistent advocates of a "war of annihilation," joined Konoe's Cabinet as Home Minister, thereby gaining a voice in the Liaison Conferences. At his first Conference on December 14, a day after the fall of Nanking, Suetsugu maintained that "unless the peace conditions are very much stiffened, our people are going to be dissatisfied and so are our soldiers at the front."† This recourse to the

---

* The Liaison Conferences (Renraku Kaigi) had been instituted only a month before as a means of bringing together the Government's top-ranking civilian and military leaders. The general staffs of the Army and Navy and the two service ministries were represented on them.

† Harada, 6: 187. The "public opinion" rationale was not entirely a contrived one. Baron Harada's journal entry for November 19, 1937, records an example of the "expectations" of the people—in this case a prominent businessman, who warned Harada that in view of the great sacrifices Japan had made in the war, "there will be terrible

suggestion of an Army and citizenry out of control and liable to radical action, a well-known device in this period, was not allowed to pass unchallenged. Konoe rose to deny the implications of Suetsugu's remarks, and in the end Suetsugu was forced to concede that Konoe was correct. But if the specter of an uncontrollable citizenry was laid to rest, the feeling was undeniably growing among Japan's leaders that "the great sacrifices" the Government had demanded of its people required the humiliation of China, a peace settlement in other words that would make it clear Chiang Kai-shek had been vanquished. This was the sense of Konoe and his entire Cabinet in early December, even before the fall of Nanking. Now, after the Chinese defeat there, the feeling of invincibility was greatly strengthened. On December 14, the same day the Liaison Conference met, Konoe publicly stated that "the National Government had become a shadow of its former self," and that in the circumstances, "if a new regime should arise in the wake of the collapse of the National Government, Japan would have no choice but to consider concrete measures for coexistence and co-prosperity with it."[27]

Admiral Suetsugu left with Konoe a report that summarized the feelings of many in the Cabinet. In it he attacked those in the Army who were calling for peace and concessions to China: "It is bad enough that our side should be presenting peace terms, but if we [go beyond that] and show a readiness to make concessions . . . , it is obvious China will take advantage of our soft attitude all the more." The report went on: "Now, Nanking has fallen and it appears that Chiang's regime is in real trouble, but nevertheless we cannot conclude that his authority has disappeared. If we weaken our campaign a little bit, it is evident that the Chiang regime will recover again. But if we give just one more little push, it will fall. If we urge peace . . . , the Chinese will only despise us and have their morale revived."[28]

An unmistakable trend was appearing. After early December there was only a small, isolated band in the General Staff that felt a conciliatory settlement of the war was desirable. Konoe clearly shared the majority feelings about the "danger" of appearing conciliatory. "Taking an attitude very similar to that of a defeated nation and purposely showing our magnanimity is not an attitude appropriate to a nation that has been winning consecutive victories," he explained to a colleague. Any evidence of weakness would be interpreted by other nations, he

unrest if we do not go all out in securing compensation [from China]." *Ibid.*, pp. 154–55. General Kawabe also noted the "public's hard-line attitude." Indeed, in his opinion "the people were the most hard-line [*ichiban tsuyoki*] of all. The Government was next, and the Army General Staff took the weakest position in the nation." *Daihon'ei rikugun-bu*, 1: 529.

felt, as a sign that Japan was in a "precarious situation." This would have a disastrous effect on Japanese commerce and industry, bringing on among other things "a sudden fall in the value of the yen and a depreciation of Government securities."[29]

On December 22 Foreign Minister Hirota finally summoned the German Ambassador to the Foreign Office to receive the Government's reply to Chiang's message of December 3. As Hirota had hinted on December 7, the Japanese now demanded that Chiang accept a new and harsher set of terms than those transmitted to him in November.[30] The new proposals, which were deliberately made unclear at the suggestion of Admiral Suetsugu, were as follows: China must formally recognize Manchukuo, a demand that had not been included in the earlier set of terms; must agree to the creation of a demilitarized zone (of unspecified size) in North China and Inner Mongolia; must pay "due reparations," another new demand; and must agree to the establishment of a special political structure in North China in order to provide for Japanese-Chinese-Manchurian co-prosperity. Dirksen asked for clarification, but Hirota said only that, with regard to the "special political structure" in North China, what was envisioned was a regime with "broad areas of authority," and one that, furthermore, "would not necessarily be under the Government of Chiang Kai-shek."[31]

Dirksen was disconcerted by the vagueness of the terms as much as by their harshness. In coming days, he would repeatedly ask Hirota for detailed explanations, failing which, he said, the Chinese could hardly be expected to accept the terms. Meanwhile, he cabled Berlin in some disgust, indicating that he was satisfied the Japanese leaders did not expect the new terms to be accepted. Indeed, said Dirksen, they looked forward to their rejection, which would allow Japan to proceed with its war of annihilation. Far from clarifying the December 22 terms, Hirota turned them into an ultimatum: China must signify her readiness to accept them "in their entirety" by about the end of the year or Japan would be "forced to treat the present situation from an entirely different point of view."[32] Not only were the peace terms vague; even the threat was vague.

According to Col. Kawabe Torashirō, the decision to advance on Nanking had been delayed repeatedly by General Tada, who had argued that, far from hastening the surrender of Chiang, as General Matsui and others had promised, the capture of the enemy's "castle town" would render a peace settlement almost impossible.[33] Tada was under great pressure to authorize the move, however, and when his own Operations

Chief, Colonel Kawabe, joined those who were urging him to change his mind, he finally relented and on December 1 gave the order to move on Nanking. Even so, he achieved a victory of sorts, managing to insert a qualification in the order to attack to the effect that the capture of Nanking should not be allowed to "prejudice any settlement to be reached with the Nanking Government."[34]

Nevertheless, with the increasing evidence that both civilian and military leaders were determined to destroy the National Government rather than deal with it, General Tada and the other members of his staff who opposed that policy became increasingly desperate. The center of opposition was in the Operations Division's War Guidance Section, headed by Lt. Col. Horiba Kazuo. Later to become one of the most important chroniclers of the events under consideration in this book, Horiba, like his superior Kawabe, was a protégé of Ishiwara. An expert on the Soviet Union and its economic planning programs, with years of service in military missions there and in Poland, Horiba returned to Japan to work with Ishiwara on his five-year industrial expansion program for Japan and Manchuria.[35]

The decision of the Government to escalate the demands on China was bitterly opposed by Horiba's unit. "They [the expansionists] enraged us," he later recalled, "and we were determined to stand up to them, to offer ourselves as volunteers to save our country from its peril."[36] What especially outraged Horiba was his conviction that the hard-line policy of breaking with the Kuomintang Government was an effort on Konoe's part to present a tidy, resolute policy to the new session of the Diet. He was convinced, in short, that Konoe was willing to jeopardize the destiny of the nation rather than make politically difficult decisions. Horiba discussed the matter with his immediate superior, Kawabe, but found him timidly bowing to authority: "Our superiors have made their decision and now there is nothing to do but follow orders." That was to be expected, said Horiba, who found Kawabe "lacking the stomach to stand up and fight in crucial situations."[37]

Horiba carried that message back to his comrades in the War Guidance Section and found them still determined to see the matter through. They decided that Horiba should confront the Vice Minister of War, General Umezu, and impress on him the urgent necessity of returning to the original peace proposals, which Chiang had accepted as a basis for negotiations. Major Takashima would similarly visit the Vice Chief of Staff, General Tada. Horiba's assignment produced disappointing results, but General Tada was moved, either by the intensity of the appeals from his subordinates or by his own convictions, to make one last dramatic effort to prevent a rupturing of the diplomatic attempts. He took his case to the Emperor.

THE IMPERIAL CONFERENCE OF JANUARY 11

The last time an Imperial Conference (Gozen kaigi) had been used as a means of settling national policy had been in the Russo-Japanese War. Apparently Tada reasoned that the Cabinet and the military would be constrained to define a more lenient policy toward China if they were forced to discuss the solution of the China Incident in the Imperial presence. The Emperor was in fact concerned about the progress of peace negotiations, and it is likely that his concern was known to Tada. The hope was that a policy of restraint would receive Imperial sanction and thus become unchallengeable national policy. As Konoe said, "[Tada] wants to be able to check the extremely strong opinions that have been coming from Matsui and Terauchi lately, to check them by saying 'It has been settled at the Imperial Conference.' "[38]

Neither the Navy nor the Foreign Ministry wanted such a meeting; nor, evidently, did Konoe, judging from his estimate of Tada: "He's an unreasonable man. I sometimes wonder how he's got as far as he has."[39] But Konoe's motive in wishing to avoid an Imperial Conference was not simply to advance his own views on the China Incident. As the scion of the most exalted branch of the noble Fujiwara family, from which Emperors and Empresses of Japan were selected in the dawn of Japanese history, Konoe consistently attempted to relieve the Emperor of the necessity of interceding in partisan issues. Until the historic Imperial Conference ending World War II, active Imperial participation in the decision-making process was almost nonexistent.* Nevertheless, an occasional frown on the Imperial countenance or an embarrassing question put to the Cabinet could provoke great consternation and cause reconsideration of the issue that seemed to displease the Emperor.

Faced with the uncompromising demands of the General Staff, Konoe agreed to the convening of an Imperial Conference. But he first devised a scheme to ensure that it would be held without jeopardizing the sanctity of the Imperial distance: he prevailed on court officials to advise the Emperor that the policy to be presented had already been decided on by the Government, and that he therefore need make no inquiries.[40] Konoe, of course, was not only preserving the Imperial dignity, but

* David Bergamini's *Japan's Imperial Conspiracy* (New York, 1971) appeared after this book was in type, and I am therefore unable to evaluate the major revisionist theme of his book, which is summed up by the subtitle: *How Emperor Hirohito Led Japan into War Against the West.*

making certain that the General Staff could not gain the Emperor's sanction for its policies. On the contrary, the Imperial silence would be seen by all present as approval of the Government's policy. Konoe's tactics and ability to manipulate an Imperial Conference reveal much about the military's right to approach the throne: that right was plainly not as useful as it might seem at first glance. Konoe's success at manipulating the decision-making process also weakens his claim (made in his postwar memoirs) that he had struggled in vain to prevent hard-line generals from plunging Japan into war. "By transferring responsibility for the China war to a clique of militarists, Konoe misled his contemporaries and historians," writes Crowley. "He also did himself a great disservice— namely, he masked his adroit political leadership."[41]

At 2:00 P.M. on January 11, the nation's eleven highest military and civilian officials gathered in the East Room of the Imperial Palace and seated themselves at two long rectangular tables, at the head of which sat the Emperor on a raised dais. Seated closest to the Emperor were the two Chiefs of Staff, the Imperial Princes Kan'in and Fushimi. At the end of the tables, most distant from the Emperor, were the Vice Chiefs of Staff, General Tada and Adm. Koga Mineichi. Foreign Minister Hirota read for Imperial approval the "Fundamental Policy for the Disposition of the China Incident," which the Cabinet had adopted only that morning.[42] Thereupon, General Kan'in, after a cautiously understated summary of the General Staff's reservations, concluded by approving the Cabinet's decision. The time-honored Japanese concern for a consensus view had prevailed over any urgency dictated by the substance of the issues. After similarly mild reservations were delivered by others present, the 55-minute meeting came to an end, and the Emperor retired without uttering a word. The "Fundamental Policy" that emerged from the conference not only confirmed the harshest demands the expansionists had put forward, including the payment of reparations to Japan and the creation of "new political organs ... with comprehensive authority in North China," but called for the issuing of another ultimatum to China.

An Inner Cabinet meeting held two days later, on January 13, set a seventy-two-hour limit on the ultimatum. If the Kuomintang regime did not accept the terms of the "Fundamental Policy" within that period, Japan would "annihilate" it or take measures to absorb it into a new central government. That new government, whose formation would be assisted by Japan, would be one "with which Japan could negotiate the adjustment of mutual relations and cooperate to bring about the regeneration of China." The Cabinet had in fact already established this policy in a meeting December 24, and with more precision than the January 11 document, had specifically declared that the recently established Provisional Government "would be expanded and strengthened until it becomes the central influence of a rejuvenated China."[43]

THE JANUARY 15 LIAISON CONFERENCE

The "Fundamental Policy," though severe, at least provided for the transmittal to China of terms more specific than the four vague conditions Dirksen had been authorized to convey some three weeks earlier. Foreign Minister Hirota, however, failed to transmit the terms as instructed by the Imperial Conference, leaving the Chinese Foreign Minister to plead for amplification as the ultimatum period ran out. Nothing so bespeaks the Japanese Government's determination to break with Chiang as Hirota's calculated silence. Indeed, Hirota did not even notify Dirksen of the seventy-two-hour ultimatum until January 16, by which time it had expired.* At a stormy day-long Liaison Conference held on January 15, Tada warned of the disastrous implications of a protracted war and once again asked for a clarification of terms and extension of the ultimatum period, but he was finally reduced to angered silence by Navy Minister Yonai Mitsumasa, who asserted, "If the General Staff has no confidence in the Government, then either the General Staff must resign or the Government must resign."[44] There was no doubt in anyone's mind which alternative Yonai was proposing.

The intransigence of the Government was made even clearer in an exchange between Prince Kan'in and Konoe. The Prince had asked Hirota what would happen if, after a "no dealing with Chiang Kai-shek" (*Shō Kai-seki o aite ni sezu*) policy was announced, Chiang said that he wanted peace. When Hirota hesitated in his response, Konoe moved to answer the question: "There will be absolutely no dealing [with Chiang]."[45]

The January 15 Liaison Conference was a harrowing experience for Tada. His only support came from Navy Vice Chief of Staff Koga. The War Minister, Sugiyama, interpreted China's failure to respond to Japanese demands as a sign that she was stalling, and sided with the Government in calling for a break with Chiang. "This meeting," as Horiba has remarked, "demonstrated just as much of a clash between the General Staff and the War Ministry as there was between the Government and the Imperial Headquarters."[46]

During a late afternoon intermission the exhausted Tada returned to

---

* The Counselor of the German Embassy in Tokyo, however, was notified by a Foreign Office official on January 12 that Japan would "reserve her freedom of action" if no reply was received from China by January 15. Presseisen, p. 141.

tell his staff of the Government's absolute determination to break relations with the Kuomintang Government. Konoe, Sugiyama, Hirota, and others had voiced their impatience at the "insincerity" of the Chinese, the futility of further negotiations, and the need for Japan to take an unmistakably resolute stand. One group in the Army General Staff (centering around Colonel Horiba) cautioned Tada not to yield to those views. It urged Tada to use the General Staff's right of direct access to the throne (*iaku jōsō*) if all else failed, that the Emperor might be made aware of his military leaders' opposition to the plans of the Government. The Emperor, it was felt, would not condone the harsh *aite ni sezu* policy scheduled for announcement on the next day if he fully appreciated its disastrous implications. Telephone calls were made to the Military Chamberlain at the palace to determine if the feeble General Kan'in could be shuffled into position for an Imperial audience before Premier Konoe. The word came back: there was a few minutes leeway in the Imperial schedule, just enough to allow General Kan'in to be ushered in ahead of Prince Konoe.

Meanwhile, however, another group of advisers was cautioning Tada that any further opposition to the will of the Government and the drastic resort to Imperial intervention could only result in the dissolution of the Government. In the end Tada sided with this group. Unwilling to demonstrate to the enemy the deep cleavages in Japanese leadership during a time of war, he decided not to exercise the General Staff's *iaku jōsō* privilege, thereby demonstrating once again the limited utility of this much vaunted but rarely used privilege.* Accordingly, he returned to the Liaison Conference in the evening to announce that the Army General Staff reluctantly accepted the decision of the Government to cease negotiations with the Chinese National Government.† At noon on

---

* By a different version of this episode, related to me by a person whose name I am not at liberty to divulge but whose knowledge of the events is very reliable, Prince Kan'in did in fact exercise the Staff privilege. According to this source, General Kan'in was briefed on what he was to say to the Emperor and was provided with a several-page memorial written in large characters (to facilitate reading by the aged Prince), but nevertheless somehow became confused and skipped over two or three pages in his oral presentation to the throne. The Emperor, unable to understand the garbled version of the General Staff's wishes, discounted them, received Premier Konoe, and gave his consent to the *aite ni sezu* decision of the Government. Assuming this account is accurate, there are at least two reasons why it has not (to my knowledge) reached print: first, out of respect for Prince Kan'in, and second, because the General Staff was on very shaky constitutional grounds in exercising its right of access to the throne on this matter, which was essentially a political rather than a military affair.

† Horiba claims there were two intermissions during the January 15 Conference. At the earlier (noon) break, Tada told Horiba that he was determined to refuse to give the Army Staff's sanction to the *aite ni sezu* policy. By the time of the later recess, how-

the following day the *aite ni sezu* declaration was made public. Hirota immediately notified the German Ambassador that the Japanese Government appreciated the good offices of Germany but they were no longer needed.[47]

Konoe's choice of words on January 16 represented an intentional departure from the language that had been agreed on at the Imperial Conference five days before. The earlier version had specified that in the event of a Chinese rejection of the Japanese terms, "the Empire will hereafter not depend [exclusively] on them [the National Government] as partners in order to solve the Incident."[48] In the public statement Konoe made on the sixteenth, this declaration had been stiffened to read: "Hereafter, the Imperial Government will not deal with the National Government."[49] This was a significant change, both in tone and in content, in the direction of belligerence.[50] Moreover, the very use of the word *aite*, a term denoting one's opposite but often charged with hostile and insulting overtones when used in a military sense, was questioned—even by Konoe's friends. According to Konoe's adviser Inukai Ken, the offensive word was inserted by a Foreign Ministry official who drafted the document and "had a difficult time" coming up with the rude, imprecise, and nonlegal language used by Konoe. Konoe's biographer too thinks the Foreign Ministry may have formally drafted the speech, but Konoe himself maintained that the tough language was the result of pressure by the North China Area Army, which in turn was being pressured by its collaborators in the newly created Provisional Government.[51]

Whatever the origins of the sensational turn of phrase, doubts immediately arose about the use of the curiously informal phrase in a document of such crucial significance. Was Japan breaking diplomatic relations with China? Ambassador Grew talked with Hirota on the morning of January 17 and then reported to Washington that "this did not involve a specific act effecting a breach of diplomatic relations but simply meant a cessation of dealings with Hankow on the ground that the government in Hankow no longer represents China. The Minister said that there would be no immediate recognition of any regime but that the Japanese Government would await developments. The regime in North China would constitute the basic power of whatever government should actually be recognized."[52]

---

ever, Lt. Gen. Nakajima Tetsuzō of the War Ministry had prevailed on Tada to give in and accept the Government's decision. "It was emphasized that if Tada did not go along, it would mean the fall of the Government, and this would have great repercussions," writes Horiba. 1: 130.

In an official release on January 18 the Government clarified its use of the term. " 'No dealing with the Nationalist Government' has a stronger meaning than non-recognition of that Government," said the Government's "Supplementary Statement."[53] Hirota went a step further and declared in an interpellation in the Diet that the statement was "stronger even than a declaration of war."[54] Thus, formal diplomatic efforts to achieve peace came to an end. The Chinese Ambassador to Japan, who had been at his Tokyo post throughout the past six months of undeclared war, was finally called home, and Japan set about the task of creating a government with which she could "more fully act in concert."

The *aite ni sezu* declaration "clearly summed up Japan's agony," writes historian Hata Ikuhiko, referring to the inability of Japanese leaders to settle on a fruitful policy for coping with the China Incident.[55] In retrospect, it seems incredible that the task of advocating and rationalizing a moderate China policy, of seeking some peaceful solution, was assumed by such a small group of men, largely centered in the Army General Staff; and that the rest of officialdom, with the public in tow, was so indifferent to the disastrous implications of a protracted war on the mainland, so unaware of the tide of national resistance rising against the Japanese presence in China.

The small group of anti-expansionists on the General Staff found itself confronting on the one hand the naïve optimism and arrogance of those in the military who envisioned a China overwhelmed "by a single blow," and on the other the Konoe Cabinet, which, as historian Usui Katsumi says, "was from the opening of the general war [i.e., after the expansion of hostilities to Shanghai in August] consistently aggressive about military achievements and what could be secured from them."[56] As early as October 1, 1937, the Cabinet was setting the stage for the eventual failure of mediation efforts, the protraction of the war, and the creation of puppet regimes by its decision to capitalize on military success, its "decision to secure important privileges from China on the grounds that 'the people's expectations from the war were expanding as the battlefronts expanded.' "[57]

Konoe came to regret the *aite ni sezu* declaration within a few months, for it soon became evident that the Ishiwara-Horiba predictions about a protracted war and an endless drain on national resources were going to come true. The speech, Konoe was reported to have said less than half a year later, was "a pointless move."* Ironically, before the year 1938

---

* Ugaki, as told to Kamata Sawaiichirō, in Kamata, p. 270. Other evidence of Konoe's dissatisfaction with the *aite ni sezu* declaration is to be found in Yoshida

had ended, Konoe took steps to nullify the January 16 statement and find a bridge (*hashiwatashi*) to Chungking. The diplomatic bridges, however, had been destroyed by the *aite ni sezu* declaration and, as Konoe discovered, it proved far easier to burn them than to reconstruct them.

If the *aite ni sezu* declaration was "a pointless move," it was nonetheless perfectly consistent with the trend of events between July 1937 and January 1938, and it would be wrong to concentrate criticism on a few ill-chosen words while neglecting the larger issue of the policies that led to those words. Konoe and his country were undone, not by words but by a fatal blind spot in Japan's national vision. Japan could not see, or did not wish to see, the wisdom in General Ishiwara's assertion that the foes she was engaging were far more persevering than the venal warlords of yesterday. Rather than awakening at Ishiwara's alarming warning about an aroused nation that would not surrender, Japan continued to be lulled by the more agreeable picture of the enemy as a weak and isolated warlord regime, an enemy that must surely fall to a quick, mortal blow.

Tōyū, pp. 202–5, which discusses Konoe's plan to dispatch Yoshida to Chiang with a letter expressing regret for the statement; and IMTFE, Def. Doc. 2104, p. 1, in which Konoe writes: "The announcement of January 16, 1938, brought about no favorable results, a fact of which I am well aware without having anyone point it out to me. I, myself, confess it was an utter blunder."

CHAPTER FIVE

Collaboration in North China

NEARLY sixteen months elapsed between Wang Ching-wei's flight from Chungking in December 1938 and the formal inauguration of the Wang Government in Nanking on March 30, 1940. One of the chief reasons for the long delay—and one of the most irritating problems faced by the Wang Government after it was created—was the existence of several other Japanese-sponsored governments and quasi-governmental bodies in China. As these local and regional governments were brought into being one after another, they acquired territorial and fiscal jurisdictions that were carefully nurtured and expanded. Intergovernmental councils and other cooperative organs were established to facilitate liaison and joint action on matters of common interest, and they too jealously guarded their new powers. Not one but a half dozen new sets of bureaucrats were created as Kuomintang officialdom retreated west; officials, from the pettiest to the ministerial level, began to secure their empires. New channels were opened between the puppet governments and the industrial and financial circles in the great coastal cities to carry the time-honored flow of bribes and governmental favors. Others were opened—and apparently widened—to allow the new regimes to take over the customary governmental role in the underworld, from the gambling casinos in Shanghai to the poppy fields of Jehol. And still others were opened between each regime and its sponsor within the Japanese military establishment on the mainland.

From the standpoint of the various puppet regimes, these links, both organizational and personal, were vital to their very existence. Without the financial and military support of the Imperial Army they could not have been created and could not have survived. But the puppet regimes were also vital to the Japanese military, not only because they guaranteed some measure of domestic order and thus released garrison troops for other duties, but more important, because they gave Japan the silent partner she needed to effect the cherished economic schemes of the Tokyo planners and mainland Army commands. And, finally, the puppet regimes were concrete expressions of Japanese statecraft, opportunities to create institutions based on the "kingly way," which alone could combat the Kuomintang and its pernicious Three Principles of the People (*san-min chu-i*), save China from its drift toward communism, and provide an ideological basis for a harmonious—and subservient—alliance with Japan.

The task of dissolving all these new bureaucratic institutions and links in 1939 and 1940, in order to make way for a new central government, strained the considerable political skill and national prestige of Wang Ching-wei. The various regimes did not give way until a nearly endless succession of conferences had been held to "adjust the situation," and in the end the Wang regime had to make room for many strange and unwelcome political bedfellows from the despised puppet regimes. Nor did the various Japanese military and governmental organs resolve their differences without months of struggles and power plays so bold that they could not but attract the attention of diplomats and journalistic observers. A veteran reporter for the *New York Times*, with extensive contacts among the Japanese military in China, reported in 1939 a plot to assassinate Wang Ching-wei, which when trailed to its source implicated the Japanese Supreme Adviser to a rival puppet regime.[1] Relations between the various mainland Army commands were "very bad" and remained that way in spite of persistent chastising from Tokyo. The Japanese militarists in China were not only intent on creating a series of autonomous regimes there, but determined to tie those regimes closely to their individual Imperial Army commands. This process was facilitated by the extensive independence enjoyed by the various mainland commands. It was not until October 1939, when a general headquarters with authority over all Army activities on the mainland was established, that the mainland armies were checked in any substantial way. In the meantime they had ample opportunity to sponsor and nurture a number of puppet regimes, and these must properly be studied in some detail before we turn to a discussion of the later Wang government.

As early as the day after the Marco Polo Bridge Incident the Imperial Army declared that it intended to let the Nanking Government administer North China. The Army "would await the sponaneous creation of political organs by the local inhabitants" in North China, it affirmed in a policy statement by July 8.[2] And yet, as the war front expanded across North China and Chinese troops withdrew from cities and provinces, the regional administrative organs dissolved. To fill the political vacuum and especially to build up local military organizations capable of helping maintain public order, the Imperial Army sponsored the creation of local Peace Preservation Committees as it occupied North China. The first of these committees came into existence with little fanfare at the end of July 1937 in Peiping and in early August in Tientsin.

In charge of controlling the committees were the Tokumu-bu (Special Services Units) of the North China Area Army.* These units were attached to the headquarters of each Army command and were responsible for civil affairs and other political activities of the Army. They operated with a minimum of control from the commanding generals and gained a singularly unpopular reputation among Chinese because of their real and suspected interference in Chinese internal politics. As the war front spread across North China dozens of Peace Preservation Committees were set up by the Tokumu-bu, which after September 1937 were under the command of the man destined to become the foremost "puppeteer" in North China, Maj. Gen. Kita Seiichi. General Kita's philosophy of government was best summarized in the comments he allegedly made to newsmen in January 1938 apropos the newly created Provisional Government. According to the *China Weekly Review*, he said there would be practically no government regulations because the Chinese people were "impatient of tiresome regulations." Kita held that "the Chinese were peculiar to themselves," and so required neither a monarchical nor a republican form of government. "It was necessary," he concluded, "to go back to Confucian times to find a really satisfactory system for the rule of the Chinese people."[3]

Though the ad hoc character of the Peace Preservation Committees was evident from the outset, they were nevertheless the nearest thing to an organized government in North China for nearly a half a year, from July to December 1937. More completely under the control of the Japanese occupation authorities than any succeeding puppet administration, they willingly undertook to carry out far-reaching programs dictated by the Japanese. They lost no time, for example, in revising the educational system to allow for the introduction of Japanese-approved textbooks that emphasized Confucian and anti-Kuomintang sentiments.[4] In return for their cooperation, the committees were rewarded with substantial loans from the Japanese and were, at least in one case—that of the Tientsin Peace Preservation Committee— given access to important sources of revenue once earmarked for the Chinese central government.[5]

The committee leaders were typically elderly veterans of decades of po-

---

* Also occasionally referred to as Tokumu Kikan (Special Services Agencies). Though Japanese sources sometimes make a distinction between the two names, I shall hereafter refer to these organs uniformly as Tokumu-bu.

litical and military struggles in North China; many had careers stretching well back into the Ch'ing dynasty. The Chairman of the Peiping Peace Preservation Committee, Gen. Chiang Chao-tsung (the very personification of the Western image of a venerable Mandarin, judging from a *Time* magazine photograph of the day),[6] had retired from public life twenty years earlier, following his ill-advised support of an Imperial restoration attempt sponsored by the warlord Chang Hsün. Many of the leaders had had long years of experience in cooperating with Japanese mainland schemes, with careers beginning in the heyday of the pro-Japanese Anfu Clique and spanning the years down to the Hopei-Chahar Political Council. None commanded popular respect, and most were thrust into their posts from either obscure or unsavory backgrounds. It is not surprising to find the press speculating freely that these incumbents were simply being used by the Japanese until the services of men with better credentials could be secured.

The Peace Preservation Committees came into existence so rapidly and were so obviously transitional that they evoked little discussion at decision-making levels in Japan. Instead, attention was focused on the pros and cons of amalgamation of the various committees into a more formal government organization.

The order placing General Kita at the head of all Tokumu-bu activities in North China, dated September 4, 1937, charged him with "controlling and guiding Chinese organs in matters relating to political administration."[7] What those organs were to be was not explained. However, two days later the Chief of Staff of the North China Area Army handed Kita instructions, which, though more poetic than explicit, provided a clue: from these Chinese organs (presumably the Peace Preservation Committees) a "future North China government would emerge as from a mother's womb."[8] This was about the time of the Chahar campaign, a period in which Ishiwara was still striving in Tokyo to prevent just such a development. He could not have found encouraging the September 19 letter of Gen. Itagaki Seishirō, a division commander in the North China action, predicting that in spite of Ishiwara's objections, "we will establish a new North China Government once we have secured the line from Suiyuan-Taiyuan-Shihkiachwang-Tsinan-Tsingtao."[9]

The initiative in creating a new regime in North China, as Itagaki's letter indicates, was clearly in the hands of the mainland Army commands. In October General Kita reported to the Military Administration Section of the War Ministry his views on the situation in North China. His tone suggests he was not seeking instructions or advice, but notifying Tokyo what it might expect from the North China Area Army in the area of political maneuver. "What we hope to do in North China is to establish an area favorable to Japan and Manchukuo and useful for defense against communism. We have no territorial ambitions, but we cannot say that if the situation lingers on, there is no chance of our establishing something like Manchukuo here—or maybe something even more."[10] "We do not plan a committee-type regime like the Hopei-Chahar Political Council," Kita explained. He had something much more politically substantial and geographically comprehensive in mind. Provincial governments would be established first, and then "we plan to establish a 'Chinese People's Federal Government' [Chūka Minkoku Renshō Seifu]—we think we should use that name from the start." What remained to be settled, said Kita, was the question of personnel. A certain "powerful candidate" to head the new government was still being "cautious," Kita wrote, "but he will probably come out when we ask him to take over."[11]

By the end of October, the plan for a new North China regime had been taken a step further. In a "Study Concerning the Establishment of a North China Government," dated October 28, Kita argued that the North China regime should not remain a local regime but should become a "central government, which will replace the Nanking Government." A purely local or regional regime, he explained in terms borrowed from the Sung Confucianist Chu Hsi, would be deficient in *taigi meibun*, a correspondence between name and function, and thus would be unable to attract first-class Chinese collaborators. Moreover, a regional regime was "ideologically retrogressive and could therefore be overwhelmed with ease by the unification strategy of the Nanking Government."[12]

Support for Kita's views was given by the War Ministry on October 30. The Military Affairs Section advised the "expansion and strengthening of a regime in North China and the creation of a rejuvenated central government." With the restoration of peace, industrial development, and expansion of trade in North China, the Military Affairs Section foresaw a revitalization process that would spread to the entire nation. Its plan called for step-by-step progress toward a new central government: first would come the creation of "independent" provincial regimes in Hopei, Shantung, Shansi, and Chahar, next a federation of these provinces, and finally a structure linking it and similar federations to be formed in Central and South China.[13] The influential China Section of the Army General Staff also lined up in favor of the plan for a new regime in North China, and in a "study" of November 18 counseled the

formation of a "truly central government for China," which would be
pro-Japanese and anti-Communist.[14]

The North China Area Army received support from other Army
sources for its North China project with one major reservation: other
commands were adamantly opposed to the proposed regime in Peiping
becoming a central government for all of China. The most vociferous
opposition came from the Kwantung Army, which had created its own
puppet government in Inner Mongolia and had no desire to see its domains, which included large areas predominantly populated by Chinese,
fall under the jurisdiction of a rival regime or a rival Army headquarters. In addition the Kwantung Army had long been at the forefront of
a movement to keep China politically fractured. Talk of a "truly central government" for China was altogether too revolutionary for its
leaders. The gist of a study prepared by the Kwantung Army's General
Tōjō was that "we should not hasten to establish a centralized government in China lest we unnecessarily irritate various local regimes." He
proposed instead a loose federation to provide "absolutely no more than
the basic outline" of government.[15]

The Central China Area Army, which was looking forward to the
creation of its own puppet government, was also opposed to determining
North China "as the political center from the beginning."[16] The opposition of other commands was not sufficient to prevent the North China
Area Army from moving ahead with its plans to establish a government
based in Peiping, but it was no doubt instrumental in the Japanese Government's decision to withhold diplomatic recognition from that regime
and to limit the scope of its authority.

With the decision to attack Nanking in early December, General Kita
moved quickly to get his North China regime functioning before the
Central China Area Army could establish a regime in "liberated Nanking." Still at a loss for a proper leader for the new regime, he decided
to establish a provisional government and postpone the selection of a
head of state. The press had been full of speculation for months that
Kita was trying to recruit Ts'ao K'un for the post, and the rumors were
well grounded. Ts'ao, a Chihli warlord, had been elected President of
China by a bribed Parliament in 1923 and had subsequently been expelled from office. Had Kita been successful in his effort to induce Ts'ao
to serve out the unexpired years of his presidency, the puppet regime
would have had at least one nationally known figure at the helm; notori-
ety if not eminence could have been claimed. However, Ts'ao's price for
cooperation with Japan was too high. The same was true of Wu P'ei-fu,
who was even more persistently courted, especially by the veteran mainland conspirator General Doihara.

Consequently, when the Provisional Government of the Republic of China (Chung-hua Min-kuo Lin-shih Cheng-fu; Chūka Minkoku Rinji Seifu) was inaugurated on December 14, 1937, in Peiping's Chüjen-t'ang (originally built as the residence of Yüan Shih-k'ai), its roster of ministers and executives included some of the least memorable names in modern Chinese history. The highest ranking official, the head of the Executive Yüan, was Wang K'o-min, a Shanghai banker who just one week before the establishment of the Provisional Government was still in Hong Kong dickering with Kita's representatives over the terms under which the new regime would operate. Wang was unwilling to exchange an affluent retirement for the role of pawn in negotiations between the Kuomintang Government and the Japanese Government. He therefore asked and received assurance that Japan would break with the Kuomintang and deal thereafter with the new government alone.[17]

Wang was archetypical of the personnel chosen for the Provisional Government. He had begun his public service as a Manchu bureaucrat, had become associated with the Banque Industrielle de Chine in the early years of the Republic, and had returned to Government service as Finance Minister in several of the ephemeral warlord governments in Peking in the years from 1917 to 1924. Like many of his colleagues in the Provisional Government, Wang had thus reached the crest of his political career at the height of the warlord era, ten to fifteen years before the Provisional Government was created. In addition to his skills as financier, Wang was known for his beautiful and flamboyant concubine. T'ao Hsi-sheng, a long-time political confidant of Chiang Kai-shek who was a student in Peking when Wang was a Government official there, recalls that often during the performances at the Chinese opera the attention of the audience, or at least of the collegiate crowd, was frequently distracted from the stage to the balcony by the elegance and glittering jewelry of Wang's consort.[18]

Wang chose the wrong side in the warlord struggles of the 1920's and, emerging as a loser, had been unable to find a place in the Kuomintang apparatus in the following years. In December 1935, when the Hopei-Chahar Political Council was formed, Wang K'o-min was one of the members. In fact, many of the leading figures in the Provisional Government, including the Minister of Public Security, Ch'i Hsieh-yüan, and the Minister of Industries, Wang Yin-t'ai, had gained practical experience in dealing with Japan as members of that regime. All were excellent choices as spokesmen for the bitterly anti-Kuomintang posture that was a hallmark of the Provisional Government. All stayed on as leaders of the Provisional Government until it lost its formal status in 1940, and thereafter all continued to be instruments of Japanese policy in North

China until 1945. Wang K'o-min was the favorite target of the foreign press in China, which delighted in reporting such things as his donations of cash for Japanese soldiers' relief and his disgrace at being publicly denounced by members of his own family.[19]

The Provisional Government made no pretense at being based on popular mandate or election. Nor did it even hint at the possibility of elections, representative institutions, or other methods of popular control in the future. The source of its sovereignty was nothing more than a "constitution" written by a self-proclaimed committee. Structurally it resembled the Kuomintang Government, at least at the outset, in lodging power in four yüan: Executive, Legislative, Judicial, and Control. The powers of a fifth yüan, the Examination Yüan, were delegated to the Ministry of Education. Shortly after the Government was inaugurated, the Control Yüan was abolished.

The Provisional Government was also similar to the Kuomintang regime in practice, in that there was little real division of power among the branches of the government owing to an interlocking personnel system and the extensive powers granted to the Executive Yüan. The Executive Yüan, for example, decided all legislation and merely submitted its work to the Legislative Yüan (whose members were appointed by the Executive Yüan!) for approval. The Executive Yüan was clearly the center of whatever authority the Japanese advisers allowed the Government. It supervised five ministries, which significantly did not include one for either military or foreign affairs. There was in fact no serious attempt to secure international recognition for the regime, nor did Japan ever offer her own recognition. "Representatives" to Japan were appointed by the Provisional Government in 1938, but they were little more than "ambassadors of good-will." No treaties or formal state agreements were ever concluded. When negotiations were necessary they were conducted with the Japanese advisers or, at the highest level, with the Commander of the North China Area Army.

The jurisdiction of the Provisional Government, as fixed by the Inner Cabinet on December 24, extended over three full provinces, Hopei, Shantung, and Shansi, and part of a fourth, Chahar.[20] As Honan was occupied by Japan, it too was to be placed under the new regime's jurisdiction. However, the Kwantung Army had invaded Shansi from the north at the same time as the North China Area Army had moved on it from the south, below the Great Wall, and had already preempted for its Inner Mongolian regime all of North Shansi, centered on Tatung and including the vital Peiping-Suiyuan Railway, which linked the Inner Mongolian reaches with the capital. Moreover, the East Hopei

Autonomous Anti-Communist Government, accustomed to its own style of autonomy since November 1935, remained entrenched in its head-quarters at Tangshan even though it had announced its own abolition and amalgamation with the Peiping regime. It only gradually began to dissolve in 1938 after the senior officials were given key positions in the new regime.[21] The most important diminution of the Provisional Government's territory arose from the fact that it could operate only where the Japanese Army was in control, which is to say its jurisdiction was restricted largely to the major cities and railways. Thus, the Intendant of Chi-tung *tao* (the Ch'ing *tao* or circuit was revived by the Provisional Government) reported in early 1939 that he controlled only seven out of the twenty-two *hsien* (counties) in his circuit.[22] The new state was scarcely the Hua-pei Kuo the Japanese Army had long envisioned.

The proclamation of inauguration read by T'ang Erh-ho, a Japanese-trained physician and Education Minister–designate, is notable in two respects: its content gives striking evidence of the new Government's unrestrained contempt for the Kuomintang, and its style splendid testimony of the Confucian spirit of its authors. The Kuomintang, it maintained, had so abused its power that calamities had become commonplace. "The people had been deceived . . . , forced to bear the burden of back-breaking taxes . . . and yet the Party leaders persist in their shamelessness." As for the war with Japan, the Kuomintang had brought it on in the first place by a hostile attitude toward Japan, and then had not been able to prosecute it successfully, in spite of ten years of preparation, because of the "Government's disorganization and internal corruption." It was an open secret, the document said, that the "leaders who spoke of integrity and selflessness had diverted public funds to their own use and had transferred vast fortunes abroad." As a result of this loss of virtue by the leaders, the discipline of the rank and file had been undermined, and out of "bewilderment and cowardice" the Government had finally abandoned its capital.[23]

Two other themes were played on in the proclamation. The first was racial: the real tragedy of the war was that "people of two nations are killing each other—even though they are of one race." The second was anti-Communist: the Kuomintang had made agreements in the name of the Chinese people with the Communists and as a result had come to advocate Communist views to the exclusion of all others.

The themes enunciated in the December 14 proclamation were from that time repeatedly set forth and elaborated by the Provisional Government. They were woven into the philosophy of the "kingly way" (*ōdō* in Japanese, *wang-tao* in Chinese) to provide the ideological support for

a massive effort at social control. The kingly way in Confucian philosophy was the exalted ideal by which the rule of righteous monarchs
could be measured. It held forth as a model the sovereign whose training in ethical duties led him to a rule based on virtue and benevolence.
In setting the proper example of sound ethical conduct, the ruler demonstrated that he possessed the Mandate of Heaven, thus ensuring the
loyalty of his subjects and assuring social harmony. In 1938, however,
the kingly way was prescribed by the Provisional Government as an anti-
dote for many of the poisons—real or imagined—that were spreading
in modern China. In short, the kingly way of Wang K'o-min and his
associates emphasized a passive citizenry absorbing the lessons of moral
example provided by the ruler as a means of warding off the infection
of Western materialism, liberalism, and communism—"isms" that pre-
supposed an active citizenry engaged in reshaping the political and social order.

Above all, the kingly way was meant to combat Sun Yat-sen's "Three
Principles of the People" (*san-min chu-i*). Joseph Levenson, speaking of
the Japanese sponsorship of a "Ch'ing revival" in Manchukuo, writes
that "*wang-tao* was offered explicitly in opposition to *san-min chu-i* ...
which the Japanese and the Manchukuo men stigmatized as Western."[24]
Wang-tao was "offered" for the same explicit purpose in North China,
lending credence to charges that Japan wished to "Manchurianize"
North China. We have seen how the Provisional Government resurrect-
ed Ch'ing political forms (the *tao*, for example) and employed veterans
of Ch'ing bureaucratic experience; but the clearest evidence of all of its
attempted Ch'ing revival was the emphasis on *wang-tao*.*

Nor was *wang-tao* simply the preoccupation of a few tradition-minded
ideologues in China and Japan. Its inculcation throughout North China
quickly became a major function of the Provisional Government. The
principal agencies for this massive undertaking were the Education
Ministry and the Hsin-min Hui (New People's Society). The Hsin-min
Hui, which was established only a few days after the Provisional Government, was largely the brainchild of General Kita, who had serious
doubts about the ability of the elderly and unvenerated leadership of
the Provisional Government to generate much enthusiasm for *wang-tao*,
especially among the young. Kita also sponsored the adoption of new
terminology, suggesting that for purposes of public indoctrination *wang-*

* The culmination of the Ch'ing revival would have seen Emperor K'ang-te (Henry
Pu-yi) brought back to Peiping (or rather Peking, since the city would once more be
China's capital) from his palace in Hsinking, Manchukuo. According to George E.
Taylor, rumors to that effect abounded in Peiping in 1938, stimulated by news that
work on a new palace in Hsinking had ceased, and that renovation of the Forbidden
City in Peiping had begun. *Struggle*, p. 27.

tao, with its ring of antiquity, be discarded in favor of *hsin-min chu-i* (new people's principles). Ironically, the "new people" expression General Kita favored as having a modern sound that would appeal to the young was lifted from that supreme embodiment of Confucian learning, the *Ta hsüeh*.[25]

The Hsin-min Hui was an all-purpose organization designed to monopolize political expression, mobilize economic and military support for the Government, and in general transmit Japanese propaganda and culture to the people. It was patterned after the Concordia Society (Hsieh-ho Hui), which functioned in Manchukuo. It was not a mass organization loosely binding millions of members but rather a tight-knit organization in which discipline and order were achieved through the time-honored Confucian system of collective responsibility (the *pao-chia* system) and through an Orwellian complex of suborganizations.[*]

The Hsin-min Hui Chung-yang Hsün-lien-so (New People's Society's Central Training Institute) was established to train cadres to carry on the work of the Society, and the Hsin-min Hsüch-yüan (New People's College) primarily to train civil servants. After a graduation trip to Japan, the first class of the college returned to assume bureaucratic positions, principally in the Ministry of Education; undoubtedly many of the graduates were assigned to the Hsin-min model schools. The Boy Scouts gave way to the New People's Youth Corps (Hsin-min Hsiao-nien T'uan). Hsin-min hospitals cared for the sick. For entertainment one could listen to the state Hsin-min chorus singing Hsin-min anthems on Hsin-min radio stations or perhaps visit one of the many Government-run Hsin-min tea houses. The regime's organ, the *Hsin-min pao* (New People's Daily), was the source of correct doctrinal and news discussions.

The tasks assumed by the Hsin-min Hui became so comprehensive, and its chapters and staff so numerous, that it all but replaced the Provisional Government as the governing body of North China. The pervasive character of the Society was set forth by one scholarly observer as follows:

> There is almost no sphere of government activity in which the *Hsin-min Hui* does not take part; there is no province in the north, no big city under occupation, and no *hsien* without its branch. The *Hsin-min Hui* arranges the mass meetings and parades for the ccle-

---

[*] The total population of North China was estimated by American sources (in 1945) to be a little over 100,000,000. The Hsin-min Hui was estimated to have a total membership of 550,000 (as of 1943), but only 50,000 "full-fledged members," that is, people who had been in the society for a relatively long period of time and had received special training. All government officials, all school principals and heads of propaganda organizations were required to belong to the Society. United States, Office of Strategic Services, "The Puppet Governmental Bodies," p. 12.

bration of anniversaries, the fall of big cities, of anti-Communist weeks, and of all sort of other things. It sends out the orders to the schools to compel their attendance at such celebrations; it trains the youth of town and country, organizes the meetings for worshiping Confucius, for respecting ancestors, for denouncing the Kuomintang. It runs a whole experimental *hsien*, organizes cooperatives, sees to relief in distressed areas, distributes loans and seed to farmers, advises on crops and agricultural instruments, provides medical services to the villages, teaches Japanese to all and sundry, sends students to Japan, runs a school of its own, compiles textbooks, composes and distributes all kinds of propaganda, runs a broadcasting station, sends out traveling movie vans, encourages the theater, engages in censorship, holds examinations, calls conferences of family heads, provides free tea houses, conducts innumerable investigations as to social conditions, makes censuses, promotes Chinese art, controls labor, and looks after public amusements. It even imports pigs for breeding experiments. It sends out traveling libraries, and offers prizes for student essays. It delights in model villages. There is no end to its activities, no limit to its energy. From Tientsin to Taiyuanfu, from Tsinan to Paoting, the flag of the *Hsin-min Hui* (the Yang and Yin symbol) greets the traveler.[26]

As noted, the official philosophy of the Hsin-min Hui, the New People's Principles, was designed to counter the influence of Sun Yat-sen's Three Principles—that "rubbish of Western thought."[27] The *hsin-min chu-i* emphasized the Confucian virtues, attention to propriety, respect for authority, filial piety, and devotion to scholarship. The closest thing to a common denominator in the new "principles," which were never systematically (let alone logically) developed, was the theme that only Japan could guide China to her salvation and to what General Doihara called the "renaissance of Oriental culture."[28]

The chief theorist and first President of the Society, Miao Pin, a former Kuomintang revolutionary and a long-time admirer of Japan, contributed his own personal philosophy to the organization. Miao had come to feel that it was Japan's warrior ethic, *bushidō*, that accounted for the differences between the Chinese and the Japanese responses to the modern world. Only by adopting Japan's military virtues, whose origins Miao traced to the Confucian tradition, could China hope to imitate Japan's vigor and throw off her own torpor.[29] The eclecticism of the new philosophy was further demonstrated in its equal reverence for

Buddhism as a part of the common heritage of the two countries. A Buddhist university, for example, was planned for Shansi just as a Confucian one was for Shantung.[30]

If the optimistic hopes for a "renaissance of Oriental culture" never resulted in the expected mass conversion of North China to Confucianism, the Society's massive effort may have at least managed to confuse the allegiances of a large segment of the population, chiefly the older people, for whom such things as Hsin-min Hui–sponsored pilgrimages to Confucian temples and study of the *Ta hsüeh* presumably had some meaning. For the student population, however, it is difficult to imagine much enthusiasm for the transparently propagandistic essay and speech contests ("Why We Wish To Destroy the Chiang Kai-shek Government," "How China and Japan Can Be Intimate," etc.), the primary emphasis given to Japanese rather than Chinese history ("by order of the Peking Education Bureau"), the wholesale adoption of Japanese-approved textbooks, the compulsory courses in the Japanese language, the inclusion of such esoteric texts as the *I-ching* in the curriculum, or the substitution of ethics (*hsiu-shen*, "self cultivation") courses for civics (*kung-min*) courses, the latter being suspect because of their emphasis on duty to country and Chinese nationalism, which could only stand in the way of the national commitment to Sino-Japanese cooperation, the ultimate goal of the various "textbook revision committees" that flourished in North China in 1938.[31]

Lt. Col. Yamazaki Jūzaburō, who served with the North China Area Army, has pointed out some of the deficiencies of the Hsin-min Hui, which he describes as a "thought campaign aimed at the construction of a new North China." Though modeled on Manchukuo's Concordia Society, he writes, the Hsin-min Hui "failed to grasp the minds of the people in North China, who were culturally far more advanced than the people of Manchukuo." It failed, he freely admits, because it was "too bureaucratic and smacked too strongly of Japan." In the end, he says, the Hsin-min Hui "turned into a group of ideologically prostrated persons who were utterly helpless against the propaganda offensive of the Communist Party."[32]

There were two areas in which the subservient character of the North China regime was especially evident. The first was the extensive control over all governmental matters exercised by Japanese advisers. In this respect, Wang K'o-min was able to score at least a minor victory. The foreign press, normally very critical of Wang, was forced to grant that he had been "adamant against the application of the Manchukuo system to North China [and] had strongly objected to the distribution of a whole army of minor Japanese bureaucrats throughout the various departments and bureaus."[33] By June 1938 it was reporting that "Wang had his way." The host of minor advisers that had "honeycombed every department" only a few months before had "all been disposed of, and the principle of a few advisers of exceptional qualifications in the higher branches only has been carried out."[34]

An understanding concerning Japanese advisers for the Provisional Government was reached in April 1938 between Gen. Terauchi Hisaichi, Commander of the North China Area Army, and Wang K'o-min. It provided for a system of "cooperative assistance" from Japan, which meant, according to Article IV of an appendix to the agreement, "prior unreserved consultation between appropriate Japanese advisers and officials of the Provisional Government" in all matters of political administration.[35] But though the Terauchi-Wang "Agreement on Advisers" expressly called for consultation prior to the appointment of advisers, as one of those advisers put it: "When the commanding officer decides to make so-and-so an adviser, that is sufficient. His duties are prescribed, and there is no need for diplomatic agreements or the like." The same man concluded his candid assessment of the adviser system by likening the advisers to the *tsukigarō*, the senior advisers to the young nobles of feudal Japan who had a reputation for becoming more powerful than those they were supposedly serving.[36]

No amount of good intention or conciliatory behavior (assuming these uncommon traits could be found in an army of occupation) would have made the adviser system palatable. According to one Japanese observer, the biggest complaint of most of the Chinese he met was the type of adviser Japan imposed on the new administrations. Conceding that "many are grossly incompetent and . . . lack a fundamental understanding of the Chinese people," he cited the case of a Chinese friend, a bureaucrat, whose immediate superior was a Japanese man who "knew practically nothing of Chinese history, culture, or economics." But worse still, he had to "consult with him concerning even the most minor matters. He must consult with someone else before giving approval. Time is wasted and nothing gets done."[37]

When we add to this aversion of Chinese bureaucrats for Japanese advisers the contempt of the Imperial Army officers for the Chinese bureaucrats, we have the ingredients of something less than harmony and cooperation. Lieutenant Colonel Yamazaki recalls with evident distaste the quality of the administrative officials recruited to serve with the Provisional Government: "They were either pale relics of the olden days or third-raters who were shunned by both the Chinese Communist and Nationalist regimes. They were faithless and corrupt officials who reported to work merely to draw their pay. They incurred the people's ill will and resistance. Ultimately, this turned into resentment against the Japanese military, civilian officials, and residents."[38]

JAPANESE ECONOMIC POLICIES IN NORTH CHINA

We have already examined some aspects of Japanese economic policy in North China, particularly those relating to customs and tariffs. Another economic move, one that is especially revealing of Japan's purposes in creating the North China regime, was the founding in March 1938 of the Federal Reserve Bank of China in Peiping. This action was, in the words of one writer, "a formidable frontal attack on the Chinese national currency."[39] The Bank, which was under the direction of a Japanese adviser, served many important ends, but its general purpose was to separate North China's financial life from the rest of China, thereby shattering the fiscal unity and integrity the Kuomintang Government had been building since 1935. As a Tokyo business monthly put it in November 1937: "North China, like Manchukuo, will form a part of the gold yen bloc and a link in the chain of the currency system by which Imperial economies will be bound."[40]

Overruling the advice of its own Foreign Office, the Japanese Government had declined to support the British in their efforts to help China stabilize her currency and nationalize her financial institutions in 1934–36. Now, after the establishment of the Provisional Government, many in Japan felt it was within Japan's power to destroy the financial and economic institutions of the Kuomintang Government and thus hasten its surrender. The hope was that by issuing a national currency and prohibiting the use of *fa-pi* (as the national currency of the Nanking Government was called), the Federal Reserve Bank would manage to pull the allegiance of North China citizens away from the Kuomintang regime. The response in Nationalist China to the announcement of the impending creation of the Bank seemed to suggest that the financial strategy of Japan would work: there was an immediate "heavy increase" in the flight of precious capital from China and in speculation in foreign currencies.

In practice, however, the Federal Reserve Bank proved only a moderately successful weapon. When the Bank was created, the Provisional Government declared that *fa-pi* could circulate for only one year, that is, until March 1939, after which the Bank's currency alone would be valid. The new currency was immediately useful to both the Provisional

Government and the Japanese Army. By issuing its own currency the
Government could offset, at least for a time, its inability to collect tax
revenues from the guerrilla-dominated hinterland. By manipulating the
rate of exchange the Japanese Army could finance its own operating
expenses and promote its economic exploitation programs. But as a
political weapon aimed at undermining Kuomintang financial stability,
the Federal Reserve Bank notes were a disappointing failure. The currency, which had only nominal backing, fell in value as huge inflation-
ary printings swelled the volume in circulation to higher and higher
levels each month. Despite the severity of the punishments meted out to
those found holding Nationalist currency, Gresham's law proved its
validity once more: the sounder legal tender of the National Government remained in use and always commanded a premium in exchange
transactions. In certain Communist-controlled areas of North China
possession of the Federal Reserve Bank notes was forbidden by law, and
violators were executed. As a result North China citizens and Japanese
alike discovered that they could buy products from the hinterlands only
with *fa-pi*.

"The Federal Reserve Bank notes [were] refused by everyone who was
out of reach of Japanese physical coercion," notes one writer.[41] Even
those within the "reach" of the Japanese military avoided the hated currency wherever possible. Japanese businessmen in China, for example,
were reluctant to accept the Reserve Bank issue because they could not
use it to pay their Chinese creditors. Foreign banks operating in China
declared they would accept the notes against other currencies only when
the Yokohama Specie Bank adopted the same policy. The Japanese
bankers, however, steadfastly refused to do so. "The entire resources of
the Yokohama Specie Bank would be paid out for the output of the
Peiping printing presses," said the Shanghai *Finance and Commerce* in
September 1938.[42] A further blow to Japanese hopes for the Federal
Reserve Bank came when the authorities of the foreign-administered
concessions in Tientsin refused to cooperate with it. Indeed, they continued to keep their accounts on a national currency basis until December 1938, nine months after the founding of the Japanese-sponsored
Bank. As a result of all these difficulties, the *fa-pi*, far from being completely displaced by the Federal Reserve Bank currency at the end of a
year, was still commanding a premium of as much as 40 per cent some
two months later, in May 1939.[43] The already confused currency situation was made even worse by the introduction of Japanese military scrip
into North China to pay for the Army's purchases of local goods and
services. And to add still further to the confusion, Bank of Japan yen

notes and a special China issue of Bank of Korea notes were also circulating in North China by 1939.

The "reformation" of Chinese currency proved to be far more complicated and difficult than anticipated. A few years earlier it had been a simple matter to wean the Manchurians away from the depreciated and unstable *feng-p'iao* currency in circulation under the warlord Chang Hsüeh-liang. But as with so many other problems, it proved impossible to transfer the experience and successes of the Manchukuo experiment to North China. Public confidence, a very real factor in the Japanese successes in the early years of the decade, was notably lacking in the later years. As one financial analyst wrote: "After eighteen months of war and despite the loss of most of her important cities, China has maintained exchange stability to a degree previously unknown. To demand that a people abandon a depreciating and chaotic currency in favor of a more stable medium of exchange is comparatively easy; to force them to accept inconvertible and worthless notes in place of a relatively sound and stable currency is a tremendously difficult task."[44]

Opium played an increasingly important role in the financial structure of the Japanese-occupied lands after the outbreak of the war. The clandestine character of the trade makes it difficult to come up with precise figures, but the testimony of numerous observers points to a sharp increase in opium trafficking after early 1937. Among those who noted the increase was the U.S. Department of Treasury attaché in Shanghai, one of whose assignments was to report to the Commissioner of Customs on narcotics traffic in China. In April 1937 he reported that "Japanese authorities" in North Chahar were issuing notices to farmers "in the name of local *hsien* magistrates," urging them to grow "the poisonous plant" and setting forth rewards (such as exemption from land tax for minimum cultivation and exemption from military service for cultivation of five *mou*).[45] These crops, as well as those produced in other parts of Inner Mongolia and Manchukuo, were smuggled into North China by Japanese and Korean *rōnin*, who received "protection from the officials of the Japanese garrison troops in North China" in return for a percentage of the profits.[46]

The introduction of opium into North China was facilitated after the war began by the establishment of the inappropriately named Opium Prohibition Bureau (Ya-p'ien Chin-chih Chü), whose main purpose was not in fact to suppress the narcotics trade, but rather to bring it under the control of the authorities through a licensing system. The reports of the Treasury attaché to this effect were later confirmed at the postwar

Tokyo trials by both Japanese officers and Chinese puppet government officials.[47] Of particular interest in this regard is the lengthy affidavit of Mei Ssu-p'ing, Minister of the Interior and one of the most important officials in the Wang Ching-wei administration. Mei denied what he termed "the current opinion" in China, that the aim of the Japanese narcotization policy (*ma-tsui cheng-ts'e*; *masui seisaku*) was to create addicts in order to "weaken and impoverish the Chinese." The plain fact was, he said, that the Tokumu-bu found the narcotics trade a useful way to supplement the "very limited funds" they were allotted to carry on their "extensive work." Narcotics were also given or sold to "unscrupulous elements and even corrupt officials" for espionage purposes, Mei testified.*

Mei distinguished between the trade in opium (*ya-p'ien*) and the trade in other drugs (*tu-p'in*), e.g., morphine and cocaine. The one he saw as largely the function of local low-ranking officials acting on their own, the other as a highly organized affair that represented a major source of funds for the Inner Mongolian puppet government. Moreover, he asserted, it was an "open secret" that proceeds from the opium traffic were remitted to Tokyo for use as a "secret subsidiary fund" by the Japanese Government. It was not until 1943, according to Mei, that the Japanese Government took the first steps in a genuine opium suppression policy, a move that was occasioned by a sudden outburst of public resentment and student demonstrations in China. (The economic adviser the Tōjō Government sent to China in response to the crisis expressed his willingness to help the Wang regime suppress the opium trade provided it kept in mind that "opium profits were the chief source of revenue for the Mengchiang Autonomous Government [of Inner Mongolia]."[48])

NATIONAL POLICY COMPANIES

It was in the sphere of economic development, which is to say the exploitation of natural resources and the control of transportation and communications, that the Provisional Government was forced to assume the most puppet-like stance and Japanese imperialist aims were most evident. Slogans about "economic cooperation" could scarcely conceal the underlying reality in this regard.

The pilot program for economic control of North China was outlined

---

* IMTFE, Exhibit CE460, p. 3. The patronage of opium dens by Provisional Government officials wearing their badges of office reached levels high enough to excite the editorial ire of the *Hsin-min pao*, which declared in disgust that the managers of the dens had "even publicized this fact, saying in effect, 'If officials consider our den worth patronizing, why don't you?'" "Opium Profits," p. 551.

in a Military Affairs Bureau (Gunmu-kyoku) plan dated December 30, 1937.[49] It provided for a special municipal government for the city of Tsingtao, with a Chinese mayor assisted by a Japanese "supreme adviser" (selected by the Tokumu-bu) and a city council of half Chinese and half Japanese composition. Joint Sino-Japanese companies were to be formed to manage the local salt, alcohol, sugar, and tobacco industries. Consideration was to be given to the granting of tax benefits and monopoly privileges to these firms. Other jointly managed firms were to be established in Shantung province to operate the coal and iron mines and related industries. A single firm was to take over the management of all vital railways.

As Japanese occupation spread over North China it became increasingly clear that a more comprehensive scheme must be developed for the joint management the Army was counting on. Wang K'o-min was known to be especially apprehensive about Japanese insistence on complete and unchecked control of the economy in North China. "Wang is a banker and an economist first and a politician long afterwards," wrote one observer. "He definitely opposes the complete monopolization of all industrial and economic plans by the Japanese and while prepared to consent to their getting slightly more than a half-share in heavy industry, insists on the remainder being apportioned [among] the Chinese capitalists and . . . the Chinese government."[50]

To allay Wang's fears General Terauchi signed an agreement with him on March 26, 1938, providing for the establishment of a Sino-Japanese Economic Council (Nikka Keizai Kyōgikai). Five persons from each country were to be appointed to the Council, which was charged with planning the economic and industrial development of North China. Wang K'o-min himself was the Chairman; his Vice Chairman was Hirao Hachisaburō, a distinguished Japanese industrialist and former Cabinet member. According to Usui, Wang signed the agreement in the belief that economic matters would be settled through the deliberations of the Sino-Japanese Economic Council in Peiping, not through unilateral decisions handed down in Tokyo.[51]

If so, he was soon disabused of the notion. The authority of the Council was nearly emasculated from the very beginning. Indeed, on March 27, the day after the agreement with Terauchi was signed, Wang had to sign another document, an "understanding" with Terauchi stipulating that the "Supreme Economic Adviser for North China would control transportation, communications, and air routes in accordance with military necessity." Further justification for sole Japanese control of these industries was the contention that the Provisional Government had no rightful claim to ownership: most of them had been owned by the National Government, and since the Provisional Government had not yet been recognized as the sovereign successor to that regime, it had not fallen heir to the National Government's title.[52] Thus, these most important sectors of the economy were removed from the purview of the Council and eventually parceled out to joint administration by the Japanese Army and Japanese industry.

In the opening months of the war, virtually all industries related to resource development—iron, coal, electric power, and the like—in the occupied areas of North China came under the effective control of the China Development Company, which alone had the power to grant commissions to operate. Created in 1935 as an offshoot of the South Manchurian Railway Company, the China Development Company was securely under the control of the North China Area Army by 1938. The need for massive injections of capital and technical aid prompted the Company to invite major Japanese firms to join in economic development schemes, with the result that Japanese industry took over important management functions in China. Mitsui, Mitsubishi, and Ōkura moved into the coal mines; Tokyo Dentō, Nippon Denryoku, and Daidō Denryoku into the electric power field; Nihon Seitetsu, Ōkura Kōgyō, and others into the iron industry. Even important consumer product industries were penetrated by the Japanese industrialists, notably in textiles, with Tōyō Spinning and Kanebō taking over Chinese spinning factories.[53]

As the need for more coordination and central planning grew with an expanded zone of occupation and increasing military demands, the China Development Company was transformed into the North China Development Company (HokuShi Kaihatsu Kaisha). The new company was authorized by an ordinance published in April 1938 and was formally launched with a capitalization of ¥350,000,000 in November of the same year.[54] Ōtani Son'yū (the former Minister of Colonization who had fathered the plan for the giant holding company less than a year before) became its first President and immediately set about creating subsidiary companies and issuing further debentures. Where Chinese interests were concerned, as in the case of the iron mines, the owners had little choice but to accept shares in return for their equipment and property. By 1939 national policy companies with names like North China Communications Company and North China Electric Company were operating all over the occupied zone.

Still, many of them operated more in theory than in fact. Efforts to raise the capital necessary to underwrite ambitious programs of railway building, harbor construction, and the like met with little success in Japan and virtually none in China. The conflicting ambitions of the Japanese military authorities and the Japanese business community made the mainland ventures less than appealing. At a time of extreme capital shortage in Japan, the Army offered little incentive to investment; it was notoriously not as interested in seeing that profits were commensurate with risk as it was in draining off production and profits to fund its own projects. What little Chinese capital was available for investment moved even more reluctantly into the schemes of the *kokusaku kaisha*. "One must not forget," observed Taylor, "that expropriation of Chinese industrial, mining and commercial property is not a convincing method of illustrating to the Chinese bourgeoisie the benefits of economic cooperation."[55]

Thus, the economic development programs that in the long run might have benefited the imperialist victim as well as the imperialist master were frequently abandoned in favor of programs with more immediately attainable goals. It will never be known, for example, exactly what the Japanese had in mind in all of the programs for "agrarian reform" that were under consideration in early 1938. Given the social outlook of the bureaucrats in the Ministry of Industries and the Hsin-min Hui officials who would have administered them, agrarian reform probably had an uncertain future at best. But in any case, as the war dragged on there was understandably less and less emphasis on such things as model villages (except as instruments of social control), road-building, repair of river dikes, and peasant loans and relief. In late 1938 the Sino-Japanese Economic Council continued to insist on the importance of these and other long-range goals but frankly declared that the immediate concern was "to increase cotton and wheat production."[56]

It is difficult to assess how much of the failure to exploit North China successfully, even in terms of Japan's own interests, must be laid directly to Japanese ineptitude and how much to the guerrilla resistance that operated everywhere in the north, even within sight of the walls of Peiping. Japan cannot be criticized, after all, for her failure to construct the extensive railway system she had planned for North China when the track laid down in the daytime was ripped up during the night. Whatever the causes, the words of the American Information Committee in 1939 seem to present a fair picture of the wretched economic situation in occupied China: "Production, trade, and consumption . . . are far below the pre-war level. The general standard of living has been considerably lowered, and a large part of the Chinese people are living on the edge of starvation. With the war going on, the Japanese are unable to repair the economic damage they have caused or to promote new economic developments on any large scale."*

As the Committee's report suggests, the Chinese population as a whole suffered economically. In Taylor's opinion, the most significant damage, so far as the general population was concerned, was done by the "small-scale expropriators and profit seekers," numbers of whom were among the 220,000 Japanese who "embarked at Kobe to seek prosperity on the continent during the fiscal year [1939]."[57] Neither the puppet governments nor the Japanese Army could or would restrain these people. Their activities were a daily reminder to Chinese in the occupied cities that they were being treated as a conquered nation. By 1944, according to Japanese estimates, there were ten times as many Japanese nationals living in China as there were in 1937.[58] The depredations of some of these mainland Japanese were the subject of a report by an exasperated official of the Hsin-min Hui who, while conceding the necessity of military control over certain essential industries, deplored in the strongest possible terms the "willful plundering of the [Chinese] people's private businesses and the attempts to place them under the control of Japanese industry."† Pawn shops, soap factories, paint stores, and flour mills were among the businesses he cited as having been seized or forced to submit to a joint-management arrangement.

Colonel Yamazaki estimates that the number of Japanese residents in North China reached some 400,000, "not a few of [whom] were 'adventurer types' [*hito-hata gumi*]." Deploring the inability of these "adventurers" to understand the significance of the "holy war" Japan had proclaimed, Yamazaki charges them with fomenting racial antagonisms and inflaming anti-Japanese feelings among the Chinese with whom they came in day-to-day contact. "As a result," he concludes, "the ideal of a 'new construction' [*shin kensetsu*] was often distorted and demolished by these thoughtless Japanese."[59]

---

* Committee Publication 5: 28. Organized in 1937 or 1938 and headed by an American missionary, Edwin Marks, the American Information Committee prepared and disseminated to the American press documentary studies on various aspects of the Japanese occupation in China. Its members included American businessmen, missionaries, and journalists residing in China.

† *Gendai shi shiryō*, 9: 614. Koyama Sadatomo, an activist in Manchukuoan youth organizations and the Hsin-min Hui, is thought to be the author of this report. Usui summarizes Koyama's findings, which were filed after a 1938 inspection tour of occupied China, as follows: "[Japanese] who up to that time had no standing or reputation in their Chinese environment and absolutely no business experience were suddenly given a certain authority and were making huge, unjustified profits simply because they were Japanese." Koyama found this kind of "disgraceful" situation wherever he went, writes Usui. "Gen'ei," pp. 286–87.

The high-handed economic practices of the Japanese in North China not only belied Japan's promise of economic cooperation but in the end were self-defeating. In 1939 Minister of Foreign Affairs Nomura Kichisaburō complained that the *kokusaku kaisha*, which were supposedly "at the center of the economic development of North China," were "all short of machinery and consequently lagging behind schedule."[60] Under the circumstances, he felt that the "only solution" was for Japan to "do everything in her power to attract foreign investments" to that area. Ironically, dependence on foreign countries was precisely what the Army was trying to prevent with its policy of economic imperialism. According to Japanese estimates, American exports to the occupied areas of China did in fact increase nearly fourfold between the years 1938 and 1940.[61] Thus, Japan increasingly relied on Western powers—especially the United States after the outbreak of the war in Europe—for assistance in her exploitation schemes, the very schemes that later, in 1941, would prove one of the most unyielding obstacles in the negotiations between Nomura and Secretary of State Cordell Hull in Washington.

To round out this discussion of the efforts to bring about a "renaissance of Oriental culture," let me make a few, last observations.

First of all, the techniques and institutions used in North China were strikingly different from those employed elsewhere in China, so different in fact that it later became almost impossible to reconcile them in order to create a national government under Wang Ching-wei. To name only the most obvious difference between the Wang K'o-min regime and the Wang Ching-wei administration, the latter, far from attacking Sun Yat-sen, claimed that it alone was loyal to his ideals. It attacked the Kuomintang for having failed to achieve the *san-min chu-i* and styled itself the "Orthodox Kuomintang" (Cheng-t'ung Kuomintang).

When Wang Ching-wei visited Peiping in April 1940, shortly after the inauguration of his government, he was greeted by a "Manifesto" published by the *Hsin-min pao*. Referring to Wang's dedication to *san-min chu-i*, it declared: "We cannot help shivering when we think of it." Everything evil in recent Chinese history was attributed to Sun's principles: "The birth of the Chinese Communists, the formation of the Chiang Kai-shek regime, the alliance with Soviet Russia and the Communists, the surrendering to American and European interests, and the resistance to the Japanese could all be traced to the *san-min chu-i*."[62]

The substitution of *hsin-min chu-i* for *san-min chu-i* suggests the Japanese felt that North China was safe ground on which to implant, or at least to try to implant, a radically retrogressive political system and political philosophy. North China, after all, had not known anything approaching political stability since the days of the Manchu empire. On the whole, it was the south that responded to Sun's ideas of nationalism and supported the Republic; nationalism had only begun to come to life in the north. The Kuomintang had had little opportunity to transmit its ideology and organization to that area, being excluded or at least severely restricted in some provinces by the Japanese and in others by virtually autonomous warlords like Yen Hsi-shan.

The group that could be expected to offer the strongest resistance to the *wang-tao* schemes, the students and radical intelligentsia, were badly disorganized after the opening months of war. Schools had been bombed to destruction, closed, reorganized, or transferred to other locations, and when they operated at all it was usually on a severely curtailed basis. The radical resistance to Japan that had been centered in these schools in 1935 and 1936 simply did not exist there in 1938. Moreover, thanks to the Communist Party's policy of "purposefully bleed[ing] Peiping's manpower to provide qualified leaders elsewhere," the "cream of the radical young intelligentsia" had left the cities for the Communist-held bases in Shansi.[63]

In the existing political vacuum the Japanese felt that indifference was the worst fate their extensive political "reforms" would meet. The Army believed it had spent five profitable years in Manchukuo learning how to combat public apathy; there was no reason why its successes could not be transmitted south of the Wall. "Whatever may happen," wrote one puppet official, "our [North China's] spiritual home will not be in Nanking. In all things, in spirit as well as in deed, the north will be nearer to Hsinking [the capital of Manchukuo] than to Nanking."[64]

There was nothing in the Manchukuoan experience to suggest that the alien Communist philosophy would offer formidable resistance to the traditional "way" of China. Many of the military and civilian advisers to the North China regime had been assigned there from previous service in Manchukuo, and they brought with them an outlook on administration and a philosophy of government shaped in those years. Again, the remarks of Colonel Yamazaki are pertinent:

> Those personnel who had tentatively succeeded in the construction of Manchukuo took charge of the construction of North China, and with their simple way of thinking and narrow range of knowledge committed blunders in guiding local administrators, and gave orders inappropriate to the actual situation. Consequently, they would often have to issue an order in the evening to repeal an order issued in the morning of the same day. The greatest reason for their blun-

dering was that the Japanese in charge did not give thorough enough attention to the Army of the Chinese Communist Party. The Chinese Communist Party was winning the people over to its side by directing its efforts to the people and not just to the Japanese Army. Conversely, we regarded the Chinese Communists as mere bandits and placed more importance on their suppression than on activities directed at the people.[65]

A further explanation for the type of regime Japan chose to impose on North China lies in the priority that area took in her strategic thinking. Central and South China seemed far less significant than North China, and consequently many Japanese were disposed to accept a relatively independent regime south of the Yellow River. But North China had to become an intrinsic part of the Japanese Empire, in fact if not in name. The area's military significance dictated this policy: most proximate to Manchukuo, it was also most vulnerable to incursions from Communists, either Soviet- or Chinese-based, or both. And if that consideration was not enough, the economic significance of the area alone would have sufficed to dictate a policy of rigid control.

Finally, the presence in North China of the largest and most harassing concentrations of anti-Japanese guerrilla forces in the country helped dictate the character of the Japanese response there. More than anywhere else in China "pacification" in North China meant relying on strictly military techniques. The Communists' Eighth Route Army never allowed Japan the luxury of time and space to attempt more subtle programs of pacification, assuming she was prepared or willing to attempt them. The extreme military posture Japan took in North China, culminating in 1941–42 in the policy of wholesale destruction (*sankō seisaku*) of territory and population in order to deny them to the enemy, had its counterpart in a puppet government system more destructive of Chinese national interests than any other she attempted to impose.

CHAPTER SIX

Central China

IN THE YEARS prior to the Marco Polo Bridge Incident, the main thrust of Japanese expansion into China was in the area north of the Yellow River. It was there—in the Shantung peninsula, in the vital Peiping-Tientsin corridor, and in the Inner Mongolian borderlands—that the Imperial Army extended the strategic frontier of Japan and of its satellite, Manchukuo. From the Army's point of view, it was essential that the Inner Mongolian borderlands be secured to serve as a buffer between Manchukuo and the Soviet Union, with its client state in Outer Mongolia; and that North China be made autonomous to serve as a buffer between the resurgent China of the Kuomintang and Manchukuo. Needless to say, these "buffers" were not intended to be neutral no-man's-lands. Militarily they were to provide the Kwantung Army with a theater of maneuver; economically their resources were to be integrated with the production capacities of Manchukuo.

Thus, it was principally in the area north of the Yellow River that the Imperial Army, or more specifically, the Kwantung Army and the railway detachments allowed by the Boxer protocols, provoked a succession of incidents and undertook a series of campaigns—and in the end wrested the direction of Japan's China policy from the hands of statesmen and diplomats. And it was in this area that Japanese Army officers gained experience in fostering local and regional autonomy movements, in dealing with—and when possible manipulating—local warlords.

In the area south of the Yellow River, however, the pattern of Sino-Japanese relations was quite different. Remote from Manchukuo and from Japan's putative North Asian enemy, the Soviet Union, the area south of the Yellow River was considered of only secondary strategic importance by the Japanese. Moreover, in view of the Western powers' financial and commercial spheres in the great coastal cities of the area, Japan was constrained to avoid the incursions on Chinese territory and interference in domestic politics that were commonplace in North

China. Japan's goals in Central China were economic rather than military and could best be fulfilled through a complex of conciliatory techniques, commonly labeled "Shidehara diplomacy."

Foreign Minister Shidehara Kijūrō, whose approach to China set an important pattern in the late 1920's, was as forceful as the Kwantung Army generals in asserting the "visible and invisible rights" of Japan in Manchuria and Inner Mongolia.[1] He had altogether different ideas, however, about the Japanese presence in South and Central China. Even at the height of the civil war in 1927, when Japanese rights in those areas were disregarded, Shidehara advocated restraint and patience; evacuation of Japanese citizens from trouble spots was deemed preferable to a show of force. Both Shidehara and his successor, Baron Tanaka Giichi, sought to win the gratitude of the forces that would emerge dominant in Central China by avoiding interventionist schemes there. When intervention finally came, it was in the north, at Tsingtao and Tsinan in 1928. Three years later, when Japan undertook full-scale military intervention in Manchuria, she was bent simply on securing the area north of the Great Wall. Fighting spilled over into China proper only after the Chinese retaliated for the invasion of Manchuria with a very effective boycott of Japanese goods. The months of February and March 1932 saw bitter fighting around Shanghai, but it was confined to that one area, and Japan immediately solicited the help of the Western powers to bring about an early cessation of the hostilities.[2] No such mediation was sought or tolerated in Manchuria, and Japan ultimately withdrew from the League of Nations (in 1933) when that body refused to recognize the legitimacy of Manchukuo.

In the years between 1933 and 1937 the Kwantung Army overran Jehol (1933) and eastern Chahar (1935) and added those territories to the domains of Manchukuo; encouraged and helped secession-minded Mongol princes to establish a North Chahar–based government claiming sovereignty over Chahar, Suiyuan, and Ningsia (1936); and sponsored, equipped, and officered a full-scale military expedition into Suiyuan (1936). In a word, it initiated and supported autonomy movements aimed at isolating Hopei and Chahar from the rest of China.

While all of this was going on in the north, Japan's attempts to improve her position in Central China were undertaken within the framework of the international treaty and concession system that had been developing for a century. Typically, these attempts looked to greater representation on the Shanghai Municipal Council (which governed the international concessions) or a removal of restrictions on travel or business activity in the interior of China. When a series of anti-Japanese

incidents resulted in the loss of Japanese lives and property in several
Central China cities in late 1936, Japan turned to diplomacy rather than
military action to obtain redress. Neither the use nor the threatened use
of the Imperial Army figured significantly in Sino-Japanese relations in
Central China in the period 1933–36. The spread of the war from North
China to the rest of China after the Marco Polo Bridge Incident was by
no means a foregone conclusion; certainly the circumspect behavior of
the Japanese military authorities in the Shanghai area argues that Japan
wished to see the conflict confined to North China. The Japanese detachment that patrolled the streets of Japan's "defense sector" in the International Settlement of Shanghai was little more than a police force. Requests for its reinforcement were not filed until August 13—more than
five weeks after the Marco Polo Bridge Incident—and even then ran
into stiff opposition in Tokyo.[3] So weak were the Japanese forces in the
Shanghai area that one Western observer of the fighting there felt they
were still "in danger of complete annihilation" for a week after reinforcements began arriving.[4]

In surveying the different patterns of Japanese experience in China,
it is important to remember that Japan did not find in the major coastal
areas of Central China the kind of inviting political disunity she was
able to capitalize on in North China. On the contrary, in Central China,
the region that provided the original Kuomintang leadership, she confronted the core of Kuomintang financial and military strength. That
fact, coupled with the reality of Western interests and power in the
region, gave her good reason for caution. Consequently, though the Japanese military was reluctant to bargain with the Kuomintang leaders on
North China affairs, it was quite willing to deal with them on matters
relating to Central China. In early January 1938, at a time when the
Trautmann negotiations were stalemated, Gen. Matsui Iwane, the Commander of the Central China Area Army, began his own private peace
negotiations with T. V. Soong, then in Hong Kong. Matsui believed it
was essential to gain the cooperation of Kuomintang financial circles in
order to resolve Sino-Japanese differences in Central China. The negotiations, however, had barely begun when they were effectively ended
by Konoe's *aite ni sezu* declaration on January 16.[5]

THE REFORMED GOVERNMENT OF CHINA

With this background of regional differences in mind, it should not
surprise us to find that the puppet regime Japan established in Nanking
in March 1938 was significantly different from North China's Provisional Government. The Nanking regime, the so-called Reformed Gov-

ernment of the Republic of China (Chung-hua Min-kuo Wei-hsin Cheng-fu; Chūka Minkoku Ishin Seifu), was established and directed with smaller effort and for more limited purposes than the Provisional Government. The ambition for an autonomous Hua-pei Kuo, so cherished in certain quarters of the Imperial Army, had no counterpart in Central or South China; there were no dreams of a Central China-land or South China-land to fire the ambitions of the Imperial Army forces operating in those parts of China after the Marco Polo Bridge Incident.

Only a token effort was made to provide the Reformed Government with the equivalent of the Hsin-min Hui. The Ta-min Hui (Great People's Society) was but a pallid imitation, "nothing more than a propaganda organ for the Army." It made no effort to inculcate the principles of *wang-tao* so favored in the North. Insofar as it espoused a political philosophy at all, it was the doctrine of *san-min chu-i*—always interpreted to emphasize that Sun was anti-Communist and pro-Japanese. A vast reorganization effort failed to vitalize the group, and unlike the Hsin-min Hui, which survived until 1945, the Ta-min Hui was soon disbanded (in 1940).[6]

The records pertaining to the establishment of the Reformed Government are extremely scant, but by all accounts it appears there was little debate in Japan over the merits of establishing another puppet regime. The creation of a Central China regime seems to have been a foregone conclusion, in view of the Japanese commitment to a fragmented China and the rivalry between the various mainland Army headquarters. What discussion there was centered on two questions: the relationship of the Reformed Government to the Provisional Government and the degree of influence of the service arms of the Japanese military in the Reformed Government. On paper at least it was agreed that the Reformed Government should be clearly inferior to the northern regime: the Provisional Government would continue to make pretenses at being the forerunner to a central Chinese government, and the Reformed Government would have to face the prospect of being absorbed into it. As for the second question, the Japanese Navy faced special problems in Central China—control of the blockaded Yangtze, for example—and was therefore determined to place its advisers in appropriate positions in the Reformed Government. Accordingly, it asked for and received a far greater share of influence in the new government than it had been given in North China.

Details incidental to the establishment of the Reformed Government, especially those involving the recruitment of personnel, were left to the Central China Area Army, or more properly, the Central China Expeditionary Army, as it was called after February 1938. This vexing task was delegated to the "Usuda organ" (Usuda Kikan), a team of political specialists headed by Col. Usuda Kanzō. Usuda was unable to persuade the first choice, T'ang Shao-i, a retired veteran of early Republican politics and a Pan-Asian enthusiast, to head the Reformed Government. Indeed thanks to the Colonel's failure to find an appropriate candidate, the date for the inauguration of the new regime had to be pushed back several times. The mortified Usuda was said to have been reduced to "copious tears" as he explained the embarrassing delays to his superiors in Tokyo.[7] The pro-Kuomintang press in Shanghai delighted in reporting the delays and accurately speculated on the reasons—the recruitment problem and the necessity of resolving jurisdictional questions with the Provisional Government and with the puppet regime of Shanghai.*

On March 28, 1938, the Reformed Government of the Republic of China was finally inaugurated in Nanking in the presence of a large body of Imperial Army and Navy officers and amidst a plentiful display of the old Republican five-barred flags. For many months after its inauguration, however, it was forced to operate out of the New Asia Hotel in the Japanese-controlled Hongkew section of Shanghai, since the Japanese Army continued to commandeer the most important public buildings in Nanking.

The men finally selected to head the regime were of approximately the same caliber as those chosen in the north. Nearly all were veterans of the first two confusing decades of the Republican era, men who, having joined the losing side in the warlord struggles of that era, had subsequently either retired from active politics or taken unimportant posi-

---

* Created on December 5, 1937, the Shanghai government did not have jurisdiction over the French Concession or the International Settlement, which remained under the control of the Shanghai Municipal Council. The regime was known by a number of names but was commonly referred to as the Ta-tao (Great Way) regime. It was first placed under a mayor imported by the Japanese Army from Taiwan, an elusive figure named Su Hsi-wen, who was so well guarded by the Imperial Army that he was rarely seen by his constituents. Damaging disclosures by the U.S. Marine Corps detachment and the Police Department of the International Settlement helped undermine what little public confidence Su and his assistants enjoyed. They "turned out to be a bunch of second-rank racketeers and gangsters, most of whom had previous police records," according to John B. Powell's anti-Japanese *China Weekly Review* (Oct. 15, 1938). Su was replaced by Fu Hsiao-an (Fu Siao-en) in October 1938. Once the managing director of the historic China Merchants' Steam Navigation Company, Fu, as Powell put it, had "chosen the wrong horse" at the time of Chiang Kai-shek's famous Northern Expedition and had been forced to flee to refuge under the Japanese in Dairen. Twelve years later, in defiance of public threats that his ancestral tombs would be desecrated, he returned to Shanghai as mayor of the Ta-tao regime. After riding about the city in bullet-proofed safety for two years, he was hacked to death in his sleep on the night of October 10–11, 1940, evidently by his butler, who disappeared.

tions in the Kuomintang Government. Many were in their seventies and, according to one survey, none was younger than fifty years of age.[8] Many had been affiliated with the pro-Japanese Anfu Clique.

The most eminent personages the Usuda Kikan was able to recruit for service in the new regime were Liang Hung-chih, Wen Tsung-yao, Ch'en Chin-t'ao, and Ch'en Lu. Liang, the President of the Executive Yüan, was the ranking official, since as in the case of the Provisional Government a chief of state (President) was provided for but not appointed. Liang had been closely associated with the Anfu Clique and its leader, Marshal Tuan Ch'i-jui, but had gone into retirement after the Northern Expedition. By 1938 if he was known to his countrymen at all, it was as a poet and essayist.[9]

Wen Tsung-yao, the President of the Judicial Yüan, like many in the Reformed Government, had been a civil servant under the Ch'ing and had taken part in the Revolution of 1911. He had served in various posts related to foreign affairs in the first years of the Republic and had been in retirement since the early 1920's. Ch'en Chin-t'ao had also been closely involved in the earliest efforts to establish the Republic. A Yale Ph.D. whose training and competence in the field of finance had brought him to the attention of Sun Yat-sen, Ch'en had been named Minister of Finance in January 1912 and again in 1920 when Sun established his southern military regime at Canton. In 1927 Ch'en had been arrested by Nanking authorities for his suspected association with the Left Kuomintang Wuhan regime. After his release from a Kuomintang prison, he had turned to scholarly pursuits. Liang was able to persuade him to return to politics and accept the finance portfolio in the Reformed Government. He served in that post until his death in 1939.[10]

Ch'en Lu, the Foreign Minister in the Liang regime, was the only diplomat of consequence to join the Reformed Government. He had served the Ch'ing and various Republican governments in important diplomatic missions abroad. As the senior Chinese diplomat in Paris from 1920 to 1928, he had borne the brunt of numerous demonstrations (and at least one attack on his life) by Chinese students, who had looked on him as the spokesman for a corrupt and servile regime in Peking. After the organization of the National Government in Nanking in 1928, Ch'en's "effective diplomatic career came to an end," writes an authoritative biographer. His service with the Reformed Government lasted less than a year, for he was murdered by a band of Kuomintang assassins in February 1939.[11]

The Japanese found it equally difficult to recruit able personnel at lower levels of the bureaucratic structure. The Reformed Government could never be sure of the allegiance of its own personnel, who were, in the words of Paul Linebarger, "disloyal and of poor morale [and] often so corrupt that no government services—needed by Japanese civilians and army alike—could be entrusted to them."[12] A major reason for the difficulty in recruiting capable talent was the bad reputation the Japanese advisers earned as bureaucratic collaborators. "Oh, no, the Japanese do everything" was the response of a Reformed Government official to an American diplomat's questions about his official responsibilities.[13]

The Reformed Government was composed of three Yüan—Executive, Legislative, and Judicial. Under the Executive Yüan were seven ministries. The establishment of a Ministry of Foreign Affairs was curious, since the Reformed Government was never formally recognized by any foreign power, including Japan, and apparently never made any serious efforts to acquire recognition. The Provisional Government, it will be recalled, had no Foreign Ministry. Tokyo authorities attempted to clarify the situation by stating that, though the Provisional Government would eventually have control of foreign affairs, the Reformed Government would act as its "proxy" until such time as the two regimes were amalgamated.[14]

Similarly, with regard to the more immediate issue of revenue collection and distribution, Tokyo authorities endeavored to preserve the illusion that the North China regime was superior and would "control" those functions while granting "proxy" rights to the Nanking regime. Once again the arrangement was designed to last only until the amalgamation of the two regimes ended the need for "local" revenue collection and disbursement. In fact, however, the two governments never did amalgamate—even to the limited degree Japan proposed—in large measure because of disagreement over revenues.

The financial plight of both regimes was extremely severe, for they were denied access to customs receipts by Great Britain and other foreign powers, which continued to administer their collection. The damage this inflicted on the fiscal health of the two puppet regimes can be gauged by recalling that the Kuomintang Government had been deriving 53 per cent of its revenues from customs fees over the last few years.[15] On February 1, 1938, the Commander-in-Chief of Japanese forces in Central China, General Matsui, told newsmen that the soon-to-be-established regime "must draw its financial resources from the customs."[16]

In protracted negotiations with Britain during 1938 and 1939, Japan represented her client regimes in arguing for the realization of General Matsui's hopes. But at the same time she had her own interests to look out for: early in the war Britain's Sir Frederick W. Maze, Inspector-General of Customs, had taken steps to freeze the payment of Boxer indemnities and other Chinese debts to Japan, and these funds were sorely needed as Japan's war costs rose in 1938. When it came to an application of force to overcome British opposition, Japan picked the issue closest to home—unfreezing the blocked debt payments. By May 1938 funds from the Chinese customs were flowing into the Yokohama Specie Bank on orders from the Commissioner of Customs at Shanghai, who explained to the Nationalist Government that it was a matter of *force majeure*. Japan was not prepared to apply similar force on behalf of her puppets, and Britain was unwilling to yield to anything less than force.[17] Consequently, the puppet regimes continued to be denied the customs revenues that alone could have eased their financial plight.

The upshot of all this was that the two regimes became dependent on funds grudgingly supplied by Japan, extralegal income, currency manipulation, and squeeze. Japanese financial support was irregular at best. It came via clandestine accounts managed by the Tokumu-bu and various intelligence agencies, which had no dedication to the long-range financial integrity of the puppet administrations. This method of subsidization, the supply of sums for immediate tactical purposes, vastly enhanced the opportunities for bribery and corruption.

Extralegal income, for the Reformed Government, meant principally the rackets of Shanghai. Which is to say that both Japan and the Reformed Government found it expedient to make alliances with the nearly autonomous gangster empires of Shanghai, which dominated the city's lucrative underworld and in good part its total political and economic life as well. When it came to currency manipulation, Japan was somewhat more cautious in Central China than in North China. She did not, for example, try to destroy the National Government's *fa-pi* by making acceptance of the Reformed Government's currency compulsory. In fact the Reformed Government did not issue its own currency until a year or more after its inauguration, and even then, it made no serious effort to drive the *fa-pi* out of circulation. This was no North China, where, as we have seen, there was a massive attack on the entire financial structure of China in the effort to bring the area into the yen bloc.

The halfhearted measures at financial "reconstruction" undertaken in Central China are attributable in large part to Japan's relatively modest goals in that area; she was satisfied—for the time being, at least—to see Central China remain outside of the yen bloc. They are also probably attributable to a bitter lesson Japan was learning from her more radical schemes in the north: the puppet Federal Reserve Bank notes were so unpopular that even the Yokohama Specie Bank refused to accept them. Despite the repressive control machinery of the Japanese Government and the Provisional Government, *fa-pi* continued to command respect—and premiums—from Chinese and foreigners alike, to the acute embarrassment of Japan, which was maintaining that the issuing authority of the *fa-pi* was a mere local regime on the verge of collapse.

If Japan did not try to incorporate Central China willy-nilly into the yen bloc, she nevertheless exacerbated the fiscal difficulties of the Reformed Government by flooding the area with a variety of paper notes, none of which were secured against metallic or foreign exchange reserves. With these notes, usually pegged at unrealistic exchange ratios favoring Japan, the Army paid for its purchases of stores and supplies and compensated the hapless owners of the businesses and industries it seized. In 1939, when Wang Ching-wei was seeking support, one of the chief appeals he made to his countrymen was that he would do what the Reformed Government had been unable to do: induce Japan to either compensate the owners of confiscated property properly or arrange for the return of the property to its Chinese owners.

THE CENTRAL CHINA DEVELOPMENT COMPANY

From the standpoint of Japan, one of the principal ends served by the Reformed Government was validating schemes for Japanese control of industry, transportation, and communications in Central China. The sanction the Government lent to these schemes was far more illustrative of the regime's puppet character than its tolerance of the relatively scattered incidents of expropriation and confiscation we have just discussed. The grand blueprint for what was called "Sino-Japanese economic cooperation" in Central China was contained in a host of agreements signed by representatives of the Tokumu-bu and Liang Hung-chih concerning the operations of the Central China Development Company (Kachū Shinkō Kaisha) and its dozen or so subsidiary corporations.[18]

The Central China company, like its northern counterpart, was established by edict of the Japanese Government. However, it was capitalized at only ¥100,000,000 (against ¥350,000,000 for the North China company), reflecting Japan's relatively modest intentions for the new enterprise. According to the Japanese Government's official announcement of the firm's program, its "main objective . . . is the work of rehabilitation and reconstruction."[19] This was in contrast to the emphasis in North China on exploiting and processing natural resources—the iron deposits in Chahar and Shansi, the coal in Shansi and Shantung, the salt fields near Tangku and along the Gulf of Chihli. Central China had many of these same resources but in considerably smaller quanti-

ties, and the Japanese thus chose to stress rehabilitating that area's industry and obtaining control of its transportation and communication
facilities.

The task assigned to the Central China company was nonetheless staggering—at least as staggering as the war-generated destruction the company would have to deal with. Rehabilitation of the railroads alone was
an enormous project: dozens of railroad trestles and hundreds of miles
of track had been blown up or rendered inoperable, and scarcely 7 per
cent of the rolling stock was intact after the campaigns in the lower Yangtze Valley.[20]

The Central China Development Company (like the North China
company) was simply a holding company, and as such organized and
financed subsidiary firms. The names of the subsidiaries it established in
1938 bear witness to the scope of Japanese economic penetration in the
area: Shanghai Inland Navigation Company, Central China Electricity
and Waterworks Company, Central China City Motor Bus Company,
Central China Railway Company, Central China Mining Company, and
so forth. These subsidiary companies were considered to be "corporations of Chinese registry under joint Sino-Japanese management." Capital for the subsidiary companies came from three sources: the Central
China Development Company, meaning for all practical purposes the
Japanese Government; Japanese industrial firms; and the Reformed
Government. In every case, Japanese capital investment assured Japanese control of the subsidiary. The cooperation of the Reformed Government was needed to give the subsidiaries a comfortable legal framework
in which to operate—and to ensure that the Japanese company presidents would be assisted by accommodating Chinese vice presidents. Most
important, the Reformed Government was expected to charter the various subsidiary companies under monopolistic terms and with tax privileges amounting to virtually complete exemption on assets and income.
Japanese "partners" were ensured of absolute control over all important decisions affecting the operation of the companies by the terms of
an agreement signed December 15, 1938. The device used was customary
in agreements with puppet regimes: a provision for "prior consultation."
What it came down to was that, though on paper the Reformed Government had considerable supervisory authority over the new enterprises,
in fact it could exercise that power only on "consultation" with Japanese authorities. In addition, in case of "unavoidable military necessity"
the Japanese authorities were empowered by the December 15 agreement
to act first (in making demands on the "joint" companies) and notify the
Reformed Government later.[21]

The Central China Development Company is important to this study if only because it clarifies the relationship between Japan and the Reformed Government. But it is significant for several other reasons as well. Primarily it is important to our discussion because of later developments; to be precise, because when Wang Ching-wei began negotiating for his regime in 1939 he found that the work of the earlier puppet regimes was not so easily undone, and in the end agreed to accept all the arrangements to which they had assented as "faits accomplis . . . which will gradually be readjusted in accordance with developments."[22] This proved to be an unwise concession, which left Wang burdened with the thankless task of "gradually" wrenching away from Japan the privileges she had secured from Liang Hung-chih and Wang K'o-min.

Second, an analysis of the Central China company (and other schemes involving economic control over China) sheds light on the true character of the New Order for East Asia Premier Konoe announced in November 1938. The company was a concrete expression of that New Order, and by studying it one can translate the abstractions of the Konoe policy into realities and discover what "mutual aid" and "close economic cohesion" meant for China.

Third, the Central China Development Company and similar New Order schemes are important as hard evidence that Japan's intention was to end Western economic influence in China and replace it with Japanese control. Western diplomats, observing the operations of the Central China company, the closing of the Yangtze to Western commercial traffic, and the efforts of the puppet regimes to institute discriminatory exchange and taxation schemes, began to suspect Japan was not to be trusted when she proclaimed that she had no intention of excluding "third power economic activities" in China. Their suspicion was deepened by the announcement of the New Order and amply confirmed by a memorandum handed to British Ambassador Robert Craigie on December 8, 1938, in which Foreign Minister Arita Hachirō declared that under the New Order foreign interests would probably be excluded from those fields Japan considered essential for defensive, economic, or strategic purposes. Arita allowed that foreign capital would still be welcome in these fields but hinted darkly that Japan intended to exclude competitive enterprise.[23]

The activities of the Japanese-sponsored governments in China, particularly in the economic sphere, prove that Japan intended to use those regimes as "special instruments against rights of third powers."[24] For this reason, the Western powers viewed Japanese sponsorship of puppet regimes as little different from outright annexation of Chinese territory.

Indeed, the same criticism was voiced by Ishii Itarō of the Foreign Ministry, who in June 1938 advised Foreign Minister Ugaki Kazushige he had the "impression that Japanese claims to having no territorial ambitions in China belied the truth that Japan was actually waging a war of subjugation."[25] The road to Pearl Harbor was paved with the unwillingness of the Western powers to accept a New Order in East Asia that discriminated against their hundred-year-old rights and privileges, a New Order indeed that was based on Japanese monopolies.

THE UNITED COUNCIL

It is clear that some authorities in Tokyo were distressed by the fragmented China being created by the various mainland Army headquarters. From the earliest consideration of a separate regime in Central China (in late 1937), Japanese officials in China sought to assure Tokyo that the proposed regime was not intended to compete with the Provisional Government: the Reformed Government "would be so guided that in the course of its future development it will smoothly amalgamate with the North China regime."[26]

That the new regime would be transitory was understood by those who joined it and was made clear to the public in an announcement by Liang Hung-chih at the inauguration ceremony. "The Reformed Government," he declared, "is founded on the realities of the prevailing situation in the provinces of Kiangsu, Chekiang, and others. It is therefore temporary in nature and is established without any intention of contending with the administration of the Provisional Government."[27] Liang went on to promise that the union of the two governments would take place as soon as through traffic was restored on the east-west Lunghai and north-south Tientsin-Pukow railways.

Japan's Five Ministers, perhaps foreseeing the years of guerrilla action against the railway lines that lay ahead, expressed their impatience with any such deadline and, in conferences held in July 1938, resolved that the puppet regimes should be "guided [toward] incorporation into one regime as early as possible." Once this was accomplished, they explained, the new regime "would inevitably be recognized at home and abroad as the new de facto government." At the same time, the Five Ministers were adamant that the new regime should be based on the "principle of *bunji gassaku*."* The Five Ministers were thus in a quan-

---

* *Bunji gassaku* is a succint phrase used in many Japanese policy statements to describe the ideal political system for China. Unfortunately, the phrase does not translate succinctly into English. It is composed of four characters that literally mean "separate governments together work." The Japanese vision was of a China divided into sev-

dary. On the one hand they wanted a "national regime worthy of the name," and hence worthy of the respect of the Western powers, which in the summer of 1938 were undecided about their commitment to the Kuomintang regime.[28] On the other hand, they were still wedded to the concept that a fragmented China would best serve Japan's continental aims. But the officers of the Tokumu-bu in charge of relations with the puppet regimes, disdainful of the value of international diplomacy and committed to the support of their clients in the puppet governments, had no such doubts. Neither did the commanders and staffs of the mainland armies, who measured the worth of puppet regimes by their contribution to the war effort. In the end these officers "on the scene" (*genchi*) solved the problem of the Five Ministers by consistently discouraging amalgamation efforts.

The first and only significant effort at unifying the puppet regimes prior to the Wang Ching-wei experiment came shortly after the Five Ministers' Conferences of July. Direction of the effort came entirely from Japan, initially from the Five Ministers, who decided on July 15 to "guide" the Provisional and Reformed governments toward the creation of a United Council (Rengō Iinkai). Delegates of the two regimes dutifully met at the Yamato Hotel in Dairen—neutral ground—on September 9–10, 1938, to ratify the scheme and to work out the few details Japan had left to their discretion.[29] Formally inaugurated on September 22, the United Council was significantly modest in purpose and even more modest in its accomplishments, exactly in keeping with the aims of the Imperial Army officers who guided its creation. Observers noted that Imperial Army officers outnumbered the members of the United Council itself at the inauguration ceremonies; that imbalance aptly symbolized the character of the Council.[30]

If the United Council had any real authority, it lay in North China: Peiping was designated as the official seat of the Council; Wang K'o-min was appointed chairman; and the North China regime was given majority representation. The Council was given no legislative or executive functions. Its intended role as a preparatory commission working toward the creation of a "truly national government" was never realized and scarcely even tried. Its monthly meetings produced little more than angry denunciations of the Kuomintang regime for its accommodation with communism. The only real efforts under way in late 1938 to bring about a "truly national government" were made entirely independent

---

eral autonomous political units, which would work together but only in a loose, decentralized national framework. The *bunji gassaku* concept obviously ran totally counter to the goals of the Kuomintang.

of the United Council. The most promising of those efforts centered on the former warlord Wu P'ei-fu and, increasingly after December 1938, on Wang Ching-wei, neither of whom enjoyed any popularity among the delegates to the United Council.

Withal, the United Council functioned as the nearest thing to a national government in occupied China until the establishment of the Wang Ching-wei regime in March 1940. If for no other reason, it is interesting because it failed so dismally: its inability to take anything more than token steps in the direction of national unity was proof of the identity of interests between Japanese militarist and Chinese puppet. Both were at home in the manageable context of local regimes with limited objectives and well-worked-out techniques for attaining those ends. And both had reason to be apprehensive about centralist tendencies that could jeopardize their positions and goals. As Wang Ching-wei came to the fore in 1939, he was faced with the task of overcoming this resistance to national unity, a resistance that was beginning to rationalize the benefits of a politically fragmented China.

Those rationalizations can be reduced to a single proposition: China could best be administered by a government of federated states because such a system best accommodated the obvious disparity of development around the country. Different provinces were at different stages of civilization and economic development. Economic centers at Canton, Hankow, Shanghai, Peiping, and Mukden would continue to dominate regional political units but be joined in one federal government. The puppet *Hsin-min pao* elaborated on this theme:

> As to the Provisional and the Reformed Governments, conditions are very unfavorable for their amalgamation, which has been talked of for some time by the statesmen of the two governments. In the first place, the two governments differ from each other in the political and economic fields and in the field of foreign relations. This is also true among the three governments, if the Autonomous Government of the Mongolian Federation is brought into our discussion, for these governments are established on different economic bases. Each has its own political condition and each should go its own way. The Mongolian Government is the earliest of the three to have its own currency and to have the institution of an independent nation; for the old economic and political systems of this region were very simple, and it is very easy to replace them with the new, through Japanese authority. In the second place, owing to its early establishment and because of considerable serious study, the

Provisional Government has made striking progress in such ways as the establishment of the Federal Reserve Bank in the spring of 1938 and the reorganization of economic development, mainly under the North China Development Company. As for the Reformed Government, things are not so simple. There are the highly and complexly developed metropolis, Shanghai, on the delta of the Yangtze, and the Yangtze Valley where foreign influences are very complicated. New economic systems are not yet in existence and the reform of currency has not yet started. The Reformed Government is doomed to be of a slow growth, slower even than that of the Government which may be erected at Hankow after the occupation of it by the Japanese forces. Therefore, although the various governments have the same aim and go in the same direction, their real economic and political conditions are peculiar. It is impossible to put these regions under one authority.[31]

The inability of Wang Ching-wei to overcome this philosophy—or more correctly, his inability to overcome the Japanese sponsors of the philosophy—greatly weakened his claim that he had collaborated with the Japanese out of a desire to promote national unity and protect Chinese sovereignty. In collaborating with Japan, Wang in fact lent his name to imperialist schemes that were utterly contemptuous of Chinese sovereignty. But before we return to this important point, let us briefly survey the Japanese puppet regimes in Inner Mongolia.

CHAPTER SEVEN

Inner Mongolia

IN ADDITION to all its other drawbacks, the United Council could not claim, even in a purely formalistic way, to represent all of occupied China, since the Kwantung Army saw fit to prevent representatives from its Inner Mongolian puppet regime from taking part in the new body. This was more damaging to the Council than might appear at first glance, for the Inner Mongolian regime ruled over a predominantly Chinese population and included some areas—North Shansi, for example—that were almost exclusively Chinese. The Kwantung Army's actions plainly ran counter to the wishes of the Five Ministers, who had expressly declared in July 1938 that the Inner Mongolian regime should be represented in the Council.[1]

Though the Inner Mongolian puppet regime ruled over a largely Chinese population, it will not be discussed in great detail because it was not strictly speaking a Chinese puppet regime, but rather a Japanese-sponsored Mongol autonomy movement under non-Chinese leadership. All the same, its peripheral relevance to the purely Chinese collaboration governments makes a brief examination of its salient features appropriate here.[2]

In the last years of the Ch'ing dynasty, and especially in the years after the Chinese Revolution of 1911, China began to make important inroads into lands beyond the Great Wall, an area that had traditionally served as a transition zone between the fully nomadic Mongols to the north and the Chinese farmers to the south. In periods when Mongol power was strong, Chinese colonists were excluded from this area; but the Mongol tribes were weak and divided in the early 1900's. Chinese colonization of Mongol grazing land accelerated as railways penetrated the area and brought it in commercial contact with the cities of North China. Where possible land was wrenched from the control of the Mongol tribal chiefs and princes by pressure and connivance. Elsewhere Chinese superiority in modern arms spelled defeat for those who tried to resist. In either case the result was the Sinification of vast areas beyond the Wall, a process that was symbolized by the creation, in 1928, of four new provinces in what was once Mongol territory: Jehol, Chahar, Suiyuan, and Ningsia.

Though some Mongol princes and chieftains were satisfied with the titles and emoluments they received as compensation for the loss of their lands (and national dignity), others fanned Mongol resentment into a great national resistance cause. That cause fitted neatly into the plans of the Kwantung Army once it decided that its Manchurian empire had to be further safeguarded against China with a string of Mongol leagues. Accordingly, after 1932 the Army pushed its Manchurian clients into actions designed to win the support of the Mongols. Liberal policies, including guarantees against encroachment on Mongol grazing lands, were instituted in the newly created "Mongolian province" of Hsingan, which the Manchurian regime carved out of its western lands and portions of the former province of Jehol. When Pu-yi was enthroned as Emperor of Manchukuo in 1934, he held out the possibility of Mongol national reunification—under the traditional feudal arrangement of allegiance to the Manchu emperor. Though the Mongol leaders were never enthusiastic about an alliance with Manchukuo (and Japan) that was certain to have distasteful strings attached, they were able to use the threat of such an alliance to extract political concessions from the Nanking Government. The greatest of the Mongol autonomy leaders in the mid-1930's was a young prince of the West Sunid Banner of the Shilingol League, Teh Wang (Prince Teh).[3]

Teh Wang, a thirtieth-generation descendant of Genghis Khan, was a semi-Sinicized Mongol.* As a youth he was tutored by both Chinese and Mongolian scholars, but though he was familiar with the Confucian classics and a skillful calligrapher in the Chinese script, he always wore the tunic-like Mongolian costume, the *deel*, and remained a devout Lamaist. Like most Inner Mongolian princes, Teh Wang felt a strong loyalty to the Manchu royal house, and as a young man he was sympathetic to monarchist movements aimed at restoring the last Manchu ruler to the throne.

In 1934 Prince Teh was able to use Japanese offers of an autonomous alignment with Manchukuo as a lever to extract Nanking's recognition of the so-called Mongolian Local Autonomous Political Council, which was inaugurated in Pailingmiao in April of that year with Teh as its Secretary-General. From the very beginning, however, the influence of

---

* Teh Wang (or sometimes Te Wang) is an abbreviated, Sinicized version of the Mongolian "Prince Demchukdonggrub."

the Council was undercut by the Chinese, many of whom had vested interests in the regions where it was to have jurisdiction. Shortly after the Council was established, for example, Chahar provincial authorities established a new *hsien* called Hua Teh at Jabsar in violation of an agreement forbidding further Chinese encroachment on Mongol territory.* Owen Lattimore blames the "Shansi-Suiyuan interests of Yen Hsi-shan" for the efforts to prevent effective Mongolian autonomy. Lattimore's reference is to Yen's sponsorship of several autonomous councils, one for each Mongol league, with nominal power resting in the hands of men representing his "interests." These puppet Mongol princes were, in Lattimore's description, a "parody of Mongol nationalism, and tantamount to an insulting accusation against Teh Wang's sincerity." When the Nanking Government abandoned Teh Wang (in 1935) by recognizing the puppet politics of Yen, Teh turned to the Japanese for support. It was not so much that the Prince "went over" to Japan, says Lattimore, as that he had "been tied hand and foot and thrown to the Japanese."[4]

By October 1935 Maj. Gen. Doihara Kenji (at that time attached to the Kwantung Army as the Chief of the Mukden Tokumu-bu) had convinced Prince Teh there was no conflict between a Mongol autonomy movement and the Kwantung Army's strategic requirements.† By May 1936 plans for the creation of a Japanese-sponsored Mongol government were well under way. Though 1935 and 1936 saw small-scale Japanese military assistance to the Mongols, their forays into Chinese-held territories were not successful enough to justify Japan's sponsorship of a Mongol government. With the outbreak of full-scale war in July 1937, however, the situation changed rapidly.

In the opening months of the war the Kwantung Army, aided by elements of the North China Area Army and Mongol detachments, overwhelmed the provincial troops of the Suiyuan warlord Fu Tso-yi. Moving south from bases in Manchukuo and west from garrisons in the Peiping-Tientsin area, the Japanese forces quickly gained control of the vital communication link between North China and Inner Mongolia, the

---

* Changing the name of the Mongolian town of Jabsar to Hua Teh was a subtle Chinese affront to the Mongols' aspirations of autonomy, for apart from the common meaning "to influence with virtue," the characters for Hua Teh can mean "to acculturize or assimilate Teh." The subtlety did not escape Prince Teh, who returned the affront when he later established a military government there by reversing the characters to read Teh Hua, or "virtue will pervade." Hangin, p. 38.

† According to General Kawabe (p. 407) Prince Teh went to Hsinking in 1935 and expressed his "total allegiance" to the Manchukuo government. Kawabe thinks (but is not certain) the Prince received a "large sum of money" that was instrumental in persuading him to collaborate with Japan.

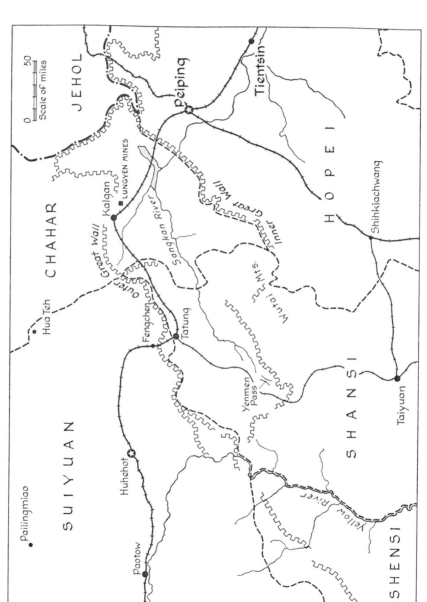

Mengchiang—Mongolian Borderlands

Peiping-Suiyuan Railway. On September 17 they followed the rail line across the Great Wall at Fengchen and exactly one month later reached the terminus at Paotow. By the end of October Japan could claim at least nominal control of all Inner Mongolia except the western reaches of Ningsia.[5]

The Tokumu-bu officers accompanying the armed forces lost no time in installing puppet regimes. The first, established at Kalgan (Changkiakow) on September 4, was the South Chahar Autonomous Government (Ch'a-nan Tzu-chih Cheng-fu; Satsu-nan Jichi Seifu). It immediately chartered a South Chahar Bank, which issued currency tied to Manchukuoan money. Soon after, on October 15, came a North Shansi Autonomous Government (Chin-pei Tzu-chih Cheng-fu; Shin-boku Jichi Seifu) in the vital transportation and coal mining center of Tatung. It should be noted that North Shansi and South Chahar are closely related geographically, both being part of the Sangkan River basin. Both regimes were centered in the small but mineral-rich area sandwiched between the inner and outer sections of the Great Wall to the north of the Wutai Mountains. Since the territory involved was overwhelmingly Chinese in population—according to Japanese estimates there were no more than 300 Mongolians in the South Chahar area and only "twenty-odd" in the North Shansi region[6]—Chinese were placed at the head of the two regimes.

The Chinese "control" was short, however, for a convocation of Mongol princes was called October 27–28 under the auspices of the Kwantung Army, and on October 29 the two regimes were incorporated into a Federated Autonomous Government of Mongolia (Meng-ku Lien-ho Tzu-chih Cheng-fu; Mōko Renmei Jichi Seifu). The new federation was headed by the senior Mongol prince, the aged Yun Wang; when he died in 1938 he was succeeded by his Vice Chairman, Teh Wang. The capital of the Federated Government was established in Huhehot, a dusty caravan town founded by the Mongol Altan Khan in the sixteenth century.* The Kwantung Army was clearly anxious to give the impression that the Federated Government was going to be dominated not by the two Chinese constituent regimes, but by the third element of the federation, itself but a loosely knit federation of Mongol leagues. In practice, of course, "adviser agreements" ensured Japanese control of both the Federated Government and its constituent units. The organic laws of each regime spelled out the virtually dictatorial powers of the Kwantung Army's supreme advisers.[7]

* Often referred to by its Chinese name, Kweisui, the city is today the capital of the Inner Mongolian Autonomous Region, which was established in 1947.

Because of such superficial features as the site of the seat of government, one is left with the impression that Japan allowed a predominantly Chinese area to slip into the hands of her Mongol allies, as the anti-Japanese press in China constantly charged. But the fact is, the Kwantung Army went out of its way to prevent such a development. For example, in response to Chinese pressure, the Army revised its plans and refused to allow Mongol troops to occupy Kalgan, concluding that Chinese fears of oppression and brigandage were justified. Similarly, favorable consideration was given to the requests of Chinese in other areas that they be subjected to a Japanese rather than a Mongol occupation. To the extent that Japanese management of the Inner Mongolian regime allowed the Mongols any exercise of ethnic superiority, it was largely a question of formalities. In every concrete and important matter, economic policy, for example, the Japanese held sway. Indeed, according to Usui, the Chinese who chose to cooperate with Japan continued to constitute an "economically oppressive force against the Mongols."[8]

Because this study is primarily concerned with Sino-Japanese collaboration, we will not further explore the question of the Mongol aspirations for autonomy and Japanese-Mongol collaboration. What does require more examination, though, because it was another of the great problems Wang Ching-wei inherited, is the Japanese disposition of South Chahar and North Shansi.

The local regimes in the two Han-Chinese provinces retained considerable autonomy and, in any case, were more tightly controlled by Hsinking (Kwantung Army Headquarters) than by Huhehot. The alienation of these economically important, purely Chinese areas from China proper must be judged as a more extreme example of *bunji gassaku* than the alienation of North China from Central China. As we have seen, the Kwantung Army tried its best to prevent the Inner Mongolian regime from participating in a purely pro forma unification under the United Council; the *gassaku* (collaboration) element of *bunji gassaku* was thus completely missing in the Federated Autonomous Government of Mongolia. The Kwantung Army's motives for retaining this area as its special preserve seem to have been almost completely economic.

The Army's decision to take a stand in North Shansi and South Chahar may be attributed to the advice the Kwantung generals received from the South Manchurian Railway Company and, more specifically, from one of its employees, Kanai Shōji. The South Manchurian Railway's activities went far beyond the scope suggested by its name. It operated so many political and economic enterprises in Manchuria that visitors could hardly tell where the government left off and the company began. The railway was also the main artery through which Japan pumped men and money into her mainland empire. Ever on the lookout for ways to improve and expand its operations, the company had underwritten ambitious research programs almost from the day it was founded in 1906, and by the 1930's the officers of the Kwantung Army were leaning heavily on the technical advice of the railway's specialists and researchers.[9] In the years immediately before the Manchurian Incident the idea of a multiracial, autonomous "State of Manchuria" began to be advocated by one of these specialists, Kanai Shōji; General Doihara, who helped to bring the idea to fruition, was "known to have been under the influence of Kanai."[10]

A man of diverse talents, Kanai was a physician (and chief of the Medical Section of the South Manchurian Railway in 1930), a bacteriologist, an economist, and according to one report "most interested in racial psychology."[11] After the Marco Polo Bridge Incident, he was summoned to the headquarters of the Kwantung Army and told to await appointment as adviser to a new "powerful and creative" Inner Mongolian regime. On August 27, 1937, when the Kwantung Army's Honda Brigade rolled into Kalgan, it was accompanied by a newly appointed Chief of the Kalgan Tokumu-bu and by bacteriologist-economist Kanai. (It was Kanai, presumably in his role as "racial psychologist," who contrived to keep Mongol troops from joining in the occupation of the city.) When the Federated Autonomous Government of Mongolia was established, Kanai became its supreme adviser.[12]

Kanai believed that the North Shansi and South Chahar areas were economically and geographically distinct from China to the south; that their more natural economic partner was Inner Mongolia, to which they were in fact connected by the Peiping-Suiyuan Railway. He later maintained that he reached this conclusion after studying the local economy and flow of goods in North Shansi, which showed that 80 per cent of the commercial traffic flowed on an east-west axis through the North Shansi center of Tatung, leaving less than 20 per cent moving north-south from Tatung to Taiyuan and the southern parts of the province.[13] The high peaks around the Yenmen Pass, at the northern edge of the Wutai Mountains, do in fact form a formidable barrier between North and South Shansi—a geographical feature that figured large in Chinese Communist strategy, it should be noted. The Communists' base area there was one of the most impregnable redoubts of Chinese resistance, to the point that though both Tatung and Taiyuan were occupied from March 1938 on, Japan was never able to gain even daytime control over the railway linking the two cities.

Rich in coal and iron, the South Chahar and North Shansi regions yielded two valuable prizes to the Japanese. The most promising of these was the Tatung coal mines, estimated to hold roughly twelve billion tons of coals; they were turned over to the South Manchurian Railway, which had some 4,000 laborers working them by the end of 1938.[14] The pricing policy for Tatung coal provides an excellent illustration of Japan's ruthless exploitation of Chinese resources. The going price for Tatung coal in the Peiping-Tientsin area was ¥1,000 per ton. In Yokohama the same ton of coal cost only ¥40. The ex-Imperial Army officer who cites these figures comments that the "majority of the Chinese living in the Tatung area simply regarded this as plundering by the Japanese Army." It provided the Communists, "who emphasized the hardships suffered by the people, with very effective propaganda," he adds.[15]

The Lungyen iron mines and smelters (in South Chahar) were the other great prize. Both were entrusted to the Fushun Collieries, a subsidiary of the South Manchurian Railway. But neither the industrial plants nor the mines were ever fully exploited. The irony was that Japan's war so strained her economy that she was never able to make effective use of the spoils she won. She was unable to come up with the capital to modernize the Lungyen iron works, which were built in 1919 but never used because of a fall in the price of iron after World War I. Nor was she able to find the funds to increase the small capacity of the existing railroads in the area. Chinese Communist harassment of transportation and communication lines also helped to prevent the area from becoming an economic asset to Japan. Insofar as the rationale for Japanese expansion was economic, the North Shansi and South Chahar experience suggested that rationale to be somewhat misguided.

The Kwantung Army did not accomplish its detachment of North Shansi and South Chahar without opposition. Both the rival North China Area Army and the War Ministry in Tokyo criticized its actions. In 1932, as one recent historical study has shown, the "complete political reconstruction of Manchuria was achieved . . . at the hands of the Kwantung Army *in defiance of government and central military leaders.*"[16] The political reconstruction of North Shansi and South Chahar was accomplished with the same defiance on the part of the Kwantung Army and the same resignation on the part of Tokyo authorities.

On August 13, 1937, approximately one week before operations in the North Shansi–South Chahar areas commenced, the Kwantung Army drew up a plan providing for its control over the South Chahar area through a Dai Tokumu Kikan (Grand Special Services Agency) located in Kalgan. General Tōjō, the Kwantung Army's Chief of Staff, submitted the plan to the War Ministry and immediately received a flat rejection from Vice Minister of War Umezu. Tōjō, not to be put off, replied that the measure was necessary if the Kwantung Army was to establish a "safe zone" adjoining Manchukuo.[17]

But the War Ministry did not relent, and on September 4 it issued its own plan, demarcating the jurisdictional boundaries of the Kwantung and North China Area armies. The Ministry proposed that the Kwantung Army's jurisdiction end at the northern side of the outer wall of the Great Wall, and that the portions of North Shansi and South Chahar sandwiched between the inner and outer walls be entrusted to the North China Area Army.[18] Both armies actually moved into the area in question, but it was the Kwantung Army that finally prevailed in violation of the War Ministry's injunctions.

On October 1 the Kwantung Army released a lengthy document that indicated the Kwantung generals intended to take matters into their own hands and present the Government with a fait accompli in the disputed area. This document spelled out in explicit detail the plan for a federation in Mengchiang,* guided by the Kwantung Army and extending as far south as the inner wall. The Army went ahead with this plan despite continuing protests from General Umezu that it would "create many problems in our relationships with all of China."[19]

The Konoe Cabinet also voiced its concern over the defiant behavior of the Kwantung Army. On December 24, 1937, it declared that the Kwantung Army's effective control of the area could not be regarded as a permanent situation; South Chahar and North Shansi would have to be returned to North China "at the proper time."[20]

The Kwantung Army was incensed at the Cabinet's position. On the day of the Cabinet meeting, the Kwantung Army Commander, General Ueda, wrote to the War Ministry saying that he had heard rumors of the position the Cabinet was going to take. To regard North Shansi and

---

* The Japanese applied the name Mengchiang (Mōkyō), which literally means Mongolian borderlands, to the area comprising North Shansi, South Chahar, and Inner Mongolia. The name was rarely used by the Chinese, even those in puppet regimes, who uniformly resented the implication that parts of Shansi and Chahar were in any sense Mongolian. The name invited confusion because the *chiang* in Mengchiang is denoted by the same character as the *chiang* in Sinkiang (in correct transliteration, Hsinchiang). Thus, many Chinese interpreted the unfamiliar term Mengchiang to signify "Mongolia and Sinkiang" and indicted Japan for an aggrandizement she never actually attempted.

South Chahar as a part of North China would be "to ignore existing realities, would cause a loss of faith in the Imperial Japanese Army and, furthermore, would destroy at its very roots all of the planning that we have been carrying out so diligently," he declared.[21] Two days later Vice Minister Umezu replied in language that left no doubt he sided with the Cabinet and strongly opposed detaching North Shansi and South Chahar from China proper. The ambitions of the Kwantung Army contained "the seeds of future troubles ... with the North China regime [the Provisional Government] and, for that matter, with China as a whole," he warned Ueda.[22]

The Kwantung Army ignored both the Cabinet decision and Umezu's warning. It had not been caught off guard by the Cabinet's resolution of December 24, as its maneuvers beforehand reveal. One month earlier it had sponsored the organization of the so-called United Committee of Mengchiang (Mōkyō Rengō Iinkai). Composed of representatives from the three constituent regimes of the Federated Autonomous Government of Mongolia, the new body was designed to have the "character of the administrative department of a central government," according to Kwantung Army directives.[23] It seems to have been concerned mainly with matters related to transportation, communications, finance, and the economy in general. The Kwantung Army's intent is clear in the secret agreements it concluded with the Committee's leaders at the time the group was formed. One of the provisions was that, regardless of any future formal agreements concerning the area, "there will be no changes whatsoever with regard to the administration of the United Committee of Mengchiang."[24]

The administrative powers of the United Committee were largely in the hands of Japanese advisers. On November 22, the very day the Committee was established, General Ueda received a letter from the leaders of the three autonomous governments of Mongolia soliciting the "leadership" of the Kwantung Army in their affairs.[25] Specifically, they asked Ueda to recommend Japanese and Manchukuoan advisers, who would be duly appointed by the Committee. The Committee would also appoint Japanese and Manchukuoan agencies "to manage important industries and transportation facilities" under its jurisdiction. The chief administrative officer of the Committee was a Director-General. Teh Wang was the first named to this post. An "understanding" provided that when the office was vacant, the Japanese Supreme Adviser would assume authority. In April 1939 Prince Teh resigned in dissatisfaction over Japanese policies, and Supreme Adviser Kanai Shōji took over the duties of the Director-General.

By means of this kind of political maneuvering, the Kwantung Army sought to accomplish in Kalgan in 1937 exactly what it had accomplished in Mukden five years earlier. In both cases it contrived to place the territories it controlled beyond the reach of the Japanese Government, with its "unreformed" party politicians and capitalists. In both cases, it succeeded. Throughout the war Mengchiang remained an almost private preserve of the mainland Army commands.

But the Army lost the support of its principal Inner Mongolian collaborator, Prince Teh. By late 1939 Teh had established contact with Chiang Kai-shek through Chiang's intelligence chief, General Tai Li. Though Teh expressed a willingness to defect to Chungking, Chiang encouraged him to remain in Inner Mongolia in ostensible collaboration with the Japanese. Teh is said to have received a secret communication from Chiang directing him to "be neither recalcitrant nor subservient" (*pu k'ang pu pei*).[26] One Japanese visitor to Inner Mongolia in late 1939 came away from an interview with Teh with the impression that "something of the spirit of Genghis Khan has been reincarnated in the Prince." "Any attempt to press [his] soul into service will not succeed," the visitor observed.[27]

CHAPTER EIGHT

1938—Various Solutions for the China Problem

IN THE many Japanese policy statements, staff papers, speeches, and conferences dealing with China in 1938, nothing is more consistently stressed by the officials charged with the solution of the China problem than the need to "unify." Advocates representing a whole spectrum of viewpoints repeatedly spoke of the need to unify thought, to unify policy, to unify actions. The word was used so often and so vaguely as to appear at first glance as one of those empty expressions favored by bureaucrats to skirt the substance of an issue. In any case, in the strained atmosphere of the late 1930's in Japan, there was a natural affinity for innocuous and ambiguous expression. Both factors may have had something to do with the emphasis on the urgency of a unified China policy. Yet that emphasis was altogether appropriate, for in 1938 Japan's China policy suffered from a disunity that threatened to paralyze attempts to bring the war to a successful conclusion, whether through negotiations or through military means. According to the Chief Secretary to the Lord Privy Seal, Marquis Matsudaira Yasumasa, the Emperor himself was chagrined at the Government's uncertain China policy in mid-1938. Matsudaira quotes the Emperor as saying, in the course of a conversation in June 1938: "Konoe visited me the other day and said, 'I would like to guide the war to an end as rapidly as possible.' Today, however, the Chief of the Army General Staff came, and he said, 'We will attack Hankow no matter what it takes.' One group says that it wants to end the war, and the other group says that it will go so far as to attack Hankow. What a pity that there is no liaison between them."[1]

The defeat of General Tada's proposals in the January 11 Imperial Conference and the promulgation of the *aite ni sezu* declaration five days later ushered in a long period in which those who held relatively moderate views were clearly on the defensive. They were ranged against a majority that was confident of Japan's ability to inflict military defeat on China, suspicious of any attempts to achieve a solution before China had been decisively "chastised," and now, in early 1938, blessed with

Imperial sanction for a war of annihilation. Only a few years before, the would-be chastisers had successfully applied military might against China in the Manchurian episode and, in 1938, they were impatient with those who called for less forceful methods. "They erred," one of their critics has written, "in advocating a reckless use of force based on the wild dream that they could solve the China problem by a policy of intimidation just as they had done before." The same writer sees the designation of the war as an "incident" as symbolic of the militarists' inability to come to grips with fundamental solutions and of the misplaced optimism that led them to think each new campaign would break the back of Chinese resistance.[2]

Still, if the hard-liners had the upper hand throughout 1938, they were nevertheless unable to expand the war with impunity. One month after the mid-January conferences, an Imperial Conference was held to decide future military strategy against China. Since the frightful breakdown of discipline in Nanking two months earlier, an "operational lull" had prevailed on the battlefields of China at the insistence of the Army General Staff. Before commencing new operations, the General Staff felt it was necessary to assess the entire military picture in China, build up support bases, and above all restore discipline in the mainland commands. Once it became clear that the Government's goal was now the annihilation of the Kuomintang regime, the General Staff set about devising strategic plans appropriate to what it felt was certain to be a protracted war (*jikyūsen*). By the end of January it had drawn up a "restrained policy for protracted war" (*shōkyoku jikyūsen*), which envisioned three stages.[3] The first stage—through the rest of 1938—would see a continuation of the operational lull in China while Japan built up her national resources. On the mainland she was to do no more than assist the puppet regimes she had created. Not until the second stage, from 1939 through 1940, were large-scale military campaigns to be countenanced against Chinese cities, including Hankow. Provided the mobilization plans of the General Staff were adopted, when the third stage began, in 1941, Japan would have an air force of ten thousand planes and a ninety-division Army capable of fighting a two-front war against both China and the Soviet Union.

The ink was not dry on the General Staff's "restraint policy" before it was challenged by a "positive policy for a protracted war" (*sekkyoku-teki jikyūsen*), the work of mainland Army commands, which protested that the prolonged period of inactivity would demoralize their troops. The North and Central China armies were both anxious to get on with the war in order to strengthen their strategic positions. The North China

Area Army was eager to move south along the Tientsin-Pukow Railway toward the vital rail junction of Hsüchou and eventually join forces with the Central China command. The Central China Expeditionary Army was dissatisfied with orders that left it in vulnerable positions on the south bank of the Yangtze and wished to cross to the northern side. In early February 1938, in violation of those orders, it began small-scale operations to the north of the Yangtze.[4] The various mainland Army headquarters were further impelled to proceed with a "positive policy" because of their secret commitments to their collaborationist clients, who naturally felt uneasy as long as the central government remained unannihilated.[5] There was also dissatisfaction in certain quarters in the Navy over the General Staff's standstill policy and a good deal of pressure for the Army to push up the Yangtze to capture such strategically valuable sites as Anking, whose air base was needed for naval air force operations.[6] Ultimately the Navy too began calling for a resumption of large-scale military activities.

Behind the restraint policy, which had the support of General Tada and Colonel Kawabe, was the conviction that the avenues for eventual reconciliation between Japan and the Kuomintang must not be completely closed, the *aite ni sezu* declaration notwithstanding. Indeed, General Tada and his Stratagem Section (Bōryaku-ka) Chief, Col. Kagesa Sadaaki, were beginning cautious exploratory talks with an official representative of Chiang Kai-shek less than a month after Konoe had declared the *aite ni sezu* policy. Tada and the other anti-expansionists had little enthusiasm for the collaboration governments and even less for the notion that Japan's destiny in East Asia should be tied to Wang K'o-min. But the mainland Army commands, supported by Foreign Minister Hirota and other Cabinet members, were bent on proving the wisdom of the *aite ni sezu* policy by eradicating the forces of the National Government as quickly as possible. Konoe, who had not yet arrived at the disenchantment with the *aite ni sezu* policy that he was to feel a few months later, offered no resistance to the "positive policy," which quickly gained the endorsement of War Minister Sugiyama and Vice Minister of War Umezu.

Once again General Tada threw the weight of the General Staff against an extension of the war, and after a stormy debate at an Imperial Conference on February 16, 1938, it appeared that the policy of restraint had won out.* In the presence of the Emperor, Tada secured an understanding for a "maintenance of the status quo and no further advances."[7]

* This meeting was a rather rare Imperial Conference of the Imperial Headquarters (Daihon'ei Gozen Kaigi), that is, an Army-Navy meeting with the Emperor, from which all civilian members of the Government were excluded.

The Emperor may have played a role in Tada's victory on February 16, for in one of his rare utterances at Imperial Conferences he questioned War Minister Sugiyama about the feasibility of a protracted war in China at a time when the Army was supposedly giving increased attention to preparations for war with the Soviet Union, and the Navy to a program of expansion. Sugiyama's consternation permitted him no more than an evasive reply to the effect that he would consult with the Government on the matter.[8] As was so often the case, however, the initiative proved to be in the field rather than at the Center. Colonel Kawabe, by this time known, in his own words, as the "dregs" of the Ishiwara "defeatist" camp, was given the impossible task of explaining the policy of restraint to the mainland commanders. He was "deluged with voices of discontent" during a mainland inspection tour in late February 1938.[9] General Tada had no choice but to replace the unpopular Kawabe on his return to Tokyo on March 1. His successor, Lt. Col. Inada Masazumi, feared that the China Incident was in danger of being "converted into another Siberian expedition"—a repetition of the costly 1918-22 fiasco that had shattered national confidence in the Imperial Army for a decade.[10] To avoid such a catastrophe, the new Operations Chief immediately scuttled the General Staff's policy of restraint in favor of a new "positive policy." That policy, in effect, simply did away with the first stage of the policy of restraint. The Army now received the go-ahead for a large-scale offensive against Hsüchou.

On March 14 a large force of Japanese troops began to move south from Shantung, and eight days later, though the Hsüchou campaign had not yet been officially authorized from Tokyo, foreign journalists in Peiping were advised by a Japanese officer that the objective of the drive was Hsüchou. On April 7 the fateful campaign finally received official sanction: the Imperial Headquarters ordered the North China Area Army to seize the Tientsin-Pukow Railway and to move as far south as the outskirts of Hsüchou, where the Central China Expeditionary Army, moving north along the same railway line, would make contact with it.[11] This pincer operation required the use of the Kwantung Army reserve forces, which to this point had been held back against the possibility of a war with the Soviet Union. From this time on, "the Kwantung Army was confronting the Russians with a bluff," Inada later conceded.[12] Those in the Army who had been urging containment of the conflict with China, first at the Yungting River, then at the Yellow River, then at the gates of Nanking, now suffered their worst defeat, for the Hsüchou campaign marked the end of efforts to localize the war. Indeed, the Imperial Headquarters order of April 7 also instructed the North China Area Army to occupy all of the Lunghai Railway as far west as Kaifeng—a task that greatly exceeded that Army's capabilities. "The result," writes Chalmers Johnson, "was anarchy, Communist intrusions, guerrilla warfare, and Japanese punitive expeditions—conditions that all contributed to Yenan's long-range success."[13]

The Japanese were not long in realizing that they had overextended themselves. Before Hsüchou could be taken, enemy forces had to be cleared from Taierhchwang, a small town about thirty-five miles northeast of the city at the terminus of a spur jutting south from the Tientsin-Pukow Railway. At first progress was rapid and resistance light, but by the end of March it was evident that the Chinese were going to make a major defense effort at Taierhchwang and several other heavily fortified cities surrounding Hsüchou. The Imperial Army suddenly found itself facing far more troops than it had anticipated—Tokyo reported that the Chinese had mobilized 190 divisions across a front that now extended some 2,000 miles. Taierhchwang, though little known to the public, was a familiar name to the military tacticians of the Chinese War College, who had long used the area around the little town for field exercises. Near Taierhchwang Chinese aircraft and mechanized units were thrown into the fray, and Japanese infantry, cut off from its own mechanized support, began to take huge casualties. For the first time in the war the Chinese began to recapture important cities from the Japanese. And for the first time in the war the feeling that the Japanese were invincible began to give way to optimism and even exhilaration as defense turned into counterattack. When friends told the U.S. Military Attaché in China, Col. Joseph W. Stilwell, that they now thought China might win the war, he agreed, "So do I."[14]

The battle for Taierhchwang raged on for eight days. Both sides claimed possession of the town at various times, but such claims were meaningless, for the town was reduced to a pile of smoldering debris after the first few days and nights of bitter hand-to-hand fighting, aerial bombardment, and artillery fire. "The nearer I came to the town," wrote an *Asahi shimbun* correspondent on April 7, "the more bodies I saw lying about, like dots on a green carpet." The Grand Canal, which flowed nearby, was said to be "running red with blood."[15] The Japanese forces finally drove the Chinese from Taierhchwang seventeen days after the first shots were fired, but few Japanese regarded the battle as a victory. The supposedly crack Itagaki Division had been humiliated, and Maj. Gen. Seya Kei, the Commander of the Second Army, which had been charged with the campaign, was retired to the reserves for having disgraced the military tradition. The Chinese generals, especially the "tiger general," Li Tsung-jen, emerged as heroes. Japanese staff officers later assessed the "signal victory" the Chinese had won and its influence on Chinese morale in strong terms: the Chinese now "began to talk boastfully about destroying the Japanese forces."[16]

Incredibly, however, the Chinese failed to preserve the forward momentum of their armies by going on the offensive. General Stilwell was baffled at the inability of the Chinese leaders to "get the idea of the offensive into their heads." Gen. Alexander von Falkenhausen, the chief German military adviser to the National Government, was said to have been "tearing his hair" at Chiang's willingness to forfeit the advantage gained at Taierhchwang. "I tell the Generalissimo to advance, to attack, to exploit his success," he complained. "But nothing is done. Soon the Japanese will have 8 to 10 divisions before Hsüchou. Then it will be too late."[17] And so it was. On May 15, less than a month after Taierhchwang fell, Japanese forces succeeded in encircling Hsüchou, and four days later they captured the city that for centuries had been regarded as a gauge of dynastic stability. When Hsüchou fell, a dynasty could not long survive.

Two contradictory results were produced by the disastrous Hsüchou campaign. On the one hand, the expansionists, unedified by any lesson that the fierce Chinese resistance might have suggested, immediately began to call for an attack on Hankow. The Imperial Headquarters had in fact already reconciled itself to the necessity of carrying the war to Hankow and Canton by the time it ordered the attack on Hsüchou; and on June 15 an Imperial Conference approved the idea. Aerial bombardment designed to break the Chinese population's will to resist began immediately.

On the other hand, the message of Taierhchwang was not wasted on some, including Premier Konoe, who at last came to agree with Ishiwara that the annihilation of the Kuomintang Government was a misguided goal. Never one known for steadfastness of purpose, Konoe now began to seek ways of backing down from the policy he had announced just four months before, and of putting the war strategy in the hands of leaders more conciliatory toward the Chiang regime. He had a degree of support in court and military (mostly Army General Staff) circles and among prominent members of the business world, who were disturbed at the economic dislocations and instability resulting from the war. Many of the financial and industrial leaders were also alarmed by the apparent trend toward closer association with the Axis powers, for they felt strongly that Japan's economic future rested on harmonious relations with Great Britain and the United States.

It is possible that the Emperor himself may also have influenced

Konoe's change of mind. Those close to the Emperor used words like "emaciated," "haggard," and "dispirited" to describe him in the spring of 1938.* There are many references in the Harada diaries suggesting that the Emperor was profoundly distrustful of the information he was receiving from his military advisers and Ministers, of their assessment of the war, and of the ability of Premier Konoe to take firm rein over the Government and bring the war to a conclusion.[18] Whatever one may say of Konoe's political behavior in the China war, concern for the well-being of the Emperor was a matter of abiding concern to him. It is inconceivable that the aristocratic Premier, whose grandfather had been Kampaku (Chief Minister) to the child Meiji Emperor seventy-five years before, would ignore the anguish the expanding war was causing the Emperor.

Konoe was also encouraged by a group of influential advisers he had gathered about him, some of them as Cabinet Councillors (Naikaku Sangi), a post he had created in October 1937 as a device for bypassing his official—and more cumbersome—Cabinet. Among the first appointed to this post was Gen. Ugaki Kazushige, who earned Konoe's confidence by declaring that he was "stripped to the waist," ready to work on a solution of the China problem.[19] Another Konoe adviser was Ozaki Hotsumi, who later became notorious for his involvement with the Soviet spy Richard Sorge. Ozaki served as a Cabinet Consultant (Naikaku Shokutaku), a position of even less official stature than that of Cabinet Councillor. Nevertheless, he held a position in Konoe's unofficial family from July 1938 to January 1939 and undoubtedly conveyed to the Premier his surpassing knowledge of Chinese affairs and his deep conviction that the policy of aggression against China was utterly destructive of Japan's best interests. In Ozaki's view the Chinese people had an unlimited capacity for resistance, and the war could be concluded only if Japan identified herself with the true interests of the nationalism that fueled the fierce Chinese resistance.[20] Konoe was also receiving advice during 1938–39 from the Shōwa Kenkyū Kai (Shōwa Research Society) and the Asameshi Kai (Breakfast Society). The Research Society was organized in 1936, at a time when Konoe was considering accepting the Premiership, by his friend Gotō Ryūnosuke. Gotō's purpose was to assemble a "brain trust" of eminent intellectuals who would research

---

* Though the Emperor was "exceedingly emaciated," the Court Chamberlain and others did not want him to go to his seaside villa to recuperate lest he be charged with setting an unheroic example for his soldiers. Harada, 6: 247. The Emperor's advisers also denied him the luxury of working in his marine biology laboratory on the grounds that such pleasurable pursuits were irresponsible in a time of austerity and sacrifice. Mosley, pp. 181–84.

problems and counsel Konoe. The Breakfast Society, formed in late 1937 after Konoe had become Premier, was an informal discussion group composed of a select inner circle of Shōwa Kenkyū Kai members. This group of educators, journalists, and politicians met two or three times a month between 1937 and 1941 over breakfast in the offices of the Cabinet or at the residence of Konoe or Prince Saionji (whose grandson, Saionji Kinkazu, was a leading member of the Society). Though the Premier did not often attend these meetings, he received reports of the discussions from his secretaries, Ushiba Tomohiko and Kishi Michizō. It is significant that in mid-1938 several members of the Breakfast Society, notably Matsumoto Shigeharu and Inukai Ken, were engaged in preliminary discussions and intrigues to settle the war through negotiations with Wang Ching-wei. Konoe was clearly at least a sympathetic listener to the counsel and activities of men who were searching for a way to end the ever-deepening conflict.

Though the groups around Konoe represented different points of view and proposed different solutions to the China problem, they were agreed generally on the inefficacy of force as a means of ending the war.* They were also fairly unanimous in their disgust with the evident weakness of the various puppet regimes in China.

As the year 1938 progressed it became increasingly clear that neither of the major puppet regimes was capable of inspiring the requisite mass

---

* It would be wrong to exaggerate the antiwar sentiments of members of these Societies, and in fact they and other Japanese intellectuals of their bent have been severely criticized by postwar writers for their generally timid and always sharply qualified objections to the China war. However disturbed Shōwa Kenkyū Kai members may have been about rampant Nipponism (*Nippon shugi*) and the racial arrogance of the Imperial Army in China, they were sympathetic to the goal of liberating East Asia from Western control. A good example of their ambivalence on the treatment of China is expressed in the 1938 article of Miki Kiyoshi, a brilliant philosopher and journalist-member of the Shōwa Kenkyū Kai. In it he condemned Japan's use of force against China, which clearly could not be occupied forever, but insisted that Japan was "not necessarily intending to force Japanese ideas on China." "This can be seen" he wrote, "from the view prevailing among Japanese leaders that the principle underlying the cultural work in North China should be Confucianism [which] "can be considered a common ideological bond between the two countries." "The China Affair," p. 608. Miki played a leading role in helping Konoe formulate the ideological principles governing the New Order in East Asia. Drafted in 1942 into the Army's Pen Corps, a unit of writers and journalists, he saw brief service in the Philippines, then decided he could not continue to use his pen to support the war. He managed to find refuge at Tokyo's Sophia University for a time but was jailed in March 1945 for violating the Peace Preservation Law—he had given food and clothing to a left-wing friend who had escaped from prison. Miki died in prison on September 26, 1945, eight days before General MacArthur ordered the Japanese authorities to release all political prisoners. For further information on the Shōwa Kenkyū Kai and Miki's career, see Piovesana; Spaulding; and Johnson, *Instance of Treason*, pp. 114–22.

allegiance for a regenerated China friendly to Japan. Neither regime could be credited with producing the defection of even marginally important figures from the Kuomintang regime. Local warlords not only had not committed their troops to either puppet regime, but were in fact rallying their men to the resistance cause in numbers that surprised and sobered Japanese strategists. By 1938 no one was confidently predicting the end of the conflict, and Japan was now forced to turn to extraordinary measures to meet the demands of the war. The National General Mobilization Law enacted in March 1938, a "carte blanche delegation of wartime legislative powers to the Cabinet," signaled the collapse of parliamentary government.[21] That in turn could easily be the first step in the direction of a military dictatorship—a development that was altogether distasteful to Konoe and many others who had gone along with the drift into full-scale war. Nevertheless a further step in that direction was taken in April, when military training became compulsory in all schools. The demands of military procurement on the economy of a singularly have-not nation were severe and growing ever more so. Raw cotton and cotton cloth were removed from the domestic market, iron was as "scarce as gold," and chemists in the Ministry of Agriculture were "tanning rat skins in their search for a leather substitute." "It is hard now to buy an iron frying pan," wrote a *New York Times* correspondent; "a month from now it will be impossible."[22] Wartime shortages of raw materials were so critical that many industries, including the important cement and shipbuilding industries, were operating at only half capacity, and the situation was getting steadily worse.[23] A recent study shows that longer work hours, deteriorating working conditions, and inadequate nutrition began to take a significant toll on the general health of the working population as early as 1938.[24] The Home Ministry advised factory owners in late 1937 that "twelve hours should be the maximum" workday, but indicated that two hours of overtime were permissible "if unavoidable." Even then the regulation was criticized as inappropriate to a wartime economy. Rest periods and dinner hours were canceled and the "14-hour working day was not at all uncommon."[25] For a few sensitive souls the prohibition of neon lights on the Ginza was a welcome product of the war—"an enlightened act by our unenlightened military government," wrote novelist Nagai Kafū in his diary.[26] But for most it was a symbol of a grim austerity that promised to become much worse before it became better.

In the end the reevaluation process that commenced at the time of the Hsüchou campaign failed to either de-escalate the war or unify

Japan's China policy. But it did engender heated discussion, a succession of new high-level proposals for the solution of the China problem, a Cabinet reorganization, an unprecedented shakeup of the War Ministry, a startling reversal of specifically declared national policy, and the creation of a new "unified" agency to handle matters related to China. And not least, it resulted in the sponsorship of several "operations" to open new channels to peace. First let us turn to the Cabinet reorganization, which put the War and Foreign ministries into new hands.

Konoe was on the verge of resigning in the wake of the disastrous Hsüchou campaign. He was apparently in ill health, and this may have contributed to his eagerness to leave office. But it is not easy to judge when Konoe took to his sick bed for reasons of health and when simply to escape the thankless responsibility of managing a nearly unmanageable national crisis.* Konoe did not thrive on the constant clashing with the military that was necessary to retain control over national affairs. He did not enjoy political controversy but considered himself above it. He was a patrician first and a politician only secondarily. "He was a *kuge* (aristocrat) above all," says one of his colleagues in the Breakfast Society.[27] No lineage in Japan was more noble than Konoe's. For centuries the Fujiwara family and its most exalted branch, the Konoe, ruled Japan, and even after its real power declined it continued to provide Japan her Empresses and other important court figures. Konoe had easy access to the throne and quite literally spoke the Emperor's language. From boyhood he had used the same stilted archaisms that made the Emperor's language barely intelligible to most Japanese. Instead of using the customary *otōsan* and *okāsan* to address his father and mother, Konoe was taught to call his parents *omōsama* and *otāsama* in the manner of the Imperial family.[28]

The virtues of the aristocratic personality combined in Konoe to make him an attractive and widely respected statesman, but the weaknesses of such a heritage rendered him a poor and indecisive leader. Nearly six feet tall, he dwarfed most Japanese. He had a commanding intellect but surprisingly little knowledge about China. He formed his closest associations among the intellectuals and aesthetes of his literary club,

---

* The Luce publications were fascinated by Konoe's hypochondria, insomnia, frailty, and preoccupation with asepsis. *Life* called him the "divine hypochondriac" (Dec. 9, 1940, p. 111); and *Time*, which featured him on its cover (July 22, 1940), calculated—on the basis of unspecified evidence—that he had "spent one-half of the days since he was 25 in bed." "In fact," *Time* stated, "his bedroom is his headquarters. He not only retires there during crises—he reads, holds conferences, sees movies, listens to the radio, eats, sleeps and worries about not sleeping there" (p. 32). For somewhat more objective assessments of the man, see Saionji, pp. 281–83; and Storry, "Konoye Fumimaro."

the Shirakaba-ha (White Birch Society), and "liked to invite scholars to lecture to him as often as possible," according to his personal secretary, Ushiba Tomohiko.[29] Among his own literary accomplishments were several translations of the works of Oscar Wilde, and it seems likely that Wilde's *The Soul of Man Under Socialism*, which he translated in 1914, struck a resonant chord in the young Prince. He agreed wholeheartedly with Wilde's contention that the purpose of life was not labor, but educated and enlightened comfort and leisure. (Indeed, the Japanese aristocracy, notable for its refined inactivity, dilettantism, and charm, had been the very embodiment of Wilde's ideal type for centuries.) The British Ambassador to Japan, Sir Robert Craigie, speaking from four years' acquaintance with Konoe, pronounced him "phlegmatic." "His expression denotes neither energy nor determination, but rather a sense of philosophic doubt. . . . His eyes are his best feature, denoting intelligence and political acumen, combined with a touch of laziness."[30] John Gunther offers the same picture: "He seems to lack energy—or perhaps he is bored," wrote the author of *Inside Asia* after a visit with Konoe in the summer of 1938. "His friends say that he makes a cult of languor," he added, citing Konoe's characteristic unpunctuality and horror of early morning (pre-11:00 A.M.) appointments.[31]

The picture of Konoe that emerges is one of a man of delicate health, reserved mien, and subtle mind, a cultivated and sophisticated man given to melancholy and brooding. To his secretary he seemed "a lonely person," "almost Hamlet-like," a man who "never trusted anyone wholeheartedly." Above all, a man wanting in leadership, Ushiba recalls, echoing the almost universal criticism of Konoe. A man, finally, who "would never say 'Nothing doing, you must do it this way' to the Army."*

During the wrangling over the National General Mobilization Law, a distraught Konoe, depressed at his inability to control the affairs of state, withdrew to his villa in the Tokyo suburb of Ogikubo on the plea of ill health. The launching of the Hsüchou campaign only increased his frustration and despondency, and at least as early as March 17 he was privately talking of resigning.[32] On March 29 he visited the Em-

---

* Interview with Ushiba, May 1970. Saionji comments (p. 281): "As a person, Konoe had many strong points. He had a sharp intuitive sense and a comparatively accurate perspective and judgment. He was not worried about petty things. Among the politicians of the time, nobody was superior to him in those respects. But in Konoe one important quality was missing. There was no might [*chikara*] . . . no ability to carry things out [*jikkōryoku*]. . . . Japan's course of action had already been determined by the Army. Its policy was the only policy of the country. The intentions of the Premier, the Emperor, etc., made no difference."

peror seeking approval for his resignation. Stating that it was "extremely difficult for a dreamer [*kūbakutaru mono*] like myself, popular but powerless, to take charge of the situation indefinitely," Konoe suggested that it would be more suitable if a "person with power" was appointed to the post.[33] In a conversation with Baron Harada Kumao two days later, Konoe disclosed what it was that had finally pushed him to resign. War Minister Sugiyama had unexpectedly flown to North China and had neither told Konoe the purpose of his mission nor informed any Cabinet member save the Navy Minister that the trip was being made. "This is the way it is in all of the Army's undertakings," Konoe told Harada. As an example, Konoe said, the Army had even insisted on its own choices to head the national policy companies in North and Central China, a truly ironical development, since an important reason for creating the companies was precisely to keep the determination of economic policy out of the hands of the Army as much as possible. "I feel exactly like a 'mannequin,' " Konoe lamented to Harada.[34]

Konoe proved unable to persevere even in his lack of perseverance, for the Emperor and Konoe's friends and advisers prevailed on him to withdraw his resignation and reorganize the Cabinet instead.[35] The reorganization, which proceeded throughout May and June, centered on Minister of Foreign Affairs Hirota and Minister of War Sugiyama. Konoe's goal was to repudiate or at least soften the *aite ni sezu* declaration, and he regarded Hirota as one of the chief architects of that policy. Sugiyama, "a good-natured, brainless, superannuated nonentity," in the words of the diplomat Kase Toshikazu, had been War Minister in little more than name for the sixteen crucial months since February 1937.[36] It is difficult to ascertain where real control over the Army resided in those months, but it is clear that it was not in the hands of Sugiyama, who was regarded by Konoe as a "robot of the expansionists."* In addition, as we have seen, Konoe was irritated by Sugiyama's reluctance to discuss important military matters with him and other civilians in the Cabinet. One of the most remarkable demonstrations of Sugiyama's

---

* From the memoirs of the Chief Cabinet Secretary, Kazami Akira, it is clear to what extent Sugiyama was manipulated by his Army subordinates. "Though it seems ridiculous," Kazami writes, "the reports of the creation of the Provisional Government came as a complete surprise to both Konoe and me. It was only through newspaper reports that we learned of [it]." When questioned earlier by Konoe on the truth of rumors of such a move, Sugiyama had consistently "replied in a noncommittal fashion, and we could never really figure out the truth." At first, Kazami states, the Cabinet was indignant at being left in the dark and tended to vent their wrath on the War Minister. Before long, however, it became evident that he had been just as uninformed as the civilian Cabinet members. He, too, had simply been "forced to give his approval to the fait accompli." *Konoe naikaku*, pp. 59, 89–90.

almost paranoiac caution in this regard occurred early in the war, when Navy Minister Yonai proposed, in a Cabinet meeting, that the Army should advance no farther into North China than the Yungting River. "What's the idea of saying such a thing in a place like this?" the War Minister scolded, intimidating the chagrined Admiral into a submissive, "I guess you're right" (*Sō ka nā*).[37]

Konoe in fact had been seeking to replace the War Minister for several months, but such a step could not be taken lightly in wartime, implying as it inevitably would a deep division over the conduct of the war. Moreover, Sugiyama did not make the job any easier for Konoe by quietly resigning; on the contrary, he resisted for several weeks all the pressure Konoe could bring to bear on him, including indirect suggestions from the palace that he step down.[38]

Nor was the choice of a successor an easy one. Every clique in the Army strained to have its candidate accepted. The anti-expansionists favored General Ishiwara or, failing him, General Tada. Konoe felt that the Tōsei-ha officers were responsible for the war and so was anxious to replace Sugiyama with someone from the rival Kōdō-ha.* Lt. Gen. Yanagawa Heisuke, for example, would have been an "extremely pleasing" choice to Konoe, but the General had been too far removed from the highest councils of war planning in the past several months.[39] The choices put forward by the expansionists included General Umezu, the Vice Minister of War, but Konoe was not on good terms with Umezu and thought that he "pulled the strings" in the expansionist camp.[40]

The final choice was Lt. Gen. Itagaki Seishirō, who like Ishiwara had begun as a strong proponent of the Manchurian adventure, then had come to favor localizing the war and bringing it to the speediest possible conclusion. Itagaki does not appear to have been the first choice of any group or clique; in fact, it was his very lack of strong factional commitments that appealed to Konoe, whose Cabinet reorganization was aimed at strengthening civilian political control over the direction of the war. In this connection, Ambassador Grew's analysis of the appointment

---

* The Kōdō-ha (Imperial Way Faction) was a loose grouping of generally young field- and even company-grade officers who, acting with great daring and independence in the early 1930's, attempted to swerve Japan in an ultranationalist direction. Their undisciplined activities, which included assassinations and attempted coups, alarmed the more conservative and mostly senior officers of the rival Tōsei-ha (Control Faction). The Tōsei-ha emerged victorious after a full-scale mutiny the Kōdō-ha organized in February 1936 failed. The usefulness of the Tōsei-ha–Kōdō-ha dichotomy in explaining the events of the 1930's in Japan has been diminished as a result of the reappraisal of James B. Crowley. For Konoe, however, the rivalry was quite important. In his memoirs, written in the final months of the war, he blames the Tōsei-ha for Japan's aggression in China and indeed for the advance into Southeast Asia that led to Pearl Harbor.

seems correct: Itagaki was favored because he both "has the confidence of the young officers in the Army and . . . believes that the Army should stay out of politics."[41]

Still, in order to secure the appointment, Konoe was forced to strike a compromise, namely, to accept the Kwantung Army's Tōjō as Vice Minister of War, a post that was almost as important as the Ministership. Konoe later attributed the failure to reach a settlement with China during this period to his new Vice Minister: "I had high hopes in Itagaki," he declared, "but I was let down because Sugiyama and Umezu left me a 'memento' in the shape of Tōjō as Vice Minister of War. I didn't realize it at the time—but Tōjō and Umezu were actually just like 'one person.'"[42]

The removal of Foreign Minister Hirota was somewhat less complicated, and Konoe was able to get a suitable candidate, Ugaki Kazushige, a General in the Army Reserves and the first non-career diplomat to hold the portfolio, without being forced into a distasteful bargain. Since Ugaki had been a Cabinet Councillor for half a year prior to this appointment, Konoe had ample time to assess his views on the China problem and was convinced that Ugaki, with a wide range of friends in high Kuomintang circles, could help him reverse the January 16 policy. But consideration of Ugaki never really hinged on his views on China, which were clearly acceptable to Konoe. The Premier's one doubt concerned Ugaki's ability to fight off the Army's dislike for him long enough to put his ideas into practice. Indeed, Ugaki did not rush to accept the post, recognizing full well that the popularity he enjoyed with the political parties, the financial world, and the public at large was not matched among the military.

A year earlier a determined group in the Army had successfully blocked Ugaki's appointment as Premier, even after he had accepted the Imperial command. His opponents never forgot or forgave him for drastically reducing the Army's strength during his tenure as Minister of War in 1925; many resented his well-known connections with political parties, and some were hostile to him for what they regarded as a betrayal of the March 1931 conspiracy to overthrow the Government.[43] Those who were advocating closer relations with the Axis in 1938 feared that Ugaki's appointment would result instead in a strengthening of ties with Great Britain, a fear that was given substance by his quick initiation of friendly talks with the British and by the warmth with which they greeted his appointment. "I liked the General from the start," the British Ambassador wrote. "It was clear that he considered one of his principal duties to be the improvement of relations with Great Britain."[44]

Aware of his insecure position, Ugaki made Sugiyama's resignation a precondition to his own entrance into the Cabinet. Moreover, he was probably instrumental in Konoe's decision to name Itagaki as Sugiyama's successor.[45]

Ugaki's views on China at once help us understand why Konoe chose him as Foreign Minister and show us the direction in which Konoe's reevaluation of the China policy was moving. Ugaki was opposed to the *aite ni sezu* declaration as an unwarranted interference in Chinese internal affairs. Shortly before becoming Foreign Minister, he wrote in his diary: "We Japanese always say that 'China for the Chinese' is what we desire, that this is our basic policy. If so, if this is to be regarded as a standard, then we should be satisfied with anyone the Chinese wish to install and maintain in office."[46]

Ugaki made it clear to Konoe he would head the Foreign Ministry only if it was understood that the *aite ni sezu* speech would be withdrawn. By that time (May 1938) Konoe was of the same mind and offered no resistance to Ugaki's demand, replying that he hoped Ugaki could somehow gracefully retract the "unwarranted" declaration.* In addition, Ugaki made his entrance into the Cabinet conditional on Konoe's acceptance of three general principles: the quick consolidation and strengthening of the Cabinet; a quick decision on a peace policy toward China; and a quick unification of diplomatic policy on China.[47]

Konoe's ready acceptance of all of Ugaki's conditions helps explain why, in historian Usui's words, the Ugaki appointment "seemed to offer a hope that a door was opening"; many felt certain that there would be a fresh approach to the solution of the China problem, and that the chances of the war dragging on were now appreciably diminished. In August Sugiyama Heisuke, a noted critic, wrote in the monthly magazine *Kaizō* (Reconstruction): "Our hopes and expectations are all wound up with Ugaki. If we do not get a 'hit' from Ugaki, who has made his appearance in the 'pinch,' we cannot be saved."[48]

ISHII ITARŌ'S "IKENSHO"

The man who provided Ugaki with the ammunition he needed to justify the destruction of the *aite ni sezu* policy was Ishii Itarō, one of the foremost China specialists in the Ministry, and Chief of its Asia

---

* Yabe, 1: 516. A remark Konoe made to Harada suggests that the initiative for retracting the declaration may have come more from Konoe than from Ugaki. Harada quotes Konoe as saying, on June 3, that he wanted Ugaki to undertake a diplomatic volte-face "because Hirota and I have concentrated too much on overthrowing Chiang Kai-shek." Harada, 7: 5.

Bureau. In June 1938 Ishii prepared for his new superior a long, thought-
ful "Ikensho" (Statement of Opinion), outlining the various alternatives
in China.[49] Like General Ishiwara, Ishii was keenly aware that Japan
would have to trim the sails of her China policy to the new winds of
nationalism in China, and his "Ikensho" is a persuasive defense of this
view. It is an uncommon document for several reasons. Unlike the
wooden, documentary style of most Foreign Office studies, it is a lively,
opinionated, almost passionate plea, a profession of the heart as much
as the mind. It bristles with pungent metaphor; the Japanese economic
policy in China, for example, was like an octopus eating its own ten-
tacles (*tako hai*), for the expansion of the yen bloc was drying up Chinese purchasing power and causing Japanese exports to China to plum-
met.[50] But above all the "Ikensho" is remarkable for its insight and
candor; it was a vigorous and forthright statement in defense of an
exceedingly unpopular view, the expression of a minority opinion that
was ahead of its day.

Ishii began by reminding Ugaki that though in the narrow sense *aite
ni sezu* meant no peace talks with the Kuomintang Government, "one
could feel some room for flexibility" because of the language used, because, that is, the declaration was couched in a vulgar or popular (*zoku-
gomi*) style rather than in official style. Inflexibility had been injected
into the declaration by Konoe and Hirota, who had taken pains to
emphasize that Japan would never discuss peace with the Kuomintang
leaders, "even if *they* proposed the peace talks."[51] Unfortunately, that
rigidity had been so praised by the "superficial voices of public opinion"
that no one could now speak out publicly against it. Ishii shifted to the
language of sumo wrestling to explain his dissatisfaction with the *aite
ni sezu* declaration. Like a *uchiyari*, the lightning quick move with which
a wrestler flips his opponent out of the ring, the policy had come as a
sudden, unexpected betrayal of expectations for peace. But all the Japanese Government had accomplished by this dramatic move was to "con-
strict its possible alternatives to react to a changing situation. All we
have is the one policy of *oshi* [pushing]." In short, the *aite ni sezu* policy
was simply the kind of flamboyant gesture a clumsy sumo wrestler might
make in the third-rate ring of some sleepy, backwater town.[52]

Supposing Japan wished to settle the Incident as soon as possible, Ishii
thought she had but four options. A further expansion of the fighting
fronts after the conclusion of the Hankow campaign was not among
them; he dismissed such a course out of hand as patently misguided. But
one option was to push the Hankow campaign through to a successful
conclusion and then establish a forward line along the Lunghai Railway

and the lower Yangtze, holding all the area to the north along the certain connecting rail lines and waterways. Though this plan might sound good, Ishii said, it had several drawbacks. If it was adopted, the Kuomintang would recover territory, thereby enhancing its popularity and prestige among the people of China. That in turn would "unsettle" the people in the occupied areas, making it all the more difficult for the occupation armies to maintain security. In addition, the Kuomintang Government would "all the more enthusiastically resort to the guerrilla tactics at which it excels."[53] Meanwhile, in the unoccupied areas the Kuomintang regime would strengthen its armies and wage a war of attrition against Japan. Ultimately, Japan would be forced to destroy these forces, which meant opening up large-scale hostilities on new fronts. And even if the worst of these predictions did not materialize, Ishii warned, the task of simply securing the occupied areas six hundred miles up the Yangtze to Hankow and maintaining communications along a network of several thousand miles of railway would cost huge amounts of men and matériel. In sum, Ishii found that this plan would "do nothing to solve the situation" and would moreover "continue to act as an obstacle to our defense in other areas" (presumably against the Soviet Union).[54] Accordingly, it had little merit in his judgment.

As a second alternative Ishii held out the establishment of a new central government, one that would combine the Provisional and Reformed Governments. The Japanese Government had in fact envisioned this action when it issued the *aite ni sezu* statement, and steps were already being taken to recruit T'ang Shao-i and Wu P'ei-fu to head the new regime. According to those who backed these two men, T'ang commanded prestige in South China and had a certain reputation within the Kuomintang that would be useful; and Wu had connections in both West and North China that would make him valuable as a collaborator. The new central government would command prestige without any special effort, its advocates maintained. Local warlords in both unoccupied and occupied areas would see which way the wind was blowing (*kaze o nozonde*) and hasten to find a haven under the roof of the new government. As a result, the Kuomintang would be abandoned. Ishii devoted the most space to a discussion of this option, which at the time appeared to have powerful backing in both civilian and military circles and indeed to be on the way to accomplishment.

Ishii argued that the second alternative overestimated the reputations of T'ang and Wu, who were but "political corpses" and "relics." To revive them would be laughable, he asserted. The Chinese would look on them as "old men who don't know when they are finished."* Far from enjoying any prestige in the minds of his countrymen, Ishii declared, T'ang was remembered as a man who had mismanaged his retirement sinecure so badly that the people of his hsien—which happened to be his native home—bodily expelled him. It was bad enough to consider collaboration with such a clay-footed hero, said Ishii, but Wu P'ei-fu was even worse. Wu's arrogant assumption that his reemergence on the scene would solve the Sino-Japanese problem must be diagnosed as a case of lingering intoxication with past glories. Those who supported collaboration with Wu contended that warlords all over China, and notably in Szechwan, would join Wu in a great anti-Chiang alliance. To be sure, Wu had strong ties with certain warlords, many of whom were unquestionably displeased with the centralization that had taken place under the Kuomintang, Ishii wrote; but it was "an error in timing" to expect that they would rise up against the Kuomintang at this juncture.[55] The warlords would move against the Kuomintang only if it was on its last legs, and at present it was far from that. In fact the National Government was keeping a close watch on the warlords, especially those in Szechwan, and if nothing else, the warlords were opportunistic. Simple loyalty to Wu would never be enough to impel them to move against the superior Kuomintang armies. In addition, the warlords still outside of Kuomintang control were so divided by jealousies and conflicts that it was unreasonable to expect them to join Wu in any united front worthy of the name. For these reasons, Ishii advised the Foreign Minister to shelve the second alternative along with the first.

Ishii gave short shrift to alternative number three, which was to have the existing collaboration regimes amalgamate with the Kuomintang Government. In the first place the Provisional and Reformed Governments were intrinsically incompatible with the Kuomintang regime because of their open hostility to Sun's Three Principles, Ishii said. Beyond that, for the Kuomintang Government to unite with regimes it had ridiculed as sham from their very inception would be tantamount to capitulation. "No matter how skilled at compromise you say the Chinese are, this is completely out of the question," Ishii asserted.[56]

The fourth and only option Ishii saw as a viable solution was to resume negotiations with the National Government. Ishii hurried to answer the oft-repeated objection to a settlement with a government that

* *Gaimushō no hyakunen,* 2: 326–26. This is perhaps too bland a translation for Ishii's pungent "old men who douse themselves in cold water like youngsters and then take ill."

had allied itself with the Communists. "If we examine the realities of the united front," he argued, "we will see that the Chinese Communist Party has simply been allowed to participate in an anti-Japanese front." A long history of bitter experience in dealing with the Chinese Communists had left the Kuomintang well aware that the Communists saw the united front as a technique to reestablish their shattered power, and consequently the National Government had been most intolerant of their activities as a party. The reports that Chou En-lai, Mao Tse-tung, and others had joined the Kuomintang, far from indicating that the Communists were about to "devour" the Kuomintang, actually demonstrated that the initiative lay with the Kuomintang.[57]

Ishii warmly praised the Kuomintang for settling its differences with the warlords of the Southwest Faction, for ending the independence movement in Fukien, and for expelling the Communist forces from Kiangsi. And in addition to its military successes, it had made laudable advances in education, finance, and economics. "Contrary to our opinions about China," Ishii said, "the Kuomintang Government has been conducting a progressive administration. The dawn of a modern nation-state in China is already here. Because of this, the strength of the Kuomintang Government has been steadily taking root in the earth of China and is capturing the minds of the people."[58]

It was "undeniable," wrote Ishii, that Chiang Kai-shek was the man responsible for the "national revival" of China. He alone had the confidence of the Chinese people: "His figure shines brighter than anyone else in the Kuomintang and the Government."[59] To try to overthrow Chiang's government or to insist on his retirement was a "wholly different" thing from "conquering local warlords like Chang Hsüeh-liang." Moreover, aside from the clear impossibility of overthrowing the Kuomintang, it was counterproductive to even try. Stability in the Far East and Sino-Japanese cooperation were Japan's often repeated ideals. Even assuming that the Kuomintang was overwhelmed, the successor regime was bound to be weak and unable to control all of China, and as a result China would fall into a state of economic and political bankruptcy. In the ensuing confusion and disorder there was one group best equipped in ideology and organization to exploit the situation, and that was the Communists. The consequence would be a China in receivership, with Japan acting as the administrator of a bankrupt country. The Imperial Army would have to suppress the hordes of disbanded soldiers wandering about the countryside. It would be faced with colossal relief projects in the areas it occupied. A massive program of propaganda and indoctrination would have to be undertaken. And, above all, Japan would have to put down the Communist armies, which might well gain the backing of the Soviet Union. In the circumstances, what chance was there that Japan might enjoy the fruits of economic progress in China? Such a situation would make a mockery of Japan's claims that she was endeavoring to bring stability to East Asia.

Japan had but one choice: to take a "broad-minded attitude" and negotiate an honorable and generous peace with China, Ishii concluded. Further, for the present at least, China and the Kuomintang were one—and Chiang was the "pivot" (*ōgi no kaname*) of the Kuomintang. To try to get Chiang to step down, to retire from politics, either in fact or merely in name, as many in Tokyo were suggesting as a minimum demand, would only damage the Japanese cause. The Chinese people would regard Chiang's retirement as a punishment administered by Japan. Moreover, the hard-line elements would never allow Chiang, on whom the "reverence of the Chinese people was focused," to resign. Rather they would drive the nation to even greater resistance. "What we must do is to rescue Chiang and attempt to use him," Ishii advised.[60]

For too long the Japanese had despised Chiang as an implacable foe, said Ishii, a hated enemy who had "used Japan as an instrument for unifying the nation." But the fact was, in late 1935, when he became President of the Executive Yüan, he had appointed pro-Japanese officials like Chang Ch'ün to the Cabinet in his concern for an amicable adjustment of Sino-Japanese relations. Ishii reminded Ugaki that the Generalissimo had also sent secret emissaries to him at the time to express his earnest wishes for better relations with Japan. "If we miss this chance, we will have no others for the next fifty or hundred years," the Generalissimo had said to the Japanese Military Attaché in China in 1936.[61] The Japanese would never cease to regret, said Ishii, that they had pushed Chiang to the point where he had to declare that China had reached the limits of her endurance. A matter for further regret was that they had regarded his "fight-to-the-end" pledge in Kuling as "nonsensical talk" instead of realizing that he was determined to carry it out.[62]

Ishii called Ugaki's attention to the fact that certain irresponsible Government authorities had been violating both the spirit and the letter of Imperial wishes. In an address to the Diet on September 4, 1937, the Emperor had declared that the only reason "my soldiers are striving loyally in spite of various difficulties [is to] urge China to reconsider and establish peace." Furthermore, Government spokesmen had expressed in the Imperial presence on January 11, 1938, their determination to "eliminate all the frictions of the past [and] reconstruct relations between Japan and China on the basis of a spirit of generosity and respect for the sovereignty and territorial integrity of China." "Perfect harmony" between the two nations was the ultimate aim of the settlement Japan would seek with China, the Emperor's Ministers had declared. Since then, however, they had been woefully remiss in their duties. They had not informed the people of these principles, and "even worse, they have not refrained from making statements that are contradictory to the decisions of the January 11 Imperial Conference."[63]

Because the authorities had ignored the spirit of the decisions made at the Imperial Conference, both the Government and the people were saying things like, "This is the golden opportunity we have been waiting for on the continent," or "It's all right to regard China as a colony even though it is an independent foreign country," or "The property of the enemy should be handled in this way or that way," or "Since we have made such big sacrifices, we should at least get control of North and Central China." All of these commonly heard expressions gave the lie to Japan's claim that she had no territorial ambitions in China. "We will subjugate China—that is the mood of Japan," wrote Ishii. Thus, far from obeying the Emperor's injunction to bring about a generous peace based on a respect for Chinese national integrity, Japan was moving in the direction of a "take-everything-you-can-get attitude" (*monotori shugi*), a "get-what-you-can-before-the-other-fellow-does attitude" (*sakidori shugi*), and a "let's-carve-up [China] attitude" (*wakemae shugi*). How could the Japanese hope to attain Sino-Japanese cooperation and peace in East Asia when there was such an enormous disparity between the decisions of the Imperial Conference and these predatory sentiments, Ishii asked.[64]

Ishii cautioned Ugaki that the Chinese were unlikely to pursue any negotiations with Japan as long as she took the attitude that China was guilty and deserved severe terms. "And even if they were to give in," he predicted, "it would lead to trouble for the next hundred years." But if, on the contrary, a powerful Japan assumed a generous attitude toward her weaker neighbor, nobody would despise her for it. Rather, the whole world would admire her "chivalrous" (*bushidōteki*) attitude. Once and for all the enduring resentment China felt toward Japan would dissolve, and a feeling of trust would be implanted in the minds of the Chinese people. Therefore, said Ishii, echoing the frequent urging of Ishiwara, Japan must offer the Chinese a "Bismarckian peace," the same kind of generous terms Bismarck had offered the Austrians at the conclusion of the Austro-Prussian War.[65] And, above all, he advised, the Government must realize that the "greatest obstacle" to peace talks was the existence of the Provisional and Reformed Governments. To allow them to continue would give rise to the same antagonisms caused by the Hopei-Chahar regime. Accordingly, Japan should set a deadline, Ishii counseled, and then let the National Government revise the status of the two regimes at its pleasure.*

Whether Japan could bring all this off, especially the renunciation of the *aite ni sezu* policy, said Ishii, was "exclusively a question of whether our governmental authorities have the courage to do so." Would they, that is, prove strong enough to carry out a fundamental change of national policy, even perhaps at the risk of their "lives," in the face of the violent popular reaction that was likely to follow?[66] If they could meet the test, it would be worth the risks, for Japan now enjoyed a "precious opportunity—the kind that comes but once in a thousand years—to adjust relations between the two countries and usher in a new era of harmony," Ishii concluded.[67]

After the new Foreign Minister studied the Ishii "Ikensho," he noted on its cover that "it largely corresponds to my own opinions."[68] In September he invited a group of journalists to a villa in Hayama to lecture them, among other things, on the history of the Austro-Prussian War. Echoing both Ishii's admiration for Bismarck and his pleas for a cancellation of the attack on Hankow, Ugaki "extolled the brilliant lesson in the military history of the world" provided by the Prussian leader and his Chief of Staff, von Moltke, who after defeating the Austrian forces in a matter of weeks, had decided not to reduce Vienna, but rather to "rein in at the ramparts of the castle and agree to a peace—a peace of nonalienation." There was an important parallel between the Prussian-Austrian and Sino-Japanese situations, Ugaki pointed out. The reason for the generous treatment of the Austrians was that Bismarck and von Moltke anticipated a war with France and wanted to keep Austria from taking the side of their enemies.[69] In the current situation the Soviet Union was the modern counterpart to France.

The Cabinet reorganization was completed in the first week of June 1938. The new Cabinet was still a coalition of diverse elements—representing court, military, and financial interests—but Konoe had managed to secure the strongest possible combination of those who were willing to commit themselves to a new approach to the solution of the

---

* *Gaimushō no hyakunen*, 2: 334. But Manchukuo was another matter. It "was more or less clear from communications through Italian channels that China is ready to recognize Manchukuo," Ishii advised Ugaki, probably "on the grounds that it is useless to try to recover lost lands." *Ibid*. The Italian embassies in China and Japan were actively engaged in mediation efforts in the early months of the war.

war, and he had successfully excluded those who were most closely associated with the intransigent policies hammered out in the Liaison and
Imperial Conferences of January. He had been able to strengthen his
hand, too, by obtaining the Emperor's approval for making the Five
Ministers' Conference the highest national policy-making organ. Thus
the Liaison Conference, which was so much at the mercy of second-level
Army and Navy officers, was officially replaced by a much more workable
conference of Konoe's own appointees, the Ministers of Army, Navy,
Foreign Affairs, and Finance. The stage seemed set for a fresh approach
to end the war with China.

The most dramatic evidence that the Ugaki appointment heralded a
new era of peace-seeking was an exchange of telegrams between Ugaki
and the one-time Chinese Foreign Minister Chang Ch'ün, a personal
friend of Ugaki's. In a gesture altogether unusual in wartime, Chang
sent a telegram to Ugaki congratulating him on his appointment, which
was an "exceedingly splendid event" and one that caused him "to rejoice
on behalf of East Asia."[70] He went on to express the hope that Ugaki
might be instrumental in reestablishing peace negotiations and suggested that Wang Ching-wei might be a suitable Chinese representative
at the peace talks.

The Japanese Foreign Minister, armed with his own convictions and
bolstered by the advice of China specialists like Ishii, lost no time in
conveying to Chang his willingness to engage in peace negotiations. In
response to the suggestion that Wang Ching-wei represent China at the
peace table, Ugaki replied that he thought not, for despite Wang's qualifications "your countrymen regard him as a leader of the pro-Japanese
faction . . . and might accuse him of selling out his country."[71] Recalling some conciliatory remarks made in Singapore by H. H. Kung, the
Generalissimo's brother-in-law, shortly after the beginning of the war,
Ugaki proposed that Kung would be an ideal representative. He was
known to be extremely close to the Generalissimo and could be expected
to speak for him. Furthermore, he did not have the pro-Japan stigma
that disqualified Wang and Chang Ch'ün himself. Kung apparently
agreed to the arrangement, for he sent his personal secretary, Ch'iao
Fu-sa, to Hong Kong to meet with the Japanese Consul General, Nakamura Toyokazu. Their first meeting took place on June 16.

The negotiations, on which both sides pinned so much hope, went on
until the first of September. Some headway was made, and at one point
a Japanese warship was readied to convey Kung to a meeting with Ugaki
in Nagasaki or someplace in Taiwan. But in spite of the extraordinary
promise of success, the negotiations finally foundered on several issues.

Early in the talks, when Kung asked for a list of Japanese terms, Ugaki replied that "despite changes in the Government, the new Cabinet and the Foreign Minister are in agreement, and Japan's foreign policy remains unchanged even though I have succeeded Hirota."[72] Nakamura later recalled that he was especially disturbed by instructions from Tokyo suggesting there would be no change in the *aite ni sezu* declaration. "I could not even begin the negotiations with such instructions," he wrote in 1956. The Consul-General flew home for discussions with Ugaki, who advised him that "Japan will drop the *aite ni sezu* banner eventually, but we can't do it now." Ishii, who was in close contact with Ugaki at this time and so in a position to comment authoritatively, later wrote that Ugaki took his adamant stand on Chiang's retirement merely as an initial bargaining tactic from which he was prepared to back down as the negotiations moved along.[73]

Ugaki's own diary, however, shows a startling change in his feelings in the few months he served as Foreign Minister. In the entry for June 28, when the negotiations with Kung were just getting under way, Ugaki showed great sympathy for Chiang and the problems he faced. "China has been bound hand and foot by the Powers for well over a hundred years," he wrote, and as a consequence the "Chinese people could not get ahead no matter how hard they strived." But in recent years China had reacted to her adversity, to the point where a "powerful trend" toward national solidarity was now sweeping over China. "Chiang Kai-shek is the one who had stepped forward to lead this trend," Ugaki recorded, but it behooved the Japanese to "take careful note of the fact that, even though we overthrow Chiang Kai-shek, this trend is going to go on as before."[74] On July 15 Ugaki set down his belief that an "Eastern community" and a long-lasting peace were possible only if Japan helped foster and strengthen Chinese nationalism rather than resisting it.[75] Two short months later, however, on the eve of his resignation as Foreign Minister, Ugaki felt that "the Chiang regime and his gang must be smashed by increasing our pressure on them."[76]

Whatever Ugaki's personal views were, the official view of the Japanese Government, as decided in the Five Ministers' Conference of July 8, was that Japanese "acceptance of the capitulation of the present central government of China" was conditional on Chiang's resignation. The Konoe Government had accepted the necessity of revising the *aite ni sezu* declaration to the extent of dealing with the Kuomintang Government in matters relating to its surrender. But the Five Ministers lacked the "courage" that Ishii had declared they would have to have if they were to completely reverse the *aite ni sezu* declaration and negotiate with Chiang himself: on July 8 they formally demanded the "resignation from public life of Chiang Kai-shek."[77]

In explaining to Nakamura that this was only a temporary expediency, Ugaki stressed that, after all, Chiang had administered the nation poorly, and as a result the Chinese people had suffered terrible misery. His retirement from public life was therefore "natural."* Nakamura disagreed: the Chinese people did not hold Chiang responsible for their defeat in the war, and therefore the demand that he resign would "cause trouble."[78]

Ugaki took a somewhat different line on Chiang's retirement in his indirect negotiations with Kung. He tied the retirement question to two other issues Kung had raised. One was the matter of indemnities. Kung asked that Japan relax her demands, contending that China simply could not afford to pay indemnities because of the great damage she had suffered in the war. The second issue Kung raised was the question of the recognition of Manchukuo. Both countries appreciated the de facto situation there, Kung said, and China in effect had tacitly recognized Manchukuo. Now it was time for Japan to recognize that the Manchukuo question was a difficult one for China to handle internally. Under the circumstances, Kung asked if Japan would not agree to drop her demands for formal Chinese recognition of Manchukuo.[79]

Ugaki's reply was that if Kung wanted the Japanese to give due consideration to China's internal problems, he should be able to appreciate the internal problem Chiang Kai-shek posed for the Japanese Government. "The Japanese people view Chiang Kai-shek as an enemy, and they have said that they will not deal with him. They bear no ill will for the Chinese people, but since it is Chiang who has been in command of the country while the present situation developed, the majority of Japanese hate him." Accordingly, said Ugaki, if China wanted concessions on the Manchukuo and indemnities questions, she would do well to "mollify Japanese feeling" on Chiang and agree to his retirement from public office. His resignation, Ugaki concluded, would "really benefit your country more than Japan," because it would create a suitable climate in Japan for the dropping of indemnities and the "silent approach" on Manchukuoan recognition.[80] These ingenious arguments failed to persuade Kung, who never so much as hinted that there was

---

* As reported by Ambassador Grew, Ugaki had remarked to British Ambassador Craigie "that Chiang Kai-shek himself is not intensely anti-Japanese but that he must bear the responsibility for the intensive anti-Japanese propaganda in the schools and elsewhere and that until he undergoes a conversion the Japanese Government cannot deal with him. Craigie interprets this as meaning 'until the Generalissimo breaks with the Communists.' " Grew to Secretary of State, Aug. 16, 1938, in *FR* 1938, 3: 263.

a remote possibility of Chiang stepping down from office. If a resignation was needed to assuage Japanese feelings, Kung said, perhaps his own might be satisfactory; he was perfectly willing to resign, he told Ugaki. (Kung had recently been appointed President of the Executive Yüan.) The gesture did not satisfy Tokyo.

Though the Chiang resignation was the principal sticking point in the negotiations, the question of North China was also a major obstacle. To Ugaki's demands for a "special zone" in North China, Kung replied with a lesson in Chinese history and geography. The Chinese people had always regarded the area outside of the Great Wall as "uncivilized" and were not overwhelmingly concerned about foreign influence there, Kung observed. China was thus willing both to give her tacit agreement to the existence of Manchukuo and to let Japan establish a special zone and garrison her troops in Inner Mongolia. But Japan had to realize, he insisted, that the area inside the Great Wall was quite a different matter. If she tried to "liberate" North China and station her troops there indefinitely, the Chinese people would assuredly become "obsessed with the notion that Japan eventually plans to annex all of China."[81]

Ugaki replied that it was ridiculous to believe Japan was trying to annex China. If she was planning to do so, why would she be seeking a zone in North China? Had not Nanking and Shanghai already fallen to Japan? The only purpose of a special zone in North China, Ugaki explained, was to provide a joint Sino-Japanese defense against communism. Inner Mongolia was the first line of that defense, and North China was the second. "All we are doing is following up on agreements I myself signed with the Tuan Ch'i-jui Government," Ugaki remarked— with some insensitivity, for the Tuan hegemony in North China at the height of the warlord era represented all that the Kuomintang regime professed to be combating, i.e., a politically fractured China and the concession of Chinese territory and sovereignty to Japan in exchange for graft and a military assistance of questionable value.[82] If Ugaki truly thought that such a response about Japanese intentions in North China would set Kung's mind at ease, it illustrates how little awareness there was, even in the minds of moderates like Ugaki, that times were changing in China.

By August reports of unfavorable Chinese reaction to Ugaki's proposals were drifting back to Tokyo, not only from Consul General Nakamura but also from various intermediaries. Chang Chi-luan, the editor of the Chungking *Ta-kung pao*, who was close to both the Generalissimo and Chang Ch'ün, was meeting with a Japanese colleague who had contacts with Ugaki. Through these meetings Ugaki learned of the Chinese determination to resist Japan as long as she continued her pressure to divide China. The journalist emphasized that sooner or later Japan must recognize two things: that China was going to become politically unified, and that the Kuomintang Government was *the* political force in China, and consequently the one with which she must deal.[83]

Ugaki's efforts to negotiate a settlement through Kung continued throughout August, but since Kung would make no concession on the issue of Chiang's resignation, the talks in Hong Kong trailed off inconclusively in early September. By that time Ugaki had lost any initiative he might have held earlier in the summer. The Hankow campaign had commenced, the Five Ministers had decided to insist on Chiang's resignation, General Doihara was working, with Tokyo's approval, to induce Wu P'ei-fu to head a new Chinese regime, Colonel Kagesa was making the initial contacts that would eventually lead to the establishment of the Wang Ching-wei regime, and perhaps worst of all from the standpoint of Ugaki's authority, the Army was moving to divest the Foreign Ministry of any control over Japan's China policy by establishing a special board for China (ultimately named the Kōain). All of these developments further reduced Ugaki's fading enthusiasm for a turnabout in China policy. The Foreign Minister was kept in the dark about some of these moves—such as the initial overtures to Wang Ching-wei's followers, which were going on at precisely the time he was talking with Kung—and was unable to control the others. But it was the usurpation of the Foreign Minister's powers by the new China board that finally impelled Ugaki to relinquish his office in September 1938.

Almost all the high officials in the Japanese Government, including the Foreign Minister, had recognized the need for some kind of a coordinating board to determine China policy.[84] Ugaki favored a body under the control of the Premier and would have limited its jurisdiction to the occupied areas of China, with overall China policy continuing to be set by the Five Ministers. In his view the chief function of such an agency was to provide liaison between the various ministries concerned with China and its principal concern, the various national policy companies operating in occupied China.

The Army had in mind something quite different. It wanted an agency with broad powers touching every aspect of Chinese life—economic, political, and cultural—and with jurisdiction over the whole of China. Somewhat inconsistently, it also wanted its Tokumu-bu to retain considerable "on-the-scene" power in matters of local administration on the mainland. On September 27 Ugaki notified the Five Ministers' Conference that, having assumed the responsibility of settling the China Incident, he could not approve a China board unless the Foreign Ministry retained the right to negotiate peace settlements with the Kuomintang Government. Opposition from both the Army and Navy ministers deadlocked the meeting, and two days later Ugaki submitted his resignation to Konoe, stating that without room to maneuver diplomatically he could not carry out his responsibilities as Foreign Minister. His resignation was accepted, and two days later, on October 1, Konoe announced the establishment of the Taishiin, a "China Board" that satisfied all of the demands of the Army. The Foreign Office, as the *Asahi* noted a few days later, had been "shorn of its fame and prestige."[85] It had less and less of a say in China policy as time went along, to the point where four years later Foreign Minister Tōgō Shigenori was told that the functions of his ministry in China were to be restricted to "pure diplomacy," which was defined as the official reception of envoys and the signing of treaties.[86]

In December the Board's name was changed to the Kōain (Asia Development Board). Though the Premier was the Board President, Army and Navy officers on the active list were its chief staff members. Among them were Lt. Gen. Yanagawa Heisuke, its Secretary-General, and Maj. Gen. Suzuki Teiichi, Chief of the Political Affairs Section, who was probably the most important member of the Board. In early 1939 the Japanese Government announced the establishment of four Kōain "liaison agencies" in Kalgan, Peiping, Shanghai, and Amoy. All were placed under the control of generals or admirals; General Kita, the chief patron of the Provisional Government, for example, was named to direct the Peiping office.

The Imperial decree establishing the Kōain gave it blanket authority to "administer political, economic, and cultural affairs in connection with the China Incident." Government statements in the press indicated, however, that the termination of hostilities would not necessarily mean the "Incident" had ended. The Government, in other words, foresaw the need for the Asia Development Board to continue functioning "until the program for the reconstruction and development of China and the economic, political, and cultural cooperation of Japan, Manchukuo, and China have been effected."[87] But the military's aim of consolidating the direction of the programs and policies in China under its own control in the Kōain was only partially realized. Though the Foreign Office was increasingly denied a role in China, the mainland Army commands and various Army and Navy groups continued to pursue independent courses of action with respect to China. Among the most promising of the independent "operations" being conducted in mid-1938 was the

effort to recruit the retired warlord Wu P'ei-fu as head of a new collaboration regime.

Throughout the summer of 1938, while Ugaki was trying to reach an
understanding with Kung and Chiang, the press in both China and
Japan speculated freely—and in general correctly—on Japanese plans
to recruit, either separately or together, three aged veterans of the warlord era to head a new collaboration government. Though there had
been some attempt in late 1937 to sound out the willingness of these
men to join in a pro-Japanese regime, the effort to enlist them was not
well organized until mid-1938. By that time, a group centered around
Col. Iwakuro Hideo, a section chief in the Army General Staff, had come
to realize that Wang K'o-min and Liang Hung-chih were incapable of
providing the leadership the Imperial Army needed if it was going to
carry out its aims in China; and that leaders of more commanding stature and eminence had to be obtained, especially if the plan to unite the
various puppet regimes into some kind of national government was
going to be pursued.[88] Iwakuro and his group therefore proposed that
a small interservice unit be created to explore the possibility of securing
the services of prominent Chinese statesmen and leaders. A Five Ministers' Conference approved the proposal on July 26, 1938, and authorized the new body to "work out important stratagems in China" and
"establish a new Central Chinese Government" in accordance with the
policies the Five Ministers were drawing up at the time.[89] Officially
named the Special Commission for China (Zai-Shi Tokubetsu Iinkai),
the new group was placed under the direct control of the Five Ministers. It eventually came to be known by a code designation, Bamboo
Agency (Take Kikan), and more commonly as the Doihara Agency in
recognition of its domination by Doihara Kenji, the archetype of the
political general.

General Doihara's skills as a battlefield commander had been called
into question earlier that year because of a disastrous rout of his troops
at Lanfeng, but his political experience in Manchuria in the early 1930's
made him eminently suitable for the task at hand.[90] To provide a sem-
blance of interservice cooperation, a Navy representative, Vice Adm.
Tsuda Shizue, was appointed to the Doihara Agency. Other members
were Col. Oseki Michisada and Maj. Gens. Wachi Takaji and Banzai
Rihachirō. The last-named is surprisingly little known to historians of
this period. Of all the "old China hands," Banzai was regarded as the
"greatest authority on China" by members of the Center. Unlike the
staff of the North China Area Army and others who insisted on the *bunji
gassaku* doctrine, he favored a strong united China. This is not to say,

1. Wang Ching-wei, 1912

2. Wang, 1930

3. L. to r.: Kao Tsung-wu, Ch'ien Ta-chün (Chiang's chief bodyguard), Chiang Kai-shek, Imai Takeo, Kita Seiichi, Amamiya Tatsumi (Japanese Military Attaché, Nanking)

4. Imai Takeo

5. Prince Teh

6. Wang and his wife, Ch'en Pi-chün, 1937

7. Ishii Itarō

8. Ishiwara Kanji just before his death in 1949

慶祝漢口陷落

華北華中完全安定

9. Poster celebrating the fall of Hankow. Circa November 1938

10. Mme. Wang, Wang, and Tseng Chung-ming read the war news in Hankow while Wang's daughter looks on

11. Official photograph taken at the inauguration of the Reorganized National Government of the Republic of China, March 30, 1940. Front row, l. to r.: Chou Fo-hai, Ch'en Ch'ün (Minister of the Interior), Ch'u Min-i, Liang Hung-chih, Ch'en Kung-po, Wang Ching-wei, Wen Tsung-yao (President of the Judicial Yüan), Wang I-t'ang, Ku Chung-shen (Vice President of the Control Yüan), Ch'u Li-ho (Vice President of the Executive Yüan), Chiang Kang-hu (Vice President of the Examination Yüan), Chu Ch'ing-lai (member of the Central Executive Committee of Wang's "Orthodox" Kuomintang), Mei Ssu-p'ing.

12. Kao Tsung-wu, Mei Ssu-p'ing, and Imai Takeo at the Chungkuang-t'ang Conference, November 1938

13. Ch'en Kung-po

14. Chou Fo-hai and his wife

15. Kagesa Sadaaki

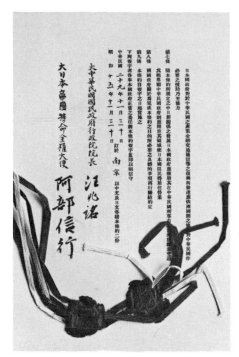

16. "Basic Treaty" between Japan and the Reorganized National Government, November 30, 1940

17. Picture of the man who tried to pass himself off as T. L. Soong in 1940. Photograph was taken through a keyhole.

18. Liang Hung-chih and Wang K'o-min, 1940

19. Wang Ching-wei, 1940

20. Poster celebrating the fall of Singapore, early 1942. Note the Wang regime pennant atop the Chinese flag.

21. March 31, 1940, the day after the inauguration of the Wang Government. Front row, l. to r.: Imai Takeo, Wang Ching-wei, Kagesa Sadaaki. Back row, l. to r.: Chou Lung-hsiang, Mei Ssu-p'ing, Inukai Ken, Chou Fo-hai, Ch'en Kung-po, Itō Yoshio.

however, that his views were as enlightened as those of Ishii Itarō. With Doihara, Banzai insisted on securing the collaboration of political troglodytes like Wu P'ei-fu.[91]

The program Doihara devised had two parts.[92] The first part called for luring the so-called Kwangsi Army, which was then assisting in the defense of Hankow, away from the Chiang camp. This task fell to General Wachi, and the plan quickly failed. Undaunted, Doihara moved ahead on the second phase of his operation: the recruitment of three important Chinese to head a new government. Of the three target individuals, two were soon eliminated. The first was Chin Yun-p'eng, an ex-Army officer who had served under Tuan Ch'i-jui as Minister of War and had finally become Premier in 1919. Toppled from office in 1921, Chin had turned from politics to business and then, in 1931, had gone into retirement as a Buddhist monk. Doihara was unable to induce Chin to abandon his holy retirement. That left T'ang Shao-i and Wu P'ei-fu. According to Doihara's constantly revised scheme, the seventy-eight-year-old T'ang was to be in charge of the civil functions of the proposed government, and Wu in charge of its military functions, including the organization of a pro-Japanese army.

Both T'ang and Wu were political veterans of the Ch'ing and warlord eras, and both had been living in retirement for several years, T'ang in Shanghai and Wu in Peiping. Wu figures so prominently in Western studies of Asian history that we need not go into his background here.[93] But T'ang's name is less well known in the West, so that we might usefully stop here to take a brief look at his background and views.[94]

T'ang went abroad in 1873 as one of the students in the first educational mission to the United States. After graduating from Columbia University, he returned to China to serve as a secretary to Yüan Shih-k'ai and, as a consequence of his association with Yüan, to rise to prominence. He served in a number of diplomatic posts under the Manchus— including that of Special Commissioner for Tibetan Affairs—and eventually became the Premier of the first Republican Government. He did not stay long in that post, however, for a stalemate developed when he was charged with financial mismanagement and his Cabinet fell in June 1912. From then until his retirement from politics in 1934, T'ang held a succession of ministerial and subministerial positions in various regimes. Unlike most of the men Japan had recruited into her puppet regimes, T'ang had served out his last years of public service in the good graces of the Kuomintang and was still in close and friendly contact with Nationalist officials in 1938.

It was because of T'ang's Pan-Asian sentiments that Doihara and his colleagues placed their hopes in him. T'ang had great respect for Japan's demonstrated military power, which "forces the so-called superior nations to shake hands with her."[95] In his view the fulfillment of both Chinese and Indian aspirations—essentially liberation from Western imperialist domination—depended on a strong Sino-Japanese alliance, an alliance that could be achieved only when Chinese patriots came to realize that distrust of Japan's strength and motives was harmful to their own national interests.

> Anti-Japanese feeling in China [he wrote in 1916] is being fanned to flames by those outside interests who do not want to see China and Japan united. . . . We have been tired of hearing that Japan is a menace to Asia. . . . We do not look at a rising Japan in the same spirit. We only wish that China and India be equally strong, that Japan hold her own on the Asiatic continent against European aggressors. Then the international nuisance, charged to Japan, but really traced to outside forces, will cease to exist in Asia.[96]

These views were not uncommon among Chinese nationalists at the time they were expressed, but T'ang still clung to them in 1938, after a decade of Japanese aggression that had left most Chinese profoundly skeptical of their neighbor's Pan-Asianism, suggesting at least one important reason for Doihara's deep interest in him. According to a Japanese Foreign Office summary of the "T'ang operation," T'ang was reluctant to cooperate with the Japanese only because he feared "that the Japanese might come to a compromise with the Chiang regime in the future or might attempt to create a purely puppet government."[97] For those reasons T'ang had steadfastly refused invitations to participate in the Reformed Government. Once Doihara arrived on the scene, however, T'ang's reluctance began to dissipate. Doihara apparently induced him to compose a "peace telegram," which would be made public as a first step in the creation of a T'ang-Wu government. But on September 30, 1938, as a draft of the telegram was being forwarded to Wu P'ei-fu for approval, T'ang was brutally assassinated. Doihara had been especially concerned about T'ang's safety because of the growing number of assassinations of persons felt to be friendly to the Japanese and had offered to provide bodyguards for the elderly T'ang, but T'ang had rejected the offer. According to Japanese sources, several of the Kuomintang's fascist Blue Shirts had gained entrance to T'ang's home in the French Concession of Shanghai during preparations for the wedding of his daughter, and one of them had sunk a hatchet in his head as he was bowing to greet his "guests." The National Government, whose henchmen were presumably responsible for the murder, issued a proclamation commending T'ang for a lifetime of meritorious service and appropriated a large sum of money for his funeral expenses.[98]

With T'ang out of the picture Doihara turned all his energies to persuading Wu P'ei-fu to abandon the Buddhist studies, poetry composition, gardening, and other refined pastimes appropriate to the retirement years of a soldier-turned-scholar. Though these efforts went on until Wu's death (on December 4, 1939), the high point of Doihara's "Wu operation" was from about November 1938 to January 1939. In order to persuade the reluctant ex-warlord to collaborate, Doihara lured an old colleague of Wu's, Chang Yen-ch'ing, away from his association with the Provisional Government, which like its sponsor, the North China Area Army, was completely hostile to the aims of the Doihara Agency.[99] With Japanese assistance, Chang set about forming "peace and national salvation" associations throughout China. The leaders of these organizations, which existed only on paper, then besieged Wu with telegrams begging him to emerge from retirement and cooperate with Japan in a movement to pacify the nation and rid it of the communism he so detested. "He was an obstinate fellow," writes Imai Takeo, who met with Wu frequently during the Wu operation. "He was always railing against communism, but it seemed that his conception of communism was that it was just the communal ownership of property and women. . . . He had absolutely no notion of the changing times. He still flattered himself that his fame had not changed at all since the magnificent warlord era, and crouched like a tiger ready to spring back into politics."[100]

It is not surprising that such a man did not examine too closely the credentials of the peace and national salvation associations that were calling for his leadership. Their "leaders," operating out of a "draft Wu" headquarters at the old soldier's former base in Kaifeng, issued statements calling for a People's Congress and similar measures in order to hasten and legitimize the return of their hero to national politics. Unaware that his support was largely the handiwork of General Doihara, Wu assembled reporters on November 30 to announce that he was organizing a Pacification Committee preparatory to establishing a new central government. In early December the Japanese press reported that Japan had appointed Wu "Chief of Pacification of the Lunghai Railway zone." Japan was about to withdraw most of her troops from North China, the reports said, so as to give Wu free rein to fight the guerrillas and muster support for the pro-Japanese regime he proposed to form.[101]

Despite a certain amount of confusion at the time, it is now apparent that Wu was never very close to accepting Doihara's assignment. Though he did not give the Japanese General a flat turndown, he insisted on concessions Doihara could not possibly agree to. He demanded, for example, that he be given a fair amount of autonomy in organizing and leading the army of his new regime, and that he be made at least nominal leader of a united government ruling all of China. These demands not only were unacceptable to the Imperial Army and the Kōain, but were repugnant to the existing puppet governments as well.[102] The Provisional Government was especially concerned over statements from the Wu camp absolving Chiang Kai-shek and the Kuomintang of any blame for the war. There was considerable fear in the North China regime that Wu might find a place for the Kuomintang in his proposed government, which would inevitably spell disaster for the fiercely anti-Kuomintang Provisional Government. As Imai puts it, the "slightest move on the part of Wu immediately gave a case of the jitters to the leaders of the Provisional Government in Peiping."[103] The Tokyo authorities passed orders on to the Provisional and Reformed Governments to cooperate with the Doihara Agency, but when leaders of the two puppet regimes met in a United Council session on January 22, 1939, they proposed that Wu's activities be restricted to Hankow (another of Wu's old bases) and Southwest China.[104]

Though the Wu operation continued throughout 1939, it could not overcome all of these obstacles. By February of that year Wu had ceased to be a major factor in puppet politics, and by the end of the year he was dead.* Upon his death, the Kuomintang Government showered honors, posthumous ranks, magnificent funeral appropriations, and personal tributes on the fallen warlord. His great loyalty in refusing to head a puppet regime was eulogized. Ironically, the Provisional Government was no less appreciative, and it too was lavish in honoring the memory of Wu—with a funeral appropriation twice as big as Chungking's.[105]

---

* Wu evidently died of complications arising from an abscessed tooth. Emergency surgery by a team of German and Japanese doctors failed to save his life but did expose the Japanese to the inevitable charge that they had murdered their patient with poison. Imai, who was in a position to know and is quite candid in such matters, says an investigation showed conclusively that the Japanese had no hand in Wu's death. Imai, *Shōwa*, p. 151.

CHAPTER NINE

The Low-Key Club

IN THE resistance-to-the-death atmosphere that prevailed in Nanking and Hankow in the first eighteen months of the war, few Chinese were willing to show open support for a conciliatory approach to the Japanese aggressors. There was considerable reluctance to speak out in favor of peace or negotiations or anything that might be interpreted—or twisted—as suggesting a slackening of the resistance effort. One group, however, was privately and cautiously beginning to question the official resistance-to-the-death slogans. This was the self-styled Low-Key Club (Ti-tiao Chü-lo-pu), so named to indicate its members' dissatisfaction with the prevailing "hysterical climate."[1] The Club met informally for lunch at the home of one of its leading members, Chou Fo-hai. Other prominent members were Kao Tsung-wu and Hu Shih.

These men were disturbed at the feverish atmosphere in China and felt that opportunists seeking public attention and favor had only to scream slogans about resistance to climb to power. In their view, China was not prepared for a long war of resistance, and consequently diplomatic channels to Japan ought to be kept open and fully explored. Hu Shih, whose association with the Club was cut short by his appointment as Ambassador to the United States in 1938, believed that "it is possible to negotiate with the Konoe Cabinet, and [that] this opportunity should not be lost."[2] Hu looked forward to a fundamental readjustment of Sino-Japanese relations that would lead to a half century of peace. More than anything else, however, it was the nagging fear that the Communists were using the united front and the war of resistance as a means of increasing their power and influence that bound the group together.

Another distinguished member of the Club was T'ao Hsi-sheng, an economic historian and former professor at Peking University. After the war broke out, T'ao, an old friend of Wang Ching-wei's and a member of his Reorganization Faction, went to Nanking to assume the first of several important posts in the Government. He became a member of the National Defense Council and the People's Political Council and acted as an adviser to Wang, who headed both organizations. Accordingly, he was in almost daily contact with Wang.

One of Wang's tasks was to handle the various peace proposals that came directly from the Japanese or indirectly through foreign diplomatic channels, including the German, British, and Italian Ambassadors. He and T'ao would discuss the merits of each proposal and then pass it on to the Generalissimo, who according to T'ao was completely preoccupied with directing the military aspects of the war effort. On occasion a plan was advanced calling for Wang to divorce himself from the Generalissimo and take a personal lead in the negotiations, but invariably, T'ao maintains, Wang refused to entertain such a notion. As a case in point, T'ao recalls that when a Japanese proposal to that effect was transmitted to Wang in the spring of 1938 by the eldest daughter of T'ang Shao-i, the political veteran the Japanese had tried to persuade to head the Reformed Government, Wang flatly rejected it and sent the woman back to Hong Kong empty-handed. In addition, T'ao claims that Wang kept the Generalissimo informed of all such proposals. "No matter what happens in the war," he reportedly told T'ao, "I will cooperate with Chiang to the end."[3]

T'ao believed that despite the Communists' participation in the war effort, their real goal was the "subjugation" of the Kuomintang. Nevertheless, the National Government was committed to a policy of cooperation, and Chiang was thus compelled to tolerate the Communists' attempts to wrest leadership from his hands. For his part, though, T'ao felt duty-bound to mobilize and keep alive an anti-Communist opposition both inside and outside the Kuomintang, and to that end he helped organize the Institute of Art and Literature (I-wen Yen-chiu Hui). The deceptively named organization had no official status, though in T'ao's words it was "actually a small bureau" of the Government. With funds supplied from "unofficial channels," the Institute "financed scholars from North China to come to Hankow to fight the Chinese Communist Party."[4]

The co-founder and Director-General of the Institute was Chou Fo-hai, the leading spokesman of those who spoke in a "low key." It was through his association with T'ao in the low-key movement that Chou came to know Wang Ching-wei, to take a major role in the negotiations leading to the creation of the Wang Government, and eventually to assume a place in that Government as its second or third most important figure.

Like many of the participants in the Wang regime, Chou had received his university education in Japan.[5] His studies at the Imperial

University at Kyoto just after World War I brought him under the influence of the economist Kawakami Hajime, then undergoing the conversion to Marxism that was to place him in the front ranks of the early left-wing movement in Japan. Perhaps because of Kawakami's influence, Chou went to Shanghai in 1921 to help found the Chinese Communist Party. He was one of the dozen delegates at the First Congress of the infant Party and was listed as a representative of Chinese students in Japan. Chou soon returned to Japan, where he spent another three years completing his education. To those who later laid his wartime collaboration with Japan to his youthful contacts with the Japanese, Chou retorted that in all his seven years there he had never formed a single Japanese friendship. Moreover (he declared in 1939), except for an occasional visit from friends with Japanese wives, he had "not received any Japanese in the past sixteen years."[6]

In 1924 Chou returned to China, this time to Canton, where the Kuomintang had established a revolutionary government. There he left the Communist Party and began teaching at the Whampoa Military Academy. As his political affiliations shifted so did his scholarly pursuits. His interest in Kropotkin gave way to scholarly studies of Sun Yat-sen, studies that attracted the attention of the Academy Director, Chiang Kai-shek, and eventually earned Chou the distinction of being the "most widely read theoretical writer of the Kuomintang."[7]

Chou rose rapidly in the ranks of the Kuomintang, thanks to his friendship with Chiang. He was scarcely thirty years old when Chiang appointed him the chief political instructor at the Central Military Academy at Nanking; in 1931 he was elected to the Central Executive Committee of the Kuomintang at its Fourth National Congress. In the faction-dominated Kuomintang Chou gradually gravitated into the CC Clique, dominated by the Ch'en brothers, Li-fu and Kuo-fu. He also began to participate in the activities of the Fu-hsing She (Regeneration Society, better known by the pejorative Blue Shirts), a semi-secret organization "founded by Whampoa zealots who felt that the KMT's civilian organization was too soft, bureaucratic, and corrupt to carry on the spirit of Sun Yat-sen."[8] Chou's special talents were in the area of political training and indoctrination, and by the time of the Marco Polo Bridge Incident he was serving as the Deputy Director of Propaganda of the Kuomintang. In addition, he had become a trusted aide-de-camp of the Generalissimo's.

Of all those who defected with Wang, Chou was clearly the one who had been closest to Chiang. "What troubled me most [about defecting from Chungking]," he reflected in 1939, "was friendship. Firstly, for more than a decade, I had topped the ladder of politics through contact with General Chiang."[9] Inukai Ken, who came to know Chou intimately during the long months of negotiations preceding the establishment of the Wang government, says he was never really certain that Chou had in fact severed all ties with Chiang, so close had the two men been. More than a suspicion always lurked in the minds of many Japanese that Chou's real function was to keep the channels between Chiang and Wang open against the day Chiang might find it expedient to make amends with Wang or vice versa. Inukai states that his own suspicions were not quieted by Chou's habit of taking old, personal letters from the Generalissimo out of his desk drawer and showing them to him when they were alone, sighing *"Natsukashii, nē,"* a wistful lament that usually suggests a desire to return home.[10]

In large measure, the story of the Wang Ching-wei peace movement begins with the Low-Key Club's Kao Tsung-wu, the Asian Bureau Chief of the Ministry of Foreign Affairs. It was Kao who launched the movement in the winter of 1937–38, and it was he who shattered it two years later. The beginnings were quiet and secretive, with each side making exploratory contacts and cautious, tentative commitments. But the end came with electrifying speed in the first week of January 1940, with Kao's sensational defection from the peace movement and his disclosure to the Hong Kong press of documents showing that the peace movement had become a one-sided instrument of Japanese imperialism.*

At the time of the Marco Polo Bridge Incident, Kao was only thirty years old.[11] He was born in China but was educated in Japan, graduating from the law faculty of Kyushu Imperial University. "He was very, very sharp and talked very well," recalls a Japanese colleague who knew him well.[12] A man of slight stature, Kao suffered from chronic tuberculosis and throughout his life was hospitalized for extended periods of time. After completing his education abroad, Kao returned to China to teach political science at Nanking Central University. Parts of his doctoral dissertation on Sino-Japanese diplomacy were published in various Chinese newspapers and magazines. The editor of one of these magazines was Li Sheng-wu, an Oxford-educated authority on international

---

* Precisely what happened in the intervening years will not be known until Kao publishes his memoirs or until the Taiwan regime allows free access to its historical archives, a permission that seems unlikely to be granted in our lifetime. According to Kao, his own account of the events will not be released until after his death. Meanwhile, he intends to guard his privacy and his recollections with extreme care for "fear of misinterpretation." Since the fateful days of January 1940 Kao has written nothing concerning the peace movement, and with the exception of our conversation in December 1969, has declined all invitations to discuss the subject with interested scholars.

law and a junior colleague of Wang Ching-wei. Li passed one of Kao's essays along to Wang, who expressed an interest in meeting the young man. Impressed with Kao, Wang, who was then Foreign Minister, invited him to join the Government to assist in the negotiations with the Japanese concerning the establishment of railway and mail communications between China proper and Manchukuo.[13] Popular opposition to these talks helped to brand Wang and those around him appeasers and brought about the climate in which his Vice Minister, T'ang Yu-jen, was assassinated, and an attempt was made on his own life. As we have seen, it also brought about the end of Wang's Government role and his retreat to Europe, purportedly to recuperate from his wounds. In the wake of these events few of Wang's close supporters remained in the Government. Kao, by this time both a supporter and a close friend of Wang's, was one of those few. Moreover, he rose rapidly to achieve the rank of Asian Bureau Chief before he was thirty years old. Kao's ability to ride out the wave of anti-appeasement protest and earn such a high rank while still so young suggests he did indeed possess the keen political talents that are often attributed to him.

In the crucial five weeks between the Marco Polo Bridge Incident and the outbreak of fighting in Shanghai, weeks in which there seemed to be a chance to prevent the North China Incident from engulfing all of China, Kao and the Low-Key Club were in an extremely "isolated" position. As Kao told Japanese contacts, anyone who took an even slightly conciliatory position was branded a traitor.[14] During much of that time, the Government was in residence at Chiang's summer capital at Kuling, in the mountains of Kiangsi province. Nationalists and Communists streamed to Kuling to discuss the proper Chinese response to the events in North China and to Tokyo's official demands that the Kuomintang regime exclude itself from the settlement of the crisis there. Many thought Chiang would continue to counsel patience in dealing with the enemy. As journalist Emily Hahn wrote, "Only a few of the highest officials were not guessing cynically that Chiang's reaction would be true to form."[15] Less than two years before he had been doing everything possible to postpone the final confrontation with Japan. "We shall not forsake peace until there is no hope for peace," he had declared at the fifth plenary session of the Kuomintang in November 1935. "We shall not talk lightly of sacrifice until we are driven to the last extremity that makes sacrifice inevitable."[16] As we have seen, from Chiang's point of view that extremity was reached in 1937. After ten days in conference with the leaders of China, he put an end to speculation by rejecting Japanese proposals for a local solution to the North China Incident and declaring the Kuomintang's firm determination to prevent any further infringement of Chinese sovereignty.

But the Low-Key Club was unwilling to concede that all hope for a negotiated settlement had faded, and in any case it doubted that China could sustain an all-out war against Japan. At Kuling Wang Ching-wei spoke for moderation, cautioning against precipitate action and pleading for five more years to reconstruct the nation and prepare for war. In private discussions Wang revealed to Kuomintang officials a "long document" that apparently shed light on the Ho-Umezu Agreement and other agreements reached in 1935. The exact contents of this mysterious document are unknown, but Hu Shih was extremely impressed with its importance and urged that it be made public in the interests of helping a negotiated peace.[17] Shortly after the conclusion of the Kuling talks, Hu attended a lunch at the home of Kao Tsung-wu along with "several braintrusters of the Nanking Government" who felt that the time was "very late" and "past mistakes" must be rectified quickly. The whole tenor of their conversations, Hu reports, was that diplomatic channels should be "positively opened," and that this task should be entrusted to Kao.[18] He hurried to recommend Kao to the Generalissimo as a "learned and responsible man"; Chiang responded that he knew Kao and was planning to see him.[19] True to his word, he met with Wang and Kao on July 31 for lengthy discussions, in the course of which Kao outlined a plan to "turn Sino-Japanese relations around one hundred and eighty degrees." Wang, according to one source, was "immediately agreeable."[20] Chiang, for his part, gave no explicit approval, but neither did he reject Kao's bold proposal.[21] This silent assent was a technique that the Generalissimo was to exhibit repeatedly in dealing with Kao's peace movement efforts. Its advantages are obvious: the Generalissimo could easily take credit for whatever diplomatic coup the bright young Foreign Office official might bring off and just as easily shrug off responsibility in the event of failure. After Sian and Kuling the Generalissimo could not afford to be "low-keyed" in public. In private, however, ambivalence had its clear rewards.

Kao rushed to report his discussions with Chiang and Wang to his longtime patron, Wu Chen-hsiu, a man about twenty years his senior who was, in the description of one acquaintance, the "Ambassador Extraordinary of the Chekiang bankers to the Nanking Government."[22] Wu was, in fact, the President of the Nanking Bankers Association and an important figure in the business community of that city. Years before, at the Military Surveying Academy in Tokyo, he had been a classmate of Chiang Kai-shek's friend and one-time (1928) Foreign Minister,

Huang Fu. Through his friendship with Huang and other Kuomintang leaders, Wu had been instrumental in advancing the careers of several protégés, including Kao. Wu had been a tireless behind-the-scenes worker for Sino-Japanese reconciliation and was deeply concerned by the worsening crisis in the summer of 1937.

Wu and Kao met on July 31, the very day of Kao's meeting with Chiang. At Wu's invitation a Japanese business colleague and friend, Nishi Yoshiaki, was present. He and Wu had become acquainted after Nishi's appointment as manager of the Nanking office of the South Manchurian Railway two years earlier. As neighbors on Kiangsu Road in Nanking, the two developed a close friendship and discovered that they shared a mutual interest in bettering relations between their countries. Nishi was a protégé of the President of the South Manchurian Railway Company, Matsuoka Yōsuke. He filed reports with Matsuoka on his peace operations (*wahei kōsaku*) and in turn was allowed to "tap the vast resources of the South Manchurian Railway freely" to meet needed expenses for the peace movement.[23] Shortly after meeting with Wu and Kao, Nishi left for Dairen to solicit the support of Matsuoka for Kao's plan. But the trip was essentially meaningless, for the fighting in Shanghai broke out while he was en route. Indeed, relations between Wu and Nishi grew strained at this point, and even more so after the atrocities in Nanking in December. By early 1938, however, they had resumed their discussions.

In the meantime, Kao had resigned his position in the Foreign Ministry shortly after the fall of Nanking, and had gone to Hong Kong for the ostensible purpose of "gathering intelligence" on the Japanese. His real mission, undertaken at the behest of Low-Key Club members Chou Fo-hai and T'ao Hsi-sheng, was to make secret contacts with citizens and officials willing to work for peace. The task required considerable travel between Hong Kong and Shanghai; Kao also made three or more trips back to Hankow between February and June 1938 to report his findings to Chou Fo-hai, who hoped that, at the very least, Kao would be able to reopen the channels to Tokyo that had been ruptured by the ill-fated Trautmann talks and the *aite ni sezu* declaration.[24]

Nearly all of those who were involved in the Kao mission, Chinese and Japanese alike, assert that the intelligence Kao gathered and forwarded back to Chou Fo-hai did not stop there but was passed on to the Generalissimo. One and all also assert that Kao's trip to Hong Kong was authorized by Chiang.[25] Any misgivings Chiang might have had about Kao exceeding his "orders" were probably laid to rest after Chiang's trusted aide, Chou Fo-hai, indicated his willingness to accept full responsibility for the mission. Chiang was undoubtedly aware that Kao was embarking on something more than an intelligence gathering expedition, but the risks of Kao's active involvement in a peace operation were probably outweighed by Chiang's feeling that Kao was ultimately loyal to him and under his control. Kao might succeed in finding influential Japanese willing to negotiate on terms acceptable to Chiang, and if he did Chiang could capitalize on the discovery. The Generalissimo was never blind to the value of a negotiated peace that could free him from his uneasy alliance with the Communists.[26]

Kao was forced to suspend his activities in late 1937 in order to recuperate from one of his frequent tuberculosis attacks, and therefore sought the assistance of a trusted subordinate, Tung Tao-ning, Chief of the First (Japan) Section of the Asia Bureau. Born in Chekiang province, Tung had spent his boyhood years in Japan and had graduated from Kyoto University. He spoke "better Japanese than the Japanese" and was a perfect example of the "Sino-Japanese man" (Nikkajin), according to a Japanese colleague in the peace movement.[27] Tung had an extensive range of acquaintances among the Japanese, and at about the time of the fall of Nanking, Kao had sent him to Shanghai to "push from behind the scenes" the Trautmann mediation efforts, and indeed to bypass the mediators by talking directly to Japanese Ambassador Kawagoe. While in Shanghai Tung received encouragement in these efforts from Wu Chen-hsiu and others in Chekiang financial circles.[28] During the previous decade, a mutually profitable relationship had developed between the bankers of Chekiang province and the Kuomintang, the bankers contributing financial support to the Kuomintang and the Kuomintang reciprocating with governmental favors. However, as the war forced the Kuomintang to retreat farther and farther inland the ties between the two groups became strained. As Fairbank has noted in assessing the post-Hankow phase of the war, the "Szechwan landlords and militarists took the place of the Shanghai bankers."[29]

The banking community was unhappy about the war on several counts, in fact. One major source of dissatisfaction was the Kuomintang's wartime practice of charging Chinese banks an approximate 10 per cent surtax on all bills of exchange. This extralegal "commission," which the Government simply appropriated, placed the Chinese banks, especially those operating in Hong Kong, in a poor competitive position and "resulted in the strange phenomenon of foreign capital enjoying an envious prosperity while Chinese capital found it necessary to battle its own Government."[30] The aggrieved banking circles apparently felt that there was little chance of improvement in wartime, and that their best hope lay in a peace movement.

Tung was also encouraged in his efforts by Nishi Yoshiaki, an old friend. In mid-January 1938, one or two days prior to the *aite ni sezu* declaration, Tung called on Nishi in his room at the Palace Hotel in Shanghai. When Tung finished conveying to Nishi his frustration at failing to find a diplomatic solution to the Sino-Japanese conflict, he was startled to hear his Japanese friend suggest that if Tung went to Tokyo, he might find certain members of the Army General Staff willing to lend a sympathetic ear to his proposals. After all, Nishi reminded Tung, he had already "crossed the Rubicon" by entering into talks with the enemy's Ambassador, Kawagoe; going to Tokyo would be "essentially the same but much more efficacious." Nishi even offered to precede Tung to Tokyo and arrange appropriate introductions.[31]

Nishi's principal acquaintance on the General Staff was Colonel Kagesa, who, unlike the "political soldiers" (*seiji gunjin*) Nishi had come to despise while working in Manchuria, was a "surpassing" person, a man who stood head and shoulders above the average Japanese officer. That had not been his first impression, Nishi admits; he had not been taken with Kagesa when first they met in 1935, Kagesa being then the Vice Military Attaché in Nanking with the "typical hard-line views" of the officer class.[32] Kagesa himself acknowledges that he was something of a "rustic samurai" with very unenlightened views of China in those days but says he began to have a change of heart with his transfer to the General Staff soon after the Marco Polo Bridge Incident.[33] Apparently at the behest of General Ishiwara, whose views of China greatly influenced him, Kagesa was made Chief of the China Section of the General Staff in August 1937. Shortly thereafter, the Stratagem Section was created for the express purpose of finding a solution to the China Incident, and Kagesa, now promoted to Colonel, was made its Chief. Nishi chanced to meet Kagesa aboard ship after his assignment to the General Staff, and in the course of renewing their acquaintanceship had been struck by Kagesa's deep respect for Chinese nationalism and determination to find a peaceful solution to the China Incident. Kagesa had come to feel, says Nishi, that Japan's "first line of defense was in supporting Chinese nationalism."[34] It almost goes without saying that in encouraging Tung Tao-ning to travel to Tokyo to explore the possibilities of peace, Nishi was pinning his hopes on Colonel Kagesa.

Within five days of his meeting with Tung, Nishi was back in Japan discussing Tung's trip with Kagesa. Kagesa immediately agreed, and on February 15 Tung arrived in Japan escorted by one of Nishi's junior colleagues, Itō Yoshio. Few details of Tung's almost three-week stay in Japan are known. We do know that in addition to talking to Colonel Kagesa, he had discussions with other officers in the Ishiwara faction of the General Staff, including Vice Chief of Staff Tada and the Chief of the China Unit (Shina-han), the then Lt. Col. Imai Takeo.[35] From this time on, Imai, like Kagesa, was to become deeply involved in the peace movement.

Kagesa admired Tung's daring in undertaking such a "dangerous" wartime mission and spoke to him of the uselessness of trying to determine responsibility for the China Incident—"as futile as counting the years of a dead child." The two agreed to work together to find a peaceful solution. Before leaving, Tung asked Kagesa to write a letter ("voluntarily") for him to take back to China. From Kagesa's memoirs, it is evident that Tung intended the letter to be read by Chiang Kai-shek. However, in consideration of the *aite ni sezu* declaration and the impropriety of a mere Section Chief writing directly to the Generalissimo, it was decided that Kagesa would write to two of his "former acquaintances," War Minister Ho Ying-ch'in and ex–Foreign Minister Chang Ch'ün.[36] In the letter (or letters—the records are not clear), Kagesa indicated his distress at the turn of events represented by the January 16 declaration, which he had vigorously opposed, and lauded the mission of Tung Tao-ning, comparing it to the historic endeavors of a Southern Sung diplomat, Wang Lun.*

The *aite ni sezu* declaration was an "unfortunate" event that made the "ultimate fate of East Asia ever more desperate," Kagesa wrote. And the Japanese were most grateful for the Tung Tao-ning mission, which was an expression of the sincerity of the Chinese people. Though it was to be hoped that Tung's work would continue, Kagesa declared, a basic solution to the Sino-Japanese problem could not be achieved by "dealing on conditions" (*jōken no torihiki*) but only by "embracing each other nakedly" (*hadaka de dakiawanebanaran*). "Dealing in conditions," that is to say, formal diplomatic negotiations, would be fruitless in the end, because China would surely demand a return to the status quo obtaining before July 1937, and that would no longer be acceptable to Japan. China must therefore trust wholeheartedly in Japan, and Japan, with her *bushidō* tradition, could not fail to respond honorably. In such a situation, Kagesa concluded, "the conditions would work themselves out."

Kagesa's disdain for the bureaucratic path to the solution of national

---

* According to Nishi, Kagesa's recondite reference to Wang Lun left the recipients of the letter puzzled and impressed. Neither Ho nor Chang could identify the not-so-celebrated historical figure who had initiated a similar peace mission some seven centuries before. Nor could the Generalissimo. Nor could the "scholarly Wang Ching-wei," adds Nishi, with evident pride in his countryman's mastery of Chinese esoterica. *Higeki no shōnin*, p. 117.

and international problems, a not uncommon attitude among the Japanese military, was matched by an exceptional sense of personal honor and loyalty, traits that are movingly testified to by those who knew him. Matsukata Saburō, a journalist who knew him well, says, "Whether things were going well or poorly in the peace movement, we were always told the complete truth by Kagesa."[37] Kagesa was eventually to become the senior military adviser to the Wang Ching-wei regime, and Wang came to rely on his frankness. Both Chinese and Japanese members of the peace movement have testified that Wang, discouraged by apparent Japanese duplicity, was often on the point of ending his collaboration with Japan, and that he persisted only because of his trust in Kagesa. As we shall see, however, Kagesa gradually became isolated from the center of power in the Army and less and less able to persuade his fellow officers to his own view: that it was in Japan's national interest to arrive at a fair settlement with Wang and encourage Chinese nationalism. The essential powerlessness of both Wang and Kagesa is a thread that winds throughout this history, and is ultimately an important key to the failure of the Wang movement. Howard Boorman characterizes Wang as a "romantic" who relied on "personal brilliance" to compensate for his lack of real political and military power.[38] Matsukata's portrait of Kagesa as a charming and magnetic figure, in whom the samurai virtues of loyalty and honor were abundantly present, complements Boorman's portrait of Wang.

On March 5 Tung departed from Tokyo in "good spirits," bearing Kagesa's letters and confident that there were important members of the General Staff who could be counted on to ease the terms of Konoe's *aite ni sezu* declaration. If the assurances he carried back to China were only the vague promises of a few personally committed Staff officers, they were nonetheless enough to sustain the hopes of the small band of Japanese and Chinese to whom he reported in Hong Kong before going on to Hankow. On hand to meet Tung at the Repulse Bay Hotel in Hong Kong were Nishi and Kao. Also present was Matsumoto Shigeharu, the South China Branch Chief of Dōmei, the semiofficial Japanese news agency.

Matsumoto, like many in the peace movement, was as much at home in China as in his native country. A cosmopolitan man, educated in several American and European universities after graduating from Tokyo Imperial University in 1923, he had represented Rengō Press and later Dōmei in Shanghai since 1933. An American acquaintance felt that Matsumoto even "looked like a Chinese . . . rather like Wang Ching-wei, and he liked to be told so, for he knew and admired Wang."[39] While studying at Yale University, Matsumoto had met one of Kao's former professors at Kyushu Imperial University; that chance meeting led him to Kao and to their lifelong friendship.[40] Matsumoto came to admire Kao enormously for his "courage" in undertaking the unpopular task of negotiating with Japan after the Marco Polo Bridge Incident. "Whenever he came to Shanghai to talk to Japanese Embassy people," Matsumoto recalls, "he came to our house on Scott Road for *misoshiru* [a Japanese soybean soup] for breakfast."[41] On such occasions, Matsumoto would give Kao the benefit of his extensive knowledge of Japanese political trends, which derived from his personal acquaintance with the Japanese leaders who were shaping those trends, including the often aloof Premier Konoe. So close in fact was Matsumoto to Konoe that he was widely regarded as the Premier's personal ambassador to China.* Much of the information Konoe received on the peace movement came via correspondence and conversations with Matsumoto.

Matsumoto also knew Colonel Kagesa, the two having been neighbors in Shanghai for a time. "We found out that my wife and his shared certain family ties, and so we became good friends," Matsumoto says. "We talked a great deal. Kagesa was always so receptive to my criticisms of the Army and Navy—I was very impressed. He would take out his notebook and say, 'What are your new orders?' He was very sincere, and so I came to love and respect him. Later, when he was transferred to the Army General Staff as Chief of the China Section, it was very convenient for me to work out some things with him."[42]

According to Imai, who was in almost constant contact with Kao from the spring of 1938 on, Kao accompanied Tung from Hong Kong back to Hankow and reported to Chou Fo-hai, who was very much encouraged by the rather meager success of Tung's mission. Kao also reported to the Generalissimo either directly or through Chou.[43] Chiang Kai-shek's response to Kao's report was to authorize Kao's return to Hong Kong. On April 16, Kao was back in Hong Kong.

Nishi reconstructs the scene of his meeting with Kao with his usual

* According to Konoe's private secretary, Ushiba Tomohiko, who was responsible for introducing Matsumoto to the Premier, "Konoe got on with Matsumoto very well. Matsumoto was one of the few who could make his views directly known to Konoe." The Premier was "very, very keen" on making Matsumoto Ambassador to the United States, Ushiba told me in an interview in 1970, but Matsumoto declined the post when it was offered, feeling that to accept it at that time would be an act of disloyalty to his superior and friend, Iwanaga Yūkichi, the President of Dōmei, who had died shortly before. Matsumoto went on to become Editor-in-Chief of Dōmei in 1940, and in postwar years has become well known to the international community in Tokyo as the Managing Director and later the Board Chairman of the International House of Japan.

penchant for detail. One suspects that Nishi hopes the reader will be impressed with the attention he gives to the complexion of Kao's face, the number of highballs consumed, and other such minutiae and will trust his accuracy on the larger questions involved. (As we shall see, Kao challenges the truth of Nishi's account.) At any rate, the scene was Room 10 (or rather the veranda of Room 10) of the Repulse Bay Hotel on the morning of the sixteenth. After Kao, Nishi, and Tung had conversed for a while, Kao indicated that he had some "very important information" to relay to Nishi and abruptly requested Tung to leave the room. Kao then related that Colonel Kagesa's letters to Chang Ch'ün and Ho Ying-ch'in had been read by the Generalissimo. The Generalissimo had been "very grateful" for the letter and had given oral instructions to Kao to convey this to the Japanese Government and to Kagesa. Kagesa should be told that "as a soldier" the Generalissimo was "deeply moved" by Kagesa's sincerity and courage. In addition, Kao was to advise Kagesa that he could "rest at ease, for I [Chiang] will never publish the letter(s)."[44] The Generalissimo had told him, Kao said, that the report Tung had brought back from Tokyo reflected the most sincere attitudes the Generalissimo had encountered in many years of negotiating with the Japanese.

As evidence of the Generalissimo's interest in this newly opened channel of negotiations, he had personally dictated to Kao the terms on which a ceasefire could be arranged. He had not spelled these terms out in detail, but had simply spoken broadly of a Japanese acknowledgment of the territorial and administrative integrity of China south of the Great Wall. As for Manchuria and Inner Mongolia, these were matters that could be negotiated at a "later date." The Generalissimo had made it clear that the reason he was willing to negotiate on these areas was his recognition that the war was in part the result of Japan's concern about her own security.[45] Chiang thus appeared willing to concede the imperative need for a Japanese-controlled anti-Soviet strategic foothold on the mainland—but only one that did not extend below the Great Wall.*

---

* Nishi, *Higeki no shōnin*, p. 136. In correspondence with me, Kao maintains that though Nishi was enthusiastically involved in the search for a Sino-Japanese peace, his account is "very far from accurate." Long conversations he supposedly had with Nishi were made out of whole cloth, Kao insists. As for the Kagesa letters, Kao says: "There were Kagesa letters, but they were not delivered." On the basis of information supplied me by David Lu, who interviewed Chang Ch'ün (Secretary-General of the Generalissimo's office on Taiwan since 1954), Chang also denies receiving any correspondence from Kagesa. I have no way of knowing which to believe, the Nishi account or the Kao-Chang denials. It is possible to impute self-serving motives to all three men. Nishi could be building a case for a noble cause in which he and his friend Kagesa participated and trying to magnify its importance by showing that not only the discredited

By this time, both Nishi and Matsumoto were urging Kao himself to go to Tokyo. Kao demurred, however, arguing that such a trip would exceed Chiang's orders. At his request Nishi agreed to undertake the mission; he left three days after Kao made his report, on April 19. Nishi's reception in Tokyo was discouraging. He had hoped that Kagesa would agree to enter into "direct" negotiations with Chiang Kai-shek, but Kagesa refused to do so.[46] Nishi's contacts in Tokyo pleaded that the political atmosphere there was too cloudy at present. The Hüschou campaign was under way during most of Nishi's stay in Japan, and this proved to be a crushing defeat for those like Kagesa and Tada who hoped to localize the conflict and ultimately to work out an accommodation with Chiang. Further exploration of the possibility of a peaceful settlement of the China problem had to be postponed until the atmosphere had cleared sufficiently to reveal the extent of the damage to the anti-expansionist cause. There were rumors that Premier Konoe was planning to reorganize his Cabinet on more favorable lines, Nishi was told. If this should happen, there would be a much better atmosphere for pushing ahead with the peace movement. Nishi thus returned to Hong Kong in mid-May with little more than assurances of continuing interest in the peace movement from various members of the General Staff. These assurances kept the peace movement alive at a time when the rapid expansion of the war fronts and the beginning of the long Hankow campaign seemed to indicate that moderate elements within the General Staff were losing ground in their efforts to keep the warfare at a quiet enough level to permit the reopening of negotiations. Without an indication of even tentative support in the Japanese high command at this time, the peace movement would almost certainly have collapsed.

Wang Ching-wei but the Generalissimo himself took an interest in it. As for Chang Ch'ün, since the peace effort we are here discussing led to the eventual defection of Wang Ching-wei, an act that has steadfastly been branded as treason by the Nationalist leaders, it is hardly surprising that Chang would deny his own or Chiang Kai-shek's involvement in the peace movement. And, finally, it can be argued that Kao, too, is protecting the reputation of the Generalissimo. To add a further note of confusion to the already murky story of the instructions Kao allegedly carried from the Generalissimo, Nishi writes that he is not sure whether the Generalissimo personally dictated the instructions (as Kao told him he did) or whether Kao drafted the instructions and then received the Generalissimo's approval, or whether Kao simply took it on himself to compose the Generalissimo's instructions without seeking the advice or the approval of the Generalissimo. (*Ibid.*, p. 137.) Nishi does not indicate why he had these doubts; I assume that it is his way of reminding the reader that on this very important question there is no unimpeachable documentary evidence, no signatures or seals of the Generalissimo, or the like. Finally, one might well have expected Kagesa to mention in his memoirs a response to his letters if he had one. But he is silent on the matter (at least in the published version of "Sozorogaki"; see my discussion of this work in the Bibliographical Note, pp. 397–98).

Nishi's mission to Tokyo marked a turning point in the peace movement. According to him, when Kao reported back to Chiang Kai-shek without any response to the peace proposals he had forwarded through Kao in April, Chiang was furious and decided that there was no alternative but all-out resistance. Accordingly, he ordered Kao to limit his activities to gathering military intelligence in Hong Kong.[47] A Kao trip to Tokyo was thus specifically enjoined by the Generalissimo, according to Nishi's account.

Nevertheless, Kao was being pressed harder and harder to undertake such a trip. Chekiang financial interests and bankers, including Ch'ien Yung-ming and Chou Tso-min, general managers of the powerful Communications Bank of China and the Kincheng Bank, respectively, urged him to go and probably offered financial assistance as well.* It may well have been Matsumoto, however, who finally persuaded Kao to make the unauthorized trip. Matsumoto recalls meeting with Kao in "about March 1938" in Kao's unheated "hiding place" in the French Concession in Shanghai.[48] (If the date is correct, the meeting took place before Nishi's unproductive trip to Tokyo.) They "shivered and talked" for two hours as Matsumoto tried to make it clear to Kao that sooner or later Japan would be forced to renounce the *aite ni sezu* declaration and deal with Chiang Kai-shek, "whether in Hankow or elsewhere." At the same time he cautioned Kao not to be impatient with Japan because it might be a "long time" before she would deal with Chiang. "In the meantime," he asked, "what is the position of Wang Ching-wei?"

Kao replied that Wang had discussed the possibility of opening up direct negotiations with Japan with Chiang about ten times, and that each time Chiang had rejected Wang's ideas. Wang was convinced there would be "no end to the increasing misery of the Chinese people, and no end to the hostilities unless negotiations were reopened," Kao said. Moreover, he firmly believed that it was necessary to cooperate with the Japanese in order to stop the expansion of the Chinese Communists.

Based upon his close association with men like Konoe, Tada, and Kagesa, Matsumoto felt confident in telling Kao that it was his feeling Tokyo would consider a "phased withdrawal of Japanese troops from the mainland," but only if Chiang would resign. Japan would accept Chiang's "temporary resignation," Matsumoto told Kao, but resign he must if there was to be peace with Japan. Kao agreed that since Chiang

---

* Inukai, *Yōsukō*, pp. 387–88. Though Inukai stresses Kao's ties to the banking community (pointing out, for instance, that Kao always used the address of the Hong Kong branch of the Communications Bank to receive coded telegrams from the Japanese participants in the peace movement), he is also careful to say that Kao was not simply acting as their agent. On the contrary, he asserts that inducing influential Chinese to join the peace movement was one of Kao's "greatest talents." *Ibid.*, p. 56.

had resigned temporarily before, there was some possibility he would do so again. He also acknowledged that there were "all kinds of anti-Chiang elements" in China, specifically naming Yen Hsi-shan, Lung Yun, and Chang Fa-k'uei. Matsumoto urged Kao to assess the possibility of temporarily bypassing Chiang and promised to "try to work out something" in Tokyo if Kao was willing to travel to Japan.

According to Nishi, Kao did not need all that much persuasion. He knew he was constrained by Chiang Kai-shek's orders to halt negotiations with the Japanese, but though he felt a deep sense of loyalty to Chiang, stronger still was his feeling that he must do something to bring about Sino-Japanese peace. Kao apparently believed or persuaded himself that Chiang's anger would pass, and that in the long run the attainment of peace would work to the benefit of the Generalissimo.[49] When Kao discussed the proposed Tokyo mission with Chou Fo-hai, he found unqualified support, and more: Chou went so far as to offer to take the entire responsibility for the trip.[50]

Until the Kuomintang archives are opened, some will continue to speculate that this is not the way it went at all, that in truth Kao's trip to Tokyo and Wang's subsequent defection were accomplished with at least the tacit approval and possibly even under the direct orders of the Generalissimo. Until evidence to the contrary accumulates, however, we are forced to rely on the memoirs and recollections of those involved in the peace movement, and they are unanimous in asserting that Kao went to Tokyo against the Generalissimo's orders.[51]

Matsumoto wrote to Kagesa in order to clear the way for Kao's trip. On the day of his scheduled departure, Kao went to Matsumoto's hotel room in Shanghai to announce that he had been having second thoughts about the trip and did not want to go. He expressed concern over the implications of the proposed temporary resignation of Chiang. He wanted assurance that Chiang would not be humiliated, that the Generalissimo "would receive very nice treatment" is the way he put it, as Matsumoto recalls. Matsumoto assured Kao that he would do his best to persuade Japanese officials to make guarantees to that effect. Kao also asked Matsumoto to be in Tokyo during his stay there, and when he said he would, Kao agreed to make the journey. Armed with official press badges and in an automobile flying the Dōmei company flag, Matsumoto and Kao passed through Japanese lines to the awaiting *Empress of Japan*.[52] Matsumoto saw Kao safely off and followed in a few days. Kao arrived in Japan in early July and remained there for approximately two weeks.

While in Tokyo Kao was introduced by Matsumoto to Inukai Ken, another prominent member of the original Wang peace movement. Inukai's father, Inukai Tsuyoshi, an important statesman and Premier at the time of the Manchurian Incident, was known as a friend of the Chinese Revolution. In a reminiscent mood shortly before his death, Tsuyoshi recalled how Sun Yat-sen had lived in the Inukai home, and how Sun and other Chinese revolutionaries had used his residence as a secret meeting place and "shared my food and clothes and even my meagre income."[53] In his *Autobiography* Sun generously acknowledged the help extended by Inukai and others to the Chinese revolutionary cause. "We must wait," Sun wrote, "for the official history of the Chinese Revolution to record in greater detail the invaluable work of our Japanese friends."[54] In 1932, Premier Inukai was assassinated by radicals angered by his conciliatory gestures to China in the midst of the Manchurian crisis. The young Inukai vowed to complete his father's unfinished tasks. Though Inukai Ken was a well-known literary figure, a sometime Diet member and a Councillor in the Ministry of Communications, his importance to the Wang peace movement derived from his father's reputation and from his own access to Konoe. Like Matsumoto, Inukai became a member of Konoe's kitchen cabinet. An avid student of Chinese affairs, he was given an office at Konoe's official residence, where he conducted research on contemporary Chinese problems. His postwar memoirs, *Yōsuko wa ima mo nagarete iru* (The Yangtze Still Flows), constitute one of the chief sources of first-hand information about the Wang movement.

As with the earlier trip of Tung Tao-ning, no official records of Kao's meetings in Japan have survived. Therefore, we must rely on the memories of the participants. Fortunately, many recorded their recollections; unfortunately, they disagree in one important respect: just how Wang's name entered the discussions.

Kagesa, writing about five years after the events, recalled that it was Kao who brought the subject up in one of the two meetings they had at Kao's inn at Hakone, in the mountains west of Tokyo.* By this account,

---

* Kao's trip to Tokyo coincided with the defection of Gen. G. S. Lyushkov, a senior officer in the Soviet Union's secret police; and the Army General Staff, worried that their paths might cross, had Kao stay in a number of commercial inns. The handling of the Kao visit in fact was altogether mystifying. On the one hand, Inukai describes the elaborate security precautions taken, mentioning clandestine meetings and secret exits from buildings, and generally suggests that Kao's presence in Japan was a carefully guarded secret. But on the other hand he pictures a full social schedule for Kao, including a large party attended by numerous Japanese dignitaries, night-club entertaining, and some dance-floor antics at the Mandarin Club—all of which seems to have been calculated to attract rather than divert attention. *Yōsukō*, pp. 77–79. According to Imai (*Shina jihen*, p. 69), in spite of the precautions taken, Kao "bumped into General Lyushkov" on at least one occasion.

Kao said that if Japan would not negotiate with Chiang, then someone else had to be found, and "the obvious person" was Wang. But it was his judgment that Wang could never hope to get his views across as long as he was still in the Government; and consequently, there was "no alternative but to force Chiang to listen to the peace overtures by launching a peace movement outside of the Government." Kagesa says he expressed his personal agreement with Kao's views and then reported back to Vice Chief of Staff Tada and "secured his agreement." At the same time, Kagesa's memoirs show he had some misgivings about Japan becoming involved in a plan that would place her under "grave obligation . . . to avoid any kind of political, economic, and of course military aggression."[55] It is clear he was unsure whether or not Japan would meet that obligation.

Imai and Inukai both suggest that Wang's name came up in a more roundabout way. According to their accounts, Kao's immediate purpose in coming to Tokyo was to find out if the *aite ni sezu* declaration still stood in the way of a rapprochement between China and Japan. In Inukai's version (which is based on what Kao told him), Imai explained to Kao that though there were many on the General Staff who disagreed with the *aite ni sezu* declaration, it was the national policy and nothing could be done about it—at least for the time being. ("A Premier's statement cannot be wiped out so easily.") Imai then went on to make the first concrete proposal of Wang as a substitute for Chiang, "as a temporary measure during this transitional period [of one or two months]." According to Inukai, Kagesa made the same proposal and added: "Once the peace movement gets on the tracks, we would shift the formal negotiations to Chiang when Wang so recommends."[56]

Of all three accounts, Imai's rings truest. While sitting in on conversations between Kao, Itagaki, and Tada, he got the "impression" that Kao "had probably already abandoned the idea of working out a solution to the Sino-Japanese incident through Chiang. Naturally, he did not push this point; it was rather that he was eagerly listening for the Japanese side to raise it."[57] Given Kao's indisputable skills as a negotiator, this kind of cautious probing seems entirely in character.

When Inukai quizzed Kao about the Generalissimo's role in his mission, he replied that Chiang thought he was gathering intelligence in Shanghai or Hong Kong. "He doesn't know about my coming to Tokyo," Kao stated flatly to Inukai. "I imagine that it would catch him completely by surprise if he heard about it."[58] What if Wang did emerge to replace Chiang in the negotiations? Inukai asked. Was there not a danger the "peace movement might become an anti-Chiang movement"?

Kao acknowledged that there was indeed such a danger, and that great caution was needed to prevent this development. Though the self-serving element in these accounts should not be discounted, their authors have all taken great pains to write of the peace movement's anxiety about stirring up the long-standing feud between Chiang and Wang and allowing the movement to degenerate into a civil war. "Chou Fo-hai has said that he is absolutely determined to oppose such a development," Kao assured Inukai.[59]

Inukai met with Kao on several occasions during his stay in Tokyo. Over scotch and soda in Kao's inn, and later, on the eve of his departure, over drinks in a Yokohama night club, the two discussed Kao's mission and the prospects of the peace movement. It is apparent from Inukai's recollections of those talks that Kao felt he was speaking on behalf of the Generalissimo and not Wang, despite his unauthorized presence in Tokyo. "I know Chiang's true feelings," he told Inukai. "Chiang would most assuredly not tell Japan, 'You must withdraw all of your troops tomorrow,' if Japan would simply agree in writing . . . to move all her troops north of the Great Wall." The details and the timing of the withdrawal from below the Wall could be left "to a secret protocol or something," Kao said.[60] He begged Inukai to try to get those points across to the proper authorities.

Inukai was prompted to ask Kao why he had consented to lead the peace movement and to undertake a mission to Tokyo that could have dire consequences for him. Kao's reply was that he disagreed with those around the Generalissimo who held that China's most pressing task was to fight Japan and that confrontation with the Communists could be postponed. He was all too aware, he told Inukai, that the Communists could capture the minds of his countrymen, especially the youth, with an appealing slogan like "Chinese must not fight Chinese." For himself, he was prepared to make "whatever sacrifice necessary to achieve peace with Japan," he told Inukai. "If that means becoming a traitor, then so be it!"[61] Kao's intense hatred and distrust of the Communists is evident in his unique analysis of the event that had triggered the war, the Marco Polo Bridge Incident. Neither the Japanese nor the Chinese garrison troops were responsible for the mysterious shots fired on the night of July 7 near Wanping, he told Inukai; they were the work of a group of Communists, "firing from a blind spot." At this writing, years later, Kao still holds to this theory, and to the vehement anticommunism he expressed in his discussion with Inukai in 1938.[62]

Kao left Tokyo convinced that there was no likelihood of Japan agreeing to open peace negotiations with Chiang in the foreseeable future, but equally convinced that there was an excellent chance she would consent to negotiate with Deputy Director-General Wang Ching-wei.* What remained to be determined were the terms under which the negotiations might begin. Though Kao was "treated royally" in Tokyo (to use Matsumoto's turn of word), he returned to China without any guarantee that Japan would make the kind of concessions Wang would need to lead a viable peace movement. Among the leaders Kao visited while in Tokyo was Saionji Kinkazu, a tireless worker in the cause of Sino-Japanese reconciliation. Kao told Saionji he was certain in his own mind that the "situation was hopeless for both Japan and China if we leave matters to those in charge of government."[63] Consequently, it was necessary for those in both countries who were really concerned about their country" to organize a peace movement capable of changing the policies of their governments. "I will go back to China and work hard," Kao told Saionji. "You do the same here."†

Kao returned to Shanghai and pondered his next move. He passed on a report of his Tokyo mission to Chou Fo-hai but decided against returning to Hankow to face the wrath of the Generalissimo and possible imprisonment for having violated Chiang's orders. In any case, there was little chance that he could persuade the Generalissimo to resign. Discouraged, exhausted, and anxious about his own future, Kao dropped out of sight for about six weeks after his return in mid-July. Kagesa and others in Tokyo were left to guess that Kao's approach to the Chinese leaders had been unsuccessful, or that perhaps he had simply been on an espionage mission after all.[64] Then, in late August, the indefatigable Matsumoto discovered the reason for Kao's disappearance: he had been hospitalized in a Shanghai sanitorium with a "touch of tuberculosis." It is possible that factors other than Kao's indisposition prompted the break in communications between Kao and the Japanese members of the peace movement, but the Japanese participants seemed satisfied with the

---

* In April 1938 an Extraordinary National Congress of the Kuomintang confirmed Chiang's preeminent position in the Party by naming him Director-General (Tsung-ts'ai). On the same occasion Wang was made Deputy Director-General.

† In 1942 Saionji was convicted of violating the Military Secrets Protection Law for disclosing certain state secrets to his close friend Ozaki Hotsumi, a key figure in the Sorge affair. The Japanese courts absolved him of subversive intent, laying his offense to simple carelessness, and consequently the aristocratic Saionji was spared the hardship of an eighteen-month imprisonment. In the postwar years Saionji has devoted himself to the task of improving Japanese relations with the People's Republic of China. He moved to Peking in 1958 and remained there for the next twelve years, writing essays on the fine points of Chinese cuisine, wines, and music, and taking an active hand in furthering Sino-Japanese trade. He played an important role in the negotiation of an informal agreement in 1963 that sends a Japanese delegation to Peking each year for bilateral trade talks.

plea of "respiratory ailments" and "mental anguish." Kao was "greatly distressed at realizing what an awkward position he had fallen into," Imai writes.[65] Kao may indeed have found himself in a position he had not anticipated: cut off from the Generalissimo without any solid assurances of support from Wang.

Both Japanese and Chinese participants in the peace movement agree that Kao's report of his Tokyo trip reached the hands of the Generalissimo. After reading the report, Chou Fo-hai first discussed it with Wang Ching-wei, who evidently was completely unaware of the Kao mission to Tokyo. Wang professed to be shocked at the news the Japanese authorities wished him to "betray Chiang" and negotiate a peace settlement. He flatly rejected the proposal and turned the report over to Chiang.[66] A few days later the Generalissimo reportedly called in Ch'en Pu-lei, his confidential assistant, and asked who had allowed Kao—"that odd character"—out of the country. Chiang's reaction to the news seems to have been more one of annoyance than rage. To Chou Fo-hai the Generalissimo simply fumed *"Huang-t'ang, huang-t'ang!"* (Absurd, absurd!)[67]

THE LOW-KEY CLUB AGAIN

Wang's summary rejection of the Japanese proposals Kao relayed in July changed to cautious interest as the year wore on. A major factor in this change was the growing dismay among knowledgeable Chinese at the dismal battlefield situation and agonizing cost of resistance. Chiang's policy of wasting the land in retreat was exacting an enormous toll. In a maneuver that simply bought a little time for the Chinese armies, for example, the dikes on the Yellow River near Chengchow were dynamited in June 1938, releasing the silt-filled waters of "China's Sorrow" to ravage three provinces before finding a new channel hundreds of miles to the north. Eleven cities and some 4,000 villages were flooded, millions of acres of farmland were submerged, two million people were left homeless, and perhaps a million Chinese died as a result of the floods and their aftermath.

Chou Fo-hai, who knew how desperate the situation was, was required as Deputy Propaganda Chief of the Kuomintang to participate in frequent press receptions in the company of the Communists Chou En-lai and Kuo Mo-jo, and found their glowing reports of battlefield successes unconscionable. "My heart was broken," he later wrote, "when I heard Messrs. Chou and Kuo's reports, which were based on false pretensions and meant only to cheat the populace."[68] Chou Fo-hai presided over the Double Ten ceremonies (commemorating the date of the 1911 Revolution) in beleaguered Hankow in 1938 and listened to Kuo make a dramatic announcement of a telephone message from the front reporting a great victory over the Japanese. He was infuriated at Kuo's subterfuge, and at the "cheating" of the wildly enthusiastic crowd. He felt, he said, that China's cause was beyond the power of rhetoric and "high tunes" to remedy.[69] How could he ask for a defense to the death of a Hankow that was already clearly doomed?

Hankow's fate was sealed, in fact, just three days after these ceremonies with the fall of the strategically important city of Hsinyang on the Peiping-Hankow Railroad on October 13. The Japanese landing on Bias Bay a day earlier, without serious opposition, similarly sealed the fate of Canton in the south. A month later, on the night of November 13, Chou's own native city, Changsha, was put to the torch and burned to the ground by its Chinese defenders in one of the most terrible scorched-earth incidents of the war. The complete truth about Changsha is still unknown—the Communists blamed the Nationalists and vice versa—but it is certain that thousands of Chinese in the refugee-swollen city perished in the four-day holocaust. It is also certain that the destruction of the city was totally unwarranted: Japanese forces were far distant from Changsha, which would not fall into Japanese hands for another six years.[70]

Wang was one of those who became increasingly distressed by the disastrous turn of events in October. He was especially incensed at the Kuomintang's handling of the defense of his home city, Canton. In a radio broadcast from there on August 9, 1939, after his defection from Chungking, he commiserated with his fellow Cantonese, who had been "repeatedly assured by both the civil and military authorities that the Japanese troops would never be able to come and take the city. . . . The main function of the authorities seemed, judging from their irresponsible optimism, just to lull the populace into a false sense of security."[71] Wang was later to justify his defection on the grounds that the struggle had become futile and the scorched-earth policy was causing "haphazard sacrifices and unnecessary sacrifices." The incendiarism by fleeing soldiers "did not halt the advance of the Japanese troops, nor in any way embarrass their positions. It merely destroyed the lives, properties, and the livelihood of the Cantonese people themselves."[72]

Was Wang motivated to criticize this kind of warfare (and eventually to defect from Chungking) by essentially humanitarian considerations and by what one writer calls his "psychopathic fear of war"?[73] His own after-the-fact explanations stress these considerations, and the emphasis on his "poetic" and "sensitive" nature in the accounts of those who were personally acquainted with him give a certain credibility to his statements. Still, it is not necessary to denigrate Wang's humanitarian concern to suggest that he had other motives for deserting Chiang as well. One that suggests itself is anticommunism.

For all of Wang's long identification with the Left Kuomintang, there is much evidence to support the contention that his "leftism" was an expediency born of the balance of political and military forces in the mid-1920's and nurtured by his personal rivalry with Chiang. Conversely, there is little evidence to suggest that Wang had any profound commitment to such "leftist" programs as land reform or to that *sine qua non* of revolutionary Marxism, the class struggle. Wang's leftism, insofar as it had anything approaching a consistent ideological basis, stood for "greater emphasis upon anti-imperialism, the constitutional phase, and the policies for the betterment of the people's livelihood, while [his opponents in the] right wing stressed the revival of China's past glory, the tutelage [role of the Kuomintang]."[74] Both Wang and his right-wing Kuomintang countrymen were elitist; he was no more willing to trust China's fate to the masses than they. One writer, noting Wang's "isolation from the masses," observes that it is "not without significance that the best-known incident in his early life [was] his attempt to assassinate the Prince Regent."[75]

In the period of the second united front, Wang's public opposition to even a temporary alliance with the Communists was well known. With his usual flare for analogy, he said he found it "pitiful" that some thought cooperation with the Communists was possible, for "such a step is tantamount to drinking poison in the hopes of quenching one's thirst."[76] After the Marco Polo Bridge Incident, public criticism of the united front was as rigorously suppressed as criticism of the resistance effort itself. Wang was nevertheless able to make at least an oblique attack on the Communists in an interesting and revealing article he published in June 1938. In it he allows that the scorched-earth policy and guerrilla warfare are useful. In fact, at first glance, he appears to find both tactics eminently desirable and to be arguing for their expanded use. For example, he concludes a compelling list of reasons in defense of the scorched-earth policy by saying: "Finally, gallant fighting and a heroic spirit of sacrifice among troops and civilians inspire those who survive with the fire of equal courage and loyalty, and will not allow the germination of a single seed which would bear fruit to comfort the puppets of our enemy."[77]

On closer inspection, however, it is clear that Wang's definition of scorched-earth techniques and guerrilla warfare amounts to a tacit condemnation of what he saw as Communist tactics and a defense instead of positional warfare. Scorched earth "means that the earth becomes scorched as a result of actual fighting. It does not mean that there must be no fighting, and that the earth should be 'scorched' without passing through the fiery ordeal of war. It is here emphatically repeated that by 'scorched earth' is meant that an area must be entirely devastated as a result of fighting."[78] Driving home his argument in words that sound familiar to Western ears, Wang goes on to say that "every inch of earth that is scorched must first be stained with the tears, sweat, and blood of the people."[79] In 1938, when he wrote the article, Wang was not in a position to charge flatly that it was the Communists who were responsible for the adoption of the scorched-earth policy he objected to, but a year later, writing from the security of his refuge in Japanese-occupied territory, he could afford to be explicit. The "scorching" of Canton was done only to conceal the cowardice of the retreating armies, he charged. Why were the Canton authorities willing to go along? "They were simply obeying the orders of Chiang Kai-shek." And why did Chiang give the order? "He was merely following the instructions of the Communist Party."[80]

Similarly, Wang's advocacy of guerrilla warfare while he was still writing from inside the Chinese lines was phrased in terms to exclude—again tacitly—the Maoist brand of guerrilla warfare: "Professional bandits, even when reorganized, must not be employed in 'guerrilla' warfare. They will avoid fighting the enemy, will avoid strong points of the enemy's lines."[81] Such avoidance was, of course, a cardinal tenet of Maoist military strategy. Again, a year later Wang was more blunt: "Unprecedentedly large tracts of land have been lost to the enemy within an unbelievably short space of time, while the guerrilla tactics adopted by the Communists have turned whatever has not been burned down into a no-man's-land. Those learned in history understand that Communist guerrilla warfare is just a euphemism for large-scale robbery."[82]

It is thus apparent that Wang's objections to the conduct of the war were not based exclusively on humanitarian considerations, but were also grounded in his anticommunism. He clearly believed that the direction of the war was slipping into the hands of the Communists, and feared the Nationalists would never be able to retrieve the initiative. He seemed particularly concerned about the Communist control of the propaganda organs of the Government in the Hankow period, and wrote at the time that "except for a few traitors here and there, every Chinese man, woman, and child realizes the necessity of offering resistance against aggression and invaders. No propaganda to this end is necessary. . . . It is much more fruitful if the people's energy is directed to practical and useful work instead of wasting time attending mass meetings and demonstrations."[83]

Developments in Europe in 1938 further discouraged Wang and the Low-Key Club, as Wang was to note in his "deathbed testament" six years later. The dismemberment of Czechoslovakia was assured at the conference table in Munich in the last days of September 1938. The Western democracies were being defeated in Europe, the will stated, and in the Far East they "were just looking on" while Japan extended her control over China. The only country to provide China aid was the Soviet Union, and the only reason for that assistance was the Soviet Union's desire to see "China brought to ruin by a policy of unending resistance to Japan." Rather than fall victim to the Soviet plot, rather than suffer enormous sacrifices and in the end lose control over China's destiny, "was it not better to bear the unbearable and conclude peace terms with Japan?" Wang supposedly rationalized in 1944.[84]

By October 1938, then, the prevailing mood of the Low-Key Club members was one of despair and desperation. It was born out of grief over the toll of human suffering that an especially cruel war was causing, chagrin over the apparent unwillingness of the Western powers to offer significant help, a sense of the futile purpose in continuing to resist the overwhelmingly superior Imperial Army, a frustration at their inability to speak out and make their views known in the clamped-down atmosphere of Hankow, a conviction that the war was moving the nation in a direction that would strengthen the hands of the Communists, of both the native and foreign (i.e., Soviet) stripe, and an impatience about getting on with national reconstruction—in cooperation with Japan if necessary and if equitable terms could be arranged. And, finally, in assessing the factors that impelled Wang to investigate the merits of allying himself with the Kao proposals, we cannot ignore the motive his detractors offer as the first and foremost consideration, namely, his personal rivalry with Chiang. Even Wang's admirers agree that the abrasion was sharp and abiding and could not but influence his decisions. To jump to the conclusion that this was the decisive factor, however, is to overlook a great many other equally if not more compelling factors.

At this point, shortly after the capitulation of Hankow and the flight of the Kuomintang Government upriver to Chungking, news of a "peace offer" based on "generous" terms reached the Low-Key Club via one of its members, Mei Ssu-p'ing, who had been in touch with Matsumoto and Imai, a contact that had been arranged by the ailing Kao. Matsumoto and Imai in turn had been in touch with Tokyo and had given

Mei assurances of a more lenient China policy then being formulated in the War Ministry. The year-long efforts of the peace movement were about to produce results.

THE NEW ORDER IN EAST ASIA

On November 3, just a few days after Mei's arrival in Chungking, a new China policy was announced in Tokyo. In a radio address to the nation, Konoe called for a "New Order in East Asia" (*Tōa shinchitsujo*),[85] based on an equal partnership between Japan and China. Japan harbored no territorial ambitions, he assured his people, and wished to bring about eternal peace in East Asia. Far from desiring territory or special privileges in China, Japan looked forward to cooperating with China against communism and the "imperialistic ambitions and rivalries of the Occidental Powers." In a move of surprising generosity, considering that his country was in the full flush of military victory, Konoe renounced Japan's claims for indemnities and promised that she would even "consider" giving up her concessions and extraterritorial privileges in China. Though the declaration noted that the "Kuomintang Government no longer exists except as a local regime," Konoe set his Government on a new course by repudiating the *aite ni sezu* statement he had made at the beginning of the year. The Kuomintang Government was welcome to participate in the New Order if it would "remold its personnel so as to translate its rebirth into fact."

On the very same day the puppet leaders Wang K'o-min and Liang Hung-chih issued their own announcement. Voicing the sentiments of the mainland Army commands, they publicly stated that Sino-Japanese peace could not be attained until the Chinese Communists were exterminated, and the Communists could not be exterminated until Chiang was overthrown.[86] Thus, though Konoe had opened the door to negotiations with the Kuomintang, the mainland Army commands—and probably Konoe himself—remained adamantly opposed to negotiating with the Generalissimo.

Konoe's New Order in East Asia was "an inevitable historical product" of the Sino-Japanese conflict, wrote Ozaki Hotsumi, Konoe's brilliant adviser on Chinese affairs. Conceding—and probably warning—that the New Order involved "many difficulties," Ozaki maintained that it had a "great potential for the future" in its recognition of the vitality of Chinese nationalism. For too long the Japanese had emphasized the feudal and colonial aspects of China and overlooked nationalism. "And yet it can be found everywhere," Ozaki wrote. "You can find it in the Kuomintang-Communist collaboration. . . . You can find it in the leaders of the puppet regimes. . . . It is evident in economic problems, in the peace question. . . . Nationalism is what has enabled China to keep fighting with all of her weaknesses. It is to be found not just at the state level but at the individual level, . . . not just among the guerrilla fighters but among the peasants who simply 'deal with the earth.' "[87] What had led to the New Order was a tardy realization on the part of the Japanese that they would never succeed in the economic organization of East Asia to their own profit by "unilateral methods."* Wringing her hands in despair over the China problem, Japan finally came up with the idea of the New Order as a means of "getting the Chinese to cooperate," Ozaki declared.[88]

Though Konoe's New Order speech left many of the most important questions dividing the two nations unanswered—there was no mention of troop withdrawal, for example—the Low-Key Club felt that it was conciliatory enough to merit further exploration and discussion. Accordingly, Wang at once ordered Mei Ssu-p'ing to return to Shanghai and initiate a new round of discussions with a view to achieving a detailed agreement on the terms of peace.

---

* Ozaki, by now allied with the Soviet spy Sorge, was the classic example of the *gisō tenkōsha* (disguised convert), the liberal or socialist Japanese intellectual who was forced to recant his beliefs in deference to the prevailing ultranationalistic atmosphere of the 1930's. This article ("Tōa Kyōdō-tai . . .") is a good illustration of how the adroit "convert," through circumlocution, euphemism, and ambiguity, managed to publish his views in the heavily censored press of the day. "Unilateral methods," for instance, was Ozaki's way of calling Japan's China policy imperialistic without resorting to a word that was a sure invitation to censorship. Another device he used to circumvent the censor was to put his own criticism in the mouths of Chinese critics. Thus, we find him writing that Konoe's policy was a "trick"—according to many Chinese. In this case Ozaki went on to placate the censor by adding (p. 329): "It is quite understandable for the Chinese to think that way because they do not understand the ideology of the Tōa Kyōdō-tai (East Asian Cooperative Body)." The term East Asian Cooperative Body was favored over the official New Order in East Asia by Ozaki and other Marxist intellectuals. Johnson, *Instance of Treason*, pp. 5–8, 119–20.

CHAPTER TEN

The Chungkuang-t'ang Conference

THE CHUNGKUANG-T'ANG (Chungkuang Mansion) was a large, Western-style house on the edge of a park in the Japanese-controlled Hongkew section of Shanghai. Scarred in the street fighting in the opening months of the China Incident, it lay abandoned until early November 1938, when repairs were hastily made, and furnishings to accommodate a party of seven or eight were rented from a nearby hotel. By November 12 the last of the arrangements was completed, the draymen and workmen had departed, and an Imperial Army officer, wearing civilian clothes, began receiving "guests." The host was Lt. Col. Imai Takeo, the head of "Operation Watanabe."* The first guest Imai received was Mei Ssu-p'ing, freshly arrived from the new Nationalist seat of government in Chungking, where he had been in contact with the Low-Key Club and Wang Ching-wei. Without waiting for the other guests, the two set out at once on the work that had brought them together: to arrive at peace terms that would be acceptable to Wang and to arrange the details of his defection from Chungking. The talks at the Chungkuang-t'ang lasted for the next eight days, concluding on November 20 with the signing of a "Conference Proceedings," which constituted the initial understanding between the Japanese Army and the Wang group.[1]

Mei Ssu-p'ing was relatively unknown to the Japanese. He was one of the few participants in the Wang movement who had never been to Japan and did not speak Japanese. Indeed, Imai was appalled to find his guest so unfamiliar with Japanese etiquette as to walk into a *tatami*-carpeted room without removing his shoes.[2] Like Kao and Chou Fo-hai, Mei was a member of the Low-Key Club. He was regarded as a follower of Ch'en Li-fu, one of the powerful heads of the Kuomintang's CC Clique, and thus, like Kao and Chou Fo-hai, did not have a long-standing association with Wang Ching-wei. Inukai considered Mei a

---

* Watanabe, a common Japanese surname, was the Army General Staff's code name for Kao Tsung-wu. Operation Watanabe (Watanabe Kōsaku) was a blanket reference for all the activities that eventually led to Wang's defection from Chungking.

"progressive," based largely on his renown as the administrator of a successful experimental hsien near Nanking, a project reportedly close to the Generalissimo's heart. Imai admired Mei as a paragon of bureaucratic incorruptibility, a man who had not used his hsien office to increase his personal wealth. Sometime in early 1938 Mei had resigned his official position and been sent by T'ao Hsi-sheng to manage the Hong Kong office of the Institute of Art and Literature. He had been in touch with Japanese members of the peace movement ever since.

In addition to Mei, the Chinese side at the Chungkuang-t'ang Conference was represented by Kao and Chou Lung-hsiang, who acted mainly as an interpreter. Imai was assisted by Itō Yoshio from the South Manchurian Railway. Kagesa Sadaaki and Inukai Ken flew to Shanghai from Tokyo as the last details were being worked out, chiefly to allow Kagesa to participate in some last-minute negotiations and to sign the "Conference Proceedings."

Five major issues preoccupied the negotiators at the Chungkuang-t'ang meeting. The official records of the conference, the memoirs of three of the participants (Imai, Kagesa, and Inukai), and Imai's official reports on Operation Watanabe allow us to piece together a fairly accurate description of the positions taken by both sides and the final compromises that were incorporated into the "Conference Proceedings" and signed on November 20.[3] Let us examine each issue as it was seen by the two sides.

The first important question was Manchukuo. It is the only issue on which the historical records do not fully agree. Imai's report of November 15, which set forth the initial positions of both sides, indicates that the Chinese were prepared to recognize the autonomy of the area. This report, which faithfully documents the numerous Chinese reservations on many other issues, states flatly that the Chinese side voiced "no objections" to the granting of recognition.[4] Inukai, however, recalls conversations with Kagesa in which they agreed that the recognition question was a major obstacle. He also recalls talking to Kao at the end of the conference and finding him "exceedingly concerned about how the recognition of Manchukuo would be handled in the [forthcoming] Konoe declaration." Kao thought that if the matter was handled improperly, the Chinese people would reject the notion, and "Wang would be forced to go into immediate exile, to Hanoi or even to France."[5] An interpretation that would reconcile the accounts of Imai and Inukai would be that there was no serious discussion over the question of recognition as such but only over the manner in which recognition would be announced by Japan. In any case, in the final document signed on November 20, the Chinese side unequivocally agreed to recognize Manchukuo. But the Japanese were unable to persuade the Chinese to accept a clause favoring a simultaneous exchange of recognition between China and Manchukuo. It was just as well the Chinese rejected the proposal, Imai conceded, since there were no Manchukuoan representatives present.[6]

The second major issue at the conference concerned China's indemnity payments to Japan. The Chinese delegates considered any kind of indemnification completely out of the question. Imai's November 15 report does not even mention the word indemnity, suggesting that neither side raised the issue in its initial proposals. By the time the final conference documents were signed on November 20, however, the Chinese were prepared to accept Japan's demand for "compensation for injuries arising out of the [China] incident sustained by Japanese citizens resident in China." In return for this concession, Japan agreed not to ask for an indemnity for "war expenses."[7] Both Inukai and Kagesa were distressed that Japan should ask for any kind of indemnity. The demand, which was pushed by the Finance Ministry in Kagesa's judgment, violated the principles that the "peace movement had proclaimed on its banners from the very beginning."[8]

The question of Japan's economic role in China was another of the critical bargaining points at the meeting. Mei, Chou Fo-hai, and Wang Ching-wei had already discussed this issue in Chungking, and Mei was now ready to declare that "China had absolutely no objections to the economic exploitation of North China by Japan and China in joint partnership."[9] In return, the Chinese wanted a promise that "there would be no Japanese industrial monopolization." Mei was also anxious to have North China identified as the area incorporating the five provinces of Hopei, Chahar, Shansi, Suiyuan, and Shantung, that is, to regain for China all of Chahar and and Suiyuan provinces, important portions of which had been placed under the jurisdiction of Teh Wang's Inner Mongolian puppet regime in 1937. In the final agreement, however, there was neither a precise definition of North China nor a specific Japanese promise to abstain from monopolization. Article IV of the "Conference Proceedings" merely provided for a "recognition of Japan's preferential rights in achieving economic collaboration and the granting of special facilities to Japan for the exploitation and use of resources in North China."[10]

The Chinese side won several major concessions with regard to the economic relationship between the two countries. An explanatory annex to the "Conference Proceedings" declared that the term preferential rights (*yūsen-ken*) in Article IV meant that Japan would enjoy most-favored-nation status—and nothing more. Imai reported on November

15 that the "Chinese side has been insistent in its desire to abolish the *'yūsen-ken'* phrase in Article IV because it would be understood within China as an encroachment against China and outside China it would encourage pressure [for like treatment] from the other powers."

These concessions expressed the mood of Imai and Kagesa as well as the wishes of the Chinese delegates. Indeed, by accepting the restricted and rather innocuous definition of preferential rights in the annex, Imai seems to have agreed in large measure with the Chinese argument. Imai also advised the General Staff that he had secured a promise of "special facilities" (*tokubetsu benri*) in the final wording of Article IV and had not insisted on the phrase "special privileges" (*tokubetsu ben'eki*), which would almost certainly meet an "unfavorable response" in China. He further deferred to the wishes of the Chinese delegates by dropping Japan's demand for the creation of a "Sino-Japanese Joint Economic Committee." The Chinese side, he reported, was fearful that such a body, responsible for all policies related to economic development, would constitute an interference in Chinese internal affairs—a fear that was fully justified by the operation of similar committees in the Provisional and Reformed Governments. Thanks to Imai's willingness to bend on this point, the final agreement simply provided for "joint consultation."[11]

Extraterritoriality was another major issue. As a result of Mei's conferences with the Wang group in Chungking, the Chinese delegates came prepared to grant Japanese nationals the right to reside and conduct business in the interior of China. In return, they expected Japan to relinquish both her extraterritorial privileges and her concessions in China. The Japanese delegates were willing to agree to the renunciation of extraterritoriality but argued that the matter of the concessions required a period of "preparation." Japan most certainly did not want to be in the position of giving up her valuable concessions while the Western powers continued to hold their prizes in Shanghai, Tientsin, and other areas, said Imai. In the end, though Mei won the extraterritoriality battle, he had to settle for a promise that Japan would consider (*kōryo*) retroceding her concessions to China.[12]

By far the thorniest question facing the Chungkuang-t'ang Conference centered on the matter of Japan's military occupation. The Japanese side professed a willingness to end the occupation of China, but it so qualified the offer as to arouse Chinese fears that for all practical purposes the proposed Wang regime would be dominated by the Japanese military. Moreover, the Wang group felt that there was only one way it could persuade the Chinese people it was acting in their best interests, namely, to show that it had been instrumental in arranging a Japanese military evacuation of China. To this end, it wanted Japan to withdraw all her troops except those in Inner Mongolia, which would remain as occupation garrisons but (at least nominally) as part of a joint anti-Communist defense force. Convinced Japan would insist on stationing troops in that area, the Wang group was anxious to bring the matter under a treaty governing the numbers, purpose, location, and duration of the Japanese garrisons. Accordingly, it proposed that an agreement on a joint Sino-Japanese defense force be subsumed under an anti-Communist defense pact similar to the Anti-Comintern Pact between Germany and Japan, "in order to avoid any misgivings on the part of the Chinese people."* In areas other than Inner Mongolia, the Chinese delegates asked that Japan "withdraw her Army immediately on the establishment of peace terms" and, further, that she stipulate exactly how long the withdrawal process would take.[13]

The Japanese position emphasized the creation of a special anti-Communist zone (*bōkyō tokushu chiiki*) in Inner Mongolia. There is little indication that Japan wished to discuss limitations on her right to station troops in that area. She envisioned an anti-Communist pact of a much more comprehensive and much more aggressively anti-Soviet character than her pact with Germany. The only concession she was willing to make to Chinese feelings was an agreement that Japanese troops would be stationed in the Inner Mongolian special anti-Communist zone for no longer than the "duration of the [Sino-Japanese] anti-Communist pact." This was a slight retreat from the original Japanese position at the Chungkuang-t'ang, which called for the stationing of troops in Inner Mongolia for a "definite"—but not precisely specified—period of time.

Two annexes to the "Conference Proceedings" went to the heart of the matter. A secret annex signed on November 20 spelled out the details of the projected anti-Communist pact. Among other things it delineated each country's military sphere in the Chinese border regions: Chinese troops were to be stationed in the Sinkiang area and Japanese troops in Inner Mongolia. In the event of war with the Soviet Union these armies would conduct joint military operations. A second, explanatory annex to the agreement provided for the stationing of Japanese troops in the Peiping-Tientsin corridor "in order to protect the lines of communication" with the anti-Communist garrisons located in the interior.[14]

---

* Imai, *Shina jihen*, p. 289. The Anti-Comintern Pact of December 1936 ostensibly provided for an exchange of information on the activities of international communism between Japan and Germany; secret clauses, however, provided that if either country should be attacked by the Soviet Union, the other would take no action of possible benefit to the aggressor.

Much more troubling to the Chinese negotiators than the Japanese demands on Inner Mongolia was the protracted period of troop withdrawal Japan insisted on for the rest of China. The Chinese side first demanded the immediate withdrawal of Japanese troops from Chinese soil as soon as a peace agreement was reached, then backed down to allow for the "completion of the withdrawal within a few months." The Japanese took the position that withdrawal could proceed no faster than the "restoration of peace" in China, and that since no one could say how the Wang regime would be received, it was impossible to set a date certain for withdrawal. Ultimately, the Japanese side agreed that the withdrawal would "commence immediately upon the 'restoration of peace' [*heiwa kokufuku*] and would be totally completed within two years after the 'restoration of public peace and order' [*chian kaifuku*]."[15] Mei and Kao considered the two-year proviso a major diplomatic victory, for to this point Japan had consistently refused to set any kind of timetable for troop withdrawal. Later, when the Japanese Government rejected the work of its negotiators by balking at the two-year clause, the Chinese side considered the action an enormous breach of faith.

In addition to discussing and working out specific peace terms, the delegates at the Chungkuang-t'ang Conference made several important decisions on the Wang regime itself, settling, among other things, how Wang's defection from Chungking would be handled, what role he would play in the peace movement after his defection, and what support he should expect from the Japanese. Two significant impressions about Wang's intentions emerge from a study of these discussions.

First, the conference records show unambiguously that the Chinese side presented proposals based on the presumption of Wang's defection and subsequent "establishment of a new government" and "organization of a new army."[16] The written record, which has been corroborated by the vivid recollections of Imai,[17] plainly does not square with the later assertions of Wang and Konoe that at the time Wang defected neither side envisioned the establishment of a government under his leadership but merely anticipated Wang would head a movement to bring about peace with Japan. There seems to me to be only two ways to explain the discrepancy: either Wang and Konoe were not honest in their later assertions, or they did not fully control their negotiators at the time and were unaware of the agreements made at the Chungkuang-t'ang. We shall return to this question later.

Second, the Chinese side hoped the new government would be established "in territory that was not occupied by the Japanese Army." Specifically, the Wang group proposed that the new government begin its rule in unoccupied Yunnan and Szechwan provinces, and then, as

Japanese troops were withdrawn, extend its authority to Kwangsi and Kwangtung provinces.[18]

The eventual failure of Wang Ching-wei to enlist the sympathy and support of the Chinese people and to escape the epithets "puppet" and "traitor" can be traced to many causes, but none is more important than the abandonment of the original plan to establish the new regime in unoccupied China. In all the discussions at the Chungkuang-t'ang and in the private utterances of Wang and his colleagues over the next year one finds a constant preoccupation with the necessity of avoiding the fate of the puppets associated with the Provisional and Reformed Governments. Wang and his followers—and not least his Japanese supporters—were determined that he not become another Liang Hung-chih or Wang K'o-min. In the case of his Japanese supporters, at least, that determination was based not only on a deep personal commitment to Wang, but also on a feeling that he alone could vitalize the yet untried New Order for East Asia.

Yet Wang's Japanese supporters also knew that his capacity to move ahead on their program for the future depended on his ability to prove that the New Order was a union of equals and not merely a disguise for Japanese imperialist intentions. Wang could best demonstrate his independence from Japan by operating from beyond Japanese-occupied territory. When Imai later discovered that Wang was considering establishing a regime in occupied territory he was astounded, and in a guarded fashion expressed to Mei and Chou Fo-hai his anxiety that Wang might follow in the footsteps of Liang and Wang K'o-min.[19]

We shall return to the reasons behind Wang's ultimate decision to establish a regime in Japanese-occupied China. What concerns us here is the expectations at the Chungkuang-t'ang Conference. It is clear from both the records of the proceedings and my conversation with Imai that the conferees were most optimistic about Wang's ability to muster wide support. Japanese sources reveal an impressive list of Chinese leaders who were considered potential allies of Wang in late 1938 or early 1939. The reasons for such assumptions varied widely. Some, like the economist Ku Meng-yü, were members of Wang's Reorganization Faction. Others, notably Kan Nai-kuang, P'eng Hsüeh-p'ei, Wang Shih-chieh, and Chang Tao-fan, were less formally tied to Wang but still close enough to be "considered members of his following."[20] But the largest number of Wang supporters would come, the Japanese assumed (wrongly, as it turned out) from the Generalissimo's many adversaries. Considerable hope was placed in the defection of one or both of the leaders of the CC Clique, Ch'en Kuo-fu and Ch'en Li-fu, to Wang's cause. Liu

Wen-hui, Teng Hsi-hou, and P'an Wen-hua, a triumvirate of Sze-chwanese warlords whose intransigent opposition to Chiang Kai-shek was well known, were also high on the list of potential Wang backers. For the same reason, the Yunnanese general Lung Yun, the Cantonese generals Chang Fa-k'uei and Ch'en Chi-t'ang, and the leader of the Kwangsi clique, Gen. Pai Ch'ung-hsi, were prominently mentioned as hopeful—and even probable—supporters of Wang. There was even talk that the War Minister, Ho Ying-ch'in, wished to join Wang.[21]

To be sure, not all of these men were expected to defect to Wang; but as the conference documents make clear, the support of certain key fig-ures, including Lung Yun and Chang Fa-k'uei, who commanded large armies, was regarded as essential if Wang was going to establish a viable government in the unoccupied southwestern provinces. Failing such a military base, the new regime could not hope to repel the armies Chiang was certain to send; nor could it assure itself a measure of independence from Japan. In the end, however, the crucial support did not mate-rialize.*

Wang's spokesmen at the Chungkuang-t'ang did more than simply conjecture about the support of certain important Chinese generals. They wanted the Japanese Army to do everything in its power to relieve the pressure on the forces they hoped to rally to their cause. Specifically, they proposed, on November 15, that the Japanese undertake campaigns against the central government on fronts scattered from Shansi to Kwangsi, beginning with an assault on the Kuomintang troops in Kwei-chow province. But care must be taken, the Chinese said, not to allow the drive on Kweichow to scatter the "Central Army" into areas where it might harass the forces loyal to Wang.[22]

For the next several months, though the Wang group made repeated requests for a variety of "diversionary attacks" (*kensei hōgeki*) aimed at

---

* For one reason or another, none of the men listed here joined Wang. Kan Nai-kuang, a Wang supporter since 1927, was Deputy Secretary-General of the Central Headquarters of the Kuomintang from 1938 to 1952. P'eng Hsüeh-p'ei was Chairman of the Board of Directors of the China National Aviation Corporation. Wang Shih-chieh, a member of the Political Science Faction, which was often at odds with Chiang's leadership, was Minister of Information. Chang Tao-fan, a prominent cul-tural figure, was a member of the Kuomintang Central Executive Committee. Also mentioned as potential supporters at one time or another were Ho Chien, Minister of the Interior; Chang Kung-ch'üan, Minister of Communications; and Ch'eng T'ien-fang, a prominent educator and Chancellor of Szechwan University. Interestingly, though Wang did not gain the support of these potential defectors, some of them were sufficiently disenchanted with Chiang Kai-shek's leadership to defect to the Communists in 1949. Two of those who stayed on the mainland were Teng Hsi-hou and Liu Wen-hui; Liu became the Minister of Forestry in the People's Government in 1959.

"intercepting" and "isolating" Chiang's forces, the Imperial Army remained unresponsive. Imai recalls: "I thought that the idea of diversionary attacks was a good one, and I argued for it with the authorities in Tokyo, but they were not really interested. All they cared about was Wang's defection—and even that was of less than secondary importance [*ni no tsugi no kangae*] to many. At any rate, after he did defect, they quickly lost interest in diversionary attacks, and so the question was never brought up again."[23] Coming at a time when Japan's strategic capabilities were badly strained, the Chinese side's requests for military assistance found little support in the Imperial Army, which had little taste for exhausting Japan's resources and manpower in the defense of a collaboration experiment that seemed incapable of generating any appreciable support on its own.

The Wang backers, however, saw this chicken-and-the-egg problem in a different light. As they viewed it, diversionary attacks by the Imperial Army were an indispensable condition for the generation of native support. There was a rich source of anti-Chiang hostility to be tapped in the persons of entrenched provincial warlords like Gen. Lung Yun, whose relations with the Generalissimo were so strained that he reportedly refused to go to Chungking unless Madame Chiang came to Kunming (capital of Lung's Yunnan province) and remained there as a hostage during his absence.[24] But however anxious Lung might have been to break with Chungking, he was well aware of the vulnerable position he was in, for one of the main preoccupations of Chiang's Central Army was "surveillance" of the troops of just such potential rebels as Lung. Chiang's troops were camped at the doorstep of Lung's headquarters and were ready to pounce at the first signs of disloyalty, Kao and Mei argued. Consequently, he would make his move only when the Central Army units were distracted from their guard duties in Yunnan.

TOKYO CONSIDERS THE CHUNGKUANG-T'ANG AGREEMENTS

On November 15, after both sides had presented their views at the Chungkuang-t'ang, Imai flew back to Tokyo for consultations with his superiors. Arrangements were made for a conference of ten or more of the highest Army officials, including War Minister Itagaki and Vice Chief of Staff Tada, to hear his report. After a two-hour meeting, lasting from 4:00 to 6:00 P.M., the ranking officers (Bureau Chiefs and above) withdrew, leaving lower-ranking Section and Unit Chiefs to discuss what had transpired in Shanghai. Imai was forced to offer repeated assurances that he was not being tricked by the Chinese and finally was able to overcome the suspicions of the officers present. Or so it seemed that day. The truth is, throughout the next year most Japanese mistrusted the motives of Wang and his colleagues, and remained constantly skeptical of Wang's continued professions that all he wanted was peace. There was an almost universal belief in Japan that Wang and Chiang were in collusion, and that the peace movement was merely a delaying tactic, an elaborate trick to weaken the Army's resolve to crush all Chinese resistance.[25]

After discussing the merits of working with Wang and his supporters and the risks of accepting responsibility for these potentially far-reaching schemes, the Section and Unit Chiefs' conference appeared to be heading toward an inconclusive end. No one present wanted to accept responsibility for the negotiations Imai was carrying on in Shanghai, or even to commit himself to support so dubious a venture as the Wang movement. At this juncture, Col. Tanaka Shin'ichi, Chief of the Military Affairs Section, suggested that they forget about individual responsibility and simply agree to accept joint responsibility. The rest of the officers concurred, and the meeting adjourned at 9:00 P.M. Armed with this support from his Staff colleagues, Imai returned to Shanghai to complete the negotiations at the Chungkuang-t'ang.

The informal and low-level consideration given to a matter of so potentially grave an importance is a striking example of a variation on the *gekohujō* theme, so characteristic of the Japanese military establishment in the 1930's. Gekokujō refers to the domination of senior military officers by their juniors. It is sometimes more narrowly translated as insubordination, a meaning that is not applicable here, for in this instance gekokujō was carried out, not in any darkly conspiratorial fashion, but in the residence, and indeed one could say at the behest, of the War Minister himself, since he and the other top-level Army officers had chosen to leave matters in the hands of their subordinates. It was also carried out at the residence of the Premier, for Kagesa and Imai took the "Conference Proceedings" to Konoe to get his reaction. Konoe listened "enthusiastically" but made no positive endorsement of the Shanghai agreements.[26] But neither did he reject them. He had been informed, and that was all the situation required.

The decision to vacate high-level responsibility was to have grave consequences for the Wang movement, for Wang and his colleagues regarded the pledges made at the Chungkuang-t'ang as emanating from the Japanese Government, and the Japanese team there as its authorized agent. But they were soon to learn otherwise, when within weeks of the conclusion of the conference, the Tokyo authorities began repudiating the agreement Imai and Kagesa signed on November 20.[27] Those agreements had no validity in international law, to be sure—there were no accredited ambassadors at the Chungkuang-t'ang—but Japan can fairly be charged with acting in bad faith. Certainly, the repudiation of the Chungkuang-t'ang agreements did not augur well for the Wang peace movement or for the New Order in East Asia.

According to Imai, the "high-level irresponsibility" that was to make the Wang movement so erratic and do so much to tarnish Japan's integrity in the eyes of both the Chinese and the Japanese participants in the movement, is easily explained:

> Nearly all my work in the peace movement [he said in our interview] was on my own and not on the basis of official orders. If it worked out well, fine. If not . . . [To complete the sentence he drew a finger across his throat in the customary Japanese gesture signifying unpleasant fates ranging from demotion to beheading]. It was the accepted practice for field-grade officers assigned to sensitive intelligence or political tasks to look for possibilities, work out the details, and take the chances *on their own*. Only then, when things were well arranged and looked promising, were high-ranking officers brought into the picture. You can call it gekokujō if you wish, but the heart of the matter was a lack of responsibility at the top.

This is the explanation of a man with unchallengeable credentials. Few officers in the Imperial Army were more experienced in arranging and directing secret operations (*kōsaku*) and plots (*bōryaku*) on the China mainland. As Imai makes clear, any interpretation of gekokujō that pictures the "superiors" as victims of their conspiratorial "juniors" is incorrect. The simple fact is that the superiors—the Bureau Chiefs and above in the Army, and the Konoe Cabinet as well—were perfectly willing to be kept uninformed about the first stages of a politically explosive project, lest it fail. It was time enough to acknowledge and take credit for a project once it began to show signs of success.

For his part, the junior officer, with his superior knowledge of the local scene, many working-level contacts, ample operating funds, and voluminous dossiers on Chinese personalities assembled from years of painstaking intelligence operations, was able to accomplish as much as his wits and daring would allow. His activities had to be kept completely secret, for any breach in security could expose his Chinese collaborators to reprisals. But there was another important reason for secrecy: a *bōryakusha* (plotter or agent) had to shield his plots from fellow Army officers involved in rival plots or counterplots. It could be very dangerous, Imai told me, for the agent whose scheme was exposed prematurely—especially if it was failing or ran contrary to the plans of another agent who had superior backing. (At this point in our conversation, Imai used the same throat-slicing gesture to indicate the consequences of indiscretion.)

Since exposure could mean that the bōryakusha would be "finished off," the number of persons privy to the details of a project was kept to an absolute minimum. If it fell through, nobody was the wiser. If it showed signs of success, however, more and more persons were allowed in on the secret, with hints of progress being passed further and further up the chain of command—but initially, at least, in guarded and unofficial fashion so as to free those in high position of official responsibility. Only when a project gained a certain degree of high-level support were recommendations passed on to ranking civilian officials—but still with great caution and discretion. Konoe, for example, would be informed, usually just sketchily and through unofficial advisers at first. If he did not slam the door on the project, the liaison between him and the responsible agent was tightened, and increasingly detailed information was funneled to him through someone like the Cabinet Secretary. Until the project reached a critical stage there was no need to use official written documents or official channels to keep Konoe informed, and there was no need for Konoe to take direct, personal responsibility for developments. And there is little evidence that he did. Here, in the system of governmental irresponsibility, lies part of the explanation for the charge of "weak diplomacy" (*nanjaku gaikō*) so commonly laid at Konoe's door. Here too is a partial explanation for the variety of simultaneous "operations"—some of which were at cross-purposes—being conducted by Japan's "China hands" in 1938.

CHAPTER ELEVEN

The Hanoi Period, December 1938-April 1939

THE DELEGATES to the Chungkuang-t'ang Conference worked out a schedule for Wang's defection from Chungking. On paper it appeared relatively uncomplicated. Wang in Chungking and the Japanese authorities in Tokyo were to study the agreements signed at the conference and then send word of their acceptance (or rejection) of the terms to agents in Shanghai and Hong Kong by December 3. If the agreements were acceptable to both sides, Wang was to leave Chungking on December 8 and make his way to Hong Kong (via Kunming). In the meantime Konoe was to make a public announcement of a new policy for "adjusting Sino-Japanese relations," an announcement that would embody, in general language, the Chungkuang-t'ang peace terms. Wang would thereupon announce his view that the National Government should accept Konoe's speech as the basis for negotiations.[1]

Both sides signaled their acceptance of the Chungkuang-t'ang agreements as planned. It would be useful to know the exact language in which the Japanese message to Wang was couched, for as we shall see there was an enormous disparity between the agreements signed at the Chungkuang-t'ang and the peace terms Japan decided on ten days later, at an Imperial Conference on November 30; unfortunately, none of the pertinent records gives us any clues. At any rate, Wang's acceptance was secretly relayed to Tokyo via Imai in Shanghai, and Konoe moved ahead with plans for his speech. He was scheduled to deliver a radio address to the nation in Osaka on December 11, and decided to use that occasion to announce the "new policy" toward China.[2]

But events took a sudden turn on December 9, when word reached Konoe that Wang had not been able to make good his escape from Chungking. Those who had been suspicious of Wang's intentions now began to feel that their mistrust had been justified. Even Imai began to wonder if he had fallen into a trap, as some of his Army colleagues had predicted; indeed he began thinking of ritual suicide, the only appropriate course if he had been deceived at the Chungkuang-t'ang. In this atmosphere of mounting suspicion, a Five Ministers' Conference was hastily convened. Foreign Minister Arita advocated going ahead with the speech regardless of Wang's whereabouts or plans, but Konoe decided that "even though it was probably a Chinese trick, he was prepared for deception; and since he had gone that far with the scheme he would go ahead and postpone his speech in accordance with the wishes of the Chinese."[3] Konoe, probably because of Imai's reports, was distrustful of Kao Tsung-wu—the "politician"—but he had come to have a certain confidence in the Wang movement because of Mei Ssu-p'ing's participation in it.[4] On the evening of the ninth Konoe told two friends that he had been forced to cancel the trip to Osaka, and that "as of tonight, I'm going to be ill."[5]

True to his words, Konoe withdrew to the seclusion of his Tekigaisō residence for several days, apparently without arousing any suspicion, despite his reputation for pleading illness to avoid awkward political situations. The public and even most of the Cabinet had no inkling of the impending change in national policy or of Japanese involvement with Wang.* It was to be several weeks before the Japanese learned the full story behind the interruption of Wang's plans.

In the weeks after the Chungkuang-t'ang meeting, Wang arranged a series of conferences at his official mansion, located on the grounds of the Chungch'ing temple. Present at these meetings were Mei Ssu-p'ing, T'ao Hsi-sheng, and Chou Fo-hai. Also present was Ch'en Kung-po. Ch'en, like Chou Fo-hai, had helped launch the Chinese Communist Party only to break with it in short order. The reasons for his leaving the Party are still debated; the one most commonly accepted is that his duties as a revolutionary conflicted with his desire to matriculate at Columbia University.[6] If so, desire prevailed, for from 1923 to 1925 he was a graduate student at Columbia. After receiving his M.A. Ch'en returned to China and quickly associated himself with Wang Ching-wei's Reorganization Faction in the Kuomintang. From that time on, his career was closely linked to Wang's. When Wang's star rose, Ch'en's rose too. When Wang went into European exile in 1936, Ch'en went to Europe; when Wang came back, Ch'en came back. At the time Wang held these conferences, Ch'en was serving in Chengtu as Chairman of the Kuomintang's Szechwan Provincial Headquarters. By all accounts he was Wang's most trusted adviser and ally.

---

* Ambassador Grew cabled the State Department from Tokyo that he was "reasonably certain" Konoe had canceled his radio broadcast because of "drastic changes" regarding Wu P'ei-fu. Grew to Secretary of State, No. 783, December 14, 1938 (U.S. Dept. of State, *Foreign Relations*, 1938, 3: 417).

Among the issues discussed at Wang's residence was the long-debated question of whether a reply to the expected Konoe announcement should be left to the Generalissimo or whether Wang should take the initiative. If we are to accept the word of Wang and his followers on the events of November–December 1938, Wang was still keeping the Generalissimo informed of the activities of the peace movement at this point and now urged him anew to make the reply to the Japanese. Chou Fo-hai tells of a meeting Chiang called to discuss the matter, at which only a few of the "many important military and civilian officials" present, including Ch'en Li-fu of the CC Clique, spoke out vigorously for a continuation of the war of resistance. According to Chou, the hard-line advocates argued that if the war of resistance was abandoned, the Communists, the Kwangsi Clique, Feng Yü-hsiang, and other anti-Kuomintang elements would use anti-Japanese slogans to build public support for their opposition to the Government, with a new eruption of civil war the inevitable result. In their view the only way to forestall that war, which they seemed to assume the Kuomintang would lose, was to continue to resist the Japanese. Furthermore, they insisted the Kuomintang had nothing to lose by this course: if the war ended in victory Chiang would be remembered as a hero, but even if it did not "our names will go down in history because we have fought against insults from abroad." No other opinions were expressed, according to Chou. Siding with the advocates of continued resistance, Chiang decided to reject the impending Konoe demarche.[7]

If the report is true, it suggests the impossible dilemma the Kuomintang felt it was caught up in. Continued resistance meant maintaining the united front and providing a sanctuary for the Communists, thereby enhancing their chances of success at war's end, the development most feared by Wang and the Low-Key Club and by Chiang himself. But the other course, bringing resistance to a halt, was even more distasteful, inviting the Kuomintang's enemies, especially the Communists, to capitalize on the charges of cowardice and appeasement. Chiang obviously found continued resistance the lesser of two evils. Wang chose the avenue of peace and answered those who accused him of giving the Communists an enormous advantage by observing that they were "by nature mischief-makers," who would make trouble whatever the Kuomintang advocated, peace or war. He preferred, he wrote in 1939, "for them to come out in the open and publicly create trouble against peace rather than see them engaged in secret manipulations and intrigues under the cloak of patriotism as is the state of affairs today."[8]

In this awkward and seemingly hopeless situation, it is not surprising to find both Chiang and Wang vacillating in late 1938, both taking cautious but noncommittal interest in the peace efforts of Kao Tsung-wu and his colleagues. The very fact that the Kuomintang appreciated the dilemma, moreover, adds substance to Wang's often repeated assertion that his defection did not represent a radical departure from the very policies Chiang himself had been weighing throughout 1938. After a visit to Tokyo in the summer of 1939, Wang returned to Shanghai to address a group of American and European journalists. At that time he declared that it was Chiang who had relieved Kao of his post in the Foreign Ministry and assigned him the task of arranging peace negotiations with Japan.

> The allegation that Mr. Kao Tsung-wu acted on his own and was without authority is therefore absolutely untrue. During the negotiations there had been many opportunities for both parties to come closely together, but they always stumbled on the question of General Chiang [retiring from office?], which caused him frequently to change his mind concerning the question of peace. My visit to Tokyo was not along a new line of approach; it was only to prevent the negotiations started by Mr. Kao Tsung-wu from breaking down.[9]

Wang claims that as soon as he heard of the Generalissimo's decision to reject the Konoe announcement he requested a meeting; and that he was still hoping to change Chiang's mind when they met on December 9, immediately after Chiang had returned from an inspection trip to Kunming.[10] "I expressed to General Executive Chiang Kai-shek the view that the difficulties now confronting China arise out of the problem of how to sustain the war; that, with regard to Japan, they arise out of the problem of how to end the war; that both countries realize their own particular difficulties as well as the difficulties of the other, and that, therefore, peace is not an impossibility."[11]

After a "great and violent debate," Chiang remained unconvinced, and the two parted. It was only then, according to Wang, that he made his final decision to defect from Chungking. Even then, he made at least one more attempt to change the Generalissimo's mind. Finally, on December 18, he saw Chiang and advised him that he was going to Chengtu to address a gathering. Whether this was intended as a deception or was meant merely to clear the Generalissimo of any responsibility or complicity in Wang's departure, we do not know.* In any event Wang left

---

* Several sources mention that Wang announced his intention to go to Chengtu, where his colleague Ch'en Kung-po was then stationed as Director of the Szechwan

Chungking a few hours later, bound, not for Chengtu, but for Hanoi. In a note to the Generalissimo, he explained that he was leaving in order to continue the policy he had advocated all along, namely "resistance together with negotiation." Foreseeing the trials of negotiation, he predicted that "your task will be the easy one, mine the difficult."[12]

Wang had secured the necessary—and hard to come by—airplane reservations through one of his protégés, P'eng Hsüeh-p'ei, the Vice Minister of Transportation. There was no indication on the tickets of who was to use them, a common security measure in wartime China and a device that allowed P'eng to maintain he "did not even dream" the tickets were for Wang's own use. With one exception Wang's household staff had opted to follow him into an uncertain exile, and in the early morning of December 18, a caravan of four automobiles, bearing servants and luggage, began the long motor trip to Hanoi. By 9:00 A.M. Madame Wang, Wang's long-time friend and personal secretary, Tseng Chung-ming, and two other members of the Wang household were at Chungking's Sanhupa Airport. To their alarm they found Gen. Chou Shih-jou, the Commander-in-Chief of the Air Force, waiting to board the same flight, but they were somewhat reassured when he displayed no suspicion at their presence at the airport. Wang himself arrived only a few minutes before the scheduled take-off. He seemed completely relaxed as he strolled around the airport for a moment before boarding the plane. Once in the air, General Chou decided to show off his skill as an aviator for the benefit of his distinguished fellow passenger. While he was forward in the pilot's compartment, Madame Wang and Tseng nervously weighed the possibility that Chou had received some last-minute alert from Chungking and was flying the plane back. But after a seeming eternity, he emerged from the cockpit and returned to his seat, giving a smart salute as he passed Wang's seat. Wang remained relaxed through the entire episode.[13]

Shortly after noon the plane arrived at its destination, Kunming, the capital of Yunnan and the headquarters of Gen. Lung Yun. There was

---

Provincial Headquarters of the Kuomintang. The Japanese Consul-General in Shanghai wired the Foreign Ministry on December 29 that Wang had been invited to Chengtu to deliver an address at Szechwan University. (Usui, "Nitchū sensō no seijiteki tenkai," p. 204.) Chiang's adviser, W. H. Donald, wrote some months after that Wang had told Chiang on December 18 "he was going to Chengtu to address a gathering." ("From Chiang's Headquarters," p. 195.) The most detailed version is supplied by Kung Te-po, who writes that Wang visited Chiang's confidant, Chang Ch'ün, shortly before his departure and told him he was going to take up Ch'en Kung-po's repeated requests that he make a speech in Chengtu. Wang asked Chang to relay his travel plans to the Generalissimo, and Chang agreed to do so. (*Wang Chao-ming,* p. 87.)

an enthusiastic airport reception, with General Lung and a band on hand to greet the Deputy Director-General. Formalities concluded, the party was led to Lung's residence, where the two men commenced a marathon discussion that went on until past midnight. No one pretends to know the exact details of their exchange, but we know enough about Wang and Lung to say with some assurance that this discussion played an important, perhaps even a decisive, role in the Wang collaboration movement. Lung, a Sinicized Lolo tribesman, was the very archetype of the Chinese warlord. The border province of Yunnan had been Lung's private domain since 1928. The Kuomintang had legitimized his rule in Yunnan by giving him the title of Governor, but in practice Lung paid little heed to the Central Government. He maintained his own army, issued his own currency, exploited the tin mines, and controlled the lucrative opium industry much as he saw fit. He was an "opium general" in the fullest sense of the word, being both addict and entrepreneur.[14]

Madame Wang had gone to Kunming earlier on the pretext of a lecture tour in order to prepare the way for Wang's arrival. Her spadework guaranteed Wang a hospitable reception in Kunming and a smooth exit out of China. Still unsettled, however, was Lung's total commitment to Wang's cause, and that was undoubtedly the matter under discussion on December 18. Evidently Wang was unable to extract a firm promise of support, for General Lung wavered for some weeks after and in the end cast his fate with Chungking.*

While Wang negotiated with General Lung, Wang's nephew Ch'en Kuo-ch'iang, an instructor at the Kunming Aviation School, made the final arrangements with Eurasian Airlines, Inc., for a charter flight to Hanoi.[15] On December 19 Wang sent a telegram to the Generalissimo saying that because his blood pressure had been adversely affected by the high altitude flying of the day before, he had decided "to remain in Kunming for another day before returning to Chungking."† The Wang

---

* General Lung's uneasy alliance with the National Government lasted until after the war when Chiang moved quickly to establish firm control over Yunnan province. Though Lung was given a nominal post in the Government, he was kept under "a close surveillance that amounted to house arrest." In late 1948 he managed to escape to Hong Kong in disguise, and in 1950 he decided to join the Communists in Peking. He was appointed to several official posts but was dismissed from them in 1958 after being accused of confiscating more than 3,000 *mou* of land from peasants. He died in 1962. Boorman, *Biographical Dictionary*, 2: 458–59.

† Quoted in Chin, *Wang cheng-ch'uan*, 5: 32. Chin gives Chou Fo-hai as the source for his information on the Kunming telegram; I have found no corroborating sources. This wire does not seem to make much sense in view of Wang's efforts to convince Chiang only a day earlier that he was going to Chengtu (which is northwest of Chungking whereas Kunming is southwest). It is possible that the Chengtu ploy was intended

party, now augmented by T'ao Hsi-sheng and Chou Fo-hai, then boarded the chartered aircraft and flew to Hanoi, arriving there the evening
of December 19.

Few of the participants in the Wang movement believe that Chiang
was unaware of Wang's plans to leave China. Even if we discount the
claims that Wang was completely candid with Chiang about his sympathy for the peace movement, it seems certain that Chiang would have
been kept well briefed by Gen. Tai Li's 100,000-man intelligence network and by his host of well-placed private informants. Chiang's confidential secretary, Ch'en Pu-lei, for one, was in close touch with many
of the members of the peace movement, especially Chou Fo-hai.[16] Wang's
long-time associates Li Sheng-wu and Ho Ping-hsien and Chou Fo-hai's
confidant Chin Hsiung-pai all insist it is inconceivable that the Generalissimo was in the dark about Wang's plans to defect and contend
that he certainly could have prevented Wang's departure if he had
wanted to. Most of the participants in the peace movement would agree.
Furthermore, the entourage that made good its "escape" to Hanoi included not only Wang himself but three well-known public figures
(Tseng Chung-ming, Chou Fo-hai, and T'ao Hsi-sheng), together with
their families, household staffs, and baggage. Whatever the truth of the
matter, to this day well-informed Japanese and Chinese persist in believing that Chiang "manipulated" Wang's departure.[17]

Chin Hsiung-pai, then a Shanghai journalist, recalls that immediately
after Wang's departure from Chungking, Shanghai newsmen with Kuomintang connections received word from the capital that Wang was not
to be attacked in the press.[18] This squares with the Generalissimo's denial on December 26, during his regular weekly memorial meeting with
his staff officers, that Wang was on a mission to discuss peace terms with
the Japanese. Insisting that Wang was in Hanoi "for medical treatment," the Generalissimo referred to his second's "meritorious service

to relieve the Generalissimo of any stigma of complicity in the event Wang's depar-
ture plans were discovered before he left Chungking; and that once in Kunming,
Wang thought Chiang might have need of another explanation of his whereabouts.
Chou Fo-hai, who had arranged to be in Kunming on business a few days before
Wang's arrival there, told Imai that he received a telegram from Ch'en Pu-lei instruct-
ing him to return to Chungking. Uncertain about how much information the Generalissimo had on Wang's plans, Chou thus had an agonizing choice: should he obey
Ch'en Pu-lei's orders, return to Chungking, and face the possibility that Chiang knew
of Wang's plans to defect and disapproved; or should he flee Kunming while he had
the chance. If he chose to flee and Chiang was not aware of Wang's plans, Chou's premature defection would probably put Chiang on to the plot and jeopardize Wang's escape. Chou shrewdly decided on a third alternative, it seems: he contacted Chiang and
was given permission to stay on in Kunming for a few extra days in order to finish his
business. Imai, *Shina jihen*, pp. 86–87.

to the state" and "expressed the hope that if Mr. Wang had his own views on national policy he should feel free to return and discuss them with members of the Government and the Party."[19]

Colonel Imai, meanwhile, had been waiting in Shanghai for word of Wang's defection. On December 21 he sent a cable to the General Staff confirming Wang's arrival in Hanoi and forwarding Wang's request that Konoe make the agreed-on speech on December 22. Konoe obliged and hastily called a press conference for the evening of the twenty-second. At that time he read a ten-minute statement outlining three "common aims," later known as Konoe's Three Principles (Konoe San Gensoku).[20] With "far-sighted Chinese who share in our ideals and aspirations," the Japanese would cooperate to bring about "neighborly amity, common defense against communism, and economic cooperation," Konoe declared. These principles were vague enough to allow Wang Ching-wei to point to Konoe's statement as evidence of a change of heart on the part of Japan. If Japan was truly willing to become a "good neighbor" (the first of the principles was usually translated into the English phrase President Franklin Roosevelt had made current in describing the role of the United States in the Western Hemisphere), there was every reason to end the war of resistance and move to the peace table. Further evidence of Japan's change of heart, Wang was to say, was to be found in Konoe's expressed willingness to negotiate with Kuomintang representatives, in effect a confirmation of Konoe's repudiation of the *aite ni sezu* declaration.[21]

Wang's public endorsements, however, concealed a bitter disappointment with the first official response of the Imperial Government to his defection. Though Konoe kept his December 22 statement brief, he went beyond vague general principles to touch on many of the questions discussed at the Chungkuang-t'ang Conference in fairly specific terms. He made it clear that he had not committed himself to the decisions reached there. He also laid himself open to charges that he cared little about the future of a collaboration movement as such but had simply been interested in encouraging Wang to defect in order to promote dissension in the Kuomintang. To the distress of both the Chinese and the Japanese participants in the Wang movement, Konoe called on China to "do away with the folly of anti-Japanism, and with resentment over Manchukuo, . . . and enter of her own will into complete diplomatic relations with Manchukuo." Even harder to swallow, however, was the absence of any mention of a time limit on the stationing of Japanese troops south of the Great Wall. Kagesa was as distressed as Wang over the omission. Using the traditional vague appeal to considerations of "troop morale," certain quarters in the Army had demanded that Konoe make no commitment on military withdrawal. From the Chinese point of view, Kagesa writes, Konoe's frequent references to an indefinite garrisoning of troops on Chinese soil "irritated the whole country [of China]."[22]

From Inukai, who was present at Konoe's official mansion the evening of December 22, we get some inkling of the pressures the Premier was under to steer clear of a troop withdrawal commitment. In a telephone conversation with Kagesa, who was attending a meeting of the Army General Staff, Inukai learned that there was vigorous opposition on the part of some Staff officers to any declaration by Konoe of a self-imposed time limit on the military occupation of China.[23] Leading the opposition were Lt. Gen. Nakajima Tetsuzō, who had just succeeded General Tada as Vice Chief of Staff a few days earlier, and Maj. Gen. Tominaga Kyōji, one of his subordinates. Tominaga was particularly outspoken in his determination to head off Konoe, declaring that he would "resolutely refuse to authorize such a disgraceful announcement." Victorious nations simply did not promise defeated nations they would withdraw troops by a certain date, Tominaga declared; any such promise would be an inexcusable insult to the valiant soldiers on the front line. Nor was he moved by the fact that commitments had been made at the Chungkuang-t'ang, he added; he did not feel bound by any of the agreements to which Kagesa had affixed his seal. The notion that the promises Imai and Kagesa made were no more than personal commitments was voiced increasingly as time went on.

According to Inukai, Konoe overheard this telephone conversation, which was conducted in a private office adjoining his own. It is illustrative of the poor communications between Konoe and the Army that the Premier learned of the Army's opposition to the Chungkuang-t'ang agreements in such an offhand manner. Just as illustrative was his response; he was unwilling—or unable—to take a firm stand against the hard-line advocates. Konoe not only rejected Inukai's suggestion that he urge the Chief of Staff to seek the Emperor's support for a declared time limit on the occupation; he responded to the idea as if he was a "disinterested third party," according to Inukai.[24]

"Please encourage Kagesa to work on the matter some more," the Premier instructed Inukai. "He's an expert on smoothing things over, isn't he?" Inukai protested that Kagesa's position in the "peace and friendship camp" (*wahei shinzen-ha*) put him "completely at crosss-purposes with Tominaga," and that he could not be expected to have much influence. Despite all urging, Konoe could not be persuaded to take any extraordinary measures to have the Chungkuang-t'ang commitment to a deadline on the Japanese occupation recognized as morally binding. As the hour for Konoe's press conference drew near—it was not held until 8:20 P.M.—Kagesa made a last desperate attempt to see him, hoping to impress on him how seriously the peace movement would be damaged if he failed to commit Japan to the terms negotiated at the Chung-kuang-t'ang. But Kagesa was denied access to Konoe by the Chief Cabinet Secretary, Kazami, and was unable to make a last-minute face-to-face appeal. By all accounts, Konoe personally prepared his December 22 declaration and kept its contents entirely secret from the various military factions that were anxiously working to influence him. It was an almost unheard-of departure from custom for a Premier to deliver so momentous a speech without first consulting his highest Cabinet officers and appropriate members of the military, but Konoe was apparently determined to demonstrate that he was not yielding to pressure from either the hard-line advocates or the "peace and friendship camp."[25]

Kagesa and Inukai grimly read the Premier's press release while Konoe was confronting the reporters. The whole reason for Chinese resistance, Kagesa later wrote, was the encroachment of Japanese troops on Chinese soil, and therefore, "if we were going to breathe life into the advocacy of peace, it was absolutely necessary for us to mention our intention of withdrawing troops."[26] Konoe's December 22 statement came close to dooming the Wang movement before it had properly begun. But Konoe had done no more than give voice to the hard-line advocates who, far from bending, had actually enlarged their demands on China while others were attempting to lay the groundwork for peace in Shanghai.

Konoe's New Order and Three Principles declarations of November and December 1938 had their roots in a policy formulation drafted by Major Horiba's War Guidance Section in 1938. For six months this document, "The Policy for New Relations," was passed on up through the various departments of the Army-Navy bureaucracy, where it was discussed, amended, and given the necessary seals of endorsement.[27] On November 30, having worked its way up to the top of the chain of command, it was brought before an Imperial Conference and given the supreme endorsement. It is in this policy statement that we find at least some explanation of the discrepancy between the spirit of the Chung-kuang-t'ang Conference and the spirit of the Konoe statement of December 22. We also find there a sharper picture of the Japanese vision of the New Order in East Asia, for "The Policy for New Relations" was written in hard, specific language as opposed to the vague pronouncements found in official public statements.

At the heart of the "Policy" was Konoe's New Order based on China,

Manchukuo, and Japan, each entity "respecting the national character" of the other two, each "respecting the territory and sovereignty" of the others. But whereas Konoe's announcement of the New Order left those phrases clouded in the studied ambiguity of diplomatic usage, the "Policy" spelled out its authors' understanding of the phrases with considerable candor. Japan would insist, it stated, that "the administrative formula of the new China be based on principles that conformed with *bunji gassaku*." In a word Japan would continue to keep China's leaders from fully uniting their country. In substance, if not necessarily in form and name, the regional, autonomous regimes in Inner Mongolia and North China (as well as the "special administrative areas" in Shanghai, Tsingtao, and Amoy) would continue to be sponsored by Japan. Japan would continue to exercise control in China through advisers, who would be assigned to any central regime that might emerge, as well as to the local regimes; and even more significantly, she would be guaranteed supreme control in Inner Mongolia and North China, where she would be allowed to maintain a "necessary" number of troops for an unlimited length of time.

In economic matters Konoe's New Order announcement spoke only of "close economic cohesion" between China and Japan, but the secret "Policy for New Relations" could afford to be more explicit. With regard to the exploitation and utilization of the resources of North China and Mengchiang, for example, the most important consideration would be the needs of Japan and Manchukuo. Here and elsewhere in China, in order to facilitate the exploitation of Chinese resources, Japan would be provided with "special privileges" (*tokubetsu ben'eki*). The phrase that was eliminated at the Chungkuang-t'ang on November 20 as totally repugnant to the Chinese was thus retained in "The Policy for New Relations" and solemnly approved in the presence of the Emperor on November 30.

In the all-important matter of troop withdrawal "The Policy" reveals a contemptuous disregard for the spirit and the letter of the Chungkuang-t'ang agreements, on the basis of which Wang was prompted to defect. It saw "a joint defense against communism" as reason enough to allow Japan to station troops at will in "important places of North China and Mengchiang." Nor was there to be a time limit on the occupation of Shanghai, Nanking, and the Hangchow delta zone, where the anti-Communist "joint defense" rationale did not apply. Japanese troops were to be maintained there "until the public peace is secured." In addition, ships were to be stationed "at specified positions along the banks of the Yangtze River" and at "specified islands on the coast of South

China." Furthermore, China would not only have to tolerate all these military installations; she would also have to shoulder all the expenses involved. Finally, wherever Japanese troops were stationed, Japan was to "reserve the right of strategic requisition and of supervision of railroads, aviation, communication, and important harbors and waterways."

Major Horiba, the principal author of "The Policy for New Relations," has since conceded that this perpetuation of the *bunji gassaku* concept reflected the "obsolete notions of the so-called 'China experts' [Shina-tsū] and ran counter to the modern trend toward national unity."[28] But in 1938 not even moderate elements in the Army—and Horiba was among them—could conceive of a solution to the China problem that did not provide for a continuation of *bunji gassaku*.

Yet even as Horiba admits the flaws of his "Policy," he asks that it be judged in the context of the time, which he feels exonerates it to some degree. As he says, those who attempted to secure governmental and imperial approval of "The Policy for New Relations" in 1938 were attempting "to formulate the goals and limits of the war."[29] This brought them into conflict with those in the Army and the government who were unwilling to consider any limitations. Impervious to the dangers that a protracted war held in store for Japan, these hard-liners were unwilling to consider any solution other than a military one—deeper and deeper penetration of Chinese territory. We have seen the difficulties General Tada and others on the Army General Staff met when they sought to prevent an expansion of the war. It was within the context of an expanding war with ill-defined goals that Horiba sought to set some limits. If the limits seem inexcusably severe to us, they may still have been the most lenient that could be obtained, as Horiba and others claim.

The acrimonious charges of weakness against the General Staff (and, in particular, against General Tada), created an atmosphere in which the moderates knew that even though they might secure official approval for a state policy containing reasonably generous peace terms, there was little chance they could see such a policy through to a successful conclusion. It is significant that Horiba was not authorized to begin his draft of a new policy until April 1938. Only after the reverses at Taierhchwang had demonstrated the terrible cost Japan would have to pay for an expanded war did some support for a changed policy toward China begin to materialize.

Horiba tells of the difficulty he had in securing a degree of support for the new policy. Discussions within the War Ministry could not even proceed until one of the most vehement hard-line advocates, Lt. Col.

Kawamoto Yoshitarō, was absent from his post. Kawamoto was "dumb-founded," writes Horiba, to find that in his absence Ministry officials had accepted the Horiba draft in principle. Horiba also met opposition in the Navy Ministry but found an ally there in the person of Lt. Comdr. Fujii Shigeru. Thanks to Fujii's support of the draft policy, he soon fell from grace and was investigated as a "heretic to naval thinking."[30]

The task of advancing the draft policy fell largely on the shoulders of Colonel Kagesa, who with the Cabinet reorganization of May–June had been transferred to the War Ministry as Chief of the Military Affairs Section, an important position that allowed him to lobby for policy formation both inside and outside the military establishment.* Kagesa, like Horiba, speaks of the resistance to the new policy in the War Ministry. The failure to demand territory and indemnities caused "not a few people in Army and Government circles" to view the policy as unacceptably weak. Indeed, Kagesa declares, this but reflected the mood of the average citizen, who felt that Japan should be given territory and power in China as "compensation for the sacrifices she had made as a result of the China Incident."[31] To settle for anything less than "territorial compensation" in such circumstances was not easy for an Army that was exceptionally concerned about its image and its "face."

Doubtless some will charge Horiba, Kagesa, and others who argue that the "Policy" was the best the moderates could get at the time with mere rationalization. There is, however, ample reason to accept their argument. Certainly, the discussions at the November 30 Imperial Conference tend to bear them out. After listening to Foreign Minister Arita read the policy statement, Baron Hiranuma Kiichirō, the President of the Privy Council, asked to be heard. Though he found the policy "appropriate on the whole," Hiranuma (who was to succeed Konoe as Premier shortly after Wang's arrival in Hanoi) thought that more attention ought to have been paid to the establishment of the new Chinese regime. There were "formal" and "real" aspects that had to be considered, he declared. In purely formal terms the regime should appear to be the product of the "spontaneous initiative of the Chinese people," but "in

---

* Kagesa's new post was more important than the organization charts of the War Ministry would indicate. In practice he performed the tasks of his immediate superior, Maj. Gen. Nakamura Akihito, the Chief of the Military Affairs Bureau (Gunmu-kyoku), who was apparently in failing health. The Chief's position in the military bureaucracy was an extremely important one. One of his principal responsibilities was liaison with other Government agencies—or as Maruyama Masao describes it, "crass political activity." Since his "task was *political* administration, he could meddle in politics; since it was political *administration*, he was free from political responsibility," writes Maruyama. *Thought and Behaviour*, p. 119.

reality it must depend on the guidance and assistance of our Government [which] should demonstrate both compassion and power." The Chinese must be made to realize that "they cannot turn against us," Hiranuma said.[32]

Among other things, Hiranuma objected to the approach to Mengchiang. He was disturbed that the "Policy" was not positive enough in declaring Japan's absolute need for an autonomous Mengchiang. To maintain that Japan demanded an autonomous Mengchiang in order to combat communism was true enough as far as it went, he conceded, "but even without the purpose of anticommunism, it may be that we will have to call for an extreme degree of autonomy [in Mengchiang]." Hiranuma had no objection to a purely formal acknowledgment of Chinese sovereignty in the area, but beyond that it would have to be kept independent of Chinese control. Yet if Japan's insistence on an autonomous Inner Mongolia was not to be based on the area's value as an anticommunist zone, then what was the justification for her demands? Hiranuma answered the unspoken question: "A consideration of Mengchiang's relationship to Manchukuo" made the autonomy of the area a strategic necessity for Japan. Foreign Minister Arita rose to put Hiranuma's mind at ease on this and other points. The "Policy" cited anticommunism as justification for Japan's right to station troops in Mengchiang, he said, but "this was meant only to indicate the most important objective." Other reasons—such as the importance of Mengchiang's mineral resources to Manchukuoan industry—were presumably involved. As to another objection Hiranuma raised, that the "Policy" perhaps envisioned a too-hasty retrocession of the international settlements, Arita assured the Baron that "it goes without saying we would do so only after having induced the various European countries to follow suit."[33]

It is impossible to read the accounts of the Imperial Conference of November 30 and the Konoe declaration of December 22 without agreeing with Imai that they were "one-sided and coercive," "grounded in the *ken'eki shisō* [the doctrine of rights and special interests] of the past," and "far removed from the things that were emphasized by Japan at the Chungkuang-t'ang talks."[34] The supreme irony is that Konoe's December 22 declaration was regarded by many as too conciliatory, as further evidence of Konoe's "weak-kneed diplomacy."

Before we turn to Wang's activities in Hanoi, we should say a brief word about Konoe's attitude toward Wang's defection from Chungking. Most accounts picture Konoe as indifferent, suspicious, and pessimistic in this regard. He clearly did not share the enthusiasm of Kagesa and his associates for Wang as Japan's best hope for a speedy settlement of the war, and so not surprisingly did not share their sense of urgency about granting Wang concessions to strengthen his position. Baron Harada, a dutiful, day-by-day chronicler of the events and gossip of Shōwa Japan, records numerous meetings with Konoe in the autumn and winter of 1938, and nowhere in his account is there a hint that Konoe placed any value on Wang as a collaborator. Konoe's private secretary confirms the Premier's lack of interest in Wang, who "must have been bitterly disappointed by Konoe's attitude toward him."[35] In short, Konoe—and others in the Government—had no clear vision of how Wang's defection was to be used by the Japanese. Cabinet Secretary Kazami, one of those closest to Konoe and one of the few civilians privy to the inner workings of Operation Watanabe, writes:

> It is a fact that Konoe never considered, never even dreamed, of establishing a new central government centered on Wang at this time [December 1938]. . . . Konoe earnestly hoped that, with Wang standing in between, acting as mediator, [Japan] might be able to talk with China and things might proceed better. That is all he hoped for. There was no reason for a Wang regime or anything like that. Moreover, in view of the [lack of] progress of the new regimes in North and Central China, talk of another new regime was something that could have had little appeal [to Konoe].[36]

As we shall see, this concept of Wang as a mediator accords very well with Wang's own statements on the subject.[37] He steadfastly maintained that his intention in defecting was not to organize a new government, but only to examine the peace proposals Tokyo was making. If Japan was sincere and promised an honorable settlement, he had planned to do his utmost to mobilize Chinese public opinion in support of a negotiated settlement of the war. If Chungking responded favorably, well and good; but whatever its response, he had had no thought of collaborating with Japan in the establishment of a new government at the time. This, Wang's own explanation of his motives in December 1938, accords with Konoe's view of Wang as a "bridge" rather than a collaborator.

It does not, however, accord with the reports Colonel Imai brought back from the Chungkuang-t'ang Conference. As we have seen, those reports suggest considerable emphasis at the meeting on the need for military support for Wang's movement as a first step toward developing a government that could challenge Chungking's authority in unoccupied China. Imai asserts that these plans were advanced by the "Chinese side." But whatever the case, his reports suggest that there was no serious discussion of the underlying premise, that both the Chinese and the Japanese present accepted the notion of a Wang regime as axiomatic.

How can the discrepancy between the Wang-as-bridge theory and the Chungkuang-t'ang documentation be resolved? Are we to believe that Imai wove his reports out of whole cloth, that the Chinese side did not make the proposals he records? Even assuming Imai saw some advantage in misrepresenting the Chinese, he could hardly have hoped that their views would remain unclarified for any length of time. The Chinese side was there to commence what promised to be a very close partnership with Imai and his colleagues, and it seems unlikely that Imai would have seen anything to be gained in the long run by so grossly misrepresenting the Chinese views.

It is possible that both Wang and Konoe left the details of the Chungkuang-t'ang discussions to their agents, though it is difficult to believe they were completely unaware of the most basic proposals discussed there, especially Wang, whose future was so deeply involved. For my part, I think the most reasonable assumption is that Wang and his followers simply prepared for two eventualities. That is, Wang did indeed plan to appeal to Chungking after his defection to accept the honorable peace terms he hoped to extract from Konoe. Yet he could hardly have ignored the possibility that his mission would fail, and almost certainly would have considered other options, exile abroad and collaboration with Japan being the two most likely. At the Chungkuang-t'ang his agents were merely exploring some of the aspects and terms incidental to collaboration. We are bound to suppose that later, as Wang lay dying, he was deeply concerned about the judgment history would assign to his name. It is hardly surprising that mindful of the unflattering stigma history usually attaches to wartime collaborators, he chose to emphasize his primary—and intended—goal in his "last will and testament" and to underplay the unintended outcome.

The first official reply from China to Japan's December 22 declaration came, not from Wang but from Chiang Kai-shek, who issued a statement rejecting Konoe's peace terms on December 26.[38] Chiang's first concern was to mute the enthusiasm of his own people, on whom Konoe's "sugar-coated words were expected to produce intoxicating effects." Konoe's call for a Sino-Japanese anti-Communist pact was nothing but his way of getting Chinese consent to Japanese garrisons on Chinese soil, Chiang declared; if China had been willing to allow that, there would have been no war in the first place.

Chiang also directed his reply at the Western powers in the hope of persuading them that Japan's New Order in East Asia threatened their interests as well as China's, and not only in China, but in all of East Asia. To be sure, Chiang had been making such appeals right along, but he had been pressing the Western governments harder and harder since the fall of Hankow and Canton. In a "strictly confidential" telegram to the State Department, U.S. Ambassador Nelson T. Johnson reported that British Ambassador Sir Archibald Clark-Kerr had conferred with the Generalissimo in Changsha on November 4–5, immediately after Konoe's New Order speech. Clark-Kerr had informed the U.S. Naval Attaché, James M. McHugh, that though the Generalissimo "had not talked threateningly," he had declared "the time had now arrived when he had to have a specific statement of Britain's intentions as well as tangible evidence to present to the people of China at the forthcoming plenary session of the Kuomintang." He had then suggested a loan to support Chinese currency "as an initial move on Britain's part." McHugh, a palace intimate, reported that it was his impression the Generalissimo "had presented an ultimatum to London." Soon after, McHugh himself talked with the Generalissimo, who told him there was reason to believe Japan would afford China "very easy peace terms in return for an about-face towards the British." McHugh responded by asking Chiang how he would sell anti-British sentiments to the Chinese people. Before he could answer, Madame Chiang interrupted to say that "the people would accept peace with Japan if the Generalissimo told them it was the best thing for China."[39] On November 19 Ambassador Grew in Tokyo sent a "strictly confidential" message to Washington reporting that his British colleague there, Sir Robert Craigie, believed "some further concrete step in support of Chiang Kai-shek will soon have to be taken by Great Britain if they wish to avoid his being driven into the Japanese camp."[40]

For the next six years, indeed almost until the last gun was fired, Chiang was to hound Great Britain and the United States with innuendo and veiled threats. But his meaning was quite clear. Without greater and greater support from the Western powers, he might find the continued struggle too burdensome for his war-weary nation. He might yield to the counsel he was receiving from various quarters that he cooperate with Japan in achieving an "Asia for the Asians." After a meeting with Madame Chiang in July 1942, Stilwell scribbled in his journal an account of yet another of her efforts to "throw a scare into us": the flat statement "China can not go on without help." The pro-Japanese activity was very strong, Madame Chiang warned him, and without more help the Chinese would be forced to "make other arrangements."[41]

In the period we are considering here, there is no more consistent theme in Sino-American relations than the threat—sometimes veiled, sometimes open—that the Chiang regime was prepared to "make other arrangements" with Japan if Western aid fell short of its demands. If the threats were "mostly bluff," as many American and British observers believed, they were nevertheless credited in the right places, from Chungking's point of view. It may be more than coincidence, then, that the first major American grant of credit to China was announced on December 16, 1938, just two days before Wang fled from Chungking. Willys Peck, Chargé at the American Embassy in Chungking, wrote that the announcement of the $25,000,000 credit had "been construed by the Chinese as indicating the commencement of action by those powers [the United States and Great Britain] to prevent Japan from achieving its aims in the Far East, and it now seems clear that this conviction has immensely stimulated and stiffened the will for prolonged resistance."[42]

As the world press speculated on Wang's whereabouts in the last days of December 1938—the Japanese news agency Dōmei reported him on his way to Europe while other journalists placed him variously in Shanghai, Hong Kong, Canton, and Hanoi—Chungking remained cautiously uncritical. According to Chou Fo-hai, it was widely believed in Chungking that Wang's departure was based purely on personal considerations, and that he would soon abandon his emphasis on peace and return to the capital.[43]

To clear up the mystery and clarify his reasons for leaving, Wang sent a lengthy telegram, dated December 29, to the Central Executive Committee of the Kuomintang. Because the future of the Wang movement was still very much in doubt, especially in view of the generally unsatisfactory terms of the Konoe declaration of December 22, many in the Wang camp were opposed to a public airing of Wang's defection at such an early stage. Mei Ssu-p'ing, however, successfully argued that it would be "unfair" to keep the message secret, and the telegram appeared in a Hong Kong newspaper on December 31.[44]

Though Wang's "peace telegram" (as it was dubbed by the Western press) was addressed to Chungking, it was meant for a Tokyo audience as well. To the Kuomintang Wang expressed his view that the recent Japanese declaration had altered the policy of January 16, that Japan was now willing to negotiate, and that Konoe's Three Principles offered a reasonable basis for negotiation. Recognizing that Konoe's second principle, "anti-Communist collaboration," appeared to contradict the Kuomintang's united-front policy and to threaten the good Sino-Soviet relations then prevailing, Wang attempted to explain it away, stating, rather lamely, that an anti-Comintern pact would not be directed against the Soviet Union, but rather was intended to "check subversive international conspiracies of Communists." As for the Chinese Communist Party, it had no reason to fear the pact as long as it kept faith with its pledge to support Sun Yat-sen's Three Principles. However, the Chinese Communists would have to "completely abandon [their] party organization and propaganda work, abolish [their] 'frontier' government, as well as [their] special military system, and be absolutely subject to the legal institutions of the Republic of China."

For the benefit of his Tokyo audience, Wang endorsed in general terms Konoe's declaration and invited Japan to match Konoe's lofty words with deeds. At the same time he made it clear that he did not accept Konoe's vagueness on the question of the stationing of Japanese troops in China. Konoe's reference to "specified points" was acceptable only if it was understood that all of those points would be "restricted to the vicinity of Inner Mongolia." Further, the garrisoning of anti-Communist troops must be limited to "a period concurrent with the contemplated anti-Communist pact." As for China proper, the Japanese Army must be withdrawn from Chinese soil "promptly and completely." In a final appeal, Wang called on Japan to "institute a pro-Chinese educational policy" so that the Japanese people and their leaders might "abandon their traditional attitude of contempt and their ideas of conquest with regard to China."

Another telegram from Wang to Chungking, this one addressed to the Standing Committee of the Kuomintang Central Executive Committee and dated December 28, was made public on January 8.[45] In it Wang revealed the substance of the discussions he had held with the Generalissimo just prior to his defection. As he had stated at the time, "peace [was] not an impossibility," since both Japan and China had come to realize how destructive the war was for both countries. Wang went on to point out that the Generalissimo had accepted the terms conveyed through Trautmann in December 1937 as a basis for negotiation, even though they "were more unfavorable and even less definite" than those Konoe had put forward on December 22, 1938. Though some assistance from the Western powers was beginning to flow into China, Wang observed, it was "by no means sufficient to have any effect on the outcome of the war"; it was substantial enough, however, to give China additional bargaining strength. Only the Chinese Communist Party stood to profit from a continuation of the war, Wang concluded.

With the publication of this telegram, the first public declarations of support for Wang were heard in Shanghai and Hong Kong. Notable among the early enthusiasts were Lin Pai-sheng, a prominent newspaper publisher and longtime Wang supporter, Fu Shih-shuo, an educator and one of the earliest members of the peace movement, and Ch'u Min-i, Wang's brother-in-law (and later his Minister of Foreign Affairs).

Imai's Operation Watanabe report of January 15 indicated some further grounds for guarded optimism regarding the Wang movement.[46] Kao had told him that large numbers of Chinese from Hong Kong and various parts of China had sent "telegrams of encouragement" to Wang. (Not a few of these people, said Kao, had taken the precaution of cabling Chungking to express their opposition to Wang.) According to Imai, a former President of Peking National University, Chiang Mon-lin, had conducted a survey among the San-min Chu-i Youth Corps, which showed 63 of 159 respondents in favor of Wang's actions as against only 25 opposed. (The others were undecided.) Imai also reported that there was third-party (Socialist) support for Wang and signs of tentative backing from Shanghai labor unions. Most encouraging of all, he thought, were the reports that a number of warlord generals, including Lung Yun, P'an Wen-hua, Teng Hsi-hou, Chang Fa-k'uei, and Liu Wen-hui, were in "smooth contact" with Wang. Further, Yunnan's pivotal Lung Yun had allowed Wang to go to Hanoi and only then had pledged his loyalty to Chiang. All this was "on the surface—just an expediency," Imai reported; Lung was playing a wait-and-see game. When a conference of provincial leaders was held in Chungking on January 10, Lung sent only a proxy. Meanwhile, Wang supporters in Hong Kong had forwarded nearly three million Chinese dollars to the Communications Bank in Yunnan on the pretext of aiding in the monetary reform of General Lung's domain.

Chungking's response to Wang's public declarations was swift but measured. On the day after the "peace telegram" was published, that is, on January 1, 1939, Wang was expelled from the Kuomintang and removed from all public offices. More severe sanctions—among them an order for his arrest—were not declared for many more months. During the early stage of Wang's exile, both sides—the Kuomintang in Chungking and the Wang group in Hanoi—cautiously avoided actions that might make reconciliation impossible. This is not to say that Wang did not receive his share of verbal abuse in Chungking. Chou En-lai, who had known Wang since World War I when they had been in France together, was quoted as saying that "in my twenty years of association with Wang I have always known him to be a quitter."[47] A longtime political rival, Wu Chih-hui, accused Wang of selling his country "for personal vanity" and asserted that he was "no longer worthy of being treated as a human being."[48] The Communist *Hsin-hua jih-pao* (New China Daily) likened him to China's most notorious traitors, including Wu San-kuei, who had betrayed the Ming to the Manchus three centuries before. But Wang looked back into China's rich history and found a precedent of his own to cite. He reminded the Chinese people of another late-Ming figure, Chang Hsien-chung, a "bandit" who had carried out scorched-earth tactics against the Manchus and had so weakened the country that it was unable to oppose the Manchu invasion from the east. Wang's comparison was particularly apt in the current situation because the "bandit" Chang hailed from Yenan.[49]

What was probably more discouraging to Wang than the reaction in China was the criticism he received in Japan. The rightist *Kokumin shimbun* (The National Newspaper), for example, responded to the "peace telegram" by saying that his "terms could not possibly be accepted by Japan as a basis for negotiation." Though Japan might be able to find some formula that respected Chinese sovereignty, the paper said, "not a single Japanese soldier now in China wants to leave the continent until and unless real peace and order are established."[50]

During the first few months of 1939, Wang had two major preoccupations: to ascertain Japan's true attitude toward his peace movement (a task that was made all the more necessary and complex by the resignation of the Konoe Government in January) and to enlist supporters in China. Chungking meanwhile played a waiting game, placing as much emphasis on dissuading Wang as on discrediting him. The National Government was well aware that Wang was becoming more and more discouraged about the prospects for his movement and by late January was considering exile to Europe; he had in fact applied to the German Embassy in Tokyo for a visa.[51] In addition, the British Embassy in Chungking "visaed [Wang] for travel in Great Britain"—but only after it had informally checked with Chiang Kai-shek and "ascertained that he had specially intervened to make a foreign tour by Wang possible."[52]

That Wang came very close to abandoning the peace movement for a self-imposed European exile was largely due to the disappointing response to his appeals for support, especially from the powerful generals of the southwestern provinces. On January 15 Imai relayed to Tokyo a report from Ch'en Kung-po: Chungking was so alarmed by the possibility of collaboration between the southwestern armies and Wang that a "punitive expedition" against the potential rebels was being considered. "The relations between Chungking and the military factions [of Kwangtung and Kwangsi provinces] can only be regarded as the quiet before the storm," Imai concluded.[53]

As it became more and more evident that the storm was not breaking, and that Chiang had succeeded in inducing the southwestern generals to stay in the Kuomintang fold, Wang's future grew increasingly bleak. The failure of the Cantonese warlord Chang Fa-k'uei, now the Commander of the Fourth War Area, to break with Chungking was especially disappointing to Wang; Chang had a long record of opposition to Chiang and had been Wang's strongest military supporter in his futile bid to form a separatist regime in Canton in 1931.

In the absence of adequate studies of the power relationships between the so-called Southwestern Faction and the Chungking regime, one can only speculate on the reasons for Chiang's success in the southwest. We have already mentioned one possible factor: America's extension of credit to Chungking at this critical point and the prospect of additional massive financial support from the United States and Great Britain. Lung, Chang, and other potential Wang allies were probably impressed by Chiang's ability to command Western support and financing, and more than a little dubious about the kind of aid Japan would give Wang. Perhaps more important, however, was the element of nationalism. An "opium general" like Lung Yun might well have been governed more by considerations of expediency and self-interest than by nationalism, but it was a mistake for Japan to have assumed that his officers and men would have followed him in a break with the central government. As Imai says in retrospect, "*They* were inspired by nationalism even if General Lung was not."[54]

This brings us to a further reason for Wang's growing pessimism during the first few months of 1939, namely, the reluctance of the Japanese to commit themselves wholeheartedly to his cause. This situation was exacerbated by Konoe's resignation less than two weeks after Wang's defection. Konoe's action was not directly related to Operation Watanabe. However, for those associated with the Wang cause it was tragically coincidental that other national issues conspired to cause Konoe to resign at this junction. Among those issues were a drastic increase in the number of small and medium business failures, a rapidly accelerating rate of inflation, and a rising tide of pro-Axis sentiment that most of Konoe's Cabinet opposed but could not counteract. As we have seen, historians have not been inclined to credit Konoe with much tenacity of purpose in the face of adversity. In January 1939 it was Wang's misfortune to become the indirect victim of the Premier's well-known "weak nerves" (to use Maruyama Masao's description).[55]

Konoe's successor, Baron Hiranuma, was not a welcome choice to the Operation Watanabe group. Kagesa and Inukai were en route to Hanoi to establish liaison with Wang when they heard a radio broadcast in Taiwan reporting the resignation of the Konoe Cabinet. Disturbed by the implications of the news broadcast, they hastened back to Tokyo to see whether Operation Watanabe still had a future. It did as it turned out; but this was not immediately apparent, for Hiranuma adopted an even more noncommittal wait-and-see attitude than his predecessor, and for several months there was little evidence that the Japanese Government was seriously interested in supporting Wang. The guiding hand of Operation Watanabe, Imai, was ordered back to Tokyo and by February was shifting his attention to other activities, including the effort to recruit Wu P'ei-fu.

In the meantime Chungking continued its efforts to encourage Wang to go abroad. Both Foreign Minister Wang Ch'ung-hui and Chiang's confidential secretary, Ch'en Pu-lei, remonstrated with Wang in Hanoi to that end. In addition, Ku Cheng-ting, a member of Wang's Reorganization Faction who had veered toward Chiang Kai-shek in recent years, was twice dispatched to Hanoi to urge Wang to return to Chungking or to go to Europe. Wang reportedly told Ku that as long as Chiang continued his unrealistic war of resistance, he would not return to Chungking. However he apparently requested a passport for travel to Europe and was on the verge of leaving in mid-March, when Ku returned from Chungking with the passport and "travel expenses."[56] But a day after Ku left Hanoi for Chungking, Wang suddenly changed his plan in response to a shattering personal tragedy.

ASSASSINATION OF TSENG CHUNG-MING

At about 2:00 A.M. on March 21, 1939, Wang's confidential secretary and close friend, Tseng Chung-ming, was murdered in the private house in which Wang and his immediate party were residing in Hanoi. The machine-gun–wielding assassins had little trouble gaining entrance to the house, which unlike all the homes Wang was to live in thereafter was only lightly guarded. It has generally been assumed that Tseng was murdered in order to intimidate Wang, but a reconstruction of the events by Chin Hsiung-pai strongly suggests that Wang himself was the intended victim; that is still the belief of the murdered man's widow. Both think that the assassins were misled by the fact that Tseng and his wife occupied the most elegantly appointed bedroom in the house while Wang slept in a bedroom "as simple as a servant's."* At any rate, whether by design or by accident, it was Tseng's bedroom the assassins sprayed with bullets, mortally wounding the cultivated translator and author. His wife, a painter of international reputation known by her maiden name, Fang Chün-pi, was wounded as well.[57]

The Wang, Tseng, and Fang families had been closely linked since 1909, when the older sisters of both Tseng and his wife had plotted with Wang to assassinate the Prince Regent. While working toward a doctorate at the University of Lyons, Tseng had kept up his studies of Chinese literature and history under Wang's tutelage. After his return to China in 1925 Tseng had served in a variety of Government posts, reaching the vice-ministerial level; in 1936 he had left Government service to become Wang's secretary. If, as some suggest, Tseng's shocking murder was intended to terrorize Wang, the plot backfired badly. Six days later, on March 27, a Hong Kong newspaper edited by his supporters carried a statement from Wang, announcing his resolution to carry forward his program of achieving a peace settlement with Japan, "not only for the sake of comforting my friends, who will never leave my mind, but, and even more so, for the sake of the nation whose existence depends on this policy."[58] Madame Tseng also issued a statement, saying "death may occur in consequence of advocating peace; we have to exchange our own death for the existence of the nation."[59]

By Wang's account, he had made up his mind to go abroad before Tseng's murder, but had served notice on Chungking that he would return "should the National Government let the present impasse drag on without coming to a definite decision." It must have been his intention to return that provoked Chungking and "caused the outrage," he sur-

---

* Chin, *Wang cheng-ch'üan,* 5: 47. Chin's account of the assassination (*ibid.,* Chaps. 187–88) is a first-rate piece of detective work based on privileged interviews with Wang's children as well as study of the appropriate documents. Chin charges Wang Lu-ch'iao and Cheng Chieh-min (a member of the Blue Shirts) with primary responsibility for the deed, and also implicates the Chinese consul in Hanoi. Cheng escaped and returned to Chungking, but Wang Lu-ch'iao and two others were captured and confessed that Wang Ching-wei was their intended victim. The assassins had taken the house next door to Wang's and for several days had peered into his house with binoculars. Since Wang frequently used the elegantly furnished room for a reception and conference room, the assassins were thoroughly convinced that it was his room. After all the evidence is in, however, Chin is still not prepared to say for certain that Wang was the intended victim. He notes, for example, that at one point in the trial the murderers claimed they had intended to murder everyone in the house. However, they were evidently unaccustomed to "midnight carnage," became "confused," and left before completing their task, he writes.

mised.[60] Madame Tseng also asserts that Wang had "definitely" decided to go abroad before the attack on her husband caused him to revise his plans.[61]

That so much should have hinged on this single event, the death of a relatively unimportant politician, murdered in circumstances that suggest he was the victim of a plot gone awry, is a striking illustration of the role of chance in history. Beyond that, Wang's dramatic response to the event, his sudden reversal of plans and decision to plunge wholeheartedly into the schemes that only days before had seemed so unpromising, tends to confirm Boorman's characterization of him as a "romantic radical," a man whose "ardent patriotism outran his political judgment."[62] In this case, it would seem his sense of grief and personal outrage also outran his political judgment.

In his March 27 announcement Wang did more than pay tribute to Tseng; he also made a sensational disclosure that greatly widened the gulf between him and Chungking. He released what purported to be the minutes of a meeting of the Standing Committee of the National Defense Council held in Hankow on December 6, 1937, to discuss the Trautmann peace terms. It was at this meeting that Vice Minister of Foreign Affairs Hsü Mo delivered his report on the meeting held four days earlier, at which Chiang's most important generals had unanimously agreed that the Japanese peace proposals forwarded through Ambassador Trautmann constituted a basis for negotiation.

According to Hsü's report, though Chiang had agreed to allow German mediation to continue, he had promptly proceeded to ignore the spirit of his generals' advice. In discussions with Ambassador Trautmann later the same day (December 2), the Generalissimo had declared that "he dared not trust Japan; treaties had been torn to pieces by Japan and words spoken not kept." Trautmann had pleaded for the adoption of "a spirit of tolerance" by the National Government and had expressed the fear that Chinese rejection of the Japanese terms would merely bring more exacting terms in the future.[63]

The point Wang was making in his disclosure was that even before the fall of Nanking, there was a consensus favoring the acceptance of Japanese terms. He did not try to blame Chiang for standing in the way of a peaceful settlement or for ruining the Trautmann mediation efforts. He merely asked the public to note that his own call for peace in the spring of 1939 was consistent with the prevailing opinion in the highest Government councils in the autumn of 1937. How much more opportune it would have been, Wang argued, for China to have come to terms with Japan in December 1937, before her armies had swept through Nanking,

Tsinan, Kaifeng, Hsüchou, Kiukiang, Canton, and Wuhan. One might reasonably suppose, he said, that Japan's peace terms would have stiffened after these military successes; that she in fact appeared to be offering to negotiate on terms no more demanding than those she had offered in 1937 called for a positive response on the part of China. Wang did not discuss specific peace terms in his March 27 statement; each point would have to be worked out in detail in future negotiations. Simply put, Wang felt that "if the terms violate national sovereignty and independence, then peace is impossible; if the terms are such as not to jeopardize the sovereignty and independence of the nation, then peace is possible."[64]

With Wang's publication of state secrets, an infuriated Chungking, constrained up to this point to tread softly because of the high national esteem in which he was held, was able to attack him openly as a traitor.* The *Ta-kung pao* retaliated with a disclosure of its own: the details of a purported secret agreement between Wang and Hiranuma (negotiated by Kao Tsung-wu). According to the paper, Wang had offered to lead "an anti–Chiang Kai-shek and anti-Communist war" provided the Japanese guaranteed to assist him by occupying Sian, Nanning, Changsha, Foochow, and other strategic points. Japan was to complete her part of the program in May and June 1939, after which Wang would cease his appeals to Chiang to engage in peace negotiations and step forward to do his part in an all-out war against Chungking. In addition, said the *Ta-kung pao*, Wang had asked the Japanese for Ch $3,000,000 per month to cover his government's expenses, plus a loan of Ch $200,000,000 to help build up an army.[65] Wang did not exactly deny the *Ta-kung pao* charges, saying only that "the allegations are beneath contempt, and I have no intention to waste my time in denying them."[66]

However dismal the prospects of the Wang movement in this period, the fact is, the Chinese side was still carrying on some negotiations with the Japanese. Kao, for example, was back in Tokyo in late January 1939 with more pleas for Japanese "diversionary attacks" to free Gens. Lung Yun, Chang Fa-k'uei, and others to join Wang's movement.[67] The *Ta-kung pao* allegations appear to have some basis in fact, though they seem to refer more to the wishes of Wang and his circle than to their actual accomplishments. As we have seen, the Wang party's desire for Japanese military attacks on strategic points was relayed through Colo-

---

* Even so it appears that Chungking continued to work behind the scenes to get Wang to reconsider his stand. David Lu speaks of personal appeals to Wang in early April from Madame Chiang Kai-shek and T. V. Soong, as well as a promise from the Generalissimo that the past would be forgotten if Wang would return to Chungking. *From the Marco Polo Bridge*, p. 84, citing unpublished material in the Japanese Foreign Office archives.

nel Imai as early as November 1938. Wang had also requested financial assistance in the exact amount mentioned by the *Ta-kung pao* as early as December 30.[68] I have found no evidence, however, that Premier Hiranuma had made firm commitments to Wang (or Kao) at the time of the *Ta-kung pao* disclosures.[69]

RESCUE FROM HANOI

When news of the Tseng assassination reached Tokyo, the Hiranuma Cabinet authorized Colonel Kagesa and Inukai Ken to go to Hanoi to see if Wang wanted to move to a safer place, to move, to be precise, under Japanese protection. Though the prosecution at the International Military Tribunal after the war was reluctant to accept Kagesa's testimony that Wang freely chose to leave Hanoi, it is altogether logical that, once having decided to lead the peace movement, he would want to return to Chinese territory.[70] Moreover, the French authorities in Hanoi were not anxious to shelter an anti-Chungking movement and were unwilling to offer Wang the protection that he was going to need in the future. At this point Wang's colleagues in Hong Kong and Shanghai had for several months been laying the groundwork for his possible return to Chinese soil. Funds were being collected, newspaper and radio support was being enlisted, pro-Wang organizations were being formed, and vital ties with the underground world—which alone could guarantee the safety of the Wang hierarchy—were being established.

Traveling under assumed names, Kagesa and Inukai arrived at Haiphong on April 16 aboard the specially chartered 5,000-ton *Hokkō-maru*; both met Wang for the first time two days later. On April 20 Kagesa asked the War Ministry to make arrangements for Wang's arrival in Shanghai. Those arrangements included secret houses with iron-covered, bullet-proof windows and iron-grilled doors in the interior.[71] A siegelike existence was about to begin for Wang.

On April 25 Wang and his party boarded a small French vessel chartered for the trip, and a day later they left Haiphong. The Japanese party left the same day on the *Hokkō-maru*. But the French ship was poorly provisioned and did not ride well in the rough seas that were soon encountered, and the Wang party was forced to transfer to the *Hokkō-maru* en route. Thus, though he sought to avoid it, Wang was escorted back to China by an officer of the Imperial Army on a Japanese ship decked out with flags to celebrate the Emperor's birthday.[72]

The nearly two weeks at sea (with a stop at Taiwan for refueling) provided Wang ample time for reflection. A melancholy poem he composed one night at sea while listening to the ticking of the ship's clock and mourning his vanished comrades and "the crushed hopes of a lifetime" measures the dark despair he felt on his return to Chinese soil.[73] Still, the trip also afforded Wang, Kagesa, and Inukai an opportunity to become acquainted with each other's views. Wang impressed on the Japanese the supreme difficulty of gaining a sympathetic audience in China for a peace settlement. Appeals for a war of resistance were manifestly patriotic, he said, but it was hard to convince anyone that the advocacy of peace could also spring from a love of China. The Chungking Government was intractable and not to be swayed by mere appeals, he declared, and so he had come to the conclusion that the establishment of a "peace government" was the only hope. "We will prove by facts that Sino-Japanese cooperation is fruitful, and then we will see which course of action public opinion will support, resistance or peace."[74] Such a course was bound to be severely criticized at first, he thought, but if Sino-Japanese cooperation should proceed well, the public would see that the war of resistance was pointless. Confronted with such a development the Chungking regime would surely see reason and move in the direction of peace.

Wang repeatedly stressed three points to Kagesa and Inukai. First, he maintained that his ultimate purpose was not to establish and direct a rival government; that was only a means to an end. His ultimate goal was reunion with Chungking. No meaningful peace settlement with Japan could be expected as long as Chungking and the Wang camp remained divided. Moreover, if his vision was correct, Wang said, if those in Chungking were finally compelled to join his movement, he would consider his purpose fulfilled and "would retire to private life without hesitation."[75]

Second, Wang stressed that he most emphatically did not wish to see his peace movement degenerate into civil war. "After we set up a government, we will have to establish armed forces," he conceded, "but by all means, I would like to see to it that those forces do not fight with Chungking and thus bring down a bloody disaster on our people." Kagesa agreed with Wang and recorded his admiration of Wang's "noble spirit" and political selflessness.[76]

Finally, Wang tried to impress on Kagesa and Inukai the importance of Japan's role: the ultimate success or failure of his movement depended on her willingness to keep faith with him and the Chinese people in the spirit of the Three Principles Konoe had enunciated. Patriotic Chinese were not going to be moved by the talk of peace, Wang said. "The advocacy of peace is only a hair's difference from the advocacy of treason. . . . Only a fair and just policy on the part of Japan can impart a luster to the peace movement."[77] Wang indicated that he was aware there were divisions among his colleagues, that there were some who had become disenchanted with the peace movement and were cautioning him about the dangers of establishing a collaboration government. The Hong Kong group, he said, included "not a few . . . who have a pessimistic view of the Japanese Government." Wang was less certain about the views of his supporters in Shanghai. In Kagesa's judgment, though Wang wanted and expected to go to Tokyo to sound out the Hiranuma Government in full detail, he was clearly siding with those who were willing to accept the risks of pinning their hopes on Japan's sincerity.[78]

Wang was correct about the division in his own camp over his next move. A minority group centered in Hong Kong favored what was coming to be known (at least among the Japanese participants in Operation Watanabe) as the Kao course. At the Chungkuang-t'ang Conference it was Kao Tsung-wu who had most vehemently insisted that the proposed Wang regime be free of Japanese control, or any suspicion of control. He had made it quite clear he would not even consider the establishment of a Wang regime unless it was located in unoccupied Chinese territory and had its own military base in the form of a native army. Otherwise, he felt the new regime would be doomed to the same fate as the other puppet regimes. Kao drove a hard bargain at the Chungkuang-t'ang Conference for these and other principles he considered essential for Wang's independence of action, and it is little wonder that both Imai and Kagesa were exasperated with his obstinacy and found Mei easier to deal with. "If it had been left up to Kao alone," Imai wrote, "we would not have gotten together from the very beginning."*

The unsatisfactory response of Konoe and Hiranuma to Wang's defection only deepened Kao's convictions. He began to discuss with British authorities in Hong Kong the possibility of Wang defecting to the Crown Colony. When that proved fruitless, he did his utmost to discourage Wang from going to occupied China. Meanwhile, he made himself even more unpopular among the Japanese by suggesting that they cease their contacts with Wang. "I loved Wang and did not wish to see him become a Japanese puppet," Kao explains today. For that reason, he claims to have sent a cable to Kagesa begging him not to go to Hanoi

---

* Imai, *Shina jihen*, p. 78. Inukai too found Mei more tractable and prepared to allow "more than Kao would have." Inukai, *Yōsukō*, p. 94. There was, however, another reason for the profound Japanese distrust of Kao: the suspicion that he was behind various press leaks on Operation Watanabe. A certain Lieutenant Colonel Ichida, a secret agent stationed in Hong Kong (and operating under the unlikely cover of a mosquito-coil salesman), maintained that information he had conveyed to Kao in the strictest confidence kept appearing in the *Ta-kung pao*. Inukai, *ibid.*, p. 139. As we shall see, Kao was eventually responsible for a massive disclosure of secret information on the Wang movement to the Chinese press.

and containing the bluntest of admonitions: "You have enough puppets already. Leave my friend alone." Not surprisingly Kao was deeply distrusted thereafter. "They [the Japanese] did their best to keep me away from Wang after that," he recalls. "When I was in Nanking, I was known as the Number One pro-Japanese. Now I suddenly became known as the Number One anti-Japanese."[79]

The chief spokesman for the other faction in the Wang camp was Chou Fo-hai. His course, the one to which Wang was being drawn, was to establish a government under Japanese jurisdiction in the expectation that Japan's self-interest must surely lead her to grant concessions to the new regime. Chou felt that "it would have a great appeal to all practical-minded Chinese" if the Wang government could prove its usefulness by securing the return to Chinese owners of the businesses, factories, and homes the Japanese Army had taken over in one form or another. Obviously, such a demonstration of the "practical utility" of Wang's political program could be more easily arranged if the regime operated from within occupied China.[80]

In a lengthy conversation in Shanghai in April 1939, Nishi and Chou discussed the merits of the two courses.[81] Chou told Nishi that he had once hoped the Japanese Army would help Wang set up an independent regime in unoccupied China; but now, since that was apparently no longer an option, he felt there was nothing to do but set up a government in occupied Nanking and carry on the peace movement from there. When Nishi expressed astonishment that a "faithful advocate of Dr. Sun Yat-sen's *san-min chu-i*" like Chou should propose such a course of action, which was tantamount to a denial of Sun's principle of nationalism, Chou replied that Nishi was idealizing the Kao course, for however independent Kao wanted the Wang regime to be, when all was said and done, its establishment was predicated on the support of the Imperial Army. Consequently, Chou concluded, there was no essential difference between his plan and Kao's.

Chou's argument was difficult to refute, but Nishi was not prepared to concede the point. Insisting that the course Chou proposed would inevitably make Wang a "captive of the Japanese Army without any appeal to your people," he suggested that Chou urge Wang to abandon the idea of establishing a government and instead promote the peace movement and "enlighten your people with speeches." Chou replied that this had been Wang's intention until recently, and perhaps still was, but for himself, he was now convinced that simply promoting the peace effort was no longer sufficient. "I appreciate your concern about our becoming captives," Chou said, "but whether or not that happens will depend on the attitude of the Japanese. Should the Japanese Government view us as its captives, peace will be impossible no matter what any of us do." Nishi's final rejoinder in the debate was a reminder that "my comrades [in the peace movement] have been trying to change our Government's attitude into the kind of an attitude you hope for. Regrettably, however, we have been far from successful. . . . If the Japanese Government was as splendid as you seem to think it is, the Sino-Japanese problems would already have been solved."[82]

From this discussion, it is clear that the Japanese participants in the peace movement were also of two minds. Nishi Yoshiaki, one of the original organizers of the movement, was waiting for the *Hokkō-maru* to dock at Keelung. For more than a year the various members of the peace movement had been referred to in correspondence by code name, and Nishi felt honored when so distinguished a man as Wang deigned to address him familiarly by his secret name—Tarō. But Wang's eminence did not deter Nishi from speaking straightforwardly to him. As a minimum condition of peace Wang should demand that Japan return all of China south of the Great Wall without any strings attached, Nishi said. If Japan was really intent on building a New Order in East Asia and "eternal Sino-Japanese peace," she could not fail to agree to such a condition; if, however, she persisted in attaching provisos to such a promise, then "as a Japanese . . . I would hope that you would attack the Japanese Government rather than the Chungking Government."[83] When Wang did not reply to this candid advice, Nishi took his case to Kagesa.

Wang had risked his career and his life by leaving Chungking with no military power behind him, relying solely on Konoe to back his cause, Nishi told Kagesa. Given the present attitude of the Japanese Government, a "peace government" simply would not work. "It is inexcusable in such a situation merely to use this elder statesman [*genrō*] of China, Wang Ching-wei."[84] If Kagesa could do nothing to prevent Wang from being so manipulated, Nishi made it clear that he would wash his hands of the peace movement. Much as he would have liked to reassure Nishi, Kagesa, who shared not only Nishi's admiration of Wang but also his misgivings about the future of a Wang regime, was helpless—and more than a little envious of Nishi's freedom to do and say what he chose. Returning from their conversation, Kagesa wistfully remarked to Inukai: "I've just been bawled out, Ken. Wouldn't it be nice to be free like Nishi?"[85]

Wang's arrival in Shanghai on May 5 marked the end of the "innocent period" of the Wang movement. Though the rhetoric of the movement continued to stress the futility of resistance and the need for peace negotiations, the "shrewd people of Shanghai knew," as one of Wang's supporters writes, "that it was only the prelude to the establishment of a government in occupied territory." In the space of a "few days," more than five hundred of the "shrewd people" reported for secret interviews at the Shanghai office of Chou Fo-hai, who began to recruit the bureaucratic talent necessary to transform the peace movement into a government. Increasingly, the primary goal of the Wang movement, whatever its rhetoric and whatever the intentions of its leader, came to be the acquisition of power.[86]

Inevitably this transition brought disillusion to those like Nishi who had been the original supporters of the Wang movement. They had regarded themselves as a third force, speaking for neither the Chinese Government nor the Japanese Government but rather for supranational Pan-Asian goals, the first of which was the realization of peace. If they did not clearly articulate their goals, they nevertheless felt, as Nishi later wrote, that the "one absolute condition for the achievement of Sino-Japanese peace was Japan's abandonment of her imperialist policies."[87] To Nishi in April 1939, Japan's treatment of Wang indicated that she was intensifying rather than abandoning her imperialist policies, and that Wang was embarking on a hopelessly doomed course of collaboration.

CHAPTER TWELVE

Discussing the Terms of Collaboration, April-September 1939

IN THE TEN months after Wang arrived in Shanghai, that is, from May 1939 until the establishment of his Reorganized National Government in March 1940, he was faced with two monumental tasks. The first was to convince Japanese authorities that it was in their interest to grant him an honorable peace settlement, one that would give viability to his new regime. The second task was to build support for his program in occupied China. The two tasks were closely related, for success in one would give him leverage with which to achieve success in the other.

Wang's principal ally in the first effort was a small group of China experts (Shina-tsū) who worked out of a Shanghai building known to the Japanese as the Plum Blossom Mansion (Baikadō). The group possessed little in the way of a formal or legal mandate, and so had no official name. Detractors who wished to emphasize that the group was dominated by Colonel Kagesa referred to it as the Kagesa Agency, but the most commonly accepted name was the Plum Blossom Agency (Ume Kikan).[1] The informal existence of the agency continued until Wang's regime was established, at which time two of its most important members, Kagesa and Inukai Ken, became the chief advisers, military and civilian, respectively, to the Wang Government. The close association between the Wang Government and Kagesa prompted—and to some extent justified—charges that Kagesa regarded the Wang operation as his private preserve.

Kagesa stated the purpose of the Plum Blossom Agency in wholly negative terms: "to see that the Wang Government was not a puppet of Japan."[2] Kagesa was distressed that some of his Army colleagues viewed the agency as just another Tokumu-bu, whose functions were precisely the creation and management of puppets.[3] He rejected and deplored both the one-sided purposes and the underhanded tactics of the Toku-mu-bu; and took pride in earning the respect of Wang, whom he came to admire greatly. I have found no reason to doubt the universal judgment of his former associates that Kagesa was an eminently honest officer who was determined to justify Wang's trust in him. Kagesa's openness with Wang extended to at least one unauthorized disclosure of secret state papers to Wang's followers, an act that earned him much criticism in the Army General Staff. But from his memoirs it is clear that he felt his role as a loyal officer of the Emperor was completely compatible with his attempts to secure for Wang the best peace terms Japan could reasonably offer. In his view, he was acting not only in the best tradition of Japan's warrior code, which compelled the victor to be honest and even generous in dealing with his foe, but also in the best interests of Japan over the long haul.

Though clearly dominated by Kagesa, the Agency included other Army officers as well as representatives of the Navy, the Foreign Ministry, and the Kōain. A number of private citizens, especially journalists and educators, also belonged to it. Its second-most-important member, Inukai Ken, though formally attached to the Kōain for administrative purposes, participated in an almost private capacity.* The other civilians, as men of considerable influence in the public media, were expected to defend Wang (in the press, for example) from "slanderous charges" put forth by Chungking agents and later by the inevitable hordes of disappointed job seekers.[4]

Kagesa stresses that the members of the Plum Blossom Agency accepted his authority "spontaneously." This seems to have been the case, for though he legally had authority only over the other Army officers, the rest of the Government members apparently followed his lead except in the few instances when they received direct orders from their parent organizations.[5] The only time this division of authority precipitated a crisis was in late 1939, when the Navy demanded that its representative, Adm. Suga Hikojirō, be allowed to negotiate independently with the Wang group on matters it considered vital to its own interests. In all other respects the Plum Blossom Agency appears to have functioned harmoniously and with a single purpose—the one assigned to it by Colonel Kagesa.

But if there was harmony within the agency, there was no harmony within Japanese officialdom as a whole. On the contrary, Kagesa and his China experts encountered an enormous tide of opposition to Wang from several quarters of the Government. Skepticism and uncertainty

---

* Inukai's service to the agency seems to have been poorly—if at all—recompensed by the paymaster. Consequently, he found it necessary to sell off part of his family's collection of Yüan dynasty scrolls to finance his work in China. Konoe helped him find a buyer for the valuable heirlooms. Inukai, *Yōsukō*, p. 204.

about Wang's intentions were at the root of much of this opposition. Even after the rift between Wang and Chungking had grown measurably deeper as a result of the assassination of Tseng, many in Japan continued to believe that Wang and Chiang were acting in collusion. Colonel Kagesa himself was not only inclined to that view, but declared later that he had hoped such was indeed the case, for though their collusion required special caution on Japan's part, Wang would be that much better a bridge between Tokyo and Chungking.[6]

The Kōain was too big and diverse by the spring of 1939 to have a unified point of view. Maj. Gen. Suzuki Teiichi, Chief of the Kōain's powerful Political Affairs Section, is credited with "initiating moves to silence those who were against the establishment of Wang's regime."[7] In general, however, the Kōain appears to have been cool to the idea of cooperating with Wang and unwilling to grant him any better terms than those offered to Japan's other mainland puppets. Kagesa and Inukai both testify to the "obstruction" the Plum Blossom Agency faced in the Kōain; others have characterized the Kōain's reaction in even stronger terms.[8] The greatest opposition to Wang came from the Kōain officers in the mainland liaison offices. Lt. Gen. Kita Seiichi, the director of the Peiping office, sponsor and protector of Wang K'o-min, was openly hostile to Wang Ching-wei, and was capable of turning his feelings into obstructive tactics and procrastination that did much to harm Wang's cause in 1939. It is probably more than coincidence that Kita was removed from his Peiping post just one month before the Wang Ching-wei regime was finally established.

In addition to the Kōain's opposition to Wang, most general officers in the Army were either indifferent or opposed to his cause. Nishi lays this to their "lack of a political sense" and contends that the military just did not know what to do with Wang and his peace proposals.[9] But that answer is far too simple. For instance, the opposition of Maj. Gen. Okamura Yasuji, Commander-in-Chief of the Eleventh Army in occupation at Hankow, was grounded in an acute political sense. The *aite ni sezu* declaration was becoming "more and more of an obstacle to a settlement of the war every day," he wrote in March 1939. The war could be settled only by dealing with Chungking, he felt, and it was a "midday dream" to presume that a "temporary" government like Wang's would have any fruitful effect on Chungking. "The effect might well be the opposite," Okamura feared.[10]

Even among those who supported Wang in the spring of 1939 there was a strong tendency toward a wait-and-see attitude. Wang might prove useful, but only if he could show a sufficient base of support to accomplish one of two purposes: to coerce Chungking into accepting Japanese peace terms or to establish a new regime that had a good chance of isolating the Chungking regime until it was no longer a significant force. Many of those who hoped Wang could accomplish the second goal saw Chungking as beset by an unmanageable amount of factional strife and tension on which Wang could usefully capitalize.

It must be stressed, however, that there was not much optimism among the General Staff strategists about a weakening of Chungking's determination to continue resistance. The most careful General Staff appraisals of the National Government in the spring of 1939 drew conclusions about its fighting strength and morale that were wholly at odds with the cavalier dismissals of the Chiang regime in official statements intended for public consumption. The frequent mention in General Staff studies of the likelihood of a "ten-year war" attests that the Army was far from convinced of its own propagandistic downgrading of Chiang as an insignificant local warlord. It is not surprising that even those in the Army who wished Wang well were skeptical of the value of any solution worked out with him alone. Many of them were convinced that a meaningful solution to the war absolutely depended on an agreement involving the Chungking regime, more or less sharing Konoe's view that Wang's value was to be measured by his willingness to act as a bridge between Tokyo and Chungking.

The support Wang was receiving at this time from the East Asia Bureau of the Foreign Office must also be regarded as less than wholehearted. Though the Foreign Office was hinting both at home and abroad that it was "Japan's resolute intention to recognize a new central regime under Wang at the appropriate time," it seems likely these statements were, as the historian Usui has observed, not so much an endorsement of Wang as an "effort to pressure the Powers into breaking off their aid to Chiang."[11]

Aware of the tenuousness of his support, Wang made a trip to Tokyo the first order of business after his arrival in Shanghai in May 1939. The Five Ministers obliged by extending him an invitation on May 12, and on June 2 he arrved in Tokyo with a small entourage, including Chou Fo-hai and Kao Tsung-wu.

Wang's request for high-level meetings in Tokyo created a climate of urgency in the War Ministry and General Staff in late May and early June. In an effort to resolve the controversy over Wang and to settle on a single workable policy, front-line commanders were called back for a series of briefings and consultations; their views having been aired, a

Five Ministers' Conference was then held on June 6, several days after Wang's arrival in Tokyo. Out of the Ministers' deliberations emerged the first comprehensive policy statement on China since Wang's defection from Chungking a half year earlier. Had Wang known the details of that policy or the extent of skepticism and indifference to his cause— some say Premier Hiranuma did not even know Wang had been invited to Tokyo—his trust in Japan would surely have been badly shaken.[12] The cordial, albeit noncommittal, reception he received in the offices of the Five Ministers in the second week in June was in sharp contrast to the harsh policy these same men had just hammered out at their meeting of the sixth.

The basic decision of the Five Ministers' Conference of June 6 was that Wang Ching-wei would be only one of the "constituent elements" of any new central government created in China. Wu P'ei-fu and the leaders of the existing regimes would have to be included. The Chungking Government would also be eligible to become a constituent element, provided it "changed its mind and reformed"; by reform was meant the abandonment of an anti-Japanese and pro-Communist policy.[13]

The Five Ministers thus did not anticipate any immediate, hasty creation of a new regime. There was much preparatory work to be completed, and during that period Wang would have to prove his usefulness by "winning over various powerful forces within the Chungking Government, and above all by winning over eminent persons within that Government."[14] Further, he would have to establish a basic pool of influence of his own, raise funds, and recruit and fully equip an army. Japan would "restrict as much as possible its outward interference" in such preparatory projects. Details of form and schedule would be settled later after consultation with Japan. The Ministers made it clear that they were giving no blanket endorsement to the idea of a new regime. They wanted time to assess the "development of the preparatory projects, especially the extent to which [Wang] can develop personnel resources [*jinteki yōso*] and fundamental power."[15]

Beyond all this, the Ministers set out in detail the *quid pro quo* for any Wang regime. First, Wang would have to agree that the "future political system of China shall conform to the principle of *bunji gassaku*," to accept, in a word, limitations on the authority of the central government. In Inner Mongolia, an "especially intensive anti-Communist zone," the central government would have no more than nominal authority. The same was true in the case of North China, which "in view of national defense and economic considerations will be made into a Sino-Japanese zone of intensive consolidation [*NisShi kyōdō ketsugō chitai*]." For purely economic reasons, the "lower reaches of the Yangtze" would also be a zone of "consolidation." As a final condition, reflecting the Imperial Navy's increased emphasis on strategic planning for an "advance to the south" and confrontation with Great Britain and the United States, Wang would have to grant Japan a "special position" in "specified islands along the South China coast."[16]

Plainly, the demands that had been set forth at the November 30, 1938, Imperial Conference had hardened (and even expanded; witness the demand for a special Japanese position along the South China coast). Neither the hardships of the prolonged war nor the patently unsatisfactory puppet regimes nor the evidence of a growing Chinese commitment to resistance had served to create any pliancy in the Japanese bargaining stance. Exactly how inflexible this position was can be seen in the "remarks" the Ministers appended to the policy statement of June 6. Orders were issued to give Wang "the impression of a bright future and Japan's complete sincerity by allowing him to carry out his wishes on [inconsequential] matters." However, on all important matters, Japan's policy was to remain absolutely unchanged, and Wang must be compelled to accept that policy in all its essentials.[17]

For the time being, Wang was to be kept in the dark about the precise demands Japan would make on him. The Ministers resolved that in their meetings with Wang, they would not discuss any controversial or divisive issues or "enter into a careful scrutiny of details," but instead would emphasize their confidence about the establishment of the New Order in East Asia and their determination to reach a just and generous settlement of the China Incident.[18] Four of the Ministers held fast to this resolution; the fifth, War Minister Itagaki, alone offered Wang something more than vague assurances of Japanese support and lavish praise for his patriotism and daring.

THE WANG-ITAGAKI TALKS

In both public and private declarations since the Marco Polo Bridge Incident Japan had declared that she had no intention of interfering in the internal affairs of China. Yet it was universally recognized that her adviser system constituted a massive interference in Chinese internal affairs. In two conversations with Itagaki, on June 11 and June 15, Wang was warned that he could expect this system to continue.

Itagaki took note of the written proposals Wang had submitted on May 28, just before his departure for Tokyo, in which he had outlined the type of government he proposed to establish and, indirectly, the kind of cooperation he sought from Japan.[19] After paying tribute to the

Provisional and Reformed Governments and predicting a glorious page for them in history, he had made it clear that he wanted them to be consigned to history as soon as possible. There could not be two governments in one China, his note declared; therefore it would be "appropriate" for the two puppet governments to declare their own dissolution "spontaneously" on the creation of his government.

Itagaki's analysis of this proposal must have been jarring to Wang, whose conversations with the other Ministers had led him to expect at least vaguely reassuring responses. It was Japan's understanding, Itagaki said, that the "designation of the Provisional and Reformed Governments *as governments* was to be discontinued" at the appropriate time. Japan, however, did not intend to allow the "substance and fact" of the two regimes to be eliminated.[20]

Wang was appalled. Since the beginning of the war he had been telling the Chinese people a peace settlement with Japan was possible provided she agreed to terms that would not jeopardize China's sovereignty. Konoe's speech of December 22 had appeared to respect China's sovereignty, and thus to offer China a way out of the war. Now, in this, his first opportunity since December 22 to discuss Konoe's abstractions in concrete terms with a Cabinet member, he learned that it was Japan's intention to preserve the substance of the hated puppet regimes she had established on the mainland. The depth of Wang's disillusion is not difficult to imagine. "In the final analysis, then, are you not talking about [Chinese] sovereignty?" Wang asked Itagaki.

Itagaki conceded that there were questions of sovereignty involved, but suggested that the whole problem might better be termed one of "political organization." He then launched into a lecture on the principle of *bunji gassaku*. Different parts of China had "special characteristics" and special significances to Japan. There were "zones that would have to be associated most closely" with Japan in the future, he said, giving Wang a nearly verbatim rendition of the *bunji gassaku* section of the Five Ministers' decision of June 6. But he carried their discussions one step further, concluding that Japan's special interests in certain parts of China made it "necessary to preserve by some sort of organization the relationships that had sprung up between Japan and the Reformed and Provisional Governments." That being the case, he told Wang, "it is my wish that you respect the substance and reality of the existing [puppet] governments."[21]

In reply Wang said that he was prepared to absorb certain elements of the two puppet regimes into a new central government, but that if Japan tried to reserve any significant degree of sovereignty to those regimes, he would have no part in the creation of a new government. He insisted that a meaningful agreement with Japan depended on the existence of a truly sovereign, united, central government in China. This was precisely what those who were committed to *bunji gassaku* did not believe, and Itagaki was firmly in that camp; he did not relent. What he had in mind, he said, was the establishment of a "political committee" with autonomous powers in North China in order to strengthen Sino-Japanese relations in that area.

Wang conceded that there were historical precedents for such a committee but pointed out that all previous measures of the sort had been viewed as temporary expedients, dictated by the lack of a strong central government. If Japan intended to leave real power vested in the puppet regimes (or successor institutions, such as the "political committee for North China"), the new regime would plainly be a sovereign central government in name only. The inevitable result would be civil turmoil in China, a struggle for jurisdiction and authority between the central regime and the regional regimes. Such a situation would be detrimental not only to China but ultimately to Japan as well, Wang declared, for he would have no chance of solving Sino-Japanese problems in the context of a divided China. If Japan was determined to leave real power in the hands of her puppet institutions, he could come to only one conclusion: that the best course was to postpone the creation of a new regime.

It is difficult to avoid the judgment that Wang's conclusion—or rather threat—was eminently correct, and that his name would be held in higher esteem today if he had remained firm. At this point in the conversation, however, another voice was heard. Colonel Kagesa, who sat in on the three-hour conference between Wang and Itagaki on June 15, intervened, urging Wang to reconsider. How could Wang have asserted earlier that the creation of a new central regime was necessary to the "solution of the situation" and now talk of a postponement? Was he going to put forth a new plan? How could he hope to acquire sufficient stature and authority to pressure the Chungking regime unless he helped to organize a new government? The institution of a new regime was of the "utmost urgency," Kagesa declared, assuring Wang that the question of jurisdiction and sovereignty was surely susceptible to solution with further study.[22]

Itagaki seconded Kagesa's assurances, but with certain "clarifications." He was not proposing that the present regimes be granted real sovereignty, he said. But at the same time Wang would have to recognize and accept the "various existing realities" in China that had arisen as the war had spread throughout the country, for instance, the "organs for regional economic development" (i.e., the giant holding companies discussed earlier). Itagaki's "assurances" were hardly reassuring for Wang, once he learned he was expected to consent to such "existing realities." What Itagaki was bluntly saying was that there could be no turning back of the clock, that Japan was not willing to yield the spoils of war. The Japanese vision of an autonomous North China was fixed and immutable.

In the end Itagaki wrung a concession from Wang that essentially emasculated his regime before it was even established: he agreed to the creation of an "administrative council" for North China with a "relatively large degree of autonomy." In return he asked that there be no infringement on the rights of his regime in Central China; Wang emphasized that he was talking about economic as well as political rights. Itagaki nodded *"kekkō desu"* (that's fine) in assent.[23] At this point the War Minister's candor seems to have left him, for he had helped adopt a policy only nine days before (at the June 6 Five Ministers' Conference) that ruled out an honest acquiescence to Wang's compromise proposal.

Before the fateful Wang-Itagaki talks had concluded, Wang gave his assent (or at least offered no serious objections) to several other of Itagaki's demands. He agreed that Chinese recognition of Manchukuo was necessary. He was sympathetic to Itagaki's complaint about Sun's *san-min chu-i*, which were "viewed as a menace in Japan," and agreed to take steps to clarify the Three Principles, especially the troubling principle of *min-sheng chu-i* (people's livelihood), which many Japanese identified with communism. Finally, he agreed to disavow the principle of "one government—one party" and to guarantee access to government positions to men outside the Kuomintang. Itagaki was entirely correct in his presumption that Wang and his colleagues, if left to their own political instincts, would attempt to "reorganize" the Kuomintang in Shanghai and grant the "reorganized and orthodox" party a virtual monopoly on governmental position and power. This was unacceptable to the Imperial Army, which demanded that Wang broaden the channels to political power and "democratize" the Party. There is no evidence that the Imperial Army felt uncomfortable in its unusual role as a champion of democracy, for its purpose was simply to guarantee positions of power in China to its own puppets, especially those in the North China regime.

Still and all, Wang's agreement to disavow the principle of "one government—one party" was little more than a formal concession, for he persisted in regarding the work of establishing a new government as the task of the Kuomintang. Increasingly this meant that he was forced to profess his belief in a number of myths. His tiny band of followers in

Shanghai, according to one of the myths, was the Orthodox Kuomintang, the guardian of Sun's Three Principles, which were being ignored and perverted by the opportunists in Chungking. This led to another myth: that the government the Orthodox Kuomintang proposed to establish on October 10, 1939 (the anniversary of the Revolution of 1911) would not be a new government but a return of the true government to its proper seat of authority. After the "return to the capital" (*huan-tu*) everything would be the same as before. The five-yüan structure of government would be preserved, and the title of President of the National Government would be reserved for the venerable Lin Sen, who had held that largely ceremonial post since 1931. Of great symbolic importance to Wang was the choice of the national flag: he insisted on using the blue sky and white sun emblem of the National Government. Though it is problematical that the Japanese authorities and Wang were even agreed on the establishment of a new regime at the time of Wang's June 1939 trip to Tokyo, the choice of a national flag became a major bone of contention during that trip—and for long after.[24]

Japan argued for the resurrection of the five-barred flag of the early Republic (and then in use by the North China puppet regime) on the grounds that disastrous errors were sure to occur if the armies of both the National Government and the new Wang government used the same flag; confused Japanese soldiers were almost certain to fire on friendly troops on occasion.

But Wang refused to accede to the wishes of the Japanese, both out of loyalty to Sun Yat-sen, who had pressed for the blue sky and white sun flag (a red field was added later) as a national emblem even before the Revolution of 1911, and out of his own desire to give the trappings of legitimacy to his regime. To the annoyance of the Japanese, the blue sky flag flew over Chinese residences in the International Settlement in Shanghai—including Wang's—after Wang's arrival there in the spring of 1939.

In Tokyo, the deadlock over the flag was finally resolved when the Japanese proposed a compromise. Wang could keep the disputed flag if he would agree to fly it below a triangular yellow pennant bearing the words "peace and national reconstruction" (*ho-p'ing, chien-kuo*) to distinguish it from the flag used by Chungking. (It was later decided to add "anticommunism" to the slogan on the pennant; thus: *fan-kung, ho-p'ing, chien-kuo.*) Wang and his colleagues resented the "strange looking compromise"—Chou Fo-hai commented that the pennant resembled a "pig's tail"—but finally accepted the Japanese solution in principle.[25] The Chinese appreciated that Japan would have difficulty enforcing the use of the pennant; as Chou pointed out to Inukai, it would be attached with cords that could easily be untied. In the months that followed, there were numerous irritations over flag protocol—to which both sides contributed their fair share, the Chinese by carrying out Chou's threat and flying their flag without the hated pennant, the Japanese by permitting puppet institutions like the Hsin-min Hui to continue flying the five-barred flag.

In many ways, and certainly during Wang's initial meeting with the Tokyo authorities, all of the resentment over Japanese interference in Chinese affairs was distilled down into this one issue. Indeed, it was only after Chou threatened to break off negotiations if Japan persisted in demanding the adoption of the five-barred flag that the Japanese offered their compromise. Chou was far from satisfied with the final agreement. "I'm going to have a hard time trying to answer my children when they ask me why the flag has been changed," he told Inukai.[26] Nothing, with the possible exception of Japan's attempts to tamper with Sun's Three Principles and reinterpret them to her own satisfaction, so aroused the patriotic indignation of both Wang and Chou as the flag issue. Wang's constant appeals to Japan for a reconsideration of her stand fell on deaf ears until 1943, when she finally dropped her demands on the despised pennant after four years of bitter contention.

The Wang trip to Tokyo generated a fresh round of acrimony in the Wang movement and widened the gulf between the Kao and Chou camps. Earlier, when Wang had summoned all of his followers to Shanghai to discuss the merits of such a trip,[27] Ch'en Kung-po, still in Hong Kong, had refused to join the parley. He had, however, sent a colleague, Ho Ping-hsien, to represent him. Ho and Chou Fo-hai had clashed at the meeting, with Chou arguing that there would be no "security" for the Wang movement until a government was established, and Ho arguing that any further participation in negotiations with the Japanese would divide the party and the country and blemish the "glorious revolutionary career" of Wang Ching-wei. Kao had also counseled Wang against the trip to Tokyo.

Wang, as we have seen, decided to go, rejecting the counsel of Kao and Ch'en Kung-po, his most trusted adviser. Both men then had to decide whether to accompany Wang on a mission that seemed to be fraught with hazard. After much painful deliberation, Kao decided to do so. "As a friend, it was not right to leave him," Kao recalls.[28] Ch'en, however, refused to make the trip and remained in neutral Hong Kong for another half-year before finally, and reluctantly, joining Wang—apparently swallowing his misgivings out of friendship and loyalty.

In Tokyo Kao was literally pushed into the background by the Japanese authorities, who resented the cautionary advice he was giving Wang. The "troublemaker" was not housed with the main body of the Wang entourage in the Tokyo suburb of Ōji, but instead was given quarters in Asakusa, several miles distant. The separation may have had something to do with the fact that Kao was recuperating from a flareup of tuberculosis, but he and Inukai both believe that he was deliberately isolated from Wang and in fact was earmarked for death by poisoning. Inukai was evidently responsible for saving Kao from that fate, but the scare did not serve to lessen Kao's growing suspicion of his Japanese hosts.[29]

If Wang learned anything at all in Tokyo, it was that the one great abiding principle of Japan's puppet politics was the principle of *bunji gassaku*. The Army representatives "indirectly" suggested to him that he would do well to visit Wang K'o-min, Liang Hung-chih, and Wu P'ei-fu on his way back to Shanghai, and he agreed to do so; if Japan would sponsor a new regime only on condition that it be a loose federation in which these men had a role, then it obviously behooved Wang to improve his relations with them.[30] Accordingly, three days after the conclusion of his talks with Itagaki, Wang left Tokyo bound for North China.

Wang's trip to North China was even more discomfiting than his Japanese trip had been. Though Wu had been in correspondence with Wang and had seemed sympathetic to his cause, he refused to see Wang. The Kōain, which had just appropriated an enormous ¥10,000,000 purse to finance the Wu Operation, was either unwilling or unable to induce Wu to talk with Wang. Like everyone else, Wu had been uncertain about Wang's defection and Chiang's complicity in it; he may have still had serious doubts.[31] Or he may have rebuffed Wang (as Wang later claimed) because he wished to be President of the new regime, an office that Wang insisted on holding for Lin Sen.[32]

The conversations Wang held with the North China puppets merely served to underscore the difficulties he could expect in a coalition with them. The talks with Wang K'o-min were especially unproductive. The two Wangs had little affection for each other. Wang Ching-wei was sharply critical of the ineffective Hsin-min Hui program to which Wang K'o-min had tied his regime; it could not counteract or placate the Peiping students, to say nothing of the Chinese Communists, Wang insisted.[33] The Wang-Wang talks were held in the presence of Wang K'o-min's principal supporters in the Imperial Army, including General Kita. With that backing and in defiance of Tokyo's wish that the Provisional Government cooperate with Wang Ching-wei, the North China puppet not only refused to support Wang, but declared that he would not participate in any regime Wang established. Once Wang Ching-wei had departed, Wang K'o-min held a press conference to announce that the Provisional Government would not support any of Wang Ching-wei's ventures,[34] thus confirming the public's suspicion that the two Wangs did not get on well together.

Japanese officials did not participate in the Wang-Liang talks, which, though apparently somewhat more amicable than the Wang-Wang talks, did not increase Wang's optimism about the prospects of coalition. From the tone of Liang's remarks, and those of his Minister of the Interior, Ch'en Ch'ün, a Kuomintang veteran, it is clear both men felt Wang Ching-wei was in collusion with Chiang. Both were anxious to convince Wang that they had not attacked the Generalissimo: had they not sent emissaries to Hankow in 1938 to clear the establishment of the Reformed Government, to assure Chiang that the new regime was purely a "temporary measure," and to let him know that everyone would "rejoice when the situation permitted [his] return to Nanking?"[35]

As noted, in 1931, at the height of internecine quarrels in the Kuomintang, Wang Ching-wei had established a short-lived separatist government in Canton with the support of the armies of Gen. Chang Fa-k'uei. In July–August 1939, after his series of unpromising talks in Tokyo, Peiping, and Nanking, Wang made a desperate attempt to renew the autonomy experiment in Canton. He and his Japanese supporters in the venture calculated that success there might enable him to sidestep some of the problems involved in collaboration with the other puppets.

It is not clear who put forth the idea in the first place, Wang or the Japanese. The Japanese authorities at the Center appear to have had no hand in creating or backing the plan. Judging by the reports Consul-General Okazaki Katsuo forwarded from Canton, the Japanese Foreign Ministry was completely in the dark.[36] Certainly the plan bore no resemblance to the Five Ministers' program of June 6, which called for a new central government based on the collaboration of Wang, Wu, and the existing regimes.

Just as the puppet regimes in North and Central China were supported by the Area Armies in their respective regions, the South China regime was to receive its principal—perhaps its only—support from the South China Expeditionary Army under the command of Lt. Gen. Andō Rikichi. Though the full role of the Plum Blossom Agency in this venture is not known, some of its members certainly attended the meetings between Wang and the South China Army officials.[37] By early August the Chinese and Japanese representatives had agreed to install a government in Canton. It was to embrace five southern and southwestern provinces and to have more authority and power than the other Chinese regimes. The South China Army, for example, planned to give Wang jurisdiction in police and security matters as well as political and economic affairs.[38] The expectation was that the regime eventually would expand into a central government for all of China. Few other particulars of the project are known; more than likely it was hastily contrived, with little attention to detail or long-range planning.

Wang traveled to his birthplace, Canton, to make a personal appeal for support. In a radio broadcast on August 9, "overwhelmed with emotion and enthusiasm," he blamed Chiang for the "haphazard sacrifices and unnecessary sufferings" of the people of Canton during the brief defense of the city some ten months before. Not only was it futile for China to continue to heed Chiang's "high-sounding words of continuing resistance" in the absence of a military force capable of defeating Japan, Wang insisted, but in the end resistance could only profit the Communists. They had "no sense of nationality" but took their orders from the Third International, which was anxious to see China's true nationalists (as well as the Japanese imperialists) exhaust themselves in combat. If China somehow won the protracted struggle with Japan, it would be the Communists who would claim the fruits of victory, and the first thing they would do would be to wreak their vengeance on their erstwhile allies.[39] This theme, that only the Communists stood to gain by a long and costly war, was repeatedly stressed by Wang and is regarded by his admirers as evidence of his political acuity and accurate reading of the future.[40]

Wang's public appeal for support was directed more to the warlord generals and their sizable armies (especially his old ally and fellow Cantonese Chang Fa-k'uei) than to the citizenry at large. In his radio address and in less open appeals Wang promised that he had already made arrangements with General Andō, and that the Chinese troops had only to support his peace proposals to achieve a just peace. In effect, if Chang and his fellow generals would surrender, their armies would not be disbanded, and they and their troops would be allowed to join Wang in governing South China. "Canton will be given back to the Cantonese," Wang promised.[41]

Wang's appeals were to no avail. The long-anticipated, or at any rate the long-hinted-at, support from the supposedly wavering generals did not materialize. By late August it was evident to Wang and the South China Army that Wang was not going to receive military assistance from

Chang Fa-k'uei, and the South China autonomous movement was quietly dropped from consideration. Shimizu Tōzō, a Foreign Ministry China specialist attached to the Plum Blossom Agency who was with Wang during his swing through South China, vividly recalls the poor reception Wang's radio appeal had.[42] Discouraged with the failure in the south, Wang returned to Shanghai and plunged into a new effort to build public support.

On August 28 Wang convened a gathering of supposed Kuomintang supporters. The meeting, heralded for several weeks by Wang's press agents as the Sixth Kuomintang Congress, proved to be one more dismal failure in an ill-starred summer of failures.

In private Wang had been emphasizing the discontent among Kuomintang leaders in Chungking and predicting that many would join his cause. He had assured Wang K'o-min, for example, that many comrades from Chungking would be among the 300 representatives expected at the Congress, and that many others, including Ch'en Li-fu of the CC Clique and Minister of War Ho Ying-ch'in, were anxious to defect but might have some difficulty in doing so. In an extravagantly optimistic estimate, Wang told the North China collaborator that from two-fifths to three-fifths of the Kuomintang troops (including those of Chang Fa-k'uei) would soon join his cause. When none of this support materialized, Wang's prestige fell sharply and his bargaining power with both Japan and the other puppets was badly crippled.

As it turned out, only 240 "representatives" of the Kuomintang participated in the creation of the "Orthodox Kuomintang" at the rump Sixth Congress. Indeed, even that disappointing figure would not have been achieved if the rolls had not been padded with the baldest kind of opportunists. One of Wang's most ardent apologists, Chin Hsiung-pai, confesses his anxiety at attending a meeting packed with "people who had no connection with Wang, people who were only yesterday shouting resistance."[43] (For that matter, Chin himself had dubious credentials; though appointed as the representative of two districts, he was not even a member of the Kuomintang.) No amount of press agentry could conceal the farcical character of the Sixth Congress; it was correctly interpreted by most observers as a rubber-stamp device for Japanese demands, even though the Japanese (or more precisely, Kagesa) respected Wang's wishes that they not interfere in the deliberations of the Congress. In fact, there were few deliberations in the scant, five-hour-long Congress, which in effect ratified the Japanese demand for a broadened (that is, extra-Kuomintang) base to the new government. Kagesa did not need to send observers or advisers to ensure that the Congress understood and complied with this demand, for as we have seen, Wang had already bowed to it some two months earlier, in his talks with Itagaki in June.

To satisfy the Japanese, Wang (and the Congress) expanded the Party's guiding organ, the Central Political Council, to include not only Kuomintang members but other "persons of outstanding virtue and great wisdom." The Congress "Manifesto" declared that the Central Political Council was to be the "highest political organ in the country" during a period of "tutelage," which would end only after the war was over.[44] The role of the Central Political Council was thus the same in the Orthodox Kuomintang and the original Kuomintang; the important difference was that the new Council would be more in keeping with the second of Sun's Principles, *min-ch'üan chu-i* (democracy) than the Chiang-led organ. Or at least in theory; to no one's real surprise, most of the virtuous and wise persons who were eventually appointed to the Central Political Council were leading figures in the Reformed and Provisional Governments.

Wang secured the Congress's approval for this measure only at the expense of considerable rancor on the part of his Kuomintang colleagues, many of whom despised the leaders of the puppet regimes. On the eve of the Congress a delegation of Orthodox Kuomintang stalwarts pleaded —in tears according to one report—that Wang dissociate himself from the "running dogs" in the existing regimes.[45] (They seem not to have felt any sense of irony in their denunciation of Liang Hung-chih and others as traitors undeserving of affiliation with the Orthodox Kuomintang in the tasks that lay ahead.) Politics was making profoundly disagreeable bedfellows out of the old puppets and the new pretenders to power. Even Wang's closest supporters conceded that much of the tension between the two groups could be laid to the haughty arrogance of Wang and his followers. As one of them, the Foreign Ministry's Ōta Ichirō, noted perplexedly, "It is impossible to understand the brash behavior of Wang and especially Wang's young lieutenants toward Wang [K'o-min] and Liang."[46]

Three weeks after the Congress closed, Wang asked Wang K'o-min and Liang Hung-chih to meet with him in Nanking in the hope of reaching an understanding on two issues: the composition and functions of the Central Political Council and the relationship of North China to the new regime. Some progress was made on the first matter. The puppet leaders agreed that Wang Ching-wei could be the Chairman of the Council and could appoint all of its members, and he in turn granted a slightly larger representation to the Reformed and Provisional Governments than he had wished.

Apart from this, however, there was little agreement at the conference.

Wang K'o-min and Liang refused outright to discuss any substantive questions on the grounds that they lacked competence and authority; nothing could be resolved, they stated, until they consulted with their respective advisers, Generals Kita and Harada, both of whom were known to be unwilling to make important concessions to Wang Ching-wei.[47] When the meetings adjourned on September 20, Wang K'o-min publicly acknowledged his gratitude for Wang Ching-wei's complimentary remarks and then artfully held them out as a justification for the continuation of North Chinese separatism and autonomy. "We are impressed by Mr. Wang Ching-wei's statement for peace," Wang K'o-min declared, "because he paid tribute to the members of this [Provisional] Government for what it has done in the past. . . . If what we have done is of benefit to the general state of affairs and the livelihood of the people, *we expect to proceed with our original intention* and attain success."[48]

T'ao Hsi-sheng and Mei Ssu-p'ing accompanied Wang to the Nanking discussions, and T'ao writes with grim irony of the Japanese Army's "protection" of the three Chinese "leaders": the streets lined with Imperial Army sentries, their motorcycle escorts by the Japanese military police, and the like. T'ao and Mei looked on the Wang-Wang-Liang discussions as a kind of mahjong game in which the players never decided on the strategy. Instead, the decisions were made by the Japanese officers (Kita, Harada, Kagesa) reaching from behind, over the shoulders of the players. Once back in Shanghai, T'ao says, "nobody liked to mention that trip." "We all felt gloomy, insulted, ashamed, and contrite."[49]

The October 1939 issue of the Tokyo journal *Chūō kōron* (Central Review), which appeared at the time of the Nanking meeting, carried an article by Wang Ching-wei in which his acute displeasure with Japan comes through all too plainly.[50] It was not yet clear, he wrote, what Japan's New Order in East Asia would mean in concrete terms. It promised to provide East Asia with the means for delivering itself from the twin enemies of Western "aggressionism" (*shinryaku shugi*) and communism. There was no question that China needed help. And just as certainly Japan, which had so successfully warded off the two evils, was capable of helping. If his Japanese readers were puzzled, then, about China's notable lack of enthusiasm for Japan's aid, he could explain it. The simple truth was, many Chinese feared Japan even more than they feared Western imperialism and communism. For them, Japan was not just another brutal force with which China had to contend; she was a "brute among brutes."

How could Japan hope to interest the Chinese in the reconstruction of East Asia, Wang asked, when her behavior forced them to contemplate the possible destruction of their own homeland? He suggested that the Japanese recall the case of the Chinese Emperor of antiquity who was mystified when a courtier defined a lean year as one in which the supply of cereals was insufficient to feed the population. Why could the people not eat meat in such circumstances? he wondered. Surely the Japanese could see, Wang hoped, that "the Chinese fear of national destruction is comparable to a lack of cereals for food, and the proposal to reconstruct East Asia no different from talk about eating meat."

CHAPTER THIRTEEN

"Everything from the Earth to the Sky"

KAGESA succeeded in returning Wang to the Sino-Japanese political stage after escorting him from Hanoi to Shanghai. But after five months of rehearsals no one could say when or indeed if the performance would begin. No one could even predict whether Wang would have the leading role. His drawing ability was being questioned by many in Japan, and Wu P'ei-fu and others were waiting in the wings. As a result, Wang's disillusion about the prospects for effective collaboration with Japan was growing rapidly.

He was disillusioned by his trip to Tokyo and his discovery of the gap between the lofty idealism of Konoe's Three Principles and the hard facts of collaboration revealed in the office of War Minister Itagaki. He was disappointed by the lack of response to his appeals for support. With the single exception of his old comrade Ch'en Kung-po, who after wavering for many indecisive months in Hong Kong finally agreed to back him in late 1939, no important person had answered his call. He was constantly vexed by the harassment he was forced to endure at the hands of the existing puppets and their Japanese advisers. He was uncomfortably aware of the efforts to bypass him by seeking direct negotiations with Chungking. Perhaps most distressing of all for a man keenly aware of his historic position in Republican China was Wang's realization that his personal motives for defecting from Chungking—undoubtedly honorable and patriotic—might not be enough to prevent his being branded a *han-chien* by his countrymen. In the face of apparently insurmountable obstacles it was the assurance and promises of Colonel Kagesa that sometimes meant the difference between Wang's perseverance and his historic tactic of retreat into exile. "Beyond a certain point," recalls journalist Matsukata Saburō, "the peace movement kept going on personal attachments alone."[1]

Kagesa's access to War Minister Itagaki and persuasive advocacy of Wang's cause combined to produce a gradual increase in pro-Wang sentiment in the Army. But even more instrumental in causing Wang's star to rise was a purely adventitious event that occurred on the remote reaches of the Khalka River, the border between Manchukuo and the Soviet Union's client state of Outer Mongolia. There, near the village of Nomonhan, six months of fighting between the Kwantung Army and the Soviet Red Army (along with their respective puppet troops) culminated in a resounding Japanese defeat in September 1939. For the first time Japan had faced an enemy that possessed modern arms and equipment and employed modern tactics. The Kwantung Army proved no match for the vastly superior Soviet artillery and tanks. Soviet transport and supply capabilities—from railheads nearly 400 miles away—caught Japanese intelligence by surprise. Soviet bomber raids into Manchukuoan territory presented an ominous threat to Japan. And, finally, the Soviet troops were of a far different mettle than the Czarist troops Japan had last faced, showing a courage and tenacity that resulted in an astounding 73 per cent casualty figure among the Japanese forces in the period between July 1 and September 16, when most of the fighting at Nomonhan occurred.[2]

We have seen the abiding preoccupation of the General Staff with the threat of the Soviet Union. From the earliest days of the war in China the General Staff strategists had sought solutions that would enable them to concentrate their attention on the threat from the north. The defeat at Nomonhan was a sobering confirmation of their apprehensions. It was also a demonstration of the dangers of runaway Army commands, acting in flagrant defiance of national policy laid down in Tokyo. War Minister Itagaki sought to turn the border clash over to the Foreign Ministry for diplomatic solution, and the General Staff adopted a policy that in essence called for "an early conclusion of the struggle, honorably or dishonorably." The Kwantung Army studied the policy and arrogantly decided to ignore it.[3]

There were even wider implications to the clashes at Nomonhan. On August 23, at the height of the warfare there, the Germans signed a non-aggression pact with the Russians, effectively freeing the Soviet Union of European responsibilities to concentrate her forces against her Asian adversary. The Axis-leaning Hiranuma Government was rocked by the betrayal of its erstwhile anti-Comintern ally and was promptly dissolved. The Cabinet that replaced it was headed by Gen. Abe Nobuyuki, who was known to be sympathetic to Wang Ching-wei. (He was later to be appointed Japan's first Ambassador to the Wang regime.)

Of more significance to the Wang cause was the subsequent shuffle of Army personnel, which saw Gen. Ueda Kenkichi, the Commander of the Kwantung Army and one of the staunchest advocates of *bunji gassaku*, relieved of his command. But the most important change of all was the reorganization of the mainland command. On September 20 the General Staff announced that the North and Central China Army commands were to be dissolved and replaced by a unified China Expeditionary Army. This was no mere efficiency measure but a move on the part of the General Staff to unify Army policy toward China by destroying the power of the regional commands. A measure of the importance placed on the creation of the unified China Expeditionary Army was the appointment of Minister of War Itagaki as its Chief of Staff. The effect of all these measures was a sudden enhancement of Wang's cause. There was renewed determination in certain Army quarters to unify Japanese policy on China and terminate the war as quickly as possible. Whether the war could best be terminated by relying on Wang or by resolving differences with Chungking was still a matter of contention, to be sure. Nevertheless, the creation of the China Expeditionary Army at least promised to diminish the threat posed to Wang by the regional army commands and their puppets.

In this connection it is interesting that at the very time Wang K'o-min and Liang Hung-chih were so obstructive in their talks with Wang Ching-wei (September 19–20), their Japanese advisers and Kagesa were meeting in Nanking. Wang K'o-min's sponsor, General Kita, was said to be "restrained" as he listened to Gen. Higuchi Sueichirō (the Chief of the Intelligence Division of the General Staff), who had flown from Tokyo to advise the assembled officers of the significance of the recent changes. The Abe Government, Higuchi told them, had endorsed Kagesa's program of supporting Wang Ching-wei "to the end."[4]

Higuchi discounted efforts at direct negotiations with Chungking: up until three months ago there were those who had favored that course, he said, but "there are none of those indiscreet people around now." Specifically, Higuchi addressed himself to intelligence reports of the mediation efforts of the American educator J. Leighton Stuart, President of Yenching University. Stuart was said to have been in touch with the Generalissimo, who had indicated that he would give his blessing to any of Wang K'o-min's attempts to achieve a peaceful solution with Japan as long as Wang Ching-wei and his followers were excluded. Higuchi's analysis was that "Stuart is a habitual liar, and [that] to ignore Wang at this time would be to discard *bushidō*."[5]

Wang defected from Chungking in December 1938. From November 1938 to November 1939 the Japanese constantly discussed and debated among themselves the details of treaties and agreements leading to a "readjustment of Sino-Japanese relations." Extensive discussions with Wang and his colleagues were conducted on the same subject, but they were always informal and inconclusive. Consequently, communications with Wang during this period were always at the level of personal discussion. Even at that level, Wang was unable to learn of Japanese intentions in any real detail. His urgent appeals for a clarification of the number and authority of Japanese advisers, for example, simply went unanswered. Agreements and understandings arrived at on the basis of private talks were manifestly unsatisfactory from Wang's point of view because they could easily be repudiated by Japan. Even when such understandings were reduced to writing and sealed (as in the case of the Chungkuang-t'ang agreements), repudiation was possible. It was a measure of both Japan's indecisiveness about the merits of supporting Wang and the division of authority in the creation of a China policy that in November 1939—almost a year after Wang's defection—Japan was still unwilling to commit herself to binding negotiations on a basic treaty, an obvious necessity if she was to recognize a new government under Wang.

The Kōain, which had prime responsibility for fixing Japan's position on such a treaty, drew up a "draft plan," in effect a detailed list of the terms Wang must bow to if Japan was to support the establishment of a new regime. Colonel Horiba of the General Staff was responsible for getting the necessary seals of approval for the plan and was also responsible for liaison with Kagesa and the Plum Blossom Agency. As concrete problems like a troop withdrawal schedule were discussed, Horiba found "the same greed that had been displayed at the time the 'Policy for New Relations' was being drafted" welling up again in various quarters.[6] The terms of the draft plan were based on the severest possible interpretation of the decisions of the Imperial Conference of November 30, 1938, supplemented by several new harsh demands. When Horiba brought the Kōain's formulations to Shanghai in October 1939, he told Kagesa he doubted that Wang could ever gain the support of the Chinese people if he accepted them. Kagesa agreed: the Kōain's draft plan was a "dirge that signaled the failure of the peace movement even before the Wang government was established."[7]

Because of the harshness of the Kōain conditions, Horiba suggested to Kagesa that he not reveal them in detail to Wang but try merely to get his assent to them in general terms. He counseled Kagesa to regard the Kōain's formulations as a reference for his use alone, and to look on the present demands as no more than an initial bargaining position. Once Wang consented to a number of generally stated demands, the Kōain's conditions could be revised by "political discussions." Accordingly, Kagesa should feel free to make "appropriate concessions to Wang."[8] The political discussions would presumably come after the inauguration of the Wang regime in ambassadorial level talks.

Kagesa and the entire Plum Blossom Agency agreed with Horiba that the Kōain draft plan spelled doom for the peace movement. Most, however, did not share Horiba's conviction that negotiations should proceed when, in the words of Shimizu Tōzō, Japan was "asking for everything—from the earth to the sky."[9] To negotiate with Wang on the basis of this kind of proposal "would be to cast doubt on Japan's sincerity and in the end would work to Japan's disadvantage," the Foreign Office China expert argued.[10] Shimizu and other members of the Agency implored Kagesa to denounce the Kōain proposal and send it back to Tokyo as a bankrupt policy; he should make it clear that even if Wang accepted the terms of the draft plan, the peace movement would be disgraced and eventually destroyed.

Kagesa rejected the advice of both Horiba and the Plum Blossom Agency dissenters. Horiba's scheme was unacceptable for a number of reasons. First, Kagesa's inclination to be completely open and frank with Wang made him instinctively rebel against it. In any case, he had already gone beyond his authority recently by showing Wang the full text of the terms set forth by the Imperial Conference of November 30, 1938, and saw no reason to change his policy of openness now.* Second, Kagesa realized that Wang was deeply skeptical of Japanese intentions (especially since he now knew the harsh details of the November 30 conference) and was unlikely to proceed any further on the basis of vaguely worded general agreements. Wang was in fact demanding more and more clarification of Japanese terms. Finally, Kagesa did not share Horiba's optimistic view that the Kōain formulations would eventually be softened in later political negotiations. On the contrary, the very fact that Colonel Horiba—a "fair and honest man"—had felt constrained to associate himself, even halfheartedly, with the Kōain demands seemed to Kagesa "proof that Japan was being overwhelmed by a narrow-minded, hard-line view."[11] Nothing to date had supported Horiba's optimism. And as we now know, the events that followed certainly did not justify it.

Though sympathetic to the arguments of his colleagues in the Plum Blossom Agency, Kagesa rejected their advice too. In the last analysis, he told them, it was not their function to create policy but to carry it out.

* On hearing of the disclosure of this document to Wang, a shocked Horiba complained that "Kagesa always treated the Chinese as comrades [*dōshi*]." *Shina jihen*, 1: 318.

There was simply no justification for a disciplined soldier to refuse to negotiate on the basis of the Kōain's orders. Therefore, what he would do, he promised his associates, was to present the Kōain plan to Wang in its entirety, listen to his objections, and then return to Tokyo to argue for a revision. Kagesa was more candid about his distress with his close friend Inukai: "I am ashamed to wear the uniform," he confessed.[12]

THE YÜ YÜAN ROAD CONFERENCES

In Wang's absence in the summer of 1939 a heavily fortified residence was prepared for him in the "extension roads" area of Shanghai, which, though outside of the boundaries of the International Settlement, received protection from Settlement police. Inside the compound at Lane 1136, Yü Yüan Road, were a dozen houses where not only Wang, but all his top advisers (including Chou Fo-hai, Mei, and T'ao) and their families lived and did much of their work. If their siegelike existence was inconvenient, it was clearly preferable to the dangers to which their comrades on the outside were exposed. Kuomintang assassins and terrorists drastically reduced the life expectancy of Wang's supporters in Shanghai and gave a special mark of courage to those who survived.*

On November 1, 1939, Colonel Kagesa, Inukai Ken, and other members of the Plum Blossom Agency arrived at 1136 Yü Yüan Road to commence two months of negotiations. The resulting "Informal Agreements" signed on December 30 represented an almost complete capitulation by Wang to Japanese demands.[13] With a few changes, the agreements were incorporated into the "Basic Treaty" of November 30, 1940, which formalized Japanese relations with the Wang regime.

The Japanese demands at the Yü Yüan Road Conferences so stretched the patience of Wang and his colleagues that the meetings frequently dissolved in acrimonious exchanges and, on at least one occasion, stalemated completely. It was only the toughmindedness of Mei Ssu-p'ing and especially Ch'en Kung-po that gained Wang the few concessions he received at the Yü Yüan Road meeting. Ch'en had joined the Wang group out of

---

* Chou Fo-hai frequently pointed out to those who claimed he defected for reasons of personal safety that life in bomb-gutted Chungking was much safer than life in Shanghai. "Plainly speaking," he wrote, "a man of my standing would have been safe anywhere [in Chungking] in case of air raids, being provided with the strongest of bomb-proof dugouts. There was ample time to make preparations when warning was given of an approaching air raid." In contrast, "my life [in Shanghai in 1939] is constantly being threatened by the Communists and the 'special service' element of the Chungking regime. As there is no warning of an approaching assassination . . . , I think the danger to life created by these terrorists is much more serious than a Japanese air raid." "Retrospect," p. 2. Chou's critics have remained unconvinced by his arguments. Kung Te-po, writing in 1963, fifteen years after Chou's death, insisted Chou had become so alarmed by Japanese air raids in Chungking that he tended to "pass water on hearing the air raid alarms." *Wang Chao-ming*, p. 54.

personal loyalty to Wang rather than in the conviction that Wang was on the right course; on the contrary, Ch'en was convinced that Wang was more poet than politician, that he tended to "look at things too optimistically," and that he had been deceived by Konoe in December 1938 and was about to be deceived again.[14] Ch'en's efforts to convince Wang to hold out for better terms and more explicit guarantees of Japanese sincerity met with only limited success. Though Wang played no role in the actual negotiations, he played a crucial role in the conferences by "soothing" the intransigent Ch'en into acquiescence. Even such firm supporters as Inukai do not deny that Wang yielded too much and, indeed, compromised away the chance of his own future success.[15] It is difficult to account for Wang's weakness with any certainty, but Ch'en's claim that Wang was temperamentally unsuited for the difficult task of bargaining with a wartime enemy is surely at least part of the answer. It also seems likely that Wang placed an unwarranted degree of trust in Kagesa, whose probity and honor were beyond doubt but whose ability to wring concessions for Wang from Tokyo was limited.[16]

Nevertheless, Kagesa did his best, and even hurried back to Tokyo during the conference stalemate (in mid-November 1939) to plead for easier terms for Wang. Suspecting that the highest echelons of the War Ministry were not fully informed of the negotiations in Shanghai, Kagesa took his case directly to Gen. Hata Shunroku, the Minister of War—and found his suspicions confirmed. Hata "knew absolutely nothing of the details" of the Yü Yüan Road talks. Kagesa found Hata sympathetic to his pleas for a relaxation of terms and "got his consent on many points." Hata would not give, however, on such critical issues as troop withdrawal and Japanese management of Chinese railroads, the second of which was looming ever larger as a sticking point in a negotiated settlement of the China war. On these questions Kagesa found that some in Tokyo were saying "we could soften the terms if we were dealing with Chungking, but we cannot do so now [that is, in negotiations with Wang]." Still, there were those who continued to insist that softer terms were impossible "even if we were dealing with Chungking."[17]

Kagesa was reluctant to identify by name the militants who opposed concessions to Wang in a journal written while he was on active wartime duty, but Colonel Horiba, in his postwar account of the same events, fixes the center of the hard-line faction in the office of the General Staff's Operations Division, commanded by Maj. Gen. Tominaga Kyōji. Tominaga's group had plumped vigorously for a rigid, hard-line interpretation of the Kōain plan and was hostile to any suggestion by Horiba that a "generous" treatment of China might be in the interest of friendly "concert" between the two nations. Tension increased between Tominaga and Horiba (who was on Tominaga's staff) as the two repeatedly tangled on the issue of troop withdrawal. Tominaga insisted on the need of a permanent garrison for the Shanghai-Nanking-Hangchow triangle and was especially adamant about the need to keep Imperial Army troops in Nanking. Horiba was finally pushed to criticize his superior for trying to violate the Imperial Conference decision of November 30, 1938, declaring that stationing troops in Nanking was "like walking with dirty shoes into the living room of your employer." For this indiscretion Horiba was thoroughly berated by the enraged Tominaga, required to sign a paper promising that he would have no further contacts with the Plum Blossom Agency, and then "kicked out" of Tominaga's office. Soon after, he was transferred to China.[18] Thus ended the influence at the Center of an important critic of what Horiba called the "policy of special privilege in China." (Tominaga, in contrast, retained considerable influence and eventually became Vice Minister of War in the Tōjō Government.)

Unlike the Chungkuang-t'ang Conference where no minutes were kept, the Yü Yüan Road Conferences have left us an almost verbatim account of each session.[19] These reports reveal in striking detail the extent to which Konoe's fine sounding Three Principles of 1938 concealed the ugly realities of collaboration with Imperial Japan. In addition to the day-by-day minutes of the meetings, we have the accounts of several of the participants in the Yü Yüan Road Conferences. After every formal daytime session, Inukai met with Chou Fo-hai, Kao Tsung-wu, and others from the Chinese side, sounded out their feelings, and reported back to Kagesa, who then prepared his bargaining strategy for the next session.

Essentially, the talks centered on five major topics: advisers, economic development, military affairs, North China, and various "special areas" (*tokushū chiiki*).[20] The first, the question of advisers, had been a Wang concern for a number of months. While in Tokyo he had petitioned Japan to refrain from appointing advisers to the central government "in order to dismiss any doubts the Chinese people might have concerning the possibility that Japan might intervene in Chinese internal administration." The proper person to negotiate differences between the two governments, he maintained, was an ambassador, not a supreme political adviser. Technical advisers were acceptable to Wang provided their functions were limited to matters of scientific technique, but they must work with Chinese officials behind the scenes and remain hidden from the public.[21] Any direct contact between the Japanese and the Chinese public was totally unacceptable.

The Japanese began to whittle away at Wang's petition in October, declaring that though they would not send any political advisers to the central government, it was "both necessary and beneficial for Sino-Japanese relations to appoint teachers, customs officials, technicians, etc., to agencies directly attached to the central government."[22] The Chinese side relented, but rather pathetically asked for an understanding that there would be no treaty obligation binding China to employ such advisers: "We will invite the not-purely-technical advisers only when *we* see the need." When Kagesa reported that he had secured this compromise from Wang, he attached an observation of his own: "The Chinese side maintains that it would be awkward for it to agree to employ such advisers in a formal treaty but it will do so in practice."[23] Still later, during the Yü Yüan Road Conferences themselves, the Chinese were pressured into agreeing to regard "financial and economic advisers" as technical advisers and hence acceptable under the previous agreements. In addition, Japan demanded almost unlimited rights to dispatch advisers of all kinds—including political advisers—to North China, Mengchiang, and "special areas of close Sino-Japanese cooperation" like Shanghai and Amoy.

Wang was also gravely concerned about keeping local and provincial governments free of the Japanese presence, and asked that no political advisers be attached to these governments. Where the Japanese Army required the cooperation of local officials before it had withdrawn, he "hoped that Japan [would] take diplomatic measures and not issue dictatorial written or oral notices." Kagesa replied that in general Japan would comply with Wang's wishes, but Wang had to understand that the appointment of Japanese advisers on the local level was "unavoidable in certain special situations and in certain areas." When Kagesa's reply was reported to the Kōain, it deplored the use of the word "unavoidable" as misguided; the Chinese should "naturally accept" such Japanese advisers. Undaunted, Kagesa notified Tokyo that in any event the Chinese "were not really expecting" Japan to accept their restrictions on the assignment of Japanese advisers to local governments.[24]

Wang had also sought to reach some understanding on economic problems while in Tokyo. Reminding his Japanese hosts that the Chungkuang-t'ang Conference had agreed economic collaboration would be "based on the principle of reciprocity and equality," he asked for the speedy return to Chinese owners of all mines and factories occupied or confiscated by the Japanese. He also asked Japan to rectify the "unreasonable situation" obtaining in many of the jointly owned enterprises, which saw Japan claiming 49 per cent ownership but failing to make good on her promise to supply capital. In addition, Wang asserted that Japan had consistently undervalued the Chinese assets in the joint ventures and asked that she take steps to revalue them "with objective standards." Finally, Wang did not wish to be saddled with the economic contracts Japan had concluded with the Reformed and Provisional Governments, many of which had been drawn up in flagrant disregard of the "principle of reciprocity and equality," and asked that he be given the opportunity to renegotiate all contracts immediately—even before the creation of a new central government.[25]

The initial reply came from the Plum Blossom Agency: Japan would "consider" some rational plan for returning mines and factories to Chinese ownership but China would have to recognize that "certain military needs arise during a war." Furthermore, some factories already had been "dealt with [*shori*] because of the presence of the enemy." As to the renegotiation of existing contracts with the Reformed and Provisional Governments, that would be permitted only in cases where China could point to a violation of "The Policy for New Relations."[26]

The Kōain's reply to the Chinese proposals was considerably tougher. The Kōain denied that any mines or property had ever been confiscated or occupied. "We have simply taken measures to protect [Chinese] property," it declared, with no apparent sense of the bitter irony in its choice of words. The properties would be returned "after discussion," the Kōain added. But this was a qualified promise at best, for the Kōain made it clear that "those [industries] related to military necessity or special circumstances [would] presumably not be returned," or if returned, would automatically be converted into joint ventures. As for the official contracts negotiated with the Reformed and Provisional Governments, they were "fair" and absolutely not subject to renegotiation.[27]

The question of special privileges (*tokubetsu ben'eki*), which the Chinese had thought settled at the Chungkuang-t'ang, was reintroduced at the Yü Yüan Road Conferences. Though the Japanese had agreed previously to renounce any claim to special privileges, the Kōain's draft specifically demanded economic privileges, especially in the exploitation of underground resources in North China and Mengchiang. Kagesa and his technical adviser Koike answered Chou's demands for a clarification of special privileges by saying that the special treatment was to apply to coal and iron "by and large . . . but in addition light metals were very important to national defense." As an example of what Japan had in mind, Koike cited the need for a revision of the Chinese laws that disallowed the introduction of foreign capital into the coal and iron industries. Mei objected that the Kōain seemed to be bent on using all of the coal and iron in North China and Mengchiang to fill Japan's needs. Since almost all of China's coal and iron came from North China, Mei complained, it would be very "troublesome" if Japan did not consider the needs of China as well. Koike's assurance that Japan did not intend to use all of the valuable underground resources was hardly reassuring to the Chinese: China could certainly use the "leftover products from blast furnaces built jointly by Japan and China," he declared.[28]

At this point Chou Fo-hai requested Kagesa to drop the demand for special privileges. Why, he asked, did Japan insist on special privileges in North China and Mengchiang when the Wang group had agreed to give her preferential rights (*yūsen-ken*) in the exploitation of resources throughout the country? It was more than a question of semantics, as is evident from Kagesa's reply. Preferential rights would not satisfy Japan, he said, citing the exploitation of coal resources as an example. If the laws governing the mining of coal forbade the granting of "facilities" to foreign nations, then Japan would be ineligible for such facilities even though she enjoyed preferential status. Kagesa argued that "preferential rights are a negative thing and what we are talking about is economic cooperation, which is something quite positive."[29] It meant, in short, granting Japan "facilities" and privileges that were totally denied to other foreign countries, explained Kagesa. Kagesa constantly found himself in the unenviable position of promoting the idea of economic cooperation to a group of Chinese who each day became more cynical about the one-sided character of the Japanese notion of cooperation. In the end he gave way to Chou's concern about the *tokubetsu ben'eki* language, which the Chinese side insisted would sound very bad in Chinese translation. The substance of the Japanese demands was little changed, however, by the substitution of *tokubetsu bengi* (special facilities) for *tokubetsu ben'eki*. As finally agreed on, the relevant clause read:

> In keeping with the spirit of joint defense and economic cooperation, China shall accord special facilities to Japan for the development of specially designated natural resources in North China and Mengchiang. . . . In other areas of China, in a spirit of economic cooperation, China will grant necessary facilities to Japan so that she may develop and utilize specially designated resources needed for national defense. However, in the use of these resources, China's needs will be considered.[30]

On the question of control of the "joint management enterprises," the final agreement granted Japan ownership rights ranging from slightly under the controlling level to 55 per cent in the case of "specially designated enterprises" (*tokutei jigyō*), which were vaguely defined as those relating to Japan's military requirements. Further Japanese economic control was ensured by Wang's recognition of Japan's right to dispatch advisers, who were to have varying degrees of control over the allocation of resources and the planning in various industries. Finally, Japan received a number of financial privileges. These privileges—the one granted with the most reluctance permitted Japan to use military scrip in China—had the effect of allowing Japan to manipulate the Chinese currencies, rates of exchange, and balance of payments to her own advantage. Mei Ssu-p'ing remarked in disgust that the 1922 Washington Conference had unfairly excluded Japan from China, and now Japan was rectifying that injustice by pushing other countries out of China. The problem was, he said, Japan's demands "might give rise to the misunderstanding that she was trying to push the Chinese out of China!" This was not simply the opinion of Mei and Wang; it was the impression that all Chinese would have when they heard of the Japanese demands, Mei held.[31]

The third major subject discussed was the disposition of Japanese troops and military advisers. In Tokyo Wang had called for an international advisory group to assist in the "planning of national defense." In a move clearly designed to minimize Japanese control over the army of his new regime, Wang proposed that half the advisers be Japanese and the other half Germans and Italians. All were to be used in military institutions or schools. Individual army units would not be allowed to engage experts "by any means whatsoever," though inspection trips to the units might be tolerated if sent by the supreme central military organs and if the foreign inspectors did not concern themselves with personnel affairs. Finally, Wang brought up the question of *fukki guntai*—Chinese forces who "returned," i.e., declared their loyalty to the new government. Wang asked that once returned troops appeared in an area, the Japanese evacuate their units and turn control over to the Chinese forces. Evidence of even a "partial" Japanese willingness to go along with such a policy would have a "great effect in attracting troops" to his cause, he pleaded.[32] Here, it would seem, was another test of Japanese sincerity.

The initial response to Wang's proposals was almost wholly negative. "The Policy for New Relations" envisioned only Japanese advisers in the mounting of a lasting defense against communism; no interference by third-party countries could be tolerated. As to Japanese advisers being assigned to field units, the Plum Blossom Agency felt China's wishes could be honored "as a general principle" but suggested there might be "specially critical areas" and "specially designated units" that would benefit from the presence of Japanese military advisers. "Could you explain 'specially critical areas' and 'specially designated units'?" came the rather doleful Chinese reply.[33]

The Chinese side at the Yü Yüan Road talks moved on to other criticisms of Japanese plans to station troops on Chinese soil. There was the question of "joint defense against communism," which in the Japanese program justified an almost permanent garrisoning of troops in large parts of China. The Chinese at the Yü Yüan Road Conferences seemed reconciled to allowing Mengchiang to suffer that fate. By this time the Japanese had so often stressed that Mengchiang was destined to become a satellite of Manchukuo, there seemed little point in challenging them on the point. But North China was another question. The Chungkuang-t'ang Conference in 1938 had authorized the stationing of the anti-Communist troops of the Imperial Army in the "Peiping-Tientsin corridor," but now, one year later, the Japanese shook off that fairly precise limitation and demanded the right to station troops at "various important points" in North China. When Chou questioned the change, Kagesa's only reply was that the situation too had changed in the past year; Red Chinese troops had fanned out all over North China. The new demand was a "shocking blow," Mei declared. T'ao Hsi-sheng indicated that the Chinese had not understood Konoe's "defense against communism" as calling for the stationing of Japanese troops on Chinese soil—with the possible exception of Mengchiang. No matter how the Japanese tried to justify the stationing of troops on Chinese soil, T'ao told Kagesa, the "Chinese people are going to regard it as an interference in Chinese internal affairs, and we will be right back where we were three years ago." Chou added that he foresaw no end to the escalation of Japanese demands if they were to be justified in terms of the "changing situation." He reminded Kagesa that the Communist New Fourth Army had recently appeared south of the Yangtze. "So, does that mean anti-Communist garrisons there, too?" asked Chou. "If you insist on rationalizing your change of demands on us in terms of the 'changing situation,' " the exasperated Chou told Kagesa, "then there can be no end to it all."[34]

In the Japanese proposal submitted at the Yü Yüan Road talks, the provision permitting the stationing of anti-Communist troops in China was placed in the same clause as the provision allowing the stationing of Japanese troops wherever necessary until peace and order were restored. This was especially galling to the Chinese. They feared that the anti-Communist garrisons would become an ugly, permanent fact of life in Mengchiang and North China, since the Japanese could not be persuaded to set a time limitation on the stationing of such troops. Now, in the same clause, Japan proposed to station troops in other parts of China—not as anti-Communist garrisons but merely as a peace-keeping force. Inevitably, the Chinese said, this juxtaposition of the two questions in the same clause suggested that Japan contemplated the right to garrison troops—under one pretext or another—all over China as long as she pleased.

Would it not be possible at least, Chou persisted, to separate the two problems in the treaty, to provide for the unlimited garrisoning of anti-Communist troops in one clause and for the "civil order" garrisons, on which there was hopefully going to be a time limit, in another clause? Kagesa demurred: "Wherever we put these clauses, they are going to be kept secret and so the people are never going to know." Chou struck back: "Of course, they're going to be secret, but the people are going to see the troops. And then somebody will have to explain." Kagesa replied that the Chinese should not regard the one kind of garrison as so different from the other. The anti-Communist garrisons would not necessarily be permanent, and "the peace preservation troops might not be so short-range," he said with his usual candor.[35]

Mei would not be put off. It was not just a matter of a difference in time, he said. "Peace preservation" had strong overtones of interference in Chinese internal politics. This provision was directed at China, whereas the anti-Communist defense proposals were presumably directed at the Soviet Union. At about this stage Kagesa's patience seems to have been wearing thin and, anyway, there was nothing more he could offer his Chinese colleagues. He responded tartly:

> Peace is fine. That's one thing. But trusting the Chinese Army, which until yesterday was fighting against us, that's another thing. Much effort and time will have to be spent before we can cooperate honestly. If we take it as an absolute principle that Japan withdraw immediately so as not to interfere in Chinese internal affairs, then what was all the bloodshed about? That's what the Japanese people will say. I understand what you mean when you talk about interference, but from our point of view, we cannot put our complete trust in Chinese armies just because the war has ended. Therefore we will have to station peace preservation troops for a while, and that will not be interference.[36]

When this frank explanation left the Chinese unmoved, Kagesa took another tack, shifting the responsibility for the peace preservation troops onto the Chinese themselves: "You used to claim that once the Wang movement began, the armies would return and the movement would have real military power. Under the present circumstances, however, that seems unlikely. There is strong criticism of Wang in influential circles for his failure to attract armies. Given this situation, it is unavoidable that Japan now assume greater responsibility for strengthening you [militarily] than she anticipated last year."[37] Wang's failure to attract military support from the restive warlord-generals was coming home to roost. There was little room for rebuttal once Kagesa had inserted the needle into the most vulnerable point in the anatomy of the Wang movement.

Withal, the Wang group did win one major point at the Yü Yüan Road Conferences. After much debate both in Shanghai and at Miyake-zaka (the headquarters of the General Staff in Tokyo), the Japanese finally agreed to a phased withdrawal of their peace preservation troops, which would begin after the restoration of peace and be concluded "within two years, during which time China would guarantee the maintenance of civil order."[38]

In his talks with Itagaki in June 1939 Wang had consented to a high degree of autonomy for North China, since it was all too clear that Japan intended to maintain and expand the special economic and military position she had held there since 1935 (when the Hopei-Chahar Political Council was established). It remained only for the negotiators at the Yü Yüan Road Conferences to decide precisely how separate North China would be and to draw its boundaries. The sections dealing with North China were among the harshest in the Kōain plan, Kagesa's guideline for the negotiations. Inukai recalls his own thought on reading the Kōain's call for virtual independence for North China: "Nowhere in the whole world was there a puppet regime" that would accept such terms.[39]

Nothing was more central to Wang's entire peace program than the view that the Chinese could achieve peace with honor if Japan would but agree to respect China's sovereignty over all her lands. On his defection he had assured the Chinese people that his reading of Konoe's Three Principles had convinced him of Japan's good faith in this regard, and for a year now he had repeatedly stressed in his public appeals that his discussions wth Japanese leaders had sustained and deepened that conviction. He thus desperately needed to be able to stand before the Chinese people with proof that his new government would have genuine control over North China. Had Japan agreed to terms that would have given him that proof, there is little doubt he would have reaped a rich harvest of public respect and support, for he would have been credited with eliminating the greatest single cause of the Sino-Japanese War. Just as certainly, Japan would have shared in Wang's enhanced prestige, and the whole history of the Wang regime—and the New Order for East Asia—might have been different.

Unfortunately for Wang, Japan did not give him the needed proof. The December 30 agreements provided that his central government would have no more than token authority in North China. Japan, meanwhile, would have extraordinary economic and military privileges there and worse yet, from Wang's point of view, would not have to answer to his government in the event of disputes over those privileges but instead would resolve any differences with a North China Political Council (Hua-pei Cheng-wu Wei-yüan-hui; Kahoku Seimu Iinkai), a new organ that would be but a thinly disguised extension of the puppet Provisional Government. Wang tried to salvage what he could. He expressed the hope that Japan would recognize his government's right to appoint the members of the Council, to veto its decisions, and to determine fiscal policy for North China. The Japanese answer was a firm no on all three counts.

Nothing is more illustrative of Japan's determination to create an independent North China than the measures taken to ensure the complete fiscal independence of the proposed North China Political Council. The Council was to be allotted a large, fixed share of China's customs fees, salt revenues, and excise taxes—essentially all the monies collected in North China. Wang could do no more than discuss a few percentage points with the Japanese negotiators. Further, the Council would be allowed to issue bonds, and the puppet-run Federal Reserve Bank of China in Peiping to continue its monetary activities, including the issuance of currency. For Wang such an abrogation of powers appropriate to a central government had to be deeply humiliating. But even more important, it created enormous problems of a practical nature. (To keep this all in perspective, however, it must be remembered that these were not new problems; China had only taken the first steps toward breaking down regional political and economic autonomy a few years before the Marco Polo Bridge Incident.)

The December 30 agreements gave other indications of the autonomy Japan foresaw for North China. The Political Council would have sole authority in several vital areas: common defense, particularly as it pertained to anticommunism and keeping order in North China; all questions arising from the garrisoning of Japanese forces in North China; all matters related to providing Japan with special facilities to exploit underground resources; the rationalization of the supply of needed materials to Japan, Manchukuo, Mengchiang, and North China; and virtually all matters related to the transportation and communications facilities of the area.[40]

Finally, the North China Political Council was to have the right to raise its own army—a so-called Pacification Army (Suiching-chün). And on the semiofficial level, the entire apparatus of the Hsin-min Hui was left intact to organize opposition to Wang's programs in the future. Later, on the occasion of Wang's first post-inaugural trip to North China, the *Hsin-min pao* created a sensation by carrying a manifesto bitterly critical of him and his attempts to revitalize Sun's Three Principles. It concluded: "Wang has promised to form a righteous government, but it is vain talk; there is no sincerity behind it."⁴¹ Similarly, when Wang continued on to the capital of Inner Mongolia, Prince Teh took pains to ignore his presence, refusing to meet him at official airport receptions and failing to observe protocol by returning his visits.⁴²

Only in the matter of the geographic demarcation of North China did Wang manage to win some concessions. The original Kōain plan called for the inclusion in North China of "that portion of Honan to the north of the old [pre-1938] Yellow River channel," as well as the vital east-west Lunghai Railway (which was just to the south of the Yellow River). Indeed, this was a relatively mild interpretation of North China, compared with that being promoted by the North China Area Army at this time. By its plan North China's boundaries were to have been extended so far south as to include "parts of Anhwei and Chekiang provinces," that is, to take in the Yangtze River Valley.⁴³ In the course of the Yü Yüan Road talks, Chou Fo-hai—"the master of compromise"—flatly declared that there was no room for compromise on the Kōain's unreal boundaries for North China. In the end Kagesa gave in, and North China was officially defined as "Hopei and Chahar provinces north to (and including) the Great Wall together with Shantung province."

North China was only one of several areas in which Japan demanded special rights at the Yü Yüan Road talks. Other areas of concern were Mengchiang, Shanghai, Amoy, and Hainan. Wang was forced to agree that Mengchiang had a "special character as a zone for close national defense and economic cooperation between Japan, China, and Manchukuo," and accordingly should have a "high degree of autonomy." The original Kōain proposal on Mengchiang eliminated all but the most perfunctory hint that the area would remain under the sovereignty of the central government. At the Yü Yüan Road talks, however, the Wang group managed to wring promises from Kagesa that the exact scope of authority of the Mengchiang regime would be fixed according to regulations drawn up by the central government. It was a slim victory at best, for in the next clause the Chinese promised to draw up such regulations only on prior consultation with Japan.⁴⁴

Because the Kōain regarded the lower reaches of the Yangtze as "a zone of especially close economic cooperation" between China and Japan, the control of Shanghai was not to be left entirely in the hands of Wang's new central government. Instead, the Kōain called for a continuation of the virtually autonomous status that had existed there since the installation of the Ta-tao regime in December 1937. The Wang government was expected to work closely with the administration of a "new Shanghai" through advisers and "liaison agents" so that it could cooperate to the fullest with Japan in matters related to the reconstruction of the city, navigation on the Yangtze, aviation, and economic and financial affairs in general.

The Chinese team at the Yü Yüan Road talks vigorously opposed Japan's efforts to remove Shanghai and the lower Yangtze from the control of the new central government. Chou, T'ao, and Mei repeatedly pressed Kagesa to explain why Japan insisted on singling out the lower Yangtze as a "special zone" or "area of intense economic cooperation." Was it not enough, they asked, that Wang had agreed to commit all of China to a policy of economic collaboration with Japan. "When you keep inserting these special items about the lower Yangtze it cannot help creating suspicion that you have some secret ambitions for that part of China," T'ao told his Japanese colleague. Giving Kagesa a lesson in recent Chinese history, T'ao pointed out that the lower Yangtze was economically the most important part of China. All of the important financial leaders were in that area, and it was precisely there that the new government of Wang would succeed or fail. "If the financial leaders of the lower Yangtze oppose us, it will mean opposition forces in the very area that is supposed to be the heart of [Wang's] government, and so it will be weak." Moreover, said T'ao, Japan was taking a grave risk, for the Western powers might well interpret her demands for special rights in the lower Yangtze as evidence of her intent to monopolize the economy of that part of China. The record of Japan's relationship with the Reformed Government would suggest that this was to be the case, T'ao observed.[45] As always, the Chinese seemed more concerned than the Japanese themselves about the perils of a Japanese collision with the Western powers.

Kagesa took umbrage at the unsolicited lecture from T'ao. "You sound like you're trying to eliminate the whole question of the lower Yangtze from our discussion. I cannot help having some doubts about your motives," he said testily. Japan had no intention of totally excluding other powers from the economic life of the lower Yangtze, he insisted. "However, before the Incident, the situation was that China would cooperate with any power except Japan. We simply want to rectify that situation."[46]

It is unnecessary to go into the complex details of the final agreement on Shanghai hammered out at the Yü Yüan Road talks. Suffice it to say that the beleaguered Wang was forced to agree to "prior consultations" with the Japanese on a broad range of economic activities and even to "intense liaison and cooperation" in cultural and educational matters. To ensure that "cooperation," Japanese liaison agents were to be employed in the social welfare, education, and police bureaus of the Shanghai Municipal Government.[47]

The city of Amoy, strategically located across the straits from Taiwan, was to be tied even more closely to Japan than Shanghai. As outlined by the Kōain in June 1939, the "Special Amoy Municipal Government" would have been almost wholly subservient to Japanese officialdom: the Mayor's appointment and dismissal were to be subject to the approval of a Japanese Commissioner; half of the City Council members were to be Japanese; if the Japanese Councilmen so desired, the Chief and Vice Chief of Police were to be Japanese; and to complete the domination, the Chief of the Kōain Amoy branch was to have veto power over all "important matters" that came before the city government. In addition, all business enterprises of any consequence were to be organized as joint ventures. The Kōain seemed intent on realizing the dream of a Japanese writer who, noting the strategic significance of Amoy to Japan, declared: "In a very real sense, it should be regarded as an extension of Taiwan, the territory of Japan."[48] Though some of the most obnoxious demands of the Kōain on Amoy were rejected by the Yü Yüan Road negotiators, enough remained to ensure that it would be turned into a city with a "distinct flavor of Japanese control."[49]

The question of Hainan was an especially irritating one for the Chinese team at Yü Yüan Road because it was a subject that had not even appeared on the agenda of the Chungkuang-t'ang Conference the year before. Since then, however, the "southward advance" strategy, aimed at British and French possessions in Southeast Asia, had begun to crystallize in the offices of the Navy Ministry in Tokyo. That strategy plainly could not succeed without naval air bases and dockyards on the South China coast, and consequently the Navy insisted that the Kōain persuade Wang to permit the virtual transformation of the island into a Japanese naval base.

Kagesa seems to have been unsympathetic with the Navy's "southward advance" strategy in general and its Hainan demands in particular.[50] As a result, the Navy relieved him of the responsibility of discussing the question by ordering its Plum Blossom Agency representative, Suga Hikojirō, a venerable Rear Admiral with a specialized knowledge of the China coast, to negotiate the question directly. Kagesa rather enigmatically confided to Wang that the reason the Navy had sent "this old man" to negotiate the Hainan question was that "it had absolutely no plausible justification" for asking for the island and thought that the good-natured Suga, who was known to be fond of Wang, would be personally appealing to the Chinese. Since Chou Fo-hai was reluctant to engage in negotiations with Suga lest he incur the wrath of heaven for speaking harshly to such a "godlike old man,"[51] the task was assigned to Ch'en Kung-po.

The six-day-long negotiating session once more revealed the deep concern of the Chinese about the danger of a southward advance provoking a war with Great Britain and ultimately the United States.[52] On many occasions Ch'en (and others in the Wang movement) attempted as best they could to dissuade Japan from moves that would involve her in a war with the Western powers. At least in part because of that fear, Ch'en resolutely refused to agree to the demands Suga presented. But the Imperial Navy—and in particular Admirals Yonai and Yamamoto Isoroku—was equally resolved to have Hainan and indeed was determined to sabotage the entire Wang collaboration program if it did not get its way. In the end, therefore, Wang ordered Ch'en to relent and grant Japan virtual free use of Hainan.[53] The portion of the Yü Yüan Road agreement intended for public consumption stipulated only that the central government would dispatch authorities to Hainan to facilitate harmonious cooperation between Japan and China. A secret annex to the agreement specified what that "cooperation" would mean. Japan not only was given free rein in the stationing of troops, the construction of naval facilities, and a host of other matters related to military needs, but also was granted the right to exploit the underground resources of the island.[54]

On November 1, shortly after Kagesa had opened the Yü Yüan Road talks by handing over to the Chinese the full text of the Kōain draft plan, T'ao Hsi-sheng summarized his understanding of the purpose of the conference. It was because Chungking had rejected peace with Japan that it "unavoidably became necessary" for the Wang group to plan the organization of a new government. But that government was only a means to an end. As the discussions went forward the negotiators on both sides of the table should keep the ultimate objective uppermost in their minds: "the collapse of the Chungking Government, which will be the means of bringing about peace." As T'ao saw it, the agreement worked out would have to guarantee Wang "persuasive power sufficient to move the Chinese people to destroy the Chungking Government." Failing that, all was lost.[55]

Far from giving Wang the vital "persuasive power" T'ao had spoken of, Japan burdened him with terms so wretched as to almost guarantee the failure of his peace experiment. From the opening moments of the discussions at Yü Yüan Road, there were signs of the disaster to come. "I must beg to ask your reconsideration of some points," Kagesa said after listening to T'ao's opening statement. Ending the war was *not* the ultimate objective of Japan's collaboration with Wang, said Kagesa. If that was her purpose, she would be satisfied to return to the status quo ante bellum. Japan's purpose in fact was a larger one, namely, the "safeguarding of East Asia [from communism]."[56] It was to this end that Japan was making her demands for special zones of intense cooperation and mutual defense. Kagesa's protestations notwithstanding, all of the Chinese negotiating team, and especially T'ao, continued to be deeply suspicious of Japan's "larger purpose" and throughout the talks bridled at each mention of special zones.

The fact that Japan had broken faith with the Chinese side by discarding the agreements made at the Chungkuang-t'ang Conference soured the atmosphere at the later talks. Kagesa confides to his diary his own surprise and disappointment when he discovered that the Kōain plan, which he was forced to use as a basis of negotiations, contained "no small number of new items," such as Hainan, the extensive Japanese management of important railways, the authority to be granted the North China Political Council, and the enlarged zones for permanent anti-Communist garrisons.[57] How much greater, then, must the disillusion and disappointment of the Wang camp have been. Kao Tsung-wu, so alienated from the Wang group by this time that he took little part in the formal discussions on Yü Yüan Road, was moved by a poetic whimsy to compose a traditional Japanese *tanka*:[58]

> The north,
> The south,
> The sea,
> And the mountains.
> None of them belongs to China.
> Where shall the Chinese people live?

By December 30, 1939, Kao's whimsy had turned to complete disenchantment. On that day, the negotiators of the Yü Yüan Road Conferences gathered at Wang's residence to toast the new year and sign the agreements they had labored over for the past two months. Both Kao and T'ao excused themselves from the bleak ceremonies on the plea of illness, and six days later the two principal founders of the Wang movement abandoned Wang.

CHAPTER FOURTEEN

"A Splendid Feast—Reserved for Chiang"

* BOTH KAO AND T'AO had begun to distrust Kagesa some months before the Yü Yüan Road talks. Kao now saw him as "just another Doihara." Both had cautioned Wang against placing any confidence in the Colonel; both had urged Wang not to sign the Yü Yüan Road agreements. Both had also become aware that Japanese suspicion of them had reached the point where their lives were endangered. T'ao had received word from friends that the dreaded Japanese-controlled security organization known as "No. 76" (from its location at 76 Jessfield Road in Shanghai) had plans to murder him and Kao, and accordingly both made plans to escape from Shanghai.[1]

The agent for their deliverance from the hands of No. 76 was Tu Yüeh-sheng, the underworld boss of Shanghai. The composite picture of Tu that emerges from a dozen or so accounts makes Fu Manchu appear saintly by comparison.[2] For naked power and complexity of character, the most important city bosses of America in the 1920's could not begin to compare to the Shanghai overlord. Tu had begun his business life as a fruit peddler but had risen through the ranks of the Green Gang in his native Shanghai to become that city's preeminent gangster.* He controlled the gambling, prostitution, narcotics, and protection rackets in a city that was notoriously rich in these activities. But Tu's ascent to political power and respectability did not begin until 1927, when his armed thugs assisted Chiang Kai-shek to root out the left-wing trade unionists and students of Shanghai. For his role in "delivering" Shanghai to Chiang (who is widely believed to have been a member of the Green Gang in his early years), Tu was lionized by the Western business community of Shanghai, decorated by Chiang, and elevated to a variety of

---

* The Green Gang (Ch'ing-pang) was the direct Shanghai descendant of the secret societies that flourished in the Yangtze River Valley for many centuries. Of the varied activities of these gangs Harold Isaacs writes: "They traded in opium and slaves. They kidnaped for ransom. They trafficked in blackmail and murder. Rare was the shopkeeper or trader or boatman, big or small, from the Yangtze's mouth to the Szechwan gorges, who did not pay them tribute." *Tragedy*, p. 142.

respectable positions in civic organizations, hospitals, schools, banks, and the like.

Slow to recognize upstart pillars of society, the British-edited *Who's Who* for China first listed Tu in 1933, at which time he was certified as a "well-known public welfare worker." If his detractors are correct, Tu's most remarkable talent was his ability to use his eminence as philanthropist and public servant for nefarious purpose. As a member of the Opium Suppression Bureau, for example, Tu expanded his control over the narcotics distribution network of Shanghai, which flourished as never before. As a member of the board of directors of the Chinese Red Cross, Tu was able to profiteer in medical supplies. At a time when the Army was being decimated by malaria, Tu's warehouses were reportedly bulging with quinine, which was sold—when the price was right—on the black-market by his agents.[3]

When the war with Japan broke out in 1937, Tu donated his bulletproof automobile to the Kuomintang general defending Shanghai, and shifted his headquarters from his magnificent mansion on the Avenue Doumer in the French Concession to Hong Kong. But despite his distance from Shanghai, he remained in firm control of the city's underworld. Among other things, he assigned certain patriotic functions to his 15,000-man private army there. One task the Green Gang undertook was to prevent prominent Chinese from participating in pro-Japanese enterprises, especially the Reformed Government. When the gangsters were unable to discourage such unpatriotic behavior with bribes—Chungking placed a half million dollars (Chinese) each month at the disposal of Tu—sterner measures were used. Scores of pro-Japanese sympathizers and collaborators were murdered by the Green Gang.

It was to Tu that Kao and T'ao turned for assistance in breaking with Wang. After being contacted by Kao, Tu flew to Chungking to see the Generalissimo. Chiang, who was in Kweilin on an inspection tour, rushed back to the capital when he heard that Tu's mission concerned Kao, and gave Tu permission to assist Kao's escape from Shanghai.[4] On New Year's Day, 1940, Kao and T'ao paid their respects at Chou Fo-hai's home, at which time Kao apparently hinted to Chou that he was leaving the Wang camp. "Both of us agreed to make separate efforts for the same goal of peace in China," Chou wrote in his diary entry for that day.[5] Three days later Kao and T'ao boarded an American President Line ship bound for Hong Kong, arriving there on January 5.

For the next sixteen days nothing was heard from the pair, who were being guarded in Kowloon by Tu's men. In fact, Hsiao T'ung-tzu, the Director of the Government's Central News Agency, was in touch with

the defectors, and on January 21 they handed over secret documents used
at the Yü Yüan Road Conferences. On that same day, the Hong Kong
Ta-kung pao carried banner headlines announcing "sensational disclosures" of "documents of a secret agreement between Wang Ching-wei and
Japan." The next day, January 22, a telegram from Kao and T'ao to
Wang was also made public. In it they declared that they no longer felt
a moral obligation to keep secret the discussions recently held in Shanghai because they had come to the conclusion that Japan was scheming
"to dismember our country and bring about its extinction." They implored Wang to "restrain the horse from falling over the precipice" and
abandon his effort.[6]

The revelation of the documents sent a shock wave through the Wang
camp. Chou Fo-hai may well have had an indication from Kao that a
defection was in the offing, but he almost certainly had no inkling that
the defectors would disclose the contents of the Yü Yüan Road negotiations. His diary entry for January 22 reads: "The two beasts, Kao and
T'ao. I vow that I will destroy them."[7]

Kao and T'ao were quickly castigated in the Wang press as disgruntled
job-seekers, and the authenticity of their disclosures was denied. There
is little to support the first charge beyond the circumstantial evidence
that both men were to be given only second-level positions in the Wang
regime. The skilled economist T'ao seems to have been slated to head
the Propaganda Ministry rather than the Ministry of Trade and Industry, as he had hoped; Wang apparently had already decided to give that
portfolio to Mei Ssu-p'ing. As for Kao, the one man who above all others
could be called the progenitor of the Wang movement and an authority
on foreign affairs, he was destined to be Deputy Minister of Foreign
Affairs under the dubious guidance of Madame Wang's brother-in-law,
Ch'u Min-i.[8] Wang's improbable first choice held degrees from French
universities in pharmacology and medicine but had practiced neither
profession; as an associate of Wang's in the National Government, the
genial Ch'u had been occupied with ceremonial functions—celebrations
in honor of Confucius's birthday, the Belgian national centenary, and so
forth. Among foreigners he was known for his eccentric preoccupations
with athletics and health: he was the editor of a popular health magazine, the inventor of a mechanical sparring partner for boxers, a pro-
moter of the traditional fighting art of *t'ai-chi-ch'üan* as a popular sport,
and an enthusiastic kite-flyer.* If Kao's defection was indeed simply a
matter of disgruntlement, it would seem to be justified, for Ch'u's ap-

---

* Emily Hahn traces Ch'u's fame as an eccentric back to his doctoral thesis: *A Study
of the Vaginal Vibrations of the Female Rabbit. China to Me,* p. 21.

pointment to the Foreign Ministership was a clear case of nepotism, and just a foretaste of things to come. Kwangtung province, for instance, virtually became the private preserve of Madame Wang, governed successively by her brother, her nephew, and, in the last months of the war, her brother-in-law Ch'u.[9]

The second charge leveled at Kao and T'ao—that the documents were not what they purported to be—was technically correct. Analysis of an English translation reveals them to be the documents Kagesa presented to the Wang group on November 1 and not the documents that finally emerged from the conferences. Thus, they do not give the Wang negotiators full marks for the concessions they were able to extract from Kagesa (regarding the boundaries of North China, for example). Nevertheless, the disclosures were widely believed and must be credited with doing enormous damage to the good name—if not the actual progress—of the Wang movement. Many of the things they revealed were intended to remain forever buried in secret protocols annexed to some future "Basic Treaty," and the disclosures represented a great propaganda victory for Chungking.

Needless to say, there was almost boundless joy all over Chungking when news of the Kao-T'ao disclosures reached the city. Chiang is said to have sent a letter to Kao applauding him as the "genius of Chekiang."[10] A few months later Kao received a passport from Chungking and sailed for the United States, where he has lived ever since. T'ao remained in Hong Kong until it was overrun by the Japanese after Pearl Harbor. After many narrow escapes from the Japanese, who not unnaturally were anxious to lay hands on him, he managed to escape from Hong Kong with the aid of Tu Yüeh-sheng.[11] By February 1942 T'ao was back in Chungking, where he joined the Generalissimo's personal staff. Soon after, he began collecting materials for Chiang's wartime book, *China's Destiny*, which he probably ghostwrote. Since 1943 T'ao has been affiliated with the *Chung-yang jih-pao* (Central Daily News), first as Editor-in-Chief and then as Chairman of the Board. He has lived in Taiwan since the Generalissimo and his supporters moved there in 1949.

With Kao's declining influence in the Wang camp in the post-Hanoi period and his defection in January 1940, the so-called Chou course became the popular view in the Wang camp. The majority was now ready to accept the principle of a collaboration regime, located in Japanese-occupied China. From the moment Wang arrived in Shanghai in May 1939 he was thrust into an arena in which two powerful, opposing forces were operating, neither of them in the least beholden to him. One was the National Government's network of secret police and intelligence agents (directed by Tai Li), which worked in concert with Tu Yüeh-sheng's Green Gang. The other was the Imperial Army's Tokumu-bu and the battalion or so of Chinese espionage agents and terrorists in its employ. As we have seen, Wang had no organized military backing. For simple survival alone, in the Shanghai of 1939, he had to ally himself with men who could protect him. In order to survive *and* build a head-quarters, recruit followers, mobilize newspaper support, organize a new government and party, *and* offer some measure of security to those who cast their fate with him, he had to ally with a group powerful enough to combat the combined forces of Tai Li and Tu Yüeh-sheng.

The Japanese Army met those qualifications, but in May 1939 Wang was not ready to accept the stigma of being protected by the Imperial Army. A story is told that illustrates how strongly he—and in this case the even more determined Madame Wang—felt about the matter. On the night of their arrival in Shanghai, Wang stayed aboard ship in order to avoid an *Asahi* reporter, who apparently had been tipped off about the trip. Meanwhile, the rest of the party was taken to the Chungkuang-t'ang, in a Japanese-controlled part of the city, to spend the night. Most of the group saw no harm in enjoying Japanese hospitality and indeed considerable advantage in the protection afforded by patrolling units of Japanese police. But Kao and Madame Wang were of another mind. Kao incurred Kagesa's displeasure by announcing that he would not re-main at the Chungkuang-t'ang but instead intended to stay with his brother in the French Concession. Madame Wang made known her dis-pleasure with the accommodations by stating flatly that she would swim across the Soochow Creek (which separated the Japanese-controlled Hon-kew section of Shanghai from the International Settlement) if her Japa-nese hosts did not give her safe conduct to the French Concession. Inukai had to smile at the picture of the "fat old lady" swimming across muddy Soochow Creek in the middle of the night, but Imai was touched by Madame Wang's "burning pride" and determination to avoid becoming a "puppet of the enemy."[12]

Once having ruled out open Japanese protection, Wang had little choice but to develop a security apparatus of his own. This task he en-trusted to Chou Fo-hai. While Wang was still in Hanoi, Chou had begun building a security system around a sinister pair of hoodlums who, with the help of Tokumu-bu agents, soon rivaled Tu Yüeh-sheng as the evil geniuses of the Shanghai underworld. Because these two thugs, Li Shih-ch'ün and Ting Mo-ts'un, came to have an all-too-important influence on the character of the Wang movement, it is worth going into their backgrounds in some detail.[13]

In 1939 Li and Ting were both in their mid- or late-thirties. Physically, there was little resemblance between Li, of rugged physique and sunny countenance, and Ting, a frozen-faced, frail, five-foot-one consumptive. Both had begun their political careers as members of the Communist Party; and both had renounced communism and joined one of Tai Li's principal espionage organizations, euphemistically known as the Central Investigation and Statistics Bureau.* In about 1938 Li fled to Hong Kong to escape "severe punishment" for certain illegal activities. The Shanghai-based Tokumu-bu of General Doihara then recruited him and shortly after that Chungking dispatched his former superior, Ting, to entice him back to Chungking. Far from succeeding, Ting was himself persuaded to defect and to join Doihara's spy apparatus. In light of this history, the two men's devotion to Wang's cause has to be seen as thoroughly grounded in self-interest and expediency.

By early 1939 Doihara had moved on to Peiping and to the unsuccessful Operation Wu P'ei-fu. The Shanghai apparatus passed into the hands of Lt. Col. Haruke Keiin, who quickly assisted Li and Ting to form a fearsome terrorist and spy ring, operating out of an old foreign-style house, No. 76 Jessfield Road, in the "Badlands" section of Shanghai. Colonel Imai, no stranger to ruthless espionage organizations, writes that Li and Ting were "bloodthirsty, forever carrying out bloody incidents." "No. 76," he says, "caused people to shudder . . . and struck terror into the hearts of the average citizen [of Shanghai]."[14]

Chou Fo-hai had been associated with Ting and Li years earlier in Nanking when all three were members of the CC Clique, and so it was not unnatural that he sought the help of his former colleagues. But in

---

* No other wartime secret police organization in Asia was as powerful or as feared as this Bureau, which operated under the Military Affairs Commission, itself directly controlled by the Generalissimo. Tai, whom Barbara Tuchman labels "China's combination of Himmler and J. Edgar Hoover" (*Stilwell*, p. 261), was despised by most American observers in wartime China, and his police apparatus was usually likened to the Gestapo. Though his agents were supposed to conduct anti-Japanese counter-espionage activities, they were much more actively engaged in suppressing Communists and anti-Chiang movements. See the Tai Li entry in the Index to the 1944 *Foreign Relations* volume for references to dispatches by Foreign Service Officer John Carter Vincent and others concerning General Tai. A more flattering appraisal of him is to be found in *A Different Kind of War* by Vice Adm. Milton A. Miles, who worked closely with Tai in the war. The panegyric nature of Miles's account is clear from this tribute he paid to Tai (who died in 1946): "Many people who were intimately familiar with China have said that if Tai Li had lived, China would not have been lost. That is possible, for he had bested the Communists before and might have been able to do so again" (p. 576).

truth, as Nishi writes, "it was not a matter of Li and Ting being 'captured' by Chou. It was precisely the opposite: Li and Ting were waiting to seize Chou."[15] With no military support and little financial support, Wang and Chou were so weak in the spring of 1939 that they were in no position to dictate terms to Li and Ting. They were forced to go hat in hand to solicit the aid that No. 76 could offer to Wang's beleaguered cause. As a result, the Wang movement became inextricably associated with the unsavory assortment of hoodlums and job-seeking politicians that streamed in and out of the well-barricaded portals of No. 76.

Wang probably never visited No. 76; but in any case it was certainly Chou who shouldered the main responsibility for liaison with Li and Ting and for interviewing and recruiting the flood of office-seekers (some of whom had been "shouting anti-Wang slogans only yesterday") who saw personal opportunity in Wang's peace crusade.[16] The low quality of personnel Chou was able to attract to Wang's cause was surely attributable, at least in part, to the fact that the Wang movement, and later the Wang Government, became virtually synonymous with No. 76. Whatever the cause, the paucity of capable, honest, and patriotic officials in Wang's regime was both a source of disappointment to him and an irritant in his relations with the Japanese. "The eyes of your countrymen are on you," Kagesa scolded Chou and the other Chinese at the Yü Yüan Road talks. Wang's followers had devoted themselves to the peace movement when they were in Chungking, Kagesa continued, but after coming to Shanghai they had changed their attitude. Now they only cared about becoming government officials. "The Wang Government should be something more than an unemployment office," he chided.[17]

The balance of terror No. 76 helped to maintain turned Shanghai into a nightmare of reprisals and counterreprisals. The Shanghai equivalent of the Biblical eye for an eye was a "banker for a banker, an editor for and editor," to cite the two most important targets of terrorist attacks. Customarily, when Chungking's Green Gang or Blue Shirts cut down a pro-Wang banker, No. 76 immediately executed a pro-Chungking banker, and indeed a supply of luckless hostages was kept on reserve in the basement cells at No. 76. Some of the Li-Ting captives managed to save themselves, however. "Usually those captured by No. 76 were shot or committed suicide, but if you said that you surrendered you were given a fairly good government post," writes one who was intimately familiar with the infamous house.[18] Those fortunate enough to have families willing to pay huge ransoms could also sometimes regain their freedom. Jabin Hsu, for example, a University of Michigan–trained official of the Chiang regime's Finance Ministry, was released when his family turned over its entire fortune—$300,000. Hsu later told an American friend that his captors had indicated he could quickly recoup his fortune by becoming an officer in the state banking system established by Wang.[19]

Ch'en Hung-shu, one of the Kuomintang's secret agents in Shanghai, surrendered to No. 76, and in return for considerations of "personal advancement," wrote an exposé, *The Inside Story of the Blue Shirts*. Among the men he named were two important leaders of Shanghai's Kuomintang underground, Wu K'ai-hsien and Chiang Po-ch'eng. Both were eventually tracked down by the Japanese secret police and turned over to No. 76. Fortunately for them, Chou Fo-hai was persuaded by Chungking to release the two prisoners.[20] This was only one of several such incidents, proving that the reign of terror in Shanghai was not always so wild and uncontrolled as it sometimes appeared. Though scores of Wang's followers were murdered in terror incidents, none of the high-ranking officials of the Wang group was killed in those attacks.

The petty feuding and factional rivalries that were spawned in the unhealthy atmosphere of No. 76 also damaged the public image and the general morale of the Wang camp. As we have seen, Wang desperately needed military support. One of the first to defect to his side was a certain General Ho T'ien-fu; but Wang had little time to rejoice at this coup, for Ho was gunned down in a "Badlands" nightclub on Christmas Eve 1939 by one of his 18 bodyguards. Though the assassin may have been bribed by Chungking, popular rumor had it that Ho had "a conflict of interest" with someone at No. 76. Ho's troops were inherited by Ting Hsi-shan, an ex-chauffeur whose task at No. 76 was to drive around Shanghai, collect graft from the numerous gambling dens controlled by No. 76, and pick up political prisoners. "In the early period of the Wang regime, practically everybody dissatisfied with Wang was picked up by Ting or by Wu Ssu-pao."[21] Wu, another of the No. 76 crew, had also been a chauffeur—in fact had driven the car of the American Chairman of the International Settlement administration for a time. With access to the municipal garage, he had profitably tapped its supplies of gasoline and tires. He had also engaged in numerous racketeering activities and had become "fat, prosperous, and arrogant." When the Wang regime was organized, Wu joined the "police" staff at No. 76 and rose to considerable power there. An American newspaperman writes of Wu's style:

> It was his custom to take the prisoners out for a walk in the evenings, the stroll ending up at a corner of the walled compound, where there were several freshly filled graves. Wu would then throw his arm affectionately over the victim's shoulder and tell him of the

benefits to be derived from joining the puppet regime or contributing a liberal sum to its support. It was hardly necessary for him to mention the consequences of refusal.[22]

The two ex-chauffeurs' careers at No. 76 were short-lived. In 1941 Ting's criminal activities came to the attention of Wang, who ordered his imprisonment; shortly thereafter he broke out of prison and fled to the interior to join the Kuomintang. Wu gained too much power too quickly at No. 76, and his career came to an abrupt end in 1941, when a dispute erupted between No. 76 and Chou Fo-hai over the distribution of the funds that flowed into No. 76. Wu lost not only his post as "police captain" but also his life. Soon after his dismissal, he was poisoned by the co-commander of No. 76, Li Shih-ch'ün.

To round out this discussion of internecine rivalry at No. 76, let us look at the closing chapter of the career of Li Shih-ch'ün. Chou Fo-hai antagonized Li by appointing a favorite to a post in a lucrative government enterprise charged with channeling Shanghai customs revenues into the treasury of the Wang regime. Soon after, a newspaper associated with Li's faction printed an editorial attacking the corrupt lives of the Wang regime's leaders, including Chou Fo-hai. Chou telephoned Li, who disclaimed any responsibility for the attack. It was the work of Hu Lan-ch'eng, Vice Minister for Political Affairs in the Ministry of Propaganda, he claimed. Though Chou was unable to fix the blame for the incident on Li, relations between the two took a sharp turn for the worse. Somewhat later, Li was invited to the home of a certain Okamura, a major in the Japanese military police force (Kempeitai), where he was treated to a Japanese delicacy called *manju*. Soon after he returned home his body began to swell and turn purple, and after twenty-four hours during which the "perspiration flowed like rain," the poisoned *manju* had done its work and death released him from his agony.*

The Kao-T'ao defections and the seamy scandals at No. 76 infuriated

* Chin, *Dōsei*, Chaps. 31–32. The co-commander at No. 76, Ting Mo-ts'un, managed to survive several attempts on his life by Chungking agents. The most spectacular involved his teenage mistress, Cheng P'in-ju, the daughter of a Chinese father and a Japanese mother. The loyalties of Miss Cheng were thought to be on the side of her mother; in fact, Chungking had recruited her and turned her into a double agent. She lured Ting into an ambush in Shanghai, but he managed to escape with his life. Unfortunately for the compassionate but reckless Miss Cheng, she had exposed her complicity in the deed by putting her calling card inscribed with a Buddhist prayer for a peaceful death for her lover in Ting's pocket. On Ting's orders she was taken to an open grave, shot, and photographed. (Photographing the remains of traitors was a device used by both sides in the Shanghai terror wars to publicize the effectiveness of counterespionage techniques.) See Inukai, *Yōsukō*, pp. 237–52; and Imai, *Shōwa*, pp. 135–37.

and demoralized the Wang camp, but it was too deeply committed to its course to falter. The momentum could be reversed only if Chungking showed serious interest in Japanese peace terms. As Tokyo watched for signals from Chungking the Plum Blossom Agency took the Wang movement a step closer to its "return to the capital" by sponsoring a meeting between Wang and the leaders of the puppet regimes. The sessions began in Tsingtao on January 23. The Five Ministers' June 1939 injunction to include Wu P'ei-fu in the new government was erased by his sudden death in December 1939; their decision not to support Wang until he had proved his worth by persuading influential Chinese to defect from Chungking had been quietly dropped in the intervening months.

The contentiousness that had marked the last Wang-Wang-Liang meeting (at Nanking, in September 1939) had dissipated by the time of the Tsingtao Conference. The Yü Yüan Road Conferences had worked out arrangements acceptable, if not entirely satisfying, to the three leaders and their Imperial Army sponsors. The Tsingtao Conference simply planned the details for the absorption of the Reformed Government into Wang's new regime (Liang, for example, became President of the Control Yüan) and for the continuation of the Provisional Government under its new name (the North China Political Council).[23]

The Tsingtao Conference cleared away the last apparent obstacles to the creation of the Wang Government, and Wang's spokesmen went so far as to announce the imminent founding of the new regime. In truth, however, the discussions at Tsingtao were of only secondary importance, for the main focus of Tokyo's attention was turned toward Chungking, which was beginning to hint that it was interested in peace negotiations. No matter how affectionately Tokyo paraded its fiancée in public, it remained privately skeptical about marriage with the Wang regime. For all of the vilification Chiang Kai-shek received in Tokyo, he remained the more alluring partner. Meanwhile, from about August 1939 on, and especially after the convocation of the Sixth Congress of the "Orthodox Kuomintang" in late August, relations between the Wang group and Chungking deteriorated so badly that any hope of Wang serving as a bridge to Chungking all but disappeared.

Wang's editorial support had begun to pay dividends and contributed to the widening breach with Chungking. Lin Pai-sheng, editor of the Shanghai daily *Nan-hua jih-pao*, excoriated the Chiang regime for doing the very thing that it found treasonable in Wang, namely, searching for a negotiated peace settlement. The difference between Chungking and Wang, Lin argued, was that Chungking pursued its goals secretly, whereas Wang took the peace issue directly to the public. And it was proper that he do so, in Lin's view, for a constitutional government must decide vital national issues like peace and war, issues that related to national survival, by appealing to the public or in constitutional bodies. No proper government should ever "prevent people from talking" or "throw into the street anyone who dares mention [peace]," wrote Lin, who himself had been brutally assaulted and shot in the eye after he declared his support for Wang in January 1939.[24] In addition to criticizing Chungking for its suppression of peace talk, Lin bore down on the issue of Chiang's putative "domination by the Communists," in effect suggesting that it was Chiang rather than Wang who was being manipulated:

> Moscow's interests of recent years have obviously lain in keeping Japan embroiled with China; hence, all her efforts have, up to the present, been directed against any conclusion of peace. Hence, again, the opposition of the Chinese Communists to all the peace efforts. How completely these gentry are subject to Moscow is evident from the declaration, immediately following the Soviet-German Non Aggression Pact, of their leader, Mao Tse-tung, that Germany was no longer China's bitter enemy. Moscow from being anti-German became pro-German, and the Chinese Communists followed suit. When Stalin says, "Turn," we all turn!
>
> The Nomonhan Agreement, concluded on September 15, between Japan and the Soviet Union, makes clearer the fact that China has all along been made the pawn of Russia in that country's long drawn out controversy with Japan. As soon as it suits Moscow to come to terms with Tokyo, Chungking is abandoned. One wonders if the Communists will, as a result, find that Japan as well as Germany is China's friend.
>
> From 1937 on, General Chiang Kai-shek has, whether wittingly or not, been playing Moscow's game. It was this domination of the Generalissimo by the Communists, themselves acting on orders from Moscow, and the consequent subordination of China's interests to those of Russia, that caused Mr. Wang to break with Chungking. Whether the Anti-Comintern Pact is dead or alive is completely irrelevant to the case, and affects Mr. Wang's position and arguments not in the least. Nor does it matter whether the Communists are for the moment the palest pink instead of the deepest red or not. They still remain tied to Moscow, and committed, should they ever get the opportunity, to the Bolshevization of the country and its subordination to Soviet-Russia. They are the compradores *par excellence* of modern Russian Imperialism.[25]

Wang's own attack on both the person and the policies of the Generalissimo was also intensified in the latter half of 1939. In a speech in Canton in August, he lashed out at Chiang for "regarding his own personal interests as far more important than the interests of the nation." At Sian, Wang declared, Chiang had "present[ed] the country to the Communist Party and the Third International as a reward for being allowed to keep his life."[26] At the Double Ten celebrations in 1939, Wang described Chiang as "an aspirant dictator [who] has not even the minimum moral and ethical qualifications of a normal human being."[27] This was not a mere escalation of slander on Wang's part; it was a self-justification based on the Confucian imperative concerning the loss of mandate by a wicked tyrant. Wang made the point explicit: "Our most urgent task today is thus the overthrow of the personal dictatorship and the purification of the political and military system of the country."[28]

Despite Wang's stepped-up campaign against the National Government, the most persistent theme in his speeches continued to be the question of "peace and national unity," as he put it. In answer to those who claimed that China was rapidly attaining the long-sought-after goal of national unity as the result of the war of resistance, Wang wrote:

> I strongly disagree with such a statement. From the dawn of history to the present day, those at the helm of State have always made it their duty to maintain domestic peace for the purpose of resisting foreign aggression, not to engage in external war for the purpose of maintaining domestic peace. An external war is a very serious matter, so how can we turn an external war into an instrument for achieving internal peace? China is engaged in a war of resistance for the purpose of maintaining her status as an independent nation; she did not go to war only to achieve national unity. I strongly object to using a war of resistance as a method of unifying the country. Moreover, as things stand today, the advocacy of peace will not affect, in the least, the unity of China, while the non-advocacy of peace may not necessarily prevent a breakup of the united front.[29]

In defending his peace policies, Wang did not argue that Japan was faultless in her China policies, but merely that somehow the "cycle of revenge" had to be terminated. In a September 1939 article, he explained what he meant by "cycle of revenge":

> For instance, Japan says: "Chinese animosity against Japan is the cause of the Mukden Incident." China says: "Japanese aggression is the cause of the Chinese animosity." Japan says: "China has to give up the policy of 'playing one barbarian against the other' before

Sino-Japanese relations could be improved." China says: "Japan has to give up her aggressive policy towards China before the Sino-Japanese relations could be improved." And so on, and so forth. They all accuse each other, expecting that the other party would take the initiative to better her attitude. This can only serve to worsen the situation.[30]

OPERATION KIRI

As the gap between Chungking and Wang widened, and as the possibility of using Wang as a bridge to Chungking dissolved in acrimonious exchanges between Chungking and Shanghai, the Japanese began to explore a fresh series of operations designed to bypass Wang and reopen direct negotiations with Chungking. By early 1940 one of these operations appeared so promising that the creation of Wang's regime was put off for some months. And even after the regime was established in March 1940, Japan refrained from formally recognizing it for more than six months in order to permit the most careful exploration of new avenues of secret diplomatic approach to Chungking. Wang's closest Japanese supporters, especially the Plum Blossom group, correctly felt that some of the avenues were blind, that they had been opened up as part of a Chungking plot to prevent Japan and Wang from working out the New Order in East Asia. Apart from these loyalists, however, there were few Japanese who were willing to take the chance of jeopardizing a possible rapprochement with Chungking by premature alliance with Wang. Moreover, though we now know that the Plum Blossom Agency was correct in seeing as spurious at least some of Chungking's interest in negotiations, no one could know for certain at the time how sincere (or insincere) Chungking was. Indeed, it is still impossible today to be certain whether the most promising of these peace efforts, the so-called Operation Kiri (*Kiri kōsaku*), was a pure hoax or a sincere peace move on the part of Chungking.[31]

Operation Kiri was the code name for a series of negotiations that began in November 1939 and lasted for nearly a year. The mysterious affair began when Lt. Col. Suzuki Takuji, while on an intelligence mission in Hong Kong, met a man who represented himself as Soong Tzu-liang (T. L. Soong), a younger brother of T. V. Soong and Soong Mei-ling (Madame Chiang Kai-shek). The Imperial Army's intelligence files, which ought to have been bulging with information on such an important figure, were wholly inadequate. When data were hastily assembled, they revealed that Soong had been the Financial Commissioner for Kwangtung some three years earlier, then had moved to Hong Kong to become the Manager of the Southwestern Transportation Company. Whenever Madame Chiang came to the Crown Colony on one of her frequent trips for medical care and respite from the arduous life in wartime Chungking, the family—including T. L.—assembled at the Sassoon Road home of Madame H. H. Kung (Soong Ai-ling). After the full implication of the potential value of a direct pipeline to the highest authorities in Chungking had simmered in Suzuki's mind, he called for Colonel Imai to join him. By February 1940 Colonel Imai, or as he was introduced, "Mr. Satō of the South Manchurian Railway," was in Hong Kong ready for his first meeting with Chiang Kai-shek's brother-in-law.

At their first meeting, Imai was acutely aware that he had no positive assurance the man before him was in fact T. L. Soong. The stranger appeared to be about forty years old, was five foot two or three inches tall, seemed courteous and well-mannered, spoke good English, and occasionally puffed on a cigar. Unfortunately, Imai relates, he could locate no one who was acquainted with T. L. Soong to see if the description fit. The man who had introduced Suzuki to T. L. was a reporter—one Chang Chih-p'ing—who had once worked for the East Hopei puppet regime and claimed to have been a classmate of T. L.'s at St. John's College in Shanghai. Imai had known Chang Chih-p'ing in the East Hopei days—but could he be trusted?

Imai took his impressions back to Tokyo and received the green light to pursue Operation Kiri in spite of the possibility of deception. The talks began in earnest in March 1940, under elaborate security arrangements, on the second floor of a Chinese business establishment in Hong Kong. Occasionally, the site of the meetings was changed to a candlelit basement in a house in Macao—"It reminded me of something from out of the Tokugawa era," Imai recalls.[32] Each evening, from 9:00 on, sometimes until dawn, Imai and two assistants (Col. Usui Shigeki and Sakata Masamōri) met and discussed peace terms with the Chinese delegation, which now included Gen. Ch'en Ch'ao-lin, from the Generalissimo's military headquarters, and Chang Yu-san, Chief Secretary to the National Defense Council. Chang did most of the talking but deferred to Ch'en on the most important questions. Soong did little more than "mediate."

The Japanese authorities, who maintained a close surveillance on all of the Chinese participants in the discussions, discovered—with the help of Chinese informants at Kai Tak Airport—that no matter how late the meetings adjourned the Chinese delegates immediately assembled for a long time and then dispatched a liaison man to the airport. Then, usually in the middle of the night, a plane left for Chungking. Another thing that encouraged Imai to believe he was really in touch with Chungking was the reports in the Hong Kong press suggesting Madame Chiang was in the Colony and was supporting certain peace talks from behind the scenes.

For a few days the negotiations proceeded smoothly, the only obstacles arising out of the efforts of one of Imai's rivals, Maj. Gen. Wachi Takaji, to sabotage the talks by revealing their existence to the Shanghai newspapers. The Japanese side learned several things as the talks progressed. First, Chungking made it clear that it would not consider any kind of collaboration (*gassaku*) with Wang. The Chiang regime was reported to be pleased at the deterioration of American-Japanese relations and attributed it in part to the fact that Japan seemed to be moving nearer to the support of a Wang regime. If Japan wanted peace, Chungking insisted, she would have to realize that the stationing of Japanese troops in North China was "absolutely out of the question." Moreover, she would have to understand that her demand for the recognition of Manchukuo caused a "great problem" for the Kuomintang Government, and would therefore have to drop that demand "for the time being." Inasmuch as Wang had already committed himself to recognizing Manchukuo, the Japanese Government had become "somewhat at ease about the Manchukuoan question," writes Imai. "We did not appreciate how much of an obstacle to peace the recognition issue was, and so we were surprised at learning Chungking's true feelings."[33]

By the time the meetings had reached this stage, plans for the creation of the Wang Government had moved ahead to the point where a date, March 26, had been set for ceremonies marking the "return of the Kuomintang government to the capital" at Nanking. So promising was Operation Kiri, however, that when Chungking asked for more time to resolve the recognition question, both the Kōain and the China Expeditionary Army Headquarters asked Tokyo to postpone the inauguration ceremonies until April 15. Tokyo, suspecting that Chungking was insincere and merely interested in embarrassing Wang (who at this stage had not been given any explanation for the repeated delays in the inauguration of his new regime), was willing to give the National Government only four more days' grace. If no reply was received from Chungking by March 30, inauguration ceremonies would take place on that day. No reply was forthcoming.

In May 1940 the Operation Kiri negotiations began anew. This time the two principal negotiators brought with them credentials signed by the Generalissimo.[34] T. L. Soong's identity, meanwhile, was still unverified. According to Imai, it was even impossible to determine how old the real T. L. Soong was. Operation Kiri investigations turned up evidence that he was born in various years between 1893 and 1899. In the hope of solving the mystery, Imai arranged a meeting in the Grand Hotel in Hong Kong between himself and Soong. Soong was carefully seated in a direct line with the keyhole, and while the two chatted Colonel Suzuki crouched at the keyhole and snapped several photographs. When the pictures were shown to Chou Fo-hai and Ch'en Kung-po, Imai was exasperated to find that one thought the man was Soong, and the other thought that he was not.

Though Chou and Ch'en privately savored the frustration of Japanese intelligence, they were not able to frustrate the effort itself, and Operation Kiri went on. It was not until 1945 that the mystery was finally cleared up. By an amazing coincidence, Sakata Masamōri, the Japanese translator for Operation Kiri, chanced to recognize "T. L. Soong" among a group of Chinese prisoners in a camp near Shanghai. Under interrogation, the man revealed that his name was Tseng Kuang, that he was a member of the Blue Shirts, and that he had indeed impersonated his look-alike six years earlier. His orders had come directly from Chiang's intelligence chief, General Tai. Eight years after the end of the war, Imai was visited by Chang Chih-p'ing, the reporter who had introduced "T. L. Soong" to Colonel Suzuki. He corroborated the impostor's story. The Generalissimo and General Tai had taken direct charge of the negotiations and had great expectations for them, according to Chang, but after word of the talks was leaked to the public, Chiang was under great pressure to break them off and finally did so in September 1940.[35]

In spite of the Chinese deception about Soong, Japanese analysts are inclined to believe that the Chinese participants in Operation Kiri were in fact in contact with Chungking, and think it altogether possible that the negotiations were as close to producing results as they seemed: by August both sides were seriously discussing a cease-fire and a meeting between General Itagaki and the Generalissimo at Changsha. In the end, Operation Kiri failed because of the Kōain's insensitivity to the Generalissimo's predicament. The Chinese negotiators insisted that Chiang truly yearned for peace with Japan, for tensions were mounting in the united front and "would become evident in August [1940]." Imai reported that in Chungking's view the announcement of an official, high-level meeting with the Japanese would precipitate an all-out civil war in China, and that the Kuomintang naturally wished to be in a position to destroy the Communists when the time came. Accordingly, it was imperative that Tokyo drop its demands for a *prior* commitment from Chungking on the recognition of Manchukuo. But the Japanese high command would not yield the point. As desperately as the Army wished for peace with China, General Itagaki told Imai, it was sticking to its "get tough" policy and would insist on the recognition of Manchukuo. On September 28, 1940, the Headquarters of the China Expeditionary Army finally decided that China was "not sincere in her desire for peace" and downgraded Operation Kiri to just another "channel for intelligence."[36]

Meanwhile, Wang and his colleagues had come to regard Operation Kiri as a serious threat. Fully informed by Kagesa of the progress of the secret talks after about June, they grew more and more gloomy as it appeared that the talks were making some headway. By July Chou Fo-hai was glumly predicting in his diary: "For a year or so after peace is achieved, Chiang might find us very important for negotiations with the Japanese, but then we will probably all be assassinated."[37] Chou's uneasiness points up one of the fundamental weaknesses of the whole Wang Ching-wei effort as conceived by Japan. The Wang movement never stood on its own feet and was never recognized as an end in itself, either before or after the creation of the new Government. Because Tokyo persisted in focusing its attention on a settlement with Chungking, Wang's regime was never allowed to develop its own goals or achieve a degree of national dignity to which Japan would pledge its support. There is nothing that so bespeaks the puppet character of the Wang regime as the indifference toward it of its sponsor and guarantor. And there is nothing that so discredited the New Order in East Asia as Japan's offhanded treatment of her first partner in that experiment.

When hopes for a direct settlement with Chungking flickered in the last days of March 1940, Tokyo allowed the Plum Blossom Agency to proceed with the installation of the Wang Government. Not much confidence was placed in the new regime, but for the moment at least Chungking inspired even less hope. There was a possibility that Tokyo might end up alienating everyone in China; the Japanese had to be careful "to avoid falling between two stools," observed Navy officer Ugaki Ten on March 16.[38]

Wang's inauguration on March 30 was a dismal affair, the plans of bureaucratic festivity makers notwithstanding. A cold, misty rain added to the already cheerless atmosphere in a city that had suffered much under the Japanese. The Imperial Army was still present in strength, and there were few Chinese who could look with indifference on the sight of Japanese soldiers guarding the approaches to modern China's most sacred shrine, the Sun Yat-sen mausoleum carved into the side of Purple Mountain. It was a pattern the Japanese Army followed throughout its occupation of China, this callous disregard of national sensibilities, expressed in countless little acts of arrogance: the renaming of streets (to detested names like Matsui, the conqueror of Nanking), the setting of Chinese clocks to Tokyo time, the engineering of giant school rallies to celebrate the capitulation of Chinese cities to Japanese forces. Now, on the day of the "return of the Kuomintang Government" to Nanking, Wang ordered the hated triangular pennant removed from the blue-sky flags flying at the inauguration ceremonies. As if to underscore Japanese determination to control even the symbols of Chinese national life, Kagesa countermanded the order and had the yellow pennants affixed before the proceedings began.

The inauguration was held in a simple hall, the most impressive Government buildings in the city having been commandeered by the Imperial Army. Japanese officials had been persuaded to stay away from the brief ceremony, which consisted of a short announcement by Wang and his introduction of his Ministers, each of whom stepped forward for a bow from the chalked circle that marked his place. Later in the day Wang received the press and issued a circumspect warning to Japan. The Reorganized Government agreed with Konoe's Three Principles, he declared. But "China must maintain the independence of her sovereignty and her national freedom before she will be able to carry out the principles of good neighbourliness, of a common anti-Comintern front and economic cooperation and, further, share in the responsibility of building up the New Order in East Asia."[39]

Wang could have been little reassured by the remarks of Suma Yakichirō, a Japanese Foreign Office spokesman who met with the press on the following day, April 1, to discuss the new regime. Replying with unintended irony to questions about the independence of Wang's regime, Suma indicated that there was no need for apprehension: it was as independent as the Government of Manchukuo.[40] Nor could Wang have been heartened by the declaration of Lin Sen, the proposed President of the Reorganized Government in whose stead Wang was "acting President." In a radio broadcast from Chungking, Lin called for the arrest of Wang as a traitor whose deeds were facilitating Japanese aggression.[41] Other Kuomintang officials in Chungking greeted Wang's elevation by burning grotesque cardboard effigies of him and his wife and collecting a reward fund to be paid to his assassin.[42]

Official greetings were sent from Tokyo, but the dispatch of Gen. Abe Nobuyuki as the official representative of the Japanese Government at the proceedings was interpreted by the Chinese press as a slight to the new regime. If the Government of Japan had been determined to express its confidence in the new regime, it should have sent Konoe or someone of similar stature rather than the inconsequential Abe. An even more pointed rebuff was the failure of Tokyo to extend diplomatic recognition to the Wang regime.

At the time of the Yü Yüan Road Conferences, Horiba had stressed to Kagesa that the demands the Japanese were making represented the full reach of Japan's conditions and, in fact, could be softened after the creation of the Wang Government. Whether Wang accepted Horiba's assurance at face value is not known. If he did it would help explain his acceptance of the harsh terms on December 30. At the same time, it would tend to justify the criticism of even his admirers that he was naïve and far too compliant. Harsh as the terms were, there was ample reason to suspect Japan might treat them as less than binding if it so suited her purpose; as with past agreements and understandings, she might simply repudiate the December 30 agreements on the grounds that they lacked official Government sanction. This was precisely what the Kōain intended to do, as Wang was to learn when he began negotiating his "Basic Treaty" with Japan in the summer of 1940.

The man designated to negotiate the treaty with Wang was Abe Nobuyuki, the General (and former Premier) who had represented the Japanese Government at Wang's inauguration. Abe, given the subambassadorial rank of Envoy Extraordinary, took his instructions from the Kōain (more specifically, from Lt. Gen. Suzuki Teiichi) rather than from the Foreign Ministry. Its orders to him were based on two fundamental premises. The first was that as long as the war lasted Wang must not expect Japan to make any concessions that might complicate military operations. General Suzuki told Foreign Minister Arita that any official discussion of compromises with Wang on military or economic matters was out of the question while hostilities continued. There is no doubt, historian Usui writes, about the type of government envisioned by the Kōain: "It was nothing more than a device for controlling occupied territory."[43]

The second premise guiding the Kōain thinking on the "adjustment of Sino-Japanese relations" was that the true key to Japan's destiny on the mainland was not the Wang regime, but the Chungking regime. "The first obligation of the new Wang central government is the peace effort with Chungking," declared the leaders of the China Expeditionary Army.[44] The Kōain agreed wholeheartedly. In March 1940 Matsumoto Sōkichi, of the Osaka *Mainichi*, asserted "that the Chungking Government still commands the support of millions of Chinese, that the majority of Chinese are anti-Japanese, and that Japan and Wang have to undertake a long propaganda battle to win any significant number of people to their cause."[45] General Suzuki echoed these sentiments in a remarkably frank assessment of Chiang and Wang to an American newsman: "We realize only too well that [Chiang] is the one outstanding man in China. We should be working through him. . . . We are aware of Wang Ching-wei's record of deserting those with whom he worked. But he is the best Japan could get under the circumstances."[46]

An important segment of the Army General Staff shared the Kōain's lack of confidence in Wang and continued to look for a direct link to Chungking. Indeed, the mood of many throughout the nation was one of profound skepticism about the wisdom of Japan's association with Wang. In a debate in the Diet, a veteran leader of the Minseitō Party, Saitō Takao, delivered a speech of rare tone and substance for that bland and passive body of legislators.[47] For two hours he excoriated the Government for its China policy. The Government, he declared, "with its grand talk of a 'holy war,' ignores realities and willfully conceals from the people the sacrifices they are forced to make. The Government uses phrases like 'international justice,' 'moral diplomacy,' 'co-prosperity,' and 'world peace,' but understanding what these phrases mean is like trying to hold a cloud in your hand."[48]

Saitō was particularly incensed about the Government's support of Wang, which Saitō feared would end all possibilities of reconciliation with Chungking. While making it clear that he held Wang in great esteem, Saitō lectured the Diet on the realities of international law and state power:

> When I stand back to examine the situation, I can't understand where [the Wang] Government is going to get power. In order to stand as a state in international law, a nation must have the ability to control itself internally and perform its responsibilities to the rest of the world. Where does it get the strength to do those things? From military power. No matter how much of a state structure you erect . . . , without military power you have nothing. This is especially evident in Chinese history—a new regime has always had superior power. . . . Chiang Kai-shek has that power, and that is the reason he was able to unify China. . . . But does the new government have that power?[49]

Answering his own question, Saitō declared that the Wang regime— "shot through with bandits and defeated stragglers"—was thoroughly incapable of establishing internal peace. Inevitably, the Japanese Government would have to make enormous sacrifices in manpower and money if it wished to prop the regime up. Saitō paid dearly for this attack. For besmirching the holy war and suggesting that the Government "should be able to do something more than simply demand sacrifices of the people," he was called before a House discipline committee and expelled from the Diet.[50] Ironically enough, pacifist Saitō's doubts about the wisdom of all-out support of Wang, if that meant burning the last bridges to Chungking, were shared in the hawkish councils of the Kōain.

The Kōain's continuing emphasis on the necessity of reaching a solution with Chungking meant that it was willing to sacrifice Wang to that end. In a word, Japan's most liberal terms were not to be presented to Wang but were to be held in reserve for future negotiations with Chungking. As Inukai saw it, the negotiations with Wang were like a banquet at which the choicest dishes were withheld from the invited guest (Wang) so that "a splendid feast" could be laid out for the uninvited guest (Chiang).[51]

FINAL NEGOTIATIONS—THE BASIC TREATY

When Abe acquainted Wang and his colleagues with the terms of the Basic Treaty as proposed by the Kōain, their initial reaction was that "Japan has extracted from the informal agreements [of December 30] everything that she wants in order to incorporate it into the forthcoming treaty. The rest will be turned into wastepaper."[52] Once the official negotiating sessions began in July the correctness of this reaction was borne out on issue after issue. For example, Wang asked Abe for an indication of the concrete steps Japan meant to take to implement her intention (declared by Konoe publicly in December 1938 and reaffirmed at the Yü Yüan Road Conferences) to retrocede the concessions and abolish her extraterritorial privileges. Abe declined to do so, pleading the precarious position of Japanese businessmen in China, who could not compete against the British imperialists, with their enormous capital resources and huge staffs of compradores. Wang tried to get several of the secret understandings in the December 30 agreements written into the Basic Treaty in order to quiet the rumors that Japan did not regard past agreements as binding. Abe refused to yield on any of these items, which in general provided for some restraints on Japanese economic activities (such as the issuance of military scrip).

Perhaps the bitterest pill of all for Wang was Abe's refusal to concede to a provision for the nationalization of China's railroads, a step that was specifically and unequivocally called for in the December 30 agreements. Wang pleaded in desperation with influential visitors from Tokyo to intercede with Premier Konoe to give the new regime the "face" it needed to stand independently. First on the list of his requests was that Japan honor her December 30 agreements by returning the railroads (at least those in the Shanghai-Nanking area) to Chinese management.[53] The Kōain adamantly refused on the grounds of "military necessity" and the "close relationship between railroads and the Imperial Army's pacification efforts." As a result, the railroads remained under joint Sino-Japanese management, which for all practical purposes meant Japanese management.

The uncompromising Abe stood fast on virtually every point of substance in negotiating the Basic Treaty with Wang. Only in matters of wording or on procedural questions did the Chinese side score some modest gains. The sometimes long-drawn-out debates over wording provide an interesting insight into the thinking of Wang—or rather of his lieutenants, since it was Chou Fo-hai and Mei Ssu-p'ing who did much of the actual negotiating. When, for example, the Japanese proposed that Article V provide for the stationing of Japanese naval units in the Yangtze "in order to preserve the common interests of the two countries," Chou asked that the "common interests" clause be changed to read "on the basis of facts established prior to the Incident." After all, said Chou, the stationing of naval units by Japan in the Yangtze was an established fact—and one approved by Chiang Kai-shek.

Chou clearly hoped the change of wording would shift the responsibility for these forces to Chungking's shoulders. Abe compromised, and the final version included both phrases as justification for the Japanese naval presence on the Yangtze.[54]

Needless to say, on the all-important question of troop withdrawal, Wang was unable to extract any concessions from Abe, and Article III of an Annexed Protocol to the Basic Treaty incorporated much of the language used in the December 30 agreement. By tying the two-year withdrawal period to demands that Wang's government guarantee "the firm establishment of peace and order during this period," the Basic Treaty provided for an occupation period of almost indefinite duration.

An exchange between Chou and Kagesa illustrates the distance between the two sides on the issue of troop withdrawal. Said Chou: "You claim that Japanese [civilians] won't come to China unless the Army is there. If you would only come as guests, then we would welcome you. But if your people feel that they won't be secure unless they have guns, then it is going to be a very awkward situation for us."[55] The Nanking Government would be expressing its approval of a permanent occupation by Japanese troops if it signed the treaty, Chou added, and this would seriously damage the new regime in the eyes of the public. Kagesa replied: "What you say about guns and guests is wrong. The Japanese want to come as guests in *haori* [formal attire] but your *zashiki* [rooms] are not in good condition. Before the Incident, Japan tried to get along with China, but the atmosphere in China was not very favorable. The peace was not very well kept there. So, the kind of guests you want— good guests—will not come unless peace and order are provided. You know that full well."[56]

On August 31 the text of the Basic Treaty was finally agreed on, and the way was clear for Japan to announce her formal recognition of the Wang regime. But once again Tokyo stalled for more time.

MORE DELAYS: OPERATION CH'IEN

On January 4, 1940, Maj. Gen. Mutō Akira, Chief of the War Ministry's Military Affairs Bureau, reflecting the deepening frustration of the Imperial Army with the never-ending conflict in China, declared that the Army was determined to end the war "during this year by whatever means." Similar signs of a do-or-die push in 1940 were evident in numerous policy statements, studies, and decisions during the year. As always, however, the Army remained ambivalent on the question of force versus persuasion. Both were to be used to end the war.[57]

Nevertheless, 1940 saw the balance shift toward an ever-widening application of force. Angered by Great Britain's sympathy for the Chinese and taking advantage of her preoccupation with the European war, Japan demanded that Britain seal the China-Burma frontier (which is to say, close the Burma Road over which a steady flow of supplies had been reaching China). The Japanese also demanded the closing of the Hong Kong frontier, and to back up that demand, sent a large force to take up positions along the borders of the New Territories. Britain responded as she had to earlier displays of Japanese belligerence: by calling on the United States to stand with her in resisting the Japanese demands. The United States responded as *she* had on similar occasions in the past: by urging Britain to stand firm while rejecting any form of joint action. Unwilling to face Japan's ire alone, Britain obliged by closing the Burma Road and the Hong Kong frontier on July 18.

Four days later Prince Konoe was invested as Premier and formed a Cabinet unanimously committed to the creation of "a high-degree defense state." What this meant, in the words of historian Robert J. C. Butow, was that a " 'high-powered government' would be inaugurated, the national general mobilization law would be more widely invoked, a wartime economic structure would be established, war materials would be stockpiled, and Japan's shipping tonnage would be expanded."[58] Lt. Gen. Tōjō Hideki was named Minister of War and Matsuoka Yōsuke Foreign Minister. On July 27, less than a week after Konoe's investiture, a Liaison Conference—the first in two years—was held. The decisions emerging from that conference "constituted a pivotal stage in the metamorphosis of the China Incident into the Greater East Asian War," writes Butow.[59] The essence of those decisions was that where diplomacy failed, Japan would "use force" (*buryoku kōshi*) to achieve her goals in Asia.

The probability that Japan would need to fall back on force was increased once she began to contemplate a Japanese-dominated economic bloc in Southeast Asia. Such a bloc was essential to sustain her military machine on the China mainland; without the resources of Indonesia, Malaya, and the Dutch East Indies, a protracted war against Chiang was almost certain to fail. This economic fact of life was underscored in July 1940, when the United States introduced a trade-licensing system aimed at Japan. That cautious first step in the direction of economic embargo began to hurt Japan badly two months later, when scrap iron was placed on the list of goods Japan could no longer obtain from the United States.

One of Matsuoka's first acts as Foreign Minister was to demand that the newly created Vichy Government in France close the border between China and Indochina and prevent the flow of supplies to the Kuomintang regime. He further demanded that Japanese forces be allowed to move into northern Indochina. Premier Pétain stalled for a month in the hope that the United States might come to the aid of the French forces in Indochina. When no help from Washington was forthcoming, Vichy weighed its chances of resisting an invasion mounted from Japan's new naval and air bases on Hainan Island and from its land bases in neighboring Kwangsi province. Finally just as Churchill had deemed it politic to yield on the Burma Road, so did Pétain on Indochina. On August 30, in an exchange of notes with Matsuoka, French Ambassador Charles Arsène-Henry agreed to discuss economic conventions and to grant military facilities to Japan in Indochina.

Meanwhile, Germany's devastating Blitzkrieg in the spring of 1940 prompted the Japanese Foreign Office to calculate that the "disintegration of the British Empire is inevitable." Matsuoka, a professed pro-American, argued that Japan, "weak and isolated" by the combined effects of the China Incident and American economic pressure, had to rely on the power of another country to see her through her crisis.[60] Germany was the logical choice, he concluded. The result was the Tripartite Pact between Italy, Germany, and Japan, which was formally signed in Berlin on September 27, 1940. But the Pact did not have the intended effect—it did not frighten the United States into passivity but instead helped speed Japanese-American relations toward the breaking point.

As the relations between Japan and the United States deteriorated, Chungking took renewed hope. On October 12 the American Ambassador in Chungking, Nelson T. Johnson, reported that Vice Minister of Foreign Affairs Hsü Mo had remarked:

> The Generalissimo and other high officials of the Chinese Government now feel there is a growing recognition in the United States and Great Britain that China's struggle is likely to have a vital effect on the future security of the two democratic powers and that the hostilities in the Far East are inseparably linked with those in Europe. China, therefore, is less receptive to peace overtures now than at any time since the commencement of hostilities.[61]

"It is safe to comment that Chinese morale is now higher than at any time since the start of the Sino-Japanese conflict," Johnson added. Further bolstering the morale of Chungking was Great Britain's announcement that she would reopen the Burma Road on October 18. In addition to the satisfaction of having quantities of gasoline, trucks, and other supplies flowing into China once again, the Chinese were given a substantial psychological boost by the reopening of contact with Burma.

This was the mood of Chungking at the time the Konoe Cabinet was formulating a new policy toward China. That policy, incorporated in a statement entitled "Essentials for Adjusting the China Incident," was formally approved at an Imperial Conference on November 13, 1940.[62] The new policy called for Japan to continue to pursue peace efforts with Chungking until the end of the year. Nevertheless, the recognition of the Wang regime, so often delayed because of the hopes placed in Operation Kiri, would take place no later than November 30. Accordingly, Matsuoka began some last-minute attempts to persuade Chungking to accept Japan's peace terms.

Matsuoka followed two routes. He first prevailed on Japan's new Axis partners to impress on Chungking the futility of continued resistance. On November 15 German Foreign Minister Joachim von Ribbentrop summoned the Chinese Ambassador in Berlin to the Foreign Office to remind him that all of Europe was under German control and to predict that the war would end by late 1940 "or by early spring [of 1941] at the latest." China, said Ribbentrop, was soon going to be without international support. She should therefore respond favorably to Matsuoka's peace overtures and take this "last opportunity" to join the Axis. If Chiang Kai-shek did not respect this advice, both Germany and Italy would be forced to follow Japan in recognizing the Wang regime, he warned.[63]

As a counterpoint to these tactics of threat and doom, Matsuoka employed conciliation in his main attempt to reach Chungking. His protégé Nishi Yoshiaki, who had been so instrumental in creating the Wang movement, now became Matsuoka's agent in reaching Chiang. In this effort Nishi used two intermediaries he had known in Nanking: Chang Ching-li, former Chief of the Financial Bureau of the Ministry of Communications, and banker Ch'ien Yung-ming, a personal friend of the Generalissimo's. As in the case of Operation Kiri, Japanese officials were in the dark during most of Operation Ch'ien, uncertain whether or not they were really in touch with the Generalissimo. In fact they were, but this was not revealed until after the war.

The two reports we have on the various terms that were discussed during Operation Ch'ien are not altogether consistent with each other;[64] but both suggest that at one point Matsuoka agreed in principle to the terms Chang Ching-li presented during a visit to Tokyo in October 1940. If this is so, Matsuoka was endorsing terms that were substantially more generous than those the Wang regime had been forced to accept. For example, instead of the two-year withdrawal period for occupation troops to which Wang had consented, Matsuoka agreed to the withdrawal of all Japanese troops sent to China after the Marco Polo Bridge Incident within six months after a cease-fire was effected. (The period could be extended to one year in accordance with a defense treaty that was contemplated.) With respect to resources, China's needs were to be given the highest priority; her requirements having been satisfied, Japan was then to have the option of buying all she needed—at the highest prevailing market prices![65]

That Matsuoka—and apparently Tōjō as well—were willing even to consider such terms as a basis for discussion with Chungking strongly supports the thesis that the Konoe Government was extremely reluctant to proceed with the signing of the Basic Treaty with the Wang regime. Inukai was evidently correct in his belief that the "choicest dishes" were being held in reserve for Chiang. Further evidence of the cool attitude of the Japanese toward Wang's government is to be found in the discussions of the Privy Council on November 20. At this time the Privy Council was largely a place of retirement for distinguished civil servants of the Emperor, but it still clung to one last vestige of power: its constitutional authority to ratify treaties. What clearly troubled the Councillors was the very idea of according Wang recognition. Count Arima Yoriyasu spoke for many of those present when he contrasted Wang with Chiang: Wang's defection had proved his "lack of integrity, and he was little trusted by the Chinese themselves [whereas] Chiang enjoyed the trust of the Chinese people because of his heroic life [*eiyūteki sonzai*]."[66] When the Council reconvened the following day, the Councillors continued to express much more interest in Chungking than in Nanking, and Foreign Minister Matsuoka tried to relieve the apprehensive mood by expressing his confidence in his own peace negotiations: "[Chungking has] approached closer to us, and the negotiations are proceeding rather smoothly." The worried Councillors were assured by Matsuoka and others that even if recognition was extended, the Imperial Government would not cease its efforts to induce Chiang to join the Wang regime.[67]

Unfortunately, from this crucial point on, the historical record on Operation Ch'ien grows murky, revealing only a frantic scurrying about by intermediaries and last desperate attempts by interested parties to forestall the signing of the Basic Treaty.[68] We are left with nothing but speculations about the reasons for the final collapse of the approach to Chiang, and the decision at a Liaison Conference on November 28 to proceed with the signing of the treaty two days later. As might be expected, those who were most intimately connected with the Wang regime attributed the entire operation to Chungking's cunning effort to delay the recognition of the Wang regime; and pressure from the Wang regime and Kagesa was surely instrumental in the November 28 decision to sign the treaty. According to one account, if last-minute delays in flight schedules between Chungking and Hong Kong had not occurred, Operation Ch'ien might have survived, and the recognition of the Wang regime might have been delayed even longer.[69]

It is quite plain Chungking used the negotiations to emphasize to the United States and Great Britain that they could withhold massive aid from China only at the risk of forcing a Sino-Japanese detente, which would free Japan to move south and imperil Western interests. While T. V. Soong and Gen. Claire Chennault were in Washington pleading for aid, the Generalissimo was keeping President Roosevelt informed of the Japanese peace overtures and German offers to act as a guarantor of Japanese terms. Ambassador Johnson in Chungking clearly feared that Chungking was on the verge of accepting Matsuoka's offer to negotiate. On November 21, less than six weeks after he had glowingly reported Chungking's high morale, Johnson was writing in a totally different vein. The Generalissimo had told him that if America did not counter the expected Axis recognition of the Wang regime by "showing a positive attitude," his war of resistance would be "gravely imperiled."[70] On November 27 Johnson cabled Washington again, reporting that Chiang appeared to him a "man who has lost confidence in his ability to contend longer with the domestic situation [and] feels he has now virtually exhausted the strength of his nation in resisting aggression, in an effort as much in the interests of Great Britain and the United States as of China, and that it is now time for the United States to come to its help."[71]

The pressure on President Roosevelt worked. On November 21, he told his advisers to expedite a loan agreement so that an announcement could be made by November 30. Consequently, as Abe and Wang were signing the Basic Treaty in Nanking, Washington was announcing the most massive China aid program yet. The United States would put $100,000,000 at Chiang's disposal; fifty modern pursuit planes were to be sent immediately, and more were promised; and steps would be taken to allow American citizens to serve in China as aviators or aviation instructors.[72] From this time forth, the fate of Wang's regime was increasingly tied to the growing American involvement in East Asia.

Chiang Kai-shek commented that the signing of the treaty in Nanking on November 30, 1940, was like the "reading of an oration over [Wang's] tomb." Wang's death, said Chiang, had come earlier in the year, with the Kao-T'ao disclosures, and his funeral had taken place at the inauguration ceremonies on March 30.[73] Those who were more kindly disposed to Wang do not deny the funereal atmosphere in Nanking at the treaty signing. According to one observer, Wang awaited Abe's arrival in front of Sun's mausoleum, where the ceremonies were scheduled. "He stood there as if in a daze, staring ahead at the white clouds that billowed over Purple Mountain, tears flowing copiously down his face, which was drawn in bitter anguish." The ceremonies, commented the same observer, "opened the curtain on a historic tragedy."[74]

There was ample reason for Wang to ponder the events leading to that day with bitterness. It had been exactly two years since the Chungkuang-t'ang Conference had opened the door to his defection from Chungking in order to create a rejuvenated China based on Sun's dictum that "without Japan there is no China; without China there is no Japan." Wang's good intentions had not been sufficient to preserve his movement from two years of miscalculations and misunderstandings, duplicity and treachery. He often spoke of the necessity of China and Japan "sharing each other's fate" (*t'ung-sheng kung-ssu*); the events of the past two years strongly suggested that the fate in store for him was not a promising one. Three weeks later Chou Fo-hai recorded in his diary how "terribly mistaken" his view of Japan had been while he was in Hankow and Chungking. "The correctness of the views of those who advocated resistance has been amply proved," the disillusioned Chou confessed.[75]

CHAPTER FIFTEEN

The Pacific War Years, 1941-1945

THOUGH IT took a while for nomenclature to mirror reality, the China Incident became the Greater East Asia War (Dai Tōa Sensō) when the bombs began dropping on Pearl Harbor on December 7, 1941. In the Imperial Rescript declaring war on the United States and Great Britain, the Emperor stated it was the "protection" offered by those countries that had enabled the Chungking regime to "continue its fratricidal opposition," and declared that "this trend of affairs would, if left unchecked, not only nullify Our Empire's efforts of many years for the sake of the stabilization of East Asia, but also endanger the very existence of Our nation. The situation being as it is, Our Empire for its existence and self-defense has no other recourse but to appeal to arms to crush every obstacle in its path."[1]

Donald Keene has described the exhilaration of Japanese intellectuals on hearing the news that the war had expanded. Hino Ashihei, whose graphic war-diary account of the fighting in China had given him an international reputation as the Erich Remarque of Japan, reported that he was overcome while listening to the radio by a vision of gods advancing over the skies of Eastern Asia. "I am sure that I was not alone in this emotion. . . . Was there anyone, I wonder, who did not weep with emotion on hearing the Rescript announcing the declaration of war?" The novelist Mushakōji Saneatsu, known as a Tolstoyan Christian and a believer in neighborly love, rejoiced that the war would provide Asians with the opportunity to eject American and British influence from their homelands and wondered at Churchill's and Roosevelt's "folly" in taking on Japan as an enemy.[2]

The Wang Government did not share such views. It was stunned by the news of Pearl Harbor. There had been no prior consultation on the Japanese decision to go to war with the United States and Great Britain, and the majority of the officials had thought a Japanese attack on the Soviet Union was a far more likely possibility than the "southward advance."

There were many reasons for this calculation, recalls one member of the Wang Government, Chin Hsiung-pai. Japan and Russia were historic enemies; the Soviet Union had extended more aid to China than any other country during the China Incident; the Japanese Army was anxious to revenge the defeats at Changkufeng and Nomonhan; anticommunism was one of the Three Principles Konoe had promulgated, and anticommunism was considered to be the "nucleus of Japanese policy"; Germany was known to be exerting great pressure on Japan to attack the Soviet Union and desist from antagonizing Britain and the United States; and surely the thought of a gigantic pincers movement against the Soviet Union, with Germany moving eastward from Europe and Japan moving westward from the Pacific—surely it was natural to think that prospect would be more appealing to Japan than the reckless gamble she actually took on December 7.[3] As Madame Wang Ching-wei reflected at her postwar treason trial, if Japan had dropped her bombs on Siberia instead of Pearl Harbor, the outcome of World War II would have been completely different, and the Wang regime might not have failed. A Chinese Nationalist diplomat, viewing things from a different perspective, once remarked to an American colleague that "your Pearl Harbor Day was our V-J Day."[4]

Chin Hsiung-pai recalls his own mixed feelings when he heard the news of December 7—or December 8, as it was in the Orient. On the one hand he perceived in it the first "ray of light" since China began its war of resistance. Japan had "created a situation from which she could not rescue herself," and eventually China would profit from Japan's blunder in attacking America. On the other hand, he saw a bleak picture for the time being. "If they [the Japanese] are successful, they will become ever more arrogant and exert more and more pressure on us; and once they begin to fail, they will make more and more demands on us," he feared.[5]

The fears of Chin and others in the Wang regime seemed confirmed in early 1942, when the Tōjō Government began pressing for the creation of a Greater East Asia Ministry. Foreign Minister Tōgō Shigenori rightly maintained that such an organ would arouse antagonism in China, but his opposition was futile; before the year was out, he had resigned and the new Ministry was in operation. The Japanese Ambassador to Nanking, Shigemitsu Mamoru, regarded as a friend and supporter of the Wang regime, was recalled and was replaced by Tani Masayuki, who was regarded as a "tea-boy" (or "yes" man, *shabōzu*) of General Tōjō. In addition Kagesa and Inukai, the chief military and civilian advisers, respectively, to the Wang regime, were withdrawn.

Inukai had become peripherally involved with the Ozaki-Sorge spy apparatus when he had divulged information on the Basic Treaty negotiations to Saionji Kinkazu and Ozaki. The reasons for Kagesa's recall are less clear. Inukai maintains that the Tōjō Government had become dissatisfied with Kagesa's "too generous" (*kandai sugiru*) treatment of Wang and had ordered his transfer, but others feel that he was simply transferred in the course of routine Army rotation.[6] At any rate, Kagesa, now a General, was ordered first to a field command in Manchukuo and later to Rabaul in the South Pacific, where he spent the last months of the war in the inglorious defense of a bastion that the Allied forces chose to bypass in their island-hopping strategy. Wang was displeased with the removal of the trusted Kagesa from Nanking and made his displeasure known to the Japanese Army—to no avail.*

Throughout 1942 Japan beseeched Wang to join her in the war against the United States and Great Britain. His condition, which was finally met, was release from the hated Basic Treaty of November 1940, including all of the secret agreements and annexes that did so much to discredit his collaboration with Japan. The regime's declaration of war on the Allies on January 9, 1943, was followed by an agreement replacing the Basic Treaty—the "Pact of Alliance," signed by Wang and Ambassador Tani on October 30, 1943. But even before the new agreement went into effect, Japan had begun divesting herself of some of the most conspicuous infringements on Chinese sovereignty by agreeing to retrocede the Japanese concessions in Hankow, Tientsin, Amoy, and other cities. In June 1943 the Japanese agreed to allow the Wang Government to assume administrative control over the International Settlement in Shanghai.

There is little need to dwell on the details of the new pact and the various agreements on the concessions, for the fact is, that though the return of the Shanghai International Settlement to Chinese control was probably the most signal success of the Wang regime, it came too late to have any important influence on either the survival of the regime or

---

* Some months after Kagesa's transfer, Wang was visited by Col. Tsuji Masanobu, one of the supreme *bōryakusha* of the Imperial Army. After chatting for a while through an interpreter, Wang ordered the interpreter from the room and proceeded to discuss confidential matters with Tsuji in the customary manner of Chinese and Japanese who do not speak each other's language—by writing. Wang complained of the senior advisers and diplomats with whom he had to work. He did not feel that he could confide in any of them, he lamented. When Tsuji asked Wang who his choice for a military adviser was, he unhesitatingly wrote out "General Kagesa." Tsuji, "Futari no Dai Tōa shidōsha," p. 214.

the credibility of Japan's promise of a New Order. Moreover, it was the Allies, not the Japanese Government, that took the lead in renouncing treaty rights in China. The Sino-American Treaty of 1903 promised such a step, but it was not until October 1942 that Secretary of State Cordell Hull finally presented the Chinese Ambassador in Washington a draft treaty fulfilling that promise. Though Shigemitsu maintains that Japan was considering such a move as early as "mid-1942,"[7] the credit for formally terminating a century of unequal treaties must go to the United States and Great Britain, both of which signed treaties with Chungking on January 11, 1943, ending their special privileges in the foreign enclaves.

It was not that Japan was simply a few months tardy in relinquishing some of her privileges, Shigemitsu reflected in his postwar memoirs, but rather that she was six years too late. If Japan had taken such steps in 1937, he wrote, there would never have been a Sino-Japanese war.[8] To which we might add, this degree of flexibility only three years earlier would have added immeasurably to the Wang regime's appeal, as it could not at this late stage. At that critical time, in the spring of 1940, before the United States had thrown her military forces into a defense of the Chiang regime, such a treaty, lending a certain integrity and merit to Japan's promise of a New Order, might have helped tip the scales in favor of Wang in his struggle with Chiang. In 1943 Japan's concessions, though satisfying to Wang, were too little and too late to bolster his regime.

Paralleling Japan's tardy gesture of friendship and respect for Chinese national feelings was her decision to adopt a "New Policy for China," which was set forth at an Imperial Conference December 21, 1942.[9] The work of Shigemitsu, this new policy was translated by the mainland Army commands into the so-called policy of well-meaning assistance (*kōteki shien*) in early 1943.[10] As the name suggests, the turn in policy represented the Army's recognition that its "supervision" and "guidance" of the Wang regime and the North China Political Council amounted to intervention in purely internal Chinese affairs. Now only indirect aid was to be offered to Chinese administrative organs, which meant the end of the Tokumu-bu. The despised Special Services Units were replaced by Renraku-bu (Liaison Units). There was something more than a change in bureaucratic nomenclature involved in the switch from Tokumu-bu to Renraku-bu. Army officers were instructed to cease using harsh or imperious language toward Chinese citizens and Government officials. Instead, a new low-profile approach characterized by "assistance, suggestion, and guidance" was to be adopted. The initiative for the policy did not come from the Army, according to one ex-officer.

> Who was behind it? We did not know for certain, but we believed that it was the will of the Emperor. If the orders had simply come from the Army, they would not have succeeded in influencing the minds and habits of Japanese officers. But when word came from the Headquarters saying it was the will of the Emperor that we should behave more respectfully toward the Chinese, that had a great influence on us. Even so, however, people don't just change overnight. The change had to come gradually. . . . If only it had been done earlier, it would have been good. For five years or more we had been following the hard policy. . . . If only we had changed, for example, when the Wang Government was established. After all, it was in the following period that the Communists became so strong.[11]

The inability to settle on a consistent and unified China policy plagued Japan just as much after the recognition of the Wang regime as it had before. Some Japanese leaders continued to call for a reconciliation with Chiang Kai-shek, and a smaller group to urge the strengthening of the Nanking regime. But the abiding ambition—illusion might be a better word—of the Imperial Army was to conquer the enemy once and for all by capitalizing on factional and regional rivalries within the Nationalist Army. Thanks to an enormously effective intelligence-gathering network, the Imperial Army seems to have been able to sniff out every hint of disaffection among the powerful regional military leaders in the Nationalist camp. Though learning of disaffection and taking advantage of it are two quite different things, at one time or another in the years between 1941 and 1945, the Imperial Army's hopes of exacerbating the tension among Chiang's military supporters focused on an impressive list of generals. In addition to those named earlier (e.g., Lung Yun, Chang Fa-k'uei, and Liu Wen-hui), the roster included Li Chi-shen, of Kwangsi; Liu Chien-hsü, of Shensi; Yü Han-mou, of Kwangtung; Hsüeh Yüeh, Commander-in-Chief of the Ninth War Zone; Sun Lien-chung, Deputy Commander-in-Chief of the First War Zone; and a host of divisional commanders.[12]

Ho Ying-ch'in, Minister of War until 1944, was the object of considerable attention, both because of his important position in the Government and because of a constant barrage of intelligence reports that suggested he was on the verge of provoking a split in the leadership in Chungking. Indeed, according to one report, the split had already occurred in early 1942.* Not only had Ho and a few other generals formed a peace party in the wartime capital, but they were said to be "conspiring with the Nanking Government to force Chiang into exile in India or Iran." After that Ho and his followers planned to come to terms with Wang Ching-wei—but only as a prelude to their taking control of the Nanking Government themselves.[13] What made the reports on Ho credible to Japan was the fact that he was probably the most aggressively anti-Communist general in Chungking. He was a prime mover in bringing about the Nationalist clash with the Communist-led New Fourth Army in January 1941, an action that came to symbolize the beginning of the end of the united front. General Ho's "obsession" with communism was well known to American Foreign Service officers in the capital, who were greatly concerned about his apparent unwillingness to press the war against Japan for fear of exhausting the forces that would be needed to destroy the Communists after the war.[14] Furthermore, the Japanese learned from Chou Fo-hai that Ho believed China would be thoroughly subordinated to the United States in the postwar years if Japan were to be completely destroyed and so had been "sending feelers to Chou to probe the possibility of a separate peace with Japan."[15]

Another important object of Japanese attention was the northern warlord Yen Hsi-shan. Few Chinese leaders better illustrate the complex love-hate feeling toward Japan in certain circles in China in the twentieth century than General Yen, for nearly forty years overlord and Governor of Shansi province. Yen, a graduate of the 1909 class of the Military Academy in Tokyo, was profoundly impressed with Japan's progress. On returning to China he carried with him a deep admiration of the Japanese for their mastery of such modern skills as X-ray technology (which he had encountered firsthand as a patient in a Japanese hospital) and for their progressive attitudes on the elimination of primitive social customs (such as teeth-blackening). But, as his biographer writes, "his admiration for the Japanese . . . was tempered by the realization that they menaced the independence of China."[16]

In the years after the Manchurian Incident Yen publicly deplored the unwillingness of the Kuomintang Government to adopt a resolute policy of national resistance. The resolute stand of his own armies to the Japa-

---

* The report came from a Chinese informant, Eugene Ch'en (Ch'en Yu-jen), via the Kōa Kikan. This agency, headed by Lt. Col. Okada Yoshimasa, was given the task of capturing and detaining important Chinese in Hong Kong after the Pacific phase of the war broke out in December 1941. Though many important figures were apprehended, the biggest prize escaped Okada's net: Madame Chiang managed to escape from the island on a small plane the Generalissimo sent for her. Akashi, "Japan's Peace Maneuvers," p. 156, citing an interview with Okada.

nese-sponsored Mongol-Manchurian invasion of Suiyuan province in 1936 prompted the *North China Herald* to remark: "Many believe that a greater mass of Chinese has been swayed by Yen's campaign against the Japanese in Suiyuan than ever before in History."[17] After the Marco Polo Bridge Incident Yen invited the Communist Eighth Route Army into his province to assist him in resisting the Japanese invaders. So determined was his defense of Taiyuan that even Gen. Chu Teh, a fierce fighter in his own right, condemned Yen for employing "suicidal tactics" against Japan.[18]

And yet by 1940 Japan felt confident enough of her ability to recruit General Yen to her cause to launch a major operation known as Tai-haku Kōsaku. Maj. Gen. Tanaka Ryūkichi, a friend of Yen's since 1928 when Japan had supported Yen in his warlord struggles with his arch-rival, Feng Yü-hsiang, was in charge of the operation in its early stages.[19] Japanese hopes seem to have been based on Yen's antagonism toward Chungking for denying him arms shipments and his growing disenchantment with his sometime comrades in the Eighth Route Army. The cooperation between Yen and the Communists in Shansi gradually dissolved until by 1944 there was open fighting between their troops. Though Yen welcomed—and evidently received—aid from Japan, the main objective of the operation, namely, a declaration of support for Japan by Yen, was never achieved.[20] According to Tanaka, Yen was convinced that the crippling of the Japanese Navy in the Battle of Midway (in the spring of 1942) foreshadowed Japan's eventual defeat in the war. After that, Yen was "unwilling to compromise himself by becoming [Japan's] ally."[21]

Another operation deserves mention, if only because of its curiosity. In 1944 a small group of General Staff intelligence officers (among them Col. Haruke Keiin, the Tokumu-bu Chief who had been instrumental in organizing the notorious No. 76 in Shanghai, now promoted to Chief of the China Section, and Maj. Gen. Arisue Seizō, Chief of the Intelligence Division) and two civilians attached to the General Staff proposed an approach to the Communists in Yenan about the possibility of a separate peace settlement. The two civilians were Sano Manabu and Nabeyama Sadachika, two early leaders of the Japanese Communist Party. Both had been arrested in 1929 for their radical activities and sentenced to life imprisonment in 1932. The following year, the pair had created an international sensation in the radical world by recanting their communist views and declaring that the Japanese Communist Party was "anti-people," "isolated from the masses," and little more than a "propaganda organ of the Soviet Union."[22] In spite of their cooperative attitude, they were not released from prison until 1943. At that time, their knowledge of international communism—both had extensive experience on Comintern assignments in China and the Soviet Union—was recognized by the Army General Staff, to which they were quickly assigned as civilians.

Nabeyama was allowed to go to North China in the spring of 1944 for two months in order to study the communist movement. On his return to Tokyo he filed a report with the Intelligence Division arguing for a negotiated peace with the Yenan Communists. The regime in Yenan, he reported, was an independent government with a defined territorial base. Echoing the reports that well-informed American diplomats in China were forwarding to Washington at exactly the same time, Nabeyama argued that "the Yenan regime was a clean and corruption-free government commanding popular respect and support."[23] Nabeyama's conclusion was that though Moscow's influence in the Shensi Soviet could not be ignored, Japan should enter into direct negotiations with Yenan anyway. Incredibly, it appears that the General Staff was actually swayed by Nabeyama's proposals and made plans to implement them, dismissing, apparently, the obvious fact that any plan to negotiate a peace settlement with Yenan, whose existence depended on its success in mobilizing patriotic resistance to Japan, was doomed to failure. The Nabeyama plan, more far-fetched perhaps than others, was but one of a wide assortment of operations aimed at rescuing the Empire from its ever-deepening crisis.

Midway, the Solomons, the Marshalls, the Gilberts, the Marianas—these names measured the disaster that was overtaking the Empire in the years 1942–44. Beginning with the battle for Guadalcanal in mid-1942, which drained three divisions from China, each major engagement in the Pacific forced troop and supply reallocations that increasingly weakened the Japanese forces on the mainland and prompted Tokyo to rethink the conditions of a peace settlement with China. Nonetheless, there is little evidence that Japan's diminished capacity to dictate peace terms was reflected in the approach she took in her negotiations with Chinese leaders. Even after the fall of Saipan in July 1944, an event that precipitated the collapse of the Tōjō Cabinet and placed Japan within range of American bombers, Japanese peace negotiators still insisted on hard-line terms that were wholly inappropriate to their country's desperate situation.

In September 1944, for example, with American forces poised for a landing in the Philippines, Gen. Ugaki Kazushige emerged from retirement to undertake a personal peace mission to China with the blessing of the new Premier, Koiso Kuniaki. But on September 5, 1944, six days before Ugaki's departure, the newly formed Supreme War Council decided on peace terms that ensured the failure of his mission.* While offering one fillip to Chungking—the return to Chinese sovereignty of Hong Kong—the new peace terms hedged on the withdrawal of Japanese troops from the mainland (to be carried out only when British and American troops were withdrawn) and, as ever, insisted on the status quo in Manchukuo.[24] In an almost preposterous gesture of conciliation, Premier Koiso suggested that Ugaki might offer Chungking "certain southern territories—for example, French Indochina"—in lieu of Manchukuo.[25] Needless to say, Ugaki's overtures elicited no response from Chungking.

Meanwhile, Wang's Reorganized Government was slowly acquiring some of the trappings if not the substance of an independent government, a process that to Wang's satisfaction was accelerated following the promulgation of the "New Policy for China" in Tokyo in late 1942. One of the projects Wang was most deeply interested in was the "rural pacification movement" (*ch'ing-hsiang yün-tung*), which was in full swing by July 1941. This movement aimed at the establishment of "model peace zones" (*mo-fan ti ho-p'ing ti-ch'ü*), areas that were to be cleared of Communist guerrillas and then restored to full economic productivity.

To achieve the necessary social control in these areas, the Wang regime fell back on the age-old system of collective responsibility known as *pao-chia*. The first step in the institution of this system was a careful census check and the establishment of basic units: each family unit constituted a *hu*; ten *hu* constituted a *chia*; ten *chia* constituted a *pao*. Leaders were appointed at each level, responsibility and authority delegated, and local militia squads created. Blockades and checkpoints were set up in each district. Identity cards were distributed and travel permits were required for all movement. Each household had to display a certificate on its front door giving information on the occupants of the house.

When the "pacification" system worked well, it constituted a formidable obstacle to guerrilla infiltration, a check on the movement and activities of the population, and even an agency for thought-control. But rural pacification was meant to accomplish more than a restoration of law and order. Wang expected the Rural Pacification Commission to promote the economic recovery of the model zones, all of which were chosen primarily on the basis of their economic wealth. Most were in

---

* The Supreme War Council (Saikō Sensō Shidō Kaigi), instituted in August 1944, expanded the Four Ministers' Conference to include the Army and Navy Chiefs of Staff.

Kiangsu, Anhwei, and Chekiang provinces, which took in the areas most tightly controlled by the Nanking regime.* The first area in which the pacification movement was initiated, for example, was the Shanghai-Nanking-Hangchow triangle in the lower Yangtze delta. All told, the rural pacification areas included lands "which once produced enough silk and rice to support the main bulk of the population in China."[26]

For several reasons the rural pacification schemes did not yield the hoped-for results. In the first place, though Wang was Chairman of the Rural Pacification Commission, he unwisely entrusted its day-to-day management to a rank opportunist, Li Shih-ch'ün (of No. 76 fame), who served as Secretary-General of the Commission until his murder. Further, as confidence in a Japanese victory declined, the common people became wary of the Reorganized Government's currency and began stockpiling commodities. A 1945 U.S. War Department report stated that the "hoarding of food and other commodities became even more prevalent in Japanese-occupied areas than in Chungking Government areas. From 1943 on the currency inflation in Japanese-occupied areas began to rival that in Chungking areas. . . . The inflation reached an acute stage during 1944; since that time it has been considerably worse than in Chungking areas."[27]

Inadequate transportation facilities also weakened the rural pacification program. The deterioration of rolling stock, Communist interdiction of rail traffic, and American air attacks on railway bridges and ports, hampered the distribution of goods in China. In addition, the very success of some of the rural pacification techniques had unanticipated effects on rural production. The blockades and checkpoints, for example, were effective in checking banditry and guerrilla infiltration, but they also impeded the exchange of goods between rural pacification areas and urban centers. Bureaucratic red tape and endless delays in granting ex-

---

* The U.S. War Department estimated that at the end of 1943 the total area of occupied China, that is, the areas behind the most advanced Japanese positions, was roughly 345,000 square miles. Of this, the Communists controlled roughly 155,000 miles, much of which was thinly populated, mountainous land in North China, and the Japanese about 82,000 square miles. The balance was regarded as no-man's-land or guerrilla areas (about 67,000 square miles) and Chungking-controlled areas (41,000 square miles). The total population in what was defined as occupied China was about 183,000,000, with an estimated 70,000,000 people living in Japanese-occupied areas, 43,000,000 in guerrilla areas, 54,000,000 in Communist-controlled base areas, and 16,000,000 in Chungking-controlled areas. Van Slyke, *Chinese Communist Movement*, pp. 116-17. According to a 1944 Japanese survey, about 5,600,000 Chinese lived in the carefully selected target areas of the rural pacification programs, approximately 21.4 per cent of whom were organized into *pao-chia*. Nishitani, *Kessen kokumin seifu*, pp. 159-60.

change permits and travel authorizations also contributed to the failure of the program.

Much of the responsibility for implementing the rural pacification program was in the hands of the Army of the Reorganized Government. Under the "New Policy for China" the responsibility for garrisoning the occupied areas was rapidly shifted from the Imperial Army to the Reorganized Government. However, the Nanking troops were put on station as peace-keeping forces, not to assist the Imperial Army by engaging the Allied armies in battle. Indeed, according to one official of the Reorganized Government, Wang refused to allow so much as a "single soldier" to cooperate with Japan in this way.[28] In a memorial to the Emperor of Japan concerning his regime's entrance into World War II, Wang said he intended to declare war to show Chungking that, contrary to its propaganda, his Reorganized Government had ample resources of men and supplies and enjoyed good morale.[29]

Most estimates put the total number of troops in the Nanking armed forces at their peak strength at the 900,000 mark, divided about half and half between army regulars and local and provincial irregulars.[30] In addition to an Air Corps, which existed only on paper, the Nanking Government had a "few small ships," donated by Japan—and this was the "Navy" over which Minister of the Navy Ch'u Min-i, Wang's brother-in-law, presided. Ch'en Kung-po and Chou Fo-hai regarded Ch'u's appointment with unconcealed levity.[31]

Many, perhaps a majority, of Wang's regular troops were Nationalist defectors. Substantial numbers of them had crossed over with Gens. Sun Liang-ch'eng, Li Ming-yang, Wu Hua-wen, Ho P'eng-chü, P'ang Ping-hsün, and Chang Lan-feng.[32] According to one member of Wang's Government, the generals who joined the Nanking Government fell into four categories: those who felt themselves victimized by the friction and competition within the Nationalist forces; those who were being attacked by both Japanese and Communist forces and decided to join Wang for survival; those who were essentially outside the Kuomintang military establishment and, lacking power, had been discriminated against; and those who discovered the gross disparity in the quality and quantity of weapons between the Imperial Army and the Nationalist Army, and simply lost hope in the war of resistance.[33]

If troops defecting from Chungking were usually welcomed by the Nanking forces, the opposite was not the case. Chiang was extremely suspicious of puppet troops who surrendered and declared their allegiance to him. Consequently, soldiers in Wang's Army who might have considered defecting to Chiang went over instead to Yenan, which made a point of welcoming them. The case of Gen. Wu Hua-wen is illustrative. Wu, who at one time commanded the Third District Army in Shantung, defected from Chungking to Nanking and then attempted to reverse himself, pledging his loyalty to Chungking once again. But the Generalissimo was unconvinced, and in the end Wu's troops "were forced" to join the Communists. Much of the Manchukuoan Army was similarly incorporated into Lin Piao's Red Army forces.

What needs to be emphasized, however, is that the line between puppet soldiers and Nationalist soldiers was often blurred, though many generals did not make a specific, public issue of their loyalties as General Wu did. Until the Imperial Army undertook the massive offensive known as Operation ICHIGO in mid-1944, most front lines were stabilized, and the war for many soldiers on both sides had become "institutionalized" in five years of relative quiet. This institutionalization was seen best in the so-called roadless areas that served as the boundaries between Nanking China and Chungking China. An American official described the life along one of these "borders" in the south of China:

> The "Roadless Area" was about twenty miles deep, in rich beautiful rice country, and the armies led an almost idyllic existence. The officers lived with their families and servants in requisitioned farmhouses, fine and large in such a fertile district, and had become wealthy by smuggling or taxing smugglers. The trade over the lines was constant, with rice, salt, and various raw materials going out; cloth, cigarettes, and luxuries coming in. A shrewd trader could make a profit of four to five hundred per cent by one trip across the front and back.[34]

The constant fraternization between the Nationalist and Nanking troops often worked to the advantage of the Nationalist Army. Comdr. Milton Miles, a U.S. Navy intelligence officer, was astounded at the willingness of the puppet troops to support Nationalist operations:

> I had heard already a little about Chinese puppet soldiers who performed many tasks for the Japanese. Such troops were common enough in the occupied areas and, serving under their own officers, they sometimes were given the responsibility for keeping order in certain Japanese-controlled communities and for attending other comparable tasks. They were fed and paid by the Japanese, of course, and were not unwilling to provide certain services. Still, they were Chinese and, at heart, were apt to retain many native loyalties. I asked [a certain Captain Tseng] if the puppet soldiers were *always*

willing to cooperate. . . . "Oh, yes," Captain Tseng replied. "They must be careful with the Japanese, of course, but sometimes, when they feel it is safe, they even invite us to dinner. The Japanese pay them and expect their loyalty but they also take them to task and punish them for any outbreak in their territory. So if they do not behave as we want them to we just move in and fire a few shots— enough to suggest that a little disorder has broken out. Then the Japanese punish them for us. It is a fine system!"*

American officials who had to weigh whether a given general deserved their support kept a sharp eye open for such behavior, which both perplexed and shocked them. Foreign Service Officer John Paton Davies assessed Gen. Ku Chu-t'ung, Commander of all Nationalist troops in the Third War Area (Chekiang), as "not particularly disloyal—or loyal— he is too busy trading with the Japanese. . . . His interests are more commercial than military or political."[35] From 1942 on, Ku was in fact in almost continuous contact with Chou Fo-hai in Nanking.

Many Nationalist generals had one trait in common, a trait that was frequently noted by American observers (and execrated by Gen. "Vinegar Joe" Stilwell): an extreme reluctance to commit their troops to battle. The allocation of rations, salaries, rifles, gasoline, and stores of various kinds was determined by troop strength. Troop strength measured the wealth of the commanding general and determined not just his military status but also his political stature. With his armies intact he was wealthy and influential. The shortsighted general who dissipated his forces in clashes with the enemy risked exchanging momentary glory for a permanent loss of political standing. He was thus understandably reluctant to engage the Japanese, a reluctance that the Japanese welcomed and encouraged. Though not all Nationalist generals should be accused of holding back their troops, those who were outside of the Generalissimo's favored Whampoa Clique well knew the precariousness of their position and worked diligently to avoid battle in order to pre-

---

* *A Different Kind of War*, p. 59. Miles is sharply critical of America's failure to take advantage of the willingness of many puppet troops to defect from Nanking. He particularly blames General Albert Wedemeyer for this error. And perhaps with some justice, for in testimony before the Senate Armed Services Committee in 1951, Wedemeyer's answers to questions about puppet troops give the impression that he had not the slightest notion of what puppet troops were, much less how they might have been exploited. After searching his memory several times, Wedemeyer finally recalled that puppet troops under "a general named Wang" had operated during the early days of the war, then added that they were never significant after he arrived in China (as Stilwell's successor, in October 1944). *Ibid.*, p. 490; U.S. Senate, 82d Congress, *Hearings, Committee on Armed Services*, pp. 2300–2301.

serve their armies. This often required an exquisite delicacy. The Cantonese general Yü Han-mou, for instance, who commanded all the Nationalist forces in unoccupied Kwangtung province, avoided open collaboration with Japan and yet managed by his "cautious tactics toward the Japanese [to keep] his seven divisions fairly intact."[36]

In any event, it was not exclusively or probably even primarily the "outsider" generals who adopted these "cautious tactics," but rather the generals in Chiang Kai-shek's own circle. Moreover, the cautious tack, which was common enough in the best of times, became endemic in the six- or seven-month period beginning in May 1944. In that month, under the impact of the do-or-die Operation ICHIGO, the Nationalist lines broke at Changsha, and the Chinese troops began a pell-mell retreat south toward the Indochina border. By November the Japanese had pushed through a corridor to the border, capturing the American base at Kweilin, the largest in China, on the way. The triumphant Imperial Army then swung west across barren Kweichow province and was advancing on the provincial capital of Kweiyang—and indeed probing the approaches to Chungking—when the Chinese lines finally held. Almost half a million Nationalist soldiers were lost, and eight provinces with a population of more than 100,000,000 fell under the control of the Japanese, before ICHIGO reached its high-water mark in December and then began to recede. It was during these disastrous months, months of widespread speculation that the Chungking Government would fall or be toppled in a coup led by Marshal Li Chi-shen, a Kwangsi warlord with a long career of opposition to Chiang, that the "cautious tactics" type of collaboration was most frequently seen.

Indeed, though we lack conclusive proof, it is impossible to ignore the wealth of circumstantial evidence from a variety of sources suggesting Chiang was so shaken by the growing momentum of Marshal Li's separatist movement that he himself was moved to go well beyond the cautious tactics stage of collaboration with the Japanese. The ICHIGO offensive cut a wide swath precisely through the territories controlled by Marshal Li and Gen. Hsüeh Yüeh, who was debating whether to throw his considerable support (twelve divisions) to Li. It is certain that at the very least the Generalissimo withheld support and reinforcements from Li and Hsüeh, who were struggling to halt the Japanese drive. The American Ambassador in Chungking, Clarence E. Gauss, who cannot be accused of any bias in favor of Li's movement since he ordered his staff to deny it the American support it needed to survive, cabled Washington in August 1944: "It is our opinion that [Li's] movement has grown out of the necessity as sent [seen?] by Li and his associates of taking action to defend that area [the southeast] from the Japs, the Central Government having signally failed to make such defense or to assist local forces with funds and equipment for that purpose."[37]

Associates of Marshal Li, the Communists, and popular gossip all suggested that Chiang had gone further than denying support to his potential rivals. As Consul Arthur Ringwalt reported from Kweilin, Li's home base, the Generalissimo supposedly had "asked the Japanese to destroy the troops of the Ninth War Zone under Hsüeh Yüeh, who he believed was in a plot against him. . . . The Japanese in conjunction with the Generalissimo are said to have delivered an ultimatum to Marshal Li and his clique that unless he dropped his plans for the consolidation of the opposition against Chungking, the Japanese would destroy his clique and all of South China."[38]

According to popular rumor the Japanese and the Generalissimo had even come to an agreement by which Chiang would be given an "inviolate refuge" in West China—the so-called Tali-Tungkwan Square—provided Chungking offered no resistance to Japanese advances elsewhere.[39] Though neither Japanese nor Nanking records positively confirm the existence of such an agreement (which would hardly have been a formal agreement in any event), the constant comings-and-goings from Nanking to Chungking of important couriers like the Kuomintang agent Wu K'ai-hsien may well have been related to such an informal agreement.[40] At any rate, the ICHIGO drive drew up just short of the Tali-Tungkwan Square. Kweilin, just outside the square, fell to Japan; Kweiyang, just inside the square, did not.

What makes the rumor of Chungking's limited collaboration with Japan and the Nanking regime credible is the desperation of Chiang's situation in late 1944. An expedient understanding of the sort could well have been instrumental in staving off the collapse of his regime. And in the months after the Japanese surrender in August 1945, such an understanding might well have given the National Government the edge in the postwar struggle for power between the Communists and the Nationalists. The dispatches of John Paton Davies, the Second Secretary at the American Embassy and one of the most trenchant analysts of the complex political scene in China, frequently emphasize this point. In December 1944 Davies prepared a lengthy memorandum summarizing the critical position Chiang was in, with both the Communists and various warlords ready to challenge his authority. Davies concluded that

> Chiang's greatest hope for domestic reascendency lies in cooperation with the Japanese-sponsored Chinese puppets. Assuming that the United States and possibly Britain will drive out or cause the with-

drawal of the Japanese from East China, the Generalissimo's surest stratagem for the repossession of the vital Yangtze valley and the southern coastal cities is collaboration with the puppets, who may be expected to attempt interregnum control between the Japanese and Chiang. The Generalissimo has therefore looked with complacency if not approval upon the "surrender" to the enemy by some of his generals and their subsequent incorporation in the puppet armies. At the same time he has maintained through Tai Li's and other secret services constant contact with the puppets. Through these channels he is able to receive and reply to Japanese peace feelers and other propositions.*

Davies made it clear that he did not believe the Generalissimo was about to capitulate to the Japanese, for "he has more to gain from us than from them." "But," he went on, "that does not mean that he wants to fight the Japanese. He wants, and may well have, a mutual non-aggression agreement with the Japanese which will give him time to recuperate for what he considers inevitable—civil war." Furthermore, the Japanese welcomed such an attitude, said Davies. "We can no longer assume that the Japanese desire to destroy Chiang and his government. The destruction of the Chiang regime would only tip the balance of power in China in favor of the Communists, whom the Japanese regard as greater enemies than Chungking. It might also bring into being a vigorously anti-Japanese coalition government."

One month later, in January 1945, Davies was reporting comments made to him by an "intelligent Chinese journalist with extensive connections among high officials." "Chiang's greatest hope for regaining control of Central and East China is through future cooperation with the puppets. . . . Hence the present contacts which Chungking maintains with Nanking and [the North China Political Council in] Peking," the journalist observed. Furthermore, he said, the Japanese knew and approved of these relationships because they did not now wish Chiang destroyed ("he is essential to them").[41]

At the time of this report the Japanese had good reason to regard Chiang as essential to them. If he was crushed, they would be exposed to the much more resolute resistance of Marshal Li and General Hsüeh, not to mention the Communists in North China, who were stronger than ever. By early 1945, however, Li's separatist plans were no longer a seri-

---

* Davies transmitted the memorandum to Harry L. Hopkins (Roosevelt's special adviser), saying in a covering note, "I think that you will be particularly interested in the sections dealing with Japan and the Puppets." U.S. Dept. of State, *Foreign Relations*, 1944, 6: 724–27.

ous threat, thanks to his military losses during Operation ICHIGO and the failure of the United States to support him. Li, who was regarded by most American observers as a progressive political force, had solicited American support for his anti-Chiang reformed government in the Southeast as early as the summer of 1944. Officials on the scene were sympathetic to his cause. Consul Ringwalt, for example, felt that if Li's plans should force a collapse of the Chungking regime, "the result may not be an unmitigated evil to China and to the cause of the allied nations."[42] Ambassador Gauss, however, presumably on orders from Washington, ordered a "hands-off policy," and the movement gradually lost its momentum.*

The true test of the usefulness of the Nanking and Japanese armies to the Nationalist cause did not come for another half year—until the last days of the war and, indeed, the first few postwar months, when they proved an important element in the power struggle between the Nationalists and the Communists. In the meantime, however, the Reorganized Government received a sharp blow with the death of its leader, Wang Ching-wei, in November 1944.

WANG'S DEATH

In November 1943 leaders of the seven regimes within the Greater East Asia Co-Prosperity Sphere assembled in Tokyo for a two-day assembly that was designed, as the Burmese representative, Ba Maw, stated, as the "first visual manifestation of the new spirit stirring in Asia."† Little hard business was conducted. Rather it was a time for eloquence and breathless expressions of confidence in Japan. "I do not think that it is an accident that this assembly has been convened in the Land of the Rising Sun," said the Indian leader Subhas Chandra Bose. "This is not the first time that the world has turned to the East for light and guidance."[43] It was also a time for gestures of good will from Tokyo. In response to Bose's paean, for example, Premier Tōjō rose to announce Japan's decision to hand over the Andaman and Nicobar Islands in the Indian Ocean to the Azad Hind. For some of the leaders it was their

---

* U.S. Dept. of State, *Foreign Relations*, 1944, 6: 505–6; and 1945, 7: 159–60. Li Chi-shen went into a Hong Kong exile in 1947 and two years later joined the Communists. He served in several important government positions in the People's Republic until his death in 1959. His would-be collaborator, Hsüeh Yüeh, never finally committed himself to Li, and despite his history of differences with the Generalissimo, found a place in the Nationalist Government on Taiwan after 1949.

† Ba Maw, *Breakthrough in Burma*, p. 338. The seven countries represented were Japan, China, India, Burma, the Philippines, Thailand, and Manchukuo. Subhas Chandra Bose, of the Azad Hind (Free India) Government, participated as an observer.

first meeting—and for some (like Jose Laurel and Ba Maw) it was their last until they met in Tokyo's Sugamo Prison after the war. Wang Ching-wei was there, "strikingly handsome, with a smile and a bow for everyone. He spoke little, but carefully chose his words, and his voice was soft and winning. You soon sensed the Chinese tragedy in his restrained demeanour and trailing words," wrote Ba Maw.[44]

What Ba Maw did not record was that Wang's health was failing. The bullet that had remained in his back since the 1935 attempt on his life had caused a serious infection, which was complicated by a long-standing liver ailment. Wang took a turn for the worse on New Year's Day 1944, and in March, accompanied by his family, was flown to Japan for surgery. The operation did no more than alleviate his pain, and from that time on Wang was physically incapacitated. For the next eight months Ch'en Kung-po served as acting President of the Reorganized Government in Nanking.

In late October, as Wang lay gravely ill in the hospital of the Imperial University of Nagoya, he sensed the end. The Chinese do not follow the Western practice of composing a last will and testament in good health but rather, believing the last will to be a potentially auspicious document, prefer to write it only when all hope for recovery is gone. Accordingly, Wang began to dictate: "It has been eight months since I came to Japan. For several days there has been a terrible fever. For a man of sixty-two, one cannot be certain of the future."* Forced to spend much of his time in a poorly heated, ill-ventilated bomb shelter in the basement—the B-29 raids began in November—Wang declined rapidly. On November 9 pneumonia set in, and late the next afternoon he died. His remains were returned to Nanking for ceremonial burial in a mausoleum near Sun Yat-sen's. But the elaborate tomb was never completed, and fourteen months later, with Chungking forces once again in possession of the capital, Wang's grave was destroyed on orders of Gen. Ho Ying-ch'in with the approval of the Generalissimo. The destruction was accomplished in secrecy—at least in as much secrecy as the detonation of 150 pounds of dynamite allowed. Wang's body was then burned and the ashes secretly disposed of.[45]

CHOU FO-HAI TAKES CHARGE

Though Wang's trusted colleague Ch'en Kung-po succeeded him as chief of state, the real authority in the Reorganized Government had already passed into the hands of Chou Fo-hai, and there it remained to

---

* Chin, "Wang Ching-wei," 159: 2. See my discussion of the authenticity of this document in the Bibliographical Note, pp. 395–97.

the end of the war. Chou held a variety of positions in the Reorganized Government, but none of an importance that would suggest his real power. Chou's power and importance derived from his versatility and surpassing skill at intrigue. For a man known in his earlier years for his theoretical insights into Sun's Three Principles, Chou seems to have been little troubled by ideological consistency or questions of high principle in his later years. Gnawing doubts about the judgment of history were left to Wang and to Ch'en Kung-po.

Chou's Japanese colleagues in the peace movement nicknamed him Hotoke, the Buddha.[46] But that defined his physical appearance only. In temperament he matched the stereotype of his native Hunan, emotional and hot-blooded, traits supposedly caused by the peppery cuisine favored by the Hunanese, Chou included. An astute commentator on modern China, the Jesuit priest O. Brière, observes that though Chou was "not without merit," he was "a restless soul, incapable of settling down."[47] As we have seen, Chou had no sooner "settled down" with the Reorganized Government than he began to question the wisdom of his defection from Chungking. Japanese arbitrariness had already driven him to "tear out his hair" in rage. At his postwar treason trial Chou declared that in the first years of the war with Japan he had "worked with Japan to try to benefit China, whereas in the last years he had worked with China to fight against Japan."[48] The statement is plainly too self-serving to stand as the final judgment on Chou—the Chinese magistrate hearing Chou's case accepted the statement with considerable reservation in passing his final judgment—but there is some truth in it.

It may well be that Chou never severed contacts with Chungking; it is certain at any rate that by early 1942 he was in smooth, almost daily communication with Chungking agents. In addition to a squad of couriers who filtered through the Japanese lines carrying messages back and forth, Chou maintained contact with Chungking via two secret radio stations. One was beamed toward the headquarters of his old friend Gen. Tai Li, the Kuomintang's Chief of Military Intelligence; the other kept him in touch with Gen. Ku Chu-t'ung, another personal friend. Since Chou could not hope to carry out the liaison without the Japanese becoming aware of it, he cleared the matter with a few officials. The Japanese were extremely skeptical at first, but Chou managed to play on personal friendships and take advantage of conflicts between the Army and the Navy to gain the necessary authorization. The persuasive Chou was even able to convince the Japanese that the radio contacts would be used to help arrange a peace settlement with Chungking.

Very few people in either the Reformed Government or the Japanese military knew the secret radio stations existed.* One of the privileged few who did know of them was the chief economic adviser to the Wang Government and Chou's trusted ally, Rear Adm. Okada Yūji.[49] Another was Chin Hsiung-pai, perhaps the closest political confidant Chou had. Chin feels that one of Chou's worst faults was his almost compulsive habit of consulting Chungking, about even the most trivial matters. Before accepting appointment as Mayor of Shanghai in late 1943, for example, he sought Chungking's approval. Chungking was evidently equally solicitous of Chou's feelings; at least its care to relay the news of his mother's death at once suggests as much.†

According to Chin, Chungking handed Chou several assignments in late 1943, that is, shortly before Wang became incapacitated. Chou was in "very high spirits" as he began to carry out his assigned tasks, which included allocating foodstuffs to the Kuomintang armies, appointing provincial governors who had Chungking's stamp of approval, making certain that Nanking's troops never clashed with troops loyal to Chiang, and in general making proper use of the funds the Nanking regime had at its disposal. (Among other things, Chou was Finance Minister and President of the National Bank.)[50]

Chou was given even greater responsibilities toward the end of the war. When an Allied landing along the China coast loomed as a possibility, he was given the job of coordinating anti-Japanese uprisings behind the Japanese lines. Once again he responded enthusiastically to his orders from Chungking. This time, however, he did not have an opportunity to demonstrate his cheerful obedience to Chungking, the success of the island-hopping strategy in the Pacific and the atomic bomb obviating the need of a costly mainland landing. Had it not been for this, "Chou would have had his chance to show his importance," writes Chin.[51]

Even so, there was still room for Chou to "show his importance." In early 1945 many in China, especially the business and financial leaders of Shanghai, feared that metropolis might be "scorched" by the withdrawing Imperial Army. And indeed Shanghai, situated as it is on a sea

---

* Chou assigned the task of day-to-day radio communications to two carefully screened Chinese. But they were plainly not screened well enough, for one of them, P'eng Sheng-mu, was a Nationalist agent. P'eng had been in Chungking's service since at least June 1939, when he accompanied Wang and Chou to Tokyo as an interpreter. Chin, *Dōsei*, pp. 105, 250.

† Chou dutifully made preparations to announce his mother's death to the Shanghai newspapers the day he received the news. When Chin advised him to wait a while lest he tip his hand on his radio communications with Chungking, the filial son told Chin to mind his own business and made the announcement as planned. Chin, *Dōsei*, p. 252.

of mud, was extremely vulnerable. An interruption of its electric power could leave the city without drainage, with an epidemic almost certain to follow in short order. There was also the possibility, of course, that the city would be set to the torch. As Foreign Service Officer John Stewart Service reported, "Both puppet and Central Government Chinese are desperately anxious to avoid warfare which may destroy their main economic centers, where many of them personally are heavy property owners and where many of their families and relatives still reside."[52] Still, Service noted, the Japanese might well be reluctant to "scorch" the city, since there were "large Japanese populations and huge economic interests which the Japanese hope to protect and preserve." The whole question was further complicated by the very real possibility that the Chinese Red Army might be in a better position to occupy Shanghai than the Nationalist forces. In assessing this complex of unknowns, Service concluded that there was "a community of interest between the Central Government, Puppets and Japanese."[53] Exactly so. And Chou Fo-hai, on the scene as Mayor of Shanghai—"the tiger's nest"—was the pivotal figure in the community. In what was probably the only direct, personal communication he undertook with his former patron, Chiang Kai-shek, Chou wrote in early 1945 that he understood the Generalissimo was planning a counterattack. For himself, he said, "I am in the tiger's nest and so operations to help the counterattack are very complicated. If we delay, we cannot make adequate preparations; if we make haste, we may reveal our hand. . . . I give priority to your orders. When the day of victory comes, I will be pleased to be subject to your severe punishment. Even if I die."*

Shanghai, Nanking, and the other great Yangtze and coastal cities were eventually turned over by puppet and Japanese troops to Chiang's forces and denied to the Communists, but the process was far from routine or quick. On August 18, 1945, three days after the Japanese surrender, the Commander-in-Chief of the China Expeditionary Army, Gen. Okamura Yasuji, set a basic post-surrender policy for his forces: to cooperate in the reconstruction of China, to assist the National Government in its efforts to unify the Chinese people, and to "resolutely chastise" the Chinese Communists if they should evidence anti-Japanese behavior.[54]

---

* Chin, *Dōsei*, pp. 270–71. Chou's letter was transmitted by the Kuomintang underground leader Chiang Po-ch'eng. The Generalissimo reportedly received the letter, was impressed by Chou's deferential attitude, and was about to write a reply when someone suggested that it would be more politic to send an oral response. *Ibid.*

Okamura ordered his Vice Chief of Staff, Major General Imai—the same Imai who had played such an important role in the early days of the Wang movement seven years earlier—to Chihkiang in Hunan to work out arrangements for the surrender of Japanese units to Nationalist authorities. When Imai stepped down from his plane at Chihkiang on August 21, he found the airfield lined with American and Chinese soldiers anxious to catch a glimpse of the first military emissary from defeated Japan. His mission led to talks between Okamura and the Vice Chief of Staff of the Nationalist Army, Leng Hsin, beginning on August 27. Leng asked for Okamura's cooperation in "securing" eight major cities: Shanghai, Nanking, Peiping, Tientsin, Wuhan, Tsingtao, Canton, and Hong Kong. Okamura agreed, but pointing to the difficulties his armies were experiencing and were likely to continue experiencing with Communist forces, which were demanding the surrender of weapons and equipment, he advised Leng to dispatch his best troops as early as possible to North China, where the situation was especially troublesome. It was his personal belief, he added, that though Japan was in for an extremely difficult future, China's future—presumably after the Communist menace was eliminated—would be "peaceful and tranquil."[55] As Usui indicates, the tone of the Okamura-Leng meetings suggests not so much a meeting of victor and vanquished as a meeting of friends cooperating against a common enemy, the Chinese Communists.[56]

As the troops of the Imperial Army and the puppet regimes set about securing China's cities on behalf of their erstwhile enemy, the Nationalists and Communists squared off for the start of what was to be four years of deadly civil war. In Shanghai Japanese troops were still armed and in a position to arrest the Americans who arrived there on September 2, eighteen days after Japan's capitulation.[57] It was several more days before Chinese Nationalist troops began arriving in Shanghai in strength, and September 9 before General Okamura signed the instruments of surrender in Nanking. On September 10 *New York Times* correspondent Tillman Durdin reported the "particularly important role" played by Chou Fo-hai in the "puppets' shift to the Kuomintang." With the encouragement of the Nationalist Government, Chou had "assumed a 'pacification' role in the Shanghai area, with what is reported to be a fairly strong and well-equipped army [and is] still fulfilling this role," wrote Durdin.[58] It was not until October 3 that Chou was arrested and flown to Chungking, along with Ting Mo-ts'un, concurrently the head of No. 76 and Wang's Minister of Welfare.

Meanwhile, as Okamura had promised, Japanese troops were clashing with Communist forces in North China rather than surrendering to them. On September 9 American Ambassador Patrick Hurley reported that the Communists' attempts to take over the Shantung-Hopei region had been stymied in the past week because Nationalist commanders had gotten Japanese and puppet "reinforcements." As a result, the Communists would probably move northward to try for control of the Tientsin-Peiping area, Hurley felt, though they appeared to have little chance of success there "because of difficulties placed upon Communists' movement by strict Japanese control of communication lines."[59]

During September and October the United States threw her weight on the side of the Nationalists by supplying transport planes to move their armies to key sectors in East and North China and, when that proved insufficient, by landing fifty thousand U.S. Marines to secure the ports and airfields of Tsingtao, Tientsin, Peiping, and Chinwangtao. These transportation centers were vital, not only to the control of North China but to the control of Manchukuo as well. (On the basis of the Yalta Agreement, the Soviet Union had occupied Manchukuo and was preventing the Nationalists from landing troops at Dairen; Chinwangtao was the North China port closest to Manchukuo.) At the end of October, some seventy-five days after the end of the war, the American Consul in Tientsin reported that the Japanese forces controlling the vital rail link from Peiping to Chinwangtao were under constant attack by the Communists. The American Marines in the area "depend almost entirely on former puppet and Japanese troops for maintenance of order in towns along the line," he cabled, adding that the situation would soon "become serious unless adequate number of Chungking troops arrive."[60]

On November 23, well over three months after the Japanese surrender, the Commanding General of the United States forces in China, Albert C. Wedemeyer, reported to his Chief of Staff that "the continued and effective disarming of Japanese by Chinese Central Government Forces is impossible for three reasons": the central government forces were being diverted to the task of opposing Chinese Communist forces; the Japanese forces were being employed by the Nationalist Government to protect communications lines and installations against the Communists; and if the Japanese were disarmed in certain areas where the Chinese Communist forces existed in strength, the Communists would move in and take over not only the areas vacated by the Japanese but also their arms and equipment.[61]

In Yenan Mao complained bitterly about the collusion of the Nationalist, puppet, and Japanese troops. Two days before the Japanese surrender he lashed out at the Generalissimo in a press release entitled "Chiang Kai-shek Is Provoking a Civil War":

> Even before the enemy's actual surrender, Chiang Kai-shek, China's fascist ringleader, autocrat and traitor to the people, had the audacity to "order" the anti-Japanese armed forces in the Liberated Areas to "stay where they are, pending further orders," that is, to tie their own hands and let the enemy attack them. No wonder this selfsame fascist ringleader dared to "order" the so-called underground forces (who are, in fact, puppet troops "saving the nation by a devious path" and Tai Li's secret police collaborating with the Japanese and puppets) as well as the other puppet troops to "be responsible for maintaining local order," while forbidding the anti-Japanese armed forces in the Liberated Areas to "take presumptuous action on their own" against enemy and puppet forces. This transposition of the enemy and the Chinese is in truth a confession by Chiang Kai-shek; it gives a vivid picture of his whole psychology, which is one of consistent collusion with the enemy and puppets and of liquidation of all those not of his ilk.*

An especially close relationship developed between Imperial Army units and the Shansi warlord Yen Hsi-shan immediately after the end of the war. Yen's relationship to Chiang Kai-shek in the thirty-four years since Yen began his control of Shansi had vacillated from open warfare at its worst (in 1930) to gruding coexistence at best. At war's end Yen was determined to prevent the Kuomintang from exercising anything more than formal authority in his province. The real challenge to his power, however, came from the Communists and, indeed, by August 1945 large chunks of Shansi had already been wrested from his control by the Communist Eighth Route Army. To meet the threat from the Communists, Yen had collaborated with Japan off and on during the war, and now, in 1945, as the threat intensified, he moved to strengthen his ties with the defeated enemy.

One of Yen's first moves was to persuade the President of the Japanese-established Shansi Industrial Company (Sansei Sangyō Kabushiki Kai-

---

* Mao, 4: 27. The "saving the nation by a devious path" phrase is explained by the editors of Mao's *Selected Works* as follows: "This refers to the dastardly practice of capitulating to Japan and fighting communism. . . . The Kuomintang reactionaries directed part of their troops and government officials to surrender to the Japanese invaders and then, as puppet troops and officials, to join the Japanese troops in attacking the Liberated Areas; this was what they cunningly named 'saving the nation by a devious path.' " *Ibid.*, p. 31.

sha) and several of the firm's technical experts to stay on in Taiyuan to assist him in an ambitious industrialization program for his economically backward province.[62] The company President and now one of Yen's chief economic advisers was none other than Kōmoto Daisaku, who in 1928 (as Colonel Kōmoto of the Kwantung Army) had arranged the assassination of Gen. Chang Tso-lin and who in 1931 had been one of the instigators of the Manchurian Incident.*

Six days after the end of the war, Yen ordered his son-in-law, Gen. Wang Ching-kuo, to the Japanese stronghold at Linfen to negotiate an agreement with the Commander of the 114th Division, Maj. Gen. Miura Saburō: Yen's forces would not disarm the Japanese troops in Shansi but instead would cooperate closely with them in "defense" against the Communist Army. Soon after, an all-volunteer force of Japanese soldiers was organized into a Special Services Corps (Tokumu-dan) and began fighting to protect Yen's provincial empire.[63]

Yen Hsi-shan, a graduate of the Japanese Military Academy and a great admirer of the Japanese Army's esprit de corps and military tradition, invited a group of Japanese officers to establish a military academy in Taiyuan to train the Chinese officers of his Shansi Army. The Japanese eagerly agreed to the flattering request. While Yen was inspecting his troops one day in early 1946 (accompanied as usual by a Japanese general in the uniform of the Imperial Army), one of his Chinese generals led the assembled soldiers in a series of ringing cheers. "Long Live the Republic of China!"—and when the tumult had died down, "Long Live the Empire of Japan!" "It was the first occasion in postwar years when 'Long Live the Empire of Japan' had been publicly proclaimed," writes the Japanese observer of the incident with obvious pride, "and it was Japanese and Chinese soldiers shouting it together."[64]

Eighteen months after the end of the war American travelers in Taiyuan observed that the streets of the city were still crowded with Japanese soldiers, dressed in Yen's uniforms but fighting under their own commanders.[65] In battle after battle with the Communists between 1945 and 1949, when Yen's grip on Shansi was finally broken by the Red Army, "Japanese soldiers comprised the mainstay of his forces."[66] When the end finally came in April 1949, the half-starved, hard-pressed troops

---

* The warlord Chang Tso-lin, known as the Old Marshal, ruled the "Three Eastern Provinces" (Manchuria) from 1919 to 1928. He proved a fairly tractable collaborator in the expansionist programs of the Japanese when they first moved into the area, but by 1928 he had grown recalcitrant. On June 3, 1928, the train in which Chang was riding was blown up in an incident engineered by Colonel Kōmoto, and he died a few days later. In 1932 Kōmoto shed his military uniform to become a Director of the South Manchurian Railway.

of Gen. Imamura Hōsaku were among the last to lay down their lives in the cause of Yen Hsi-shan.*

Still, the situation in Shansi was exceptional. Elsewhere, the repatriation of Japanese troops was accelerated, and by late 1945 they were playing less and less of a role in the civil war. Nevertheless, certain influential Imperial Army officers made it clear to Chiang that they would do everything they could to assist him in his struggle with communism. Col. Tsuji Masanobu, for example, a devoted follower of Ishiwara Kanji, an advocate of Asia for the Asiatics, and an intelligence officer with a wealth of knowledge about Japan's anti-Communist efforts in North China and Manchukuo, offered his services to Chiang in 1945. The highest-ranking Imperial Army officer to serve Chiang in the immediate postwar years was Gen. Okamura Yasuji, who was released from prison on the order of the Generalissimo. While many of his colleagues were being tried and found guilty of war crimes in the postwar trials at Manila, Djakarta, Tokyo, and other cities, Okamura was counseling the Kuomintang Government on strategy in the civil war. In January 1949, when a Shanghai court officially exonerated Okamura, who had carried out the policy of "kill all, burn all, destroy all" (*sankō seisaku*) in North China less than seven years earlier, a furious Mao declared: "We tell you gentlemen of Nanking frankly: you are war criminals, you will be brought to trial."†

THE FATE OF THE CHINESE COLLABORATORS

At least as early as January 1944 the Chungking Government hinted (at a press conference for foreign correspondents) that in certain cases of "extenuating circumstances," members of the Wang regime would be dealt with liberally and even pardoned.[67] That forecast was borne out after the war: most low-ranking bureaucrats and even some ministerial level officials were merely detained in a kind of comfortable imprisonment until 1949 and then released. During the detention period these "prisoners" were allowed free contact with each other and with the out-

---

* General Imamura swallowed poison rather than surrender to the Communists. Yen indicated he too was ready to swallow the "bitter tea" rather than surrender to the Communists, and a *Life* magazine photograph (Nov. 22, 1948, p. 41) shows him displaying a box of cyanide capsules reserved for his use and the use of his family. However, he found an alternative to surrender or suicide: he reconciled his differences with Chiang Kai-shek and fled to Taiwan with him in late 1949. He died there in 1960. Gillin, *Warlord*, pp. 287–88.

† Mao, 4: 327. Tsuji and Okamura returned to Japan in 1949. Okamura became active in veterans' organizations and continued his support of the Kuomintang regime after its move to Taiwan. Tsuji was elected to the Diet in 1952. He disappeared mysteriously in 1961 while on a trip to Hanoi to cover the war in Indochina for the *Asahi*.

side. One of them, Li Sheng-wu, Wang's Minister of Education, says he and his fellow prisoners "got the feeling that the Kuomintang Government did not intend at first to execute *anyone*." He blames the change in attitude on the part of the Government on the wife of Miao Pin. Miao, the first President of the Hsin-min Hui, had joined Wang's regime as Vice President of the Examination Yüan. In 1945 he had gone on a peace mission to Tokyo, representing himself as an emissary of Chungking. It is uncertain whether he did in fact represent the National Government, but in any event the Supreme War Council was suspicious, and the mission failed.[68] According to Li, Madame Miao "foolishly" published documents that implicated high Chungking officials in her husband's peace effort. "The documents apparently embarrassed somebody," Li explains, "because it was only a short time later that the executions of Miao, Ch'en Kung-po, and the others began." They were executed on specific orders, according to Ho Ping-hsien.[69]

Let us see, then, what became of the leading collaborators.

As noted, despite his yeoman service in Shanghai in the closing days of the war, Chou Fo-hai was soon arrested. Gen. Tai Li took personal charge of the prisoner and accompanied him back to Chungking, where he was placed under house arrest with his family. Tai, Chou's personal friend and the main link between him and Chungking, was the only person save the Generalissimo himself in a position to intercede in Chou's behalf. Unfortunately for Chou, General Tai was killed in an airplane crash on March 17, 1946. His death may have been as damaging to the cause of Chou and the other main collaborators as the alleged disclosures of Madame Miao (though it should be noted that in this period the National Government was being assailed by the Communist press for its slowness in bringing the collaborators to trial, which may have helped press the Government into action).[70] For whatever reason, the Government began to hand down indictments within two weeks of General Tai's death, and Chou and Miao Pin were among the first to be tried. Chou was sentenced to death, but in one of the few orders of executive clemency Chiang issued in these cases, Chou's sentence was commuted to life imprisonment.[71] The clemency order declared that Chou had returned his allegiance to the National Government in 1944. He died in prison of a heart attack in February 1948.

Ch'en Kung-po fled from Nanking to Kyoto in fear of his life the day after the Japanese surrendered. He remained there in hiding for about two months and then, in October, was returned to Nanking for detention and trial. Along with other leaders of the Wang regime, he was tried for treason in the spring of 1946 in Soochow. His vigorous self-defense concluded with the assertion that not a single day had passed in which the Wang Government had failed to struggle with the Japanese. On April 5 he was sentenced to death, and two months later he was executed by a firing squad.

Liang Hung-chih, the former head of the Reformed Government and the President of the Control Yüan in the Wang regime, went into hiding but was captured with his mistress, tried, and executed. Wang K'o-min, the head of the Provisional Government and later Chairman of the North China Political Council, died in a Peiping prison in December 1945 while awaiting trial. Wang I-t'ang, who also served as the Chairman of the North China Political Council (from 1940 to 1943) was executed in September 1946. Among the other leading collaborators who were executed were Mei Ssu-p'ing, Lin Pai-sheng, and Ch'u Min-i. Chin Hsiung-pai calculated that about 2,720 civilian and military leaders of the Wang regime were executed and another 2,300 (including Madame Wang Ching-wei) were sentenced to life imprisonment.[72]

Some collaborators never got to court but were the victims of vigilante justice. Ch'en Ch'un-yu (described in press accounts as the Chief of the Japanese secret police in Hangchow), was taken by a crowd in September 1945, was paraded through the streets, and then was quickly executed.[73] Such incidents, however, were more common in the countryside than in the cities. In villages liberated by Communist troops, the cadre customarily used summary public trials of the local gentry to break the iron grip this class held on village life and set the stage for agrarian reform and eventual collectivization. One of the most frequent charges leveled at the landlords was collaboration with the Japanese. And indeed, there was often substance to the charge; in order to protect their privileged economic status, many rich landlords had undoubtedly developed pro-Japanese sympathies. Nor is it so surprising, after all, that the propertied classes in the "liberated areas," given a choice between collaborating with the enemy and submitting to the Communists' soak-the-rich policy, chose the unpatriotic option; it was largely against these landlords that the often furious wrath of the "people's courts" was directed.

Yet collaboration with the enemy was only one—and probably not the chief—grievance in a complex of grievances the poor peasants had nurtured for a lifetime against their often despotic landlords. American newsman Jack Belden's accounts of the vicious punishment meted out to the landlord of Stone Wall Village in Shansi reveal how genuine and many those grievances were. There, in return for a preferential grain tax from the local Japanese Army commander, the landlord had regularly entertained Japanese officers at his table (exacting the necessary food from his tenants), conscripted young men to work in the Japanese labor corps, coerced women to satisfy the sexual needs of the Japanese officers, and in general used the Japanese as a club to threaten anyone who resisted his iron-fisted control over the village.[74] Judging from Belden's accounts of the "speaking bitterness" sessions, which were the usual prelude to the execution of hated gentry, the villagers were not incensed by the act of collaboration itself. Their anger was not directed at the landlord's unpatriotic acts, and there were no charges about such things as betrayal of country. Collaboration was simply seen as one more device to reinforce the landlords' age-old tyranny over the peasants, and it was this tyranny that provoked the wrathful lynchings in the countryside.

In areas not under Communist control, grievances against collaborators were sometimes completely ignored. The most flagrant case involved the Governor (1934–41) of Fukien province, Ch'en Yi. From at least 1940 on, patriotic Chinese and especially Overseas Chinese (many of whose ancestral homes were in Fukien) were outspokenly critical of Ch'en Yi's graft-ridden, repressive administration and of his refusal to break his ties with Japan and commit the province to all-out resistance.[75] In August 1941 Chiang Kai-shek finally responded to demands that Ch'en be removed from office and ordered him to Chungking—not, however, to disgrace or punish him but to appoint him Secretary-General of the Executive Yüan.

In October 1945 Ch'en came under bitter attack from the Fukienese as a collaborator and a "lawless warlord despised by all the people."[76] Charged with the arrest and death of thousands of anti-Japanese and with inviting the South Manchurian Railway to exploit the mines in Fukien, Ch'en not only was not held accountable, but was appointed Governor of Taiwan, only just liberated from a half century of Japanese control. The announcement of this appointment provoked a spectacular display of outrage, with Fukienese and Taiwanese alike flooding Chungking with letters begging the Generalissimo to reconsider. "There was an undercurrent of disbelief," writes an American diplomat stationed on Taiwan in the immediate postwar years. "Now at last the Japanese were defeated, and the Government was allied with the most powerful country in the world—the United States of America. There had been so much talk of the future and reform. And now this."[77] Chiang ignored the protests, believing Ch'en to be the most logical choice for the post both because of his experience with things Japanese and because of his experience in Fukien, which is opposite Taiwan and the original home of a large percentage of the island's population.

Ch'en's year-and-a-half rule over Taiwan further tarnished his reputation and transformed the Kuomintang from liberator to despoiler in the eyes of most of the Taiwanese. The Japanese administration of the island, though harsh and at times repressive, was at least efficient and free from corruption. The Taiwanese, who had gained certain benefits under the Japanese colonial rule (such as a literacy rate of about 80 per cent, second only to Japan and considerably higher than the mainland), quickly became disenchanted with their new masters, who were more arrogant, not so competent, and far less honest than their old ones.[78] In February 1947 the Taiwanese disaffection escalated into huge protest demonstrations that threatened to blossom into a full-scale revolt until Ch'en Yi launched a suppression campaign of a ferocity the islanders had never experienced under Japanese rule. By the time the mass round-ups and executions had come to an end, "several thousand Taiwanese were massacred, including virtually all of the small group of leaders with modern education, administrative experience, and political maturity."[79] General Wedemeyer reported to the Secretary of State in August 1947 that the Taiwanese feared "the Central Government contemplates bleeding their island to support the tottering and corrupt Nanking machine and I think their fears well founded. . . . Many were forced to feel that conditions under autocratic rule [of Japan] were preferable."*

* U.S. Dept. of State, *United States Relations with China*, p. 309. The Generalissimo could no longer ignore the protests over Ch'en's governorship and recalled him in April 1947. A year later he was appointed Governor of Chekiang. In early 1950 Chiang ordered his execution—on the grounds that he was a Communist conspirator!

CHAPTER SIXTEEN

An Assessment

THE TWO years that elapsed between Wang's flight from Chungking in December 1938 and the signing of the Sino-Japanese Basic Treaty in November 1940 was a period of almost unrelieved failure and capitulation for Wang. Wang made the mistake of assuming that the Chinese political world was "split exactly in half," and it proved not to be.[1] His peace movement failed to sway the minds of the Chungking Government, failed to produce defections of pivotal leaders to his cause, failed to win the backing of Overseas Chinese communities in Southeast Asia, and failed to secure the support of any of the supposedly wavering warlord generals. Japan compounded Wang's error by assuming that "anti-Chiang" somehow implied "pro-Japanese," or could be converted into "pro-Japanese" without too much difficulty. But far from heightening the tensions and clique rivalry that might have weakened Chungking's ability and determination to prosecute the war, Wang watched helplessly from Hanoi and Shanghai as the Generalissimo, his hand strengthened by Western aid and promises of further aid, brought dissidents into the fold. The coalition between the Nationalists and the Communists, if something less than a model united front, continued to work fairly well until the New Fourth Army Incident in early 1941.

In short, China became unified and committed to resistance as never before, and Wang became increasingly alienated from the prevailing mood of the country. From all accounts, before the murder of his personal secretary and friend by Kuomintang agents in March 1939, he was on the verge of conceding his failure and going into exile. But that crime enraged him and rekindled his determination to defy Chungking's efforts to intimidate him.

From the day he returned to Chinese soil from Hanoi, in the company of Japanese Imperial Army officers and on board a Japanese vessel, until the establishment of his Reorganized National Government in March 1940, Wang relinquished to Japan a vast measure of Chinese sovereignty—the very thing he had so often vowed not to do. He agreed to the adviser system, which gave the Japanese effective control over almost all levels of government. He recognized the independence of Manchukuo and the autonomy of Mengchiang (including lands below the Great Wall). By his acquiescence in the creation of the North China Political Council, he cooperated in Japan's efforts to autonomize, under her own tight control, the historic heartland of China and tie that vitally important area to her strategic purposes. Even in the lower Yangtze valley, an area close to his own capital where his regime supposedly had some measure of independence, he gave in to Japanese demands for military, economic, and political privileges.

In sum, there was never an unoccupied China analogous to the unoccupied France that the Vichy regime was wresting from its conquerors at approximately the same time. As we have seen, the initial understanding between Wang's colleagues and the Imperial Army General Staff provided for the establishment of a regime in the unoccupied provinces of South China. We need not recapitulate here how and why that plan fell through. But it is worth emphasizing again that the agreement to establish the regime in occupied rather than unoccupied territory had important implications for the character and purpose of the regime. As Kao Tsung-wu and other Wang followers early realized, it meant that the Wang regime had laid itself open to essentially unanswerable charges of subservience to Japan.

Whether he intended to or not, Wang in effect lent the great prestige of his own name (and the not so great prestige of his Reorganized Government) to the *bunji gassaku* program of Japan's most determined continental expansionists, a program that clearly belied the claims of those who insisted Japan was distressed at China's weakness and disunity and favored a strong and unified country capable of repelling the encroachments of foreign powers, particularly the Soviet Union and Great Britain. It was a program so contemptuous of Chinese nationalism that Wang's even tacit acceptance of it foredoomed the failure of his regime. It was a program that made Wang's promise of a "rejuvenated China" a preposterous deceit. Wang's defenders may be correct in asserting that he and his colleagues did not really commit themselves to Japanese programs but only deceived the Japanese into thinking they did. Maybe so. But that does not mean the counterargument has any less force to it: that Wang, by virtue of his eminence in China, assuredly divided and confused his own people by an even equivocal support of Japan.

There were, to be sure, Japanese who advocated a much more lenient policy toward Wang. Many of these men were in the debt of Gen. Ishiwara Kanji for their strategic outlook, the view that the real threat to

Japan was the Soviet Union. Reconciliation with China was an imperative of that concept, for Japan dared not face the Soviet Union with a
hostile China at her back. In order to reconcile and stabilize the relationship between China and Japan, Ishiwara proposed to build an East
Asia League that would serve the interests of both countries. Based on
equality and mutual assistance, this loose association would ensure Japan the security and economic strength she needed to defend herself
against the Soviet Union. Ishiwara held that by disavowing aggrandizement and the fruits of past aggression (an aggression that he, paradoxically, had helped to generate), Japan would have no difficulty in inducing China to support the League.* Its purposes were thus not only compatible with but beneficial to the growth of Chinese nationalism, for
China as well as Japan would be strengthened by the League and in a
position to defend herself against imperialism, whether from the Soviet
Union or from the West.

The Japanese most intimately and consistently associated with Wang's
collaboration with their country, men like Inukai Ken and Kagesa Sadaaki, considered themselves disciples of Ishiwara. Bent on building the
Wang regime around Ishiwara's concepts, they sought to reduce Japanese demands on Wang and to grant him sufficient concessions to free
him of the puppet stigma and enable him to establish a genuinely independent and viable regime. Given Kagesa's important position and contacts in the Army's hierarchy and Inukai's association with the Premier,
Wang had some reason to be optimistic about their ability to produce
what they promised. That optimism, as it turned out, was not justified.
The failure of Kagesa, Inukai, and others to induce the Japanese leaders
to rein in their demands doomed both the Wang collaboration experiment and Japan's larger Pan-Asian goals to failure.

We have suggested that one of the principal reasons for the failure of
the Kagesa-Inukai efforts was the abiding and widespread feeling in offi-

---

* I have tended throughout this book to award high praise to Ishiwara for his uncommon respect of the strength of Chinese nationalism and, though this is deserved
praise, it should not blind us to some questionable elements in Ishiwara's thinking.
He was proposing, after all, that the General Staff dictate national policy, a proposal
that, as Crowley points out (*Japan's Quest*, p. 394), "would deny the legitimacy of the
power of the cabinet and premier to decide official policy." Secondly, we must remember that Ishiwara wanted peace with China not as an end but as a means—to wage
the inevitable war with the Soviet Union. Finally, given Ishiwara's hatred of communism, he would surely have found unacceptable any solution to the China Incident
that did not provide for the total extirpation of communism in China. One can only
guess where Ishiwara's ideas would have led Japan, but a General Staff dictatorship,
a second Russo-Japanese war, and Japanese involvement in a renewed civil war in
China do not add up to a felicitous fate for Japan.

cial circles in Japan that Chungking was too important to ignore, that there could be no meaningful settlement of the Sino-Japanese conflict unless Chungking was a party to that settlement. In light of Chiang's status in the eyes of the Chinese and the well-known personal conflict between him and Wang, it was impossible to avoid the conclusion that any association with Wang, not to say total collaboration, must prolong the war with China. Consequently, the literature of the period is replete with metaphors suggesting, as Inukai chose to put it, that Wang was merely an unwelcome guest and Chiang the honored (if delayed) guest for whom the feast would be spread. Though General Imai greatly admired Wang, he was frank to concede that collaboration with Wang was "not exactly like running into the Buddha in hell."[2] Thus, even those most committed to Wang's cause were sensitive to the necessity of somehow reaching an agreement with Chungking, and so wavered between supporting his regime as an end in itself and using him as a bridge to the Nationalist Government.

There are other things that help to explain the failure of the Ishiwara-Kagesa-Inukai vision of Sino-Japanese cooperation. The most obvious is that the *bunji gassaku* policies of the Japanese militarists thwarted the rising nationalistic aspirations of the Chinese people. No Chinese leader could hope to build a following by associating himself with the dismemberment of his nation, and yet Japan demanded of her Chinese allies that they not only tolerate the Manchukuoan and North Chinese puppet regimes but openly endorse them. How could students in Peiping's schools have failed to hate Japan after being forced to participate in giant track marathons to celebrate the capitulation of the Wuhan triangle in late 1938? What must those students (and their teachers) have thought as they gathered for an athletic meet in 1939, with the five-barred flag of the Provisional Government waving overhead, observing (in the Oriental version of the Nazis' Nuremberg spectacle) a massive human formation shaping the graphs Tung-Ya-Hsin-Chih-Hsü, A New Order in East Asia? Could they not see for themselves, as historian Usui has written, that "it was the Japanese Army and not the Provisional Government that was ruling occupied China"?[3] And how many Chinese collaborators must have shared the experience of the Chinese journalist who decided he could no longer stomach collaboration after attending a conference that was called on to pass a resolution thanking the Imperial Army for its role in the creation of Manchukuo?[4]

And yet Japan's determination to hold onto her spoils never flagged. Not even those leaders most sympathetic to Chinese nationalism considered relinquishing Manchukuo. Nowhere in Ishii's "Ikensho" was such a proposal made. Certainly nowhere in Ishiwara's anti-Government speeches is anything of the sort suggested. On the contrary, Ishiwara argued (correctly) that Manchuria was basically not a Chinese land but a land of Manchurians, Mongols, and Koreans that had been colonized by China. Japan had moved into it in order to save it from falling into the hands of the West, and now it was simply "a joint Sino-Japanese colony."[5] In none of the peace operations we have surveyed was the relinquishment of Manchukuo a consideration. So far as I know, such a concession was not seriously considered until July 1945—and even then it did not have the backing of Tokyo.* In any case, at that point Chungking was in no mood to negotiate a separate peace with Japan. Less than a month later Soviet troops poured over the Manchurian border and ended Japanese options once and for all.

A more basic reason for the failure of the collaboration experiments to bear fruit was what historian Oka Yoshitake calls the "psychological isolation" of Japan from the rest of Asia.[6] That isolation, Oka holds, developed because Japanese nationalism sprang from a unique source. The nationalism of the Japanese had an artificial quality in the sense that it was instilled in the citizenry by the Government. Chinese nationalism, in contrast, grew out of a very real—and bitter—century of experience, and therefore had great vitality and depth. In short, the Japanese, failing a history of humiliation at the hands of foreigners, could not fully appreciate the feelings of those of their Asian neighbors who had. Only this psychological deficiency can explain how Japan could insist on the resignation of Chiang Kai-shek as a condition for an armistice—and persist in that demand oblivious to the advice of Ishii Itarō and the many others who recognized that Chiang was a powerful symbol of a new national mood. Blinding herself to that fact, Japan imposed her will on Wang, stripped him and his regime of patriotic appeal by her exactions, and then expected him to regain that appeal by posing with her as co-liberators of a country oppressed by Soviet and Western imperialism. The monumental conceit embodied in that expectation can only be explained in terms of a monumental "psychological isolation" from Chinese nationalism. The depth of irony in that expectation was appreciated by few Japanese and by most Chinese.

The preceding forty-odd years had seen many Japanese-sponsored "Pan-Asian" programs, but few that met the requirement of genuine

---

* This was another of the many secret operations conducted by General Imai. In this case he attempted to negotiate a peace settlement (on the authority of Gen. Okamura Yasuji, Commander-in-Chief of the mainland forces) with Gen. Ho Chu-kuo, Deputy Commander of the Tenth War Zone. Interview with Imai; Imai, *Kindai no sensō*, pp. 336–38.

equality set forth by General Ishiwara.[7] All too many of Ishiwara's colleagues were caught in the snare of their own circular reasoning about Pan-Asianism. For them, Pan-Asianism bestowed on Japan the obligation to thwart Soviet and capitalist expansion into China; but to carry out that emancipating mission, she herself had to expand into China and acquire a strategic power base. Such concepts of Pan-Asianism developed in the minds of Japanese at best only half-liberated from thought patterns deriving from their country's past history. A feudal society inclines its people to think in terms of hierarchy, not equality. Need we ask which nation the Japanese Pan-Asianists thought should be at the top of the hierarchy? The contrast in the Chinese and Japanese responses to Western imperialism and Soviet Bolshevism provided the answer. China's response had been weak and Japan's had been strong; if the twin blights were to be eradicated from Asia it was obvious that the direction of the task could not be entrusted to China. To many Japanese, China did not have even the minimum requirements for leadership in such a crusade because she was not a genuine polity. "China is a society, but she is not a nation," wrote Maj. Gen. Sakai Ryū, Chief of Staff of the Japanese forces in North China in 1937. "Or rather," he goes on, "it would be fair to say that China is a society of bandits." "The Chinese people are bacteria infesting world civilization," he adds in language that was far from uncommon among Japanese militarists.[8]

A uniquely Japanese manifestation of the relative positions assigned to Japan and China in the Pan-Asian hierarchy—and a concept especially menacing to China—was the belief in *tenshoku* (divine mission). According to this fanatical notion, Japan was entitled, nay compelled, to save China whether she wanted to be saved or not. General Matsui's scarcely credible justification of the war in China before the International Military Tribunal becomes plausible only if one understands the dictates of tenshoku:

> The struggle between Japan and China was always a fight between brothers within the "Asian family." . . . It has been my belief during all these years that we must regard this struggle as a method of making the Chinese undergo self-reflection. We do not do this because we hate them, but on the contrary because we love them too much. It is just the same as in a family when an elder brother has taken all that he can stand from his ill-behaved younger brother and has to chastise him in order to make him behave properly.[9]

That the behavior of the Japanese soldier and civilian in China did not always meet the standards of decency suggested by Matsui's "elder brother" phrase is an issue we need not belabor.[10] The postwar Tokyo trials provided evidence enough to document the scale of atrocities visited on the Chinese by their elder brothers, but that evidence did not explain the reason for the inhumanity—if, indeed, wartime inhumanity can be explained. Since, however, the brutish behavior of the Japanese mainland garrisons contributed so greatly to the frustrations of those, like Wang, who wished to cast the Japanese in the best possible light, we cannot pass over this point without a comment or two.

Surely part of the breakdown in discipline of the Japanese armies can be explained by the absence in the Japanese social system of a generalized code of ethical behavior, one that would provide ethical dictates to the peasant in his home village and to the same peasant after he had donned an Army uniform and been sent to garrison a Chinese city. At home the Japanese is guided—very nearly smothered—by rules of social conduct so detailed and demanding as to provide the solution to nearly every social or moral situation that confronts him. He needs only to follow the rules and customs he has been taught since childhood to ensure both his own tranquility and that of his society. When the Japanese was likely to run amok was when he found himself in a situation for which the rule book provided no answers, in a situation outside of the boundaries of the code that governed his customary behavior. "The Japanese who ventures out beyond the boundaries of his rule book is more completely lost than those of us who live by more generalized precepts and fewer exact rules," writes Edwin O. Reischauer.[11] The "familiar situational guideposts" of the Japanese work well enough under ordinary circumstances and, indeed, probably create "less friction and strain than our own more individualistic code of conduct," says Reischauer, but their ethical code "seems to break down more completely than our more generalized ethics when confronted with the unexpected, throwing the Japanese back on their unguided instincts."

Japanese writers prefer to emphasize the baneful effects of Army life on the Japanese soldier of all ranks. Noma Hiroshi's postwar novel about the Imperial Army in World War II, *Shinkū Chitai* (Zone of Emptiness), depicts the Army as a dehumanized organization built on the repression of natural desires. Based on his own experiences he writes a chilling account of injustices, savage rivalries among officers for promotions, corruption, and, above all, brutality. Sociologist Tsurumi Kazuko describes the "relentless destruction of privacy and the extensive use of violence" as methods of "negative affect socialization." "Anger and contempt were maximized in the socializing agents, while distress, fear, and humiliation were maximized in the persons socialized," she writes.[12] The aim of the socialization process was to inhibit the soldier from thinking, doing, or even feeling anything of his own volition—in short to create the "zone of emptiness" Noma described in his novel. Only when that was done could the soldier be "socialized for death"— which is to say, made to accept death willingly.

Maruyama Masao maintains that the atrocities committed by Japanese forces in China and other countries represented the "transfer of oppression." Oppressed and brutalized by their superiors, the soldiers managed to find a kind of psychological compensation in oppressing and brutalizing whoever they could. Without relieving the senior officers of ultimate responsibility for the atrocities in China, Maruyama points out that it was the rank-and-file soldier who perpetrated these crimes. Given the nature of Japanese society, he concludes, it is scarcely surprising that soldiers "who in ordinary civilian or military life have no object to which they can transfer oppression should, when they find themselves in this position, be driven by an explosive impulse to free themselves at a stroke from the pressure that has been hanging over them."[13]

Leaving aside the rape and plunder, it is worth noting that the Japanese "elder brother" in China was as prone as any other soldier to incorporate racial slurs into his everyday vocabulary. The Japanese "Chankoro" is the equivalent of the English-language "Chink" and was used with the same contemptuous overtones. In Hino Ashihei's war reportage (translated into English as *War and Soldiers*), "Chankoro" could be the objects of contempt regardless of whether they resisted the Japanese or welcomed them. Hino writes of his surprise at being greeted with smiles by the inhabitants of certain towns during the brief Hangchow campaign in late 1937:

> Such a thing could never be if any enemy occupied Japanese towns, and the men, women and even children would never forget that they were enemies and would be hostile to the very end. Japanese would sooner die than be friendly with an enemy. We would be friendly with Chinese individuals and indeed came to love them. But how could we help despising them as a nation when they would sell their smiles and flattery to an enemy for the price of their own skins when the destiny of their nation [was] in the balance. To us soldiers, they were pitiful, spineless people.[14]

It is not difficult to see how such attitudes of national superiority— or the fixation on chauvinistic slogans (like *kokui hatsuyō*, enhancing the national prestige) as statements of ultimate national goals—could frustrate the dreams of Pan-Asianists like Ishiwara. Shigemitsu Mamoru, decrying the wartime preoccupation with glory in his country, writes:

"Unhappy Japan! She not only misunderstood; she was impatient and intolerant of restraint. Always it was 'glory' that mattered. In national policy, in the plan of campaign, it was 'glory' that decided. This it was that molded the mentality of the people in time of war. It was splendid, but endurance and wisdom would have been more valuable."[15]

Nor is it difficult to appreciate the problem Wang Ching-wei faced in selling the Pan-Asian sentiments of Sun Yat-sen to the Chinese people. All the allure of Wang's oratorical skill could not conceal the fact that the Japan of 1940 was not the Japan that had befriended Sun and assisted the Nationalist cause in the early years of the century. In November 1924, only a few months before his death, Sun was in Japan on the last of many trips to that country. In the last major address he was to give to the Japanese, he spoke on the subject of Pan-Asianism. Contrasting Oriental culture, which was based on benevolence, justice, and morality, or the rule of right, with the Occidental rule of might, Sun threw down a challenge to his Japanese audience: "Japan today has become acquainted with Western civilization of the rule of Might, but retains the characteristics of the Oriental civilization of the rule of Right. Now the question remains whether Japan will be the hawk of the Western civilization of the rule of Might or the tower of strength of the Orient. This is the choice which lies before the people of Japan."[16]

The failure of Kagesa, Inukai, and their colleagues to meet the challenge posed by Sun, their failure to secure concessions for Wang that would have enabled him to stand in a position of equality with Japan, confirms that the hierarchic brand of Pan-Asianism had gained a powerful grip on the Japanese mind since 1924. In November 1938, however, when Wang was preparing to defect from Chungking, Konoe had merely given a name to his version of Pan-Asianism—the New Order in East Asia. It remained to be seen how the abstractions of his speech would be converted into hard policy. It is easy enough in hindsight to see that the New Order would turn out as it did, with Japan dominating her Pan-Asian partners. At the time, however, there was reason to believe that the New Order offered some hope for a genuine partnership—not because Konoe and his advisers were deeply committed to a truly equal partnership (though some undoubtedly were) but because they wished to check Japan's military cliques and end the war that was so disastrously draining the strength of Japan. That it was the members of the Kōain rather than Konoe and his advisers who interpreted the New Order had terrible implications for Wang. As Gen. Kita Seiichi, one of the guiding lights of the Kōain, later declared, with a directness not often heard at the war crimes trials, the function of the Kōain was simply "to Japanize China."[17]

Let us cite one last reason for the failure of the Ishiwara concept of Pan-Asian equality to take hold: the simple fact that the most powerful segment of the military did not share Ishiwara's basic assumptions. To be sure, Gens. Tōjō Hideki, Tanaka Shin'ichi, Tominaga Kyōji, Sugiyama Gen, and the others in that circle did share Ishiwara's concern about the Soviet Union. But they came to a completely different conclusion: China should not be befriended and thus neutralized but should be annihilated and thus neutralized.

In the latter half of 1937 and in 1938 Japan gradually committed herself to the policy of annihilation, ignoring the warnings of Ishiwara. As one reads the records of the various meetings held to determine high state policy—the Imperial Conferences, Liaison Conferences, Four and Five Ministers' Conferences—one is struck with the absence of an effective leader, the uninspired analysis of great problems, and, above all, the shortsightedness of the planning. In a word, the evidence is overwhelming that Japan drifted into the mainland quagmire exactly as Ishiwara had predicted. Many Japanese, insiders and outsiders alike, have commented on this process. Maruyama Masao writes of the inability of Japan's leaders "to regulate the means in terms of clearly perceived objectives," so that "the use of brute force to carry out policy became more and more commonplace, until finally there was no turning back."[18] Konoe offered this pathetic epitaph in 1945: "The situation was such that they [the Army] were pushed on by developments and went on, gradually extending themselves. Herein [lay] the great danger of the China Incident."[19]

Konoe characteristically places the onus of responsibility on the Army, when in fact, as we have seen, the annihilation policy received the unqualified endorsement of his Cabinet in January 1938. If Konoe had civilian advisers like Ozaki Hotsumi to sound the alarm about the dangers of a war with China, he also had advisers like Nagai Ryūtarō, a man with "impeccable credentials as the kind of enlightened civilian moderate often characterized as liberal."[20] Even moderates like Nagai could rationalize the policy of annihilating Kuomintang China by arguing that Japan's real enemy was not the Chinese people but "the unholy alliance between the white imperialists and their puppet [Chiang Kai-shek] in Nanking."* Konoe was not unmindful of the dangers of protracted war, but the intoxicating appeals to Japan's mission were sufficient to deaden his sensitivity to those dangers.

Of interest to the historian are the deep roots in Japanese history of

---

* Duus, "Nagai Ryūtarō and the 'White Peril,'" p. 46. Nagai held various portfolios in the first Konoe Cabinet and served as a special ambassador to the Wang Ching-wei regime in 1942. He came to believe that the traditional political parties

the view that Japan's defense required the annihilation—or at least the conquest—of China. At least as early as the eighteenth century writers like the arms expert and defense strategist Hayashi Shihei (1738–93) were portraying China—and Russia—as a menace to Japan and calling for a vigorous policy of expansionism to counter the danger. In 1823 the remarkable Satō Shin'en (1769–1850), physician, pharmacologist, astronomer, and one of the earliest exponents of Western military science, wrote a book entitled *Kondō Hisaku* (A Secret Plan of Absorption) that emphasized the dangers to which a weakened China exposed Japan.[21] It was not that China herself threatened Japan; it was that China had allowed the real menace to Japan, England, to get a foothold in Asia. As Satō saw it, Japan should respond by seizing part of China as a bulwark against further British expansion.

Not surprisingly, the picture of China as a menace (albeit indirect) to Japan and as a contemptibly weak and corrupt nation came into sharper focus with the defeat of the Chinese Empire in the Opium War (1839–42). From then on, the castigation of China by such influential thinkers as Aizawa Seishisai (1782–1863), Yokoi Shōnan (1809–1869), Fukuzawa Yūkichi (1833–1901), and Tokutomi Sohō (1863–1957) became increasingly shrill. What delayed the Japanese assault on China and her protectorate Korea was not doubt about the need or inevitability of such a move but debate over timing and preparedness. Japan dared not move until she had thrown off the feudal divisiveness of the past, acquired a strong sense of nationhood, and learned well the secrets of Western military superiority. By the 1880's many felt that those goals had been accomplished, and in the meantime the spectacle of China's humiliation and defeat had loomed ever larger.

At this point a lofty sense of rectitude was injected into the thinking of the expansionists. Expansion into China was now proposed not in the name of narrow reasons of national self-interest, but in the name of safeguarding civilization—though there was by no means unanimity over precisely which civilization was to be saved, "modern civilizaton" or Oriental civilization. The great educator and popularizer of Western doctrines of liberalism, Fukuzawa Yūkichi, constantly emphasized this theme. "Our country must not fail to protect it [China] militarily, guide it culturally, and show it the way to arrive at the stage of modern civili-

---

were incapable of mobilizing the energies of the nation to meet the extraordinary needs of wartime Japan and joined Konoe in pressing for their dissolution (including his own party, the Minseitō) in favor of one all-embracing political organization. The result was the Imperial Rule Assistance Association (Taisei Yokusankai), created in 1940, with which he remained affiliated until his death in 1944.

zation," he wrote in 1881. Moreover, if it proved unavoidable, "our country may even threaten [China] by force to ensure its progress."[22] In 1885 Fukuzawa wrote a brief but justifiably famous essay in his newspaper, *Jiji shimpō* (News of the Times). The essay, "Datsu-A ron," as the title suggests, called for Japan's "withdrawal from Asia," that is, for Japan's renunciation of her Asian heritage in favor of an all-out dedication to modernization on Western models. Along with such a dedication went the necessity of abandoning any thought of civilizing the hopelessly backward Chinese and Koreans. "We need not be especially cordial to China and Korea just because they are our immediate neighbors. We would do better to treat them in the same way as do the Western nations," Fukuzawa wrote.[23] Here, in Fukuzawa's "Datsu-A ron," Matsumoto Sannosuke finds the very seeds of Japanese aggression against China. "It is . . . undeniable that this thesis served to justify and encourage Japan's imperialistic advances into the Asian continent in the subsequent decades," he writes.[24]

Tokutomi Sohō, like Fukuzawa an important spokesman for things progressive and Western, used the editorial columns of his influential newspaper, *Kokumin no tomo* (*The Nation's Friend* was its English subtitle), to justify the war with China that finally came in August 1894. Japan was on the threshold of becoming "Greater Japan" (Dainaru Nihon), a nation on the move throughout Asia and the South Pacific, he wrote in the year before the First Sino-Japanese War. Nor was the purpose of the expansion he advocated merely to develop trade or plant colonies, said Tokutomi, "but [even more] in showing off national power to the world." "In every respect, it is China that prevents us from expanding our own national power," he wrote shortly before the war broke out. "When we try to establish 'Greater Japan,' we find the cause of great troubles confronting the foreign policy of our country in China, not in Europe."[25] When a proper provocation for war with China was discovered in the summer of 1894, Tokutomi was delighted, for it meant an opportunity for Japan "to take her place alongside the other great expansionist powers of the world."[26] And when the "splendid little war" he favored finally erupted, Tokutomi's exhilaration knew no bounds. In an editorial issued soon after the war began, he corrected those who thought that it was being fought to establish a huge indemnity. Japan was simply "fighting to determine once and for all [her] position in the world," he wrote, adding: "If our country achieves a brilliant victory, all previous misconceptions will be dispelled. The true nature of our country and of our national character will suddenly emerge like the sun breaking through a dense fog."[27]

Meiji Japan's foremost Christian scholar, Uchimura Kanzō (1861–1930), though later known for his pacifism, shared this feeling of mission at the outbreak of the war and proclaimed it a "historical necessity." Invoking classical, Biblical, and European history to prove that the "Corean War" (as he called it) was a "righteous war," Uchimura argued: "The Corean War is to decide whether Progress shall be the law in the East, as it has long been in the West, or whether Retrogression, fostered once by the Persian Empire; then by Carthage, and again by Spain, and now at last (last in world's history, we hope) by the Manchurian Empire of China, shall possess the Orient forever."[28]

The war with China was a succession of easy triumphs for the Japanese. It was immensely popular at home—so many old samurai wished to join the fray that the Emperor had to issue a special rescript ordering them to remain at their jobs. Whatever feelings of cultural affinity and indebtedness the Japanese might once have felt toward the Middle Kingdom dissolved as the nation reveled in self-pride and scorn for China. Donald Keene has compiled a veritable catalog of the popular songs, plays, poems, and *nishiki-e* (colored wood-block prints) that celebrated the brief war. Invariably the Chinese are portrayed in the *nishiki-e* as craven, subhuman creatures totally devoid of dignity, reason, and honor. Songs pilloried the Chinese leader Li Hung-chang ("Li, Li, flat-nosed Li Hung-chang . . ."). One asked, "What is it rolling before the prince's horse?" and contemptuously answered, "That is the pumpkin-head of a Chinaman, don't you know?"[29] On hearing of the declaration of war the distinguished poet Yosano Hiroshi (Tekkan) (1873–1935) recalled the infamous *mimuzuka*, the mound of Chinese soldiers' ears the sixteenth-century Japanese leader Hideyoshi had raised during the war with Korea:

> What need we yield
> To ancient glories?
> The time is near
> When again we shall build
> A mound of ears.[30]

It is true, of course, that many Japanese did not share these anti-Chinese sentiments at the time, and it is also true that by the 1930's much had happened in China to shake the Japanese loose from their contempt for China. But the predisposition was there, and we have seen how rare it was for an Ishii or an Ishiwara to challenge the time-honored view of China as weak and therefore, paradoxically, menacing to Japan. And we have also seen how little heeded was their counsel. Nor did defeat in World War II entirely end the preoccupation of some Japanese with the need for annihilating China. Tsurumi Kazuko cites an example of the persistence of this view in the final testament of a lieutenant general who was soon to be executed for war crimes. "After my physical death, my true spirit will soar in the sky and will never rest until it achieves its revenge for Japan's defeat.... The reconstruction of our Emperor's country will require the destruction of America and the conquest of China. As long as our country is under pressure either from America or from China, its rehabilitation will fall short of the realization of Greater Japan's world destiny."[31]

At the opening of this book, I accepted the opinion of Tsunoda Jun that an understanding of the "aborted outcome of the efforts" of men like Ishiwara Kanji and Inukai Ken (I would include Ishii Itarō) was crucial to an understanding of the Sino-Japanese War. Ba Maw, Japan's principal collaborator in Burma, has speculated what might have happened had their efforts not been "aborted." In his recently published memoirs, he laments the tragic consequences of Japan's "betrayal" of her Asian allies and collaborators. How different everything might have been, he writes, for both Japan and Asia, if Japan had not been betrayed by her militarists and their "racial fantasies."

> Had her Asian instincts been true, had she only been faithful to the concept of Asia for the Asians that she herself had proclaimed at the beginning of the war, Japan's fate would have been very different. No military defeat could then have robbed her of the trust and gratitude of half of Asia or even more, and that would have mattered a great deal in finding for her a new, great, and abiding place in a postwar world in which Asia was coming into her own.[32]

WANG'S MOTIVES

Shimizu Tōzō, the Foreign Ministry China specialist attached to the Plum Blossom Agency, once remarked that whenever Wang Ching-wei appeared at social or ceremonial functions attended by Japanese diplomats and military officers, the Japanese "all looked insignificant by comparison."[33] Wang's commanding presence served to inspire his followers, but it could not diminish the toll that six long years of wartime collaboration gradually took on their lives. The desperate situation the Wang regime found itself in after America's entry into the war broke the spirit of many of the participants and gave rise to a live-for-today outlook on life. "There was lots of drinking," writes Chin Hsiung-pai, and "Li Shih-ch'ün, Mei Ssu-p'ing, Ch'en Kung-po, Chou Fo-hai—everyone except for Wang himself—had affairs with women."[34] Wang's private life remained above reproach and even his harshest critics could not direct at him the charges of profiteering and dissipation that were commonly leveled against his subordinates. His home was simple and lacked the expensive touches one might expect in the home of so illustrious a man. Wang liked to have dinner guests, but the fare was always "very plain Western food," and he would usually dine at one table with his wife and children while the guests dined at another. According to one anecdote, Madame Wang once purchased some Western tableware that Wang mistakenly supposed to be expensive. In a rage he broke all the pieces and chided his wife: "How can you waste money on such things at a time like this?"[35]

The periods of rage came more and more frequently for the normally placid Wang as the strains of his collaboration intensified. He would often explode in the middle of a meeting, banging his fist on the table, looking for a chair or another object to throw, and when he found none, taking his anger out on someone present—usually his brother-in-law, Ch'u Min-i. One of these highly emotional scenes occurred in 1943, when Wang learned that his subordinates planned to put a number of captured Nationalist soldiers the Japanese had turned over to them in a prisoner-of-war camp. With tears of rage flowing down his cheeks, Wang upbraided his colleagues for their lack of patriotism. It was understandable that Japan should wish to treat the soldiers as enemies and prisoners of war, he said, but after all, these men had risked their lives for "our country," so how could their fellow Chinese possibly think of treating them with anything less than respect?[36] The impossible dilemma of wartime collaboration was summed up in such incidents—and in the words of advice Wang gave his son shortly after the Pacific War began. Realizing what American participation in the war portended for Japan and for himself, Wang prepared his son for the worst. If China was saved, if she survived, then his life and honor would be lost, and his family and house destroyed. "You must have the courage to meet this future," Wang told his son.[37]

When Wang defected from Chungking, he could not have been unmindful of the judgment history accorded to collaborators. He himself had denounced Pu-yi (who was not even a Han Chinese) as a "traitor" for collaborating with Japan's schemes in Manchukuo.[38] He must surely have known his political opponents and his countrymen in general would throw his own words up to him, pronouncements like this, of 1934: "China [will] take an inflexible stand against any step implying, or savouring of, recognition of 'Manchukuo.' "[39] Or like this, made in the same year: "Since September 18, 1931, when Japan launched her treacherous attack on Mukden, we have stubbornly refused, at all costs, to sign treaties derogatory to China's national honour and sovereign rights. We are prepared to suffer now in order that the future may bring us less suffering."[40] Or this, just a year before his defection: "Are we willing to become puppets? If we are not, the only way open is to make the supreme sacrifice. . . . Individual sacrifice is not enough. The Chinese people must see to it that none of their compatriots live to become puppets."[41]

If Wang was truly convinced that his people were being exploited and mauled at the hands of the Japanese aggressors, how could he possibly explain away his collaboration with them? It is tempting to believe that his collaboration was based entirely on miscalculation, on the assumption Japan would win the war; and that he then became the prisoner of this assumption, continuing his collaboration long after it had become clear that it would serve neither his country's nor his own interests.

In Wang's purported last testament, the argument is made that it was *because* of the depredations against his people—not in spite of them—that Wang negotiated and eventually collaborated with Japan.[42] The document concedes that Wang negotiated from a weak bargaining position ("I was empty handed") but argues that his collaboration was justified precisely because of his weakness and the weakness of China. China's situation in December 1938 seemed desperate: significant support from foreign friends was problematical at best, and in the meantime China's most important territory was occupied by a ruthless enemy and the rest was being ravaged by the scorched-earth policy of hopelessly inept defenders. The desperate plight called for a desperate move. Chiang could not advocate peace or compromise with the enemy because his responsibility was military defense of the homeland, and the nation's "blustery" mood would never countenance such an action from him. "So, rather than him, me." Admittedly, Wang's weakness—unlike Chiang, he had no armies—gave him little reason to be optimistic about his mission, but at the very least, by negotiating with the enemy, he could take advantage of conflicts within the Japanese military and try to reach more rational minds (such as the Emperor).

> The reason that I sullied my good name and disregarded my glorious past record of dedicating myself to state affairs for forty years was because at a time of national emergency, we cannot preserve the life of our state unless we depend upon our wits. If we can take

advantage of the enemy's lack of caution and restore territory and console the homeless people—if I could do that—I don't care how difficult the remainder of my life might be. Understanding people will feel sympathy for my difficulties and will not accuse my policies as being unjust.[43]

As the desperate Japanese came to think that Wang might be influential enough to secure peace, he was increasingly able to "secure some protection for my countrymen," to delay the enemy's attacks, to "compete" with Japan for possession of China's commodities and resources. For Wang, therefore, becoming a collaborator and signing agreements and treaties was a way of competing—above all, competing for control of Chinese sovereignty. When the war was over, after all, the treaties would become mere "wastepaper"—assuming an Allied victory (as he was finally forced to do).

NANKING AND VICHY

The ingredients in Wang's decision to collaborate are much like those that moved the French collaborators, Pierre Laval and Marshal Pétain, to work with the Germans. By comparing him with them we can better assess the motives, accomplishments, and peculiarities of the Chinese experience.

The anti-British bias of the French collaborators (the feeling that the British were selfish imperialists who were ready to fight to the last French soldier) was shared by Wang and his colleagues. Thus, resentful though they were at the failure of the British (and the Americans) to come to the aid of China, they took great national pride and satisfaction in joining in the effort to eject the Western imperialists from East Asia. In both the French and the Chinese cases the anti-British indignation of the collaborators was directed not only at the British themselves but also at their own countrymen for their excessive military and especially economic reliance on Britain and America. The shrill charges of some of Wang's colleagues that Chiang Kai-shek was a puppet of Britain (and the Soviet Union) may be discounted as propaganda or evidence of a guilty conscience, but the calm, measured analysis of the collaborator T'ao Hsi-sheng, a respected economist of international reputation, must be considered criticism of a different order. Discussing the defects of Chinese industrialism, T'ao writes:

> The amount of national capital in industry, beyond "compradore capitalism," is negligible. Even this small amount of national capital has to rely on foreign capital directly or indirectly. Thus Chinese

industrialists cannot read the signs of international issues. What is more, they lack an independent and self-assertive national standpoint. When any problem arises they are wondering and hesitating as to what attitude the foreign capitalists will adopt. If the problem is a big one they depend on international assistance, otherwise they have to go to the foreign Concessions in China for assistance or protection. Therefore the interests of the industrialists are not in harmony with those of the general populace. For not all the populace can rely for their living on foreign countries or on the foreign Settlements. The wealthy industrialists however can make their profits in Great Britain and America or in Shanghai and Hong Kong. . . . China as a weak nation, in adopting a policy of being "friendly to distant countries and hostile to neighbours" will inevitably bring about a situation which is summed up in the proverb, "Water from afar cannot extinguish a fire nearby."[44]

A second major similarity in the outlook of the French and Chinese collaborators, and an important cause of the appeasement sentiment in both countries, was the bogy raised by a perceived menace from the left. The formation of the Popular Front in France in the winter of 1935–36 and of the United Front in China the following winter frightened rightists in both countries into believing that their nations were in danger of being taken over by left wing coalitions more or less dominated by Moscow. A slogan in currency in France in this period summarized that fear: "Better Hitler Than Blum." (Leon Blum, a Socialist, headed the first Cabinet produced by the Popular Front.)

Though this slogan had no precise equivalent in China, it requires little imagination to impute the slogan "Better Japan Than Mao" to Wang and his colleagues. ("Better Tokyo Than Moscow" is probably more apt, since Mao's power was just beginning to be recognized in the period of the United Front and, in any case, Wang and his colleagues felt that the ultimate threat to China came from Moscow rather than Yenan.) In France the anti-Communist mood of the collaborators and would-be appeasers diminished while the German-Soviet Non-Aggression Pact was in force (1939–41) and the French Communists began working with the Fifth Column to undermine French resistance efforts. But there was no comparable diminution of anti-Communist sentiment among the Wang group. On the contrary, as we have seen, Wang and his associates became more and more persuaded as the war progressed that only the Chinese Communists (and their Moscow "masters") could emerge as victors.

Both French and Chinese collaborators displayed the one great talent that is the hallmark of accomplished collaboration—fence-straddling. Thus, with the appropriate substitution of proper names (e.g., Japanese for German, Kuomintang for Third Republic), historian Gordon Wright's description of Pierre Laval can serve equally well as a description of Wang Ching-wei or Chou Fo-hai. The Laval of 1942 was vastly different from the Laval of 1940, Wright notes.

> Then he had been convinced of an imminent German victory, and he had sought to win for France a favorable place in the New Order. Now [in 1942] the outcome of the struggle was no longer sure, and his altered purpose was, by dissembling and delay, to evade German exactions and to preserve some semblance of French autonomy. As time went by he even developed the idea of bringing about a peaceful transition from Vichy to a restored Third Republic. This new role that he chose in 1942 was played until August 1944, with considerable skill and cunning, though with steadily decreasing power to shape the course of events.[45]

The will attributed to Wang reveals accomplishments and concerns similar to those of Laval (and others as well). It asks the Chinese to remember that Wang had openly lectured on the doctrines of Sun Yat-sen and on behalf of the Kuomintang's revival, that he had adhered to the precepts of the Central Military Academy, that he had not allowed Japan to promote the use in Chinese schools of textbooks depicting the Chinese as "slaves," and that he had kept alive the memory of the two great Sung patriots Yüeh Fei and Wen T'ien-hsiang in the classrooms.* It also defended such slogans as *t'ung-sheng kung-ssu* ("sharing each other's fate"), which the Japanese had broadcast widely as evidence of Wang's approval of their aims in China. The slogans were chosen carefully, the will maintained: all had had currency before the war started, and some were artful variations on patriotic anti-Manchu slogans dating back to the end of the Ch'ing.[46]

---

* American intelligence agents were impressed with Wang's accomplishments in the realm of education. In a report dated September 26, 1944, the O.S.S. noted that in the schools of Canton, where Wang's influence was greatest, "very few" of the teachers propagandized for the enemy and, as a result, "for the most part, the students remain uncontaminated, hating the Japanese." "As a whole," the report concludes, "the educational system has not been too greatly affected by the enemy." United States, Office of Strategic Services, *Programs*, 2: 15. Wang's Education Minister, Li Sheng-wu, was in fact exonerated at his postwar trial largely because of the difference between the textbooks adopted by the Liang Hung-chih regime and those used by the Wang Government. Ch'en Kung-po also made the textbook issue a major part of his defense at his postwar trial. Chin, *Dōsei*, p. 402.

Though the Wang self-defense presented in the will may strike some Western readers as a retreat into abstraction and weak rationalization, it has a uniquely Chinese quality. Preserving the doctrines of the esteemed Sun, honoring the memory of age-old patriots, cleansing the textbooks of subversive content, and keeping alive the Confucian heritage—Wang undoubtedly would have felt that such accomplishments would have the ring of genuine merit in the ears of his countrymen as they assessed his collaboration years. And always, in all his writings during the collaboration period, Wang appealed to historical precedent to prove he was safely within the bounds of an ancient and honorable tradition that raised collaboration with wartime enemies to the same exalted dignity as resistance to wartime enemies.

Throughout China's long history she had learned to be flexible in responding to threats from the often militarily superior "barbarians" beyond her frontiers. Even when it was impossible to control the barbarians by force of arms, it was still possible to protect Chinese culture and the Confucian way of life by "using barbarians to check barbarians" (*i-i chih-i*), by appeasement techniques (*chi-mi*, i.e., keeping the barbarians under loose rein), and, if the situation was desperate enough, by dispatching tribute missions to placate the intruders.[47] Nor were patriotic Chinese statesmen precluded from resorting to more drastic options, such as the ceding of Chinese territory and even active collaboration with the enemy, if these methods were deemed necessary to preserve China from the full fury of savage peoples yet to be transformed by the civilizing grace of the Confucian Classics. Wang could find ample historical evidence to suggest the prudence of such policies, for often the alien enemies "came and were transformed" (*lai-hua*) by the superior blessings of Chinese civilization. The apparent inevitability of the Sinicization of barbarian peoples—regardless of their military strength—allowed the Chinese to develop a complacent, even sanguine, attitude toward collaboration. "In the historical experience of China . . . collaboration with alien enemies has always been a common phenomenon," writes historian Lin Han-sheng. "It has actually enriched China's culture and enlarged her territory and influence."[48]

All of this is not to say that the Wang group welcomed comparison with every appeaser and collaborator in Chinese history. Ch'en Kung-po, for example, disavowed the efforts of his trial prosecutors to link Wang with two of China's best-known collaborators, Chang Pang-ch'ang and Liu Yü, Sung dynasty officials who renounced their allegiance to the Emperor in order to serve the Tartar invaders in the twelfth century.[49] For his part, Wang preferred to compare himself with Chang Chih-tung and Li Hung-chang, who during the Boxer Rebellion in 1900 had pursued a conciliatory policy toward the Western imperialists, thereby risking censure and impeachment for "currying favor with the barbarians" and disobeying the orders of the Throne. In Wang's view the cautious and prudent statesmanship of Chang and Li ought to be judged against the heroic but essentially futile resistance policies of Gen. Nieh Shih-ch'eng, who lost his life while leading his troops against the forces of the foreigners. "True, there were loyal and brave soldiers and citizens," Wang wrote in 1939, "and yet the most they could do was to follow into the footsteps of Admiral [sic] Nieh Shih-ch'eng. Faithful unto death they were, but their death could not save the fate of the nation."[50]

Wang's Western clothes, years of residence abroad, easy familarity with Western ways, and sophisticated knowledge of modern affairs belied his Confucian background. He was a *hsiu-ts'ai* ("flowering talent," i.e., he had passed the first hurdles in the traditional examination system) before he began his modern studies in political science in Tokyo, and his writings reveal a profound Confucian strain. In "Confucius and China's Moral Relationships," an essay written in 1941 in honor of the sage's birthday, Wang criticized those who found the ancient Confucian precepts wanting and looked abroad to Communist Russia or capitalist Britain and America for solutions to China's ills. These countries could not provide answers to China's problems; they were the source of her problems. Wang attributed China's weakness, her "state of unrest and bewilderment" in the nineteenth century, to two closely related factors. The first was the relentless efforts of the missionary movement to wean the "lower classes" away from their native ways. "They founded hospitals and performed charitable activities in order, by imperceptible degrees, to win the heart of the poorer classes. A little later, the missionaries adopted the native, common language in preaching the Gospel. . . . In this way the Chinese indigenous culture was undermined among the lower classes."[51] The second reason for China's weakness was that the educated classes, though impervious to the influence of the missionaries, became enamored with Western science. "It goes without saying," wrote Wang, "that when the upper classes, who constituted the bulwark of the nation, lost confidence in their own culture, there was a grave crisis."[52] Those who "scoff" at China, Wang said sternly, "have forgotten what constitutes a nation. Next in importance to blood ties and language is culture. To look down upon your own culture is to look down upon your own race and nation."[53]

For Wang, the best in Chinese culture was embodied in the ethical precepts of Confucianism. Thus, by turning back to Confucius China could achieve the "moral rehabilitation" and spirit of national unity she needed to repel the foreign influences that had brought her so much misery. In Wang's denunciation of Western imperialism and Soviet communism, in his faith in the revitalizing powers of the Confucian Classics, and in his specific endorsement of the New Life Movement, we see the ideological affinity between him and his archrival, Chiang Kai-shek. There is no sentiment in Wang's 1941 essay on Confucius that is not present in Chiang's *China's Destiny*, published two years later. Ironically, if there is a difference in tone, it is the Chiang work that seems the more viciously and indiscriminately anti-Western. In it "Chiang heaped on foreigners the blame for warlordism, prostitution, gun-running, opium smoking, gangsterism, and all the bloody chaos at the birth of the Chinese Republic [and] bewailed the influence of foreign missionaries and their universities on Chinese culture."*

Wang's writings, whether political tracts or poetry, uniformly reflect the sensibilities and outlook of the *chün-tzu*, the superior man. Nothing is more central to the Confucian ideal of the superior man than the notion of the efficacy of personal rectitude—"If the Emperor behaves righteously, his ministers will behave righteously; if the ministers behave righteously," etc. Wang's entire career and the esteem in which he was held in China attest to the fact that his deficiencies in the area of political consistency were compensated for by personal integrity and courage of a high order. Confidence in the integrity of his own moral position, especially as the loyal disciple and interpreter of Sun Yat-sen, and an awareness of the power of his personal magnetism combined to produce in Wang the same stubborn perseverance that characterized Wen T'ienhsiang, whose memory Wang revered. Both Wang and his Sung model Wen were thus guilty of "irrational behavior," but it was irrational behavior in the best Confucian tradition. As historian Frederick W. Mote has said of Wen, he remained "loyal to the principle of loyalty when he knew his cause was hopeless, even lacking the sanction of Heaven."[54] The very name Wang chose for himself in his youth, "Ching-wei," suggested the heroic dimensions of the career that followed. (The name, it

* White and Jacoby, *Thunder Out of China*, p. 126. The 1943 edition of *China's Destiny* was a Chinese-language version, *Chung-kuo chih ming-yün*. As noted earlier, T'ao Hsi-sheng is widely regarded as the ghost-writer of this work, which was Chiang's first attempt at an extended political analysis of China. The unbridled xenophobia in the original version prompted a torrent of official protests from China's wartime allies, who resented being tarred with the same brush Chiang used on imperialistic Japan. Apparently as a result of the protests, the book was withdrawn from circulation after a first printing of a half million copies. Though portions of the 1943 edition were translated into English in 1944, an authorized—and revised—English-language edition was not published until 1947.

will be recalled, referred to a legendary bird of extraordinary persistence, a virtue Wang wished to imitate in his resolution to overthrow the Manchus.)

Once again, a comparison with Laval, this time on the level of personality, holds true. Allowing for the absence of any Confucian wellsprings in the character of Laval, there are interesting similarities that belie the customary notion of puppets as mindless and manipulable. Historian Geoffrey Warner's description of Laval applies equally well to Wang: "[Laval was] burdened with idées fixes and an unbounded faith in his own ability, and blessed, unfortunately, with a very real power of persuasion."[55] The awesome, thankless task of attempting effective collaboration with powerful victor nations was not one for the pusillanimous. On the contrary, an Olympian or imperious stereotype would more accurately fit many of the leading collaborators. The novelist Céline referred to Pétain as the "last King of France" and he did in fact use the royal plural—"We Philippe Pétain"—as one to the manner born.[56] At his treason trial, Vidkun Quisling boasted that he "grew up among Viking graves, between Bible history and old Saga tales. . . . The name Quisling . . . is an ancient Nordic name and it indicates one who is a side branch of the royal family."[57] As for Wang, Kao Tsung-wu calls him a "great and courageous man because he had the strength to do what he thought was right no matter how unpopular it was."[58]

WANG AND THE CHINESE COMMUNISTS

The desecration of Wang Ching-wei's tomb in January 1946 symbolized Chiang Kai-shek's apparent triumph over his long-time political rival. But Chiang's victory was destined to be short-lived. As Wang had foreseen, the Chinese Communists emerged from the war as a greatly strengthened challenger to the Kuomintang. The Red Army, which had a strength of perhaps 50,000 on the eve of the Marco Polo Bridge Incident, consisted of half a million disciplined regulars at war's end. Starting with little more than a toehold in the sparsely populated, arid hill country of northern Shensi province in 1937, the Communists expanded westward into mountain-ringed Shansi and from there spilled out into the North China Plain and even into Central China; by the end of the war they controlled nineteen guerrilla base areas with a total population of 70 to 90 million.[59] At that point, the Communists had only to sustain their momentum, build on the patriotic sentiment they had mobilized during the war of resistance, and capitalize on the blundering and corruption of the Kuomintang to achieve their revolutionary victory

of 1949. From his grave, the symbolic grave, not the desecrated ferro-
concrete mausoleum, Wang was able to see the victory of his rival Chiang
dissolve into an ignominious retreat to Taiwan in the space of only
four years.

Are Wang's followers therefore justified in casting him in the role of
prophet? I would say not, for though he had certainly foreseen that the
Communists would reap the harvest from a prolonged war with Japan,
his insight ended there. His warnings in the years after 1938 about the
menace of communism sound shrill and demagogic. He invariably emphasized the Communists' malevolent cunning, their heavy-handed use
of force, their disregard for the welfare of the people, and above all,
their unpatriotic motives for resisting Japan. One looks in vain for some
glimmer of appreciation that the Eighth Route Army was winning the
countryside because its behavior there contrasted so sharply with that of
the Nationalist soldiers, who earned a dismal reputation as plunderers,
rapists, and extortionists. Wang's ill-fated Rural Pacification Program
suggests that he was not oblivious to the need for rural reform, but the
steps taken must be judged as half-hearted when measured against
China's needs. One looks in vain in Wang's speeches and writings for a
sign of awareness that the Communists were winning the people over
because vast numbers of them preferred the Communists' social and
economic reform programs, limited though they were in the early years
of the war with Japan, to the age-old evils of high rents, high interest
rates, and high taxes, which continued to keep the peasants in the Nationalist-controlled areas in unrelieved misery.[60] Wang must have been
aware, as most foreign observers certainly were, that a disproportion-
ately heavy burden of the war fell on the poor peasant families. While
the sons of the rich often bribed their way out of military service or became officers and grew wealthy through the misappropriation of funds
or blackmarket activities, the sons and fathers of the poor were roped
together and dragged away to recruitment centers, where they became
the expendable and exploited victims of their own officers. "If men were
ever delivered tied up for army duty in the Communist areas, I never
saw it," writes Col. David D. Barrett, an American officer with extensive
experience in both Communist- and Nationalist-controlled areas.[61]

Wang warns that the Communists will profit from the war, but nowhere do we find that he senses the key to their ability to profit from
the war: their talent for first making resistance a truly popular, patriotic cause and then preempting that cause. Instead, what we find is a
litany of distortions and banalities and, above all, the unshakable con-

viction that the Communists "have no sense of nationality and do not carry out any instructions other than those issued by the Third International."[62] In September 1939 Wang wrote:

> Patriotism is alien to Communism; the Communists do not pay any allegiance to the country to which they legally belong. . . . In my bitter experience, gained since the outbreak of the Sino-Japanese hostilities, the Communist elements in our midst, in advocating the policy of resistance, have done so only at the order of the Comintern, in order to further the interests of the Comintern, to which the interests of China have to be subordinated. For the Chinese Communists owe allegiance only to Moscow, not to the country they legally belong to [and] their source of inspiration is Moscow; it is Moscow who controls their thought and their action.[63]

In the same month, Wang's rump Sixth National Congress of the Kuomintang declared that the Communists were making use of the war to "put into execution their policy of ruining the middle and lower-middle classes, rendering the majority of the general population jobless and homeless, so that, poverty-stricken, they could be easily utilized by the Communists." It was also the policy of the Communists to "render the masses ignorant by illegally suppressing the freedom of thought and of expression, for if the nation is intellectually bankrupt, the people can be made to follow more blindly." In this way, the Congress stated, the Communists hoped to replace the National Government with their "Border Government," and ultimately to convert the country "into a Soviet China, forever a protectorate of the U.S.S.R."[64]

There is good reason to temper our criticism of such an assessment. It was widely assumed in 1939 that the Kremlin and Yenan were linked in an indissoluble superior-inferior relationship, and in fact it was not until the Sino-Soviet conflict of the late 1950's that the existence of a Sinicized form of communism became fully appreciated. Furthermore, in 1938, when Wang defected from Chungking, and in 1939, when he was writing extensively in an effort to muster support, many of the reform programs that were to win such popularity for the Chinese Communists were only in their infancy; historians still debate the extent and influence of those programs in the early years of the Sino-Japanese War.[65] But all of this is a bit beside the point, which is that Wang seriously erred in seeing nothing but "depredations" in the Communists' social and economic undertakings and in underestimating Mao's ability to meld nationalism and communism in the crucible of a war of resistance.

He failed to gauge the needs of the Chinese people, and he failed to read the patriotic pulse of the nation. So, it might be added, did his rival Chiang Kai-shek. Miscalculations of such an order are fatal in those who presume to lead great nations and, accordingly, both Wang and Chiang forfeited the role of leader to Mao Tse-tung.

A NEED FOR AMBIVALENCE

The task Wang set himself in the mid-1930's was considerably more difficult than his earlier goal of overthrowing the Manchus. Wang's advocacy of conciliation with Japan in the years before the Marco Polo Bridge Incident was based not on exoneration of Japan but on an awareness of China's appalling weakness and disunity. He put forth programs to correct those flaws, but in the meantime advocated negotiation and, if necessary, concession. He nearly paid with his life for his concessions when an assassin's bullet struck him down in November 1935. From then on, the national mood became ever more hostile to appeasement, and Wang himself was increasingly isolated from the sources of power. With the growth in 1938 of a small but potentially influential peace movement, with channels to the offices of the Premier in Tokyo and, more importantly, to the Japanese General Staff, Wang seized the opportunity to defect from Chungking and explore the possibility of reconciliation with Japan elsewhere. For once even his critics could not accuse him of a lack of consistency in his policies. Still less, in my opinion, was there warrant for charges of expediency or venality. The message Wang left for Chiang, to the effect that he would henceforth bear the heavier burden and Chiang the lighter, may or may not have touched the Generalissimo, but it is quite clear Wang carried heavy burdens indeed in the remaining six years of his life.

Wang did not survive the war, did not live to defend himself at the postwar trials at which almost all of his colleagues were sentenced to death. His widow, Ch'en Pi-chün, however, survived both the war and the postwar trials. This extraordinarily self-willed woman, who had been as much a part of Wang's political life as his personal life from the last days of the Manchu dynasty, when they shared bomb-planting escapades in Peking, refused to follow the advice of relatives and retire from political activities after Wang's death. It was clear by then that the Japanese were going to lose the war and her family urged her to withdraw from the Government on the chance that such a move would prompt Chungking to treat her with leniency at the inevitable postwar treason trials. Madame Wang replied that though she had no doubts about the outcome of the war, she felt obliged to remain politically active to do what she might to prevent the Japanese from wreaking their vengeance on occupied China.

At her trial in Soochow in the spring of 1946, Madame Wang vehemently defended her husband and excoriated her captors. How could Wang have sold out the country, she asked rhetorically. It was clearly impossible for him to sell the areas that were under the control of Chungking; and as for the areas under the control of Nanking, they were "lost territories that were occupied by the Japanese." Her husband, she boasted, had not lost an inch of Chinese territory. What he had done was to *take back* territory that treacherous, high-ranking Army officers had abandoned in order to escape to safety. Wang had to do *something* to meet the needs of the "deserted populace." "Now more than ever," she declared, "I express my heartfelt admiration for the deceased Wang Ching-wei's flawless labor on behalf of the salvation of his country."[66] Far from recanting, she "thumped on the table and in a loud voice cross-examined the prosecutor" to the evident satisfaction of an applauding audience. At the conclusion of the brief hearing, "scores of spectators besieged Madame Wang for autographs, which she readily gave."[67] Her next two years were spent in a Kuomintang prison in Soochow; she fell into the hands of the Communists when they took Soochow in 1948 and spent the final eleven years of her life languishing in poor health in the Ward Road Jail in Shanghai.[68]

By sketching in the personality, outlook, motives, and accomplishments of Wang (and other collaborators), I have tried to diminish the paradox in the seemingly abrupt transition of Wang from patriot to puppet. Historians are rightly suspicious of discontinuity. I believe, however, that this apparent example of discontinuity is resolved by simply taking the effort to defuse the explosive connotation of puppet and the only slightly less pejorative collaborator.

The Asian collaborators of recent history have run the gamut from the faceless and mindless Pu-yi in Manchukuo to the larger-than-life national hero Sukarno in Indonesia. Their conduct deserves judgment by sounder standards than the epithet puppet suggests. This is not of course to say that we must suspend that judgment. It is only to say that the topic of wartime collaboration is by nature full of ambiguities, ambiguities that Laval recognized when he told friends: "If my policy succeeds there won't be enough stones in France to put up statues to me; if it fails, I'll be hanged."[69] Indeed, the problem that faced China in

Wang's day, a China victimized for a century by aggression and encroachments from so many quarters, was an ambiguity in itself: it was not so much a question of how China could deliver herself from all of her enemies as a question of which enemy threatened her the least. In assessing collaborators caught up in such ambiguities, I believe that there is need for a healthy ambivalence, the kind of ambivalence that undoubtedly gripped the applauding spectators at the trial of the traitor Madame Wang Ching-wei.

Notes

Notes

Complete authors' names, titles, and publication data are given in the Bibliography, pp. 401–15. The following abbreviations are used in the notes:

CWR   *China Weekly Review.*
DGFP   *Documents on German Foreign Policy, 1918–1945.*
DR   *Daihon'ei rikugunbu.*
FR   *Foreign Relations of the United States, Diplomatic Papers.*
GH   *Gaimushō no hyakunen.*
GSS   *Gendai shi shiryō.*
IMTFE   International Military Tribunal for the Far East.
JAS   *Journal of Asian Studies.*
MFA   Ministry of Foreign Affairs (of Japan).
NSGT   Hata Ikuhito, "Nitchū sensō no gunjiteki tenkai."
NSST   Usui Katsumi, "Nitchū sensō no seijiteki tenkai."
OA   *Oriental Affairs.*
PT   *People's Tribune.*
TSM   *Taiheiyō sensō e no michi.*

CHAPTER ONE

1. John K. Fairbank, Edwin O. Reischauer, and Albert M. Craig, *East Asia: The Modern Transformation* (Boston, 1965).

2. Tsunoda, "Kaidai," p. 422.   3. Linebarger, p. 208.

4. Fairbank, p. 72.   5. Recto, p. 94.

6. Laurel, p. 16.   7. Wurfel, p. 697.

8. Steinberg, "Jose P. Laurel," p. 662. The best surveys of the Japanese occupation of the Philippines are Steinberg's *Philippine Collaboration in World War II* (Ann Arbor, Mich., 1967) and Theodore Friend, *Between Two Empires: The Ordeal of the Philippines, 1929–1946* (New Haven, Conn., 1965).

9. Koentjaraningrat, p. 3.

10. Sukarno, p. 179. A valuable interpretive study of the Japanese occupation of Indonesia is Harry J. Benda, *The Crescent and the Rising Sun* (The Hague, 1958). Also valuable is a collection of documents edited by Benda and others: *Japanese Military Administration in Indonesia: Selected Documents* (New Haven, Conn., [1965]).

11. Kahin, p. 557.   12. *Ibid.*

13. Lebra, pp. 46–47.   14. Ba Maw, p. 142.

15. *Ibid.*, p. 275.   16. *Ibid.*, p. 185.

17. For representative expressions of this view, see Tanaka Kanaye; and Ohkura.

18. Aisin-Gioro Pu Yi (Henry Pu-yi), *From Emperor to Citizen* (2 vols.; Peking, 1964).

19. *Ibid.*, 2: 275.

20. Lockhart (Counselor of Embassy, Peiping) to Secretary of State, Nov. 5, 1938. *FR* 1938, 2: 372.

21. I am indebted to Professor Van Slyke for this and many other comments he made while reading my manuscript in its thesis stage.

CHAPTER TWO

1. See also Shirley; Lin Han-sheng, *Wang*; T'ang, *Wang*; and Boorman, "Wang."

2. Gasster, "Reform," p. 76.

3. Interview with Matsumoto.

4. Saionji, p. 289. Shortly before his death in 1944 Wang told Saionji the reason he chose this name.

5. Pu Yi, 1: 34. The Hsüan-t'ung Emperor became the puppet Emperor of Manchukuo, K'ang-te, better known in the West as Henry Pu-yi.

6. Gunther, p. 263.

7. *Ibid.*; Smedley, p. 103.

8. Shirley, p. 47.

9. For details, see Scalapino and Yu. Wang did not become a "Class C" member, which would have required abstinence from liquor.

10. Imai, *Shōwa*, p. 142.

11. Wu is the best source on this event.

12. Isaacs, pp. 92–93.

13. Chiang, p. 29.

14. Payne, p. 58, citing a Chiang speech.

15. Jerome Ch'en, "Left Wing," pp. 556–63, discusses Sun's will.

16. Loh, p. 448.

17. Tong, p. 149.

18. Wang Ching-wei, *China's Problems*, pp. 13–23.

19. Payne, p. 157. 20. Chiang, pp. 41–42.

21. Payne, p. 156. 22. Chiang, p. 42.

23. Han, *Mortal Flower*, p. 179. 24. Israel, p. 82.

25. *Ibid.*, p. 83. 26. Clubb, p. 172.

27. Quoted in Lin Han-sheng, *Wang*, p. 143.

28. *Ibid.*, pp. 132, 135. Paraphrase.

29. Wang Ching-wei, *China's Problems*, pp. 116–17.

30. *Ibid.*, p. 116.

31. *Ibid.*

32. *Ibid.*, pp. 113–14.

33. Sun's remarks, made in 1917, in full context were as follows: "Should China desire an ally, she should not look beyond Japan and the United States of America. The relationship between China and Japan is one of common existence or extinction. *Without Japan there would be no China; without China there would be no Japan.*" (Emphasis in original.) Sun, *China and Japan*, p. 113.

34. Shimada, pp. 71–72.
35. Nishi, p. 250.
36. Shimada, p. 118, gives details concerning the Ch'in-Doihara Agreement.
37. *Ibid.*, p. 135.   38. Han, *Mortal Flower*, p. 376.
39. Shimada, pp. 172–73.   40. IMTFE, Document CE393.
41. Shimada, p. 172, contains a table illustrating some of the discriminatory customs rates.
42. For example, see Borg, pp. 178–80.
43. Hata, *Nitchū senso chi*, p. 66.
44. Shimada, p. 162.
45. The implications of the Sian Incident are well treated in Van Slyke, *Enemies and Friends*, Ch. 5.
46. Grew, p. 193.

CHAPTER THREE

1. Hata, *Nitchū senso shi*, p. 257. For organizational charts showing the relationship between the various units being discussed here, see *ibid.*, pp. 200, 347–52.
2. The notebooks and essays of Ishiwara appear in Tsunoda, *Ishiwara Kanji shiryō: senso shiron.*
3. Ogata Sadako, pp. 42–43.
4. *Ibid.*, p. 43.
5. See Horiba, 1: 65–78, for the economic surveys prepared by Ishiwara and his staff. His second volume is devoted entirely to statistical studies relating to the Japanese economy in the war years.
6. The apocalyptic war, sometimes referred to by Ishiwara as the "war of annihilation" (*semmetsu senso*), is discussed in Seki Hiroharu, pp. 366–67. A valuable interpretive study of Ishiwara is Nishina, "Manshūkoku." Collections of primary sources written by or directly related to Ishiwara are available in GSS, 8: 665–778; GSS, 9: 722–74; and Tsunoda, *Ishiwara Kanji shiryō: kokubō ronsaku.* See also Boyle, "The Road," pp. 279–82.
7. Tsunoda, *Ishiwara Kanji shiryō: kokubō ronsaku*, p. 202. From a document of Ishiwara's dated Jan. 6, 1937.
8. *Ibid.*, p. 198.
9. Crowley, *Japan's Quest*, p. 321, citing IMTFE documentation.
10. Ishii, *Gaikōkan*, p. 273.
11. Hata, *Nitchū senso shi*, p. 120, citing memoirs of Gen. Imamura Hitoshi. Tanaka Ryūkichi also discusses this ironic turn of events in *Nihon gumbatsu*, p. 82.
12. NSST, p. 117, citing unpublished documents in the Senshishitsu (War History Archives).
13. The interview between Ishiwara and Prince (Captain) Takeda (who was assigned to a historical research project in the Army) is printed in full in Tsunoda, *Ishiwara Kanji shiryō: kokubō ronsaku*, pp. 433–52.
14. Hahn, *The Soong Sisters*, pp. 241–44, contains an English translation of the Kuling speech. The Kuling Conferences are often referred to as the Lushan Conferences (from the Lushan Mountains where Kuling is located).
15. Ishii, "Ikensho," p. 323. *Hikaremono no kouta*, which I have translated

as "bluff," refers to a "tune hummed by an arrested man being dragged away" by the authorities. It suggests feigned nonchalance.

16. *GSS*, 10: xxvi-xxvii.

17. Suda, pp. 266–67; *DR*, 1: 452–53. General Sugiyama, for example, was reported to have "made a sour face" on hearing of the plan for Konoe to fly to China. According to Ishiwara, opposition also came from Gens. Homma Masaharu and Kasahara Yukio.

18. Saionji, p. 272. Saionji's description of Ishiwara as a "nuisance" literally reads a "bump over the eye" (*me no ue no tankobu*).

19. Imamura, 2: 284.

20. Imai, *Shōwa*, pp. 117–18. Gen. Satō Kenryō, a colleague of Mutō, maintains that Mutō personally claimed credit for forcing Ishiwara's transfer. NSGT, p. 365.

21. Usui, "Shiryō Kaisetsu," p. xxvii.

22. Hattori, p. 100.

23. "Tai jikyoku shori yōkō." Text in Hata, *Nitchū sensō shi*, pp. 340–41.

24. In the same week the Army General Staff drew up its own "Essential Points Concerning the Management of the North China Incident" (HokuShi jihen shori yōkō), in which the "chastisement" spirit is notably absent. Text in Horiba, 1: 98–101.

25. Crowley, *Japan's Quest*, p. 376.

26. Johnson, *Peasant Nationalism*, p. 37.

27. Imai, *Shina jihen*, p. 97.

28. Saionji, pp. 282–83; Yabe, 1: 422.

29. NSGT, p. 33, citing Senshishitsu archives.

30. Tsunoda, *Ishiwara Kanji shiryō: kokubō ronsaku*, pp. 249–51.

31. *Ibid.*, p. 252.

32. *Ibid.*

33. *Ibid.*

34. *Ibid.*, p. 430. From an Ishiwara manuscript dated Nov. 18, 1940.

35. *Ibid.*, p. 461.

36. Interview with Yamazaki Jūzaburō.

37. NSST, p. 117, citing an unpublished Ishiwara manuscript in the Senshishitsu, probably written in late 1937 or early 1938.

38. From General Kawabe's "Tai-Shi chūō seiken hōsaku" (Policy Regarding the Central Government in China), in *GSS*, 9: 49–50.

39. Ohkura, p. 132.

40. Tsunoda, "Kaidai," pp. 422–23.

41. Interview with Matsukata.

CHAPTER FOUR

1. An English translation of the "Outline" (Shina jihen taisho yōkō) may be found in IMTFE, Def. Doc. 2507. My somewhat freer translation is based on the Japanese text in Gaimushō, *Nihon gaikō*, 2: 370–72.

2. NSST, pp. 114–15, citing unpublished material in the MFA archives. Ōta was the China Section Chief of the East Asian Bureau of the MFA at the time.

3. *Ibid.*, p. 119.

4. "HokuShi keizai kaihatsu yōkō-an," cited in NSST, p. 120.

5. Ōtani's plan was contained in a memorandum forwarded to Foreign Minister Hirota. Cited in *ibid.*, pp. 119–20.

6. Cited in *ibid.*, p. 120.

7. "HokuShi keizai kaihatsu hōshin," summarized in *ibid.*, pp. 120–21. The document was issued on Dec. 16.

8. Maxon, p. 124.

9. Horiba, 1: 116.

10. Harada, 6: 119, quoting his telephone conversation with Aoki Kazuo, Vice Minister of the Board, Oct. 18, 1937.

11. Good English-language accounts of this subject may be found in Clifford; Borg; and Arthur N. Young.

12. NSST, p. 116.

13. Saionji, p. 274.

14. Crowley, *Japan's Quest*, pp. 342–45.

15. Dirksen to German Ministry of Foreign Affairs, *DGFP*, 1: 778–79. For a fuller discussion of the Trautmann talks, see Presseisen; James T. C. Liu; and Jones, pp. 53–70. I am indebted to Jones for most of the citations from the German archives.

16. For the text of the terms, see NSST, pp. 125–26. Though there was no mention of an autonomous regime in North China, the November 5 terms expressed Japan's "hope that the chief administrative officer in the area would be friendly to Japan."

17. Saionji, pp. 275–76.

18. *DGFP*, 1: 780–81.

19. Arthur N. Young, p. 16.

20. Borg, p. 441, citing Crew's unpublished diary, entry for Nov. 12, 1937.

21. Wang Ching-wei, "Facts," p. 62. 22. *Ibid.*, pp. 66–67.

23. *DGFP*, 1: 790. 24. Horiba, 1: 115.

25. From his "Tai-Shina chūō seiken hōsaku" (Policy Regarding the Central Government of China), in GSS, 9: 49–50.

26. Dirksen to German Ministry of Foreign Affairs, Dec. 7, 1937, *DGFP*, 1: 799.

27. Crowley, *Japan's Quest*, p. 359, quoting *International Gleanings*, Jan. 15, 1938, p. 3.

28. GSS, 9: 104–5. This document was found among Konoe's papers by Tsunoda Jun. Though it is unsigned, Tsunoda is certain from internal evidence that its author was Suetsugu. Interview with Tsunoda.

29. Harada, 6: 210.

30. The terms are listed in GH, 2: 286. A list in Jones, p. 65, deriving from German sources, is somewhat variant.

31. GH, 2: 287.

32. Dirksen to German Ministry of Foreign Affairs, Dec. 22, 1937, *DGFP*, 1: 802–3.

33. Kawabe, p. 437.

34. Crowley, *Japan's Quest*, p. 358, quoting Gaimushō archives.

35. Biographical data on Horiba taken from intro. (by Inaba Masao and Hara Shirō) to Horiba, 1: 3–7.

36. *Ibid.*, p. 117.

37. *Ibid.*, pp. 116–18.   38. Harada, 6: 203.
39. *Ibid.*   40. IMTFE, Doc. 3090.
41. Crowley, *Japan's Quest*, p. 393.
42. "Shina jihen shori konpon hōshin," cited in Horiba, 1: 123.
43. *Ibid.*, p. 136. See also Ishii, *Gaikōkan*, p. 302.
44. Yabe, 1: 468.   45. *Ibid.*
46. Horiba, 1: 130.   47. Jones, p. 69.
48. *"Teikoku wa jigo kore o aite to suru jihen kaiketsu ni kitai o kakezu ...."* Horiba, 1: 123.
49. *"Teikoku seifu wa jigo kokumin seifu o aite to sezu...."* The text of the January 16 statement may be found in Gaimushō, *Nihon gaikō*, 2: 386. An English translation was printed in the *New York Times*, Jan. 16, 1938.
50. NSGT, p. 40.
51. Inukai, p. 41; Yabe, 1: 469. Yabe accepts the notion of pressure from the North China Area Army but rejects the idea that Army officials were acting on behalf of the puppet Wang K'o-min. That was only their "rationale," he writes; they had already made up their mind that Japan must break with Chiang. On the language used in the *aite ni sezu* declaration, see *GH*, 2: 228.
52. U.S. Dept. of State, *Papers: Japan, 1931–1941*, 1: 438.
53. Gaimushō, *Nihon gaikō*, 2: 387.
54. Shigemitsu, *Shōwa*, 2: 183.   55. NSGT, p. 41.
56. Usui, "Shiryō kaisetsu," p. xxix.   57. *Ibid.*

CHAPTER FIVE

1. Abend, p. 313. The adviser was Maj. Gen. Harada Kumakichi. The activities of Harada, who was Chief of the Central China Area Army's Tokumu-bu at the time the Provisional Government was established, and of his assistant, Col. Kusumoto Sanetaka, are discussed in IMTFE, Pros. Doc. 2203, pp. 1, 7. Both men were instrumental in the creation of a rival regime, the Nanking-based Reformed Government. For other examples of rivalry between mainland Army commands, see Goette, p. 61; Harada, 6: 95–98; and Coox, "Effects," p. 60. I have relied also on interviews with ex-Army officer Yamazaki Jūzaburō, who stresses the "bad feelings" between the North and Central China armies.
2. Imai, *Kindai*, p. 116.   3. *CWR*, Jan. 22, 1938, p. 207.
4. Meng, p. 125.   5. NSST, p. 130.
6. *Time*, Sept. 13, 1937, p. 17. 7. GSS, 9: 41.
8. *Ibid.*   9. NSGT, p. 27.
10. Gens. Kita and Nemoto Hiroshi to Gen. Tanaka Shin'ichi, Oct. 18, 1937. DR, 1: 514.
11. *Ibid.*, pp. 513–14.   12. NSST, p. 131.
13. *Ibid.*   14. *Ibid.*
15. Hq., Kwantung Army, "Shinkō Shina kensetsu hōsaku taikō" (Outline of a Plan for the Construction of a Rejuvenated China), GSS, 9: 234–36.
16. IMTFE, Pros. Doc. 2203, p. 1.
17. Nashimoto, Ch. 6; Yabe, 1: 469. Nashimoto was an economic adviser to the Provisional Government, and his book is one of the best firsthand accounts of the regime by a Japanese.
18. Interview with T'ao.

19. For example, see *CWR*, May 14, 1938, p. 300; and *CWR*, Nov. 19, 1938, p. 370.

20. Horiba, 1: 136.

21. *OA*, 9 (1938): 115.

22. Taylor, p. 33.

23. Aoki, 3: 213–15.

24. Levenson, p. 133.

25. Maruyama Shizuo, pp. 60–61.

26. Taylor, p. 71.

27. *Ibid.*, p. 210, citing Hsin-min Hui "mottoes . . . offered to householders who wished to use them" (as New Year's decorations).

28. Doihara, p. 116.

29. Mote, p. 190. citing Miao's *Wu-te lun* (On the military virtues).

30. Conroy, "Japan's War: Ideological Somersault," p. 372.

31. Taylor, pp. 93, 224–25; Bisson, pp. 311–13.

32. Yamazaki, 113: 50.

33. *OA*, 9 (1938): 114.

34. *Ibid.*, p. 340.

35. Usui, "Gen'ei," p. 286. A complete text of the Wang K'o-min–Terauchi agreement can be found on microfilm at the Library of Congress, *Archives in the Japanese Ministry of Foreign Affairs*, Reel 356, S1.6.1.1–7, pp. 153 et seq.

36. NSST, p. 134. The adviser quoted was Yuzawa Michio, former Vice Minister of Home Affairs.

37. American Information Committee, Publ. 8: 29.

38. Yamazaki, 113: 50.

39. W. Y. Lin, p. 31.

40. Arthur N. Young, p. 65, citing the *Oriental Economist* (Tokyo).

41. Stein, p. 236.

42. Cited in Arthur N. Young, p. 67.

43. Stein, p. 236.

44. W. Y. Lin, p. 35.

45. IMTFE, Exhibit CE393, Report, U.S. Treasury Attaché, Shanghai, April 7, 1937.

46. *Ibid.*, Exhibit CE399, Report, U.S. Treasury Attaché, Shanghai, Jan. 13, 1937.

47. See, for example, the testimony of Harada Kumakichi, a Tokumu-bu officer, *ibid.*, Exhibit CE423; and the affidavit of Mei Ssu-p'ing, a cabinet member in the Wang Ching-wei regime, Exhibit CE460.

48. IMTFE, Exhibit CE460, p. 5. The Mengchiang regime is discussed in Chap. 7.

49. Santō oyobi Seitō hōmen shori yōkō-an" (Essentials of the Draft Plan for Managing the Shantung and Tsingtao Sectors), cited in NSST, pp. 132–33.

50. *OA*, 9 (1938): 339.

51. NSST, p. 134.

52. Taylor, p. 134.

53. NSST, p. 156.

54. *Tokyo Gazette*, 18 (Dec. 1938): 2.

55. Taylor, p. 148.

56. *Ibid.*, p. 155.

57. *Japan Chronicle*, June 1, 1939, cited in Taylor, p. 149.

58. Johnson, *Peasant Nationalism*, p. 44.

59. Yamazaki, 113: 52.

60. NSST, p. 188.

61. *GSS*, 9: xxxii.

62. *OA*, 13 (1940): 245.

63. Israel, p. 179.

64. *OA*, 12 (1939): 306.

65. Yamazaki, 113: 54.

CHAPTER SIX

1. Iriye, *After Imperialism*, p. 111.   2. Ogata Sadako, p. 143.
3. Crowley, *Japan's Quest*, p. 344.   4. Snow, *Battle*, p. 49.
5. Maruyama Shizuo, pp. 65–67.
6. For a good description of Ta-min Hui activities, see *ibid.*, pp. 70–74.
7. Tajiri Akiyoshi (Consul-General, Hong Kong) to MFA, Tokyo, March 1, 1938. NSST, p. 136.
8. *CWR*, April 2, 1938, p. 119.
9. *OA*, 9 (1938): 197. See also the biographical sketch in Boorman, *Biographical Dictionary*, 2: 351–53.
10. Boorman, *Biographical Dictionary*, 1: 170–72.
11. *Ibid.*, p. 213.   12. Linebarger, p. 196.
13. *FR* 1938, 3: 311.   14. *OA*, 9 (1938): 276.
15. Y. C. Wang, p. 457.   16. Arthur N. Young, p. 89.
17. *Ibid.*, pp. 86–96.
18. *CWR*, March 16, 1940, pp. 82–86, gives an English translation of the texts of several of these agreements; it is based on disclosures made by Kao Tsung-wu and T'ao Hsi-sheng, who defected from the Wang Ching-wei movement in January 1940.
19. *Tokyo Gazette*, 18 (Dec. 1938): 2.
20. NSST, p. 135.
21. *CWR*, March 16, 1940, p. 186.
22. Horiba, 1: 326. To Wang's distress, the number of economic agreements proliferated enormously in the months just before the creation of his regime in March 1940. See the complaints of Wang's chief lieutenant, Chou Fo-hai, to Japanese authorities in *GSS*, 13: 255.
23. Great Britain, *Documents*, 8: 323.
24. Michael, "Significance," p. 408.
25. Cited in Usui, "Gen'ei," p. 287.   26. *GSS*, 13: 127.
27. *FR* 1938, 3: 130.   28. *TSM*, 8: 265.
29. Japanese control of the agenda and substance of the Dairen meetings is indicated in a secret report, dated Aug. 20, 1938, from the chief of the Navy's Tokumu-bu in Shanghai to his superiors in Toyko. *GSS*, 13: 165.
30. *OA*, 10 (1938): 295.
31. Cited in Taylor, p. 179. See also the discussion of a "Manifesto" issued by a meeting held under the auspices of the Reformed Government in Nanking, in *North China Herald*, Dec. 7, 1938, p. 402.

CHAPTER SEVEN

1. *TSM*, 8: 265.
2. For a fuller discussion of Japan's activities in Inner Mongolia in this period, see Kurihara. Documents pertaining to the puppet regimes in Inner Mongolia are contained in *GSS*, 9: 107–84.
3. Boorman, *Biographical Dictionary*, 2: 6–10, has a biographical sketch of Prince Teh. I have also relied on information presented at the Association for Asian Studies meeting in Washington, D.C., March 29, 1971, by Gombojab Hangin (John G. Hangin), a former administrative assistant to Prince Teh.

4. Lattimore, pp. 437–38.

5. Hata, *Nitchū sensō shi*, pp. 274–78, discusses the military aspects of the campaigns in Inner Mongolia.

6. Imai, *Kindai no sensō*, p. 122.

7. NSST, p. 142.

8. *Ibid.*, p. 143.

9. John Young, *Research Activities*, pp. 3–11.

10. Ogata Sadako, p. 76.

11. *CWR*, April 29, 1939, p. 258, citing the *Tokyo hanashi*, April 1939.

12. NSST, pp. 139–40.

13. *Ibid.*, p. 141, citing a series of articles by Kanai in the *Mainichi shimbun* (Shinano ed.), March 11–May 1, 1961.

14. Ahlers, p. 302.

15. Yamazaki, 113: 54.

16. Ogata Sadako, p. 178.

17. *GSS*, 9: 112–13.

18. *Ibid.*, p. 116. Though Usui, apparently discussing this same plan, attributes its authorship to the Kwantung generals (NSST, p. 140), the authors of *GSS* "presume" that it was composed by the War Ministry. It seems unlikely that the Kwantung Army had a hand in it.

19. *GSS*, 9: 171.

20. NSST, p. 144.

21. *Ibid.*

22. *GSS*, 9: 171.

23. NSST, p. 143.

24. *GSS*, 9: 167–68.

25. *Ibid.*, pp. 168–69. Cf. the similar letter from Henry Pu-yi to Gen. Honjō Shigeru (CIC, Kwantung Army in 1932) requesting advisers and other help, in Ogata Sadako, pp. 123–28.

26. Hangin, p. 39.

27. Itō, p. 206.

CHAPTER EIGHT

1. Harada, 7: 8.

2. Imai, *Shina jihen*, p. 97.

3. NSGT, pp. 42–43; Horiba, 1: 142–47.

4. Imai, *Kindai no sensō*, pp. 134–35.

5. Hata, *Nitchū sensō shi*, p. 152.

6. Kawabe, p. 453; Harada, 6: 248.

7. Hata, *Nitchū sensō shi*, p. 153.

8. Harada, 6: 248.

9. Kawabe, p. 445.

10. NSGT, p. 44.

11. Hata, *Nitchū sensō shi*, p. 290.

12. Coox, "Effects," p. 60. See Hata, *Nitchū sensō shi*, pp. 289–90, for evidence that extensive use of reserves was *not* required at this time.

13. Johnson, *Peasant Nationalism*, p. 37.

14. Tuchman, p. 186.

15. *OA*, 9 (1938): 265–66.

16. Lt. Gens. Shimoyama Takuma and Hashimoto Gun, cited in Johnson, *Peasant Nationalism*, p. 36.

17. Tuchman, pp. 186–87.

18. See, for example, Harada, 6: 248, on the Emperor's dissatisfaction with War Minister Sugiyama; 7: 32, on the Emperor's chief aide-de-camp, "who never transmits what he should to the Emperor and vice versa"; 7: 51–52, on the Emperor's alleged scolding of War Minister Itagaki for the Army's "fre-

quent uses of sneaky methods . . . and disobedience of orders from the central authorities"; and 7: 97–98, on the indecisiveness of the Army General Staff.

19. Ugaki, *Ugaki nikki,* p. 300.

20. For excellent summaries of Ozaki's views of China and his associations with the "Konoe circle," see Johnson, *Instance;* and Storry and Deakin, *Case of Richard Sorge.* Extensive documentation on Ozaki has been brought together by the editors of *GSS,* the first three volumes of which are devoted to the Sorge Affair (Soruge *jiken*).

21. Yanaga, p. 534.

22. *New York Times,* July 31, 1938, p. 27, cited in Coox, *Year,* p. 133. Coox also contains a list of austerities imposed on the Emperor. Among other things, he was forced to substitute native sake for foreign wines, to replace foreign tobacco with Japanese cigars and cigarettes, and to use only silver crests (rather than the customary gold) on Imperial gifts and cards. *Ibid.,* quoting the *Asahi shimbun,* July 4, 1938, p. 11.

23. Tsuru, p. 194.

24. *Ibid.,* pp. 214–16.

25. *Ibid.,* p. 215.

26. Seidensticker, p. 154.

27. Interview with Matsukata.

28. Tsurumi, p. 57.

29. Interview with Ushiba.

30. Craigie, p. 60.

31. Gunther, p. 68.

32. Harada, 6: 265.

33. *Ibid.,* p. 270.

34. *Ibid.,* pp. 270–71.

35. Yabe, 1: 496.

36. Kase, p. 111; Kazami, p. 59.

37. Yabe, 1: 422.

38. *Ibid.,* p. 502.

39. *Ibid.,* pp. 502–3.

40. *Ibid.,* p. 509.

41. Grew, p. 248, diary entry of June 21, 1938.

42. Shigemitsu, *Gaikō,* pp. 134–35. I am indebted to Alvin D. Coox's study *Year of the Tiger* for this and the previous reference.

43. Storry, *Double Patriots,* pp. 60–63.

44. Craigie, p. 61.

45. Harada, 6: 330–32.

46. NSST, p. 146. Usui here quotes from an entry in Ugaki's diary that I am unable to find in the new edition edited by Tsunoda. Usui's version, however, closely conforms to entries in the Tsunoda edition for April 24 and May 5, 1938. (Tsunoda, *Ugaki Kazushige nikki,* 2: 1235–36.) Curiously, an earlier, one-volume version of the diary edited by Ugaki himself omits this and many other interesting entries regarding his views on China. (See Ugaki Kazushige, *Ugaki nikki.*) The Tsunoda edition, for example, includes entries for April 26 and May 18, 1938, both excluded from the Ugaki-edited work, in which Ugaki ruminates on the relationship between the Communists and the Nationalists— "a case of sleeping in the same bed but having different dreams (*dōshō imu*)." (Tsunoda, *Ugaki Kazushige nikki,* 2: 1233, 1237.)

47. Ugaki, *Ugaki nikki,* pp. 313–14.

48. Sugiyama Heisuke, p. 115.

49. The text of this important document can be found in *GH,* 2: 315–37. Its full title is "Kongo no jihen taisaku ni tsuite kōan" (Plan for Countermeasures for the Present Incident).

50. *Ibid.,* p. 319.

51. *Ibid.,* p. 316.

52. *Ibid.*, pp. 315, 327. Rustic third-rate ring would be a closer translation of Ishii's language: *inaka no miya sumo.*

53. *Ibid.*, pp. 324–25.
54. *Ibid.*, p. 325.
55. *Ibid.*, p. 326.
56. *Ibid.*
57. *Ibid.*, p. 327.
58. *Ibid.*, p. 328.
59. *Ibid.*
60. *Ibid.*, pp. 328, 333–34.

61. *Ibid.*, p. 329. The Attaché was Gen. Isogai Rensuke. Ishii also told Ugaki that according to a reliable source, in the period when Ugaki was Governor-General of Korea (1931–36), he had several secret meetings with Chiang's emissaries, all sent to relay the Generalissimo's "earnest wishes" for better Sino-Japanese relations. "From this, we should know the intentions that are at the bottom of his [Chiang's] heart," Ishii advised Ugaki. *Ibid.*

62. *Ibid.*
63. *Ibid.*, pp. 331–32.
64. *Ibid.*, p. 332.
65. *Ibid.*, p. 333.
66. *Ibid.*, p. 330.
67. *Ibid.*, p. 332.

68. *Ibid.*, p. 315.

69. Coox, *Year,* citing "Hayama kaidan" (Hayama Ghost Story) in *Asahi shimbun,* Aug. 14, 1963, p. 1.

70. Ugaki, *Ugaki nikki,* pp. 326–27.
71. *Ibid.*, p. 327.
72. *Ibid.*, p. 329.
73. Nakamura, p. 262.
74. Ugaki, *Ugaki nikki,* p. 316.
75. *Ibid.*, p. 318.

76. Tsunoda, *Ugaki Kazushige nikki,* 2: 1262, entry for Sept. 27, 1938. This is one of the entries suppressed in the earlier edition of the Ugaki diaries.

77. *TSM,* 8: 264.
78. Nakamura, pp. 262–63.
79. Ugaki, *Ugaki nikki,* pp. 329–30.
80. *Ibid.*, p. 332.
81. *Ibid.*, p. 330.
82. *Ibid.*, p. 331.
83. Usui, *Nitchū sensō,* pp. 77–78.

84. My discussion of the Kōain is based on Baba, "Kōain."

85. *Asahi shimbun,* Oct. 6, 1938.

86. IMTFE, *Proceedings,* p. 35757.

87. *FR* 1938, 3: 433, citing "press reports of Government statements."

88. Maruyama Shizuo, pp. 75–77.

89. *TSM,* 8: 266.

90. For a good discussion of Doihara's political activities in Manchukuo, see Ogata Sadako, pp. 67, 75–76.

91. Interview with Imai.

92. Imai, *Shōwa,* pp. 146–51.

93. For general background material on Wu P'ei-fu, see Soter; and Boorman, *Biographical Dictionary,* 3: 444–50.

94. Biographic data on T'ang taken principally from *CWR,* Oct. 8, 1938, pp. 174–75; *OA,* 10 (1938): 335–36; and Boorman, *Biographical Dictionary,* 3: 232–36.

95. *OA,* 10 (1938): 336–37.
96. *Ibid.*
97. IMTFE, Doc. 2203, p. 6.
98. Maruyama Shizuo, pp. 79–80.

99. Chang Yen-ch'ing was the Vice Chairman of the Hsin-min Hui. See Imai, *Shōwa,* pp. 149–51, for details of Chang's pro-Wu activities.

100. *Ibid.*, pp. 148–49.

101. *CWR,* Feb. 4, 1939, p. 312; and Feb. 11, 1939, p. 330. See Barger for a

good account of the confusion surrounding Wu's "acceptance" of the role of "Chief of Pacification" by a firsthand observer.

102. See IMTFE, Pros. Doc. 1005–22. This is a three-page summary (signed by James T. C. Liu) of a longer handwritten report on Wu P'ei-fu and the Doihara Agency by Hayashide Kenjirō, a staff member of the Japanese Embassy in Peiping. The difficulty in communications between Wu and Doihara may account in part for their failure to reach agreement. Though Doihara was in almost constant contact with Wu, he was never able to meet with him personally because Wu was kept under constant surveillance by Kuomintang agents in the late 1930's. Consequently, all communications had to flow through third parties. Okano, p. 1149.

103. Imai, *Shina jihen*, p. 99.

104. IMTFE, Pros. Doc. 1005–22, p. 2.

105. *CWR*, Dec. 16, 1939, p. 100.

CHAPTER NINE

1. My information on the Low-Key Club is based on interviews with its survivors and those who knew its members personally: Kao Tsung-wu, T'ao Hsi-sheng, Chin Hsiung-pai, Ho Ping-hsien, and Li Sheng-wu. There are fleeting references to the Club in Inukai, pp. 377–78; and Chin, *Wang cheng-ch'üan*, 5: 9 and *passim*.

2. Lin Han-sheng, *Wang Ching-wei*, p. 220, quoting excerpts from Dr. Hu's diary. Entry for Aug. 6, 1937.

3. T'ao, "Luan-liu," pp. 165–66.

4. *Ibid.*, p. 166; interview with T'ao.

5. Biographic data on Chou Fo-hai taken from Boorman, *Biographical Dictionary*, 1: 405–9; Inukai, pp. 376–84; and Yoshida Tōyū's intro. to Chou Fo-hai, *Shū Fukkai nikki*, pp. 1–34.

6. Chou Fo-hai, "Retrospect," p. 1.

7. Boorman, *Biographical Dictionary*, 1: 405.

8. Israel, p. 97.

9. Chou Fo-hai, "Retrospect," p. 15.

10. Inukai, p. 378.

11. Biographic data on Kao taken from Inukai, pp. 385–92 and *passim*; Imai, *Shina jihen*, p. 72; and Nishi, pp. 74–76. Records on Kao's date of birth vary. According to a contemporary biographic dictionary (Tōa mondai chōsa-kai, eds., *Saikin Shina yōjin den*, p. 59), he was born in 1906, whereas a biographic sketch written by a colleague in the peace movement indicates he was born in 1907 (Nishi, p. 406).

12. Saionji, p. 284.

13. Interview with Li.

14. NSST, p. 116.

15. Hahn, *Soong Sisters*, p. 240.

16. *GH* 2: 322–23.

17. Lin Han-sheng, *Wang Ching-wei*, p. 218, citing Hu's diary entries for July 25 and July 27, 1937.

18. *Ibid.*, pp. 218–19, Hu's diary entry for July 30, 1937.

19. *Ibid.*, pp. 219–20, Hu's diary entry for July 31, 1937. Imai states that Kao was very close to the Generalissimo, and that Chiang had even taken an official role in Kao's wedding. Imai, *Shōwa*, pp. 125–26. Chinese who knew Kao well deny that the two were ever that close. Interviews with Ho and Li.

20. Nishi, p. 76.

21. *Ibid.*

22. Inukai, p. 230. For biographic data on Wu Chen-hsiu, see Nishi, pp. 26–30.

23. Inukai, p. 77.

24. Imai, *Shina jihen*, pp. 66–69.

25. *Ibid.*, p. 66. Also, Nishi, pp. 134–36; Chin, *Wang cheng-ch'üan*, 5: *passim*; and interviews with Ho and Li.

26. Yoshida Tōyū suggests this in his intro. to Chou Fo-hai's diary (Chou Fo-hai, *Shū Fukkai nikki*, pp. 1–34); and Hata concurs in *Nitchū sensō shi*, pp. 154–55.

27. Nishi, pp. 92–93.

28. *Ibid.*, pp. 90–98; Imai, *Shina jihen*, p. 66.

29. Fairbank, p. 221. For a discussion of the Kuomintang's relationship with Chekiang financial institutions, see Y. C. Wang, *Chinese Intellectuals*, Chaps. 13–14.

30. Inukai, pp. 75–76, 386–87.

31. Nishi, pp. 95–97.

32. *Ibid.*, p. 102.

33. Inukai, pp. 125–26.

34. Nishi, p. 104.

35. Kagesa, "Sozorogaki," pp. 358–59; Imai, *Shina jihen*, p. 66.

36. Portions—but not the same portions—of the letter(s) are included in Kagesa, "Sozorogaki," p. 359, and Nishi, p. 116. Imai, *Shina jihen*, p. 67, and Nishi, p. 135, both indicate that the letter(s) reached their destination and were read by the Generalissimo.

37. Interview with Matsukata. See also the remarks Matsukata made at memorial services for Kagesa (who died in 1948), as reported in Inukai, pp. 126–27.

38. Boorman, "Wang," pp. 317–18.

39. Hahn, *China to Me*, pp. 44–45.

40. Nishi, p. 125; correspondence with Matsumoto, September 1971.

41. Interview with Matsumoto.

42. *Ibid.*

43. Imai, *Shina jihen*, p. 67. See Boyle, "Japan's Puppet Regimes," p. 239, for further details.

44. Nishi, p. 135.

45. *Ibid.*, pp. 135–36.

46. *Ibid.*, p. 178.

47. *Ibid.*, pp. 185–86.

48. The version of the meeting presented here is Matsumoto's, as told to me in an interview in 1969.

49. Nishi, p. 186.

50. Inukai, p. 387.

51. Imai, *Shina jihen*, p. 68–69; Inukai, pp. 46–47.

52. Interview with Matsumoto.

53. Inukai Tsuyoshi intro. to Kawakami, p. vii.

54. Quoted in Sharman, p. 154.

55. Kagesa, "Sozorogaki," p. 359.

56. Inukai, p. 49.

57. Imai, *Shina jihen*, p. 69.

58. Inukai, pp. 46–47, 387.

59. *Ibid.*, p. 51; Kagesa, "Sozorogaki," pp. 364–67.

60. Inukai, p. 61.

61. *Ibid.*, pp. 44, 72.

62. *Ibid.*, p. 91; interview with Kao.

63. Saionji, p. 284.

64. Kagesa, "Sozorogaki," p. 359.

65. Imai, *Shina jihen*, p. 68; Yabe, 1: 578; interview with Matsumoto.

66. T'ao Hsi-sheng, "Luan-liu," p. 166; Imai, *Shina jihen*, p. 69.

67. Imai, *Shina jihen*, pp. 69–70; Chin, *Wang cheng-ch'üan*, 5: 9. "Odd character" is *ayashikaran yatsu* in Imai's Japanese translation.

68. Chou Fo-hai, "Retrospect," p. 11.

69. *Ibid.*

70. See Boorman, *Biographical Dictionary*, 1: 42–43 (entry for Chang Chih-chung); and Lin Han-sheng, *Wang Ching-wei*, pp. 299–302, on the subject of responsibility for the burning of Changsha.

71. Wang Ching-wei, "Towards," p. 9.

72. *Ibid.*, p. 10.

73. Stuart, p. 115.

74. Jerome Ch'en, "Left Wing," p. 570. James Shirley also emphasizes this point in his thesis on Wang, p. 88. Chin Hsiung-pai, an admirer of Wang, offers the following anecdote as an illustration of Wang's ideological expediency. Asked in 1927 to justify the policies of his Hankow regime, first joining with the Communists and then breaking away from them, Wang supposedly replied: "Why do we join with the Communists? It is because we respect the *doctrines* bequeathed us by our leader [Sun Yat-sen]. Why then, you ask, did we split with the Communists? That was out of respect for the *spirit* of our leader." (Emphasis added.) Chin, *Dōsei*, p. 109.

75. Rosinger, p. 273.

76. Quoted in Durkee, p. 88.

77. Wang Ching-wei, "Guerrilla Warfare," p. 210.

78. *Ibid.*

79. *Ibid.*, p. 211.

80. Wang Ching-wei, "Towards," p. 10.

81. Wang Ching-wei, "Guerrilla Warfare," p. 212.

82. Wang Ching-wei, "The Truth," p. 70.

83. Wang Ching-wei, "Guerrilla Warfare," p. 215.

84. Chin, "Wang," 159: 3.

85. U.S. Dept. of State, *Papers: Japan, 1931–1941*, 1: 477–78.

86. *FR* 1938, 3: 368–89.

87. Ozaki, pp. 324–26.

88. *Ibid.*, p. 328.

CHAPTER TEN

1. "Conference Proceedings" is my short form for the full title: "Nikka kyōgi kiroku oyobi dō ryōkai jikō narabi Nikka himitsu kyōgi kiroku" (Sino-Japanese Conference Proceedings and Items of Understanding Together with the Proceedings of Secret Sino-Japanese Conferences). The full text is presented in Imai, *Shina jihen*, pp. 293–98.

2. Imai, *Shōwa*, pp. 124–25. Other information on Mei based on Inukai, p. 87; Chin, *Wang cheng-ch'üan*, 5: 9–10; Yabe, 1: 577–79; and interview with T'ao.

3. Imai forwarded five reports on Operation Watanabe from Shanghai to the Army General Staff between Nov. 15, 1938, and Feb. 1, 1939. These reports are printed in full in his *Shina jihen*, pp. 286–305. All but the second report are printed in *TSM*, 8: 275–84. These reports, together with Imai's comments on

them (in *Shina jihen*, pp. 78–95; and my interview with him) constitute the basic sources for the information in this chapter.

4. Imai, *Shina jihen*, p. 289.

5. Inukai, pp. 93, 96–97.

6. Imai, *Shina jihen*, pp. 295–96.

7. *Ibid.*, p. 294.

8. Inukai, p. 95.

9. Imai, *Shina jihen*, p. 289.

10. *Ibid.*, pp. 293–94.

11. *Ibid.*, pp. 294–96.

12. *Ibid.*, p. 294.

13. *Ibid.*, p. 289.

14. *Ibid.*, pp. 294–95.

15. Imai, *Shina jihen*, p. 296.

16. *Ibid.*, pp. 83, 288.

17. Interview with Imai.

18. Imai, *Shina jihen*, pp. 83, 288.

19. *Ibid.*, p. 96.

20. *Ibid.*, p. 93.

21. *Ibid.*, pp. 84, 93, 303; IMTFE, Doc. 1519-H, pp. 9–10. See also the *CWR* report that Ch'en Li-fu had joined Wang's entourage in Hanoi (Jan. 14, 1939, p. 201).

22. Imai, *Shina jihen*, p. 288.

23. Interview with Imai.

24. Tuchman, p. 316.

25. Imai, *Shina jihen*, pp. 78–79.

26. Interview with Imai.

27. Inukai, p. 100; Imai, *Shina jihen*, p. 103; Hata, *Nitchū sensō shi*, p. 155; Horiba, 1: 317–19.

CHAPTER ELEVEN

1. Imai, *Shina jihen*, pp. 297–98. A more detailed account of the planned timetable can be found in Lin Han-sheng, *Wang Ching-wei*, pp. 311–12.

2. Yabe, 1: 588–89.

3. *Ibid.*

4. Harada, 7: 233–34. Imai and Kagesa shared an admiration for Mei and a distrust of Kao, whom they considered "insincere." Kagesa, "Sozorogaki," p. 379; Imai, *Shina jihen*, p. 78.

5. Yabe, 1: 588.

6. Another reason was certainly his continued support of the warlord Ch'en Chiung-ming, a Party enemy. See Wilbur, pp. 461–65.

7. Chin, *Dōsei*, pp. 22–23, 57–58.

8. Wang Ching-wei, "Facts," p. 66.

9. Wang Ching-wei, "Aims," p. 23.

10. Some Japanese sources hold that Chiang's unexpected return to the capital forced Wang to change his plans. Imai, *Shina jihen*, pp. 86–87. Other sources that bear on this question are Donald (Chiang's adviser), pp. 194–95; Chin, *Dōsei*, pp. 24–28 (based on talks with Chou Fo-hai); and Boyle, "Japan's Puppet Regimes," pp. 278–80.

11. Wang Ching-wei, "Why," p. 59. See also Ch'en Pu-lei's account of the Dec. 9, 1938, meeting in his *Hui-i lu* (Memoirs), p. 108, part of which is translated in Lin Han-sheng, *Wang Ching-wei*, p. 315.

12. Chin, *Wang cheng-ch'üan*, 5: 98.

13. *Ibid.*, p. 31.

14. *Ibid.*, Chap. 186; Boorman, *Biographical Dictionary*, 2: 457–59.

15. Chin, *Wang cheng-ch'üan*, 5: 27. Chou Fo-hai told Imai that the aircraft was "borrowed by General Lung Yun." Imai, *Shina jihen*, p. 87.

16. Chin, *Dōsei*, p. 270; Inukai, p. 47. The papers and diaries of Ch'en Pu-lei (who committed suicide in 1948) would undoubtedly throw much light on the

Wang defection. According to Chin Hsiung-pai, these papers are in the possession of Ch'en's brother, a newspaper reporter for a Hong Kong newspaper stationed in Manila. Interview with Chin.

17. Interviews with Li, Ho, and Chin. Chin uses the phrase *shuang huang*
to describe the feelings of "in-the-know" Shanghai newsmen in 1939 about the
relationship between Chiang and Wang. His reference is to a theater act in
which two comedians talk simultaneously, mouthing their words in perfect syn-
chronization.

18. Interview with Chin.

19. *FR* 1938, 3: 436.

20. As Konoe's third major policy statement on the China war in 1938, the
December 22 statement is frequently referred to as the Number Three Statement (Dai-sanji Seimei). The other statements were the January 16 *aite ni sezu*
declaration and the November 3 announcement of the New Order in East Asia.
An English translation of the December 22 statement can be found in U.S.
Dept. of State, *Papers: Japan, 1931–1941*, 1: 482–83. The Japanese text is printed in Gaimushō, *Nihon gaikō*, 2: 470. Konoe's Three Principles invited comparison with the Three Principles Foreign Minister Hirota enunciated in October 1935. See Crowley, *Japan's Quest*, p. 230.

21. Wang Ching-wei, "Peace Proposals," p. 56; "Why," p. 59.

22. Kagesa, "Sozorogaki," p. 362.   23. Inukai, pp. 100–104.

24. *Ibid.*, p. 101.   25. *Ibid.*, pp. 101–2.

26. Kagesa, "Sozorogaki," p. 362.

27. The full title of the document is "NisShi shin kankei chōsei hōshin" (The
Policy for Adjusting the New Relations Between Japan and China). My discussion of this policy is based on an English translation in IMTFE, Pros. Doc.
2178-C, and the original Japanese text in Horiba, 1: 191–94. This document, the
main part of which is a *besshi* (annex) entitled "NisShi shin kankei chōsei
yōkō" (Essential Points Concerning the Adjustment of the New Relations Between Japan and China), is often confused with another policy bearing that
name. Though the second policy, which was approved more than a year later,
on Dec. 30, 1939, was in general based on the first, there is considerable difference between them. The text of the later document is printed in *TSM*, 8:
286–94.

28. Horiba, 1: 193.   29. *Ibid.*

30. *Ibid.*, p. 196.   31. Kagesa, "Sozorogaki," p. 360.

32. Horiba, 1: 224–27, contains the complete text of Hiranuma's remarks.

33. *Ibid.*, p. 228.

34. Imai, *Shina jihen*, p. 90, and *Shōwa*, p. 128.

35. Interview with Ushiba.

36. Kazami, p. 178.

37. I have used two sources for Wang's statements: his conversations with
Kagesa and Inukai in April–May 1939, as recorded in Kagesa, "Sozorogaki,"
pp. 365–67; and what purports to be his last will and testament in Chin,
"Wang," 159: 3–4, 15. The authenticity of Wang's will is discussed in the Bibliographical Note on pp. 395–400.

38. See text in *OA*, 11 (1939): 97–99.

39. Johnson, Chungking, to Sec. of State, No. 547, Nov. 16, 1938. U.S. Archives, 793.94/14365.

40. Grew, Tokyo, to Sec. of State, No. 741, Nov. 19, 1938. U.S. Archives, 793.94/14373.

41. White, *Stilwell Papers*, p. 104.

42. *FR* 1938, 3: 435.

43. Chin, *Dōsei*, p. 32.

44. Wang Ching-wei, "Peace Proposals" is an English translation of the Dec. 29 message. In Chinese the telegram is frequently referred to as the *yen-tien*, a telegraphic code designation. In Japanese it is usually referred to as the *heiwa dempō* (peace telegram).

45. Wang Ching-wei, "Why" is an English translation of the message released on Jan. 8, 1939.

46. Imai, *Shina jihen*, pp. 302–4.

47. *CWR*, Jan. 7, 1939, p. 174.

48. Quoted in Lin Han-sheng, *Wang Ching-wei*, p. 338. See Chin, *Wang chong-ch'iian*, 5; ch. 185, for a detailed account of the relationship between Wang and the scholar and educator Wu Chih-hui (1864–1953), one of the "four elder statesmen of the Kuomintang."

49. Wang Ching-wei, "Freedom," p. 188.

50. *Kokumin shimbun*, Jan. 10, 1939.

51. NSST, p. 207.

52. Peck, Chargé in Chungking, to Sec. of State, No. 60, Jan. 30, 1939. U.S. Archives, 793.94/14651. Baron Harada's journal contains the exact text of this telegram with the notation that the Imperial Navy had "received" the message. Harada, 7: 287, entry of Feb. 15, 1939.

53. Imai, *Shina jihen*, p. 303.

54. Interview with Imai.

55. Maruyama Masao, p. 97.

56. Miwa, p. 129; Chin, *Dōsei*, pp. 33–34.

57. In addition to Chin's account, I have relied on Kung Te-po, p. 88. I am also grateful to Madame Tseng for sharing her recollections of the murder and its aftermath with my wife in an interview in Boston in July 1970.

58. Wang Ching-wei, "Facts," p. 61. See also Wang's touching tribute, "In Memory of Dr. Tseng Chung-ming."

59. T'ang, *Fundamentals*, p. 49.

60. Wang Ching-wei, "Facts," p. 67.

61. Interview with Madame Tseng.

62. Boorman, "Wang," pp. 317–18.

63. Wang Ching-wei, "Facts."

64. *Ibid.*, p. 65.

65. *CWR*, April 15, 1939, p. 203.

66. *OA*, 11 (1939): p. 276.

67. Nishi, pp. 239–42.

68. Imai, *Shina jihen*, p. 304.

69. Lu asserts that the Foreign Ministry archives "confirm that such an agreement existed on an informal basis" (p. 85).

70. IMTFE, *Proceedings*, pp. 24043 *et seq*. (Kagesa cross-examination). The bulk of the depositions, testimony, cross-examination, etc., of Kagesa during the course of the Tribunal are to be found in *ibid.*, pp. 23790–24141, and in Def. Doc. 1282. In addition, see Pros. Exhibits Nos. 1005-1 to 1005-23, which are largely concerned with Japanese relations with Wang Ching-wei in the period April 1939–July 1939, i.e., immediately before and after his flight from Hanoi to Shanghai. I discuss the usefulness of the Kagesa testimony in the Bibliographical Note on pp. 395–400.

71. IMTFE, Pros. Exhibit 1005-6.

72. Kung Te-po, Chap. 9. See also IMTFE, *Proceedings,* pp. 24055 *et seq.*
73. Chin, *Wang cheng-ch'üan,* 5: 91.
74. Kagesa, "Sozorogaki," p. 365. Inukai, pp. 162–64, also contains an account of the conversations at sea.
75. Kagesa, "Sozorogaki," p. 366.   76. *Ibid.*
77. *Ibid.*   78. *Ibid.*
79. Interview with Kao.   80. Inukai, p. 165.
81. Nishi, pp. 243–49.   82. *Ibid.*
83. *Ibid.,* pp. 256–60.   84. Inukai, p. 165.
85. *Ibid.,* p. 166.   86. Chin, *Dōsei,* pp. 52–54.
87. Tsunoda, "Kaidai," p. 423.

CHAPTER TWELVE

1. The name of the mansion in Chinese is Meihua-t'ang. See Kagesa, "Sozorogaki," pp. 373–74, for a discussion of the Plum Blossom Agency.
2. *Ibid.,* p. 374.
3. *Ibid.;* Inukai, p. 204.
4. Kagesa, "Sozorogaki," p. 376. One of the members, for instance, was Kamio Shigeru, an *Asahi* correspondent. For examples of his journalistic coverage of the Wang movement, see his two articles "Wang Ching-wei and the Peace Movement" and "Wang Ching-wei vs. Chungking."
5. Kagesa, "Sozorogaki," p. 374.
6. *Ibid.,* p. 363.
7. Lu, p. 87.
8. Inukai, p. 206; Kagesa, "Sozorogaki," p. 378; Horiba, 1: 239.
9. Nishi, p. 227.   10. Inaba, p. 339.
11. NSST, p. 209.   12. Shigemitsu, *Shōwa,* 1: 208.
13. *TSM,* 8: 270. A valuable commentary on the Five Ministers' Conference and the decisions of June 6, 1939, can be found in Horiba, 1: 261–65.
14. Horiba, 1: 263.   15. *Ibid.*
16. *Ibid.,* pp. 262–63.   17. *Ibid.,* pp. 263–64.
18. *Ibid.*
19. The official Japanese translation of the May 28 proposals, "Jikyoku shūshū ni kansuru gutaiteki benpō" (Concrete Proposals Concerning the Handling of the Situation), is set forth in Imai, *Shina jihen,* pp. 306–10.
20. *GSS,* 9: 656–57. Emphasis added. This quote comes from what appears to be a stenographic account of portions of the Wang-Itagaki conversations of June 11 and June 15, 1939, *ibid.,* pp. 652–59.
21. *Ibid.,* pp. 657–58.
22. *Ibid.,* p. 657.
23. *Ibid.,* pp. 658–59.
24. The issue of the flag is discussed in Inukai, pp. 191–95; Kagesa, "Sozorogaki," p. 368; Imai, *Shina jihen,* pp. 95, 97; and Johnson, *Peasant Nationalism,* pp. 47–48.
25. Inukai, p. 195.
26. *Ibid.*
27. Discussed in Chin, *Wang cheng-ch'üan,* 5: 95–96.
28. Interview with Kao.
29. Interview with Kao; Inukai, pp. 171–73.

30. IMTFE, Doc. 1519-H, p. 4.
31. NSST, p. 211.
32. IMTFE, Doc. 1519-H, p. 6.
33. NSST, p. 211, citing unpublished material in MFA archives.
34. Lu, p. 82. See also Nashimoto, p. 115.
35. NSST, p. 212, citing unpublished material in MFA archives.
36. See, for example, Okazaki to Foreign Minister Arita, July 12, 1939, in IMTFE, Doc. 1519-I, p. 1.
37. NSST, p. 213.
38. Hara (Deputy Chief, Tokumu-bu, South China) to Ugaki (Chief, First Section, Military Affairs Bureau, Navy), Aug. [30], 1939, *GSS*, 13: 246. In NSST, p. 213, Usui discusses another important source on the plans for a South China autonomous government: "Shūdan to Takeuchi-gawa to no kyōgi jikō" (Essential Items of the Conference Between Takeuchi [Wang Ching-wei] and the [Army] Group). Takeuchi, a common Japanese surname, was the code name for Wang.
39. Wang Ching-wei, "Towards," pp. 10–12.
40. See, for example, Chin, *Dōsei*, pp. 56–58.
41. Wang Ching-wei, "Towards," p. 12.
42. Interview with Shimizu.
43. Chin, *Dōsei*, p. 55.
44. For the full text, see *People's Tribune* (Shanghai), 27 (1939): 107–16.
45. Chin, *Dōsei*, p. 73.
46. NSST, p. 215, citing unpublished material in MFA archives.
47. *Ibid.*, p. 214; Kagesa, "Sozorogaki," p. 376; T'ao, "Luan liu," pp. 170–71.
48. *CWR*, Sept. 30, 1939, p. 174. Emphasis added.
49. T'ao, "Luan-liu," p. 171.
50. Wang Ching-wei, "Nippon ni yosu."

CHAPTER THIRTEEN

1. Interview with Matsukata.
2. Hayashi Saburō, p. 15.
3. *GSS*, 10: 80–81; Katsu H. Young, p. 93.
4. NSST, p. 214, citing unpublished material in MFA archives.
5. *Ibid.*
6. Horiba, 1: 317.
7. Kagesa, "Sozorogaki," p. 378.
8. Horiba, 1: 319; Kagesa, "Sozorogaki," p. 376.
9. Interview with Shimizu.   10. Kagesa, "Sozorogaki," p. 377.
11. *Ibid.*   12. Inukai, p. 197.
13. The official title of the December 30 document is "NisShi shin kankei chōsei ni kansuru kyōgi shorui" (Conference Documents Relating to the Adjustment of Sino-Japanese Relations). They are printed in *TSM*, 8: 286–95.
14. Nashimoto, pp. 125–27.
15. Inukai, p. 282.
16. See, for example, T'ao Hsi-sheng's account of how Kagesa was able to persuade Wang to continue the Yü Yüan Road talks after Wang had "made up his mind" to discontinue negotiations. "Luan-liu," pp. 172–73.
17. Inukai, p. 273; Kagesa, "Sozorogaki," p. 379.

18. Horiba, 1: 319–20.

19. *GSS*, 13: 249–315.

20. See *ibid.*, pp. 316–35, for the give-and-take between the Chinese and the Japanese on various important issues before the Yü Yüan talks. The documents therein are a Chinese position paper (with an intro. by Wang, dated June 13, 1939), a Japanese reply (dated Oct. 24, 1939), a Chinese reply to the Japanese reply (undated), and a Kōain commentary on the paper and replies (dated Nov. 1, 1939).

21. *Ibid.*, p. 318.

22. *Ibid.*

23. *Ibid.*, p. 319.

24. *Ibid.*, pp. 320–21.

25. *Ibid.*, pp. 325–26.

26. *Ibid.*

27. *Ibid.*

28. *Ibid.*, p. 264.

29. *Ibid.*, p. 265.

30. *TSM*, 8: 287.

31. *GSS*, 13: 254.

32. *Ibid.*, pp. 322–25.

33. *Ibid.*, p. 324.

34. *Ibid.*, p. 259.

35. *Ibid.*, pp. 257–58.

36. *Ibid.*, p. 258.

37. *Ibid.*, p. 259.

38. *TSM*, 8: 287.

39. Inukai, p. 267.

40. *TSM*, 8: 288.

41. Steiger, pp. 466–67.

42. Hangin, pp. 20–21.

43. NSST, p. 215.

44. *TSM*, 8: 289.

45. *GSS*, 13: 253–54.

46. *Ibid.*, p. 254.

47. *TSM*, 8: 290–91.

48. Ogata Noboru, p. 296.

49. NSST, pp. 220–21.

50. Inukai, p. 278.

51. *Ibid.*, p. 280.

52. Records of the Suga-Ch'en meetings are printed in *GSS*, 13: 302–15.

53. Inukai, pp. 278–80.

54. *TSM*, 8: 294.

55. *GSS*, 13: 251–52.

56. *Ibid.*, p. 252.

57. Kagesa, "Sozorogaki," p. 376.

58. Cited in Inukai, p. 267.

CHAPTER FOURTEEN

1. Interviews with Kao and T'ao.

2. The best accounts are in Y. C. Wang, "Tu Yueh-sheng"; and Boorman, *Biographical Dictionary*, 3: 328–30. Tu's name is found in a variety of transliterations in English-language publications, e.g., Dou Yu-seng, Tu Yu-sen.

3. Han, *Birdless Summer*, p. 84.

4. See Chin, *Wang cheng-ch'üan*, 5: Chs. 182, 198–99, on the Kao-T'ao-Tu contacts.

5. Chou Fo-hai, *Shū Fukkai nikki*, p. 36.

6. An English translation of the documents and the Kao-T'ao telegrams is printed in *CWR*, Feb. 3, 1940, pp. 341–44, under the headline "Wang Ching-wei Sells Out."

7. Chou Fo-hai, *Shū Fukkai nikki*, p. 52.

8. Chin, *Dōsei*, pp. 71–72.

9. Boorman, *Biographical Dictionary*, 1: 220.

10. Chin, *Wang cheng-ch'üan*, 5: 114.

11. T'ao, "Luan-liu," pp. 177–93.

12. Inukai, pp. 169–70; Imai, *Shōwa*, p. 130.

13. In addition to the sources cited in the course of the text discussion that follows, see Chin, *Dōsei*, pp. 49–52; and Haruke, *passim*.

14. Imai, *Shōwa*, p. 135.

15. Nishi, p. 252.

16. Chin, *Dōsei*, p. 52. Chin discusses Chou's recruitment tactics and their results on pp. 47–54.

17. Inukai, pp. 268–69. 18. Chin, *Dōsei*, p. 149.

19. Powell, p. 335. 20. Chin, *Dōsei*, Ch. 35.

21. *Ibid.*, p. 197. 22. Powell, p. 336.

23. Conference records and *gokuhi* (top secret) Plum Blossom Agency reports on the Tsingtao Conference may be found in the Library of Congress, *Archives in the Japanese Ministry of Foreign Affairs*, Reels 491–93, S1.1.1.0-27, pp. 5580–5645.

24. Lin Han-sheng, *Wang Ching-wei*, p. 342.

25. Lin Pai-sheng, p. 41.

26. Wang Ching-wei, "Towards," p. 11.

27. T'ang, *Fundamentals*, p. 88.

28. *Ibid.*

29. Wang Ching-wei, "Facts," p. 65.

30. Wang, "Sino-Japanese Relationships," p. 5.

31. My discussion of *Kiri kōsaku* (literally, Operation Paulownia) is based on the documentation, primarily records of conversations between Colonel Imai and various Chinese negotiators, in Imai, *Shina jihen*, pp. 112–50, 326–75. Other sources used are Imai, *Shōwa*, pp. 152–64; Chin, *Dōsei*, pp. 66–67; NSST, pp. 229–37; and Chou Fo-hai, *Shū Fukkai nikki*, *passim*. Among the other operations under way in 1940 were the Stuart Operation (involving the American educator John Leighton Stuart); and *Ran kōsaku* (Operation Orchid). See Imai, *Nitchū sensō shi*, pp. 159–60, for brief discussions of both.

32. Imai, *Shōwa*, p. 161. The Tokugawa Period lasted from 1600 to 1867.

33. *Ibid.*, p. 158.

34. Chou Fo-hai had his doubts about the authenticity of the seal and signature used on the accreditation documents. *Shū Fukkai nikki*, p. 169, entry for July 18, 1940. See also Imai, *Shina jihen*, p. 137, on this point.

35. According to Chang Chih-p'ing, one of the sources of pressure on the Generalissimo was the Chinese Ambassador to the United States, Hu Shih. Imai received further corroboration of the involvement of the Generalissimo and Tai Li in Operation Kiri in 1955, when he received a letter from the impostor himself. Imai, *Shina jihen*, pp. 149–50.

36. NSST, pp. 234–47.

37. Chou Fo-hai, *Shū Fukkai nikki*, p. 166, entry of July 14, 1940.

38. NSST, p. 233.

39. *People's Tribune* (Shanghai), 28 (1940): 301.

40. *Far Eastern Review*, 36 (1940): 127.

41. Aoki, 3: 310–11. 42. *CWR*, April 6, 1940, p. 200.

43. NSST, p. 224. 44. *Ibid.*, p. 223.

45. Matsumoto Sōkichi, p. 113. 46. Goette, p. 126.

47. The full text of Saitō's speech is printed in GSS, 13: 336–44.

48. *Ibid.*, p. 338.

49. *Ibid.*, p. 339.

50. *Ibid.*, pp. 339, 343. The last-quoted remarks brought applause and cries of "Hear! Hear!" from his fellow Dietmen.

51. Inukai, p. 318.
52. NSST, p. 225, citing unpublished material in MFA archives.
53. Interrogation of Saionji Kinkazu in connection with the trial of Ozaki Hotsumi et al. *GSS*, 3: 490.
54. Yano papers. The nearest thing to a stenographic record of the negotiations on the Basic Treaty (*Kihon jōyaku*) is a set of notes taken by a Foreign Ministry official, Yano Seiki. See my discussion of this source in the Bibliographical Note, p. 400.

55. *Ibid.*   56. *Ibid.*
57. NSST, p. 228.   58. Butow, pp. 143, 152.
59. *Ibid.*, p. 153.   60. Lu, p. 115.
61. *FR* 1940, 4: 424.
62. "Shina jihen shori yōkō," in Gaimushō, *Nihon gaikō*, 2: 464–65.
63. Grew to Sec. of State, Nov. 25, 1940, in *FR* 1940, 4: 444–46.
64. See the firsthand account by Nishi, pp. 272 *et seq.*; and a good summary in NSST, pp. 232–44.
65. NSST, p. 242.
66. Horiba, 1: 507.
67. *Ibid.*, pp. 509–10.
68. *TSM*, 8: 302–5; Chou Fo-hai, *Shū Fukkai nikki*, pp. 248–56.
69. Lin Han-sheng, *Wang Ching-wei*, pp. 456–57.
70. *FR* 1940, 4: 440.
71. *Ibid.*, p. 447.
72. Feis, p. 135.
73. *China Quarterly* (Chungking), 5 (1940): 936.
74. Chin, *Dōsei*, p. 112.
75. Chou Fo-hai, *Shū Fukkai nikki*, p. 267.

CHAPTER FIFTEEN

1. Maki, p. 105.
2. Keene, "Japanese Writers," p. 212.
3. Chin, *Dōsei*, pp. 168–71.
4. *Ibid.*, p. 168.
5. *Ibid.*
6. Inukai, p. 129. Imai and Rear Adm. Okada Yūji, for example, see nothing political in Kagesa's transfer; interviews, 1970.
7. Shigemitsu, *Shōwa*, 2: 169.
8. *Ibid.*, p. 167.
9. "Tai-Chū shin seisaku," which is the informal title. The full title is "Dai Tōa sensō kansui no tame no tai-Shi shori kompon hōshin" (Basic Policy for Dealing with China in Order to End the Greater East Asia War). Text in Gaimushō, *Nihon gaikō*, 2: 580–81; discussed in Imai, *Kindai no sensō*, pp. 281–84.
10. Discussed in Yamazaki, 113: 49; interview with Yamazaki.
11. Interview with Yamazaki.
12. Akashi, "Japan's Peace Maneuvers," *passim.* I am indebted to Professor Akashi for allowing me to cite his unpublished manuscript on the subject of wartime peace movements. On Hsüeh Yüeh, see Cohen, "Who Fought the Japanese?" pp. 113–14.

13. Akashi, "Japan's Peace Maneuvers," p. 17, citing unpublished *Hata nisshi* (diary of Gen. Hata Shunroku).

14. See, for example, *FR* 1942, 4: 212; and report of O. Edmund Clubb in *FR* 1944, 6: 786.

15. Akashi, "Japan's Peace Maneuvers," p. 63.

16. Gillin, p. 11.

17. *Ibid.*, p. 236, citing *North China Herald*, Dec. 16, 1936.

18. *Ibid.*, p. 272.

19. Maruyama Shizuo, pp. 171–72. For documents on the operation, see *GSS*, 13: 449–521.

20. Hirano, p. 199, cited by Gillin, p. 282.

21. Tanaka Ryūkichi, *Hai-in*, p. 18, cited by Gillin, p. 280.

22. Takabatake, p. 166.

23. Akashi, "Japan's Peace Maneuvers," p. 68.

24. Imai, *Kindai no sensō*, pp. 327–28.

25. Ugaki, *Ugaki nikki*, p. 385.

26. Li Ngoc, p. 176. See Johnson, *Peasant Nationalism*, pp. 61–67, 210–12, for a discussion of model zones and *pao-chia*.

27. Van Slyke, ed., *Chinese Communist Movement*, pp. 121–22.

28. Chin, *Dōsei*, p. 175.

29. Wang Ching-wei, "Ō shuseki."

30. Chinese Communist Party estimate, cited in *FR* 1945, 7: 222. See also U.S. War Dept. estimate in Van Slyke, *Chinese Communist Movement*, p. 96; and Chin, *Dōsei*, p. 194. Chin estimates 600,000 regular troops.

31. Chin, *Dōsei*, p. 188.

32. *Ibid.*, p. 210. *FR* 1945, 7: 128–29, describes most of these generals as followers of Gen. Feng Yu-hsiang.

33. Chin, *Dōsei*, p. 210.

34. Peck, p. 573.

35. *FR* 1945, 7: 160. See also Chin, *Dōsei*, p. 194.

36. *FR* 1945, 7: 199.

37. *FR* 1944, 6: 510. See also Tuchman, pp. 472–73.

38. Ringwalt to Gauss, Aug. 10, 1944. *FR* 1944, 6: 151.

39. Peck, pp. 580–81.   40. Chin, *Dōsei*, pp. 147–53.

41. *FR* 1945, 7: 161.   42. *FR* 1944, 6: 151, 414–15.

43. Ba Maw, p. 345.   44. *Ibid.*, p. 338.

45. Chin, *Wang cheng-ch'üan*, 5: Chap. 202.

46. Inukai, pp. 18, 376–84.

47. Brière, p. 21.

48. Chin, *Dōsei*, p. 164.

49. Interview with Okada. See Chin, *Dōsei*, Chap. 57, for a discussion of the secret radio communication system.

50. Chin, *Dōsei*, pp. 215 *et seq.*

51. *Ibid.*, p. 217.

52. *FR* 1945, 7: 52–53. Dated Feb. 23, 1945.

53. *Ibid.*

54. Usui, *Nitchū sensō*, p. 188; Imai, *Kindai no sensō*, pp. 364–68.

55. Usui, *Nitchū sensō*, pp. 189–90.

56. *Ibid.*, p. 190.

57. Miles, p. 531.
58. *New York Times*, Sept. 10, 1945, p. 4.
59. *FR* 1945, 7: 553.
60. *Ibid.*, p. 599. "Japanese troops" bracketed in the original.
61. *Ibid.*, p. 663.
62. Jōno, pp. 281–82.
63. Usui, *Nitchū sensō*, pp. 197–98; Imai, *Kindai no sensō*, p. 370.
64. Jōno, p. 298.
65. Gillin, p. 285, citing articles in the *New York Times*, Feb. 13, 1946, and Feb. 10, 1947.
66. *Ibid.*, p. 286, citing Hirano, p. 210.
67. *FR* 1944, 6: 319, 333.
68. See Fishel; and Imai, *Shōwa*, pp. 174–80.
69. Interviews with Ho and Li.
70. See, for example, *New York Times*, March 26, 1946, p. 18.
71. Chin, *Dōsei*, pp. 455–56. Chin holds that Chiang relented after an interview with Chou's tearful wife, which was arranged by Chou's friend Ch'en Pu-lei.
72. Lin Han-sheng, *Wang Ching-wei*, p. 490, citing Chin, *Wang cheng-ch'üan*.
73. *New York Times*, Sept. 27, 1945, p. 5.
74. Belden, *passim* and especially Chap. 30. See also Chao Shu-li's novel *Changes in Li Village*.
75. See, for example, the account of the campaign of Tan Kah Kee (Chairman of the Nanyang Overseas Chinese General Association) to oust Ch'en Yi as Governor of Fukien, in Akashi, pp. 74–81. See also the biographical sketches of Tan Kah Kee (under Ch'en Chia-keng, the Wade-Giles romanization) and Ch'en Yi in Boorman, *Biographical Dictionary*, 1: 165–70 and 251–54; and Kerr, pp. 53–56.
76. *New York Times*, Oct. 22, 1945, p. 2.
77. Kerr, p. 56.
78. Mancall, p. 2. For a balanced discussion of the Japanese accomplishments during Japan's half-century overlordship of Taiwan, see Eto.
79. Boorman, *Biographical Dictionary*, 1: 253.

CHAPTER SIXTEEN

1. Interview with Imai.   2. Imai, *Shina jihen*, p. 97.
3. Usui, "Gen'ei," p. 285.   4. Chin, *Dōsei*, pp. 220–22.
5. Tsunoda, *Ishiwara Kanji shiryō: kokubō ronsaku*, pp. 246–47. From a May 10, 1938, speech to Manchurian students studying in Tokyo.
6. Morris, p. 38.
7. In recent years, Japanese scholars have devoted much attention to analyzing Japanese Pan-Asian concepts and programs. See, for example, the published versions of two roundtable discussions listed in the Bibliography under Hayashi et al.; and Takeuchi. See also Oka; Mayo; Iriye, *Across*; and Jansen, "Japanese Views."
8. Quoted in Hata, *Nitchū sensō shi*, p. 246.
9. Cited in Maruyama Masao, p. 95.
10. See Dull and Umemura, pp. 6–7 ("Atrocities"), for a guide to IMTFE documentation concerning this subject.

11. Reischauer, pp. 139–41.

12. Tsurumi Kazuko, p. 116. See especially Chapter 3, "Socialization for Death: Moral Education at School and in the Army" on this subject.

13. Maruyama Masao, p. 19.

14. From an unsigned review in *OA*, April 1940, p. 217. Hino Ashihei was the pen-name of Tamai Katsunori.

15. Shigemitsu, *Japan and Her Destiny*, p. 270.

16. Sun, p. 151.

17. IMTFE, Exhibit CE835, p. 8.

18. Maruyama Masao, "Japan's Wartime Leaders," *Orient/West* (Tokyo), 5 (1962): 41, cited in Coox, *Year*.

19. Konoe, "Memoirs," p. 4015.

20. Duus, "Nagai Ryūtarō and the 'White Peril,' " p. 41. See also Matsumoto Sannosuke, "Significance," for a valuable commentary on Duus; and Duus, "Nagai Ryūtarō: The Tactical Dilemmas of Reform" for a more extended study of Nagai.

21. Norman, p. 38.

22. Matsumoto Sannosuke, "Yukichi Fukuzawa," p. 167, citing Fukuzawa's *Jiji shōgen* (A Critique of the Trends of the Times).

23. *Ibid.*, p. 169.

24. *Ibid.*

25. Miyakawa and Igeta, p. 519, citing Tokutomi's "Shina ron" (An Essay on China), which appeared in *Kokumin no tomo*, no. 230.

26. Pyle, p. 173, citing Tokutomi's editorial of July 23, 1894.

27. *Ibid.*, citing Tokutomi's editorial of Sept. 13, 1894.

28. Keene, "The Sino-Japanese War of 1894–95," p. 128, citing *Uchimura Kanzō zenshū* (The Complete Works of Uchimura Kanzō).

29. *Ibid.*, p. 134.   30. *Ibid.*, p. 127.

31. Tsurumi Kazuko, p. 156.   32. Ba Maw, p. 185.

33. Chin, *Dōsei*, p. 289.   34. *Ibid.*, p. 288.

35. *Ibid.*, p. 290.

36. *Ibid.*, p. 166. Yang, p. 148, reports a similar incident in which students were arrested after circulating leaflets denouncing Wang as a traitor.

37. Chin, *Dōsei*, p. 290.

38. T'ang, *Puppet State*, p. 28, citing Wang speech of March 1, 1934.

39. *Ibid.*

40. Wang Ching-wei, *China's Problems*, p. 112.

41. *CWR*, April 6, 1940, p. 179.

42. Chin, "Wang Ching-wei."

43. *Ibid.*, 159: 4.

44. T'ao, "Sino-Japanese," pp. 150–51.

45. Wright, p. 516.

46. Chin, "Wang Ching-wei," 159: 4.

47. See Yang; and Schwartz on the importance of these techniques in Sino-barbarian relations.

48. Lin Han-sheng, "A Case Study," p. 1.

49. Chin, *Dōsei*, p. 390.

50. Wang Ching-wei, "Sino-Japanese Relationships," p. 6.

51. Wang Ching-wei, "Confucius," p. 263.

52. *Ibid.*

53. *Ibid.*, p. 266.

54. Mote, "Confucian Eremitism," p. 234.

55. Warner, p. 827.   56. Roy, p. 172.

57. Hewins, p. 21.   58. Interview with Kao.

59. Johnson, *Peasant Nationalism*, p. 73; Fairbank, p. 235. If militia were to be included in the 1945 strength of the Red Army, its growth would be even more impressive.

60. See Selden for an excellent study of the Communists' programs.

61. Barrett, p. 86. Barrett can scarcely be regarded as a Communist sympathizer—"Red China is the bitterest enemy we have in the world today" he writes—but his fascinating monograph is replete with comparisons (usually unflattering to Chiang's troops) between the Nationalist and Communist armies during the war years.

62. Wang Ching-wei, "Sino-Japanese Relationships," p. 6.

63. *Ibid.*, "The European War," pp. 102–3.

64. *Ibid.*, "Towards," p. 4.

65. See, for example, Gillin's review of Johnson's *Peasant Nationalism* in *JAS*, 23 (1964): 269–89.

66. Inukai, p. 369; Imai, *Shina jihen*, p. 253; Chin, *Wang cheng-ch'üan*, 4: Chaps. 161–63.

67. *South China Morning Post* (Hong Kong), April 18, 1946, p. 1.

68. Boorman, *Biographical Dictionary*, 1: 220. Edgar Snow's statement (*Other Side*, p. 547) that Madame Wang was still alive in 1961 and a prisoner in the Ward Road Jail appears to have been in error.

69. Wright, p. 518.

Glossary

Aite ni sezu 相手にせず Short form for Konoe's Jan. 16, 1938, "no dealing [with Chiang Kai-shek]" declaration

Bunji gassaku 分治合作 Japan's policy of keeping China politically fractured into regional units

Ch'ing-hsiang yün-tung 清郷運動 Wang Ching-wei's rural pacification movement

Chungkuang-t'ang 重光堂 Chungkuang mansion, the site of the November 1938 conference in Shanghai that led to Wang's defection

Gekokujō 下剋上 Domination of senior military officers by their juniors

Iaku jōsō 帷幄上奏 Right of access to the throne enjoyed by ranking Japanese military officers

Kiri kōsaku 桐工作 Operation Kiri, involving T. L. Soong's impostor

Kokusaku kaisha 國策會社 National policy companies

Luan-liu 潮流 *Cross Currents,* the memoirs of T'ao Hsi-sheng

Mengchiang/Mōkyō 蒙疆 The Mongolian Borderlands

"Sozorogaki" 曾走路我記 "A Rambling Discourse," the memoirs of Gen. Kagesa Sadaaki

Tai-haku kōsaku 對伯工作 The operation aimed at enlisting the collaboration of Yen Hsi-shan

Ti-tiao Chü-lo-pu 低調倶樂部 The Low-Key Club

Tokubetsu ben'eki 特別便益 Special privileges

Tokubetsu bengi 特別便宜 Special facilities

Tokubetsu benri 特別便利 Special facilities

Tokumu-bu 特務部 Special services units. Also, *Tokumu kikan* 特務機關 Special services agencies

T'ung-sheng kung-ssu 同生共死 Wang's slogan "sharing each other's fate"

Ume kikan 梅機關 Plum Blossom Agency, headed by General Kagesa

Watanabe kōsaku 渡邊工作 Operation Watanabe, aimed at enlisting the collaboration of Wang Ching-wei

Yen-tien 豔電 Wang's Dec. 29, 1938, "peace telegram" to Chungking

Bibliographical Note

WHEN WANG Ching-wei's body was brought back to China after his death in Nagoya, Japan, in November 1944, many people asked Madame Wang if her husband had left a last political will and testament to guide his followers. Her answer was always an unequivocal "no." Other relatives and close friends who visited the bedridden leader frequently in his last months also agreed that he had neither left a political testament nor discussed one with anyone. There the matter rested until 1964, when *Ch'un-ch'iu*, a Hong Kong monthly, published what purported to be the "last minute feelings" of Wang.

The story of the *Ch'un-ch'iu* disclosures began in the autumn of 1963 with the arrival of a letter at the magazine's offices addressed to Chu Tzu-chia, a Hong Kong–based journalist and sometime contributor. The magazine carelessly allowed the letter to gather dust until February 8, 1964, when Chu happened to drop into the office. He opened the envelope, marked only with the return address of a Hong Kong insurance company, to find a four-and-a-half-page brushwork document that purported to be Wang's last will, though it was clearly not in his hand. A second sheet, which did appear to be in his hand-writing, bore seven characters in beautiful, cursive script: "Last-minute feelings, Chao-ming." Also enclosed was a piece of plain, yellow notepaper bearing the Kowloon address of Wang's eldest son and the instruction, "Please deliver." There was no message as such for Chu Tzu-chia himself.

"Chu Tzu-chia" is a pseudonym for Chin Hsiung-pai, a former subministerial member of the Wang Government and a close colleague of Chou Fo-hai. Chin's *Wang cheng-ch'üan ti k'ai-ch'ang yü shou-ch'ang*, discussed below, constitutes an important source on the events I have discussed in this book. Chin recalls that he read the long four-and-a-half-page, five-thousand-character document many times before he was finally convinced of its authenticity. He endeavored to track down its anonymous sender but without success; the only clue—the insurance company—proved to be no help. Since the address of Wang's son was correct and the document could easily have gone directly to him, Chin concluded that he was supposed to make the will public before sending it on to Wang's son. Accordingly, he released it to *Ch'un-ch'iu*, which published it in full in the February 1964 issue. (See Chin, "Wang Ching-wei.")

The purported will, which I have cited several times, especially in the concluding chapter, is dated October 1944—with a place for the day of the month left blank. It opens with the statement that Wang is dictating the testament to his wife, that he expects her to hand it to "a certain person," unnamed, for safekeeping, and that it should be published "at an appropriate time in the future, perhaps upon the twentieth anniversary of my death." According to Chinese reckoning, that anniversary was reached in November 1963—approximately the time the letter to Chin Hsiung-pai was posted.

The printing of the alleged will touched off a controversy over its authenticity, and at this writing, eight years later, no one has proved it either genuine or spurious. Opinion is divided among Wang's followers and the Chinese and Japanese members of his collaboration movement. About one-third of those I have consulted regard the document as genuine, another third denounce it as a sham, and the others, after studying and restudying the document, frankly concede that they are uncertain.

Many of Wang's closest associates examined the document before its publication, decided it was surely not written by him, and urged Chin not to release it. Some of these men are certainly in an excellent position to testify to the authenticity of the document, notably Ho Ping-hsien and Li Sheng-wu. Ho, who was a confidant of both Ch'en Kung-po and Wang for some twenty years, is a diligent student of Wang's writings, which he has been carefully compiling and analyzing for many years. Li, another long-time associate of Wang's, is still close enough to Wang's children to be called "Uncle." Both men vehemently and categorically rule out any possibility of the alleged will being written or even authorized by Wang. In both style and content, they say, it betrays a hand that is not Wang's. They also cannot believe that the existence of such a document could have escaped the notice of someone like Ch'en Kung-po, who traveled to Japan to be at Wang's side two or three times in his last months. And they believe that as close as they were to Ch'en, he would surely have informed them of the will. They concede that they are at a loss to explain the motives of the real author and disclaim any knowledge of his identity. However, when pressed to reveal their "best guess," they offer one name with guarded reservation—that of Lung Yü-sheng, a poet of some eminence, now deceased. Lung, whose poetry was admired by Mao Tse-tung as well as Wang, tutored Wang's children and was known to have a writing style much like his. (Interviews with Ho and Li, March 1970.)

One month after the alleged will was printed, Chin Hsiung-pai published an article in the same journal presenting the views of believers (including himself) and disbelievers. In it Chin writes (in what is plainly an understatement) that Wang's eldest son, Wang Meng-chin, was dubious about the authenticity of the will. (Ho and Li assert that Wang's entire family not only rejects the will but begged that it not be published.) Chin reported Wang Meng-chin as marshaling several arguments against the document: he was with his father almost constantly in his last months and could not possibly have been unaware of the dictation of a five-thousand-word will; in any case, if his father had chosen to dictate a will, he would not have dictated it to Madame Wang but to Meng-chin himself; the "anniversary of my death" phrase in the opening statement does not ring true, for Wang Ching-wei was always a revolutionary spirit and abhorred anything that smacked of formality, especially if it was directed at himself or his family, and would never have encouraged anyone to remember the anniversary of his death; since it was not Wang's style to explain or justify his behavior, any will he left would have been concerned with guiding his followers' future steps rather than explaining his own past actions; and, finally,

Meng-chin himself had asked his mother to urge his father to write a will, but she had declined to do so in order to avoid "upsetting" her ailing husband.

Chin Hsiung-pai rejects Meng-chin's arguments, declaring that both the style and the content of the document reveal Wang's hand. The charge that Wang could not have written it without others knowing about it is easily answered, Chin says, by assuming Wang wrote it before his trip to Japan. As the end drew near, he simply made certain last-minute revisions and dated the document October 1944. Indeed, Meng-chin himself seems to concede that the will might have been written in late 1943 while his father was recuperating in Peiping. (Chin, "Wang Ching-wei," 160: 4.)

Hu Lan-ch'eng, Political Vice Minister in the Ministry of Propaganda and a long-time Wang associate, acknowledges that Meng-chin was "extremely unhappy" about the publication of the will, but argues that "it can by no means be regarded as a forgery." According to Hu, Wang's close friend Yen Chia-pao told him that "without a doubt there are many points of historical truth in the will." (Correspondence with Hu, 1970.)

A Japanese translation of the will was published by the *Mainichi* newspapers on April 29, 1964. On May 2 *Mainichi* followed up with the comments of two of Wang's closest Japanese associates, Imai Takeo and Shimizu Tōzō. Both accepted the will as genuine without reservation, Imai referring to it as a "great historical discovery." Little comment has been made on the will in America. Professor Lin Han-sheng, of Sonoma State College, has noted that though the authenticity of the document is still debated by scholars, he has "not been able to uncover any valid reasons for considering it a forgery" and finds the style of the document "distinctively Wang's own." (See his *Wang Ching-wei and the Japanese Peace Efforts*, pp. 13–14.)

In preparing this study, I have relied largely on the recollections, both oral and written, of the chief participants in the various Sino-Japanese collaboration movements. I believe that the most useful and reliable source in this regard is Gen. Imai Takeo. Though Imai had a very personal and extensive involvement in the collaboration movements, there is little evidence of bias in his works. He is not only candid but writes with a professional historian's concern for detail and documentation. The same care for precision is to be found in Col. Horiba Kazuo's long study (780 pages, plus a volume of statistics). Horiba, however, was not as directly involved in the collaboration projects as Imai, especially after 1939. Moreover, he is often preoccupied with showing how he and some of his fellow officers on the Army General Staff constantly endeavored to find a "moral" solution to the Sino-Japanese crisis. It is not that one doubts him; it is only that one never knows precisely what "moral" means.*

Gen. Kagesa Sadaaki's "Sozorogaki" is another major source on the development of the Wang Ching-wei movement. Written in 1943 when Kagesa was stationed at Rabaul, "Sozorogaki" gives us a clear insight into the motives and

---

* "Moral" thus appears to be an "amuletic" word, to use the terminology of Tsurumi Shunsuke in his classic study—a word that asserts nothing but is chosen and used for its protective qualities much as one uses an amulet. Tsurumi's work first appeared in 1946 (*Shisō no kagaku*, issue no. 1). An English translation was published in the *Bulletin of the School of Oriental and African Studies* (18 [1956]: 514–33).

frustrations of one of the Japanese leaders of the Wang movement. Kagesa begins his "Sozorogaki"—his rambling discourse—with the disclaimer that having no access to records, he is forced to dictate the work from memory. As a result, it contains numerous inaccuracies, chiefly in dating. On the whole, however, these errors do not detract from the value of the long document. Portions of the "Sozorogaki" were included in the deposition Kagesa gave at the International Military Tribunal for the Far East, but he carefully excluded those sections that put the Imperial Army in an unfavorable light. For example, in a long passage in "Sozorogaki," he gives a detailed account of conversations Wang Ching-wei held with various Government leaders during his June 1939 trip to Tokyo, including the talk in which War Minister Itagaki outlined what the policy of *bunji gassaku* held in store for China. Passages like this were deftly omitted by Kagesa at the postwar trials. (Cf. "Sozorogaki," p. 371, with Kagesa deposition, p. 15.) Unfortunately, "Sozorogaki," though vastly superior to the trial documentation, is also a condensation. I am informed by a source close to the General's family that they insisted on deletions in the original manuscript and will not permit publication of the full document until some time in the future. The *Gendai shi shiryō* version, unfortunately, does not even indicate where the excisions were made.

The memoirs of Nishi Yoshiaki and Inukai Ken, though valuable, are flawed by the extensive quoting of long three- and four-way conversations that occurred in 1938. Since neither tape recorders nor stenographers were present at these conversations, one must assume both authors have taken a certain license. Kao Tsung-wu, for one, not only denies that he said certain things Nishi attributes to him, but states flatly that whole conversations were created out of thin air. (Interview, 1969.) Nevertheless, both Nishi and Inukai seem to have kept journals, and where their accounts can be cross-checked for accuracy, they square reasonably well. Nishi's account is especially detailed, to the point of giving room numbers in Hong Kong's Repulse Bay Hotel, a favorite rendezvous for the "third force" members in 1938. (The management of the hotel, unmindful of the historical importance of Room 10, has long since changed the room-numbering system, thus denying at least one historian the pleasure of reliving a small slice of history.)

Inukai was a polished and respected writer before he began to play a role in the Wang movement, and his experienced hand is reflected in the gracious and urbane prose style of his *Yōsukō wa ima mo nagarete iru*. None of the members of the Wang movement give us the ambiance of that movement so successfully as the cosmopolitan yet very Eastern Inukai. A word of warning: the reader of *Yōsukō* should know at the outset that Inukai insists on using aliases for two of the chief figures in his account "because of his fear of embarrassing" the principals (*Yōsukō*, p. 5). I doubt that I am breaching any professional code by identifying Kao Tsung-wu as Inukai's K'ang Shao-wu and T'ao Hsi-sheng as his Chuang Chih-cheng. Why Inukai should attempt to disguise the names of the two is a little puzzling, for he presents very flattering accounts of their motives. (Both men, it will be recalled, supported Wang's defection from Chungking and then abandoned the movement in 1940.) It is all the more puzzling because K'ang (Kao) reportedly indicated that Inukai and Matsumoto Shigeharu were the only ones who knew the real story of his involvement in the peace movement and asked Inukai to "write the truth about it" before Kao died (*Yōsukō*, p. 18).

The memoirs of Chinese participants in the collaboration movements that I have found most useful are T'ao Hsi-sheng's "Luan-liu" and Chin Hsiung-pai's five-volume study, *Wang cheng-ch'üan ti k'ai-ch'ang yü shou-ch'ang*. "Luan-liu" (the title is derived from an ancient song in which the death of a man who had tried to cross a treacherous stream is mourned by his widow) is brief and pointed. Chin's work, by contrast, is a thousand pages long and discursive. Its interest derives mainly from Chin's direct personal involvement with many of the events and figures he writes about, especially Chou Fo-hai. Like all of the Chinese accounts of the Wang movement, Chin's suffers from a lack of documentation, a deficiency that will not be corrected to any significant degree until the Kuomintang regime in Taiwan releases the material in its archives on the sensitive issue of wartime collaboration. Still, Chin does his best to compensate for this deficiency by doggedly seeking out available documentary sources and interviewing survivors of the collaboration movements as well as combing his own memory. The result is a collection of firsthand accounts of fascinating episodes and personalities with the accent on intrigue, personal rivalries, and sensational exposé. Chin does not recoil from passing judgment on the motives of the men he writes about, and his is the work to consult for a counterpoint to Inukai's flattering portrayal of Kao and T'ao, for whom Chin has only the greatest contempt.

In addition, mention should be made of Chou Fo-hai's diary. Though I cite a Japanese translation, the original Chinese version was published in Hong Kong in 1955: *Chou Fo-hai jih-chi*. Chou was a conscientious diarist, and it is regrettable that only the 1940 portion of his journal has been published. Near the end of the war he placed seven volumes of his diary, covering the years from 1939 to 1945, in a Shanghai bank. These volumes were confiscated by Nationalist intelligence authorities, who refused to turn them over to Chou's widow, undoubtedly in the fear that they would reveal the extent of the clandestine contacts between Kuomintang officials and members of the Wang Government. One of the Nationalist officials in charge of the "Office of Traitors' Property," a certain Teng Pao-kuang, eventually defected to the Communists, and it is believed that the leak of the 1940 volume can be traced to him. (Boorman, *Biographical Dictionary*, 2: 409.)

To move from the subject of memoirs and firsthand accounts to documentary sources, let me say at the start that the 1960's saw the publication in Japan of an immense body of historical material, sparing the student of the Sino-Japanese War untold hours of work in the Foreign Ministry and Senshishitsu archives. This publications bonanza is all the more gratifying because it is so difficult to gain access to these collections—normally a matter of competency and "connections." For the young scholar especially, the development of the right connections (*tsukiai*) can be a challenging introduction to Japanese social mores, but it can also take eleven months of a twelve-month research grant to get the right doors to open.

The most useful of the documentary sources published in the last decade are the five *Nitchū sensō* volumes (3,600 pages) in the *Gendai shi shiryō* series of the Misuzu Publishing Company; the two *Gaimushō no hyakunen* volumes

(2,700 pages) of the Hara Publishing Company; the documentary annex (Vol. 8; 600 pages) to the *Taiheiyō sensō e no michi* series; and the seven volumes of Misuzu and Hara containing the diaries and papers of Ishiwara Kanji, Ugaki Kazushige, Sugiyama Gen, and Okamura Yasuji (over 4,000 pages). It will be a long time before Western scholars have exhausted these valuable historical documents, none of which, alas, is indexed.

One important source of information on the Sino-Japanese wartime collaboration that has not yet found its way into print is the collection of documents I refer to as the "Yano papers." Only recently discovered, these papers are the notes and summaries of conversations prepared by Yano Seiki, a Foreign Ministry official. Most pertain to the negotiations on the Basic Treaty in mid-1940. They are now preserved at the Kokumin Gaikō Kaikan in Tokyo, a semiofficial agency of the Foreign Ministry.

There is no comprehensive treatment of Sino-Japanese wartime collaboration in any language. The Usui and Hata contributions to Volume 4 of the *Taiheiyō sensō e no michi* series, however, are a good place to begin. The cutoff date in the case of both studies is 1941; for the post-1941 period the scholar is virtually on his own, though the studies of Akashi Yoji may rectify this discrepancy in the near future. The unpublished doctoral dissertation of Lin Han-sheng, *Wang Ching-wei and the Japanese Peace Efforts*, contains a wealth of information on the subject of Sino-Japanese collaboration, but here too the principal focus is on the years before 1941.

For further bibliographical guidance, one should first consult Frederick W. Mote's *Japanese-Sponsored Governments in China, 1937–1945*. Though published almost twenty years ago, this model of bibliographical thoroughness will always be useful; it is well arranged and extensively annotated. For a discussion of Chinese sources, including the writings of Wang Ching-wei, Ch'en Kung-po, and Chou Fo-hai, the reader is referred to the first chapter of Lin Han-sheng's dissertation. Finally, an extensive bibliography of Wang's writings, compiled by Ho Ping-hsien, is on file in the Lou Henry Hoover Library at Stanford, Calif.

Bibliography

Abend, Hallett. *My Life in China, 1926–1941*. New York, 1943.

Ahlers, John. "A Made-in-Japan 'Genghis Khan,'" *China Weekly Review*, Feb. 4, 1939, pp. 302–3.

Akashi Yoji. "Japan's Peace Maneuvers with the Chungking Government." Unpub. manuscript.

————. *The Nanyang Chinese National Salvation Movement, 1937–1941*. Research Publication No. 5, East Asian Series. Lawrence, Kans., 1970.

American Information Committee. [Publications.] Shanghai, 1938–40. Especially No. 5, "China Exploitation Company Unlimited: A First Hand Study of Japanese Economic Cooperation," Aug. 1939; and No. 8, "Japan's Puppets on the Chinese Stage," Jan. 1940.

Aoki Tokuzō. *Taiheiyō sensō zenshi* (Historical Background to the Pacific War). 6 vols. Tokyo, 1953.

Ba Maw. *Breakthrough in Burma: Memoirs of a Revolution, 1939–1946*. New Haven, Conn. 1968.

Baba Akira, "Kōain setchi mondai" (Some Questions Concerning the Establishment of the Kōain), *Gaimushō chōsa geppō*, 7 (1966): 46–83.

Barger, H. H. "Marshal Wu P'ei-fu," *China Journal* (Shanghai), 30 (1939): 133–38.

Barrett, David D. *Dixie Mission: The United States Army Observer Group in Yenan, 1944*. China Research Monographs, no. 6. Berkeley, Calif., 1970.

Belden, Jack. *China Shakes the World*. New York, 1949.

Benda, Harry J. *The Crescent and the Rising Sun*. The Hague, 1958.

————, James K. Irikura, and Kōichi Kishi. *Japanese Military Administration in Indonesia: Selected Documents*. New Haven, Conn., [1965].

Bisson, T. A. *Japan in China*. New York, 1938.

Boorman, Howard L., ed. *Biographical Dictionary of Republican China*. 4 vols. New York, 1967–71.

————. "Wang Ching-wei: A Political Profile," in Hsüeh Chün-tu, ed., *Revolutionary Leaders in Modern China*, pp. 295–319. New York, 1971.

Borg, Dorothy. *The United States and the Far Eastern Crisis of 1933–1938*. Cambridge, Mass., 1964.

Bose, Subhas Chandra. *The Indian Struggle, 1935–1942*. Calcutta, 1952.

Boyle, John H. "An Incident Becomes a War: Konoe's *Aite ni Sezu* Declaration," *Japan Interpreter* (Tokyo), 6 (1970): 309–25.

————. *Japan's Puppet Regimes in China, 1937–1941*. Ph.D. Diss., Stanford, Calif., 1968.

———. "The Road to Sino-Japanese Collaboration: The Background to the Defection of Wang Ching-wei," *Monumenta Nipponica*, 25 (1970): 267–301.

Brière, O., *Fifty Years of Chinese Philosophy, 1898–1948*, New York, 1965.

Butow, Robert J. C. *Tojo and the Coming of the War*. Princeton, N.J., 1961.

Chao Shu-li. *Changes in Li Village*. Peking, 1958.

Ch'en, Jerome. "The Last Emperor of China," *Bulletin of the School of Oriental and African Studies*, 28 (1965): 337–55.

———. "The Left Wing Kuomintang: A Definition," *Bulletin of the School of Oriental and African Studies*, 25 (1962): 557–73.

Ch'en Kung-po. "The Basis of Sino-Japanese Cooperation," in T'ang Leang-li, ed., *Fundamentals of National Salvation*, pp. 273–96. Shanghai, 1942.

———. *The Communist Movement in China*. Ed. with introd. by C. Martin Wilbur. Columbia Univ. East Asian Institute Series, No. 7, Sept. 1960. (Originally submitted as M. A. thesis, Columbia Univ., 1924.)

Chiang Kai-shek. *Soviet Russia in China: A Summing-up at Seventy*. Rev. abridged ed. New York, 1965.

Chin Hsiung-pai [Chu Tzu-chia]. *Dōsei kyōshi no jittai* (The Realities of Co-existence). Trans. from the Chinese by Ikeda Atsunori. Tokyo, 1960. This is a revised and slightly abridged version of the following entry.

———. *Wang cheng-ch'üan ti k'ai-ch'ang yü shou-ch'ang* (The Beginning and the End of the Drama of the Wang Regime). 5 vols. Hong Kong, 1959–64.

———. "Wang Ching-wei tui-kuoshih i-shu shou-tz'u fa-piao" (The First Publication of Wang Ching-wei's Last Testament to His Country), *Ch'un-ch'iu* (Hong Kong), 159–60 (Feb.–March 1964): 2–15, 2–4.

China Institute of International Affairs, ed. *A Collection of Documents with a Prefatory Note*. Shanghai, 1939. Especially No. 2, pp. 1–7, Wang Ching-wei, "Sino-Japanese Relationships: My Conception and Aims"; No. 2, pp. 8–13, Wang Ching-wei, "Towards the Realization of Peace with Honour"; No. 3, pp. 1–13, "Manifesto of the Sixth National Congress of the ["Orthodox"] Kuomintang"; No. 3, pp. 21–35, Wang Ching-wei, "The Aims of the Peace Movement"; and No. 4, pp. 1–20, Chou Fo-hai, "Retrospect and Prospect."

China, National Government, Ministry of Education, comp. *Agreements Between Wang Ching-wei and Japan*. Chungking, 1943.

———, Ministry of Information, comp. *China Handbook, 1937–1943*. New York, 1943.

———. *The Collected Wartime Messages of Generalissimo Chiang Kai-shek, 1937–1945*. 2 vols. New York, 1946.

Chou Fo-hai. "Retrospect and Prospect," in China Institute of International Affairs, ed., listed above.

———. *Shū Fukkai nikki* (Diaries of Chou Fo-hai). Ed. and trans. from the Chinese by Yoshida Tōyū. Tokyo, 1953.

Chu Tzu-chia (pseud.). See Chin Hsiung-pai.

Clifford, Nicholas R. *Retreat from China: British Policy in the Far East, 1937–1941*. Seattle, Wash., 1967.

Clubb, O. Edmund. *Twentieth Century China*. New York, 1964.

Cohen, Warren. "Who Fought the Japanese in Hunan? Some Views of China's War Effort," *Journal of Asian Studies*, 27 (1967): 111–15.

Conroy, F. Hilary. "Japan's War in China: Historical Parallel to Vietnam?," *Pacific Affairs*, 43 (1970): 61–72.

———. "Japan's War in China: An Ideological Somersault," *Pacific Historical Review*, 21 (1952): 367–79.

Coox, Alvin D. "Effects of Attrition on National War Effort: The Japanese Army Experience in China, 1937–1938," *Military Affairs*, 32 (1968): 57–62.

———. *Year of the Tiger*. Tokyo, 1964.

Craigie, Sir Robert. *Behind the Japanese Mask*. London, 1946.

Crowley, James B. "Japanese Army Factionalism in the Early 1930's," *Journal of Asian Studies*, 21 (1962): 309–26.

———. *Japan's China Policy, 1931–1938*. Ph.D. Diss., Univ. of Mich., 1960.

———. *Japan's Quest for Autonomy*. Princeton, N.J., 1966.

———. "A New Deal for Japan and Asia: One Road to Pearl Harbor," in James B. Crowley, ed., *Modern East Asia: Essays in Interpretation*, pp. 235–64. New York, 1970.

Daihon'ei rikugun-bu (Army Division of the Imperial General Headquarters). Bōei-chō, Bōei kenshūsho, au. and comp. 2 vols. Tokyo, 1967–68.

Documents on German Foreign Policy, 1918–1945: From the Archives of the German Foreign Ministry. Series D. 9 vols. Washington, D.C., 1949–56.

Doihara Kenji. "Taishi kokumin kōryō no konkan" (The Basis of Japan's Policy towards China), *Chūō kōron* 614 (Nov. 1938): 116–24.

Donald, W. H. "From Chiang's Headquarters," *Asia* (New York), 39 (1939): 193–96.

Dull, Paul S., and Michael Takaaki Umemura. *The Tokyo Trials: A Functional Index to the Proceedings of the International Military Tribunal for the Far East*. Ann Arbor, Mich., 1962.

Durkee, Travers A. *Wang Ching-wei and Japan*. M.A. thesis, Stanford Univ., 1949.

Duus, Peter. "Nagai Ryūtarō: The Tactical Dilemmas of Reform," in Albert M. Craig and Donald H. Shively, eds., *Personality in Japanese History*, pp. 339–424. Berkeley, Calif., 1970.

———. "Nagai Ryūtarō and the 'White Peril,' 1905–1944," *Journal of Asian Studies*, 31 (1971): 41–48.

Eguchi Bokuro et al. *Taiheiyō sensō shi* (History of the Pacific War). 6 vols. Tokyo, 1952.

Eto Shinkichi. "An Outline of Formosan History," in Mark Mancall, ed., *Formosa Today*, pp. 43–58. New York, 1964.

Fairbank, John K. *The United States and China*. 2d ed. New York, 1958.

——— and Masataka Banno. *The Japanese Studies of Modern China*. Tokyo, 1955.

Feis, Herbert. *The Road to Pearl Harbor*. Princeton, N.J., 1950.

Fishel, Wesley R. "A Japanese Peace Maneuver in 1944," *Far Eastern Quarterly*, 13 (1949): 387–97.

Foreign Relations of the United States: Diplomatic Papers. See United States, Department of State.

Friend, Theodore. *Between Two Empires: The Ordeal of the Philippines, 1929–1946*. New Haven, Conn., 1965.

Fujiwara Akira. *Gunji shi* (History of the Military). Tokyo, 1961.

Gaimushō. *Nihon gaikō nenpyō narabini shuyō bunsho, 1840–1945* (A Chronological Table of Japanese Foreign Policy and Important Documents). 2 vols. Tokyo, 1955.

Gaimushō no hyakunen (One Hundred Years of the Ministry of Foreign Affairs). Gaimushō hyakunen shi hensan iinkai, eds. 2 vols. Tokyo, 1969.

Gasster, Michael. *Chinese Intellectuals and the Revolution of 1911.* Seattle, Wash., 1968.

————. "Reform and Revolution in China's Political Modernization," in Mary C. Wright, ed., *China in Revolution: The First Phase, 1900–1913,* pp. 67–96. New Haven, Conn., 1968.

Gendai shi shiryō (Modern Historical Materials). Misuzu shobō, eds. 43 vols. Tokyo, 1962–70. Especially Vols. 1–3, *Soruge jiken* (The Sorge Affair); Vols. 8–10, 12–13, *Nitchū sensō* (The Sino-Japanese War); and Vol. 37, *Daihon'ei* (Imperial Headquarters).

Germany, Foreign Ministry. See *Documents on German Foreign Policy.*

Gillin, Donald G. *Warlord: Yen Hsi-shan in Shansi Province, 1911–1949.* Princeton, N.J., 1967.

Giniger, Henry. "Petain—of Verdun, of Vichy, of History," *New York Times Magazine,* Nov. 16, 1964, pp. 96–99.

Goette, John. *Japan Fights for Asia.* New York, 1943.

Great Britain, Foreign Office. *Documents on British Foreign Policy, 1919–1939.* 2d series, Vols. 8–9. London, 1960–65.

Grew, Joseph C. *Ten Years in Japan.* New York, 1944.

Gunther, John. *Inside Asia.* New York, 1939.

Hackett, Roger. "The Military," in Robert E. Ward and Dankwart A. Rustow, eds., *Political Modernization in Japan and Turkey,* pp. 328–88. Princeton, N.J., 1964.

Hahn, Emily. *China to Me.* New York, 1944.

————. *The Soong Sisters.* New York, 1941.

Han Suyin. *Birdless Summer.* New York, 1968.

————. *A Mortal Flower.* New York, 1966.

Hangin, Gombojab (John G. Hangin). "Prince Demchugdongrub (De Wang), Leading Inner Mongolian Nationalist—Reminiscences by a Former Administrative Assistant." Unpub. manuscript based on a paper presented at the Association for Asian Studies meeting, Washington, D.C., March 29, 1971.

Harada Kumao. *Saionji kō to seikyoku* (Prince Saionji and the Political Situation). 9 vols. Tokyo, 1952–56.

Haruke, Keiin (Yasutane). *Bōryaku no Shanhai* (Shanghai Intrigue). Tokyo, 1951.

Hata Ikuhito. "Nitchū sensō no gunjiteki tenkai" (Military Developments in the Sino-Japanese War), in *Taiheiyō sensō e no michi,* 4: 3–110, listed below.

————. *Nitchū sensō shi* (History of the Sino-Japanese War). Tokyo, 1961.

Hattori Takushirō. *Dai Tōa sensō* (The Great East Asian War). 4th (one-vol.) ed. Tokyo, 1966.

Hayashi Fusao et al. "Dai Tōa sensō o naze minaosu no ka?" (Why Are We Reassessing the Great East Asian War?), *Ushio,* Feb. 1964, pp. 66–94.

Hayashi Saburō (in collaboration with Alvin D. Coox). *Kōgun: The Japanese Army in the Pacific War.* Quantico, Va., 1959.

Hewins, Ralph. *Quisling: Prophet Without Honour.* London, 1965.

Hillam, Ray C. "Counterinsurgency: Lessons from the Early Chinese and Japanese Experience against the Communists," *Orbis* (Univ. of Penna.) 12 (1968): 226–46.

Himerareta Shōwa shi (A Secret History of the Shōwa Era). *Chisei*, eds. Special issue. Dec. 1956.

Hirano Reiji. *Manshū no imbōsha: Kōmoto Daisaku no unmeiteki no ashioto* (The Manchurian Intriguer: The Fateful Trail of Kōmoto Daisaku). Tokyo, 1959.

Ho Ping-hsien. Correspondence with author. 1969–71.

Horiba Kazuo. *Shina jihen sensō shidō shi* (Operational History of the China Incident). 2 vols. Tokyo, 1962.

Hu Lan-ch'eng. Correspondence with author. 1970.

Hull, Cordell. *Memoirs.* 2 vols. New York, 1948.

Ike Nobutaka. *Japan's Decision for War.* Stanford, Calif., 1967.

Imai Takeo. *Kindai no sensō: Chūgoku to no arasoi* (Modern Wars: The Struggles with China). Tokyo, 1966.

———. *Shina jihen no kaisō* (Reminiscences of the China Incident). Tokyo, 1964.

———. *Shōwa no bōryaku* (Shōwa Intrigues). Tokyo, 1967.

———. "Tai-Ka wahei kōsaku shi" (Peace Operations against China), in *Himerareta Shōwa shi*, pp. 250–58, listed above.

——— and Shimizu Tōzō. "Ō Chōmei kōsaku kaisō" (Recollections of the Wang Chao-ming Operation), in Tokyo TV Channel 12 News Bureau, eds., *Shōgen: Watakushi no Shōwa shi* (Eyewitnesses' Accounts of Shōwa History), 2: 268–77. Tokyo, 1969. (From a television broadcast on Nov. 18, 1966.)

Imamura Hitoshi. *Imamura Taishō kaisōroku* (Memoirs of General Imamura). 4 vols. Tokyo, 1960.

Inaba Masao, ed. *Okamura Yasuji Taishō* (General Okamura Yasuji). Tokyo, 1970.

International Military Tribunal for the Far East. Tokyo, 1946–49. Analyses of documentary evidence; documents; exhibits; and *Record of the Proceedings.*

Inukai Ken. *Yōsukō wa ima mo nagarete iru* (The Yangtze Still Flows). Tokyo, 1961.

Iriye Akira. *Across the Pacific: An Inner History of American-East Relations.* New York, 1967.

———. *After Imperialism: The Search for a New Order in the Far East, 1921–1931.* Cambridge, Mass., 1965.

———. "Japanese Imperialism and Aggression: Reconsiderations" (review article), *Journal of Asian Studies*, 22 (1963): 103–13.

———. "Japan's Foreign Policies between the Wars—Sources and Interpretations" (review article), *Journal of Asian Studies*, 26 (1967): 677–82.

Isaacs, Harold R. *The Tragedy of the Chinese Revolution.* 2d ed. Stanford, Calif., 1961.

Ishida Takeshi. "Beyond the Traditional Concept of Peace in Different Cultures," *Journal of Peace Research* (Oslo), Feb. 1969, pp. 133–45.

Ishii Itarō. *Gaikōkan no isshō* (The Life of a Diplomat). Tokyo, 1960.

———. "Ikensho" (Statement of Opinion), in *Gaimushō no hyakunen*, 2: 315–

37, listed above. The formal title of the "Ikensho" is "Kongo no jihen tai-saku ni tsuite no kōan" (Some Ideas Concerning the Handling of the Present Situation).

Ishin seifu gaishi hensan iinkai. *Chūka minkoku ishin seifu gaishi* (An Informal History of the Reformed Government of the Republic of China). Tokyo, 1940. ("For private distribution.")

Ishiwara Kanji. See entries under Tsunoda Jun, ed.

Israel, John. *Student Nationalism in China, 1927–37.* Stanford, Calif., 1966.

Itō Kinjirō. "Toku-Ō no kinjō to shinsei Mōko" (Prince Teh's Present Situation and the New Mongolia), *Chūō kōron,* 627 (Nov. 1939): 198–206.

Jansen, Marius B. *The Japanese and Sun Yat-sen.* Cambridge, Mass., 1954.

———. "Japanese Views of China during the Meiji Period," in Albert Feuerwerker et al., eds., *Approaches to Modern Chinese History,* pp. 163–89. Berkeley, Calif., 1967.

———. "Modernization and Foreign Policy in Meiji Japan," in Robert E. Ward, ed., *Political Development in Modern Japan,* pp. 149–88. Princeton, N.J., 1968.

Japan, Ministry of Foreign Affairs. *See* Gaimushō.

Johnson, Chalmers. *An Instance of Treason: Ozaki Hotsumi and the Sorge Spy Ring.* Stanford, Calif., 1964.

———. *Peasant Nationalism and Communist Power.* Stanford, Calif., 1962.

Jones, F. C. *Japan's New Order in East Asia: Its Rise and Fall, 1937–1945.* New York, 1954.

Jōno Hiroshi. "Sansei dokuritsu senki" (A Record of the Independence War in Shansi), in Aochi Shin, ed., *Tairiku o kakeru yume* (Dreams of the Continent), pp. 265–304. Tokyo, 1969.

Kagesa Sadaaki. International Military Tribual for the Far East, Defense Document No. 1282 (Kagesa deposition).

———. International Military Tribunal for the Far East, Exhibit CE 2721 ("Record of the Proceedings of the Commission Taking the Deposition of Kagesa Sadaaki at First National Hospital, Tokyo, Japan, May 22–23, 1947").

———. "Sozorogaki" (A Rambling Discourse), in *Gendai shi shiryō,* 13: 349–98, listed above. (Written in 1943.)

Kahin, George McT. "Indonesia," in G. M. Kahin, ed., *Major Governments of Asia,* pp. 535–700. Ithaca, N.Y., 1963.

Kaji Wataru, ed. *Hansen shiryō* (Antiwar Materials). Tokyo, 1964.

Kamata Sawaiichirō. *Shōrai seidan* (Tales Whispered Among the Pines). Tokyo, 1951.

Kamio Shigeru. "Wang Ching-wei and the Peace Movement," *Contemporary Japan,* 8 (1939): 1061–1069.

———. "Wang Ching-wei vs. Chungking," *Contemporary Japan,* 9 (1940): 378–86.

Kao Tsung-wu. Correspondence with author, 1969–71.

Kase Toshikazu. *Journey to the Missouri.* New Haven, Conn., 1950.

Kawabe Torashirō. "Kawabe Torashirō shōshō kaisō ōdōroku" (Records of an Interview [conducted by Prince Tsuneyoshi] with Major General Kawabe Torashirō), in *Gendai shi shiryō,* 12: 401–56, listed above. (The interview was conducted in 1940.)

Kawakami, K. K. *Japan Speaks on the Sino-Japanese Crisis.* New York, 1932.

Kazami Akira. *Konoe naikaku* (The Konoe Cabinets). Tokyo, 1951.

Keene, Donald. "Japanese Writers and the Greater East Asia War," *Journal of Asian Studies,* 23 (1964): 209–25.

———. "The Sino-Japanese War of 1894–95 and Its Cultural Effects in Japan," in Donald H. Shively, ed., *Tradition and Modernization in Japanese Culture,* pp. 121–75. Princeton, N.J., 1971.

Kerr, George H. *Formosa Betrayed.* Boston, 1965.

Koentjaraningrat. "Indonesian Image of Japan," *Bulletin* (of the International House of Japan), Dec. 1969, pp. 1–23. (From a lecture given Nov. 4, 1969.)

Konoe Fumimaro. "Memoirs of Prince Konoye," in United States Congress, 79th Congress, Joint Committee on the Investigation of the Pearl Harbor Attack, ed., *Pearl Harbor Attack, Hearings Before the Joint Committee on the Investigation of the Pearl Harbor Attack,* exhibit 173, pp. 3985–4029. Washington, D.C., 1945–46.

———. *Ushinawareshi seiji: Konoe Fumimaro Kō no shuki* (A Lost Political Cause: The Notes of Prince Konoe Fumimaro). Tokyo, 1946. Some claim the author of this book is Ushiba Tomohiko, Konoe's personal secretary.

Koo, T. K. "Economic Documents Relating to the Genesis of the Japanese-Sponsored Regime in North China," *Far Eastern Quarterly,* 6 (1946): 65–77.

Kublin, Hyman. "The Evolution of Japanese Colonialism," *Comparative Studies in Society and History,* 2 (1959): 67–84.

Kung Te-po. *Wang Chao-ming hsiang-ti mai-kuo mi-shih* (A Secret History of Wang Chao-ming's Surrender and Treason). N.p., n.d. [? Taiwan, 1963].

Kurihara Ken. *Man-Mō seisaku shi no ichimen* (Aspects of Japanese Policy Toward Manchuria and Mongolia). Tokyo, 1966.

Lattimore, Owen. *Studies in Frontier History.* London, 1962.

Laurel, Jose P. *War Memoirs of Dr. Jose P. Laurel.* Manila, 1962.

Lebra, Joyce. "Japanese Policy and the Indian National Army," *Asian Studies* (Manila), 7 (1969): 31–49.

Levenson, Joseph R. *Confucian China and Its Modern Fate: The Problem of Monarchical Decay.* Berkeley, Calif., 1964.

Li Ngoc. *The Later Career of Wang Ching-wei with Special Reference to His National Government's Cooperation with Japan, 1938–1945.* M.A. thesis, Hong Kong Univ., 1966.

Lin Han-sheng. "A Case Study of Chinese Collaboration: The Nanking Government, 1940–1945." Unpublished manuscript.

———. *Wang Ching-wei and the Japanese Peace Efforts.* Ph.D. Diss., Univ. of Penna., 1967.

Lin Pai-sheng. "The Peace Movement in China," *People's Tribune,* 27 (1939): 37–42.

Lin, W. Y. "The Sino-Japanese Currency War," *Amerasia,* 3 (1939): 30–36.

Linebarger, Paul M. *The China of Chiang Kai-shek.* Boston, 1941.

Liu, F. F. *A Military History of Modern China.* Princeton, N.J., 1956.

Liu, James T. C. "German Mediation in the Sino-Japanese War," *Journal of Asian Studies,* 8 (1949): 157–71.

Loh, Pichon P. Y. "The Politics of Chiang Kai-shek: A Reappraisal," *Journal of Asian Studies,* 25 (1966): 431–51.

Lu, David. *From the Marco Polo Bridge to Pearl Harbor*. Washington, D.C., 1961.

Maki, John M. *Conflict and Tension in the Far East: Key Documents, 1894–1960*. Seattle, Wash., 1961.

Mancall, Mark. "Taiwan, Island of Resignation and Despair," in Mancall, ed., *Formosa Today*, pp. 1–42.

Mao Tse-tung. *Selected Works of Mao Tse-tung*. 4 vols. Peking, 1961–65.

Maruyama Masao. *Thought and Behaviour in Modern Japanese Politics*. Ed. and trans. by Ivan Morris. London, 1963.

Maruyama Shizuo. *Ushinawaretaru kiroku* (Lost Records). Tokyo, 1950.

Masutani Shōzō. *Kessen kokumin seifu* (The Nationalist Government at War). Tokyo, 1944.

Matsumoto Sannosuke. "The Significance of Nationalism in Modern Japanese Thought: Some Theoretical Problems," *Journal of Asian Studies*, 31 (1971): 49–56.

———. "Yukichi Fukuzawa: His Conception of Civilization and View of Asia," *The Developing Economies* (Tokyo), 5 (1967): 156–90.

Matsumoto Sōkichi. "Shina minshū no dōkō ni tsuite" (Trends Among the Chinese People), *Gaikō jihō*, 846 (Mar. 1, 1940): 107–18.

Maung Maung, ed. *Aung San of Burma*. The Hague, 1962.

Maxon, Yale C. *Control of Japanese Foreign Policy*. Berkeley, Calif., 1957.

Mayo, Marlene J. "Attitudes Toward Asia and the Beginning of Japanese Empire," in Grant Goodman, comp., *Imperial Japan and Asia*, pp. 6–27. New York, 1967.

Mei Ssu-p'ing. "The Price of a Vacillating Policy," *People's Tribune*, 27 (1939): 239–42.

Meng, C. Y. W. "Peace Preservation Committee—Japan's Set-up in North China," *China Weekly Review*, Jan. 1, 1928, pp. 125–26.

Miao Pin. *Wu-te lun* (On the Military Virtues). N.p., 1935.

Michael, Franz. "The Significance of Puppet Governments," *Pacific Affairs*, 12 (1939): 400–412.

———. "What 'Puppets' Mean," *Pacific Affairs*, 12 (1939): 377–85.

Miki Kiyoshi. "The China Affair and Japanese Thought," *Contemporary Japan*, 6 (1938): 601–10.

Miles, Milton E. *A Different Kind of War*. New York, 1967.

Miwa Kimitada. "The Wang Ching-wei Regime and Japanese Efforts to Terminate the China Conflict," in Joseph Roggendorf, ed., *Studies in Japanese Culture: Tradition and Experiment*, pp. 122–42. Tokyo, 1963.

Miyakawa Tōru and Igeta Takeru. "Soho Tokutomi," *The Developing Economies* (Tokyo), 5 (1967): 512–26.

Mori Kyōzō. *Kyokutō kokusai gunji saiban kiroku: mokuroku oyobi sakuin* (Catalog and Index of the International Military Tribunal for the Far East). Tokyo, 1953.

Morishima Morindo. *Imbō, ansatsu, guntō: ichi gaikōkan no kaisō* (Conspiracies, Assassinations, and Swords: The Recollections of a Diplomat). Tokyo, 1946.

Morley, James. "Checklist of Seized Japanese Records in the National Archives," *Far Eastern Quarterly*, 9 (1950): 306–33.

Morris, Ivan. *Nationalism and the Right Wing in Japan*. London, 1960.

Mosley, Leonard. *Hirohito: Emperor of Japan*. New York, 1966.

Mote, Frederick W. "Confucian Eremitism in the Yüan Period," in Arthur F. Wright, ed., *The Confucian Persuasion*, pp. 202–40. Stanford, Calif., 1960.

———. *Japanese-Sponsored Governments in China, 1937–45*. Stanford, Calif., 1954.

Nakamura Toyokazu. "Shirarezaru Ugaki-Kō himitsu kaidan" (The Unknown Secret Talks between Ugaki and [H. H.] Kung), in *Himerareta Shōwa shi*, pp. 261–65, listed above.

Nashimoto Yūhei. *Chūgoku no naka no Nihonjin* (The Japanese in China). Tokyo, 1958.

Nishi Yoshiaki. *Higeki no shōnin: Nikka wahei kōsaku hisshi* (Witness to a Tragedy: A Secret History of the Sino-Japanese Peace Movement). Tokyo, 1962. (Printed for private distribution.)

Nishina Gorō. "Manshūoku no kensetsusha—Ishiwara Kanji to Asahara Kenzō (The Builders of Manchukuo—Ishiwara Kanji and Asahara Kenzō), in *Tenkō*, 3: 160–200, listed below.

Nishitani Shōzō. *Kessen kokumin seifu* (The National Government at War). Tokyo, 1944.

Norman, E. Herbert. *Japan's Emergence as a Modern State*. New York, 1940.

Nu, U. *Burma Under the Japanese*. London, 1954.

Ogata Noboru. "Kōain renraku-bu to yon chōkan" (The Kōain's Liaison Offices and Their Four Officers-in-Charge), *Kaizō*, 21, 4 (April 1939): 292–96.

Ogata Sadako. *Defiance in Manchuria: The Making of Japanese Foreign Policy, 1931–1932*. Berkeley, Calif., 1964.

Ohkura Kimmochi. "The Reconstruction of East Asia and the Soviet Union," *Contemporary Japan*, 8 (1939): 131–34.

Ohno, K. *The Japanese Attempts to Negotiate Peace Between 1937 and 1945, and an Analysis of the Reasons for Their Failure*. B. Litt. Diss., Oxford, 1960–61.

Oka Yoshitake. "Kokuminteki dokuritsu to kokka risei" (National Independence and the Reason of State), in *Kindai Nihon shisō shi kōza* (Studies in Modern Japanese Intellectual History), 8: 9–38. Tokyo, 1961.

Okamura Yasuji. See Inaba Masao.

Okano Masujirō. *Go Haifu* (Wu P'ei-fu). Tokyo, 1939. (Printed for private distribution.)

"Opium Profits in North China," *Asia* (New York), 40 (1940): 551–54. ("By a correspondent in North China.")

Orient Yearbook. Tokyo, 1942.

Ozaki Hotsumi. "Tōa kyōdō-tai no rinen to sono seiritsu no kakkanteki kiso" (The Idea of an 'East Asian Cooperative Body' and the Objective Basis for Its Realization), in Takeuchi Yoshimi, ed., *Ajiya shugi* (Asianism), pp. 322–35. Tokyo, 1963. (Reprinted from *Chūō kōron*, 616 (Jan. 1939): 4–18.)

Payne, Robert. *Chiang Kai-shek*. New York, 1969.

Peck, Graham. *Two Kinds of Time*. Boston, 1950.

Piovesana, Gino K. "Miki Kiyoshi: Representative Thinker of an Anguished Generation," in Joseph Roggendorf, ed., *Studies in Japanese Culture: Tradition and Experiment*, pp. 143–61. Tokyo, 1963.

Powell, John. *My Twenty-five Years in China.* New York, 1945.

Presseisen, Ernest L. *Germany and Japan: A Study in Totalitarian Diplomacy, 1933–1941.* The Hague, 1958.

Pu Yi, Aisin-Gioro (Henry Pu-yi). *From Emperor to Citizen.* 2 vols. Peking, 1964.

Pyle, Kenneth B. *The New Generation in Meiji Japan: Problems of Cultural Identity, 1885–1895.* Stanford, Calif., 1969.

Recto, Claro M. *Three Years of Enemy Occupation.* Manila, 1946.

Reischauer, Edwin O. *The United States and Japan.* 3d ed. Cambridge, Mass., 1965.

Rosinger, Lawrence K. "Wang Ching-wei—The Technique of a Traitor," *Amerasia,* 4 (1940): 271–75.

Roy, Jules. *The Trial of Marshal Pétain.* New York, 1966.

Rōyama Masamichi. *Foreign Policy of Japan, 1914–1939.* Tokyo, 1941.

Saigō Kōsaku. *Ishiwara Kanji.* Tokyo, 1937.

Saionji Kinkazu. "Kizoku no taijō" (Departing the Nobility), in Imai Seiichi, ed., *Shōwa no dōran* (Upheavals of the Shōwa Era), pp. 268–329. Tokyo, 1969.

Sawada Ken. *Wang Chao-ming.* Tokyo, 1939.

Scalapino, Robert A., and George T. Yu. *The Chinese Anarchist Movement.* Berkeley, Calif., 1961.

Schwartz, Benjamin I. "The Chinese Perception of World Order, Past and Present," in John K. Fairbank, ed., *The Chinese World Order,* pp. 276–88. Cambridge, Mass., 1968.

Seidensticker, Edward. *Kafū the Scribbler: The Life and Times of Nagai Kafū, 1879–1959.* Stanford, Calif., 1965.

Seki Hiroharu. "Manshū jihen zenshi" (Prelude to the Manchurian Crisis), in *Taiheiyō sensō e no michi,* 1: 287–440, listed below.

Selden, Mark. *The Yenan Way in Revolutionary China.* Cambridge, Mass., 1971.

Sharman, Lyon. *Sun Yat-sen: His Life and Its Meaning.* New York, 1934.

Shieh, Milton J. T. (Milton Jan-tze Shieh). *The Kuomintang: Selected Historical Documents,* Jamaica, N.Y., 1970.

Shigemitsu Mamoru. *Gaikō kaisōroku* (Diplomatic Reminiscences). Tokyo, 1953.

———. *Shōwa no dōran* (Upheavals of the Shōwa Era). 2 vols. Tokyo, 1952. An abridged English translation exists: *Japan and Her Destiny.* New York, 1958.

Shimada Toshihiko. "Kahoku kōsaku to kokkō chōsei" (North China Activities and the Adjustment of Diplomatic Relations), in *Taiheiyō sensō e no michi,* 3: 3–244.

Shiota Shōbei. " 'Ubawareta' hitobito: senjika no Chōsenjin" (A 'Ravaged' People: The Koreans in World War II), in *Asahi jānaru,* ed., *Shōwa shi no shunkan* (Moments of Shōwa History), 1: 341–50. Tokyo, 1966. My translation of this article is also available in *Japan Interpreter,* 7 (1971): 43–53.

Shirato Ichirō. *Japanese Sources on the History of the Chinese Communist Movement.* Columbia University East Asian Institute Series, No. 2, Nov. 1953.

Shiratori Toshio. "Tairiku seisaku no bunkashiteki igi" (The Significance of Our Continental Policy to Cultural History), *Kaizō*, 19, 11 (Nov. 1937): 76–80.

Shirley, James R. *Political Conflict in the Kuomintang: The Career of Wang Ching-wei to 1932*. Ph.D. Diss., Univ. of Calif. (Berkeley), 1962.

Smedley, Agnes. *The Great Road: The Life and Times of Chu Teh*. New York, 1956.

Snow, Edgar. *The Battle for Asia*. New York, 1941.

————. *The Other Side of the River: Red China Today*. New York, 1961.

Soter, Paul Richard. *Wu P'ei-fu: Case Study of a Chinese Warlord*. Ph.D. Diss., Harvard, 1958.

Spaulding, Robert M., Jr. "Japan's 'New Bureaucrats,' 1932–45," in George M. Wilson, ed., *Crisis Politics in Prewar Japan*, pp. 51–70. Tokyo, 1970.

Steiger, G. Nye. "Japan Fails to End Stalemate," *Events*, 7 (1940): 465–69.

Stein, Guenther. "Economic Notes," *Amerasia*, 3 (1939): 234–40.

Steinberg, David. "Jose P. Laurel: A 'Collaborator' Misunderstood," *Journal of Asian Studies*, 24 (1965): 651–65.

————. *Philippine Collaboration in World War II*. Ann Arbor, Mich., 1967.

Storry, G. R. *The Double Patriots: A Study of Japanese Nationalism*. Boston, 1957.

————. "Konoye Fumimaro, The Last of the Fujiwara," *St. Anthony's Papers*, 7: 9–23. London, 1960.

———— and F. W. Deakin. *The Case of Richard Sorge*. New York, 1966.

Stuart, John Leighton. *Fifty Years in China: The Memoirs of John Leighton Stuart*. New York, 1954.

Suda Teiichi. "Nitchū mondai ni shōgai o kakete" (A Life Spent on the Sino-Japanese Problem), *Sekai*, 207 (March 1963): 264–72.

Sugiyama Gen. *Sugiyama Memo* (Sugiyama Papers). 2 vols. Tokyo, 1967.

Sugiyama Heisuke. "Ugaki shin gaisō" (The New Foreign Minister Ugaki), *Kaizō*, 22 (1938): 113–21.

Sukarno. *Sukarno: An Autobiography* (As Told to Cindy Adams), New York, 1965.

Sun Yat-sen. *China and Japan: Natural Friends—Unnatural Enemies*. Ed. by T'ang Leang-li. Shanghai, 1941.

Taiheiyō sensō e no michi: kaisen gaikō shi (The Road to the Pacific War: A Diplomatic History of the Prewar Years). Nihon kokusai seiji gakkai, Taiheiyō sensō gen'in kenkyū-bu, eds. 8 vols. Tokyo, 1962–63. Especially Vol. 1, *Manshū jihen zen'ya* (The Eve of the Manchurian Incident); Vol. 3, *Nitchū sensō: jō* (The Sino-Japanese War: Part 1); Vol. 4, *Nitchū sensō: ge* (The Sino-Japanese War: Part 2); and Vol. 8, *Bekkan: shiryōhen* (Annex: Collection of Documents).

Takabatake Michitoshi. "Ikkoku shakai shugisha: Sano Manabu to Nabeyama Sadachika" (Advocates of Socialism in One State: Sano Manabu and Nabeyama Sadachika), in *Tenkō*, 1: 164–200, listed below.

Takagi Rikurō. "Wang Ching-wei's Peace Proposal," *Contemporary Japan*, 8 (1939): 134–38.

Takeuchi Yoshimi. "Dai Tōa kyōeiken no rinen to genjitsu" (The Concepts and Realities of the Greater East Asia Co-Prosperity Sphere), *Shisō no kagaku*, 21 (Dec. 1963): 2–19.

Tanaka Kanaye. "The Kuomintang versus the Communist Party," *Contemporary Japan*, 10 (1939): 97–101.

Tanaka Ryūkichi. *Hai-in o tsuku: gumbatsu sennō no jissō* (The Cause of Defeat Revealed: The Truth About Domineering Militarists). Tokyo, 1956.

———. *Nihon gumbatsu antō shi* (A History of Factional Strife Among the Japanese Military). Tokyo, 1947.

T'ang Leang-li. *China, Facts and Fancies.* Shanghai, 1936.

———. *The Puppet State of "Manchukuo."* Shanghai, 1935.

———. *Wang Ching-wei: A Political Biography.* Peiping, 1931.

———, ed. *Fundamentals of National Salvation: A Symposium by Wang Ching-wei and Others.* Shanghai, 1942.

T'ao Hsi-sheng. "Luan-liu" (Cross Currents), in *Chuan-chi wen-hsüeh* (Biographic Literature), 2: 165–94. Taipei, 1964.

———. "Sino-Japanese Economic Relations," *People's Tribune*, 27 (1939): 146–52.

Taylor, George E. *The Struggle for North China.* New York, 1940.

Tenkō (Conversion). Shisō no kagaku kenkyū kai, eds. 3 vols. Tokyo, 1959–62.

Tōa mondai chōsa kai, eds. *Saikin Shina yōjin den* (Biographies of Important People in Recent China). Osaka, 1941.

Tōgō Shigenori. *Jidai no ichimen* (*One Aspect of an Era*). Tokyo, 1952. An abridged English translation exists: *The Cause of Japan.* New York, 1956.

Tong, Hollington K. *Chiang Kai-shek.* Taipei, 1953.

Tsuji Masanobu. "Futari no Dai Tōa shidōsha: Ishiwara Kanji to Ō Chōmei" (Two Leaders of Greater East Asia: Ishiwara Kanji and Wang Chao-ming), in *Himerareta Shōwa shi*, pp. 209–17, listed above.

Tsunoda Jun. "Kaidai" (Bibliographical Notes), in *Taiheiyō sensō e no michi*, 4: 418–26.

———, ed. *Ishiwara Kanji shiryō: kokubō ronsaku* (Historical Materials on Ishiwara Kanji: On National Defense). Tokyo, 1967.

———. *Ishiwara Kanji shiryō: sensō shiron* (Historical Materials on Ishiwara Kanji: On Theories of Battle). Tokyo, 1968.

———, ed. *Ugaki Kazushige nikki* (The Diaries of Ugaki Kazushige). 2 vols. Tokyo, 1968–70.

Tsuru Shigeto. *Essays on the Japanese Economy.* Tokyo, 1958.

Tsurumi Kazuko. *Social Change and the Individual: Japan Before and After Defeat in World War II.* Princeton, N.J., 1970.

Tsurumi Shunsuke. "Yokusan undō no sekkeisha" (The Planners of the Yokusan Movement), in *Tenkō*, 2: 53–120, listed above.

Tuchman, Barbara. *Stilwell and the American Experience in China.* New York, 1971.

Ugaki Kazushige. *Ugaki nikki* (Ugaki Diary). Tokyo, 1954. See also listing under Tsunoda Jun, ed.

United States, Department of State. *Foreign Relations of the United States: Diplomatic Papers.* 1937, Vols. 3, 4; 1938, Vols. 3, 4; 1939, Vols. 3, 4; 1940, Vol. 4; 1941, Vol. 4; 1942, *China*; 1943, *China*; 1944, Vol. 6; and 1945, Vol. 7. Washington, D.C., 1949–69.

———. *Papers Relating to the Foreign Relations of the United States: Japan, 1931–1941.* 2 vols. Washington, D.C., 1943.

————. *United States Relations with China.* Washington, D.C., 1949. (The China White Paper.)

————, Office of Strategic Services, comp. *Biographies of Puppet China.* Mimeo. Honolulu, 1945. (Compiled from short-wave intercepts of Radio Tokyo, 1941–45.)

————. *Programs of Japan in China.* 3 vols. Honolulu, 1945.

————. "The Puppet Governmental Bodies of Occupied North China." Mimeo. N.p., 1945.

Usui Katsumi. "Gen'ei o ou mono: Tōa shinchitsujo" (Pursuing an Illusion: The New Order in East Asia), in *Asahi jānaru,* ed., *Shōwa shi no shunkan* (Moments of Shōwa History), 1: 285–93. Tokyo, 1966. My translation of this article is also available in *Japan Interpreter,* 6 (1970): 326–37.

————. *Nitchū sensō* (The Sino-Japanese War). Tokyo, 1967.

————. "Nitchū sensō no seijiteki tenkai" (Political Developments in the Sino-Japanese War), in *Taiheiyō sensō e no michi,* 4: 113–256, listed above.

————. "Shiryō kaisetsu" (Bibliographic Analysis), intro. to *Gendai shi shiryō,* 9: xxiii–xl, listed above.

Uyehara, Cecil H., comp. *Checklist of Archives in the Japanese Ministry of Foreign Affairs, Tokyo, Japan, 1868–1945; Microfilmed for the Library of Congress, 1949–1951.* Washington, D.C., 1954.

Van Slyke, Lyman P. *Enemies and Friends: The United Front in Chinese Communist History.* Stanford, Calif., 1967.

————, ed. *The Chinese Communist Movement: A Report of the United States War Department.* Stanford, Calif., 1968.

Wang Ching-wei. "The Aims of the Peace Movement," in China Institute of International Affairs, ed., listed above.

————. *China's Problems and Their Solution.* Shanghai, 1934.

————. "Confucius and China's Moral Rehabilitation," in T'ang Leang-li, ed., *Fundamentals of National Salvation,* pp. 261–69. Shanghai, 1942.

————. "The European War and China's Future," *People's Tribune,* 27 (1939): 101–4.

————. "Facts About the Peace Proposals," *People's Tribune,* 27 (1939): 60–67.

————. "Freedom and Equality in the New Order," in T'ang Leang-li, ed., *Fundamentals of National Salvation,* pp. 185–88. Shanghai, 1942. (Wang's New Year's Message, Jan. 1, 1941.)

————. "Guerrilla Warfare on the Scorched Earth," *People's Tribune,* 21 (1938): 209–16.

————. "In Memory of Dr. Tseng Chung-ming," in T'ang Leang-li, ed., *Fundamentals of National Salvation,* pp. 44–49. Shanghai, 1942. (Dated April 6, 1939, Hanoi.)

————. Last testament. See Chin Hsiung-pai, "Wang Ching-wei . . . ," listed above.

————. "Nippon ni yosu: Chūgoku to Tōa" (Leaning on Japan: China and East Asia), *Chūō kōron,* no. 625 (Oct. 1939): 476–80.

————. "Ō shuseki teishutsu oboegaki" (Memorial Presented by Chairman Wang [to the Emperor of Japan]). N.d. Hoover East Asia Library #2991.5/3138.

————. "The Peace Proposals of December 29, 1938," *People's Tribune,* 27

(1939): 55–59. (Wire from Wang to Chiang Kai-shek and members of the KMT Central Executive Committee. Hanoi, Dec. 29, 1938.)

———. *Poems of Wang Ching-wei*. Trans. Seyuan Shu. London, 1938.

———. "Sino-Japanese Relationships," in China Institute of International Affairs, ed., listed above.

———. "Towards the Realization of Peace with Honour," in China Institute of International Affairs, ed., listed above.

———. "The Truth about Resistance," *People's Tribune*, 27 (1939): 68–73.

———. "Why China Should End the War," *People's Tribune*, 27 (1939): 59–60. (Letter from Wang to Standing Committee of the KMT Central Executive Committee. Hanoi, Dec. 28, 1938.)

Wang, Y. C. *Chinese Intellectuals and the West, 1872–1949*. Chapel Hill, N.C., 1966.

———. "Tu Yueh-sheng (1885–1951): A Tentative Political Biography," *Journal of Asian Studies*, 26 (1967): 433–55.

Warner, Geoffrey. "The Decline and Fall of Pierre Laval," *History Today*, 11 (1961): 817–27.

Weile, David. "North China Independence—with Qualifications," *Amerasia*, 4 (1940): 76–82.

White, Theodore H., ed. *The Stilwell Papers*. New York, 1948.

——— and Annalee Jacoby. *Thunder out of China*. New York, 1961.

Wilbur, C. Martin. "The Variegated Career of Ch'en Kung-po," in Hsüeh Chün-tu, ed., *Revolutionary Leaders of Modern China*, pp. 455–70. New York, 1971.

Woodhead, H. G. W., ed. *The China Year Book*. Various editions, 1930–40. Shanghai.

Wright, Gordon. *France in Modern Times: 1760 to Present*. New York, 1966.

Wu Tien-wei. "Chiang Kai-shek's March Twentieth Coup d'Etat of 1926," *Journal of Asian Studies*, 27 (1968): 585–602.

Wurfel, David. "The Philippines," in George McT. Kahin, ed., *Government and Politics of Southeast Asia*, pp. 679–769. Ithaca, N.Y., 1964.

Yabe Teiji. *Konoe Fumimaro*. 2 vols. Tokyo, 1952.

Yamazaki Jūzaburō. "HokuShi ni okeru Chūkyō no yūgeki-sen" (Chinese Communist Guerrilla Warfare in North China), *Kambu gakkō kiji*, 3 parts, 113–15 (Feb.–April 1963). (Based on lectures delivered by Yamazaki at the Staff College of the Japan Ground Self Defense Forces in Nov. 1962.)

Yanaga Chitoshi. *Japan Since Perry*. New York, 1949.

Yang I-chou. *Taiheiyō sensō zen'ya* (On the Eve of the Pacific War). Tokyo, 1970.

Yang Lien-sheng. "Historical Notes on the Chinese World Order," in John K. Fairbank, ed., *The Chinese World Order*, pp. 20–33. Cambridge, Mass., 1968.

Yano Seiki. Yano papers (in Japanese).

Yomiuri Shimbun, eds., *Shōwa shi no tennō* (The Emperor in Shōwa History). 14 vols. Tokyo, 1967–71. Especially Vol. 14: 77–405 (on Ch'en Kung-po).

Yoshida Tōyū. *Futatsu no kuni ni kakeru hashi* (A Bridge Between Two Countries). Tokyo, 1958.

Young, Arthur N. *China and the Helping Hand, 1937–1945*. Cambridge, Mass., 1963.

Young, John. *Check List on Microfilm Reproductions of Selected Archives of the Japanese Army, Navy, and Other Government Agencies, 1868–1945.* Washington, D.C., 1959.

————. *The Research Activities of the South Manchurian Railway Company, 1907–1945.* New York, 1966.

Young, Katsu H. "The Nomonhan Incident: Imperial Japan and the Soviet Union," *Monumenta Nipponica,* 22 (1967): 82–102.

INTERVIEWS

Chang Chia-ao (Chang Kia-ngau). Oct. 1967, Stanford, Calif.

Ch'en Chün-hui. March 1970, Hong Kong.

Chin Hsiung-pai (Chu Tzu-chia, Y. B. King). March–April 1970, Hong Kong, Tokyo.

Fang Chün-pi (Madame Tseng Chung-ming). July 1970, Boston.

Ho Ping-hsien. March 1970, Hong Kong.

Imai Takeo. Jan. 1970, Tokyo.

Kao Tsung-wu. Dec. 1969, Washington, D.C.

Li Sheng-wu. March 1970, Hong Kong.

Lu, Dr. J. I. March 1970, Hong Kong.

Matsukata Yoshisaburō (Saburō). Feb. 1970, Tokyo.

Matsumoto Shigeharu. Oct. 1969, Tokyo.

Okada Yūji. May 1970, Yokohama.

Shimizu Tōzō. Feb. 1970, Tokyo.

T'ao Hsi-sheng. March 1971, Taipei.

Tsunoda Jun. Jan.–June 1970, Tokyo.

Ushiba Tomohiko. May 1970, Tokyo.

Yamazaki Jūzaburō. Jan.–April 1970, Tokyo.

Index

Index